MOSCOW DIARY

MOSCOW DIARY

VELJKO MIĆUNOVIĆ

Translated by David Floyd
Introduction by George Kennan

DOUBLEDAY & COMPANY, INC., GARDEN CITY, NEW YORK   1980

ISBN: 0-385-14574-8
Library of Congress Catalog Card Number 79-7077
Translation and Introduction Copyright © 1980 by Doubleday & Company, Inc.
All Rights Reserved
Printed in the United States of America
First Edition

CONTENTS

CONTENTS

AUTHOR'S PREFACE
to English Edition

At the beginning of March 1956 after having been appointed Yugoslav ambassador to the Soviet Union I started making notes in connection with my new job. By the end of the month, after I had arrived in Moscow, I was already writing from day to day about practically all the important questions I came up against in the course of my new duties, and primarily about what was happening in Yugoslav-Soviet relations. The result was a collection of detailed notes made during the three years of my first period of service in the Soviet Union. The public was informed at the time about the great majority of the questions dealt with here, although some of them are also written about in this book in greater detail. When I came later to arrange the material, I also cut it down in length.

In the period dealt with here many important events took place which I write about from my Moscow angle: the Twentieth Congress of the Communist party of the Soviet Union and Khrushchev's secret speech condemning Stalin, the Moscow Declaration about restoring cooperation between the CPSU and the League of Communists of Yugoslavia, the Soviet armed intervention in Hungary, the political liquidation of the Molotov-Kaganovich-Malenkov group followed by the removal of Marshal Zhukov, the launching of the first Soviet earth satellite, the Moscow conference of Communist parties and the adoption of the Twelve-party Declaration, the execution of Imre Nagy and his comrades, the Seventh Congress of the LCY and its new program. As can be seen, there were more than enough events to fill a whole epoch, yet they all took place in the period of less than three years which I spent in Moscow.

Many of the details of which I wrote at the time were not of lasting importance and are probably of less interest to the reader today. Even while I was preparing the Yugoslav edition I tried to shorten or to cut out altogether the less interesting details. In arranging the text for publication outside Yugoslavia I have made further cuts in an effort to relieve the non-Yugoslav reader of details which, in a narrower sense, concern only Yugoslav policy or what was happening in that connection in

Yugoslav-Soviet relations twenty years ago. What remained after all these cuts has preserved some of its topicality and represents an authentic testimony concerning the events it deals with from someone who participated in some of them, and this, I hope, will be of interest to the reader today.

February 1978   Veljko Mićunović

INTRODUCTION
by Professor George Kennan
Former U. S. Ambassador to Yugoslavia

Following the dramatic break between the Soviet Union and Yugoslavia in 1948, which resulted in Yugoslavia's expulsion from the Soviet bloc, official relations between the two countries remained for several years on the lowest possible level short of a total rupture of diplomatic contact. Only low-ranking chargés d'affaires were maintained in the two capitals. These unfortunate officials, together with their subordinate staffs, were obliged to sweat out their unpleasant missions as best they could, isolated and officially ostracized, living as semiprisoners in their closely guarded residences. The death of Stalin, in 1953, produced a certain limited improvement in this situation; but much remained to be talked out between the two regimes before their relations could be—to use the favored expression of the time—normalized.

Of all the men around Stalin it had been Nikita Khrushchev who most regretted the breach with the Yugoslavs and was most anxious to see it repaired. He was well aware that a socialist Yugoslavia, operating independently in defiance of the Kremlin's authority, could not fail to exercise an unsettling influence on the other Eastern European regimes. The Kremlin feared that the leaders of these regimes would begin to ask themselves why it should be possible for Yugoslavia to enjoy this independence with impunity, whereas they themselves were obliged to accept a position of subordination.

When in the aftermath of Stalin's death, then, Khrushchev succeeded in consolidating a position of ascendancy among the late dictator's heirs, one of his first tasks was that of repairing the breach with the Yugoslavs. It was to this end that he undertook his dramatic "journey to Canossa": his visit, that is, to Yugoslavia and meeting with Tito, in May–June 1955.

The upshot of this meeting was the signing of the so-called Belgrade Declaration, defining the basis on which, thenceforth, relations between the two governments would be conducted. The Belgrade Declaration was a high-minded document, speaking of such things as "respect for the sovereignty, integrity, and equality of states in their relations with each other," of peaceful coexistence among nations "irrespective of ideological differences and of differences in their social systems," and of noninterference in the other's internal affairs "for any reason." This document provided a satisfactory basis for the resumption of normal relations and it cleared the way for the exchange of new high-level ambassadors.

It was important to the Yugoslavs that the man selected to represent them in Moscow should be someone who enjoyed Tito's complete personal confidence, who occupied a sufficiently high position in the Yugoslav party hierarchy to command respect in Moscow, and who was fitted for such a task by the personal qualities that position demanded. The combination of these requirements was found in the person of Veljko Mićunović, author of the diaries reproduced in this volume.

As onetime "partisan"—a comrade-in-arms of Tito, that is, in the recent struggle against the Germans—and as a respected and high-ranking member of the Yugoslav Communist party with extensive experience in both the Ministry of Interior and the Foreign Office, Mićunović was well prepared for his new position. It was, to be sure, his first regular diplomatic post; and he had never before been in the Soviet Union. But he was (and is), as all his friends were (and are) aware, a man of outstanding personal qualities: He was in the prime of life, was loyal, straightforward, honest, courageous, and intelligent. Further, he had a disarmingly quiet and engaging personality. But if any of the Russians thought he could be manipulated by them, they were decidedly mistaken, for he was no one's fool, and could be hard when hardness was needed. A native of Montenegro, he shared the traditional inclination of his people to view Russia as a friend. But he also shared the Montenegrins' quick pride and intuition; and with that, a ready sensitivity to situations and personalities, not to mention slights and efforts to deceive or entrap. For the post he was now to occupy, the Yugoslavs could scarcely have made a better choice.

Mićunović set out for Moscow in March 1956, on the first of his two tours of duty in that capital. (The second, not treated in these diaries, would take place in the late 1960s.) He was to remain there, on this first occasion, for approximately two and a half years. And what years, from the standpoint of Yugoslav-Soviet relations, these turned out to be! They were marked by a seemingly never-ending series of dramatic events, each of high significance for both parties, each destined to put to the test, once again, the soundness of the new relationship that had now been established.

A week before Mićunović's arrival, Khrushchev had given his famous "secret speech," in which he revealed and denounced a portion (but only a portion) of Stalin's cruelties and excesses. As Mićunović arrived, the news of this sensational event was seeping through the Soviet political establishment. The reaction to it there was of great importance to the Yugoslavs.

Then Tito himself came to the U.S.S.R. to negotiate a new basis for relations at the party, as distinct from the governmental, level.

A week after Tito's departure came the outbreak of disorders in Poland—an event which strained Soviet-Polish relations to the utmost, very nearly led to a massive Soviet military intervention, and constituted the first severe test of Soviet hegemony in Eastern Europe. This incident was, of course, only the prelude to the more serious insurrection which broke out some weeks later in Hungary, an event which involved both Yugoslavs and Russians and led to a full-scale Soviet military intervention, with far-reaching consequences for the entire situation in Eastern Europe.

In June of the following year (1957) the internal political crisis in Moscow culminated in the sudden, unprecedented, and dramatic removal of Molotov, Malenkov, Kaganovich, and other Stalin aides from their positions of leadership within the Soviet Communist party. Four months later, Marshal Zhukov was dismissed. In the autumn of that year, the great international Communist gathering in Moscow, which marked the fortieth anniversary of the Russian Revolution, proved to be a test of the Kremlin's relations with all the other Communist parties of the world, not excluding Yugoslavia, and marked the beginning (though few noticed it at the time) of the historic estrangement between Moscow and Peking.

In April 1958 the scene shifted to Yugoslavia, where the Seventh Congress of the Yugoslav Communist party (now called the League of Communists) adopted a new party program, highly unpalatable to Soviet ideological and political tastes. A few weeks later Imre Nagy, the last leader of the Hungarian rebellion, and several of his associates were executed in Hungary. This event was of particular significance from the Yugoslav standpoint, since it was the Yugoslavs who had initially given Nagy asylum in their diplomatic mission in Budapest and had released him from their custody only on the understanding that his physical safety would be assured.

Every one of these events, with the possible exception of Zhukov's removal, had its repercussions on the sensitive area of Soviet-Yugoslav relations. The Yugoslavs were not on principle hostile to the Soviet Union but were determined to go their own way. They were firmly disinclined to recognize a form of Soviet leadership which they knew, on the basis of bitter experience, could easily develop into domination. Khrushchev was equally persistent in his efforts to persuade them to accept that leadership, since he knew that nothing could more greatly strengthen Soviet prestige among the Communist parties and regimes across the world. At stake, in short, was the issue of whether an independent socialist state, ideologically close to the Soviet Union but resistant to its authority, could find a stable and satisfactory relationship to it—a relationship no worse, at least, than that enjoyed by the nonsocialist powers.

The tussle lasted the entire three years of Mićunović's mission. It involved a seemingly endless series of tilts and tensions—discussions, estrangements, reconciliations, pressures, and maneuvers between the two parties. At the focal point of all these tests of strength stood Mićunović. In the era of what might be called diplomacy by diplomatic reception, it was he who confronted Khrushchev almost daily at these social events. There, under the fascinated gaze of the assembled diplomats and foreign correspondents, he was obliged to hold his own against Khrushchev's attacks and enticements. Further, it was Mićunović who had to accompany Tito on his various visits to the Soviet Union and to share with him the task of resisting Khrushchev's stormy efforts of persuasion. At other times, Mićunović was obliged to face the Soviet statesman alone and to withstand similar pressures for hours on end, sometimes for entire days or nights.

He stood his ground stoutly. In the end, Khrushchev's efforts to bully and cajole the Yugoslavs into renouncing their recalcitrance and returning to the fold failed. Yugoslavia refused to part with a single jot of its independence. But Mićunović, despite many unpleasant moments and many trials of patience, developed a certain affection for Khrushchev as a person. Crude, ebullient, even brutal in some respects, Khrushchev was nevertheless a warm human being, who loved and needed communication; and Mićunović, being neither a rival in the Soviet heirarchy nor a "bourgeois" diplomat with whom all real intimacy was ideologically precluded, constituted a unique target for Khrushchev's earthy loquaciousness.

On the other hand, Mićunović was always aware that Khrushchev was practically alone among the Soviet leaders in his intense efforts to lure the Yugoslavians back into the fold. Nowhere else in his entourage was there manifested anything resembling the same enthusiasm for such an effort; more often, it was reserved behavior, guarded words, sometimes even ill-concealed antagonism, that came to the fore in those quarters. Mićunović was aware also of the precariousness of Khrushchev's position in the Soviet party: of the bizarre quality of a portion of his behavior, of the frequent impulsiveness and frivolity of his dispositions; of his habit of riding roughshod over the views of his colleagues; of his growing vulnerability to the sort of hostile conspiracy that was to prove, in 1964, his undoing.

Mićunović had to walk warily, therefore, even under the heaviest pressure. He could not permit himself to be taken by storm under the influence of a single personality. He had at all times to bear in mind that in the last analysis it was a great bureaucratic structure of power, not the tendencies of any single individual, with which he and his country had primarily to deal.

It is precisely in this respect—as an illustration of the nature of the regime to which he was accredited—that the Mićunović memoirs have their greatest value. Mićunović's account stands second to none as an intimate and searching illumination of Soviet diplomacy within the confines of the Communist "camp"—a diplomacy veiled by the habits of secrecy to which the Soviet leadership was, and is, addicted. But the value of Mićunović's account does not lie in this alone. It stands as proof that the annoyances and frustrations which have caused many "bourgeois" diplomats and journalists to end their Moscow assignments in frustration and bitterness are not really the reflection of any special suspicion or hostility directed at them as representatives of the detested bourgeois world. These annoyances and frustrations were scarcely smaller in the case of a "socialist" diplomat. There is in this fact a lesson which the Soviet leaders will themselves do well to ponder; for it suggests that a good portion of the frictions which seem always, sooner or later, to have attended the relations of the Soviet Union with other governments have been rooted not in the objective political or ideological differences which divide the Soviet state from other societies, but rather in certain Soviet habits and principles of action, inherited from precedents of earlier decades. Until they can correct these traits in their own political personality, these leaders must always expect their foreign relations to be subjected to a strain greater than any normal differences could alone justify.

George Kennan
Princeton, N.J.
March 1979

INTRODUCTION
by David Floyd

The "Moscow diary" of Veljko Mićunović covers the two and a half years from March 1956 to October 1958 when he served his first period as ambassador to the Soviet Union. It was a period of exceptional interest in both Soviet and world affairs because of a remarkable combination of circumstances, events, and personalities. It is that which makes the diary a document of unique value for the historian, the student of Soviet affairs, and the general reader.

In 1956 the problem of the succession to Stalin, who had died in 1953, was still unresolved, in terms both of policy and of persons. The Soviet population was in fact only just beginning to recover from the shock of the dictator's death and to emerge cautiously from the darkness of the Stalin era. Just before Mićunović arrived in Moscow, Khrushchev, as First Secretary of the Soviet Communist party, had in a speech to the party's Twentieth Congress made the first dramatic move to dissociate himself and the party from the horrors of Stalin's rule and had committed the Kremlin to a policy of "de-Stalinization"—a vague, muted promise of something better for the Soviet people. It was also Khrushchev's way of throwing down the gauntlet to the "Stalinists," who still dominated the Politburo, and of making his bid for personal power. That struggle continued in the Kremlin until the middle of 1957, when Khrushchev ousted Molotov and the "antiparty group" from the leadership, and in the spring of 1958 he took over the government as well as the party.

Meanwhile equally momentous events were taking place in the world outside. Sensing the instability in the Kremlin, the peoples of Russia's East European empire grew restless, and in October 1956 a popular uprising took place in Hungary and a major crisis developed in Poland. In the Middle East Nasser's nationalization of the Suez Canal and Western intervention produced a crisis of another kind. In October 1957 the Russians launched their first earth satellite. It was a busy time for statesmen and diplomats.

Mićunović was able to observe Khrushchev and the other Soviet leaders, as they battled with each other and with the world outside, at closer quarters than any "outsider" was able to do, because he was treated as a Communist (which he was and is) and as a "comrade" and therefore in a different category from anyone outside the Communist ranks. True, he was still eyed with some suspicion as the representative of "revisionist" Yugoslavia and confidant of the independent-minded Tito, and it could not be said that he was admitted to the innermost sanctums or councils of the Kremlin. But he had regular contact, both formal and informal, with most of the Soviet leaders and enjoyed the special confidence of Khrushchev himself. He seems to have been treated better even than the ambassadors of the most loyal Communist states of Eastern Europe. He was closer to the Soviet leaders than any other observer who has subsequently been able or willing to recount his experiences. He thus had a unique view of what sort of people the men in the Kremlin are, how they think and work, and how Soviet policy is made.

By far the most important element in this unique situation was Nikita Khrushchev himself, whose strange character, with its mixture of Stalinism and anti-Stalinism, dogma and common sense, brutality and humor, emerges clearly from the pages of the diary. If a man so untypical in many ways of Soviet leaders had not been in power in Russia at the time, Mićunović's years in Moscow would have been of far less interest. Unlike his main rivals, Molotov and Malenkov, Khrushchev had not risen to the top of the Soviet party *apparat* at Stalin's side: Away from Moscow in the Ukraine he had cultivated his own style of leadership in direct contact with the people. His earthy, outgoing manner was in complete contrast to that of the desk-bound bureaucrats like Malenkov, and he used his talents as a speaker and a practical politician to the full. As anyone knows who spent any time in Moscow when Khrushchev was in power, he was a man who enjoyed the cut and thrust of public debate and was volatile in his reactions to criticism and comment. Unfortunately, there were few in his immediate entourage or among the Moscow diplomats with the courage or ability to take him on.

Mićunović was not so inhibited. Without overstepping the bounds of diplomatic propriety, he soon learned how to disagree with Khrushchev, and he never hesitated to argue with him or criticize Soviet actions when he thought it justified. In this way, having the indispensable advantage of speaking fluent Russian, as well as a mind that worked just as quickly as Khrushchev's, Mićunović established a relationship with the Soviet leader such as no other diplomat from East or West ever had. Khrushchev seems to have welcomed and respected Mićunović's stubborn defense of his own and his government's views, so that, throughout all the ups and downs of Moscow-Belgrade relations, even when they were at their worst, personal relations between the two men always remained good.

There was, however, yet another factor which contributed to the uniqueness of Mićunović's position, and that was the unusual relationship which had developed between Russia and Yugoslavia. In 1948, as a result of Tito's refusal to be turned into a Russian "satellite" like the other countries of Eastern Europe, Stalin had "excommunicated" him and the Yugoslav Communists and imposed a political and economic boycott on Yugoslavia which lasted right up until his death in 1953. Stalin's successors chose to regard this as one of the dictator's senile aberrations and soon began making approaches with a view to restoring normal relations with Yugoslavia, and Khrushchev's visit to Yugoslavia in 1955 paved the way for a resumption of interstate relations, as a result of which Mićunović was appointed to Moscow in 1956.

But there was something less than complete understanding between the Russians and the Yugoslavs concerning the nature of their new relations. The Russians still regarded Yugoslavia in principle as a "socialist" country—that is, a country ruled exclusively by a Communist party, belonging to the "international Communist movement," and owing exclusive allegiance to Moscow. They thought that, having themselves eaten humble pie (as they saw it) in 1955, it was now up to the Yugoslavs as good Communists to return to the fold on the same footing as the members of the East European "socialist camp."

Tito and his party saw things differently. Having weathered the Stalinist storm from 1948 to 1953 without abandoning their socialist faith or their independence, they were quite ready to be on good terms with the Russians and even to admit a closer affinity to the East than to the West. But they had no intention of surrendering their hard-won independence and of exposing themselves to a repetition of the disastrous economic boycott of 1948.

These two differing points of view were the basis for the "special relationship" between the Russians and Yugoslavs. They both wanted for their own reasons to be in good relations, but on their own terms. This was the situation Mićunović had to handle, on the basis of Tito's rather uncertain directive: Don't quarrel with the Russians, but don't give in on matters of principle. But it was this situation which provided Mićunović with a unique vantage point from which to observe the Kremlin at work.

As he makes clear, Mićunović himself was an "insider," in the sense that he was a lifelong Marxist and an admirer of the Soviet Union, even if his admiration had been tempered by his wartime and postwar experiences of dealing with the Russians. He wanted his country to be in good relations with Russia, but not at any price and certainly not at the price of surrendering any element of Yugoslavia's independence. He emerges from the pages of his diary as a fervent patriot but also as a highly skillful diplomat and a sympathetic observer of the Soviet scene, though not so sympathetic as to be blinded to Russia's faults.

Mićunović returned to Moscow in 1969 for a second period as ambassador and, as he recounts in the postscript to this book, it then became apparent how great were the privileges he had enjoyed when Khrushchev was in power. By then Khrushchev had been cast onto the political scrap heap and practically all the doors which had been open to Mićunović in Khrushchev's day were as firmly closed as they were to his "capitalist" colleagues. He was not able even to make a private call on the former leader with whom he had been on such good terms only ten years previously. Khrushchev's successors had clearly made up their minds that the Yugoslav ambassador was not "one of them" and that they did not want an outsider observing them at close quarters.

* * *

What emerges from the pages of this diary, it seems to me, more clearly than from any other account of life at the center of Soviet power, is the way the Soviet leaders really look at the rest of the world, their friends and their enemies, and each other. For once we seem to hear the men in the Kremlin discussing policy and world affairs as they presumably do among themselves, with a minimum of ideological dressing.

We learn, for example, just how tenuous Khrushchev and the others felt Russia's grip was on the countries of Eastern Europe, how greatly they feared that one or other of their acquisitions in Eastern Europe would break out of the Soviet embrace, and how exaggerated was their belief in the West's plans to "roll back" their European empire. In 1958 we have Mikoyan complaining that America "cherished the illusion that it could change the social and political system established in Eastern Europe," while Khrushchev was insisting that "recognition of the present status quo in Eastern Europe is an indispensable condition for any negotiations—and that should at last be clear to the West." Fear of possible attempts by the West to "turn the clock back" (as the Russians saw it) in Eastern Europe pervades the whole book. At Mićunović's very first meeting with him in April 1956 Khrushchev told him he was expecting "difficulties with the West"—"because the West would take advantage of the situation in the Soviet Union to reduce Soviet prestige in the world and provoke trouble in the Soviet Union itself."

When in 1956 the Poles began to give signs of restlessness under Russian rule, Khrushchev could see in this only evidence that there were "anti-Soviet elements" in Poland who wanted "to go to the West and break up the camp." It was, of course, all the work of the American Secretary of State, John Foster Dulles, and Khrushchev warned Tito through Mićunović that the Russians were ready to use all means at their disposal to end the crisis in Hungary, because they "could not at any price allow a breakthrough in the camp [i.e., Eastern Europe]—which is what the West is trying to achieve."

Because he could see the world only as being divided into two hostile and potentially warring camps, Khrushchev was inevitably preoccupied with the question of Soviet strength, political and economic, but above all military. One of his principal criteria in deciding policy was whether it would persuade the West that Russia was weak or strong. Commenting on his denunciation of Stalin, he defended his action on the grounds that "the capitalists will realize that we are strong since we are able to break with Stalin in this decisive way: anyone who is weak would not undertake anything of that kind." Similarly, following his dismissal of Marshal Zhukov, Khrushchev told Mićunović that "foreigners would see that the Soviet party was strong, taking the sort of decisions that only a really strong person takes." He turned down a suggestion by Mićunović that the Soviet Government should renounce further nuclear testing unilaterally on the grounds that "it would be interpreted by the world as a sign of weakness, in that the Soviet Government would appear to have yielded to public opinion." Toward the end of his stay Mićunović was forced to conclude that "for the Russians a conciliatory attitude is a sign of weakness, just as the violence of the language used in the articles published in their press and the arrogance of their behavior are signs of strength."

When the Russians scored their propaganda victory by launching the first earth satellite, Khrushchev was overjoyed and boastful. But when the Americans replied with *their* "sputnik" Khrushchev swung to the other extreme and was cross and dejected. On another occasion Mićunović reflected sadly that "military strength is unfortunately still the first beneficiary and main indicator of the progress of science and technology in the Soviet Union."

Despite his denunciation of Stalin, Khrushchev continued to express his admiration for his predecessor and more than once revealed himself as being no less crude in his handling of affairs in a crisis. When "demoralized elements" in Georgia became restless in 1956 and demonstrated on the streets of Tbilisi, "we intervened very firmly and where necessary used troops and quickly restored order," he said. There had been "only a few" dead and wounded. When Mićunović told Khrushchev he thought the execution of the former Hungarian leader Imre Nagy had been an "irreparable mistake," Khrushchev replied that he personally approved the execution and would have done the same.

Nowhere, however, did Khrushchev's respect for, and fear of, force in domestic affairs become as evident as in his treatment of Marshal Zhukov, the World War II commander whose support had been decisive in ensuring Khrushchev's defeat of the "antiparty group" in 1957. It had come to Khrushchev's ears that Zhukov had dared to say in the course of the political crisis that if it became necessary he would himself use the Army to settle accounts with Molotov and Malenkov. To that, once the crisis was over, Khrushchev's reaction was: "If in June he threatened to call on the Army to intervene and 'restore order,' that means he could use the troops today against Molotov and Malenkov and tomorrow against someone else." Khrushchev was taking no chances, and Zhukov was banished.

Observed at close quarters, the Soviet leaders appear to have had very little respect for each other. In Khrushchev's eyes Bulganin, for ten years a member of the ruling Politburo, who served also as Soviet Prime Minister and Minister of Defense, was "a fool," an idiot and incompetent. Voroshilov, for many years Soviet head of state, appears as a senile figure scarcely aware of what was going on around him. Malenkov was accused by Khrushchev of having strangled one of the Leningrad party leaders with his own hands. The "antiparty group" accused Khrushchev of having their homes and offices "bugged."

The most sinister figure to emerge from the pages of the diary is that of Mikhail Suslov, the *éminence grise* of the Kremlin who was playing a key role behind the scenes in Khrushchev's day and continues to do so today in the Brezhnev regime. Mićunović's encounter with this awesome character in April 1958 is one of the most dramatic episodes described in these pages. But there are also some unforgettably comic scenes: Voroshilov telling the Shah of Iran's ambassador how the Bolsheviks had dealt with *their* monarch; Khrushchev bringing out from his pocket notes of an anecdote in doubtful taste at a reception in the Kremlin; the West German ambassador, following a demonstration staged outside his embassy, found "sitting dumbly on a heap of faded illusions."

However crude their treatment of others, the Soviet leaders revealed themselves as highly sensitive to anything affecting their own dignity. Thus the action of the Yugoslav press in cutting a report of a speech by Khrushchev led to a temporary crisis in Soviet-Yugoslav relations. Tito's suggestion in his Pula speech that the Soviet leaders were divided into Stalinists and anti-Stalinists rankled for many months with Khrushchev, until he finally rid himself of the Stalinists. Another remark of Tito's— that trade between Russia and Yugoslavia was to their "mutual benefit"— touched Khrushchev on the raw and contributed to the Russians' refusal of economic aid to Yugoslavia. A cartoon in the Belgrade *Politika* which Khrushchev took to depict him and Nasser together provoked another diplomatic crisis, until Mićunović pointed out that it was a caricature of President Eisenhower and not of Khrushchev.

*　　*　　*

The main theme running through the diary is naturally that of Soviet-Yugoslav relations. The diary is above all the story of how Mićunović tried to establish friendly relations with the Russians on a basis of real equality and to make the Soviet leaders understand the difference between friendship, or good relations, and subordination. I do not think he would claim to have had much success in his efforts. As he concluded on leaving Moscow, "Nobody, not even Khrushchev, can change his spots, and that is why we have in him to deal with the old and the new in one person." But the Yugoslavs themselves also recognized that they could change nothing in the Soviet Union and would have to carry on in the same way—"periodically lapsing into a state of crisis." That is, of course, what has happened with relations between Moscow and Belgrade ever since. If there are any who still believe that the rift between the Russians and Yugoslavs was a "put-up job," they should shed those illusions after reading this diary.

* * *

Another personality we get to know in these pages is that of Mićunović himself. He comes across as what he really is: a fervent patriot, a sincere Marxist socialist, a shrewd politician and diplomat, and a man never afraid to speak his mind, whether to the Soviet leaders in the Kremlin or to his own superiors in Belgrade. He was no "career diplomat" in the Western sense. After a childhood in Montenegro he soon joined the Communist student movement and then as a young man he was drawn into the Partisan war as one of the leaders of the resistance in Montenegro. Soon after the war he became a member of the Yugoslav Government in Belgrade as Deputy Minister of the Interior. In 1951 he was transferred to the Foreign Ministry as a Deputy Minister. When in 1948 Stalin pronounced his anathema on Yugoslavia, Mićunović did not hesitate in his loyalty to Tito. And later, as ambassador to Moscow, he simply continued fighting the same battles as he had fought all his life: for the "new Yugoslavia" and for his country's independence and rights. Tito, an excellent judge of men, did not err when he chose Mićunović to carry out the difficult task of restoring relations with the Russians without yielding to them in matters of principle. It would be difficult, Mićunović said. That's why I'm sending you, Tito replied with a smile. Mićunović did not let Tito down, although it is clear that he did not always agree with what Belgrade was doing. Nor did Belgrade always follow his advice.

* * *

Nearly twenty years passed before Mićunović decided to edit his diary for publication, and the questions inevitably arise: Why did he delay so long, and why did he choose to publish anyway? While it is customary for statesmen and diplomats in the West to make their memoirs and diaries available after they have retired from public life, it is very rare for Communist leaders to do the same. In the Soviet Union a few World War II marshals were allowed to put their names to heavily censored and largely unrevealing war memoirs, Mikoyan published a rather colorless account of part of his career, and an American publisher produced a book purporting to be the "reminiscences" of Khrushchev. But we have still not seen—and will probably never see—the memoirs of, for example, Molotov, whose career spanned the Russian Revolution and World War II and could certainly have much of interest to say, if he were permitted to say it. In Yugoslavia, however, Communist leaders, including Tito himself, have been much freer in their writings about their past, and several veterans of the Partisan war and the conflict with Stalin have told their stories in books.

Mićunović was doubtless inhibited from publishing his diary for some years because of the positions he continued to hold—he was ambassador to the United States from 1962 to 1967 and again to the Soviet Union from 1969 to 1971, after which he was made a member of the Presidency of Yugoslavia. In 1974, however, he suffered a stroke which left his right arm paralyzed and took him out of active politics. That gave him time to turn to his diaries and begin editing them, despite his disability, which he overcame by learning to write with his left hand and by using a typewriter. In the meantime relations between Moscow and Belgrade had stabilized, the Yugoslavs had lost any illusions they may have had about Russian intentions, and there no longer seemed to be any good reason why the truth about his years in Moscow should not be told, especially, as Mićunović points out, for the benefit of the younger generation in Yugoslavia itself. To those who have criticized him for publishing the diaries now he said:[1]

"There is the question of whether one should write about all this now and risk causing harm to some country or politician by talking about what was at the time in some respects a sort of 'internal' affair between Yugoslavia and the Soviet Union. On reflection I came to the conclusion that one ought now to write about the events of that time and about the people who played a part in them, although it means writing about party and government leaders of different countries. I think it necessary to write about them as about other mortals and to explain as clearly as possible the attitudes they took up, to quote where possible what they said in support of their views, what they expected to follow from their own and other people's actions, and, in short, to show as truthfully as possible how they carried out the policy they stood for. I believe that to write about

[1] In an interview published in the Serbian literary periodical *Kniževna Reč* on May 10, 1978.

people in that way is to separate myth from reality—and myths often serve to conceal the essence of what really happened. When written about in that way people appear more normal and more real—brought down to earth."

Asked what he thought of a Soviet official's description of his book as "anti-Soviet," Mićunović said:

"In Yugoslavia we do not go in for writing anti-Soviet books. I do not see how the facts set out in this book can be regarded by anyone as being 'pro' or 'anti.' If it comes to that I think the book could be regarded as 'pro-Yugoslav,' but something which is pro-Yugoslav ought not to be regarded *a priori* as being anti-Soviet. It is of course an old Soviet practice to label something anti-Soviet in advance, irrespective of what it really is, simply because it does not suit the official circles in Moscow and they wish to discredit it."

Mićunović considers that the whole concept of "anti-Sovietism" (which is still regularly applied to dissidents in Russia today) was a product of the early years of the Soviet regime and now quite outdated. "They behave in Moscow today as though nothing had changed and as if it were still sufficient simply to label someone 'anti-Soviet' to demonstrate the incorrectness of his views," he said.

"It looks as though the people in Moscow have forgotten that the official policy of the Soviet Communist party and of the Soviet Government was for many years extremely *anti-Yugoslav*, despite the fact that there had been a successful socialist revolution in Yugoslavia and that Communists were in power in our country. Official Soviet policy later became sharply anti-Chinese and has remained so for many years, to this very day. More recently Soviet policy has declared itself opposed to Euro-Communism. And yet Moscow goes on talking about other people's anti-Sovietism."

What about the effect of the book on relations between Yugoslavia and the Soviet Union? Mićunović was asked. He replied:

"If relations between states were to depend on what books were written in them the world would look very different today." It was hardly credible that a government could make a political issue out of the publication of a book in another country, he said. "That would imply that people in a given country should write only the sort of books which another government approved of and that the government of that country was responsible for everything written in it. That in turn would mean accepting the view that *The Moscow Years*[2] was written and published by the most official circles in Yugoslavia."

But, Mićunović insists, that was not the case. *The Moscow Years* was

[2] The present *Moscow Diary*.

solely the work of its author and was published by a highly respected Yugoslav publishing house "without any involvement of any department of state or of the party in any form." The publishing house (Liber, the Zagreb University publishers) had acted "within the bounds of its competence, strictly observing the legal provisions governing such matters now in force in our self-governing system in Yugoslavia."

The Soviet Government did indeed make its displeasure known and tried hard to prevent the appearance of the diary in the West. But its protests were brushed aside. Despite what Mićunović says about publishing freedom in Yugoslavia, it would no doubt have been possible for the Yugoslav authorities to bring pressure to bear on the publishers. But they didn't. I do not know whether the appearance of *The Moscow Years* was simply the result of a combination of publishing enterprise and a lack of "vigilance" on the part of officialdom, or whether it had the approval of Tito himself. What is certain, however, is that in 1977, when the book appeared in Yugoslav bookshops, the atmosphere in Yugoslavia was entirely appropriate for the reception of such a book.

Its appearance created something of a sensation in Yugoslavia and in the world outside. The first edition was quickly bought up and further printings were ordered. At no point was it withdrawn from the bookshops, as was reported at the time. Russian protests served only to stress the importance of the book and to underline the validity of the picture it gives of life at the top in Moscow. One of the shrewdest comments on the book came from a highly placed Soviet official who said: "Now you can see why we had to get rid of him!"—meaning Khrushchev.

TRANSLATOR'S NOTE

In rendering Slavonic proper names into English the translator is always faced with the problem of how best to transliterate them. In this book I have had to deal with names in both Russian and Serbo-Croat. I have decided to transliterate the Russian names in the generally accepted way—Khrushchev, Kaganovich—but to leave the Yugoslav proper names in their original Croat form with diacritical marks, which are very simple to understand. Ć and č both equal *ch*; š equals *sh*, and ž equals *zh* or the French *j*. So Mićunović is pronounced Michunovich, Koliševski is Kolishevski, and Ranković is Rankovich.

A few words must be said about terminology. It has been impossible to avoid using a certain amount of what is Communist jargon, though I have reduced it to a minimum. Mićunović himself has simplified things a great deal by talking about "the Russians" and "Russia" instead of "the Soviet people," "the Soviets," or "the Soviet Union"—and he has explained in a footnote why he has done so. I have extended somewhat his use of the simpler terms and have sometimes used "the Kremlin" to mean the small group of men at the top of the Soviet regime. I have used some abbreviations, such as CPSU, LCY, where I thought they would be immediately intelligible. I have not always been able to find a satisfactory substitute for "the socialist camp," which is Communist shorthand for the group of countries ruled by Communist parties dependent upon Moscow, and which therefore includes Outer Mongolia and Cuba. I have occasionally substituted the term "Eastern Europe" or "the countries of Eastern Europe." But I have also let either "the socialist camp" or simply "the camp" stand in many places.

Finally I must say something about the text in general. It will be clear to the reader that the diary entries make no claim to be a work of literature, though they have been edited and polished. They consist of notes written at the time, often in haste, and many bear the signs of being the actual reports which Mićunović sent back to Belgrade. This produced problems in dealing with the tenses and their sequence and also in rendering the accounts of conversations. Mićunović would sometimes begin his entry in the present tense and lapse into the past. He would sometimes report a conversation in indirect speech, but mix it with passages in direct speech. After consulting with him I have put those passages of direct speech which he believes to be close to what was actually said in quotation marks. Elsewhere I have left the passages out of quotes.

MOSCOW DIARY

CHAPTER ONE

APPOINTED TO MOSCOW

On March 5, 1953, when the conflict between Yugoslavia and Russia was still at its height and relations between the two countries were at their lowest, the man who had provoked the conflict, Joseph Stalin, died and the possibility emerged of change in the Soviet Union and in Soviet relations with the rest of the world. Stalin's successors moved very quickly to ease tensions and remove points of conflict, and they were soon putting out feelers concerning the restoration of normal diplomatic relations with Belgrade. Cautiously, Tito agreed and in July ambassadors were exchanged once again. But the process of "normalization" proceeded slowly until in May 1955 the Russians announced that they had agreed to send a delegation, led by Nikita Khrushchev, to Belgrade to discuss the further improvement of relations. The meeting, which took place at the end of May, resulted in the signing of the Belgrade Declaration, which was intended formally to end the Soviet-Yugoslav dispute and to establish the principles on which the two Communist countries would conduct their relations in future. Veljko Mićunović, then an Undersecretary in the Yugoslav Foreign Ministry, was a member of his country's delegation at the talks. Later that year he was chosen by President Tito to be ambassador in Moscow. Before he could take up his post, however, another major event shook the Communist world and opened up vastly better prospects for his embassy to Russia: At the Twentieth Congress of the Soviet Communist party Khrushchev made his "secret" speech condemning Stalin and his crimes.

1

Belgrade, March 7, 1956

In a couple of weeks' time I have to set out for Moscow to take up my post as Yugoslav ambassador to the Soviet Union. President Tito and the leaders of our country decided to send me there following the restoration of normal relations between Yugoslavia and the Soviet Union.

I have no idea what exactly awaits me in Moscow. I have been working on Yugoslav-Soviet relations in various government departments for ten years now, since 1946, and my comrades believe I have sufficient knowledge of the work awaiting me in Moscow for them to be able to rely on me. Until quite recently I thought the same. But as the day of my departure approaches Russia looks to me more and more like a high mountain in the mist, of which I know nothing.

Behind this lies a special factor which is not connected with the nervousness which all travelers experience before setting out on a journey. There is an essential difference, as far as my position is concerned, between what I have been doing in the course of the last ten years and the work awaiting me in Moscow. Here I have been a member of an enormous Yugoslav collective which in the nature of things enables the individual to display the greatest personal initiative while at the same time guarding him against making major political mistakes in his work. There existed numerous filters both "above" and "below" which functioned well in the process of taking decisions on questions concerning Yugoslav-Soviet relations. In our system hundreds and thousands of people took part in that process, which as a rule made it practically impossible for anyone to get politically "out of line." But now, for me, it's all going to be very different. In Moscow I shall be in a forward position and no longer a mere observer of what is going on.

We and the Russians now need a different sort of people from those of whom we have both had plenty in the last few years. What we need now is people of whom we can be sure that they will carry out the policy of normalization which we solemnly proclaimed last June and who will know how to work in a new way and to get rid of the old habits. Millions of Yugoslavs, practically the whole population, have been involved for years in our resistance to the aggressive policy of the Soviet Union. We have thousands of people who distinguished themselves in that battle. I am myself basically one of the "experts" of that kind, but we now need a different kind of expert capable of cooperating with the Russians just as successfully as they were in waging a political battle against them.

I think that in this respect our position is, for many reasons, much better than the Russians'. It was they who forced the conflict on us, not the other way round. From the very first day of the conflict, while Stalin was still alive and even later, Yugoslavia proposed several times that the conflict should be ended and that cooperation should be established on the basis of equality, independence, and mutual respect. But we had to hold out for many years, until Stalin died and for more than two years afterward until his successors accepted the Yugoslav proposals.

Finally, Yugoslavia is a small peace-loving country, while the Soviet Union is one of the two world superpowers, and our basic concepts and feelings about equality and cooperation between countries are different. With small states, such as Yugoslavia, that feeling is very developed, mainly because of the misfortune of being small. With great powers such as the Soviet Union the feeling for equality is stunted, or they hardly have it at all; they don't need it precisely because they are great.

Everything in Yugoslav-Soviet relations is now on trial on both sides. We have got to restore cooperation and trust between us. Friendship between states, as between people, is easier to establish than to maintain. Friendship, whether between people or between states, is especially difficult to restore if it has been abused and trampled on by one of the partners as Stalin did in 1948 to Yugoslavia. That is why the normalization of Yugoslav-Soviet relations advanced by such short steps and so slowly and why so much time passed before our "reconciliation" was achieved in June of last year.

The Belgrade Declaration, signed on June 2, 1955, by the Soviet Prime Minister, Nikolai Bulganin,[1] and President Tito, included the following provisions:

> In examining the questions about which the talks took place and for the purpose of strengthening confidence and cooperation between the peoples, both governments proceed from the following principles:
>
> The indivisibility of peace, upon which collective security can alone be based;
>
> respect for the sovereignty, independence, integrity, and equality of states in their relations with each other and in relations with other states;
>
> the recognition and development of peaceful coexistence between nations, irrespective of ideological differences and of differences in their social systems, which implies the cooperation of all states in the field of international relations in general and especially in economic and cultural relations;
>
> observance of the principle of mutual respect and of noninterference in internal affairs for any reason—whether of an economic, political, or ideological nature—because questions of the internal structure, of different social systems, and of different ways of advancing to socialism are exclusively a matter for the peoples of the individual countries;
>
> the development of bilateral and international economic cooperation

[1] Nikolai A. Bulganin, 1895–1975. Soviet statesman. Marshal. Member of Politburo, CPSU, 1948–59; Minister of Defense, 1953–55; Prime Minister, 1955–58.

and the removal of all those factors in economic relations which hinder the exchange of goods and retard the development of productive forces in the world and within national economies;

the cessation of all forms of propaganda and misinformation as well as other actions which spread distrust and hinder in any way the creation of an atmosphere for constructive international cooperation and peaceful co-existence between nations;

the condemnation of any act of aggression and any attempt to establish political or economic domination over other countries;

recognition of the fact that the policy of military blocs increases international tension, undermines confidence between peoples, and increases the danger of war.

* * *

What personal relations between us had been like is revealed by the fact that the Russians ceased even to talk to us in Belgrade, in Moscow, at the United Nations, or in any of the places and political gatherings at which we met from the autumn of 1949. They did not even shake hands when they met our representatives. The only exception to this was when notes of protest were handed in and rejected in the foreign ministries in Belgrade and Moscow from 1949 to 1953, which was practically the only work done by the group of low-level officials who remained behind in our embassy in Moscow and in the Soviet embassy in Belgrade.

Since the Russians[2] inflicted these relations on us for many years, I don't think we have to be surprised at the reaction of our chargé d'affaires in Moscow, D. Djurić, two or three days after Stalin's death on March 5, 1953. One of the Soviet Deputy Ministers of Foreign Affairs, Yakov Malik,[3] offered his hand to Djurić who was in a group of foreign diplomats expressing condolences to Malik on the occasion of their great loss. The fact that Malik shook his hand was reported by Djurić in a ciphered telegram to the Yugoslav Government, because it really was an event for an official Soviet representative to shake hands with a representative of Yugoslavia in public.

Belgrade, March 10, 1956

The Soviet Government will certainly not be pleased at the Yugoslav Government's decision to appoint me ambassador in Moscow. The Rus-

[2] *Author's note:* The reader will come across the terms "Russians," "Russia," and "Russian" in this book in various contexts. Although they are sometimes inadequate, these widely used colloquial terms are to be found in these pages because of the nature of diary entries, and for the sake of authenticity they have not been changed. The reader should not read into this anything except the colloquial use of the terms.
[3] Yakov Malik, b. 1906. Soviet diplomat. Deputy Foreign Minister, 1946–53 and from 1960; Soviet representative on U. N. Security Council, 1948–53; Ambassador to Britain, 1953–60.

sians always divide Communist leaders in other countries, and especially in Yugoslavia, into pro- and anti-Soviet. I feel that in the Soviet view I have long belonged to the latter group, although I think the Russians are wrong in this.

Even when I was a child in my native village of Velestov in Montenegro, Russia was the first country I came to know as a friend and "defender of the Montenegrins." Later I learned from books how, from the time of Peter the Great and Catherine right up to the October Revolution, Tsarist Russia helped Montenegro as the first free country in the Balkans to be a loyal ally of the Russian empire. Early in life I also learned that many generations of Montenegrins had considered themselves throughout their lives not only devoted friends of Russia but also the most loyal subjects of the Russian Tsars in whom they saw their mighty defender through centuries of struggle for emancipation from the Ottoman empire. That was all in the distant past, hundreds of years before the appearance of Marx and later Lenin and Communists in our society.

The generation to which I belonged could only be, and was in fact, doubly Russophile, because it grew up in that deep, centuries-old pro-Russian tradition in Montenegro, linked for hundreds of years with its "Russian protector." Those links acquired new content and strength and experienced a sort of renaissance through the victory of the October Revolution in Russia. It is not surprising, therefore, that the ideas proclaimed by the Revolution and our Communist party were accepted so quickly and on such a large scale in Montenegro even in the days when the Civil War was still raging in Russia. The leaders of the movement in Montenegro were from among the intelligentsia and the students. At that time we had practically no working class.

In the political climate which developed later I joined the illegal Communist party of Yugoslavia in my eighteenth year when I was attending Cetinje secondary school in 1934. But I won't go further into that. I will simply say that from that time right up to our first conflicts with representatives of the Soviet Government immediately after World War II, like the vast majority of Yugoslav Communists, I had felt the Soviet Union to be my second homeland, regarding it almost as something exalted and holy. I thought and spoke of Stalin[4] with no less enthusiasm than did millions of his followers in the Soviet Union and the rest of the world. I recall a telegram which I sent to Stalin as political commissar of the Lovćen partisan detachment on November 7, 1942, at the height of the war in Yugoslavia and the Soviet Union against the fascist invaders.

[4] Iosif V. Stalin, 1879–1953. Soviet statesman. Member of Politburo, CPSU, 1919–53; General Secretary, CPSU, 1922–53.

In both content and style it was like a believer addressing his God: To Thee, Almighty, Creator . . . and so on, like an oath or a prayer.

However, my enthusiasm was undermined even during the war and especially just after it ended. Quite a long time before our clash with the Russians I was having increasingly unpleasant official meetings in Belgrade with representatives of the Soviet State Security Service.[5] In that field quite early on the Russians gave signs of the storm that was to hit our country in 1948, although we were not at the time able to read them correctly.

When at the end of June 1948[6] news swept round the world of a major political sensation—that Stalin had expelled Yugoslavia from the "community of socialist states" and from the "family" of world Communist parties—we held our famous Fifth Congress of the Communist party in Yugoslavia. It was something like the general mobilization which a country undertakes only when it is faced with a war. I made a speech at that congress which was not altogether in line with the speeches of our party leaders. It was one-sided and bitter. But what I considered to be the weakest aspect of my speech—its bitterness toward the Soviet Union—received stormy applause and was well received by the Congress. Next day we learned that Soviet officials were taking my speech as a proof that Yugoslavia had adopted the anti-Soviet policy of which they had long been accusing us.

Belgrade, March 12, 1956

Everything I wrote down yesterday seems to me today to be rather exaggerated; and the fact that my thoughts keep carrying me back into the past is not a good sign, in my opinion.

We and the Russians have solemnly buried the hatchet, agreed to restore normal relations between our two countries, and set down in black and white in the Belgrade Declaration a new political basis for relations between our states now and in the future. But the question is: How do the Russians see it, since the Belgrade Declaration was written by a Yugoslav hand? The Russians signed it along with us, but as time goes on,

[5] From 1951 Mićunović was Assistant Secretary of State for Foreign Affairs in the Yugoslav Government and responsible for relations with the Russians.
[6] This refers to the publication on June 28, 1948, of the "Cominform Resolution," which denounced Tito and the Yugoslav Communists and expelled the Yugoslav Communist party from the international Communist movement. The "Cominform" was properly known as the "Information Bureau of the Communist Parties," created by Stalin in 1947 to facilitate Soviet control of the principal Communist parties of Europe. It consisted at the outset of the Communist parties of Bulgaria, Czechoslovakia, Hungary, Poland, Romania, and Yugoslavia, as well as of the French and Italian Communist parties. Its first headquarters were in Belgrade.

it becomes increasingly clear that we and they still have different ideas about it, although we solemnly signed the same document.

By following current Soviet policy it is not difficult to detect what those differences are. We regard the Belgrade Declaration as a sort of socialist Magna Carta which is to apply to Yugoslavia's relations with the Soviet Union, as well as with other socialist states, perhaps not for as long as the English one but at any rate for many years. But the Russians seem to look on this document as they would on any other ephemeral agreement concerning relations between two countries, as not having any special or lasting significance.

We consider that with the Belgrade Declaration Yugoslavia took a major step toward achieving equality and independence in its relations with the Soviet Union, "the first and leading country of socialism," not only for itself but also, even if only potentially, for the other socialist countries. But, to judge by the Russians' behavior, they think differently, and believe they can conduct one policy toward socialist Yugoslavia and a different, even opposite, one toward the other socialist states.

From what we can gather, the Russians consider the Belgrade Declaration a weak document, because it bears a "state" and not a "party" character, and they think it ought to be replaced as soon as possible by another, better document to be drawn up in Moscow by Soviet officials in the spirit of "Marxism-Leninism" and "proletarian internationalism," which the Belgrade Declaration, in the Russians' view, is very far from being. They signed it so as not to return to Moscow empty-handed, but it is significant that, although Khrushchev[7] led the Soviet delegation, he refused to sign it. It was signed instead by Bulganin as Prime Minister.

Belgrade, March 13, 1956

What is the attitude of the Western powers and other countries toward the normalization of Yugoslav-Soviet relations? Certain countries in the West probably wished that the conflict between us and the Russians would never end. Russia also cherished similar hopes with regard to our relations with, for example, the United States or any other state in the western hemisphere. The reasons for such a point of view on the part of the Russians and the Americans are easy to grasp. Nor is it difficult to understand the politics behind the support which the West extended to us after 1948. Our fundamental interests led us to ask for help and support to defend ourselves against Stalin's aggressive pressure on Yugoslavia

[7] Nikita S. Khrushchev, 1894–1971. Soviet statesman and Stalin's successor as leader of the Soviet Union. Member of Politburo, CPSU, 1939–64; First Secretary, CPSU, 1953–64; Prime Minister, 1958–64.

on all sides and to accept any help which would contribute to the defense of our sovereignty and independence. The West, on the other hand, had an interest in extending us such aid as we were able to accept.

This went on for several years, as did our conflict with the Soviet Union. And because that conflict went on for so long the Western powers seemed to become accustomed to it as a sort of permanent factor in international relations.

Now a change has come about in Yugoslavia's relations with the Soviet Union and this has had a disturbing effect on the policy which the Western and other powers adopted with regard to this international question. The signing of the Belgrade Declaration has suddenly dried up a source which had been expected to provide material for "long-term exploitation" in the battle between East and West. The Western states found themselves in the position of having to "re-form on the march," first of all in their relations with the Soviet Union and "world communism" but also with Yugoslavia, because it is also a part of what is called "world communism."

I write about this primarily because it now seems to us in Belgrade that the Western countries are moving very cautiously in their efforts to determine the real extent to which relations between the Russians and us have been normalized and to arrive at a fresh assessment of what may happen along that road. The Western powers, with which we now have good and extensive relations as a result of our conflict with the Soviet Union, will now examine under a microscope everything that goes on between Belgrade and Moscow. The West will now watch very closely to see whether Yugoslavia abandons its independent position and whether our rapprochement with Moscow means that Yugoslavia is moving gradually back again into the Soviet political orbit.

The Russians apply what appear to be the opposite, but which are in fact similar, standards in their assessment of our policy. They consider that any real improvement in our relations with them can come about only to the extent that there is a worsening of our relations with the West. The fact is that, when discussing with us the normalization of our relations, the Russians were extremely careful not to offer a single word of criticism of our relations with the West and the United States. On the contrary, they gave the impression that they had no criticisms to make of Yugoslavia's policy in this connection. Khrushchev himself went furthest in this. On two occasions he said that they not only had no objections to the credits we are taking from the United States and the West but that the Soviet Union itself was ready to take such credits, meaning credits without political strings.

We are not quite sure that the Russians really think like this. We are more inclined to see in it a further sign of the great interest Khrushchev's delegation had in bringing our talks to a successful conclusion. For our part we were certain that the talks were certainly not the occasion for the Russians to criticize Yugoslavia's policy in any way, since they had come to Belgrade to convince us of the change in Soviet policy and not to try to change Yugoslav policy.

It was obviously essential for the Russians to have the "Yugoslav clearance" before they could take any further steps in the formation of Soviet foreign policy after Stalin. It was only after the "reconciliation" with Yugoslavia that Khrushchev and Bulganin made their first official visit to India and other countries in Asia. There is no doubt that in New Delhi Khrushchev made very successful use of the results of his visit to Belgrade, because the normalization of relations with Yugoslavia was a clear indication of a change for the better in Soviet policy toward India as well and at the same time toward the other, new states in Asia and Africa.

It will undoubtedly be difficult for us to achieve any fundamental improvement of our relations with the Russians if they continue making it conditional on a worsening of our relations with the West. That would mean that the Russians are still not ready to accept Yugoslavia for what it is. For us the difficulties are bound to increase, since the West may also make conditions in one way or the other. We shall have to swim against the stream in both cases. If we reduce the pressure from the Soviet side by improving our relations with them, it may result in increased pressure from the West, which we must avoid. We shall not have done much to consolidate Yugoslavia's international position in the way of further strengthening our independence if we replace pressure from the East by pressure from the West.

The trouble is that the leading powers in the East and the West do not really admit the possibility that a small country can be independent in foreign policy and have good relations simultaneously with East and West. If Yugoslavia should succeed in achieving that, there would probably be many other states following the same policy of independence of both the military blocs which dominate international relations today. Such a prospect is a threat to the present policy of the blocs. In this lies the special dimension of the foreign policy we have been pursuing.

Belgrade, March 14, 1956

Last night we had a party in our government club on Avramović Street to mark my departure for the Soviet Union. There were ten comrades present, including Kardelj,[8] Ranković,[9] and Koča Popović.[10] It was an entirely private affair. The presence of some of our most distinguished personalities, who gladly accepted my invitation, is the best indication of how much interest our top leaders are taking in relations with the Soviet Union and in my work in Moscow.

As was to be expected, the main topic in the course of the evening was the news we had received from Moscow. The main item was the Twentieth Congress of the Soviet Communist party or, more precisely, Khrushchev's secret speech[11] criticizing Stalin. After the Twentieth Congress the Russians sent us in confidence the text of Khrushchev's speech, and this month we had a special meeting of our Central Committee at which the speech was read out. It is very long and took a long time to read, but it was listened to with unusual attention. The meeting was attended by more than a hundred people. We voted unanimously to approve the speech and declared it to be of historical importance.

Believe it or not, it now seems to some among us as though the Russians are beginning to take the path which the Yugoslavs opened up long ago. There are some among us who are inclined to think that everything, not only in our relations with the Russians but also in the "world Communist movement," now depends primarily on what direction we Yugoslavs take! It is obvious that there has been prevailing among us a mood of growing satisfaction and optimism which has often led us to behave like participants in a difficult battle which we won not only for ourselves but for others, too.

[8] Edvard Kardelj, 1910–79. Yugoslav statesman. Member of Politburo, Yugoslav Communist party, since 1938; Foreign Minister, 1948–53; Chairman, Federal Assembly, 1963–67. Member of the Presidency of the League of Communists and of the Yugoslav Republic until his death.

[9] Aleksandar Ranković, b. 1909. Yugoslav Communist official, for many years head of the security police. Member of Politburo, Yugoslav Communist party, 1940–66; Secretary of its Central Committee, 1945–66; Minister for Internal Affairs, 1946–54; Vice-president of the Republic, 1963–66. In 1966 he was dismissed from all his government and party posts and pensioned off for allegedly holding views and acting contrary to the policy of the party. He lives quietly but at liberty in Belgrade.

[10] Koča Popović, b. 1908. Yugoslav statesman, now retired from public life. Partisan commander; Chief of Staff of Yugoslav Army, 1945–53; Foreign Minister, 1953–65; Vice-president of the Republic, 1966–67.

[11] On February 25, 1956, at the end of the Twentieth Congress of the CPSU, Khrushchev, First Secretary, addressed a closed session on the subject of "the cult of personality and its consequences." The text of his speech was not published in the report of the Congress, but it was read out to closed meetings of party members and was shown in strict confidence to certain foreign delegates to the Congress, as a result of which a complete text was received in Washington and quickly released by the State Department. It was found to contain an outspoken, if only partial, denunciation of Stalin and his abuse of power, and came be known as Khrushchev's "secret speech." It was the first time anyone in the Soviet Union had criticized Stalin in public for some twenty years. The speech has still not been published in the Soviet Union, nor is it acknowledged that it was ever made.

We spent quite a long time discussing why Khrushchev's speech had not been published, so that the most important event at the Twentieth Congress of the CPSU remained secret and hidden from the citizens of the Soviet Union and the world at large. Can one talk of a change in the policy of the Soviet party and government when the Soviet public does not know what happened at the Congress or of what the change consists? What does it really amount to if Stalin is condemned at a closed session of the CPSU Congress while speakers at that same Congress insist that the policy of the CPSU was invariably correct, which means that Stalin's policy was also correct, since he led the Soviet Communist party and state for thirty years, right up to his death?

Some of those present at the party argued that, with the greatest respect for the political significance of Khrushchev's secret speech, we ought to act on the official and publicly proclaimed policy of the Soviet Union, on what the Soviet leaders actually do, and not on a secret speech made at closed sessions of the Twentieth Congress. There have been many cases in Moscow in the past when they said one thing in secret and did something different in public to us and to others, both before the conflict with us and after it. After all, in his secret speech Khrushchev did not condemn Stalin as he deserved to be condemned, but limited his criticisms and his condemnation of Stalin mainly to certain instances of the "violation of socialist legality" and even then only in the Soviet Union itself.

Not even in secret did Khrushchev mention the millions of completely innocent Soviet citizens whom the Soviet leaders sent to their death; he spoke mainly about a few outstanding individuals, high officials of the CPSU who were executed for nothing. Khrushchev did not say a single word about the fact that the Soviet Union had imposed the very same system of executing innocent and decent people, high officials of party and government, on all the countries of Eastern Europe under Soviet domination. Now the Russians are giving the impression that they recognize the "independence and equality" of those states by liquidating some distinguished Communists. It would be better if each country established who was responsible for the crimes "independently" of the Russians. But even at the Twentieth Congress the Russians whitewashed Stalin as far as crimes committed in the Eastern European countries of "people's democracy" were concerned.

These and many similar topics and comments made up our conversation at last night's party. There was a good deal of talk about the top leaders of the Communist parties and governments in Albania, Bulgaria, Hungary, Czechoslovakia, and other countries of Eastern Europe who were murdered in the course of Stalin's efforts to subjugate Yugoslavia.

11

We had defended ourselves from the Soviet Union, but the Russians had in exchange imposed Stalinism in its worst form on the countries of "people's democracy." The Russians had lost Yugoslavia, but they had Stalinized the camp.

When in the course of our farewell party criticisms and reservations with regard to Khrushchev's secret speech and doubts about future Soviet policy seemed to dominate the very lively discussion, it was Kardelj who intervened most often to warn us against going too far. Too critical an attitude could result in our making a mistaken assessment both of Khrushchev's secret speech and of the whole Congress. That Khrushchev had not made a deeper and more far-reaching criticism of Stalin, as we in Yugoslavia had failed to do years ago, meant that Khrushchev could not go further than he did. That was the reality of the present political situation in the Soviet Union, and it was not just a question of whether Khrushchev did nor did not realize that the problem as a whole went far beyond what he said about Stalin. What we should be surprised at was Khrushchev's political courage and strength in saying what he said about Stalin; we should not criticize him for not saying more.

We agreed that it would have been better if Khrushchev had made his speech in public, though that should not be allowed to reduce its political importance. Summing up the situation in the Soviet Union and especially among the top people, we agreed that the dilemma which faced the Russians was simply whether to make such a speech in secret or not make it at all, and not whether the speech should be secret or public. The speech could be made only behind closed doors.

In the course of the evening there was plenty of talk about my work in Moscow. The prevailing view was that following the Twentieth Congress of the CPSU, my basic task had been made appreciably easier. Although made in secret, the condemnation of Stalin was already widely known in the Soviet Union. It would be impossible to keep it secret. Khrushchev was not in a position to publish it in the newspapers, but millions of party members certainly knew about the speech already. Yugoslavia now has much more scope for action in the Soviet Union and in the world Communist movement than the most optimistic among us had foreseen before the Twentieth Congress. Our Central Committee has already sent a letter to the Central Committee of the CPSU telling them of our unanimous support for the decisions of the Twentieth Congress. I am going to Moscow with messages from Tito to Khrushchev couched in the warmest terms concerning the further development of Yugoslav-Soviet relations. Could one have expected anything more? As it has turned out, I am exceptionally lucky to be setting out for Moscow in such circumstances; I could wish for nothing better.

Belgrade, March 23, 1956

At my last meeting with Comrade Tito in his study at 15 Užička Street in Belgrade I insisted that we should agree on something like a general rule to serve as a guide for all of us without distinction in our dealings with the Russians, in Moscow as well as in Belgrade, in diplomatic relations and in trade relations, in party matters and in every other field. Tito brought our conversation to an end with the conclusion that I was not to get into a conflict or to quarrel with the Russians insofar as it depended on me. But I was also not to give in to them on matters of major political importance, and I would be in a good position to help put this rule into practice.

I told Comrade Tito that it would be of the greatest importance if we all managed to behave in that way. I personally was afraid that the Russians would maintain constant pressure and demand concessions from us. I was supposed neither to give way to them nor to quarrel with them; but refusal to give way usually led to a quarrel. Tito laughed and said that was why they were sending me to Moscow. I said that, if I really had to choose, I would not make any concessions, though it might lead to a quarrel, but not because I would seek it. In the end we agreed that, if we were not to have a greater choice, the quarreling should be left to the Russians, but that we should not give way.

I also discussed with Tito the visit he is to make to the Soviet Union in two months' time. It will be his first visit to Russia since the outbreak of the quarrel eight years ago. It is very important politically, not only for us and the Russians but even further afield. Tito asked that, quite apart from my regular reports to the government and the State Secretariat for Foreign Affairs, I should keep him personally informed whenever I thought it necessary. As for his official visit to Moscow, Tito said that we should now leave everything to the Russians, and that before the visit I would have to come to Belgrade for consultation.

Then I discussed with him how the history of our economic relations with the Russians had been no less dramatic than the history of our political relations. For the Russians, today as in the past, all trade is directly in the service of politics. We are afraid that it will be the same with the credit for our aluminum industry.

By canceling unilaterally all trade agreements with Yugoslavia and then imposing an economic blockade after 1948 the Russians inflicted great material harm on our country. I reminded Comrade Tito that we had discussed this last year with Khrushchev's delegation and had passed on to the Russians some very large figures concerning the extent of the direct and indirect losses which the Russians had caused us. Khrushchev refused to include this matter in our talks, saying he was not going to "pay us reparations" even if the figures we presented had been much smaller than they were. On the following day the Russians handed us their own figures for Yugoslavia's debts to the Soviet Union, in which the main item was for the captured weapons which the Soviet Union delivered to our Army before 1948. The Russians' figures were even bigger than ours. Our "economic file" on the talks with Khrushchev resembled the usual record of quarrels between states on such matters, whereas the Russians read out their claim from a single sheet of paper. It was obvious that they had drawn it up overnight in Belgrade after we put forward our demands.

After coming to the conclusion that there would be no agreement we had left this question open and turned to other matters. This exerted a certain pressure on the Russians and increased their fears that they would not reach agreement with us, so that they were rather more disposed to accept some of our political demands. Later we accepted a Soviet proposal that we should write off our financial claims against each other from the past.

On the way to Moscow, March 24, 1956

At about ten o'clock in the morning I arrived at the little airport at Zemun[12] to board a Soviet aircraft, a two-engine Ilyushin-14. This is a sort of Soviet version of a small passenger plane like the American Dakota. It was unfortunately going to take the whole day to fly from Belgrade to Moscow. I had already said good-bye to the members of my family and to my closest friends and advised them not to come to the airport at Zemun, and they agreed. I expected to be seen off officially by one or two representatives of the Foreign Secretariat and a similar number of people from the Soviet embassy, and no one else. To my surprise I found the tiny building of the little airport full of my friends, although I had already said good-bye to most of them. Conspicuous among them was a group of Yugoslav Army generals, compatriots of mine from Montenegro, famous commanders and political commissars from our national liberation war who had turned up in uniform straight from their offices. They were apparently not interested in our rules of protocol, and it was all the same to them that those rules did not provide for their presence in uniform at Zemun Airport on this occasion. The representatives of the Foreign Secretariat and the Soviet embassy were quite submerged in this mass of Yugoslav officials.

I was very touched by such a send-off. It was as though both I and the comrades who were seeing me off had returned for a moment to the best

12 Zemun: a suburb of Belgrade.

days of our war and revolution, when relations between us were direct and natural, and mutual trust was unlimited, as it can be only between people who have fought together and who were ready at any moment to give their lives for our common idea—and for each other.

Although we have already been in power in Yugoslavia for ten years and although power spoils people more quickly than anything, attacks their morale, and ruins relations between them, personal relationships between us have not yet become rigidly hierarchical in every field. The long years of conflict with Stalin after the war probably helped us more than anything else to preserve some human qualities from the war period and our youth and to slow down the process of deterioration, with the result, as you see, that there can still be sudden, spontaneous outbursts of those qualities which were the best in us but which are steadily fading into the past. Something of this was apparent in the quite irregular reversion to Partisan ways as I was seen off at Zemun on March 24, 1956.

For me it meant something else of a political nature. At least that is the impression I have. Although those present were people in leading positions in our government, party, and armed forces, who are today well informed about our policy toward the Soviet Union, I had the feeling that a number of them hoped sincerely for a rapid improvement in our relations with the Russians. As though nothing should now be allowed to stand in the way! None of them said this to me, but I could feel it. I could sense something similar at the farewell party that was given for me a few days ago in Belgrade, although in a different way and to a far lesser degree. We have all of us become aware, consciously and subconsciously, of the role our country plays in the policy of the new leadership of the Soviet Union, as well as of our own desire for the best possible development of Yugoslav-Soviet relations.

On the way to Moscow, March 24, 1956

Raif Dizdarević, who has been appointed First Secretary in our embassy, is traveling with me. He has already served a good apprenticeship in the field of our relations with countries of the socialist camp. He spent three years in Sofia, and at a most difficult time.

He told me the other day that, apart from all the other forms of harassment to which he was regularly exposed as the diplomatic representative of Yugoslavia, the Bulgarian authorities fixed up some apparatus in the room above his bedroom which automatically struck the floor above his head roughly every ten seconds, night and day, twenty-four hours a day, for months on end. Raif says that he knew very well that there was nobody living in the apartment above him, that there was some automatic device there, and that there was no sense in reacting as though there was somebody living overhead. All the same, he was unable to restrain himself, particularly in the middle of the night, from grabbing anything that came to hand and answering the bangs from the machine set up by Bulgarian police by blows against the ceiling of his room. Thus the device invented by the Bulgarian police proved effective.

Raif deserves to have his years of service in Sofia reckoned as military service or even more. After Sofia Moscow will probably seem to him like Paris. I am in a worse position, since I have never been to Bulgaria or Eastern Europe, and Moscow is my first permanent post abroad.

There are also a dozen Soviet citizens in the plane. They appear to be employees of various Soviet economic organizations having dealings with foreign countries. I tried to exchange greetings with some of them when they happened to glance my way. I wanted to get to know them and talk to them, and not only because they were fellow travelers who were to spend the whole day in the little cabin of the plane. I thought to myself: These are the first Soviet citizens whom I have come across in my new job. And they will be interested in talking on any topic with the new Yugoslav ambassador on his way to Moscow to restore friendship between our countries. I had no success. The Soviet citizens maintained their silence. And, since it made Dizdarević and me feel awkward to be talking just to each other, the Russians imposed silence on both of us as well.

We arrived in Lvov at 2 P.M., and I stepped for the first time in my life on Soviet soil. I was surprised at myself, because not only did I not experience any emotion, I did not feel anything at all at my first encounter with the "land of the Soviets"—yet that encounter had for years been my life's ambition and my most cherished dream. Yesterday's dream had, you see, become a reality, and I don't have anything to say about it. Can Stalin really have reduced us to such a state that even Yugoslav Communists, who for decades felt that the Soviet Union was their own country should feel simply like tourists, foreigners arriving in a foreign country, when they first set foot on the "land of the Soviets"?

A Russian leads us from the plane to the airport building, and I ask one of the Soviet cabin crew when approximately we would arrive in Moscow. He does not reply. I ask another one; he says it will be announced "some time or other." They put us in a room set aside for international travelers where there is nobody except the dozen Russians from our plane and us two Yugoslavs. They offer us lunch. There is only one dish— *kuritsa* (chicken). I don't want to eat anything, and certainly not the *kuritsa*, which is cold and you can't tell whether it had—"some time or other"—been roasted or boiled. The waitress serving us sees that I haven't touched the food duly set before me. No doubt she has been told who I am. She tells me I can have a *yaysto* (an egg) if I don't like the *kuritsa*.

16

All the time there are men in uniform moving around the dozen passengers. The uniforms are of various colors: green, gray, olive green, and blue. The men are all busy doing something, coming and going, while we passengers sit silently at our tables. It seems to me as though I have arrived in a country where there is a war still going on. I try to work out why there is such an atmosphere and reproach myself for reacting in this way on my first encounter with the "land of the Soviets." Lvov Airport (I tell myself) is on the Soviet frontier; foreign travelers from the West and the rest of the world pass through here into the Soviet Union, and that is why there are extra Soviet police on guard. But I don't know how to explain why the airport in Lvov is equipped with so many powerful loudspeakers which continually blare out Russian songs and marches and nearly split our eardrums. But for that it would be quiet, because there is practically no traffic passing through.

Then I reflected on the fact that Lvov was not really a Russian city and that this was still not Russia. Nor was it the Ukraine. Stalin took this city off the Poles on the basis of his pact with Hitler for the partition of Poland in 1939, the fourth time in that country's history that it had been divided between its powerful German neighbors in the west and the Russians in the east. Even today the Soviet-Polish frontier follows exactly the same line as Stalin and Hitler agreed on secretly back in 1939, after which Hitler was able to launch the second world war. Hitler's defeat and Stalin's victory and the proclamation of a socialist Poland have done nothing to change the frontier between the Soviet Union and Poland which Moscow and Berlin fixed by secret agreement back in 1939. I am amazed that the public is so little aware of such an important fact. There are very few people in Yugoslavia today who remember it, and those who did know have forgotten it.

The Russians, it seems, will never have enough territory or space, even though Russia is at least twice as big in area as the largest states in the world, such as China and the United States. In World War II alone the Russians increased their vast territory by something like two or three Yugoslavias. First of all, interpreting in their own way the pact with Hitler following the partition of Poland, they "swallowed up" the three Baltic states—Estonia, Latvia, and Lithuania. Then they went to war against Finland, from which at the end of the world war they seized territories which had been Finnish and not Russian. Then they changed to their own advantage their frontiers in the Carpathians with Czechoslovakia, from which they detached Ruthenia, and those with Romania, from which they annexed Bessarabia and the northern Bukovina. Then, at the end of the war, they abolished eastern Prussia and included part of it in Russia as a separate region, to the capital of which, the German city of

Königsberg, they gave the Russian name of Kaliningrad. There were no longer any Germans there.

Later the Russians extended their territories in Asia and the Pacific. When Japan was already on the brink of defeat in its struggle with a powerful enemy in the form of the United States of America, Stalin declared war on Japan and, in the course of a conflict which lasted only a week, not only took back from the defeated Japanese all the territories which Tsar Nicholas II had lost in the Russo-Japanese war of 1904 but also annexed fresh Japanese territories to the Soviet Union—the islands of the Kuril Archipelago. By so doing the Russians turned the Sea of Okhotsk into a sort of *mare nostrum,* and even today the Russians continue to hold on to these Japanese territories. The Japanese kept the territories which they took from Tsar Nicholas II for forty years. In all probability the Russians will hold on for at least as long to the territories which they seized from the Japanese in the last war.

The great powers in the West, victors in World War II, have remained, as far as territory is concerned, within their own national frontiers. Those who had a colonial empire have mostly lost their colonial possessions or are going to lose them very soon. The Soviet Union alone succeeded in extending its national territory, both in the west and in the east. And so the state which was already the biggest became still bigger, while its smaller neighbors became even smaller. To say nothing of the fact that the Soviet Union drew into its orbit seven European socialist states with about 80 million Europeans. And in Europe from time immemorial land and people had been more precious than in other continents right up to this last war.

The airport in Kiev was very much like the one in Lvov. But it seems to me that Kiev Airport was considerably larger and, since everything was the same as in Lvov, everything I have described already was all the more striking. In Kiev as in Lvov, in a central position in the airport building there were enormous portraits of Stalin in very bright colors and in gold wherever it was possible to gild them. In his marshal's uniform and from his Olympian heights, Stalin continued to look out from the walls into the far distance above our heads as though the Twentieth Congress of the CPSU had never taken place and Khrushchev's secret speech had never been pronounced.

We arrived in Vnukovo Airport in Moscow at nine o'clock in the evening and were met by the head of the Protocol Department of the Soviet Foreign Ministry, Molochkov.[13] The reception was friendly. Molochkov is obviously very good at his job. From the very outset he managed to

---

[13] Fedor Molochkov, b. 1906. Soviet diplomat. Head of Protocol Department, Foreign Ministry, 1947–50 and from 1955; Soviet Minister to Switzerland, 1950–55.

create an atmosphere as though we were old acquaintances. He himself makes a good impression and offered to be of assistance to me the very next day. Also there to greet me were the diplomatic staff of our embassy in Moscow, most of whom I knew already. Meeting them reminded me of the very touching "partisan" send-off I had been given at Zemun. Then we set out in the darkness on the long journey from Vnukovo Airport to the Yugoslav embassy in Moscow, in Krasnaya Presnya, one of the oldest districts of Moscow, which saw some of the bitterest fighting in the Russian Revolution of 1905. It was a cold March night. Moscow was enveloped in darkness.

The comrades from our embassy drew my attention to the fact that we were getting near the Kremlin and that even at night there was something to be seen. Its towers and walls were well illuminated and looked very impressive, although from the car I could see only a part of it. But even this first sight of the Kremlin did not interrupt the flow of the conversation which we embarked on immediately after leaving Vnukovo Airport. The comrades from the embassy told me in detail how a network of Soviet secret gadgets and "bugging" devices had recently been discovered and destroyed in our embassy. Nineteen microphones had been found, connected by wires installed underneath the parquet floors in all the rooms and in some places in the ceilings between the plaster and the concrete. Two microphones were found in each of the large rooms in our embassy; but in the smaller rooms one was sufficient. They told me that the whole building was "wired for sound," starting with the ambassador's bedroom.

The concealed arrangements for eavesdropping on us were technically rather out of date, but to all appearances they worked very well. We have been in this building now for some ten years. Before us the Japanese had it; they left the building when the Russians declared war on Japan. Then the Russians moved the Yugoslavs in and went on listening in to them as they had to the Japanese. The Russians may already have fixed up a new, more up-to-date bugging arrangement. In any case I am now, from the day of my arrival, going to have the Soviet police at my gate, and probably more of them than my predecessors in Moscow, despite our "reconciliation." The Russians probably know that it was I who, three months ago, sent to Moscow a team of people from the State Security Service to carry out a thorough inspection of our embassy building to defeat any bugging devices. There was quite a lot of talk about this in Belgrade and it could easily have reached the Russians' ears.

With regard to our general approach and attitude to the Russians I told the comrades that Comrade Tito had said that "we should not quarrel with the Russians, but we should not give in to them." It certainly won't be easy to stick to this rule, and it will not be a simple matter to judge when we should quarrel with them so as not to make concessions and when we should make concessions so as not to quarrel. Nor is it very satisfactory that I shall more often than not have to decide about this myself, here, poised over the rift between Belgrade and Moscow.

CHAPTER TWO

MEETING THE SOVIET LEADERS

At his first meetings with Khrushchev and other Soviet leaders and from his first sampling of public opinion in the Soviet Union Mićunović finds to his surprise that support for Khrushchev and the policy of "de-Stalinization" is less than he thought. Khrushchev appears to be in a minority in the Presidium of the Communist party, and there is reaction in the ranks of the party against his speech denouncing Stalin. The outlook for Soviet-Yugoslav relations is consequently less bright than had been thought.

Moscow, March 27, 1956

Yesterday I called on Molochkov, head of the Protocol Department of the Soviet Foreign Ministry, and agreed with him a list of the Soviet leaders whom I would like to see once I have delivered my letters of accreditation. Molochkov left it all to me, his duty amounting simply to making a note of the names I read out, though I thought I would have to agree the list with him. He did not add or remove a single name on the short list I dictated to him.

Only an hour or two after my conversation with Molochkov I had a call from the Soviet Foreign Ministry to say that Molotov,[1] the Foreign Minister, would receive me next day at ten o'clock. We regarded this as a piece of good news, because we would not have been surprised if we had had to wait a week to be received by Molotov. There were times, just before our conflict with the Soviet Union, when members of our govern-

---

[1] Vyacheslav M. Molotov, b. 1890. Soviet statesman. Member of Politburo, CPSU, 1926–57; Secretary, Central Committee, CPSU, 1921–36; Foreign Minister, 1939–49 and 1953–56. In 1957 dismissed from all senior posts in party and government as member of "antiparty group." Ambassador to Outer Mongolia, 1957–60; Soviet representative on International Atomic Energy Conference in Vienna, 1960–62. Now living in retirement.

ment had waited here a month to be received. Comrade Milentije Popović,[2] for example, waited more than a month for Mikoyan,[3] his Soviet counterpart in the government, to receive him. Mikoyan was always "busy," while Milentije went every evening to a Moscow theater and waited to be received.

There was a good atmosphere at the meeting with Molotov. The conversation was spontaneous, at times even cordial, as if it were a chat between old acquaintances who had not seen each other for a long time. There was not the slightest hint that we had been involved for ten years in an ideological and political war which Molotov himself had started as the joint author and signatory of the threatening letters which he and Stalin sent to the Yugoslav leaders then in 1948. Although I was in no hurry to hand over my letters of accreditation, Molotov promised to speak to Voroshilov[4] the very next day and insist that the matter should be dealt with as soon as possible.

Molotov was of the opinion that relations between us were making good progress and that practically everything we had agreed with the Soviet delegation in Belgrade last year had been resolved, but said that if there was still anything unresolved we could clear it up very quickly. ·

I did not disagree with him, although I was of the opposite opinion. Molotov made himself quite clear when he spoke of the Belgrade Declaration as something already put into practice in the course of the past few months, from which it followed that we should now prepare a new political foundation for our relations. Although I considered that in essence we had not even begun to put the declaration into effect, I kept silent and agreed with Molotov.

My first meeting with Molotov was clearly not the occasion for talking about the past or about the condemnation of Stalin at their Twentieth Party Congress. For thirty years Molotov had been Stalin's closest associate and along with him an initiator of the aggressive policy of the Soviet Union aimed at subjugating Yugoslavia. In Belgrade we heard that Molotov had opposed the policy of normalizing relations between Yugoslavia and the Soviet Union initiated by Khrushchev. Even if Molotov had raised this question, I would not have thought this the occasion to rub salt into the wounds.

Molotov referred to the Twentieth Congress as proof of the unity and

[2] Milentije Popović, 1913–71. Served as both Minister of Foreign Trade and Minister of Finance in the Yugoslav Government. Member of Executive Committee, League of Communists, from 1966.

[3] Anastas I. Mikoyan, b. 1895. Soviet statesman. Member of Politburo, CPSU, 1935–66; Deputy Prime Minister, 1937–64; Chairman, Presidium of Supreme Soviet, 1964–65. Now living in retirement.

[4] Kliment E. Voroshilov, 1881–1970. Soviet statesman. Marshal. Member of Politburo, CPSU, 1926–60; Minister of Defense, 1925–40; Deputy Prime Minister, 1940–53; Chairman, Presidium of Supreme Soviet, 1953–60.

strength of the Soviet Union. I agreed with him and told him that we in Yugoslavia had declared the unanimous support of our party for the congress resolution, as we had informed the Central Committee of the Communist party of the Soviet Union officially. I told Molotov that in Belgrade we hoped that the political course laid down by the Twentieth Congress of the CPSU would have the effect of improving the situation in Europe, abating the cold war and normalizing international relations.

Molotov received my linking of the Twentieth Congress with international relations (and not with Khrushchev's secret speech about Stalin) with evident relief and interrupted me to say that he fully agreed with my views and that the Soviet Government would undertake further steps in that direction.

The conversation with Molotov lasted about half an hour. I am happy to record that this first meeting with him made a very favorable impression on me. Molotov is already in his seventies and spent thirty years at Stalin's elbow as his closest associate. He was in fact the executor of Stalin's policies and not his collaborator, because Stalin had no need for collaborators. He succeeded not only in surviving but in remaining after the great tyrant's death among the top leaders of the Soviet Union. It appears to have turned out to his advantage that in the last years of Stalin's life he too began to fall into disfavor.

I was left with the impression that although Molotov is Minister of Foreign Affairs he does not hold in his hands the main threads of Soviet foreign policy, at least as far as Yugoslavia is concerned. Although the normalization of our relations with the Russians last year represented a major move by the Soviet Union in foreign policy, Molotov played no part in it personally, nor was he among the Soviet representatives who traveled to Belgrade. In the conversation with me, apart from two or three routine phrases, he had nothing to say about this. We were informed that Molotov had been opposed to sending a Soviet delegation to Belgrade. He had agreed with the restoration of normal interstate relations with Yugoslavia; but in his opinion the Yugoslavs should have gone to Moscow to discuss the matter and not waited for the Russians to come to them cap in hand.

Bearing all this in mind, I considered that this was not the moment to be overenthusiastic about our "reconciliation" with the Russians. Instead of discussing our affairs, we talked more about West European Social Democrats.

Moscow, March 29, 1956

On the very next day after my call on Molotov I was received by Marshal Voroshilov, the nominal head of the Soviet state, to deliver my letters of accreditation. Such prompt attention by the Soviet leaders was beyond anything I had hoped for. It is all going very well, but when things go too well, there is a possibility that things won't turn out so well in the end.

I altered the text of my speech at the Voroshilov reception, and I think I improved it a little, because the text I received from the Foreign Secretariat in Belgrade was far too dry and colorless, strictly according to pattern and written in a sort of legal language. I thought it would be better, by making some slight improvements in the text, to respond to the exceptional attention shown me here.

The ceremony of presenting my letters of accreditation struck me as being both simple and solemn at the same time. The solemnity probably comes about of its own accord. It all takes place in the Kremlin, and for the majority of new ambassadors it is probably the first time they set foot inside the place, which would be a special experience even without the accreditation ceremony.

The Kremlin is very impressive. It is larger, more complex in its structure, and much better preserved than I had thought. As far as I could see on this first visit, it struck me as being very unusual in the way it brings together, next to each other, different architectural styles of various periods in both the East and the West. The tall towers around the Kremlin remind one of the East and Asia, almost of military camps and invading hordes. The royal palaces and chambers recall another world, the West and Europe. And the churches with their gilded cupolas rising high above it all recall the ancient, Orthodox, Imperial Russia.

At various periods in the course of many centuries all sorts of architects from Russia and abroad built on this spot structures of timber, stone, brick, glass, lead, iron, and gold, and so in their way recorded the history of "Mother Russia," which is still ruled from here in the spirit of the old Russian saying: "Who rules the Kremlin rules Russia." The correctness of this saying was confirmed in the time of Stalin's autocratic rule with more force than in the time of the Tsars, back as far as the reign of Ivan Grozny.[5] After the October Revolution Lenin transferred the capital of Russia from Petrograd to Moscow, not in order to cut himself off from the people behind the walls and towers of the Kremlin, but because Petrograd was right on the frontier and might at any moment be occupied by the hostile west. In the few years which remained to him as leader of the first socialist country in the world Lenin opened the gates of the Kremlin to the citizens of Moscow and of Russia. His successor, Stalin, after asserting his own unlimited power over Russia, closed the gates again and ruled Russia and the "world Communist movement" for

[5] Tsar Ivan IV, 1530–84, known as "the Terrible."

24

all of thirty years, until his death, from within the walls, the towers, the churches, and the palaces.

Unlike Molotov, who carefully avoided making any reference to the long conflict between Yugoslavia and the Soviet Union, Voroshilov raised the subject right away and straightforwardly, without any beating about the bush. He said that it was "impossible" for anyone today to understand how such terrible and frightful things could happen between us, that it should never occur again, that Yugoslavs and Russians were real brothers, that they had fought and died together in the most difficult times when they had been thousands of kilometers apart from each other, that the Yugoslav comrades had suffered terrible unjust attacks by the Russians, and that much harm had been done. In his conversation he made frequent references to God in various combinations: in God's name, for God's sake, God knows, and so forth.

Voroshilov asked me where I came from. When he heard me say that I was a Montenegrin, he was simply overjoyed. He asked me with some hesitation whether the Montenegrins belonged to the Orthodox faith. When I confirmed that they are Orthodox, explained that Montenegro is on the dividing line between the Moslem and Catholic worlds, and that the Montenegrins are therefore "genuine Orthodox," Voroshilov's face lit up as though he had received a piece of unexpected good news. He seized me by the hand and assured me that everything between us would now be different and better and that all obstacles in the way of our friendship had been removed. He did not ask me whether I was a member of the Central Committee of the Communist party in Yugoslavia, but whether, as a Montenegrin, I belonged to the Orthodox Church. The latter was more important to him, it appears, than the former.

When I told Voroshilov that there were altogether only about 400,000 Montenegrins, he was seriously disappointed. I made a slight "concession" and said there were actually up to half a million of us but that we were spread all over Yugoslavia, and that Belgrade, in Serbia, was the largest Montenegrin city. This was too complicated for Voroshilov, who remained disappointed at the small number of Montenegrins. He questioned me two or three times whether he had heard correctly that I had said there were no more than 400,000 of us.

Voroshilov is in very good form physically. He is one of the few Soviet leaders today who became long ago, even at the time of the October Revolution and the Civil War, a legend in the popular imagination. At the Twentieth Congress of the Soviet Communist party last month he was again elected a member of the small circle of ten people who lead the Soviet Union, of which he is the nominal head of state. His personal contribution to the formation of the new, post-Stalin policy of the Soviet

Union is probably very limited. Even if he put his weight behind the new anti-Stalinist policy, his efforts might be more of a hindrance than a help to those who are really carrying out the new policy. Voroshilov has long since outlived his political time. But his name remains popular with the broad masses of the people in the Soviet Union and can still do a lot to help or hinder others to achieve something. That's the way it is in a society and system in which legend and myth are mixed with reality, insofar as it suits those who make the reality.

Although my meetings with Molotov and Voroshilov do not mean that I have really begun my work in Moscow, it is significant that the meetings were arranged so quickly and that they went off so well, whatever may happen on this slippery Yugoslav-Soviet path in the future.

Moscow, April 2, 1956

On March 29 I requested, through Molochkov, the head of Protocol at the Soviet Foreign Ministry, to be received first by Bulganin, Soviet Prime Minister, and then by Khrushchev, First Secretary of the CPSU. But the Russians have changed the order and informed me that Khrushchev could receive me today, April 2, saying nothing about my request to see Bulganin. Although this change didn't please me much, I accepted nevertheless a decision taken by the Soviet side. This begins now to look like the beginning of my real work in Moscow, since the Russians are taking decisions to suit themselves without reference to my requests.

Khrushchev received me at three in the afternoon in the Central Committee building on Kuibyshev Street in the center of Moscow. As I waited, perhaps no more than a minute, for Khrushchev to invite me in, I cast my eyes over the walls of the office of his private secretary. There hung portraits of Lenin and Stalin, facing one another, and I thought to myself: If Stalin's portrait is still hanging in Khrushchev's office, what is happening in the rest of the Soviet Union? If Khrushchev is not yet able to get rid of Stalin from his office in Moscow, how can he be removed from Russia? My reflections were interrupted by one of the staff who slipped silently out of Khrushchev's office and invited me to go in. I met Khrushchev where he stood beside a very large desk covered with a green cloth. The greeting was cordial. Khrushchev bid me welcome, said we were old acquaintances and that we would therefore work together all the better. He then left it to me to speak, and I said in a dozen sentences what was required by the occasion. I conveyed greetings from our Central Committee, the government, and Comrade Tito, and our sincere congratulations on the results of the Twentieth Congress, saying that we considered that it marked a turning point of historic significance not only for the Soviet Union but also for socialism in the world. I reminded Khrushchev of Kardelj's official statement to this effect a few days ago. Khrushchev said he had read the statement and agreed with it.

I did not intend at the very beginning to refer to the secret speech and the condemnation of Stalin. It seemed to me better to leave this subject to Khrushchev. But he remained silent, and it seemed to me as if he thought I had not yet said all I needed to say. So I went on to thank him on behalf of our Central Committee and Comrade Tito for having let us have a copy of the secret speech on Stalin, which had been read out at a closed session of our Central Committee and had been unanimously approved as an act of far-reaching historic importance. We considered that it was not just a matter of telling the truth about Stalin, but that it involved a general break with the past and the opening up of new and broader perspectives for the further advance of socialism in the Soviet Union and the world at large.

In Yugoslavia, I continued, we had long since outlived and disposed of all dilemmas concerning Stalin. Therefore, when today we approved unanimously the Twentieth Congress and his speech about Stalin, we did not act out of any narrow, selfish Yugoslav motives. It was not that. We looked at the whole matter in a wider context and not in the light only of Yugoslav-Soviet relations in Stalinist times, although we were pleased that in his speech Khrushchev had condemned Stalin's policy toward Yugoslavia. I told Khrushchev that I had had several opportunities of talking to Comrade Tito, that he attached historic significance to his speech condemning Stalin and thoroughly approved of the general political line adopted by the Twentieth Congress.

It seemed to me that Khrushchev had only been waiting for this statement of mine to take the floor immediately afterward. He said that they had been faced with a historic dilemma: to condemn Stalin or not. They were concerned about the difficulties which would result primarily in the Soviet Union itself and which would be part of the political struggle to follow here. "We shall also have difficulties abroad," Khrushchev said. "But the capitalists will realize that we are strong since we are able to break with Stalin in this decisive way; anyone who is weak would not undertake anything of that kind."

"We debated this question for a long time," Khrushchev said. The Central Committee of the party was unanimous, but the Presidium was not. That was understandable, since several of the members had been close to Stalin for many long years. But even that was not the main issue; it was a question of different interpretations of the present situation and of the perspectives ahead. Finally all the members of the Presidium agreed that Stalin should be condemned at the Twentieth Congress.

Khrushchev is sure that all difficulties will be overcome and that they will come out of this battle far stronger politically for having condemned Stalin.

Khrushchev made a brief excursion into history to explain to me why Stalin sent him to the Ukraine in 1938 after the liquidation of the Ukrainian Politburo members Kosior[6] and Postyshev.[7] Khrushchev said that right up to 1929 he alone of the ruling Russians had lived in the Ukraine, that he spoke Ukrainian, and that Stalin knew him well from his work in Moscow and had confidence in him. Of Kosior Khrushchev had only the best to say, but added that he was too easygoing and by nature a gentle person, while the difficulties in the Ukraine were enormous, and Stalin decided that the Ukrainian party needed to be led by a tough person. "Stalin liquidated Kosior because he was too soft and Postyshev because he was tough and that's the way he was with Stalin," Khrushchev said. "Both of them were very honest men and Communists with excellent records, yet see how they finished up. They have now been rehabilitated at the Twentieth Congress, but you can't raise the dead from their graves."

At that time, Khrushchev continued, Stalin, the "genius," had thought up one of those slogans which had the force of law in the Soviet Union. At some conference in the thirties he declared that "little people" could do things of the greatest importance for the country. This idea spread throughout Russia and was continually being reaffirmed as a new law of Marxism-Leninism discovered by Stalin. Thousands of "small people" emerged and began to perform their "great services." In fact, the slogan was an invitation to Soviet citizens to denounce and accuse one another.

The result of this was, Khrushchev said, that false accusations were made against thousands of good Communists and honest people. It was even done anonymously, although some of the "little people" signed their denunciations. In this way a new profession was created in the Soviet Union. As an example of the "little Soviet people" whom Stalin mobilized at the time of the great purges, Khrushchev told me some detail about a woman in Kiev. She alone, Khrushchev said, and those who used her, had on their consciences, as far as could be ascertained later, the execution of some eight thousand people.

Khrushchev told me that he had spoken with Stalin about this woman and had told him frankly his opinion that it was a case of a very sick per-

[6] Stanislav Kosior, 1889–1939. Soviet Communist official of Polish origin. First Secretary of Communist Party of the Ukraine, 1928–38; Member of Politburo, CPSU, 1930–38. Arrested 1938, executed 1939.
[7] Pavel Postyshev, 1887–1939. Soviet Communist official. Secretary, Central Committee, CPSU, 1930–33; Member of Politburo, CPSU, 1933–37. Arrested in purge and executed 1939.

son. He told Stalin of scenes in the streets of Kiev when people, especially officers, against whom the woman was particularly spiteful, would rush to the other side of the street so as not to meet her. "If you could only have seen how Stalin looked as I told him that," Khruschchev said and, after a brief pause, went on: "The question may be asked today, and it is being asked in the Soviet Union in some places, where were *we*, the members of the present Presidium and Central Committee of the CPSU, and what were *we* doing when all this was going on? Why did we let it happen, why did we remain silent about all the things that we now produce in condemnation of Stalin?" Khrushchev referred to the catastrophe of the Central Committee of the CPSU elected at the Seventeenth Congress. About 70 percent of the members of the Central Committee elected at the Congress were liquidated with or without the benefit of a trial. It was all accompanied by thousands of party conferences up and down the country singing Stalin's praises. Khrushchev argued that it would have been exactly the same if a few of those who remained alive and were now leading the party and government had opposed Stalin and his mad ways. The only difference would have been that the number of Communists killed would have been greater, but only by a hundredth part of 1 percent. That is all that would have happened, he said.

I was ready on my part to bring the meeting to an end and simply raise the question of Tito's visit, and I began to thank Khrushchev for his friendly reception, but at that point he proposed that we drink tea, saying that conversation flows more easily over tea. While we were waiting for it to be brought, Khrushchev said he wanted to acquaint me with the situation in the country following the Twentieth Congress and the condemnation of Stalin. He said there had been disturbances in Georgia, about which I had probably heard something. Demoralized elements in Georgia had taken advantage of the third anniversary of Stalin's death to provoke disorder and demonstrations in Tbilisi. Anti-Soviet speeches had been made in public places. "We intervened very sharply," Khrushchev said. "And we used troops where necessary and quickly restored order."

Why was it in Georgia that this happened, Khrushchev asked, when Stalin, though himself a Georgian, had been neither particularly nasty to the Georgians nor particularly nice? If it were a question of percentages, Stalin had killed more Georgians than Russians or members of any other of the peoples of the Soviet Union. Only the "Volga Germans," the Tatars, the Chechen, and a few other national minorities had suffered toward the end of World War II worse than the Georgians.[8] Stalin could

---

[8] The Volga Germans are descendants of German farmers invited to settle in Russia in the eighteenth century by Catherine the Great. Under the Soviet regime they enjoyed the status of an "autonomous republic." In September 1941 Stalin decreed that the whole population of the republic, probably amounting to more than 400,000 peo-

not be considered in any sense to have been a protector of the Georgians.

Toward the end of Stalin's life the situation changed, thanks not to Stalin but to Beria,[9] Khrushchev said. Beria was a fanatical Georgian nationalist who was at the same time the executioner of some Georgians and the protector of others. Nobody could do anything in Georgia without Beria and certainly not against him. The execution of Beria and now the condemnation of Stalin demoralized certain groups of people in Georgia, the only place where there had been any resistance. Now there is peace and quiet there, people have turned sullen, "a few" were killed or wounded, they all now admitted the error of their ways, repented, and were making promises, but we shan't be caught off our guard, Khrushchev said.

He was sure that they were going to have trouble with the West as well, because the West would take advantage of the new situation in the Soviet Union to reduce Soviet prestige in the world and to provoke discord in the country itself. We discussed some public statements which had already been made in that sense. The most reactionary circles were now pretending hypocritically to regret that Stalin had been condemned in Moscow and were even beginning to praise him, saying that with Stalin they were able "to come to terms easily and knew where they stood," which was no longer possible in relations with the Soviet Union. The suggestion was that there was no longer any certainty about what was going to happen tomorrow here.

The Russians had been obliged to act in this way with regard to Stalin, Khrushchev said. He had been leading the Soviet Union to disaster. As he advanced in years the sick, perverted side of his character took over. Borne down by age and sickness, in the final years of his life Stalin learned about Russia and the world from films which were made specially for him, and he ruled the country in the belief that everything in the Soviet Union was prospering, Khrushchev said.

They had had talks here, Khrushchev continued, with all the Communist parties belonging to the Cominform[10] before and during the Twentieth Congress and they decided to dissolve the organization. But the ques-

---

ple, were to be transported to Siberia and Central Asia, from where they have not been permitted to return. In 1943 and 1944 a similar fate befell other, indigenous national minority peoples living in the Northern Caucasus and the Crimea—the Crimean Tatars, the Chechen, the Ingush, the Karachai, the Balkars, and the Kalmucks—all of whom were alleged to have collaborated with the German invading forces. The total number of peoples thus deported is estimated to be in the region of 1,250,000.

[9] Lavrenti P. Beria, 1899–1953. Soviet Communist official and Stalin's last police chief. Member of Politburo, CPSU, 1946–53; People's Commissar and Minister for Internal Affairs, 1946–53. Arrested June 1953 and believed executed the same year.

[10] See p. 6, footnote 6.

tion remained: What next? They had to have some kind of organization for cooperation between the Communist parties. The West was also organized. Above all they must have a new organization for cooperation between the Communist parties now in power in Eastern Europe, and there was also the question of cooperation between the Western European Communist parties. Khrushchev assured me that he had rejected the idea of proposing a link between the Communist parties of Western Europe. "Let the Europeans decide that," he said. "They don't need Russian advice, they know best what to do." That was why Thorez[11] had been in Rome recently to talk with Togliatti.[12] Whatever the French and Italian Communists agreed to, that's the way it would be.

There was a similar problem in the case of Asia, where he had sent Mikoyan, who also had "other jobs to do." He would discuss the matter with the Chinese and others. What the Chinese thought was very important. Moreover the question of cooperation with the Communist parties of both Americas should also be settled in some way. Those parties were weak and small, and their links with the CPSU were much weaker than they were said to be in the West. Khrushchev said that the formation of four new regional organizations of Communist parties seemed to suggest itself: two for Europe, one each for Asia and America. He did not refer to Africa or the Arab world. Khrushchev spoke to me about this so that I could pass it on to Tito.

After thanking Khrushchev for his remarks, I said that all this was completely new to me and that I could not tell him what they thought about it in Belgrade or what might be the attitude of our leaders. At the same time I was free to give him my own immediate reaction, although I was not sufficiently familiar with the subject. I thought that it would certainly not be a good idea for us, immediately after dissolving the Cominform, to set up a new and similar international organization of Communist parties. And not just one organization but three or four in the place of the one Cominform which Stalin had set up and which had died politically even while Stalin was still alive.

In the new conditions collaboration between the Communist parties, and beginning with the Soviet and Yugoslav parties, should be voluntary, free, and in a spirit of equality, without the involvement of any international organizations to direct or control it. Contacts and joint actions would come about naturally according to the interests of one or the other side or of both sides. As for us Yugoslavs I was sure that the existence of the old Cominform or the creation of a new one would be a major obsta-

[11] Maurice Thorez, 1900–64. French Communist leader. Secretary-General, French Communist party, 1930–64.
[12] Palmiro Togliatti, 1893–1964. Italian Communist leader. Secretary-General, Italian Communist party, 1926–64.

cle to normal party cooperation both with the Russians and with the others.

Emphasizing once again that I was speaking entirely on my own behalf, I said we would be giving the West another chance to accuse communism of being more aggressive now than it had been in Stalin's time if we were to organize four new Cominforms in place of the one we had had. Khrushchev cut me off with the statement that we should not be afraid of a battle with the bourgeoisie, a battle that we would have to launch when the situation demanded it of us. He went on to say that there still existed the possibility of war or of the forcible overthrow, from outside or inside, of the government in one of the socialist countries of Europe, for example. We ought to unite all our forces and to have a suitable organization, Khrushchev said. For the French and Italian Communists it was a quite different matter, but for the countries of Eastern Europe a new organization was essential. As an argument in support of linking the CPSU with all the Communist parties in the world Khrushchev cited the Communist party of Indonesia. He said that in that country millions of people vote for the Communist party, yet we have no links at all with it. Is that really right?

This part of the conversation was the most important politically. But it remained inconclusive. Although I spoke only in my own name, it seems to me I sowed some doubts in Khrushchev's mind with regard to his general idea of setting up new, regional organizations of Communist parties. But I didn't have the least effect on him as far as the "socialist camp" is concerned. The Russians regard Eastern Europe as their own internal affair and, to judge from all the evidence, they will not need anybody's approval, and certainly not the Yugoslavs', for any solutions they may decide on.

The conversation lasted nearly four hours! I had been ready to leave, and to leave quite satisfied, after fifteen or twenty minutes, but it lasted so much longer because of Khrushchev's interest in the conversation. During those four hours nobody entered his office and there was not a single call on any of the many telephones on his desk.

Moscow, April 3, 1956

This afternoon I was received by Bulganin, the Soviet Prime Minister. He has an office in the Kremlin, and everything seemed more formal than yesterday with Khrushchev, although he has the most important position. The conversation was again very long, although nothing was said on either side that was particularly new or much different from what was said yesterday by Khrushchev. As the conversation took the same course as yesterday and the same questions were raised, so the comments were the same. Bulganin produced some interesting details about some things, as for example when he informed me about the demonstrations in Georgia he told me appreciably more than did Khrushchev, though Khrushchev was much more talkative.

Bulganin said that the events in Georgia had developed into an anti-Soviet action and that the disorders had lasted for two or three days. There had been one slogan demanding "Down with Soviet power" and another in praise of Stalin. Bulganin said that he, Khrushchev, and Mikoyan were specially attacked. There were shouts of "Down with Bulganin" and "Molotov for Prime Minister." The demonstrators wanted to release Stalin's son, the former general Vasili Stalin,[13] who Bulganin said was a good-for-nothing ruined by drink, now in prison but not for political reasons. The Georgians knew that Vasili Stalin had been arrested and used the fact to mobilize people and get them out onto the streets. The authorities had intervened vigorously with troops and had restored order; there were dead and wounded. Bulganin said he was telling me all this in confidence, as one comrade to another, that these matters were politically very delicate for the Soviet Union, but that he wanted me to know what had really happened in Georgia. It was clear from the conversation with Bulganin as a whole that there was complete agreement between him and Khrushchev on all the matters touched on, in other words that Khrushchev is personality number one in the Soviet leadership.

Pravda and all the principal Soviet newspapers on sale in Moscow yesterday reported on their front pages my meetings with Khrushchev and Bulganin. My earlier calls on Voroshilov and Molotov were also reported very prominently. All this has created an atmosphere warmer than normal, which does not correspond with the real state of Yugoslav-Soviet relations. It doesn't seem to me a good thing for a new ambassador to take up his duties with such a lot of fuss, especially when it concerns a Yugoslav ambassador in Moscow. It would be better if everything were quieter and more normal. As it is, it is scarcely surprising that the Soviet public and the majority of the observers here imagine that something new and important is taking place between Yugoslavia and the Soviet Union. This impression must suit the Russians very well if they surround the new Yugoslav ambassador with such attention two months before Tito's visit to Moscow.

[13] Vasili Stalin. Stalin had two sons, of whom the elder one, Yakov, by his first wife, Catherine Svanidze, is believed to have died in a German prisoner-of-war camp toward the end of World War II. The younger son, Vasili, was born to Stalin's second wife, Nadezhda Alliluyeva, and became a general in the Soviet Air Force. He survived the war and his father, and died in 1962 after leading for many years a very drunken and dissipated life. His sister Svetlana escaped from the Soviet Union in 1967 and now lives in America.

As I looked again through my notes on the conversation with Bulganin, I found particularly interesting what he said about the slogans shouted by the demonstrators in Tbilisi: "Down with Bulganin" and "Molotov for Prime Minister." Here in Moscow they ordered troops to open fire on Soviet citizens who were demanding to have Molotov as Prime Minister. And all this was taking place after the Twentieth Congress of the CPSU. Apart from Bulganin the demonstrators also demanded the removal of Khrushchev and Mikoyan. This prompts some reflections about the situation among the Soviet leaders, and the picture does not look as rosy as Khrushchev indicated to me the day before yesterday. There can be no doubt that Bulganin had decided in advance to tell me about Molotov and the disorders in Georgia, and that it was no accident that the demonstrators demanded Molotov as Prime Minister. The political sense was also obvious in Bulganin's mentioning of only Khrushchev and Mikoyan, apart from himself, as being on the other, opposite side. He made no reference at all to any of the other ten members and candidate members of the Presidium. This all came out as part of the description of what the demonstrators had done in Tbilisi, and not, of course, as in any way reflecting the views of anybody here. But it is not difficult to guess that this is not just a question of what the demonstrators had in mind.

Moscow, April 6, 1956

At a reception in the Czechoslovak embassy last night I was introduced to and had a talk with Kaganovich,[14] a member of the Presidium of the CPSU. But the conversation, as well as the speech he delivered later in the presence of some fifteen hundred guests including the Moscow diplomatic corps, left an unpleasant impression. Kaganovich spoke entirely in the old manner, adopting the attitude of an "elder brother," as they used to say here in Stalin's time.

He behaved similarly in his conversation with me. He had no comment to make on what I said about the favorable development of our relations, the good prospects for the future, the very good and friendly reception I had met with in Moscow, and our support for the Twentieth Congress of the CPSU. Kaganovich said only that Tito should come here and that they would resolve with him the question of cooperation between our parties and all other problems—"and in a proper Marxist-Leninist way."

Kaganovich's speech evoked various commentaries among the diplomatic corps. He stressed that Czechoslovakia was a cultured, industrially developed European country, that this was true, because he had been

[14] Lazar M. Kaganovich, b. 1893. Soviet Communist official. Member of Politburo, CPSU, 1930–57. Dismissed from leading positions as member of "antiparty group" in 1957 and has since been living in retirement.

there and seen with his own eyes, that the Czechs were building socialism all right and were manufacturing all sorts of machines. Only he couldn't remember what machines to mention, and just said vaguely that the Czechs made machines and bicycles! Then he stressed that there could be no socialism without the "camp," then affirmed that socialism could be built by parliamentary means as had been shown in Czechoslovakia, that the Soviet Union was for peace but that it also knew how to fight, and more of that sort of stuff. The only thing lacking was that he should also say something in praise of Stalin. It was clear that Kaganovich was not able to grasp what was going on or to understand the Twentieth Congress, from which he is probably far from being in sympathy.

The Czechoslovak embassy has only recently been built and is bigger than any other embassy in Moscow. The Czechs invite to such receptions about two thousand people, while the majority of the other embassies can scarcely invite a tenth of that number. Consequently Kaganovich had last night an exceptionally large audience. He was for nearly thirty years close to Stalin in the Soviet leadership and on that basis has retained his place in the new Presidium after the Twentieth Congress. It is difficult to fit all this together and explain it. The potential political strength of the new course and the Congress appears to us to be enormous, but listening to Kaganovich last night you might have thought that the Twentieth Congress had never taken place.

Moscow, April 18, 1956

Here in Moscow we Yugoslavs have nothing which might be called an intelligence service, even of the most primitive kind. We are forbidden to travel outside Moscow except with special permission from the Soviet Government. Soviet citizens do not dare to invite any of us to their homes or for a "cup of tea," let alone to lunch or dinner.

In official contacts with us the Russians mostly do not wish to talk about Khrushchev's secret speech or his condemnation of Stalin. I have already made more than fifteen calls on Soviet leaders and top officials, but only Khrushchev and Bulganin spoke about the speech. In numerous contacts with Russians, apart from some rare exceptions, members of our embassy staff are unable to discuss it because the Russians will say nothing. In our casual contacts with Soviet citizens it is also very difficult to talk about it because the Russians as a rule avoid the subject. Not exactly the best of signs!

When some members of our staff have had the opportunity to ask some Russians directly about the condemnation of Stalin, they have usually received replies to the effect that all this is very difficult for them, that they don't know why it was necessary, that they grew up with Stalin as leader of the Soviet Union, that with him they were victorious in the worst war that Russia ever fought, that they had made out of Stalin a genius and a god, which they now had to destroy with their own hands, and so forth. So far we have not come upon a single case where a Soviet citizen has spoken of the condemnation of Stalin with a sense of personal satisfaction or with the conviction that it was necessary to act in this way (apart, of course, from Khrushchev and Bulganin).

We have reports that fifteen days ago, the Presidium of the CPSU ordered that there were to be no more of the closed party meetings in the Soviet Union at which Khrushchev's secret speech has been read out. These meetings started up the day after the Twentieth Congress. As far as we can learn, the Khrushchev speech was well received at the first meetings, but immediately afterward it appeared that the speech was bringing confusion and discord into the party over Stalin. It seemed as though this was the only question in the Soviet Union today and that the Twentieth Congress had been held only because of Stalin. The political program of the Congress was brushed aside, as though it had never existed.

It is already becoming apparent that the fact that Khrushchev's speech was kept secret is not helping acceptance of the new course, since Russia has in some way eventually to approve it. People naturally ask why the speech was not published. This works to Khrushchev's disadvantage because people naturally come to the conclusion that there is something fishy about it. Confusion becomes further confused. There were many instances where people at the first meetings received the speech with enthusiasm. Even while the meeting was taking place they removed Stalin's pictures from the walls, threw them down, and tore them up, probably in the expectation that this would be the overt and official policy of the new Soviet leadership and that there were going to be changes in the country in all spheres. Instead of that there arrived a directive from Moscow to put an end to it all, that Stalin's pictures and busts were not to be touched, that no more party meetings were to be held, and "the people began to cool down." And the pictures of Stalin remained where they were, including Khrushchev's office.

A couple of days ago, at the funeral of the Soviet minister Yudin[15] at the Kremlin wall, in the presence of members of the Presidium, of the Soviet Government, and of foreign diplomats, one of the official speakers singled out as a special achievement of the late minister his building of the Moscow automobile factory "named after Stalin" and the Moscow li-

[15] Pavel A. Yudin, 1902–56. Soviet Minister for the Building Materials Industry.

brary "named after Lenin." And that was reported in *Pravda*, with its circulation of many millions: Stalin together with Lenin!

There can be no question but that only the Presidium could decide to do that and did in fact decide it. But none of this strengthens the position of Khrushchev or promotes the new course. It is also clear that it all indicates a certain retreat on Khrushchev's part, to the advantage of people who do not agree with him, including people in the Presidium of the Central Committee.

Moscow, April 20, 1956

The other day I received a visit from one our old emigrants, Mesić, who spent nearly twenty years in Stalin's camps in the Arctic regions. He was rehabilitated last year. He condemns Stalin, but at the same time he has his doubts about the correctness of the new course. It seems to me as though the atmosphere he encountered in Moscow confused and shook him. He told me that the people in the Far North, when they heard about Khrushchev's secret speech, immediately tore down Stalin's pictures and threw them away. Here in Moscow he found Stalin's portraits everywhere as though nothing had happened. He was also shaken by his conversations with Russians, old Bolsheviks, and former prisoners whom he met here and who have been rehabilitated. I talked with him for about two hours. It seems as though here in Moscow—and after the Twentieth Congress!—the personal morale which he brought with him from the Arctic after twenty years of hard labor has started to decline!

I think there are grounds for believing that the Presidium has decided to make the first, even if only tactical, "minor" adjustments to the campaign about Stalin. It is obvious that the indecisiveness and hesitation as well as the "secrecy" with regard to the new course pretty quickly turned into a retreat. The opponents of the new course have taken care of the rest, and by all accounts they are very strong even in the Presidium of the Central Committee, so that the wave produced by the Twentieth Congress has broken on the Stalinist shore of the Soviet system and society. Now it is rolling back and is already carrying with it something of what was brought to the surface.

In such a climate as this the attitude of the Communist party of China, which is, as far as I know, fundamentally in favor of Stalin, and consequently against Khrushchev, is well received. In various circles Soviet citizens prefer the Chinese statement to Khrushchev's speech. They say that the Chinese are objective, tactful, balanced, and truthful, and wise—which cannot be heard said about Khrushchev. Chinese policy is wise because in a Chinese way they take the view that it would be better if the present Soviet leaders worked differently from Stalin and better than he did, rather than condemning him after his death in secret speeches and then continuing to behave exactly as he did.

Moscow, April 22, 1956

It appears that some of the party leaders were involved in the riots in Georgia. Because of national feelings some people in Georgia who were previously against Stalin are now defending him. Stalin was far more of a Russian than a Georgian. Now that he has been rejected by the Russians, the Georgians have taken him over, and the Russians turn machine guns on the Georgians.

We also have information that allegedly throughout the Soviet Union this whole business is being represented as a sort of confrontation between the personalities of Stalin and Khrushchev. Whoever is doing this is acting rather skillfully, since he is obscuring the essence of the matter, making it impossible to discuss the system and society, and may be hoping that the comparison will not work out at all to the advantage of Khrushchev. That means today that the comparison works to the advantage of one of Stalin's successors who most resembles Stalin, who was closer to him than Khrushchev, and who today does not condemn the departed leader as Khrushchev has done. That is why the Georgians raised the slogan: "Molotov for leader." We have heard that there were similar slogans in favor of Malenkov.

At the same time criticism and reproaches directed at Khrushchev are being spread around. It is being said that he is coarse, unbalanced, too direct and impolite, and that such a person cannot be the leader of a great country like the Soviet Union. To judge by a "poll" we have taken, the people here still prefer people like Molotov and Malenkov, who appear bigger to Soviet people insofar as they are more remote from them. After having spent their whole lives in the Kremlin close to Stalin, Molotov and Malenkov are thought fit to be Stalin's successors, unlike Khrushchev, whom they all know well and who is just like them.

I reminded Belgrade to study the official statements by the TASS[16] agency to the effect that all fifteen members and candidate members of the Presidium went collectively to pay their respects to the mortal remains of Minister Yudin in the Hall of Columns near the Kremlin, and that they repeated the performance at a conference of young building workers in the Kremlin, where, once again, all fifteen of them turned up! Such unusual physical demonstrations of the collective nature of the So-

[16] Telegrafnoye Agenstvo Sovetskogo Soyuza—the state-controlled news agency in the Soviet Union.

viet leadership and of its political unity achieve the opposite effect. I thought that even by Soviet standards it would be sufficient for one or two members to be present on behalf of the Presidium. I don't know how to explain it. In any case, these demonstrations can scarcely be proof of political unity in the Kremlin!

CHAPTER THREE

MAY DAY 1956.
THE KREMLIN AND THE DIPLOMATS

At a "secret" lunch in the Kremlin on May Day Mićunović finds himself drawn into the inner circle of Soviet leaders and is able to study their personalities and mutual relations at close quarters. He finds them much divided among themselves. He also finds it difficult to understand the Soviet leaders' idea of what reciprocity means in relations between Moscow and Belgrade.

Moscow, May 2, 1956

Yesterday I attended the May Day parade on Red Square. Throughout April millions of people here have been caught up in the preparations for this holiday. The party and the Soviet Government are probably doing everything in their power to make May 1, 1956, a really great occasion, so that this May Day parade may surpass all previous ones. It is the first May Day parade since the Twentieth Congress, and it will probably serve as an indication of how the people are taking the new policy of de-Stalinization. We Yugoslavs, like all the other foreigners, have also been involved in the May Day celebrations, though not in the same way as the Russians. There is a substantial difference, because while the Russians work hard preparing for the occasion, we simply watch what the Russians are doing and try to draw political conclusions.

One is struck by the fact that as part of the preparations many Moscow citizens have been painting the facades of their houses, though mainly on the outskirts of Moscow, not in the center. The farther you go into the outskirts, the more painting of houses you see. Nobody repairs the buildings, but they are all busy painting them.

The Soviet authorities organize grandiose demonstrations and parades

40

of this kind better than many other countries in the world. I am not sure whether the Chinese can be considered worthy rivals to the Russians in this respect. The Soviet talent for organizing gigantic parades like this one is reflected primarily in the discipline which prevails among those who take part in the parade in Moscow, and that means hundreds of thousands of Muscovites. They are out on the streets from late on April 30 and wait patiently for hours at the allotted place until they can move off, at the very minute and at the exact place, to join the main procession near Red Square so as to march those five hundred meters in front of the tomb of Lenin and Stalin.

Long before the first of May all the embassies in Moscow were sending people scurrying round the city gathering information about the decorations, the portraits of the leaders, the order in which they are put up, the number of portraits of Lenin and of Stalin, the slogans, the size of them and what they say. Some foreigners here appear to me to be very experienced at this business. Some of them have assured me that it is of significance for assessing Soviet policy toward a country to see whether the slogan relating to that country is displayed across a whole street or only attached to the facade of a building. As for the order in which portraits of the present Soviet leaders are displayed in the city, they say that there can be no mistakes here—it is all "pure mathematics." If someone's portrait is missing, that person is finished. Political relationships in the Presidium of the Central Committee can be established precisely by noting whose portraits are closer and whose farther away from that of the First Secretary, Khrushchev.

The parade begins with a march-past of military units of the Soviet armed forces. The Minister of Defense, Marshal G. K. Zhukov,[1] reviews the troops. He stands in an open ZIS[2] limousine, wearing a mass of orders and medals, running from each of his shoulders down to his waist. The automobile moves slowly and smoothly around Red Square, and Marshal Zhukov, weighed down by years and probably hundreds of medals, stands firm and erect, thanks to a special fixture in the automobile which he holds on to with his left hand while keeping the other at the salute.

On our tribune one is struck by the exceptional "activity" on the part of the foreign military attachés.[3] They behave badly and even insultingly

[1] Georgi K. Zhukov, 1896–1974. Marshal of the Soviet Union. Chief of General Staff of Red Army, 1941; commanded the Western Front in defense of Moscow, 1941–42; deputy to Stalin as Commander in Chief of Soviet Armed Forces, 1942; commanded Soviet forces which occupied Berlin in 1945; Minister of Defense, 1955–57; Member of Presidium, CPSU, 1956–57.
[2] "ZIS" stands for *zavod imeni Stalina*—"the 'Stalin' factory" in Moscow which was for long the main Soviet automobile plant.
[3] The May Day parade is one of the rare occasions when foreign military attachés are able to come within reasonable range of Soviet weapons. They usually take advantage of the opportunity to indulge in photography.

toward the Russians. As soon as the detachments of the Soviet Army have passed through, the majority of them leave the tribune.

All the ambassadors except those from the "camp" and Yugoslavia left the tribune before midday. I remained there for another two and a half hours waiting for the end of the parade. After that I had to attend a lunch in the Kremlin to which I had been invited on behalf of the Soviet Government and the Central Committee of the CPSU by Molotov's first deputy, V. V. Kuznetzov.[4]

Moscow, May 3, 1956

I am carrying on with the notes which I started to make yesterday about the May Day parade and the "secret" lunch in the Kremlin.

Ambassadors from the countries of the "camp" and myself among them found ourselves in the central Kremlin palace in the company, it seemed, of more than a hundred members of the Central Committee of the CPSU, headed by its Presidium. At the head of an enormous table were the members of the Presidium with Khrushchev in the middle and the ambassadors of the socialist states among them. I was given a fairly good place, between two members of the Presidium, Mikoyan on my right and Saburov[5] on my left.

The lunch in the Kremlin lasted practically as long as the parade outside the Kremlin. The host and central figure was Khrushchev. He made twelve or maybe fifteen improvised speeches in the course of the lunch. The first toast was to the Soviet Communist party and to Marxism-Leninism, by which the party is now guided. The second toast was to the citizens of Moscow, the May Day parade, and the Soviet people. The third was to the Soviet Army. The fourth was to the Soviet working class, the fifth to the Soviet Communist youth organization, the sixth to the brotherhood of the Soviet peoples, and so on. Khrushchev raised one toast to cooperation between the peoples and the preservation of peace in the world.

He toasted Yugoslavia quite early on. He said the present leaders of the Soviet Union were people who looked the truth straight in the face and that the greatest blame for the conflict with Yugoslavia lay with them, the Soviet Union.

[4] Vasili V. Kuznetzov, b. 1901. Soviet Communist official and diplomat. Chairman, Soviet Trade Union Organization, 1944–53; Deputy Foreign Minister and Ambassador to China, 1953–55; First Deputy Foreign Minister from 1955; Candidate Member of Politburo, CPSU, and First Deputy Chairman, Presidium of Supreme Soviet, since 1977.
[5] Maksim Z. Saburov, b. 1900. Soviet Communist official. Member of Politburo, CPSU, 1952–57. Fell into disgrace, was made manager of a factory, and disappeared from public life.

This they had put right and this was "our greatest victory," Khrushchev said and went on to say that Tito would soon arrive in the Soviet Union, which was proof that relations between the Soviet Union and Yugoslavia were now on the right road. That this was so was confirmed by my presence at the main table, he said, and at this they all applauded loudly and stopped only when I rose to thank them. Khrushchev concluded by saying that all the conditions had now been created for "genuine" unity of all the brotherly socialist countries in Europe, meaning Yugoslavia as well. The mistakes of the past would never be repeated because the leaders of the Soviet Union would in future act in a "Leninist" manner.

When he came to talk about Stalin, Khrushchev started going into details. He said there had been a good deal of discussion on this subject in the Presidium, and he pointed at Molotov, who was sitting near him. In the silence which suddenly prevailed Khrushchev went on to say that Vyacheslav Mikhailovich was an honest Communist. At that Bulganin cut in to tell him to carry on about Stalin, and Khrushchev complied, speaking about the contempt Stalin had for people, that a human being meant absolutely nothing to him, that Stalin cared nothing for the opinion of the party, that he relied on whims and his unhealthy instincts, and that by abusing his power he had done much evil in the Soviet Union.

Presumably in order to correct his reference to Molotov, Khrushchev returned to that subject and said that in the last years of his life Stalin had begun to suspect Molotov of being an agent of American imperialism—and Vyacheslav Mikhailovich, said Khrushchev, had to make frequent visits to the United States. He went on in this manner, saying that Stalin also suspected Voroshilov of being an agent of British imperialism, although Kliment Yefremovich had never been in Great Britain. "And Stalin demanded of me that I should organize actions against the Jews in Moscow," Khrushchev said angrily. It seemed to me that Khrushchev was about to utter some bad swear words but he restrained himself and shouted: "Just imagine, comrades, even my illiterate father never joined the reactionaries or the anti-Semites, but Stalin demanded that I, a member of the Politburo, should do so!"

Then, in a burst of real enthusiasm, Khrushchev said the time had come to restore to Lenin his place in Soviet society, that they would continue Lenin's work, and that the Soviet people were full of enthusiasm for that. Then he said he was already an old man, that he might depart at any moment, and that was the reason why, as a Communist and a human being, he had been obliged to tell the truth about Stalin. Before he departs this world, he said, everyone has to give an account of what he has done and how he did it. Of himself he said he was not afraid of death, that individuals were not important, the only thing that mattered was the party. The depth of feeling in Khrushchev's remarks was shared by most of those present and burst out into spontaneous and stormy applause!

When he felt he had exhausted the domestic themes, of which Stalin was the central one, Khrushchev turned to the question of the "camp" and immediately started to criticize the present situation in Poland. Some of the leaders there were now turning their backs on the Soviet Union, were looking to the West, and wanted to split Poland off from the "fraternal community," he said. We are going to fight against that, Khrushchev shouted, banging his fist on the table. Pointing at the Polish ambassador, Levikowski, he went on: "You have your sovereignty, but what you are doing today in Poland is against your sovereignty and against socialism. We deeply regret the death of Bierut,[6] who was a Communist-internationalist, while Ochab[7] has allowed antisocialist elements to have their own way in Poland. They need to have their knuckles rapped." Apart from his favorable remarks about Yugoslavia and his critical reference to Poland, Khrushchev did not refer to any of the other socialist countries.

I don't believe that anybody in Poland, as far as the Communists are concerned, is thinking of leaving the "camp" and "going to the West," as Khrushchev accused them of doing at the lunch. But, to my great surprise, Polish Ambassador Levikowski supported him and even amplified his remarks in this sense. Following the results of World War II the Poles have nowhere to go "in the West." Khrushchev knows that perfectly well, and yet he attacked the Poles in such a violent way. It is quite a different matter if the Poles want to improve their relations with the East, with the Russians. Instead of taking the initiative in the spirit of the Twentieth Congress and changing Stalin's policy toward the Poles and other nations in the "camp," Khrushchev accuses the Poles when they try to do it themselves on the basis of what he said in his speech about Stalin.

It is interesting that, when he talked about the "camp," though in fact only about Poland, Khrushchev spoke of it as though it were an internal Soviet affair and not as though it concerned another country and the Soviet Union's relations with another state. Khrushchev said they would not permit any innovations in this connection and that they would oppose anybody who tried to introduce changes into relations between the Soviet Union and the "camp." On this matter I think Khrushchev should be taken at his word. There is good reason to believe that the Russians are

[6] Bolesław Bierut, 1892–1956. Polish Communist leader. Secretary-General, Polish Communist party, 1948–56; President of Poland, 1947–48.
[7] Edward Ochab, b. 1906. Polish Communist official. Member of Politburo, Polish Communist party, from 1954. In March 1956 he succeeded Bierut as Secretary of the party, but during the political crisis of October the same year he resigned in favor of Władysław Gomulka and was later ousted from the leadership.

prepared to use force to keep the "camp" under their complete control. This has probably long been the agreed policy of the present Presidium, and Khrushchev only put it into words at the May Day lunch when the vast majority of the Russians present supported him. It was in fact more like a formal meeting of the Central Committee of the CPSU than a lunch.

Bulganin and Mikoyan behaved as though they were closest to Khrushchev in the present circumstances. They alone would supplement Khrushchev's remarks with audible comments of their own and would indicate their approval in a way that could be heard by the hundred or so people present, after which there was usually some applause.

Molotov, Malenkov, and Kaganovich remained passive and throughout the lunch seemed unable to share in the festive atmosphere, particularly Molotov and Malenkov. I was particularly struck by the behavior of Molotov, who was closest to me at the table. At times it seemed to me that Khrushchev was touching him on the raw by what he said, especially when he spoke about Stalin and Stalin's suspicion of Molotov as an "agent of American imperialism." The only time when Molotov behaved differently was when Khrushchev spoke about Yugoslavia: He then rose and asked us to drink to friendship between Yugoslavia and the Soviet Union.

In spite of all the assertions to the contrary I had the impression that this small group of people who now rule Russia are far from being politically united. It seemed to me at times that some members of the Presidium not only do not agree among themselves politically but that as people they simply cannot stand each other any longer. It should not be forgotten that it all took place in the presence of a hundred or more top Soviet officials, a large group of Soviet marshals, and ten ambassadors from the socialist countries. I believe the majority of those people could tell that Molotov and Malenkov felt uncomfortable at the formal lunch at which the role of *khozyayin*[8] was played with such relish and ebullience by Khrushchev.

Moscow, May 7, 1956

The first anniversary of the signing of the Belgrade Declaration is approaching. Here they regard the document as having already been put into practice and even overtaken by events. As far as we can judge, the Soviet side is preparing to replace the Belgrade Declaration with something new to be signed in Moscow next month on the occasion of Tito's visit. It is a question of establishing relations and developing cooperation

[8] *Khozyayin* means "host" or "master" and is the word used to refer to Stalin in his lifetime.

between our two Communist parties, to which they attach priority here, considering, as in the past, that our relations have not been normalized so long as there is not collaboration between our parties.

On the Yugoslav side there is no objection to cooperation with the Russians through party channels as well as in other ways. The question is on what principles that cooperation is to be based, whether the independence and equal rights of each Communist party will be respected or whether, as in the past, it will be based on the theory of the "elder brother" in the "Communist family" into which we, according to the Soviet way of thinking, are supposed to return. We did not have time to reach agreement on this last year and postponed talks about establishing cooperation between the parties until a later date. That moment is now approaching, and the question will be at the center of our talks next month during Tito's visit.

The question of the Yugoslav émigrés in the Soviet Union,[9] although not in itself so important, will again be raised in the forthcoming talks in Moscow when we come to determine to what extent the Belgrade Declaration has already been put into effect and in what ways it has not begun to be carried out. Apart from that, we cannot permit the Soviet Government to continue to treat these deserters, a large number of whom are in the service of the Soviet state security (KGB), as "Communist-internationalists," as Khrushchev tried to do last year in Belgrade. So long as the Soviet Union adopts such an attitude toward these émigrés of ours it will not be possible to consider that relations between Yugoslavia and the Soviet Union have been completely normalized. Responsibility for such a situation will lie entirely with the Soviet authorities.

What is the real issue here? It is a question of a few hundred émigrés who, after the failure of Stalin's aggressive policy toward Yugoslavia, fled to the Soviet Union and are still there now. They were all very well received in the Soviet Union. The Soviet authorities gave them not only political asylum but Soviet citizenship as well and then government employment, often in very sensitive places including the Soviet Army, the party apparatus, and the State Security Service. The émigrés had their own press financed by the Soviet Government and their own regular radio broadcasts beamed into Yugoslavia. They were active from 1948 until quite recently. Radio Moscow's Yugoslav broadcasts are being written and produced by a group of ten of these émigrés today as they were in Stalin's time. The restoration of normal interstate relations between Yugoslavia and the Soviet Union last year has not changed much in this respect.

It is something quite new in the history of relations between socialist

[9] Yugoslav Communists who disagreed with Tito's resistance to Stalin in 1948 and sought asylum in Russia.

states for the citizens of a socialist country who are also members of the Communist party of that country—officers, state and party officials of that country—to betray their country, in this case Yugoslavia, at the invitation of another socialist country, in this case the Soviet Union, and to place themselves in the service of a great socialist state which was pursuing an aggressive policy toward a small socialist state. By behaving in this way the "first and greatest land of socialism" has introduced into the history of relations between socialist countries yet another issue which the development of relations between us has put on the agenda. It is a question of creating their own secret contacts, their own fifth column, in another socialist country, a question of recruiting agents for their own intelligence service, and the attempt to make out of Communists in one socialist country disloyal citizens and traitors to their own socialist homeland.

Moscow, May 10, 1956

One of the matters which is hindering Yugoslav-Soviet relations is the work of the so-called information services operating in each of our countries. For a whole year we have been raising this problem with the Soviet Government. But we have had no success, because the Russians interpret reciprocity in their own original way. Soviet newspaper correspondents are free to travel from one end to the other of Yugoslavia; we have no censorship; the Soviet Union has a permanent reading room and exhibition in the Soviet House of Culture in Belgrade, which is a center for Soviet news and propaganda activity. The House of Culture contains a library which is available free to Yugoslav visitors and is supplied regularly with new books from Moscow. There are also free showings of Soviet films, so that the Soviet House of Culture even became a competitor of the commercial cinemas! In the course of a year between 300,000 and 400,000 Belgrade people pass through the House of Culture.

In Moscow we have absolutely nothing. Our journalists do not have the right to travel freely outside Moscow, they are subjected to censorship, and we are not permitted to put up a single photograph of Yugoslavia in the window or on the wall of our embassy building.

We cannot even discuss with the Russians the showing of a Yugoslav film in Moscow unless it has been written into the agreement on cultural cooperation concluded with the Soviet Government for a period of two years.

When we discuss this with them, the Russians always repeat that the situation is perfectly normal, because they are treated like everybody else in Yugoslavia, and the same applies to the Yugoslavs in the Soviet Union. No discrimination either in Belgrade or in Moscow! The Soviet Government does not permit any country, including Yugoslavia, to carry on such activity here. Our government permits other countries to engage in such activity and so they are naturally under an obligation to permit the Soviet Union to do so as well. In this way, according to the Soviet interpretation, complete reciprocity has been established!

Apart from these questions, each of which is in its own way very instructive for the real state of our relations with the Soviet Union, there is now at the very center of those relations the question of developing economic cooperation between us. In this field the most important question is that of a Soviet credit for the construction of a new aluminum industry in Yugoslavia.

From the very beginning of our talks on this question last May and June the Russians were very cautious. No firm undertaking was given by the Soviet side about the size of the credit. At the same time we were told that they were ready to finance the production of 200,000 tons of aluminum, and we were reckoning on a soviet credit of nearly $200 million just for the first phase of our new aluminum plants in Montenegro.

We were interested even last year in signing an agreement on Soviet credits for constructing a new alumnium industry in Yugoslavia, but the Russians were in no hurry. The talks dragged on, primarily, I believe, because the Russians were not satisfied with the Belgrade Declaration and the political results they had achieved in Yugoslavia. Now they are linking the question of a credit for our aluminum with Tito's visit to the Soviet Union. Bulganin spoke about this on April 3. Now the Russians are hedging, will not talk about the size of the credit, and are saying it all depends on further negotiations.

Last year the question of the aluminum credits was exploited very skillfully by the Soviet side, and that made it much easier politically for the Russians to bring the talks to a successful conclusion. Now it looks as though the Russians again intend to exploit this question as their main "ideological argument." Be that as it may, it seems to me a bad thing that the Russians are linking ideology and aluminum credits in this way. It will not be a good thing if the question of these credits is at the center of our political talks with the Russians. It may turn out that ideology is exchanged for aluminum—in other words, that there will be no aluminum if we do not agree to "ideological unity" with the Russians.

Moscow, May 15, 1956

I will put down my first impressions of my meetings with some members of the diplomatic corps here.

The ambassadors of the countries of "people's democracy" in Moscow seem to be in an even worse state than their colleagues in Belgrade. When

I meet them, we usually simply exchange greetings and a couple of sentences about the climate or the weather; we do not discuss politics, especially the politics of the "people's democracies" or the Soviet Union. They also refrain from asking me anything about Yugoslav politics.

I have the impression that my colleagues from the countries of the "camp" or the governments which they represent here are not only confused by what is happening on the "socialist front" but are also scared because they do not know what it all may lead to in the Soviet Union and in their own countries.

I paid a visit on the British ambassador in Moscow, Sir William Hayter,[10] and I must say that I learned more from him about the present relations between Great Britain and the Soviet Union and about the forthcoming visit by Khrushchev and Bulganin to London than from all ten of Molotov's deputies whom I have met in the last few days and who are preparing the visit. Although I did not put any specific questions to him, Hayter spoke with me in the way that inspires confidence and obliges an interlocutor to behave similarly.

The French ambassador, Maurice Dejean, has more to say in favor of the new Soviet policy than the majority of his Western colleagues. In this context the French ambassador also approves Yugoslavia's policy. Apart from that, Dejean confirmed that relations with Moscow were especially important for France. It seems to me that Belgrade still remains somewhere on the periphery of France's political interests.

The United States ambassador, Charles Bohlen,[11] enjoys the reputation here of being a "Sovietologist" not only among foreign diplomats but even in Soviet academic circles. Bohlen has been dealing with Russia for a quarter of a century now, from the time when diplomatic relations were first established between America and the Soviet Union more than twenty years ago. As representative of the leading power in the NATO bloc Ambassador Bohlen occupies an exceptional position here.

Of Stalin Bohlen said that he was a gifted statesman for Russian conditions and in view of the country's traditions. For him Stalinism does not exist as a doctrine. It was simply that Stalin ruled Russia in the name of communism just as the Tsars had ruled it for centuries in the name of something else. The Russian people knew no system of government other than dictatorship and autocracy.

Bohlen gave me his opinion that things would very soon change for the better in this country. He points out that even after Stalin the leaders of the Soviet Union are not in a position to abandon the rules which Stalin

[10] Sir William Hayter, b. 1906. British diplomat. Ambassador to the Soviet Union, 1953–57. Warden of New College, Oxford, 1958–76. Retired.
[11] Charles Bohlen, 1904–74. American diplomat. Ambassador to the Soviet Union, 1953–57, and to Paris, 1962–68.

introduced into Russia's political life. In confirmation of this Bohlen cites the liquidation of Beria by Stalin's successors. He was accused of being an "agent of imperialism" and not of being Stalin's most loyal servant.

Discussing the Twentieth Congress of the CPSU Bohlen says that things would have been different if Khrushchev's speech had been made public in the country. Because it has remained a secret here, it is possible to manipulate it, Bohlen says.

The Norwegian ambassador, Brodland, I know from Belgrade, where he was for several years a successful ambassador of his country. I have frequently been a guest in his house, and in Belgrade Ambassador Brodland and I easily found a common language. It seemed to me that, although he was not a socialist, he was well disposed toward our Yugoslav socialism and an opponent of the Soviet kind. I had the impression that Brodland was sometimes more critical of the Soviet Union than was his own government.

My meeting with him was friendly. He knew that we had discovered a Russian bugging system in our embassy. He told me they had made a similar discovery and asked me how many microphones we had found. I told him: exactly nineteen. They had twenty-three, which means that they were better "wired for sound." I commented jokingly that that's the way it should be because they belong to NATO and, apart from that, their embassy building is bigger than ours.

The ambassador of the People's Republic of China, Liu Siao, gave me a very friendly welcome. But however attentive he was to me with his hospitality, he was even more careful not to touch on any political topic with me. He was not interested in relations between Yugoslavia and the Soviet Union, probably because I might then be interested in relations between China and the Soviet Union. Nor would he get involved in a conversation about the Twentieth Congress. As far as we can gather, China has reservations about the Congress, particularly about Khrushchev's Stalin speech, which is the most important thing.

The Chinese ambassador is a member of the Central Committee of the Chinese Communist party. The conversation with him was useful, but he does not wish now to discuss what we and the Chinese are most interested in politically with regard to the Soviet Union. It is a pity that Liu Siao speaks no foreign language and that you can't talk to him at all if he is not interested in talking. He makes a virtue of this shortcoming of his, so that when he is not interested in having a conversation, he doesn't bring with him any of his three interpreters. He simply shakes hands and mutters something like O-ha or A-ha, bows, and smiles. Maybe this novel Chinese diplomatic technique is not such a bad idea.

I had a meeting with the Italian ambassador. His name is Mario di Stefano. He was Mussolini's governor in occupied Montenegro in 1942. I believe that there were more Montenegrin partisans shot in that year than in the remaining three years of our liberation war. Such a man is now ambassador of the Republic of Italy in the Soviet Union.

He knew that I was a Montenegrin and he had made some preparations for the meeting with me. He knew that I had been one of the leaders of the Lovćen partisan detachment in the old Montenegro, where he had had his occupation headquarters in the town of Cetinje. He asked me whether I was in Montenegro in 1942. I told him that 1942 was the only year I was not in Montenegro because I left Montenegro in June 1942 with the Montenegrin partisans. In fact I was only about ten kilometers away from him in the hills around Cetinje, where I was operating illegally as a member of the party leadership for Montenegro, Boka, and Sandjak. The Central Committee of the Yugoslav Communist party decided to send me back into occupied territory so that I was on the spot and able to follow everything going on at that time.

Di Stefano assured me that he had "protected the Montenegrins in 1942" and that was why Tito had not declared him a war criminal. I replied that the partisans in Yugoslavia were unable to have a proper administration or archives and that in this connection they had probably made a lot of mistakes. He pretended not to have understood me and carried on in his own way.

I remember my wife, Miška, talking about an Italian fascist governor called Di Stefano, who from time to time acted both as police investigator and as a supreme judge in cases when Montenegrins were arrested. And Miška herself was among the arrested people whom Di Stefano questioned in Cetinje prison. She was then just a young girl and had been arrested as a child because her two brothers had been with the partisans from the first day of the uprising in Montenegro on July 13, 1941. One brother, Ljubo, a medical student and member of the Yugoslav Communist party, was killed in a battle with the Italians at Plevlja on December 1, 1941. Her other brother, Ivo, also a member of the Communist party, a law student who fought in the ranks of our glorious First Proletarian Brigade, was killed in a battle with the Germans the following year. It was not sufficient for the Italian occupation force that two sons had died, so they threw their parents, and their sisters, Miška among them, into prison as well.

Moscow, May 21, 1956

At the suggestion of the Soviet authorities I spoke on Moscow television and radio on May 18 about the state of Yugoslav-Soviet relations and the future outlook. What I said was not in the least interesting except in that it gave our official view of relations between us.

If I had to sum up my speech, I think it might be said that it showed we were "content with little" as far as Yugoslav-Soviet relations are concerned. They were depicted in fairly rosy colors, but realistically, with the stress on the improvement of relations in the future. I accepted certain Soviet commentaries on our relations but also stressed the Yugoslav point of view on some questions. I don't expect the Russians to be very pleased with our views.

CHAPTER FOUR

TITO IN RUSSIA

*On his first visit to Russia since his clash with Stalin in 1948
Tito is given a warm welcome and finds Khrushchev and
the Soviet leaders apparently eager to forget the past, admit
their faults, and restore the best of relations with Yugoslavia. A banquet given by Tito for the Soviet leaders gener-
ates a mood of general euphoria and creates the impression
that Soviet-Yugoslav relations have returned to normal on
the party level.*

Moscow, May 25, 1956

I spent two days in Belgrade in connection with Tito's forthcoming visit to the Soviet Union. There is exceptional interest in the visit
in Yugoslavia. Some of our people believe that we shall not find these
talks with the Russians much easier than last year's. Yugoslav foreign policy is once again being put to the test. We are all anxious that Tito's visit
to Russia should be as successful as is possible in the present circumstances.

As with the conflict with Stalin in 1948, so with the present new relations with the Soviet Union: They have not been of our choosing. It
could be said simply that events moved in that direction. Now all the results which we have achieved so far are being tested and it is all taking
place in Moscow on an open political stage before the whole world. People will now once again be able to judge whether our conflict with the
Soviet Union and our "reconciliation" with the Russians were simply
passing episodes and incidents or whether it is a question of a new and
lasting phenomenon in the development of socialism, as we believe.

It is my opinion that the Russians are also very interested in the success
of Tito's visit, though naturally on the terms which they have in mind.
They have planned a magnificent program for Tito. I don't know exactly

what may happen, but that the visit should not be a success is simply unthinkable, above all for the Russians themselves. Because what would happen then? The negotiations in Moscow will probably be difficult. They may produce extreme and opposite stands: from the greatest friendship and "unity" all the way to threats and the danger of a fresh conflict. However that may be, I believe there still remains room for some kind of agreement which will be imposed on the Russians and us by force of circumstances. In the present talks with the Russians, as in those we had last year, the decisive factor is our internal situation. If that remains stable, as it has been, and if there exists complete confidence and understanding between our leaders and the people as there has also been for the last fifteen years and as I believe still exists, then I believe there is no need to doubt that we can be successful in the forthcoming negotiations with the Russians.

But the improvement of our relations with the Soviet Union would be seriously reduced in value, and to our disadvantage, if it resulted in a worsening of our relations with the West and the United States of America. It is of fundamental and lasting importance for Yugoslavia to have good relations with both sides and not an improvement in relations with one side at the expense of worsened relations with the other. In that case our country would be like a man who tried to show how steadily he could stand on one leg. In the modern world a state which finds itself in such a situation can hardly talk about its stability.

As for our relations with the West and America, it is not just a question of our economic and financial interest in Western and American credits, in Western technology, in American wheat, or in the military aid which Yugoslavia still receives from the United States, although all that is of great importance to us. Yugoslavia is today, as far as our economy is concerned, in a similar situation with relation to the West to the one it was in previously in relation to the Soviet Union and the East. Then the Soviet Union and the East unilaterally and from one day to the next canceled more than forty international agreements and suddenly applied a total economic blockade against our country. In the past such measures had been applied only with regard to states upon which war had been declared. Despite enormous material losses Yugoslavia withstood Stalin's economic blockade. Even after the "reconciliation" the Russians have not compensated us for it by so much as a kopek. I don't know what on earth would happen if the West now suddenly shifted course and broke off economic links with Yugoslavia. I don't believe it's going to happen, any more than I believe that a country even bigger, more advanced, and richer than Yugoslavia could withstand yet another economic blockade.

It cannot be a good thing for a small state, and certainly not for socialist Yugoslavia, to get involved in the rivalries and settling of accounts between great powers. Yugoslavia is not in such a position because it is internally strong, and any country which has internal stability has a sort of immunity against being used by the great powers as a pawn in their settling of accounts among themselves.

The Soviet leaders are now preparing to do everything in their power to limit the effect of Yugoslavia as an independent socialist factor in Europe, since they can no longer eliminate it altogether. The Russians have no intention of once again, as happened last year, appearing to back Yugoslavia's independence as a socialist state. Any Soviet participation in confirming Yugoslavia's emergent independence would only increase the Russians' difficulties in their relations with the other socialist countries, especially in Europe. To recognize Yugoslavia's equal status and independence also in matters of ideology and at the same time continue to deny that same equality and independence to the countries of the "camp" —these two things can hardly go together or last very long as a policy.

Moscow, May 26, 1956

From my conversations with Bulganin and then with the British ambassador, Hayter, I got the impression that neither the Russians nor the British expected very much to come out of the exchange of views which took place during the Russian visit to Great Britain. Still, the visit was in itself a major political event and has been at the center of political attention for the last month.

What is particularly important, I think, is that by going on a friendly visit to Britain, Khrushchev and the other Soviet leaders have been for the first time in a great country which considers itself one of the pillars of Western civilization. Stalin ruled Russia with unlimited power for thirty years, and practically the whole of that time, from the October Revolution to his death, he spent within the Kremlin walls. Khrushchev set out on this trip only two months after condemning Stalin at the Twentieth Congress. Maybe it is here that one should see the special dimension and significance of Khrushchev's visit to London, irrespective of the meager results of the Soviet-British talks. Maybe our forthcoming negotiations with the Russians will be easier thanks to the fact that the Russians have just been on a visit to Britain?

Moscow, May 27, 1956

We have learned from Soviet sources that Mollet[1] had a bad effect on the already unfavorable atmosphere by his behavior while he was here. In

[1] Guy Mollet, leader of the French Socialist party and French Prime Minister in 1956.

talks and during lunches and dinners with the Russians he always began and ended his speeches with statements about France being a loyal and dependable member of the Western military alliance. It was as though Moscow was the place where, in dealings with the Russians, the French Prime Minister had to demonstrate his loyalty to the NATO bloc. The Russians also gained a bad impression from the fact that Guy Mollet limited his stay in the Soviet Union to only three days. And it didn't help much that the Minister of Foreign Affairs, Christian Pineau, stayed on another four days after his chief had left.

As with the Russians' visit to Great Britain, the visit of the French to the Soviet Union has not led to any significant changes in the political climate in Europe. Something has been done, however, simply by virtue of the fact that such visits and talks between leading statesmen of the great powers are taking place again, though we are still far from seeing any real changes for the better in international relations. The Russians have invited the British to visit Moscow, the French have invited the Russians to go to Paris, and the talks will be continued. It appears that for the time being there is no better way of developing peaceful cooperation between states than along this narrow, winding path leading to the sort of meetings and talks which I have described and in which we shall be involved next week.

Moscow, May 28, 1956

None of the Soviet leaders, not even Khrushchev himself, is thinking of making any immediate or substantial social or political changes in the system which Stalin bequeathed them. At the Twentieth Congress, apart from the speech in which he condemned Stalin, Khrushchev made another speech, which was the main political report on behalf of the Soviet leadership. In it he argued openly not only that there was nothing to be changed in the system in this country but that it was the best system history has ever known. The political line of the Soviet Communist party had, apparently, always been correct, even though it was laid down until his death by none other than Stalin. There are many reasons for believing that even the greatest anti-Stalinists here—in our understanding of the term—are counting at best only on some limited and gradual economic and other reforms in the Soviet Union which will be introduced step by step over the years. It is as though they take the view here that the system is faultless, that there can be no question of changing it, and that one can talk only of making it even better.

Some questions in connection with Yugoslavia are presented in Moscow in roughly the following way: Khrushchev condemned Stalin, against whom Yugoslavia had waged a desperate political battle. In particular Khrushchev condemned Stalin's aggressive policy against Yugoslavia. So he is depicted as having come out definitely on Yugoslavia's side in that historic conflict, so that Yugoslavia for its part should now respond to Khrushchev by changing its policy toward the Soviet Union.

If Khrushchev succeeded now in bringing Yugoslavia back again onto the side of the Soviet Union after all the dramatic events which have taken place between us, this alone would not only change substantially the political situation in the Soviet Union and the "camp" but would also change the situation in Europe to the Soviet advantage. They think here that this would be an achievement of historical significance on a world scale for Khrushchev as the architect of a new Soviet political course and the author of a policy of "de-Stalinization."

We have good reasons to support Khrushchev's policy, but the nature of our support and its limits are predetermined. In any case the limits can be set only by us and not by the Russians. The greater the illusions on the Soviet side in this respect, and the tougher the demands they make on us, the weaker and more limited can be our support for them. The Russians' maximalist demands, such as the one concerning "ideological unity," which in simpler terms means our inclusion in the "camp," can only force us into an open conflict with Khrushchev—irrespective of whether it will benefit the Stalinists or anti-Stalinists in Russia. A particular difficulty remains in the fact that the Russians believe that the situation in the "camp" would change substantially for the better if Yugoslavia were brought into it. This seems to me like believing that bad apples in a basket will become sound if you add a sound one to them. But it's exactly the opposite: The sound ones in the basket will also go bad.

Moscow, May 30, 1956

People from our protocol and security services have carried out their part of the work here successfully in connection with Tito's visit. Collaboration with the Soviet services was very satisfactory. The Russians had actually done all that was necessary, and the Yugoslavs only carried out a sort of check and acquainted themselves with what had been done. As far as the safety of important guests is concerned, the Soviet Union is probably the safest country in the world.

Our protocol officials had a good deal more to do than did the people from the security service. They had to go over again all the points on the program, of which there are a great many because Tito is staying in the Soviet Union for nearly three weeks. They also had to coordinate different views on certain matters of protocol. With the Russians, for example, Khrushchev represents the party, Bulganin the government, and Voroshilov the state. So it had to be agreed, for example, that on the drive from the Kiev railway station to Tito's residence with Muscovites lining the streets, Tito would be accompanied in the open automobile both by Khrushchev as leader of the party and by Voroshilov as head of state.

I consider it especially important to acquaint Belgrade with the atmosphere prevailing here in connection with Tito's visit. After the condemnation of Stalin at the Twentieth Congress there was a good deal of optimism in Belgrade concerning internal developments in the Soviet Union. But events here have not followed the course which some comrades expected. I personally think Khrushchev himself was surprised, so what can one say if some Yugoslav optimists have been surprised as well?

If the process of de-Stalinization had got under way in the Soviet Union, even if only hesitantly, in the spirit of the Twentieth Congress, then the Yugoslavs would have done their utmost, quite deliberately and spontaneously, to assist the process. As it is, it may turn out that Khrushchev's difficulties will not have the effect of making the Russians "softer" in their talks with us. I fear that Khrushchev will be "harder" because he is not strong and will be all the more demanding of Yugoslav support and in the form the Russians want it.

One of the ways in which the Russians are strong and we are weak concerns the Yugoslav need for modern military equipment and weapons for our Army. But if the aluminum credits have been a matter of such political importance in our relations with the Soviet Union for a whole year now, it is not difficult to imagine the sort of political role that will be played by our eventual request for, and Soviet promises about, modern Soviet weapons for our Army. Our position in this field is by no means satisfactory because immediately after the war we based the equipment of our armed forces on two main factors: our own domestic production, mainly of light weapons, and the purchase of heavy weapons from the Soviet Union. The first factor remains and has become increasingly important, but the second disappeared in 1948. The Soviet heavy armament which we had is becoming obsolete because for ten years now we have not been able at any price to buy a single screw or spare part in Russia or in Eastern Europe for the maintenance of our tanks, guns, and aircraft of Soviet manufacture. The question of resuming our "military trade" with the Soviet Union has not yet been put on the agenda and the Russians are not yet using this very effective trump card in their relations with Yugoslavia. But that moment is steadily approaching and it will be upon us during Tito's visit, although there have not yet been any formal talks about it.

Yugoslavia still receives American military aid on the basis of an agreement we signed with the United States Government some years ago. We sought to obtain weapons wherever we could, not in order to attack anyone, but only to defend ourselves from threats from the East. We were ready to buy armaments from anyone who was ready to sell them to us. The agreement with the United States Government is still in force. If our relations with the Soviet Union are stabilized on the present course, we shall no longer have any need for American military aid. But if we refuse American military aid, we shall not do so to replace it by Soviet aid. We continue to have a major interest in being free to purchase arms as well as other goods in both the United States and the Soviet Union.

Ungeni, June 2, 1956

I traveled down to the Soviet-Romanian frontier to meet President Tito and the Yugoslav delegation. The Yugoslavs decided to travel to Moscow by train and not in one of our tiny Yugoslav planes. And they chose a good route—through Romania and not through Hungary, which is the usual route from Belgrade to Moscow.

Our relations with Romania have been traditionally good and friendly. But the long history of friendly relations between Yugoslavia and Romania was seriously interrupted after World War II when Stalin involved Romania in the conduct of his aggressive policy against Yugoslavia.

Tito arrived together with his wife, Jovanka,[2] and our delegation at the frontier station of Ungeni exactly on time. The official Soviet escorting party which arrived from Moscow was led by Nikolai Pegov,[3] secretary of the Presidium of the Supreme Soviet and a member of the Central Committee of the CPSU. The welcome was exceptionally cordial and friendly. There was an artillery salute, military bands playing, and a Soviet military guard of honor. Huge portraits of the principal guest and the Yugoslav and Soviet flags and banners in bright colors transformed the appearance of the little village on the Soviet-Romanian frontier, which had probably never witnessed such a spectacle before.

Tito has brought our most distinguished state and party leaders with him. There are not many of them, in accordance with what Mikoyan advised me a month ago but they are of the highest level. They are comrades Kardelj, Koča Popović, Mijalko Todorović, Jakov Blažević, Joža Vilfan, and a group of our leading experts on subjects of special importance in our relations with the Russians. But one can't help noticing that

[2] Jovanka Broz (Budisavlević), b. 1925. President Tito's fourth wife, whom he married officially in 1952 but from whom he has been separated since June 1977.
[3] Nikolai M. Pegov, b. 1905. Soviet Communist official. Secretary, Presidium of the Supreme Soviet, 1952–56; Ambassador to Iran, 1956–63; to Algeria, 1964–67; and to India, 1967–73. A Deputy Foreign Minister from 1973.

our delegation contains no representative of our Ministry of National Defense.

At the railside stations which we passed through in Moldavia and the Ukraine and next day on the way through Russia everything went off in the best possible way. We were greeted everywhere by masses of Soviet citizens who gave the impression of being genuinely pleased and enthusiastic. These spontaneous demonstrations by Soviet citizens along the way affected all of us, including Comrade Tito. Something else which contributed to the gradual warming up of the atmosphere was the fact that we were crossing the areas where the Soviet-German front had been at the beginning and again at the end of the war and which had suffered so badly, first in the course of Hitler's invasion of the region and later even more during the German withdrawal. This was the most frequent subject of conversation during which Pegov and the other Soviet officials were untiring in providing facts and figures about the enormous human casualities and material losses which the people suffered in the areas we were traveling through.

Moscow, June 3, 1956

The welcome in Moscow was on a very high level. The whole Presidium of the Soviet Communist party was there, along with ministers of the Soviet Government, Soviet military leaders, and members of the diplomatic corps in Moscow. There was the obligatory Soviet guard of honor and a military band blaring out and echoing round the high arches of the Kiev station. Somewhere in the neighborhood could be heard the sound of an artillery salute in honor of our head of state. All this fuss and noise must impress the thousands of people living in the neighborhood, who react to it in their own way. That sort of thing doesn't happen every day at the Kiev station.

Moscow, June 4, 1956

We visited the agricultural exhibition. It is in such an exhibition that Soviet agriculture looks its best. In practice agriculture remains, forty years after the October Revolution, the Achilles' heel of the Soviet economy. The Soviet Union has not yet achieved the agricultural output of the days of the last Russian Tsar. To judge by the amount of produce he obtains from his own little patch of land and which he is allowed to dispose of privately, the Soviet farmer is probably to be reckoned among the most productive agricultural producers in the world. But to judge by what is produced by the Soviet collective and state farms with their vast areas of land cultivated on principles laid down by Stalin, the Soviet

Union is among the least productive countries in the world as far as agriculture is concerned.

Khrushchev now has an opportunity to return to his first love—agriculture—and, after forty years' experience with so little success, to open up the prospect of a better future for Soviet agriculture. Khrushchev is concentrating on the reclamation of the virgin lands in Kazakhstan, Siberia, and Central Asia. The idea is to bring under cultivation and to populate vast areas, bigger than the total arable lands of countries the size of Yugoslavia. It is an undertaking of gigantic dimensions which must involve whole generations and huge financial resources, and even so there is still a danger that the whole plan will come to nothing and will suffer from chronic low productivity and inefficiency.

It remains to be seen what will happen to Khrushchev's idea of a "return to Lenin" in Soviet agriculture. There are still about a hundred million people working on Soviet farms, which is about half, if not more, of the population of the Soviet Union. Even in Yugoslavia agriculture is not exactly blooming. What must Soviet farming be like? Socialism and agriculture still do not get on very well together, to their mutual harm.

There were happenings on the streets of Moscow yesterday such as have not taken place in living memory. During one of our trips by car across Moscow Khrushchev and Tito decided to take a walk down Gorky Street, in the center of the city. The column of automobiles suddenly stopped, and Khrushchev and Tito, and I as well, because I was in their automobile, set out on foot in the direction of the Kremlin. We were quickly surrounded by a crowd of Moscow people who happened to be passing. It seemed to me as though in only a couple of minutes several thousand people had gathered. It turned into a spontaneous demonstration and finally brought the traffic to a halt. In order to avoid the crush on the street Tito and Khrushchev went into a shop selling cakes and ice cream. The customers we found inside the shop started to move away, but Khrushchev asked everyone to stay where they were. Khrushchev and Tito ordered ice cream. But when it came to paying for them, it turned out that neither Khrushchev nor Tito had a single kopek in his pocket. Khrushchev behaved in the confectioners as though he were a regular customer and knew personally all the people who served us as well as the customers.

No doubt this "dropping in for an ice cream" on Gorky Street will cause a sensation. After this "adventure" Khrushchev, who was in the best of moods, proposed to Tito that they should go to Lomonosov University on the Lenin Hills, from where you get the best panorama of "greater Moscow," and Tito agreed. When we arrived there, the sun was going down in the west and with its last rays was turning Moscow gold and lighting it up in bright colors. Khrushchev explained to Tito where things were in the vast area of the city which we were looking down on. He also described the plans they have for building complete new districts in Moscow.

Moscow, June 6, 1956

We paid separate protocol visits on Khrushchev and Bulganin. But first of all we called on Voroshilov. We visited them all with our "full complement." The most important subject in the talks with Bulganin was the question, which he raised, of Soviet credits for the Yugoslav aluminum industry. With Voroshilov the talk was cordial, probably because it was much more concerned with the distant past than the present time. On the visit to Khrushchev he did not mention either the aluminum or any other question connected with our relations as Bulganin did. Unlike Bulganin and Voroshilov, Khrushchev was completely alone. He talked to us among other things about Stalin, the mistakes he had made in the field of theory and the serious crimes he had committed in practice. Khrushchev cited many examples, starting with Stalin's theory about the "sharpening of the class struggle under socialism," and then about Stalin's mistakes and serious failures in the field of agriculture and his attitude to the peasantry—and today that means "more than half Russia," Khrushchev said. Our host also talked about Beria. Although it is already nearly three years since the liquidation of Beria, people here seem to feel some obligation to go on producing proof that they were right to execute him.

It appears that the long interrogation of Beria resulted in the compilation of political documentation of gigantic dimensions and horrible contents, such as had probably never before been brought together in the Soviet Union. Not a single word of it has been published here. Stalin liquidated Beria's predecessors, Yezhov and Yagoda,[4] summarily, while Khrushchev subjected Beria and his collaborators to intensive interrogation for several months. I have no hard information about this, but I imagine that Khrushchev composed his secret speech about Stalin at the Twentieth Congress partly on the basis of the material produced during the interrogation of Beria.

All the gala performances which the Russians are putting on in honor of Tito are attended by Molotov, who immediately before Tito's arrival was suddenly removed from the post of Soviet Foreign Minister. Molotov's removal was seen as a real sensation and received world public-

---

[4] Genrikh Yagoda, 1891–1938. People's Commissar for Internal Affairs—i.e., head of the secret police—under Stalin from 1934 to 1936, when he was replaced by Nikolai Yezhov (1895–?1939). Yagoda was sentenced to death in the show trial of 1938 and shot. Yezhov carried out the Great Purge, known as the "Yezhovshchina," but fell from grace in 1938 and disappeared. His ultimate fate is not known; it is assumed that he was also shot.

ity. He appeared to have lost the post of Foreign Minister because of Yugoslavia. This encouraged every kind of speculation, especially in the West, to the effect that the last obstacle had now been removed to the final inclusion of Yugoslavia in the Soviet political orbit since the Yugoslavs had received no less a gift than the removal of Molotov. We know nothing of the real reasons for this sudden change in the Soviet leadership.

Moscow, June 7, 1956

We have had the first official talks between our two delegations. We started "at the shallow end"—international relations. This is by far the easier part of the talks. The Soviet delegation consisted of: Khrushchev, Voroshilov, Bulganin, Molotov, Mikoyan, Shepilov,[5] Kuznetzov, Firyubin,[6] and Ilichev.[7] On the other side of the table the Yugoslav delegation headed by Comrade Tito was almost as large. So there were nearly twenty people altogether. In such a large gathering you cannot get down to major issues with the Russians. With them the most important matters are usually discussed in a very small circle, and the most delicate ones between two people. And so it was on this occasion: There were no real negotiations.

As a mark of hospitality the Russians let Tito speak first. He expounded our general attitude on certain major issues in Europe and the world. He explained in particular some aspects of our foreign policy which please the Russians least: the Balkan Pact with Greece and Turkey, the American military aid which Yugoslavia still receives, and our policy toward a divided Germany. And he devoted special attention to the question of our relations with Albania and Bulgaria, as neighboring countries, but without going into the question of the "camp." I consider Tito was very moderate in what he said, because much more could be said, here and elsewhere, about the anti-Yugoslav policy being conducted by state and party leaders in Albania and Bulgaria.

Replying to Tito's exposé, Khrushchev dealt with subjects in the same order. He tried to take Enver Hoxha's[8] part without backing him com-

[5] Dmitri T. Shepilov, b. 1905. Soviet Communist official. Editor of *Pravda*, 1954–55; Secretary, Central Committee, CPSU, 1955–57; Foreign Minister, 1956–57. Dismissed from all posts in 1957 and vanished from public life.
[6] Nikolai P. Firyubin, b. 1908. Soviet Communist official and diplomat. Ambassador to Czechoslovakia, 1955; Ambassador to Yugoslavia, 1955–57; Deputy Foreign Minister, 1957; Secretary-General to Political Advisory Council of Warsaw Pact, 1966.
[7] Leonid F. Ilichev, b. 1906. Soviet Communist official and diplomat. Deputy Foreign Minister, 1965. Later responsible for long-drawn-out frontier negotiations with China.
[8] Enver Hoxha, b. 1908. Secretary-General, Albanian Communist party, since 1943.

pletely, saying he was only recounting what the Albanian Government had told them. It was clear to us that the Russians did not wish on this occasion to go seriously into the question of our relations with Albania or Bulgaria or with the other countries of the "camp." So at these first talks everything remained as it was. The Russians continued to regard the question of the "camp" as their own internal problem: It is a question of their allies, and Yugoslavia continues to refuse Soviet mediation as far as our relations with the countries of the "camp" are concerned. While we were still at the table and assessing the Russians' position as set forth by Khrushchev, we agreed not to go further into this question with the Russians. We will go into it with the Albanians, the Bulgars, and the others in the "camp" without Moscow as an intermediary.

We also discussed Hungary, the Russians more than we, because it is presumably clear to the Russians that Yugoslavia is not in a position to improve its relations with Hungary so long as Rákosi[9] and his crew remain in charge. The Russians told us that the internal situation in Hungary is becoming ever more complicated and more serious and that M. A. Suslov[10] is going to Budapest tomorrow to discuss with the Hungarian leaders how to extract themselves from their internal crisis. Following this statement the Russians expected us to say something in support of Suslov's mission to Budapest. But we knew nothing about it, apart from the few sentences which Khrushchev had spoken, so there was no comment from our side.

I was amazed when I heard Khrushchev say that Suslov was going on a special political mission to Hungary. He is known to us and to others for the missions he carried out on orders from Stalin and the Cominform in 1948 and 1949, when he signed the resolution against Yugoslavia.

Not only does Suslov not talk to diplomatic representatives in Moscow: He rarely even shakes hands with them. He appears only at Presidium receptions in the Kremlin and at receptions given by some of the East European countries. We have heard that he was against changing Stalin's policy toward Yugoslavia and opposed sending the Khrushchev delegation to Belgrade in May last year. I reckon the Russians could not have made a worse choice or have found a less competent representative than Suslov to send to Hungary.

With reference to Yugoslavia's foreign policy Khrushchev said that the Soviet Union had no comments to make and that they respected all the arguments that Tito had produced. Khrushchev had in mind here relations with the West and not with the "camp." He said the Soviet Union

[9] Mátyás Rákosi, 1892–1971. Hungarian Communist leader. From 1945 to 1956 was leader of Hungarian Communist party and dictator of Hungary.
[10] Mikhail A. Suslov, b. 1902. Soviet Communist official. A Secretary of the Central Committee of the CPSU since 1947; editor of *Pravda*, 1949–50; Member of Politburo, CPSU, from 1955.

would also be ready to accept credits from the United States without, of course, any political conditions, as was the case with the credits Yugoslavia was receiving. With regard to our recognition of Eastern Germany Khrushchev said it would be of the greatest importance but that the Russians were not pressing us because we would best decide the matter ourselves.

Tito and Kardelj and the rest of our delegation were very pleased. We had not expected such understanding on the Soviet side. Not a word was said at today's talks about cooperation between our Communist parties. That has been left for the end of the visit and is the most important question.

Moscow, June 8, 1956

The night before last Tito gave a dinner in honor of the Soviet leaders at the Spiridonovka[11] house. The whole Presidium of the Soviet Communist party was present. I believe the occasion will remain an unforgettable memory for all the participants. Although it was just one of the events in the program, the dinner at the Spiridonovka turned out to be something quite different and far more important. It was something like a meeting of a combined party organization, the members of which were ten Soviet party leaders headed by Khrushchev and the same number of Yugoslavs headed by Tito, and the main subject on the agenda might best have been described as "criticism and self-criticism," or rather Soviet self-criticism, without any criticism from the Yugoslav side.

Tito raised a toast to the guests, speaking fluently in Russian and without a written text. Like a good host he did not utter a single word of criticism of the Soviet Union in connection with our conflict and all the harm done to Yugoslavia. He said that Yugoslav Communists had a profound faith in the CPSU and had been convinced that the quarrel between us would be liquidated, and so it had turned out. Tito allotted credit for that equally between the Yugoslav and Soviet Communists and peoples, stressed the historic significance of the Twentieth Congress, and congratulated the Central Committee of the CPSU, which, he said, bore tremendous responsibility not only for the Soviet Union but for the further advance of socialism in the world.

With this carefully judged tribute to the present Soviet leaders, instead of indulging in any criticism of the Soviet Union, Tito seemed to have surprised the Russians, because it fitted in exactly with the theory now being put around by the Soviet leaders about the "Leninist core" which always existed in the CPSU and which allegedly continued to play a role throughout Stalin's time, unaffected by the "cult of personality." When

[11] Mansion formerly belonging to Morozov, Russian industrialist.

this appears to have been confirmed by no less a person than Tito, is there any need to seek any other evidence in Russia or elsewhere that the theory of the "Leninist core" is really true and that the members of the "core" were and still are the very people sitting at the table with us at the dinner in the Spiridonovka?

Tito was followed by Khrushchev, Voroshilov, Bulganin, Mikoyan, Kaganovich, and finally Molotov. By the number of speakers on the Soviet side and even more by what they said it is clear that no rules of protocol were observed, although the dinner was formally an official function. All the Soviet leaders seemed to be competing among themselves to see who could condemn Stalin's policy against Yugoslavia in the sharpest terms, including their own part in carrying out that policy, and who could lay the greatest stress on the many virtues and historic achievements of the Yugoslavs.

You could tell from Khrushchev's behavior that he was in the best of moods and that he considered what was taking place around the table at Spiridonovka far more important than the official talks which we had had that same morning. And Khrushchev has good reason for that. In one speech after another the most distinguished members of the Presidium talked about the difficulties which had beset our past relations, took the blame on themselves, and made promises about the policy toward Yugoslavia which they were going to support in the future. Khrushchev did not take excessive advantage of his position as "first among equals" (as he did at the Kremlin lunch on May 1), agreed with members of the Presidium who would speak and when, and was the first to applaud what individual members of the Presidium said in their self-criticism in relation to Yugoslavia.

About the speeches by Bulganin and Mikoyan I will say only that they were on a very high level, which is not so easy when such people speak on one and the same subject. Bulganin was more categorical in his criticism of the past and of the responsibility of the Soviet side than was Mikoyan, who differed somewhat in tone and vocabulary from the others, although there was nothing to take exception to. Kaganovich's was the loudest as far as the delivery was concerned, and the emptiest with regard to content. It seemed to me that even the Soviet leaders could hardly wait for Kaganovich to finish his speech. They were presumably afraid lest he say something out of place and so ruin the excellent atmosphere, because, unlike the others, he talked about the might of the Soviet Union in the old familiar terms. I had the impression that even the Russians were relieved when Kaganovich ended his speech and raised his glass to Tito's health.

A very special impression was made on me and, I believe, on the majority of those present, both Yugoslavs and Russians, by Molotov's speech. It seemed as though he was not going to speak at all, since all the other members of the Presidium had spoken, the dinner was drawing to an end, and the Russians might at any moment have got up from the table and started to take their leave. It was at this moment that Molotov asked Tito, as the host, for the floor and spoke for ten or fifteen minutes. He was critical of Soviet policy, and of his own policy, toward Yugoslavia in the past. And he was equally convincing and gave an impression of sincerity when he spoke in the most positive terms about the Soviet Union's present policy toward our country.

Molotov also spoke well, in my opinion, about the present international situation. His speech was listened to with the greatest attention not only by us but by the Soviet side as well. None of the Russians interrupted him as had been the case with most of the other Soviet speakers including Khrushchev.

Tito did not reply to this veritable firework display of speeches by the Soviet side, though they lasted a long time. Kardelj replied along the lines of Tito's speech. It was well received by the Russians, who seemed surprised that Kardelj had so many good things to say about the present Soviet policy and the Soviet leaders.

The dinner broke up at about an hour past midnight. It is difficult for me to decide who was the more pleased, the Yugoslavs or the Russians. As I noted at the beginning, the dinner turned into a sort of party meeting, and maybe the Russians consider that that was the best way to raise, if not to resolve, some of the most important questions which were to be dealt with during Tito's visit.

CHAPTER FIVE

THE MOSCOW DECLARATION

*On visits to Leningrad and Stalingrad Tito is given an en-
thusiastic welcome by the population, but rather too enthusiastic for the taste of the Soviet leaders who are disappointed at the Yugoslavs' continued resistance to their
demands. Khrushchev takes steps to counter Tito's influence
in Eastern Europe. The Moscow Declaration on interparty
relations signed at the end of the visit is suppressed by the
Russians. On the way home Tito is given a great reception
by the Romanians in Bucharest. Shortly afterward trouble
breaks out in the Polish city of Poznań.*

Moscow, June 9, 1956

Tito's first trip outside Moscow was a visit to Leningrad. I think
the Russians did well to send our people first to Leningrad. Even if the
city on the Neva, cradle of the October Revolution, had not had such a
long and glorious history, the exploits of the people of Leningrad during
World War II, the sacrifices and suffering they went through during
the thousand days of Hitler's blockade,[1] and the heroism they displayed
at that terrible time cannot fail to stir the emotions of everyone who
visits Leningrad.

On the way there I asked the Russians who came with us about the
number of Leningrad people who perished in the war. No one could give
me a definite figure. I believe it hasn't yet been officially stated here. Nor
has any memorial been erected or a common grave arranged. It is not really surprising, since the greater part of European Russia, as well as the

[1] Leningrad was besieged by the German forces from September 1941 to January
1944, a total of 872 days. The total number of people who died in the city from military operations and starvation exceeded 1 million. •

Ukraine and Byelorussia, suffered a similar fate and there are thousands of collective graves and memorials to be taken care of throughout the European part of the Soviet Union. We were told that there are plans to erect a suitable memorial to those who died in Leningrad.

The visit to Leningrad was the best choice for other reasons, too. It was in Leningrad after the war that Stalin resumed his practices of the thirties and summarily executed Leningrad's most distinguished Communists, among them a Soviet Deputy Prime Minister and chairman of the State Planning Commission, Voznesensky.[2] Can one imagine anything more frightful, even for Stalin? Immediately after the war he chose Leningrad as the place to resume his criminal practices, against the leaders of this city of heroes and martyrs on the Neva!

Tito's visit to Leningrad consequently acquired an even greater political significance, and not for us Yugoslavs alone. Tito was accompanied by the Soviet Prime Minister, Bulganin. We received such a welcome from the people of the city as no one could ever forget. I can't give precise figures, but I don't think I exaggerate if I say that we were greeted on the streets by more than a million people. Then we had a meeting in one of the biggest factories, where Tito's speech was well received. Leningrad was in a festive mood practically throughout the two days we were there. Every time we had a meeting with the local authorities or the people of Leningrad, and wherever we appeared—at the theater, in the art galleries, or on the streets—we were greeted as friends, with warmth and sincerity.

The celebrations in Leningrad were in a way linked with Yugoslavia, which was a victim of Stalin's foreign policy, just as Leningrad had been a victim of his domestic policy. It was in this city, with the murder of Kirov[3] back in 1934, that Stalin embarked on his policy of terror which resulted in the destruction of millions of innocent people.

Sochi, June 14, 1956

The journey to southern Russia began with some events which had not been planned. The visit to Stalingrad[4] was something quite out of the

[2] Nikolai A. Voznesensky, 1903–50. Soviet Communist official. Chairman, State Planning Commission, 1938; member of Politburo, CPSU, 1947–50. Executed as a member of the "Leningrad group."

[3] Sergei M. Kirov, 1886–1934. Soviet Communist official. Leader of the Leningrad Communist party organization, 1926; member of Politburo, CPSU, 1930. His assassination in 1934, believed to have been engineered by Stalin, marked the beginning of a massive campaign of arrests and executions involving hundreds of thousands of people.

[4] Until 1925 known as Tsaritsyn, from 1925 to 1961 as Stalingrad, and since as Volgograd.

ordinary. When Tito and Khrushchev left their cars and set off toward the hill called Mamayev Kurgan, famous for the battles which took place there in the last war, the crowd swept aside the strong police cordon which was supposed to keep order and to clear a way for us between the lines of people. There was indescribable confusion, and complete disorder prevailed, so that at one point Khrushchev and Tito could scarcely manage to force a way for themselves through the crowd. It was really quite unpleasant, although the disorder was the result of the people's great enthusiasm. The Russians, especially the security officers, were far more alarmed than we were.

On Mamayev Kurgan Khrushchev explained to us particular phases of the battle for Stalingrad. He had been a member of the Military Council on this front, so he had no need for experts. I asked Marshal Yeremenko,[5] who commanded the Soviet forces here, how many Russians had perished in the Stalingrad battle. After long reflection he said it was difficult to say exactly—maybe up to a million if you took the whole Stalingrad operation, which lasted about half a year. More Germans perished than Russians, Marshal Yeremenko said. Concerning the equipment of the Russian troops, who surrounded and destroyed Hitler's Sixth Army, Marshal Yeremenko said that the fighting equipment was almost entirely of Soviet manufacture.

There is still no memorial to the Soviet troops who fell at Stalingrad. On Mamayev Kurgan we came across a pile of metal, Russian or German shells, still lying there although the war ended eleven years ago. Khrushchev told us that the whole hill was going to be turned into a memorial worthy of this great Soviet victory.

While we were busy on Mamayev Kurgan listening to stories about the battle for Stalingrad, the Russians had called up large military units because, to the great surprise of the Soviet leaders, the security organs had shown themselves incapable of maintaining order in the city. We returned through lines of military trucks parked close together for mile after mile along the streets we passed through. It was the same on the city squares, where it had been made physically impossible for a crowd of more than a thousand people to gather in one place.

When we spoke with the Russians about the unusual welcome accorded to Tito and the Yugoslavs by hundreds of thousands of people, it was apparent that the Soviet displeasure with what had happened was not due to the tremendous confusion which arose or because of any threat to the safety of the important guests, Yugoslav and Soviet. I think the main reason for their displeasure was the fact that the people, carried away by

[5] Andrei I. Yeremenko, 1892–1970. Marshal of the Soviet Union. One of the principal commanders on the Russian front in World War II who took part in the battles for Moscow and Stalingrad.

their enthusiasm and spontaneous desire to greet the Yugoslavs, behaved in a way which had not been seen for decades in the Soviet Union. The Russians' displeasure increased whenever individuals, Yugoslav or Russian, commented on this. It demonstrated better than anything else how great Yugoslavia's prestige is in this country. The Yugoslavs who spoke in this sense and with the best of intentions to Khrushchev and Mikoyan about their enthusiastic welcome in Stalingrad only increased the Russians' resentment. That is why when we arrived in Sochi, Novorossisk, and other places in the south nothing similar happened. We were welcomed everywhere in a friendly way, but there were no more explosions of popular enthusiasm.

During our stay in Sochi there was time for rest and talks. Khrushchev and Mikoyan were constantly in Tito's company along with Kardelj, and there were plenty of opportunities for coming to terms with the Russians on all the questions on which agreement is possible, so that it may not be necessary actually to have any long negotiations at the end in Moscow. We reached agreement with the Russians on interstate relations without difficulty. They were very restrained, giving the impression that they were making concessions by not objecting to our relations with the United States and the West or to our policy toward Eastern Germany and the Balkan Pact. They probably do this so as to be able to ask for real and important concessions on questions concerning ideology and the "camp."

The question of Soviet credits for the building of a Yugoslav aluminum industry was not discussed in detail. It was agreed that there should be separate talks about it at government level. The Russians will still say nothing about the size of the credit, and since they are not pleased with our political stand on the question of "ideological unity" they will certainly show their dissatisfaction in the form of a further reduction of the aluminum credit. Ever since last year the size of the credit has been getting steadily smaller.

Without any pressure from the Soviet side we decided ourselves to accept a "tough" statement on the question of Germany. This will probably give the impression to the public that Yugoslavia has "drawn closer to the Soviet Union." But in essence that is not the case. Khrushchev stated explicitly that the Soviet Union had no comments to make about our policy on Germany, that our recognition of the East German state was exclusively our own affair, and that we knew best what to do. This attitude of Khrushchev's, and not Soviet pressure, made it easier for us to decide ourselves on a formulation which appears, though wrongly, like a concession on our part to the Russians. Needless to say, this was received with satisfaction by the Russians. They saw in it one of the first successes for themselves in their talks with us.

Sochi, June 15, 1956

We are having ever more doubts about whether the visit is going to end as smoothly as it began. This also includes the few optimists among us who thought otherwise because of the exceptionally friendly attitude of the Russians at the beginning. For this reason we have decided that, before we enter into talks with the Russians, we will shorten our draft declaration on party cooperation, which our delegation brought from Belgrade, but which will be totally unacceptable to the Soviet leaders. Not because it is quite a long document—the Russians are in fact fond of lengthy official statements—but because our draft sets out the Yugoslav view of the principles that should govern cooperation between our Communist parties. We shall not change this in the new, shorter draft, but the very fact that it is shorter will mean that there are less points of difference with the Russians.

We expect there to be serious differences between the two delegations on the question of the "socialist camp." We clashed over this already at a meeting between our delegations before we set off on this trip to the south. It was quite clear that for the Russians the main object of Tito's visit is to try and revert to the old situation in relations between Yugoslavia and the Soviet Union. I have already noted that we have entirely different views on these problems. Soviet ambitions are far less realistic than ours. We are interested in establishing cooperation between our party and the Soviet Communist party. We shall not set any conditions for that cooperation except those on the basis of which alone cooperation is possible: equality, independence, and equal rights. That will be difficult to refuse.

Moscow, June 18, 1956

We returned to Moscow and had the meeting for which both sides had been waiting with impatience. The Soviet delegation refused to accept our shortened draft of the document which was intended to resolve the question of party cooperation. It is not difficult to guess what the Soviet reaction would have been if we had handed them the long Yugoslav "socialist charter" which the comrades brought from Belgrade. The most stubborn opponent of our draft was Khrushchev, followed by Mikoyan and rather less vigorously by Bulganin. Khrushchev mentioned the possibility of our signing two documents, one for Communists and the other for the rest. The first would probably have been an internal document, but Khrushchev wasn't entirely clear on that point. But we did not accept this and insisted on having only one document which had to be made public. The Russians were not particularly impressed by our arguments; they consider that confirmation of the policy of the Twentieth Congress should take a different form from the one we favor.

We were able to act in this way and assume all the political risks which might have resulted from a "failure" of Tito's visit, because we are not dependent on the Russians in either domestic or foreign policy. In fact we were obliged to act in this way because the great majority of Yugoslavs support our independent foreign policy. We were very anxious to reach agreement with the Russians, but we had no intention whatsoever of jeopardizing the internal unity of our country by not standing firm. We do not have the slightest need to seek in Moscow any kind of support for Yugoslavia's internal stability. A state which seeks support abroad for its stability at home is in fact only demonstrating that it is on the way to losing both its internal stability and its independence in foreign relations.

Our refusal to assume any obligations with regard to the "camp" or to sign anything about "ideological unity" had a very bad effect on the Russians. They stubbornly refused to accept our draft of a joint communiqué, so it was agreed that Kardelj and Mikoyan should try to draw up a different joint statement as soon as possible, because Tito is leaving Moscow in a couple of days. We kept repeating our arguments and producing new ones, each in support of his own views, but it didn't help. It became clear that there were going to be no concessions on our side, and the Soviet delegation showed no inclination to alter its stand either.

Moscow, June 19, 1956

Today we had a great friendship meeting in the Dinamo sports stadium in Moscow. Tito and Khrushchev made important political speeches, from which it appeared that our agreement with the Russians is much greater than it is in reality. This will make it easier for us to have a short, unpretentious communiqué on party cooperation. It has been agreed that the Yugoslav and the Soviet press will print the complete texts of Khrushchev's and Tito's speeches. The people of Moscow who gathered in Dinamo Stadium gave Tito and the Yugoslavs a very friendly reception, but the fact is that the tens of thousands of people who applauded us hadn't the slightest idea of how great the differences are between Yugoslavs and Russians on the fundamental questions we have been discussing.

Moscow, June 20, 1956

Last night the Presidium gave a farewell dinner. The atmosphere was good, but nothing like what it was at the Spiridonovka house a fortnight ago. We were then at the beginning and today we are at the end of the visit, and now we can see more clearly the difference between wishes and reality. To judge by the Russians' behavior there is nothing left for them to do, for the time being at any rate, but to express satisfaction with the results of Tito's visit, although they are, in my opinion, really disappointed. They invested a great deal in this visit, but their investments have not paid off.

Tito awarded Yugoslav decorations to Marshal Zhukov and a group of ten senior Soviet officers and wartime commanders in the Soviet Army. Marshal Zhukov received the highest Yugoslav military decoration, the Order of Freedom, and the other ten officers—marshals Timoshenko, Koniev, Malinovsky, Moskalenko, Sokolovsky,[6] and a group of distinguished Soviet generals—received the Partisan Star.

The official receptions connected with Tito's visit—both the Soviet reception in the Kremlin and our reception in the Sovietskaya Hotel—were attended by more than a thousand people, including the diplomatic corps. A number of ambassadors—the American Bohlen, the Frenchman Dejean, the Swede Sulman, and the Indian Menon, and some others—asked for separate meetings with Tito. I was in favor of agreeing to this, although it didn't suit the Russians.

We agreed finally on a joint text of a document on party cooperation and signed it formally in St. George's Hall, the most luxurious hall in the Kremlin. At the same time we signed a joint communiqué on interstate cooperation. The document on cooperation between our parties is modest in scope, although it is called the Moscow Declaration. It contains no reference either to "ideological unity" or to the "socialist camp," and is in fact in accordance with basic Yugoslav views. Although the Moscow Declaration is shorter than the Belgrade Declaration and seems less pretentious and less precise in content, it is a document of major importance. I would point out only that the Soviet leaders have not signed such a declaration with any other Communist party in the world since World War II.

I hear that a great reception is being prepared in Bucharest for Tito and the Yugoslavs on their way back from Moscow. They say there is

[6] Marshal Semen K. Timoshenko (1895–1970) commanded a cavalry division in the Civil War, 1919, but did not distinguish himself in the field in World War II; Marshal Ivan Koniev (1897–1973) was a leading commander in World War II and became Commander in Chief of the Warsaw Pact forces in 1955; Marshal Rodion Malinovsky (1898–1967) commanded the Soviet forces which drove the German armies out of Romania, Hungary, Austria, and Czechoslovakia at the end of World War II and was Minister of Defense, 1957–67; Marshal Kirill Moskalenko (b. 1902) was put in command of Russia's strategic rocket forces in 1960 and in 1962 became Chief Inspector of the Soviet Army; Marshal Vasili Sokolovsky (1897–1968) commanded the Soviet Occupation Forces in Germany from 1946 until he was made Chief of the General Staff in 1952.

to be a mass meeting in Bucharest at which Tito and Gheorghiu-Dej[7] are to speak. I am not sure whether the Russians counted on this. Though the Yugoslavs have kept quiet about it, the Romanians have certainly not made such a mistake and have probably informed the Russians about everything. I accompanied Tito, his wife Jovanka and the Yugoslav delegation to the Romanian-Soviet frontier at Ungeni where they entered the Soviet Union. When I took my leave of Tito he was surprised, because he thought I was going with them to Belgrade. I would certainly have liked to go with them to Yugoslavia after everything that has happened in the last three weeks, but I had to return to my regular job. As we parted Tito said that it would now be easier for me to work in the Soviet Union. I agreed.

Moscow, June 26, 1956

Tito's return through Romania was a triumphal progress. In Bucharest a mass political meeting was held in the main city square, at which Tito and the leader of the Romanian Communist party, Gheorghiu-Dej, spoke. Only two days after the signing of the Moscow Declaration Tito was addressing a meeting of more than 200,000 people in the capital of Romania! It came about, so to speak, by chance, on the way back to Belgrade, but it was an event the enormous political importance of which cannot be overestimated for us, for the Russians, or for the Romanians. For them it was something out of the blue while for us it was just what we wanted. As far as their relations with the Soviet Union are concerned, the Romanians consider they are "covered" politically, because by welcoming Tito in this way they are only celebrating the Soviet-Yugoslav agreements. The new agreements about party cooperation between Yugoslavia and the Soviet Union give Romania and the other countries of the "camp" greater room for maneuver in their struggle for independence and equality in relations with the Soviet Union.

The welcome in Belgrade was the crowning point of Tito's remarkable journey. At a meeting of more than 200,000 people Tito spoke in the very highest terms of the agreements which we had signed in Moscow. After Tito's speeches in Bucharest and Belgrade people here and abroad are more convinced than ever that a further important step has taken place toward bringing Yugoslavia and the Soviet Union closer together.

The Russians probably have different views on all this. After returning to Moscow I learned that the Russians had had a meeting here of representatives of countries of the "camp" even before Tito was back in Belgrade. It was attended by party leaders from Eastern Europe whom

[7] Gheorghe Gheorghiu-Dej, 1901–65. Romanian Communist leader. Secretary-General, Romanian Communist party, 1945–65.

the Russians had summoned to tell them, among other things, about the results of the Tito visit. This haste confirms the correctness of our earlier assessment that for the Russians the question of Eastern Europe was the main issue in the political program they arranged for us.

The Moscow meeting of representatives of the countries of the "camp" was presided over by M. Rákosi. The main item on the agenda was relations and cooperation between the Communist parties following the dissolution of the Cominform. Khrushchev was the main speaker, and he expounded the view of the CPSU that there was no need to create any new international organization of Communist parties to replace the Cominform. All the Eastern European representatives agreed with Khrushchev at once without any discussion, and Rákosi, presiding, wanted to be the first to speak, and on behalf of the rest. But Khrushchev would not agree to that and demanded that each of them should speak only in the name of his own party. Khrushchev then proposed that they should arrange for the publication of a theoretical journal which would be the unofficial organ of the Communist parties which collaborated in it. This was also agreed unanimously. The journal will not have its editorial office in Moscow but in Czechoslovakia. This is meant to be a sign of equality, and it is better for the Russians because they thus acquire a new and important Soviet institution in a country of the "camp."

Not one of the East European leaders at this meeting made any reference to the Moscow Declaration, although it was published here only two days before the meeting! To ignore the Moscow Declaration in this way only the day after it was signed can be an indication only of Soviet dissatisfaction with the document. In any case the Russians have thus made it quite clear to the leaders of Eastern Europe that what they have signed with Tito has no bearing on Soviet policy toward the countries and Communist parties of the "camp." Nobody had any questions or any comment to make.

Moscow, June 30, 1956

Only a week after the signing of the Moscow Declaration there was disorder and bloodshed in the Polish city of Poznań. As far as we can make out here, the leaders of the clash between the people and the authorities were actually workers. It started with strikes. The authorities brought out troops and tanks. It is said that there were many dead and wounded among the demonstrators.

The events in Poland came as a great shock to the Russians. They see in this the beginning of the counterrevolution which, as they put it here, the West, led by the United States, has organized with the object of splitting the "camp" and separating Poland and the other socialist states from the Soviet Union. We have not been able to find anybody among the Russians who interprets the bloodshed in Poznań otherwise than as an "imperialist plot." None of the officials associates the Poles' discontent with the régime which Stalin imposed on Poland. You can even hear comments in Moscow to the effect that the people responsible are those who condemned Stalin.

One should not be surprised at such an interpretation of events which best suits the Stalinists politically and is psychologically in line with the attitude of the average official. After all, Khrushchev himself recently adopted a similar position when he threatened the Poles, accused them of wanting to "go to the West," and warned everyone in Poland and in the "camp" as a whole not to try and change the present relations. The preservation of the "camp" and Soviet domination over it is an imperative of the new Soviet foreign policy as it was of the old one. The policy of de-Stalinization does not only not permit the disintegration of the "camp"; it counts on its further consolidation.

In the view of the Soviet leaders the policy of de-Stalinization is strictly an internal affair of the Soviet party and government, actually of the Presidium of the party, which measures out doses of the new political medicine like a pharmacist. But for three months now they have not been able to hit on the right amount and they keep on writing new prescriptions.

It is possible in Moscow to proclaim a theory opposing the "cult of personality" and on that basis to build a sort of new, post-Stalin policy, even if it has its ups and downs and zigzags. It is quite a different matter when it comes to a country of Eastern Europe whose state frontiers are also a demarcation line between the Soviet and the Western armies. It is possible in the Soviet Union to exercise strict control over internal events and to adjust the process of de-Stalinization step by step. But in the countries of Eastern Europe that is not possible, because the first steps may lead to an explosion and very serious crises, with unforeseeable consequences. In Poznań it started with a protest meeting of workers in some factory. Within an hour it had turned into a mass demonstration involving tens of thousands of Polish citizens. Then the army arrived to defend the socialist system with tanks. This bloodshed in Poznań has convinced the Russians of the need for the strictest control over, and the most careful application of, the process of de-Stalinization. If he is allowed just "one spoonful" more, the patient himself may suffer.

Moscow, July 1, 1956

Perhaps the Russians think that there would have been no crisis in the "camp" and no Poznań if, ten days ago, we had accepted the idea of "ideological unity" and signed an undertaking to carry out toward the "camp" the sort of policy which suits the Russians. According to this twisted logic, we are responsible for having stubbornly defended our own independence and for fighting for equality in relations with the Soviet Union, because by so doing we prompt others to strive for the same things. But the Soviet Union is not considered responsible for having restricted the independence and equality of other socialist countries and its allies. The present picture is less favorable than it was three months ago.

Moscow, July 3, 1956

The whole Soviet press for June 30, 1956, published a declaration of the Soviet Communist party entitled, "On Overcoming the Cult of Personality and Its Consequences." It is a long document taking up nearly half of every Soviet newspaper, and it is published as a decree of the Central Committee and is connected with Khrushchev's secret speech about Stalin at the Twentieth Congress. On June 4, 1956, the Americans published the complete text of Khrushchev's speech. It was not a newspaper or the American intelligence service which did this but the State Department, which accepted full responsibility on behalf of the United States Government for the authenticity of the text. There has probably not been anything like it in relations between Russia and America for many years. This move by the Americans produced a worldwide reaction. Practically every country in the world, except those where Communists are in power, is talking about Khrushchev's secret speech on the basis of the American official version. Now we have a paradoxical situation with regard to the freedom of information for people under socialism: Khrushchev's secret speech has been published throughout the world in all major languages, and it is only in the "socialist camp" that it is still treated as a state secret.

In view of what had happened the Russians realized that they had to publish in Moscow some version of the secret speech, and so they produced the "decree," which in fact supplements and amends the secret speech.

I believe the Russians had prepared the "decree" about Stalin even before Tito's visit to the Soviet Union. I think they waited to see the results of the visit and decided the basic political line of the "decree" accordingly. Our refusal to abandon our independent position caused disappointment on the Soviet side, primarily for Khrushchev, who had personally invested more in the Tito visit than in any other Soviet political move in the spring of 1956. Maybe that is why the "decree" on Stalin is now worse than it might otherwise have been.

The "decree" is addressed not only to Communists and the "camp" but also partly to the governments and the public of Western states. The Russians still insist on the old Soviet view that the world is divided into two antagonistic blocs, and they demand strict unity on the part of all Communist parties in the struggle against capitalism, which, they claim, is preparing to destroy the revolutionary movements and their achievements by force. There is nothing said in the "decree" about the need for international unity of the working class and all progressive forces or about the need for cooperation between Communists and Social Democrats, and there is nothing at all said about the policy of coexistence and peace in the world. As for the Communists in the Soviet Union and Eastern Europe, they are given strict instructions about what can and what cannot be changed in Moscow's present policy. The state and party apparatus in the Soviet Union and Eastern Europe not only appeals for order and discipline; it appears to be put in a state of alert.

There are some other illustrations of how the wind is beginning to blow here. Along with the "decree" the Russians have now come out with public criticism of Togliatti, leader of the Italian Communist party. Only ten days ago Khrushchev and Mikoyan told us that they had no objections to the statements which Togliatti made in support of the Twentieth Congress and in favor of the policy of de-Stalinization, and that they were ready to publish it all here. Instead they have now attacked Togliatti in *Pravda!*

Although the "decree" says that the Soviet Union will continue the present, which must mean the new, policy, the stress falls too frequently on attitudes taken from the old policy. A particular weakness for us, as well as for others and, I believe, for the Russians, too, is that it ignores the Moscow Declaration, because if there is anything new and progressive in Soviet policy toward Communist parties and socialist countries it is in that very declaration which Tito and Khrushchev signed ten days ago. Although the Russians now need to produce evidence in favor of their new policy, they are at the moment embarrassed by this most important piece of evidence, and it looks as though they are already sorry they signed that declaration with the Yugoslavs.

Moscow, July 5, 1956

We had a talk with the Americans. They are worse disposed toward us now than they were three months ago when I arrived in Moscow. They seem to have been upset by the three weeks of Yugoslav-Soviet celebrations which took place here last month. Yet behind all the show, which may often be misleading, there took place the restoration of normal relations between the Yugoslav and Soviet Communist parties and the establishment of cooperation between them—and that is a new and important political fact.

It seems that the Americans are also not pleased by the fact that Yugoslavia has chosen to have a completely new basis for its cooperation with the Russians. Perhaps they are not ready to understand or to accept the fact that a superpower or, let us say, a super-Communist party like the CPSU can cooperate on a voluntary, equal, and independent basis with a Communist party of a small "Communist country" like Yugoslavia. It seems as though for the Americans it is the natural state of affairs for cooperation between Communist parties of small socialist countries and the Communist party of a great socialist country to lead to subordination. Nothing can change this, not even the text of the Moscow Declaration signed by Tito and Khrushchev. That is simply words, and in politics words, even the finest, cannot be what is most important.

However that may be, the fact remains that the atmosphere at my meetings with the Americans in Moscow is less agreeable than at any time in the last few years. We now have a very odd state of affairs: The Russians are displeased because they didn't achieve anything with Yugoslavia. The Americans are displeased because they think the Russians achieved too much. Whichever way you look at it, both the Russians and the Americans are cross—and with the Yugoslavs!

American diplomats in Moscow bestirred themselves and became very active following the events in Poland. They don't show the slightest concern about Soviet accusations that it was all the result of a "plot by American imperialism." American newsmen here say that the United States would accept any international inquiry into the causes of those events and would accept in advance any findings of an international commission which looked into the matter. Our general impression is that the Americans are pleased with what is happening. The crisis has erupted in the Soviet Union and in the Warsaw Pact, and not in America or in the NATO bloc.

CHAPTER SIX

CRISIS IN HUNGARY

The handling of a speech by Khrushchev in the Yugoslav press produces a crisis in Mićunović's relations with the Soviet leaders and gives him his first sample of the extent of Russian sensitivity. It also reveals indirectly the strength of latent anti-Yugoslav feeling in the Soviet Presidium. Khrushchev mishandles the developing crisis in Hungary.

Moscow, July 7, 1956

The Soviet Government gave a reception last night in the Kremlin in honor of Prince Norodom Sihanouk,[1] who is here leading a Cambodian delegation. When I saw a suitable opportunity, I went up to Khrushchev to speak to him. Molotov and Voroshilov were with him, and they all became very grim when I approached, exchanging greetings with me reluctantly and barely within the limits of propriety. They were so ill disposed that I thought it would be better to move away at once, but Khrushchev detained me, saying he had "certain things" to tell me.

They could not have imagined, he said, that Yugoslavia would do anything like what it had done with regard to the Soviet Union and him personally. I was taken aback and asked what had happened.

Khrushchev said that the Yugoslav press had censored his speech at Dinamo Stadium in Moscow despite the agreement with Tito that our press and the Soviet press would publish the full texts of both speeches. We in Yugoslavia had broken the agreement and censored his speech, so that in Yugoslavia people didn't know what Khrushchev had said, while in the Soviet Union they had acted in accordance with the formal agreement and had published the complete text of Tito's speech.

Khrushchev seemed to be really upset and angry. Molotov and Voroshilov looked worried, as though something terrible had happened to

[1] Prince Norodom Sihanouk. Cambodian Head of State, 1960–70.

change suddenly and fundamentally relations between Yugoslavia and the Soviet Union. Khrushchev kept making ever worse accusations against Yugoslavia. He said they had thought of writing a note of protest to our Central Committee, which was responsible for it all. They hadn't written the letter, but they hadn't dropped the idea, for it was a very serious matter and no accident. They had treated Tito with the utmost sincerity and the greatest respect and in return we had broken agreements in the crudest way. Furious and almost threatening, Khrushchev declared that they were not going to let anybody play about with them.

I was astonished. I knew nothing about this mistake on the part of the Yugoslav press, although I regularly receive our newspapers here and had glanced through them. I hadn't read the texts of Tito's or Khrushchev's speech in the papers, either Soviet or Yugoslav, because I had listened to both of them at the meeting. I was surprised that Khrushchev attached greater importance to what was more or less a technical slip on the part of the Yugoslav press than to all the results of Tito's visit. I was amazed at the language and tone he adopted.

I told Khrushchev, Molotov, and Voroshilov that I was learning about it for the first time from them, that I was very surprised that they were connecting this mistake by our press with our leaders and Tito, that Tito was still in the Soviet Union when our press reported the meeting and speeches in Dinamo Stadium, and that our leaders could not have any connection with it all. I reminded them that Tito had on at least ten occasions in the Soviet Union, then in Romania and again in Belgrade, spoken very highly about the Soviet Union and about his visit, that this had received worldwide publicity, and that it was of no importance whether some Yugoslav newspaper fifteen days ago published its own shortened version of Tito or Khrushchev at the June 19 meeting. I agreed entirely with Khrushchev's reproaches concerning the incorrect behavior of the Yugoslav press, but I thought that no political significance should be attached to it. Nobody, either in the Soviet Union or in Yugoslavia or in the outside world, had even noticed it, and yet this evening it appeared to be the most important matter connected with Tito's visit to the Soviet Union. It was not easy to understand this attitude.

I had no success with what I said, although it seemed to me that all the arguments were on my side. Khrushchev stuck to his guns. A few paces away from us stood Bulganin, Mikoyan, Malenkov,[2] and other members of the Presidium. None of them came up to us. When Khrushchev said

[2] Georgi M. Malenkov, b. 1902. Soviet Communist official. Member of Politburo, CPSU, 1946–57; Prime Minister, 1953–55. Dismissed as member of "antiparty group" in 1957 and disappeared from public view.

he didn't know how to explain such "conduct by Yugoslavia toward the Soviet Union and him personally," Voroshilov said that there was perhaps "still some Djilas"[3] among us, at which point Khrushchev cut him off.

After Molotov and Voroshilov had shaken hands with me and moved away, Khrushchev went on to say that there were still things which were not clear in relations between us and that what had happened was not accidental. When I asked him what he had in mind, Khrushchev replied that I understood very well what he meant. When I told him that I really didn't understand either what he had said or this evening's conversation from the very outset, Khrushchev said he couldn't tell me any more now but hoped that the time would come when he could.

Again getting excited, Khrushchev ended the conversation with the following statement: "You personally know very well what I have done here in connection with Yugoslavia, yet your press behaves to me in this way. All the members of the Presidium received reports about it. Your press published only a third of the official text of my speech, while the Soviet press printed the complete text of Tito's speech. Now the Presidium is looking at me. They are not saying anything yet but they've got their eyes on me now because of what you have done."

On my way home I tried to fit the pieces together and to explain in some way Khrushchev's strange behavior and the way the Soviet leaders had dramatized the whole affair. In view of the agreement, Khrushchev is right when he criticizes what the Yugoslav press did. But he is not at all in the right when he seeks to find in this mistake by our press, made three weeks ago, something like evidence that Yugoslavia is "violating agreements with Moscow."

For some reason or other Khrushchev or someone else in the Soviet leadership feels the need to provoke this storm in a teacup and to find some excuse for making such grave accusations against Yugoslavia. It is all the worse when Khrushchev does it in front of witnesses. One of them, Voroshilov, asked me if I knew what they would have done if the Poles, Hungarians, Czechs, or others had done something similar. When I said I really didn't know what the Russians would have done and waited for Voroshilov's answer, Khrushchev did not allow him to say what he was thinking.

[3] Milovan Djilas, b. 1911. Member of Politburo, Yugoslav Communist party, from 1938; Vice-president, Federal Executive Council, and President, National Assembly, 1953. One of the architects with Tito of the Communist regime in Yugoslavia, Djilas was dismissed from all his posts in 1954 for his "antiparty" activities and views. He was twice sentenced to prison for his public statements critical of the regime. Author of many political and literary works, including *The New Class* (1958), *Conversations with Stalin* (1966), and his war memoirs, *Wartime* (1977).

Moscow, July 8, 1956

The matter which Khrushchev spoke to me about last night was discussed as a special item on the agenda at a meeting of the Presidium of the Soviet Communist party! All the members of the Presidium received the material: copies of the Soviet *Pravda* and of the Yugoslav *Borba*. Two thirds of Khrushchev's speech in *Pravda* was underlined in red pencil to show exactly how much *Borba* and the rest of the Yugoslav press had left out of the speech. I had never realized that the top Soviet leaders concerned themselves with such matters. They needed this counting of lines simply to provide some formal basis for the Russian accusations. The Russians have really been looking for an excuse to worsen their relations with Yugoslavia.

I don't believe that Khrushchev is the initiator of this new tension in relations with Yugoslavia. After Molotov and Voroshilov left us yesterday Khrushchev gave me to understand that he had not started this quarrel with us of his own will but was acting in accordance with a decision of the Presidium. The reason for the worsening of relations is not, of course, the "censoring" of his speech, but Moscow's general attitude to the events which have taken place since Tito's visit.

At a time when the Soviet Union's relations with the rest of the world are worsening all round, Yugoslavia can certainly not be an exception.

I proposed that we should try to put things right by publishing at government expense a booklet about Tito's visit to Russia for mass distribution and said that the booklet should include the full text of Khrushchev's speech at the "friendship" meeting in Moscow on June 19. Even if there hadn't been this unexpected row with the Russians, I think we have good reason to publicize further the results of Tito's visit to the Soviet Union.

Moscow, July 10, 1956

Yesterday evening I met Khrushchev at a reception for Kim Il Sung, President of North Korea. Finding him in a much better mood than he was three days ago I asked him what he had in mind when he told me that there were still "unpleasant things" in relations between Yugoslavia and the Soviet Union and said that I was asking him as the ambassador of Yugoslavia and was completely at his disposal to try and remove all the things which were "unclear" and which still remained from our past relations, which had been really unpleasant. I said it was not that there were things which were unclear in our relations but that there were very clear differences and disagreements on many questions. I considered it a very good thing that we should speak frankly to each other about them. Differences in point of view were in no sense "unpleasant things." But Khrushchev wasn't prepared to get involved in a conversation on this subject. He repeated what he had told me three days previously: that the time would come for him to tell me more about it. From what he had to say about Yugoslavia's relations with the countries of the West being very good while the Soviet Union's relations with the same countries were not good at all and that many Yugoslavs continued to regard the Soviet Union in the old way, I got the impression that, when Khrushchev talks about "unpleasant things," he has in mind some conversations which Yugoslavs have had with Western diplomats.

They continue to collect here all sorts of reports about Yugoslavia, not only from Belgrade and Moscow but from the world at large. Whether or not the Soviet intelligence service is operating now "in a Leninist way" and differently from the way it operated in Stalin's day, the Soviet leaders continue to be supplied with every kind of document attacking Yugoslavia, whether it is produced in Eastern Europe or in America. If someone in Moscow is collecting only unfavorable statements made by some Yugoslavs about the Soviet Union in various parts of the world, it is not difficult to imagine what a pile of "anti-Soviet" reports can be built up in the course of a single week.

Everything that any Yugoslav has said against the Soviet Union is taken here, when it suits them, as though that individual is speaking for the Central Committee of our party and our government. These reports about our "anti-Sovietism" are now increasing in number, especially at the present time. It seems that they have come finally to the conclusion that Tito's visit served us as a means of further asserting Yugoslavia's independent policy, and the Russians are cross with themselves for having contributed to this.

Moscow, July 13, 1956

Today is the fifteenth anniversary of the armed uprising against the Italian fascist occupation forces in my native Montenegro. I am far away from my native land, and I can join in my countrymen's celebrations only in my thoughts. Here in Moscow we shall not mark this glorious occasion with any special celebrations. The armed rising in Montenegro fifteen years ago was the first armed uprising of a nation, in the true sense of these words, in Yugoslavia or in Europe in 1941.

In the course of only a few days of armed struggle in the middle of July 1941 the people of little Montenegro, having risen in revolt and led by the Communists, put out of action more than four thousand Italian officers and men. In many European countries monuments have been erected in places where a single Nazi was killed or a single patriot and member of a resistance movement in an occupied country perished. In one place alone, in one day and in a single battle, the Montenegrin partisans annihilated a complete Italian battalion of about 800 men, at the battle of Košćele, near Cetinje on July 15, 1941. Thus one of the smallest peoples in occupied Europe fought the biggest battle against fascism in the summer of 1941. If any of the bigger nations of Europe had become involved in such a battle after taking up arms against the fascist invaders, it would have been written about in every history of World War II. In fact, there is, on the way to Cetinje, at the spot where this glorious battle took place, a small, hardly noticeable memorial plaque. Such is the fate of great exploits when they are performed by a small people.

But this is not the time for me to record how through their armed uprising in 1941 the Montenegrins, like the other peoples of Yugoslavia, helped the Russians when things were going so badly for them, while Russia, though a great country, was not able either then or in the next three years of fighting, to be of direct assistance to our struggle in any way whatsoever. Fifteen years later the Russians still keep silent about this or identify Yugoslavia and its contribution to the victory over fascism with that made by any other country of Eastern Europe. But the majority of those countries were wartime allies of Hitler. Perhaps the time will come when they will tell the real truth about this in Russia, too.

Moscow, July 14, 1956

Last night Khrushchev told me that following a conversation between Tito and their ambassador in Belgrade we can consider the incident concerning our press closed. Thank goodness for that!

Khrushchev then turned to events in Poland. He attacked very strongly the "anti-Soviet elements" there, who were trying to follow Yugoslavia's example although they had no right to do so. They were all, in Poland, in Hungary, and elsewhere, Khrushchev said, now quoting Yugoslavia, although it had nothing to do with Yugoslavia, because Yugoslavia was something quite different. In fact they wanted to go to the West and break up the "camp." Behind it all stood the United States, spurred on by Dulles,[4] who in Khrushchev's opinion had gone a lot further this time than they in Moscow could have thought possible. The Russians now intended publicly to call the United States to book and to say frankly in the Soviet press what the Americans were up to. From what the Russians were doing the Americans had drawn the wrong conclusion that the Soviet Union was weak. "We shall show them that they've made a great mistake," Khrushchev said.

[4] John Foster Dulles, 1888–1959. American statesman. Secretary of State, 1953–59.

With the qualification that I was hearing about all this for the first time and that I didn't know what was going to be published here against America, I said I did not think it would be a good thing to view the present situation exclusively in the light of the events and troubles in Poland. Khrushchev cut me off, took me by the hand, and said: "Blood has been shed there." I said that that was, unfortunately, true, but that it was equally true that it was a question of a single event in one city and that that event might have its own specific causes, quite independently of Dulles's anti-Communist policy. It seemed to me that it would be good for Dulles and bad for the Soviet Union and the other socialist countries if the Russians now suddenly sought to sharpen the conflict. With the reservation that I was expressing only my own views, I told Khrushchev that other, opposite alternatives should be considered. There were plenty of them if one started by establishing precisely why the workers of Poznań revolted and why the authorities acted as they did. I could not believe that the Polish workers or the workers in other socialist countries wanted to restore capitalism or were rebelling at Dulles's instigation, whether or not the United States Government was pleased with what had happened in Poland.

Khrushchev said he understood very well what I was saying, that the Soviet Union would continue the policy of the Twentieth Congress, but would at the same time "show the enemies" that the Soviet Union was powerful and afraid of no one. This time the West had dared to provoke a revolt in Poland, tomorrow it would be somewhere else; they thought the time had come to change the results of World War II. "We must give them a rap over the knuckles," Khrushchev said. The policy of peaceful coexistence wouldn't suffer because of that. On the contrary. Imperialism accepted that policy only if socialism were strong. Imperialism would not coexist with a weak socialism.

As has always been the case till now, a tougher Soviet policy toward the West results in a tougher policy at home, in the Soviet Union, and in Eastern Europe. Soviet disappointment with Tito's visit and the blowing up of the insignificant affair with our press all fits in with this. I fear that we have not yet seen the end of this, since it seems at the moment that the cold Siberian winds have started to blow again here.

Moscow, July 15, 1956

In the latter part of his conversation Khrushchev asked me to tell Tito the following: that the situation in Hungary was very complicated. Suslov had been there and had reported back to the Presidium. The Russians had decided to give Rákosi their energetic support! Khrushchev said that they well knew how difficult his position was, but they also knew that everything Rákosi had done was on instructions from Stalin. Rákosi was no more to blame than they were here in Moscow. Rákosi couldn't say this publicly today any more than the Russians could. That was why after Suslov had reported back they had decided to back Rákosi! I don't think it surprising that such a proposal should come from Suslov.

Khrushchev told me that the Hungarians had rehabilitated László Rajk,[5] who had perished though he was guiltless. I made no comment on this, although it is more than obvious that Rákosi cannot rehabilitate Rajk and remain the leader of Hungary. Khrushchev criticized the Hungarians for having expelled Imre Nagy[6] from the party. He said they had not asked the Russians about it. Nagy should have been left in the party, where he would now have been very useful. They had no other choice but to support Rákosi, and Khrushchev wanted Tito to understand the situation properly, because he feared another conflict might arise between Yugoslavia and the Soviet Union over Hungary and Soviet support for Rákosi. Mikoyan had left Moscow a few days ago to "reach agreement with the Hungarian comrades."

I thought the conversation was over and said that I would inform Tito by telegram that same evening about everything he had said, and I was about to take my leave. But Khrushchev kept me back and said: If the situation in Hungary gets still worse, we here have decided to use all means at our disposal to bring the crisis to an end. Khrushchev said he was telling me this in confidence, that such a situation had not yet arisen and that maybe it wouldn't arise, but that he wanted to inform Tito in good time about the internal decisions which had been taken here. He also said that the Soviet Union could not at any price allow a "breach in the front" in Eastern Europe, and that was just what the West was working for.

It was clear that Khrushchev was threatening us Yugoslavs and not just the Hungarians, as it was also clear that they had decided to use force in Hungary if the situation became more serious. By all accounts Suslov did his best to deepen and sharpen the crisis, instead of reducing it and making a better solution possible. Now they threaten us with the use of the Soviet Army in Hungary and invite Yugoslavia "to understand them properly"—and remain silent.

[5] László Rajk. Hungarian Communist leader. Minister of Internal Affairs, 1945; Foreign Minister, 1948. Executed in 1949 for "Titoism." Rehabilitated and reburied in 1956.
[6] Imre Nagy. One of the founders of the Hungarian Communist party, Nagy spent fifteen years in Moscow after the collapse of the Hungarian "Soviet Republic" in 1920. He returned to Hungary after World War II to become Minister of Agriculture in 1945 and Prime Minister in 1953. In 1955 he was dismissed for his "errors," only to be made Prime Minister again in the crisis of 1956.

Presumably to soften the effect of these threats, because he could not have failed to notice my surprise and disagreement, Khrushchev told me that they had had very good talks with the Italians in the last few days. Togliatti was a "devoted and honest Communist," Khrushchev said, having apparently forgotten that only a fortnight ago Togliatti was severely criticized in *Pravda*. Then Khrushchev informed me that Ochab and Cyrankiewicz[7] had paid a secret visit to Moscow, that the Russians were going to give the Poles substantial economic aid, that things in Poland were now quieter, that Poznań had another, good side, and that the Polish leaders were responsible for what had happened. It didn't worry Khrushchev that he had recently given me completely opposite views on the same subjects. To support his argument Khrushchev told me of instances where the rebellious workers in Poznań had prevented bandits from the Armia Krajowa[8] from shooting a Polish officer who had jumped out of his tank when it was set on fire by the demonstrators. The bandits seized him and put him up against a wall, but the workers—although they were in revolt—prevented the execution.

Perhaps it seemed to Khrushchev that he had talked too much about Hungary and too much in favor of our Yugoslav attitude to Poznań, so he started to tell me about fresh charges being made against Yugoslavia by Enver Hoxha. He said Hoxha had written to him a few days ago and accused Yugoslavia of continuing to try and overthrow the lawful government of Albania. He claimed that our new minister there, Arso Milatović, was bringing people from the opposition, enemies of Enver Hoxha and the Albanian Government, together.

At this point I could remain silent no longer. I told Khrushchev that for a number of years I had personally been handling our relations with Albania, even during Stalin's lifetime, when the Albanians were killing our officers and soldiers on the frontier and committing every kind of crime against Yugoslavia, as well as later, right up to my departure for Moscow. Both before and after 1948[9] we had consistently defended Albania's integrity and sovereignty, even though its leaders, led by Hoxha, had conducted a hostile policy toward Yugoslavia. Even in Stalin's day we made it quite clear to all Albania's enemies in the West that any attempt on their part to violate Albania's sovereignty and integrity would be regarded by us as an attack on Yugoslavia's own sovereignty and integrity, whether or not Hoxha was pursuing a hostile policy toward us.

[7] Joseph Cyrankiewicz, b. 1911. Secretary-General, Polish Socialist party, 1945–48; Member of Politburo, Polish Communist party, from 1948; Prime Minister, 1947–52 and 1954–70.
[8] Armia Krajowa, or A. K.—the "Home Army," the non-Communist resistance movement in wartime Poland.
[9] I.e., after the Cominform Resolution. Hoxha then sided with Moscow.

Hoxha could thank Yugoslavia first of all, and not Stalin, that Albania was an independent country today, as well as for the fact that Enver Hoxha was today in power. We offer him the restoration of normal relations on the principles of equality of rights, respect for sovereignty and territorial integrity, and recognition of the interests of both parties. Hoxha turns this down, because it suits him better to act in the old Stalinist way and to go on intriguing in Moscow against Yugoslavia. I also rejected the charges made against our minister, Arso Milatović, whom I know very well personally. What Hoxha says against him is, in my opinion, devoid of any foundation. I begged Khrushchev to ask for a report from the Soviet embassy in Tirana about how Yugoslav diplomats in Tirana live and the sort of humiliation and maltreatment they are exposed to.

What I said seemed to make an impression. Khrushchev climbed down, said he had never been in Albania, that he didn't know the country or its leaders except Enver Hoxha "a little," that he was telling me all this only "as one comrade to another," and that the Soviet Union wanted to see an improvement in relations between Yugoslavia and Albania. I was still depressed by what he had told me about the results of Suslov's mission to Budapest, Soviet support for Rákosi, and their intention to use "all means" in Hungary, which sounded rather like a threat to Yugoslavia as well.

Moscow, July 16, 1956

At a reception at the French embassy I had not intended to approach Khrushchev. He was the principal guest, surrounded with the greatest attention by the French ambassador. But he sent one of his interpreters to inform me that he would like to talk to me if I would "stay longer at the reception." Shortly after that Khrushchev went round the guests exchanging greetings with a large number of foreign ambassadors, and when he came to me he stayed to talk, as usual with no one else present.

Khrushchev said he wanted to give me the results so far of Mikoyan's talks in Budapest. He said everything went off much better than they had hoped and that the "Hungarian comrades" had decided that Rákosi should resign. Rákosi himself had been present at the meetings in Budapest and he was "fully in agreement with this decision." Khrushchev expected that they had thus taken a decisive step toward a political solution of the internal crisis in Hungary. He asked me to pass this on to Tito and assured me that he had come to the French reception in order to tell me about it.

Bulganin came up to us, fighting his way through the dense crowd of guests. We continued the conversation about Mikoyan's stay in Hungary and established the fact that he was now "on holiday" near the Yugoslav-Hungarian frontier. Khrushchev said that Mikoyan greatly enjoyed traveling and that after his "holiday" in Hungary he might go to Yugoslavia. It is clear that the Russians want Mikoyan to go to Yugoslavia after having "resolved" the crisis in Hungary. It would appear to the world as though the Russians had secretly agreed with the Yugoslavs about resolving the crisis, although we knew nothing about what was going on, except what Khrushchev told me. Three days ago he was telling me that they had decided to give full support to Rákosi "by all means."

Contradictions like this and the adoption of contrary positions on one and the same question does not say much for the state of affairs not only in Hungary but among the Soviet leaders either. The Russians behaved similarly toward Poland. First of all, long before Poznań, they threatened the Poles, then they behaved very belligerently because of Poznań, and immediately afterward, irrespective of everything they had been saying, they gave the Poles large-scale economic aid!

Both Khrushchev and Bulganin displayed lively interest in a Mikoyan visit to Yugoslavia, straight from Hungary. They obviously need to create the impression in the world that Yugoslavia played a part in the Soviet resolution of the Hungarian crisis.

I advised Belgrade to accept a brief visit by Mikoyan, although it is being wished on us.

Moscow, July 20, 1956

Belgrade was slow in replying to the Soviet request and my telegram about Mikoyan's visit, and the Russians are becoming ever more impatient. So the Soviet Foreign Ministry sent me the passports of the crew of Mikoyan's plane. I issued the visas on my own responsibility, although I realized that Belgrade did not like having Mikoyan arrive in such circumstances.

At the same time as they press for Mikoyan to visit Yugoslavia, or actually to return to the Soviet Union through Belgrade, the Russians are still behaving badly in connection with the aluminum credits to Yugoslavia. This question dogs our relations with the Soviet Union like a shadow for the second year now, and as time passes Soviet behavior gets steadily worse. They are now putting forward political conditions. They have already reduced the credit by a quarter of the original amount and are demanding the inclusion of Eastern Germany as a creditor and that the East German Government should sign the agreement along with the Soviet Union and Yugoslavia. Comrade Avdo Humo, the member of our government who has been here negotiating with the Russians for nearly two months, has been informed about this by Belgrade. In Belgrade they have agreed to include in the bilateral agreement with the Soviet Union a paragraph saying that Eastern Germany will participate in the credit. But this first concession of ours to the Russians was not sufficient.

The East Germans had no serious objections to our arguments that East Germany ought not to be a cosignatory of international agreements on credits, because there are certain international rules which they and we must comply with. Our countries do not yet have diplomatic relations and therefore cannot sign these or any other interstate agreements at the government level. The Russians have behaved worse than the representatives of East Germany. To our reference to international law and practice the Russians opposed "Marxism-Leninism" and "proletarian internationalism."

Two days ago a communiqué was published here about talks between the Soviet Government and the government of Eastern Germany, whose delegation was led by Otto Grotewohl.[10] The Russians are giving new and important credits to Eastern Germany. At the same time they are reducing for the third time the credits they promised to Yugoslavia. The whole game is very obvious: The Russians give the Germans the credits which they promised us and ask us to accept East Germany as a cosignatory and creditor on the basis of Soviet funds which the Russians have given them instead of us. And all this is being performed in front of our very eyes. East Germany has not yet even tried to meet any of its obligations to Yugoslavia arising from the war or from the ten years since the war, yet the Russians now try to put Yugoslavia in the position of being a debtor to East Germany!

In conversation with me at a reception in the East German embassy Walter Ulbricht[11] tried openly to exert pressure on us in support of this Soviet policy. He reproached us for failing to recognize Eastern Germany. It was, he said, our "international duty." I told Ulbricht that they had not recognized Yugoslavia as a socialist country up to yesterday, but that our socialism hadn't suffered as a result. And the East Germans would not suffer because of our failure to recognize them. We would recognize them when the time came for it, and let each of us stick to his "proletarian internationalism" as previously. It was not a very pleasant conversation. Even during the reception I heard that both Ulbricht and the Russians were displeased with what had been said.

[10] Otto Grotewohl, 1894–1964. German Communist leader. Prime Minister of the German Democratic Republic from 1949.
[11] Walter Ulbricht, 1893–1973. German Communist leader. From 1935 a member of the Politburo of the German Communist party and Secretary-General of the party after its fusion with the Socialist party from 1950 to 1971.

Moscow, July 22, 1956

The other day I had V. V. Kuznetzov, First Deputy Foreign Minister of the Soviet Union, to lunch. He told me some interesting details about the recent visit of the Shah of Persia. The Russians had prepared some surprises with the object of impressing him with Soviet technical and scientific advances, in other words with Soviet military power. Military strength is, unfortunately, still the first beneficiary and the main indicator of the progress of science and technology in the Soviet Union.

At the end of his stay here they showed the Shah "secretly" in the Kremlin a film of a test explosion of a Soviet hydrogen bomb. They told him in advance only that he was going to see a Soviet documentary film about Soviet achievements "in the scientific field." Then the Russians insisted on maximum secrecy and asked the Shah not to bring more than two or three people with him, saying that there would be one or two people present from the Soviet side, that the whole affair was exceptionally confidential, and that they were showing the film to him as the sovereign of a neighboring country. According to Kuznetzov the Shah was "simply amazed" when the film came to an end, was unable to conceal his emotion, and kept repeating that we must all fight for peace, that another war was unthinkable because it would mean a general catastrophe, and so forth. From what Kuznetzov said it seems to me this film had a greater effect on the Shah of Persia than a week of talks in Moscow.

I did not tell Kuznetzov that we too, Tito and the Yugoslavs, had been shown the same film last month. And the Russians had behaved to Tito in a similar way. They told me personally that it concerned a secret and highly confidential matter, asked me to see that only two or three Yugoslavs accompanied him, and that I could be present as a member of the Central Committee of the Yugoslav League of Communists, which I took to mean that I would not have been able to attend "as a diplomat." We did indeed regard this as a special sign of confidence toward Yugoslavia. From the conversation with Kuznetzov I see that the Russians show the same film and in the same version to other distinguished guests.

I believe this Soviet diplomatic device may produce results. At night they show distinguished foreign guests in the Kremlin, on a strictly confidential basis, films of Soviet hydrogen bombs exploding, and the next day they conduct negotiations with the same guests about mutual cooperation and the preservation of peace.

Moscow, July 27, 1956

After repeating my request I have received a cabled report from Belgrade about Mikoyan's "visit." Our people are extremely disappointed in the talks with Mikoyan and his report on the solution of the political crisis in Hungary. Mikoyan told Tito and the other Yugoslavs only what was already known from the Soviet and Hungarian press.

The day after the report from Belgrade I received cabled instructions from our government to sign the agreement on credits with the governments of the Soviet Union and Eastern Germany. This decision by Belgrade was a surprise for me. I had advised against accepting this kind of agreement because it was a question of granting credits on political conditions imposed by the Soviet side. To be quite honest, the decisive factor for me was not whether we should or should not accept East Germany as a participant in the business. If it had been possible to arrange a similar economic agreement with East Germany, I would have been for such an agreement, but I wanted us and the East Germans to do it in the right way, since our states are not in diplomatic relations. What bothered me was that we were accepting open political pressure by the Russians in connection with East Germany. I began to be a little afraid that it would only increase the Soviet appetite for exerting fresh pressure on Yugoslavia. Today they have succeeded in this over Eastern Germany; tomorrow they will put even greater pressures on us in some other connection.

Moscow, July 28, 1956

We have been informed that the Soviet Presidium has issued a secret letter to party members about Tito's visit to the Soviet Union. We hear that Bulganin, the Soviet Prime Minister, is criticized explicitly for having, in his speech as host at the beginning of June 1956, called Tito a "Communist-Leninist." I don't know whether the Russians have sent this secret letter to the Central Committees of the Communist parties of Eastern Europe. If they have, then it would make this move on the part of the Presidium even worse.

We learn that Soviet people, Communists, and others who welcomed Tito with enthusiasm and sincerely applauded the new Yugoslav-Soviet rapprochement are disappointed with the Presidium's letter. Comments such as this are to be heard: If we are not on good terms with the Yugoslavs now, we never will be.

I told colleagues in the embassy that no one should say anything to Belgrade yet about the Presidium's secret letter. We agreed to try to get our hands on a text before informing Belgrade. If our information about the letter on Tito's visit turns out to be correct, then the Kremlin's attitude toward Yugoslavia is worse than even some pessimists among us imagined.

CHAPTER SEVEN

CRISIS OVER SUEZ

A strange way to treat guests—and an unfriendly way to exploit Yugoslav émigrés. Nasser's nationalization of the Suez Canal provokes a major international crisis and pushes Soviet-Yugoslav relations into the background for a time. Khrushchev proposes to make a "private" visit to Yugoslavia and to entertain Tito in the Crimea so that they can talk over their differences.

Moscow, August 8, 1956

Following Tito's return from the Soviet Union the atmosphere in Yugoslavia was very favorable for the expansion of cooperation with the Russians in all fields. Our government is encouraging everybody who can help in any way to establish contacts or promote cooperation with the Soviet Union, with the result that we are now having a veritable invasion of Yugoslav delegations of every kind. Two or three of them arrive every day, even by the same train.

At the moment there is a Yugoslav agricultural delegation, led by Ljupčo Arsov, although we and the Russians cannot learn much from each other as far as agriculture is concerned. The social and economic relations in the Soviet Union in this field are quite the opposite of those in Yugoslavia. The Russians are probably appalled at Yugoslavia's policy, because we dissolved our farming cooperatives four years ago and returned the land to the peasants, while the Yugoslavs are shocked by the inefficiency and low productivity of Soviet agriculture based on the forced collectivization of the land. But perhaps it is not a bad thing to exchange even this kind of experience of different ways of building socialism.

There are two other members of the Politburo of the Yugoslav League of Communists now in Moscow, comrades Lazar Koliševski[1] and Blažo Jovanović.[2] They have come here for a sort of official, or compulsory, annual holiday. They naturally counted on having meetings and conversations with the top Soviet party leaders, but this is not happening. So these two senior party officials of ours spend their time surrounded by Soviet party and police officials and having no contacts of any kind. The Russians have made their relations with them even worse by offering them large sums of money. It was just the usual Soviet practice on such occasions of ensuring that "our guests are able to buy souvenirs in the Soviet Union," including objects of considerable commercial value. Although our comrades expressed their amazement and displeasure at the Soviet offer and refused to take the money, the Russians left the envelopes bulging with rubles in their rooms. This went on for several days. Finally the Russians took the money away after having thus spoiled the stay in the Soviet Union of our two Yugoslav officials.

For the last ten years the Russians have made it a practice to invite high officials of countries of the "socialist camp" for their annual holidays and to send their own people to those countries in exchange. I don't know how it works out for them: The Russians probably have a better time in the countries of Eastern Europe than the people from those countries have in Russia. I know that comrades Koliševski and Jovanović had a bad time here. They told me they would never have come if they had known how they were going to be treated. We discussed these compulsory holidays as well as the exchange of numerous delegations with the Russians when Tito was here last June. The Russians were very insistent about it, probably thinking that by means of such an exchange of delegations they will strengthen their positions in Yugoslavia and influence those of our people who come here. It seems as though it does not occur to the Russians that the result of these unprepared visits by our people to Russia may be the reverse of what they expect. There is no reason to expect that every Yugoslav will be carried away by the mere fact of arriving in the Soviet Union or that he will be pleased and delighted with everything he sees here.

Moscow, August 9, 1956

To keep relations between us in the spirit of the agreement we reached in Moscow in June it has been decided that Tito should invite Khrushchev for a private visit to Yugoslavia.

[1] Lazar Koliševski, b. 1914. Secretary, Communist party of Macedonia, 1943–63; member of the top leadership of the Yugoslav Communist party since 1948.
[2] Blažo Jovanović, b. 1907. Secretary, Communist party of Montenegro, 1945–63; member of the top leadership of the Yugoslav Communist party since 1954.

When I received instructions from Belgrade to invite him as Tito's personal guest, Khrushchev was not in Moscow. He was off on one of his campaigns around the country, this time the campaign "for bread"—the grain harvest. To judge from the Soviet press, radio, and television and by Khrushchev's travels, the harvest in the Soviet Union is the most important event of the year. It is like a state of emergency or a sort of general mobilization. The campaign goes on for weeks and months, never leaving the front pages of the newspapers, which from June onward proclaim the harvest as task number one for the state and the party. Hundreds of thousands of skilled workers are mobilized, railway timetables are changed, heavy machinery is transported great distances across Russia, and for weeks all the means of communication carry instructions from the party and government to tens of millions of people engaged in the harvest campaign. When this enormous effort is added up, it is scarcely surprising that Soviet grain costs more than anyone else's.

I waited for Khruschchev to return, and when he didn't appear I went to see Bulganin and told him of Tito's invitation. He appeared surprised. He said he would inform Khrushchev the same day. The Presidium fixes when its members shall go on holiday, and Khrushchev is taking his annual leave at the beginning of September.

Moscow, August 10, 1956

As a rule the question of our émigrés in the Soviet Union always comes to the surface when there is a worsening of Yugoslav-Soviet relations. And so it was following Tito's visit.

Tito spent nearly three weeks in the Soviet Union. There was plenty of time for him to receive Soviet, foreign, and Yugoslav delegations, as in fact he did. But it was not until June 20, when Tito was already preparing to leave Moscow, that the Russians asked him to receive a delegation from our émigrés. We told them they should have mentioned it sooner. The Russians seem to have counted on getting such a reply, because they put us in a situation where we couldn't reply otherwise. But they did not hesitate to go further. They then asked Tito to receive a delegation of Yugoslav émigrés in Kiev on his way back home. When Tito said it wouldn't be possible, that there would be no time for it, the Russians said they would provide the émigrés with a plane so that they could reach Kiev before Tito did!

And so a delegation of our émigré-deserters was received, and I was present at the meeting. Tito was very clear in his interpretation of the convention which we signed with the Soviet Government last May. It was left to each individual to whom the convention applied freely to make up his own mind. Our émigrés in the Soviet Union, like all

Yugoslav citizens in any other country, enjoy Yugoslavia's legal protection. Whoever wants to return to Yugoslavia is free to do so. For those who do not want to return, that is their own affair.

One might have expected the delegation of émigrés, which the Soviet Government had forced on us contrary to all the normal rules of behavior, would appreciate the efforts which the Yugoslav Government was making in good faith to solve their problems once and for all. It turned out quite the reverse. The group of émigrés tried to use the meeting with Tito to promote a campaign in the Soviet Union against accepting the convention. They needed the meeting with Tito only in order, with the approval and help of the Soviet authorities, to wage a campaign against the return of any of our émigrés to Yugoslavia.

The principal demands in this campaign are: a general amnesty for all the deserters and then a guarantee in advance by the Yugoslav Government that all those who become officers in the Soviet Army should be accepted into the Yugoslav Army with the same ranks and functions as they have here. They demand similar guarantees with regard to the provision of accommodation in Yugoslavia, and of employment for the wives of those of our émigrés who are Soviet citizens, with the provision that they should all retain their Soviet citizenship until Yugoslavia carries out the very last of their demands. In short, the leaders of the Yugoslav deserters, with, of course, the Russians' agreement, are demanding that we should now reward them for having betrayed their country in 1948 and subsequently.

Moscow, August 11, 1956

In the course of the last ten days such important things have taken place in the international field as to force into the background for the moment not only Yugoslav-Soviet relations but many other questions as well. I refer to the decision of Egyptian President Nasser to nationalize the Suez Canal.

This question inevitably became problem number one for Yugoslav foreign policy, too. Nasser made this surprise move as soon as he returned from Yugoslavia, where for a week he had been having talks with Tito in private. Nehru was also in Yugoslavia at the time, and it appears to the whole world that Nasser must have informed Tito and Nehru about this important move and that he had the backing of the tripartite meeting in Yugoslavia when he unexpectedly proclaimed the nationalization of the Suez Canal on July 26. From some of my meetings with British and French diplomats in Moscow I have the impression that they not only suspect us of knowing in advance of the nationalization of the canal but believe that we encouraged Nasser to take this step.

I asked Belgrade for information and received the reply that Nasser had not indicated to Tito by a single word that he was even thinking of nationalizing Suez. The Yugoslav Government was taken by surprise when they learned about it from the radio and press on July 26. They presume in Belgrade that Nasser said nothing to Nehru either. I think Nasser took this decision some time before he returned from the meeting in Yugoslavia. The American refusal of a loan for building the Aswan Dam[3] undoubtedly hastened Nasser's decision to nationalize the canal.

As far as I can judge from talking to Khrushchev and top officials in the Soviet Foreign Ministry, the Russians are delighted with the news of the nationalization of Suez. This springs from their conviction that the West is constantly interested in the political difficulties and crises in the Soviet Union and Eastern Europe. Now the ground is burning beneath their feet in the West. The West will have to leave the Soviet Union and the "camp" in peace, at least for a time, in order to protect its interests in the Middle East and the privileges which it has preserved from early colonial days. For ten years now the Russians have not admitted that the West has any right to get involved in any crises in Eastern Germany, Hungary, Poland, or elsewhere in the "camp." But the Russians will not ask the British or French to agree to their taking part in the solution of the crisis over Suez. They think that right belongs to the Soviet Union.

By nationalizing Suez Nasser has caused serious problems, threatening what many of the Western powers consider to be their "vital interests," although Nasser has acted in accordance with the vital interests of Egypt, asserting the sovereign rights of his country. In the past and until very recently such moves by a small and undeveloped country to abolish privileges enjoyed by great powers on its national territory would lead almost automatically to war. Nasser displayed exceptional courage in taking this step. Now the strength has to be found to back up the courage displayed.

The Soviet Union is the only great power which firmly supports Egypt. Yugoslavia is on Nasser's side without the slightest reservation, and the Russians are now showing ever greater interest in contacts and cooperation with us over the Suez crisis. I had a long conversation about Suez with the First Deputy Foreign Minister, V. V. Kuznetzov, and with the minister's assistant, V. Semenov.[4] The first question both of them asked was: Did Nasser tell Tito in advance of his intentions? The Rus-

[3] After long negotiations the United States Government informed the Egyptian Government on July 19, 1956, that American participation in the financing of the projected Aswan High Dam was "not feasible in the present circumstances." The British Government and the World Bank also withdrew, and the work was eventually carried out with the assistance of the Soviet Union.
[4] Vladimir S. Semenov, b. 1911. Soviet diplomat. Political adviser to the Soviet Military Administration in Germany, 1945–53; Soviet Ambassador to the German Democratic Republic, 1953–54; Deputy Foreign Minister, 1955.

sians spoke of their own surprise and assured me that the Soviet Government had learned about it all from the radio and the press.

Moscow, August 16, 1956

Contact has been established between representatives of the Soviet and Yugoslav armed forces. The Russians are acting with quite a deal of tact. They make use of various anniversaries in the Soviet Army to invite Yugoslavs. They also invite the Americans and British as former wartime allies. Last month they invited representatives of our Air Force to attend the celebration of Soviet Air Force Day. Generals Viktor Bubanj[5] and Vicko Antić were here, and were well received by the Russians. Now the Soviet Government has invited a delegation from our Navy to attend a similar occasion.

It is a pity the Russians haven't invited the British and Americans for Soviet Navy Day. They both sent very strong delegations for Soviet Air Force Day and it all went off very well. Then the crisis blew up over Suez and the Russians invited no representatives of the navies of the Western powers. If nobody else, I think the British should have been present in view of the colossal efforts, courage, and sacrifices that were incurred by the British in maintaining the northern sea route from the Atlantic to Murmansk and in shipping from America precious supplies as aid to Russia during the war. But what is happening now and what is going to happen in the future are more important now than what happened in the past.

Moscow, August 19, 1956

A few days ago I had a call from Boris Ponomarev[6] in the Central Committee of the CPSU. It was about the handing over of Yugoslav archives which are now in Moscow. I had hoped that Ponomarev would hand over to me our party archives or at least some of them. But instead he gave me only a part of the purely administrative archives of the former Yugoslav monarchy, about five thousand items. There is no point in my opening them and looking at them in Moscow. That has been done by the Soviet authorities in the course of the last ten years, and they have removed everything of interest to them. These archives were taken by the Nazis from Yugoslavia during the war, and they later fell into the hands of the Russians who transferred them from Germany to Moscow.

[5] Viktor Bubanj, b. 1918. Colonel General. Chief of Staff of the Yugoslav Army.
[6] Boris N. Ponomarev, b. 1905. Soviet Communist official and historian. Since 1961 a Secretary of the Central Committee, CPSU, and since 1972 a Candidate Member of the Politburo.

It seems to me the Russians have begun at the "shallow end" to fulfill the Tito-Khrushchev agreement on archives.

Ponomarev has his office in the Central Committee building on Kuibyshev Street, next to Khrushchev's office. As we talked to him a huge portrait of Stalin stared down on us from the wall. Ponomarev doesn't appear to be particularly well disposed toward Yugoslavia, nor does he give the impression of a man who wishes to solve the question of the archives.

Moscow, August 20, 1956

I received instructions today from Belgrade to invite, on Tito's behalf, the Soviet head of state, Voroshilov, for an official visit to Yugoslavia. Our people propose next month or October for the visit. Although I am beginning to get used here to all kinds of surprises from various directions, all the same this excessive haste on the part of the Yugoslavs amazed me. Tito has not yet received a reply to his invitation to Khrushchev for a private visit to Yugoslavia. Yet our people are now planning to invite Voroshilov as well! I told Belgrade why I thought this decision by our government was wrong.

In the first place, our invitation is premature, coming only two or three months after Tito's official visit to Russia. This does not accord with our practice or with the Russians', or with the behavior of most countries in such matters. In the second place, one of the reasons given in our government's instructions was that Khrushchev will be in Yugoslavia in September so that, while he is there, he can join Voroshilov's official delegation! I consider this unacceptable to the Russians and to us. Khrushchev is the real head of the CPSU and the Soviet Union, and Voroshilov is only the nominal head of the Soviet state.

Thirdly, I asked our government to allow time to take its course, so that we should not propose an official visit by the head of the Soviet state until we have carried out at least one of the agreements reached by Tito and Khrushchev two months ago. I don't understand why our people are in such a hurry. I recommended spring or summer of next year as the time to invite Voroshilov.

Moscow, August 23, 1956

At a reception at the Romanian embassy today Khrushchev told me he was going on holiday to the Crimea on September 1. He would stay there for a time with his family and then go to Yugoslavia in the middle of September "to see Tito." He also told me that in June they had intended to show Tito some modern Soviet weapons. But there hadn't been time.

102

He would invite Tito to return with him from Belgrade to the Crimea where they could, among other things, go hunting and have a rest. Tito's going to the Crimea is obviously a condition for Khrushchev's going to Yugoslavia. We could announce Tito's visit or not, as we pleased, Khrushchev said. He thought of suggesting that Tito should spend about a week in the Crimea, and he and his wife could be accompanied by other Yugoslav leaders. He would invite me and my wife, and, he said, a week's stay in the Crimea wouldn't do us any harm. He was not saying anything to the Soviet ambassador in Belgrade, which was why he was telling me about it here. He would go to Yugoslavia alone, without any official party.

I consider this good news, and I said I was sure that in private talks he would reach agreement with Tito on everything during his stay in Yugoslavia.

Apart from that, Khrushchev put on a real performance at this modest reception. As soon as he had exchanged greetings with the British ambassador, Sir William Hayter, and the French ambassador, M. Maurice Dejean, Khrushchev started to attack them in very sharp terms for British and French policy over Suez. He spoke in a very loud voice, and the rest of us formed a circle round the "field of battle," listening in silence to this strange conversation between Khrushchev and the two Western ambassadors.

The two ambassadors together were not able to cope with the aggressive Khrushchev. It suited him very well that neither of them had a good command of Russian. The British ambassador tried to speak Russian, perhaps out of respect for Khrushchev. But, as soon as he could make out from the first few words what Hayter wanted to say, Khrushchev would interrupt him and attack British policy even more sharply. The Frenchman spoke through an interpreter, but that didn't help. Khrushchev would interrupt the interpreter as soon as he had grasped the essence of what the Frenchman was saying. This lasted for a good fifteen minutes, to the greatest satisfaction of the ambassadors of the Arab countries, the approval of the ambassadors from Eastern Europe, and the silence of the rest.

Khrushchev's main themes were: The three great powers threaten to wage a new colonial war against Egypt. But Egypt has on its side international law and the whole of progressive humanity. It was time the West understood that the days of such colonial wars were over, never to return. We were now living in a quite different epoch. The Egyptians and millions of people in Africa and Asia had worked for the colonialists, primarily for the British and French, for centuries. But history had put an end to that, yet London and Paris were still behaving as they did in the past.

The three Western powers, Khrushchev said, had better know that

103

Egypt would not be left alone in an armed battle if the West launched it. If his son decided to go as a volunteer and take up arms to defend Egypt's just cause, Khrushchev would give him his blessing.

This was the punch line of Khrushchev's remarks in the presence of about a hundred witnesses of all kinds from all parts of the world. The British ambassador was upset to hear such talk and soon left the Romanian embassy. The Frenchman stayed on a little longer.

Khrushchev's statement about giving his blessing to his son as a volunteer to go and fight in Egypt was taken by us to mean that the Presidium had taken a decision about its readiness to involve the Soviet Union in Egypt by means of "volunteers" and not by declaring war. This new form of military intervention has already been tried out in Korea, when the Chinese sent more than a million troops under the label of "volunteers," led by Chinese marshals and generals.

Moscow, August 30, 1956

At a Kremlin reception last night Khrushchev asked me whether I had had a reply from Belgrade to his proposal of a week ago for an exchange of private visits between him and Tito. Unfortunately I had had no reply, but I didn't want to admit it, so I told Khrushchev that Tito would be free in the middle of September. Khrushchev was obviously displeased that there was no reply.

I complained to Belgrade at the failure to reply to Khrushchev's proposal, and we then received one in a matter of hours. Tito accepts all Khrushchev's suggestions. He asks me to work out the details with the Russians.

Khrushchev is very well informed about Suez. He knows everything I have told the Soviet Foreign Ministry and that Nasser had said nothing to Tito about his intention to nationalize the Suez Canal. Khrushchev assured me that Nasser had not told the Soviet Union anything in advance either. He attaches great importance to Yugoslavia because our relations with Nasser are "closer." He informed me that Nasser had already approached the Russians for military aid. They will send him practically everything he asks for, taking it out of Soviet military stocks. There is not enough time to manufacture weapons for Nasser now: He needs help at once and not in a year's time, Khrushchev said. Nor should one criticize Nasser now although there are grounds for reproaching him. The question is how to help him.

CHAPTER EIGHT

A SECRET LETTER ABOUT YUGOSLAVIA

*The leaders of the Soviet Communist party distribute a
confidential letter to its members and to the Communist
parties of Eastern Europe to counteract the effect of Tito's
visit to Russia and give their own interpretation of the Moscow Declaration. At the same time Khrushchev arrives in
Yugoslavia with his family.*

Moscow, September 1, 1956

The Soviet Communist party's newspaper *Pravda* yesterday
printed an article about the trial and sentencing in Belgrade of two
Yugoslav "Cominform" émigrés and former Communists. They were
people who deserted from Yugoslavia, emigrated to the East, and put
themselves at the service of Stalin's aggressive policy against Yugoslavia.
The sentences were pretty stiff: One got eight years of hard labor and
the other four years. The *Pravda* article is very bad, assessing the whole
of our policy now "in practice" exclusively in the light of this one incident. It points out that the two Communists returned recently to Yugoslavia, and voluntarily. They believed that the question of our "Communist emigration" in the East had been "resolved finally and justly" and
that since none of our émigrés had committed any "antistate acts" none
of them would be brought to trial. *Pravda* says nothing, of course, about
how Communists from one socialist country could emigrate to another
one and from there carry on antistate activity against their own country.

About a hundred of these émigrés have returned so far. Not one of
them had been brought to trial, although every one of them has committed some offense against his country, some more and some less serious.
Pravda says nothing about that. If they were to reveal here that not one
of the hundred returned émigrés had been tried, the Russians would lose
the confidence of the several hundred émigrés they are still keeping here.

The *Pravda* article gives the false impression that only these two men have returned to Yugoslavia and that both have been sentenced to hard labor.

I called on the First Deputy Minister of Foreign Affairs, Kuznetzov, with whom I had discussed this very question not so long ago. I protested at what *Pravda* had written, and Kuznetzov tried to agree with me and with *Pravda* at the same time.

The trial took place just a month ago, yet *Pravda* writes about it only now, so there's something fishy going on. It's all the more surprising in view of the fact the Khrushchev is going to Yugoslavia as Tito's personal guest in ten days' time. A host ought not to create a bad atmosphere when he is expecting a guest, but a guest also has similar obligations. In any case I think *Pravda* should get the reply it deserves and immediately, before Khrushchev arrives on his "private" visit to Yugoslavia.

Moscow, September 3, 1956

Just as we expected, the *Pravda* article about the "trial of Communists in Yugoslavia" had a considerable effect on the Soviet public. On Moscow's busiest streets there are covered bulletin boards on which each day's copy of *Pravda* and the other Soviet newspapers are displayed. The Russians never fail to put the papers up, a practice handed down from the time of the October Revolution, when there was something to read in *Pravda* and there were not enough copies to go round. Today *Pravda* is printed in millions of copies and costs only three kopeks. Everyone who wants to read it can buy it, and normally nobody stops in front of these bulletin boards. But today it was different. Groups of people were standing at the boards, reading and commenting on the article about the "trial of Communists in Yugoslavia." There was considerable interest in it. We sent a lot of comrades from the embassy to stand next to the people and pretend to read the article. The comments by the Soviet citizens were unfavorable to Yugoslavia. I will quote some of them: "We gave Tito a good welcome here, and he goes and sentences Communists to prison." "To sentence friends of the Soviet Union in Yugoslavia is proof of Yugoslav insincerity toward the Soviet Union." "Djilas walks around freely in Yugoslavia and draws a big state pension, while Tito sends friends of the Soviet Union to prison." "There's been an amnesty for Ustaše and Četniks[1] in Yugoslavia, but internationalists are sent to prison." "General Franco grants an amnesty for Spanish Communists—Tito sentences his to hard labor."

It is sufficient to have just one "reader" in a group of people for all the

[1] *Ustaše*—Croat nationalists. *Četniks*—Serbian nationalists, followers of General Draža Mihailović.

anti-Yugoslav comments to be spread around. In this way thousands of people in Moscow are affected and their hostility toward Yugoslavia encouraged. People don't really know what it is all about and simply accept these comments in favor of the "Communists-internationalists." We have no means either through *Pravda* or through any other medium of telling the Soviet people what it is really about. If some government's policy clashes with Soviet policy, then that government and its country are usually the victims of disinformation in the Soviet press.

Moscow, September 6, 1956

For a long time now we have been trying to get at the truth about the Presidium's secret letter about Yugoslavia. From various sources we finally put together a detailed account of this document, mainly from people who are friendly toward us politically—foreign Communists from Europe who are living here and a few individual Russians.

We have no intelligence service in the Soviet Union or any people of that kind working for us. We don't do that sort of thing here, in accordance with a decision taken in Belgrade banning Yugoslav intelligence operations in the Soviet Union and the countries of Eastern Europe. The Russians were informed of this last year during talks about restoring normal relations between Yugoslavia and the Soviet Union. Khrushchev informed us of something similar concerning Soviet operations in our country so that, officially, we are supposed to have reciprocal relations in this special field.

Our movements are restricted to the area of "greater Moscow," which is twenty to twenty-five miles across. On all the roads out of Moscow at the limit of this zone there are barriers and police posts. This system was established a long time ago, in the first years of Stalin's rule, has been perfected in the course of time, and functions perfectly even today. None of us can leave Moscow by car without previous permission from the Soviet Government. In practice we move around in an area about ten kilometers across, between our apartments, the embassies, and Soviet Government offices. In Yugoslavia Soviet diplomats move about freely from one end of the country to the other.

Moscow, September 7, 1956

The Presidium's secret letter is entitled "Information Concerning Talks Between Delegations of the Soviet Union and Yugoslavia." On the first page there is a warning: "To be destroyed on the spot within a month after being received by republican, regional, city, and district committees of the CPSU." The letter consists of four sections, the first and second being devoted to our interstate relations, which are discussed in a fairly calm manner, adding very little to what has been published here, although the language and tone of the letter are more reserved than in the official Yugoslav-Soviet communiqué.

The fourth and last section is the longest and deals with "ideological questions" and interparty relations. This is the real reason for the letter being written, according to what they say at the meetings where the letter is read out. They say the Yugoslavs proposed their own draft declaration on interparty relations but that it was rejected by the Soviet side on the grounds that it was opportunist and acceptable to Social Democrats but not to Communists. It says that the Soviet delegation warned that there were still people in leading positions in Yugoslavia who still looked on our relations in the old way and dared to slander the Soviet Union and the CPSU. It then sets out how the Soviet delegation intervened in the matter of our relations with Albania and Bulgaria, and says that Tito appreciated this and said that Yugoslavia would continue to improve relations with those countries.

It says in conclusion, and this seems to be the main point of the letter, that there are quite a few ideological questions on which the two parties have very different views, because the Yugoslavs continue to stick to their own opinions. In this connection the letter concludes in roughly the following way: The Central Committee of the CPSU considers that for Comrade Bulganin, at the official lunch in Moscow on June 5, 1956, to describe Tito as a Communist-Leninist was premature, because such a description might hinder the rapprochement between Yugoslavia and the Soviet Union on ideological questions and also confuse members of the CPSU and of the fraternal Communist parties.

By means of their secret letter the Russians have given their own interpretation of, or have disassociated themselves from, some of the points made in the agreements which they signed with us on June 20. Yugoslavia is still presented as simply one of the objects of Soviet foreign policy and not as an independent and equal partner of the Soviet Union. The differences between us are attributed to our mistakes and to economic dependence on the West, and particular stress is put on Western Germany and the United States, which are the Soviet Union's worst enemies. The Russians repeat the old Soviet thesis about the division of Yugoslav leaders into "pro-Soviet" and "anti-Soviet," which is a particularly dangerous form of Russian interference in our internal affairs. The Moscow Declaration is not referred to at all; in fact, the Soviet letter is a repudiation of it. Members of the CPSU are warned that they should look on that document as a sort of diplomatic gesture on the part of the Soviet Union and not as an agreed basis for relations between our two Communist parties. The question of the "camp" is also discussed, again suggesting that Yugoslavia has promised to "improve."

From various sides we have information that the secret letter has only increased confusion in the Soviet Communist party. As far as we can judge I think it is right to say that the letter has done more to demoralize and depress the members of the CPSU, especially in those circles which know how to read between the lines, than it has done to elucidate anything for them. Comments can now be heard among Soviet Communists that it is the letter which represents the true policy of the Soviet Union toward Yugoslavia and not the document which the Soviet Government and the Central Committee of the CPSU solemnly signed with Tito in Moscow at the end of June.

The Soviet leaders also sent the letter to the countries of Eastern Europe, where there are quite a few people who will be pleased by this Soviet criticism of Yugoslavia. In fact, it was to please them that the Presidium's letter was written. In this way the Russians want to show that all the reservations they had with regard to Yugoslavia are still in force, and although this is supposed to improve the Russians' public attitude toward Yugoslavia, I believe it will do most harm to the Russians themselves. If it were possible to change countries by means of such "secret letters," the world would look a different place.

Moscow, September 9, 1956

The Russians probably know that we have learned about the letter and that Belgrade knows about it, too. Few things can remain secret today, especially if millions of people are informed of the "secret" as in the case of their letter about Tito, the criticism of Bulganin and Yugoslav policy. This "secret" has been handled here in much the same way as the "secret" speech by Khrushchev about Stalin at the Twentieth Congress. When there is such concern for secrecy, it must mean that the Russians feel an urgent political need to make clear their reservations about Yugoslav-Soviet agreements and about Tito personally.

Since the official negotiations between Yugoslavia and the Soviet Union have not given the desired results, the Russians are now trying to put this right through Khrushchev's "personal diplomacy" during his private visit to Yugoslavia. If he succeeds, then the visit will have been justified. If he doesn't succeed, then it will be said that the visit was a private one anyway and no interstate talks were planned. It is difficult to believe that Khrushchev will not have at least some success.

If, however, no success is achieved in Belgrade, or if the talks are not entirely successful, there will remain the talks in the Crimea immediately afterward which the Russians can plan in accordance with the results achieved during Khrushchev's "private" visit to Yugoslavia this month.

Moscow, September 13, 1956

In the course of preparing a brief for Belgrade in connection with Khrushchev's "private" visit to Yugoslavia I had to gather everything that the Soviet Communist party and government have done since the Twentieth Congress in domestic policy, especially in the economy.

The Soviet Government is also carrying out a partial demobilization and is making much of the way it is reducing the size of the Soviet armed forces. In the first place they are probably reducing the size of the land forces and are doing much less to reduce other branches of the forces. The reduction is the result of the increased nuclear strength and firepower of the Soviet Army and not of a "peace-loving" policy on the part of the Soviet Government, although they make propaganda use of it in this sense.

Moscow, September 19, 1956

Radio Belgrade announced today that Khrushchev had arrived in Yugoslavia with some members of his family and would remain there for about a week. No Soviet officials, either from the party or from the government, went with him. Khrushchev has thus taken a risk if the "private" visit should end in failure. But if it succeeds it will be all the more valuable to him. Radio Belgrade gave the news in a very friendly manner. Although it is a private visit, interest in it is somehow even greater. One can go on a private visit and on vacation only to a friend, whereas one can go on an official visit to anyone. From the very outset foreigners here are voicing their suspicions about the visit, which took them by surprise. There was nothing in Moscow's relations with us during the summer to suggest that Khrushchev would go on a friendly "private" visit to our country. It now appears that some of the diplomats here were in too great a hurry to draw negative conclusions about the state of Yugoslav-Soviet relations, and now they are puzzled.

Moscow, September 24, 1956

On the question of the Soviet Union's relations with the socialists of Western Europe I told Belgrade that the Russians are being too one-sided in their efforts to exploit the Suez crisis as a means of exposing the socialists in France and in the West in general. This sort of one-sided tactic benefits in the end the most reactionary circles in the West. I think it would be better for the Russians, too, if the Soviet press occasionally said a friendly word about the Social Democrats, who have behaved relatively well over the Suez question and differently from the French Government. We have similar examples in the Scandinavian countries, in Belgium, Italy, and in France itself.

The Soviet press has not published in any form the statement by John Foster Dulles that the United States will not resort to force to open a way through the Suez Canal which he made in connection with the Anglo-French formation of a "users' association." But the whole of the world's press published this statement by the American Secretary of State as an American declaration opposing the use of force in the Suez crisis.

CHAPTER NINE

TITO AND KHRUSHCHEV IN THE CRIMEA

Tito visits the Crimea for a "hunting party" and talks with Khrushchev, who tries to involve him in the crisis in Hungary. Visits to Moscow by a Yugoslav military delegation and a group of Orthodox Church dignitaries go off successfully.

Yalta, September 28, 1956

Khrushchev has returned from Yugoslavia and appears very pleased with the job he has done. He arrived yesterday by plane, accompanied by President Tito and Tito's wife, Jovanka. Khrushchev's wife, Nina Petrovna, and other members of his family are here. Voroshilov is here, too, and Bulganin is somewhere nearby. Among the others who have arrived at Khrushchev's invitation are Marshal Grechko,[1] Leonid Brezhnev,[2] Yekaterina Furtseva,[3] and Aleksei Kirichenko,[4] some of them with their wives. Aleksandar Ranković and Djuro Pucar[5] are with Tito.

In view of the fact that Khrushchev doesn't want to let things "cool off," the Russians insist on going straight from the hunting trip in Yugoslavia to organize another one in Russia. Things appear now to be going better for the Russians than they did in June during Tito's official

[1] Andrei A. Grechko, 1903–76. Marshal of the Soviet Union. Commander in Chief, Warsaw Pact forces, 1960–67; Minister of Defense, 1967–76; Member of Politburo, CPSU, 1973–76.
[2] Leonid I. Brezhnev, b. 1906. Soviet Communist official. A Secretary of the Central Committte, CPSU, since 1956; Member of Politburo, CPSU, 1957; Secretary-General, CPSU, since 1954; Chairman, Presidium of Supreme Soviet, 1977. Marshal of the Soviet Union, 1976.
[3] Yekaterina A. Furtseva, 1910–74. Soviet Communist official. Member of Politburo, CPSU, 1957–61—the first woman to reach such a position in the Soviet regime. Minister for Culture from 1960.
[4] Aleksei I. Kirichenko, b. 1908. Soviet Communist official. Member of Politburo, CPSU, 1955–60. Has since disappeared from public life.
[5] Djuro Pucar, 1899–1979. Yugoslav Communist official. Member of the top leadership of the Yugoslav Communist party from 1952.

visit. Since Voroshilov, the nominal head of state, the Soviet Prime Minister, Bulganin, and other Soviet leaders are going to join us, the whole affair will appear just as official as the June visit. But then everything was done in a strictly official way and ended with the publication of joint communiqués. It won't be like that this time. But it would be better if this kind of contact and discussion ended with some kind of communiqué for public consumption. It can look rather bad for a country like ours if no official communiqué is issued. But what sort of communiqué can you issue about a hunting party?

I traveled down from Moscow with Miška. In the Crimea, at Simferopol Airport, we waited for the guests from Yugoslavia. The weather down here is rather cool and Miška tends to feel the cold, and she complained to me about it in the night. Next day the woman who was looking after us, as soon as she saw us and before we had had time to say anything to her but good morning, turned to Miška and said: "You felt cold in the night, and I've already told them to bring you another blanket." It was obvious that "walls have ears." It is sufficient for us to talk to each other in our room for our wishes to be fulfilled.

This evening we received a report from our embassy in Moscow about the way the Chinese national day was celebrated. The Russians organized two special meetings, but the top Soviet leaders did not turn up either at the meetings or at the reception which the Chinese embassy gave in Moscow. The reception was attended by a large number of people, especially "ordinary people," as though the Russians wanted to make up in numbers for the absence of "top people." The behavior of both hosts and guests was noticeably cold and lacking in enthusiasm. Mikoyan proposed a toast, but only three quarters of an hour after a speech of welcome by the Chinese chargé d'affaires, who gave the reception because the ambassador, Liu Siao, is in Peking. This too is symptomatic.

Mikoyan's speech was formal and cool, very different from similar speeches in Eastern European embassies. The toast was short, with Mikoyan putting too much emphasis on the need to preserve Soviet-Chinese unity. I have the impression that that unity has run into difficulties. Three or four minutes after the speech the Russian leaders left the hall, and the other Soviet guests left ten minutes later.

In the Crimea, September 30, 1956

Yesterday we had an informal lunch in one of the former palaces of the Tsars in Yalta. All the Russians I have mentioned were present. Khrushchev has brought down here a lot of those among the present Soviet leaders who have his personal confidence and with whom he has worked together either in Moscow or in the Ukraine. Tito and our leaders know very few of them and are meeting the majority of them here for the first time.

At the lunch the Russians proposed a lot of toasts, and practically every one of the Russians present spoke, while Khrushchev and Bulganin spoke more than once. On our side there were speeches by Tito, Ranković, and Pucar. The latter proposed a toast of which I can't say that it pleased the Russians very much. He spoke with unconcealed irony about "Comrade Stalin" and his death. I had the impression that referring to Stalin in this way did not please the Russians. Khrushchev asked me who Pucar was, and I told him simply that he was one of the most outstanding Communists in Yugoslavia.

There was no shortage of alcohol during the lunch, and the Russians were able to take it better than our people. Among the Russians it seemed to have the greatest effect on Bulganin. Khrushchev drank like the rest but remained completely in control of himself. Old Voroshilov was not feeling well at the end of the lunch and was unable to keep up with the others.

After leaving the table the guests spread out around the rooms in the palace. I stayed with Bulganin. There were opponents of a rapprochement and honest cooperation between us on their side as well as on ours, Bulganin said. In Yugoslavia they were mostly lower down, in the state and party organizations, whereas in the Soviet Union they were, unfortunately, at the top. He didn't say whom he had in mind, but he was clearly thinking of particular members of the Presidium and it is not difficult to guess who some of them are. In any case Bulganin gave me to understand that there are more than one of them. This was the first time that Bulganin or any of the Russians had spoken openly in this way about this question and had said straight out that there were people in the Soviet leadership opposed to cooperation and friendship with us.

He said that he had also in his time had "to say some unpleasant things against Yugoslavia." I interrupted him here and said that we in Yugoslavia knew that he had been, along with Khrushchev, an initiator of the new policy toward Yugoslavia and among those most responsible for the positive changes which had taken place in the Soviet Union. Bulganin squeezed my hand several times and talked about the "unpleasant things" again. I gathered he was thinking about the speech he made in Sofia in 1949 where he was sent on Stalin's special instructions. He said he had been ordered exactly what to say and how to say it. I tried to pass onto something else, but Bulganin went on to say that in 1955 he had on his own initiative proposed that they should go to Yugoslavia. "I said we should go to Belgrade or anywhere else if we thought we could correct the mistakes we had made," he said.

There were in the Yugoslav Foreign Ministry, Bulganin said, opponents of sincere Yugoslav-Soviet cooperation and friendship and they were very active. He then asked about a number of senior officials in our ministry whose names he pronounced with difficulty. He asked me whether I knew them well and when I confirmed that I did Bulganin went on to say that the Russians had documents in their hands which showed that these people were working not only against friendship between us but also against Comrade Tito, of whose policy toward the Soviet Union and the socialist camp they disapproved. These people were saying that the Yugoslav Foreign Ministry was responsible for the country's foreign policy. It would be unfortunate for our relations if that was the case and our foreign policy depended on such people. They could do us great harm, Bulganin said, because people like those officials in the Yugoslav Foreign Ministry had no confidence in Tito. They were not loyal to him in other matters, too. I might not believe this, he said, but they had proof of what he was telling me as a comrade and a friend.

It passed through my mind that on the eve of the Cominform resolution of 1948, the Russians had used much worse language about Vladimir Velebit,[6] then an assistant to our Minister of Foreign Affairs. Although he was completely innocent, as a gesture to Stalin and Molotov, Velebit was transferred from the position of assistant to the Foreign Minister to a job in the tourist industry!

I judged it pointless to argue with Bulganin. Bearing in mind the state he was in at the moment, it would have been useless to get involved in an argument. In his cups he had told me what he thought when sober. If I had replied to him as he deserved it would have led to an incident which would have been difficult later to correct. Or Bulganin would have had to say he didn't know what he had said to me or that I wasn't telling the truth. In any case it would have been impossible to put the matter right. So I passed it all over in silence and I did not even report what Bulganin had said.

In the course of the conversation Bulganin often referred to the telegrams which I send from Moscow to Belgrade. As he did so he would take me by the hand and say: "Don't put that in your telegrams" or "A lot depends on what you say in your telegrams." The Russians have a habit of saying this to an ambassador even when they haven't been drinking: It is their way of suggesting that a foreign ambassador and his reports are to blame for everything. At times it seems to me as though their intelligence service has got hold of our cipher and is reading my telegrams.

[6] Vladimir Velebit, b. 1907. Yugoslav Communist official, diplomat. In their letters to the Yugoslav Communist party which preceded the breach in June 1948 the Russians called Velebit "the English spy." He was dropped temporarily from the Foreign Ministry, but later served as ambassador in Italy and Britain.

In the Crimea, October 2, 1956

Khrushchev has been in his element for the last few days. I don't believe he went shooting often in Stalin's day, but he is a keen and quite competent shot. I believe Yugoslav officials go shooting more often than he and the other Soviet leaders do, so that they are more experienced at the sport. It also seems to me that the shoots in Yugoslavia are better organized than here in Russia. Our people agreed with Khrushchev that Yugoslavia would send to Moscow some of our game wardens to help the Russians organize the hunting areas here. Khrushchev commented that, since Yugoslavia was an advanced country in this field, it should extend this form of technical aid to the Soviet Union. We probably devote much more attention to hunting than they do in Russia. So it looks as though socialism is going to restore to the hunt its former feudal splendor.

One day at about eleven o'clock in the morning we were surprised to see Erno Geroe, first secretary of the Hungarian Communist party, suddenly emerge from the next room in the house where we normally lunched when Khrushchev was the host, as was most often the case during our stay in the Crimea. Geroe was in the company of two or three other people who looked more like Hungarians than Russians. We had not had the slightest hint that he was arriving in the Crimea; at any rate no one had told me about it. This reveals the other side of our present "hunt" in the Crimea, as well as Khrushchev's "holiday" trip to Yugoslavia. The situation in Hungary has for long been the weakest point in the socialist camp. The Russians have tried several times this year to resolve the internal crisis and had finally to agree to Rákosi's resignation, since the Hungarians themselves could no longer put up with him. It looks as though we were responsible with the Russians for choosing Geroe in Rákosi's place and are now confirming the new situation, though we are in fact learning about it all only after the Russians have carried out their decisions.

Whether the Russians' behavior pleases us or not, we now have no choice but to receive Geroe as though we had agreed in advance to a meeting in the Crimea. This will all be announced publicly, and only afterward shall we be able to consider what to do next.

* * *

To try to sum up that situation now: It seems to me that, during his private visit to Yugoslavia and Tito's stay in the Crimea, during which he behaved differently from the way he did in June, Khrushchev has been more successful than he was three months ago. He probably considers it an especial success that it has been agreed here that the Hungarians are to visit Yugoslavia in ten days' time. That is bound to be an important event for Hungary and for our relations with the camp as a whole. It is also of no little importance that Khrushchev and Tito have had the opportunity for more than ten days running to talk to each other without an intermediary. This is the first time anything like this has happened in the history of Yugoslav-Soviet relations.

Moscow, October 8, 1956

As soon as I returned to Moscow I wrote to Comrade Ranković and suggested that I should go to Belgrade as soon as possible for talks with senior officials, because it had been impossible to do so in the Crimea. I don't know what impressions our leaders took away from the Crimea, nor what matters may have been agreed with the Russians, nor do I know in detail what has been agreed with the Hungarians. I don't know any of the political conclusions which our people have come to following Khrushchev's stay in Yugoslavia, nor do I know whether they have been confirmed or elaborated during the visit to the Crimea. Comrade Tito said we would have a chance to talk in the Crimea and at his suggestion I put off certain duties I had in Moscow, but we didn't get round to a conversation in the Crimea after all.

Moscow, October 12, 1956

The Suez crisis has continued to develop and was the subject of discussions with Khrushchev both in September in Yugoslavia and later in October during Tito's stay in the Crimea. Neither we nor the Russians had reckoned on the worst happening, that is to say the use of force by the great powers of Western Europe and Israel against Egypt. We examined various possibilities of support and aid for Nasser, whose situation was considered to be very difficult.

Foreign diplomats here are very busy seeking information about what happened in the Crimea and in Yugoslavia. In the few days since I returned from the Crimea I have had meetings with the ambassadors of Norway, Canada, Austria, France, Argentina, Hungary, Greece, Egypt, and some other countries, at their request. I also had a long talk with the correspondent of the New York *Times*, Jordan, who asked to see me.

A certain number of the people we talk to now assume that we are having difficulties in our relations with the Soviet Union and that they are the result of Soviet policy. They know about the Presidium's secret letter concerning Tito's official visit to the Soviet Union, which has become a political sensation. Most of the people we talk to take the letter as proof that the Russians are playing a double game in relations with Yugoslavia.

Some ambassadors are putting round the idea that military matters were also discussed in the Crimea, thus explaining the presence of Marshal Grechko. But this idea has so far not found many takers. Everyone attaches special importance to the unexpected presence of Geroe and the Hungarians in Yalta. Most foreigners here conclude that we had agreed with the Hungarians to meet them in the Crimea, which is certainly not the case, or they say the Russians and Hungarians took us by surprise with the visit. It seems to me that neither view does us much good.

Moscow, October 13, 1956

There is considerable interest among the diplomats in the presence here of a Yugoslav military delegation led by General Jakšić. Some foreigners are inclined to link his visit to the Soviet Union with recent developments in our relations with the Russians.

The day before yesterday I met Marshal Zhukov at a reception and had a long conversation with him. His first words were to tell me that he was going to receive our military delegation. He was interested in who was in it and what impressions they had of the Soviet Union so far. The marshal left me with the impression that he was genuinely pleased to have our delegation here. So far it has been well received by the Russians. Interest in the delegation among the diplomats is growing. Some Western diplomats are particularly sensitive about the establishment of military links between Yugoslavia and the Soviet Union.

Moscow, October 14, 1956

For the last few days we have had yet another delegation from Yugoslavia here on an official visit—a delegation of the Serbian Orthodox Church which has come at the invitation of the Russian Patriarch Alexius.[7] The delegation, led by the Patriarch of the Serbian Orthodox Church, Vikentiji Prodanov, is made up of a group of Serbian priests and bishops. The average age of the delegation seems to me to be about seventy, or perhaps it just seems so because they all have long gray hair and beards which make them look older than they are. The Russian Patriarch Alexius is a person of some consequence in the Soviet Union who has had an interesting career, particularly during World War II which caught

[7] Alexius (lay name Sergei Simansky), 1877–1970. Patriarch of the Russian Orthodox Church, 1945–70.

him in Leningrad, where he lived through the thousand terrible days of Hitler's blockade.

I met the leader of our delegation, the Patriarch Vikentiji Prodanov, for the first time here in Moscow. He made a good impression as a patriot and a person genuinely ready to do what he could to promote the interests of his country in spite of the fact that it was now being run by Communists who were opposed to all religion and all churches, including his own Orthodox Church. Patriarch Prodanov quite rightly took the view that his mission here was not only ecclesiastical but also political. The truth is that everything must be done to gain the confidence of the Russian Patriarch. The Russian Church was for many centuries the protector of the Orthodox churches among the Balkan Slavs, and these traditional links have not faded altogether in Yugoslavia, but it is also true that the delegation should not do anything to weaken the confidence which the Church enjoys with the government in Yugoslavia.

One morning Patriarch Prodanov requested a meeting with me and asked if, at practically any price—because I had turned him down on the first occasion—he could read me the speech which he was going to make in a couple of days' time at a formal lunch with the Russian Patriarch Alexius. He told me that the occasion would be attended by about twenty Russian church dignitaries and that the Soviet Government would be represented by the chairman of the sort of commission for religious affairs which we also have. Patriarch Alexius is going to invite me to the lunch, too. At Prodanov's insistence I read his speech and returned it to him saying that it was very good and that I had no comments to make on it.

I attended the Russian Patriarch's lunch. There were about thirty Russian church dignitaries and, at the main table, members of our delegation with the ambassador of "Communist Yugoslavia" among them. The Russians looked very imposing, with their long beards and their hair down their backs, of more than average height and build, especially one or two of them, their black robes reaching to the ground and making them look even taller. I don't think that even the Bolshoi Theater in Moscow, for all the enormous resources and talent it disposes of, could have staged a better group of Orthodox dignitaries.

The two patriarchs made speeches appropriate to the occasion. The Russian speech was carefully worded and no doubt approved by the authorities, even if it wasn't actually written by them. Before this unusual lunch began the Russian Patriarch Alexius invited all those present to stand and instructed Father Nikolai, from Minsk in Byelorussia, I believe, to say grace, which he chanted in a magnificent thundering bass voice which made the very glasses ring. Then they all crossed themselves, except me. I very nearly did the same but as I was clasping one hand in the other I could not move in time to perform a gesture, which, however unimportant, would have had repercussions in Belgrade.

A few days ago I gave a reception in our embassy for the Russian Patriarch to mark the visit of our church delegation to the Soviet Union. The Russian dignitaries, led by the Patriarch, all turned up, and the reception went off in a much more cordial spirit than when we hold similar occasions for officials of the Soviet Foreign Ministry or other official representatives of the Soviet Government. The Russian guests felt free and easy with us, and nobody tried to extract or to conceal any secrets, as always happens when we are with Soviet Government, and especially diplomatic, officials. Russian and Serbian priests seemed to understand each other more easily and better than Yugoslav and Soviet Communists do.

Finally I must record the fact that our churchmen were received by the Soviet Prime Minister Bulganin, that the Soviet Foreign Ministry, in the person of Deputy Minister Fedorenko, took part in all the formal occasions, and that, as far as the meeting with Bulganin was concerned, it could not be said that the Church was separated from the State either in the Soviet Union or in Yugoslavia. In this case the Church was acting in the service of the State rather than being separated from it. As for the reception by Bulganin, I can say that the Russians, meaning the Central Committee and the government, received our priests better than they received the members of the Executive Committee of our party, Blažo Jovanović and Lazar Koliševski, who, because they were not received by Bulganin, returned dissatisfied to Yugoslavia.

It was interesting to note that the Russian bishops and priests keep on forgetting Tito's name and did not mention him in their toasts, and our bishops keep correcting them. The Russians tried to persuade the Yugoslav delegation to accept cash and to go around the Moscow shops to buy anything they wanted, for their church or for themselves. Our priests turned this down, saying they had enough money and would buy what they needed. Our priests did not like to remain alone or to talk for long with their hosts without their colleagues. The only exception to this is the Russian priest from Belgrade, Tarasiev, who behaves so that you might think he represents not only the Russian Orthodox community in Belgrade but also some other, much more powerful "secular" Soviet organizations in our country.[8] Our bishops were for that reason obliged to warn him publicly. The Russians were so attentive that they transported our delegation back to Belgrade in their most luxurious railway coaches.

[8] Meaning the secret police.

Moscow, October 15, 1956

The Soviet press has so far ignored events in Hungary connected with the rehabilitation and reburial of László Rajk, who, though innocent, perished as a result of the Stalinist trial directed against Yugoslavia seven years ago. They also write nothing about steps to rehabilitate the other innocent victims. It is apparently a very sensitive subject for the Russians.

We hear that the Russians are displeased with the course of events in Hungary. The initiative is steadily slipping out of the hands of the authorities and into the hands of the people. Special Soviet-Hungarian talks took place on this subject in the Kremlin ten days ago. Mikoyan and Suslov were present on the Soviet side—they are specialists of a sort for Hungary, because they have been there several times on various political missions.

Moscow, October 18, 1956

From our press, which we receive here with some delay, we learn that a Hungarian delegation led by Geroe has been in Yugoslavia for some days. The new Hungarian leaders were in a hurry to go to Yugoslavia as soon as possible and announce the restoration of normal relations with our country. They think that through Yugoslavia they will be able to improve their political standing in their own country. So do the Russians, under whose guidance this is taking place. Perhaps the Hungarians' visit to Yugoslavia will strengthen Geroe's position at home, but it will certainly not help raise our prestige. I don't know what public opinion in Yugoslavia thinks about the Hungarian visit and I know even less about the reaction of the Hungarian public, which has become rather restless following the steps taken in Budapest to rehabilitate Rajk and the other Hungarians who were executed.

Diplomats here are telling all sorts of stories about the situation in Hungary, mostly unfavorable to the Soviet Government. Comparisons are being made between the rehabilitation of Rajk and the rehabilitations being carried out in the Soviet Union. But there is a substantial difference. When Rajk was reburied in Budapest, speeches were made and everything took place in public and in the presence of vast crowds of people. In Russia the rehabilitations are carried out more or less in secret and the population plays no part at all in the process, and scarcely knows it is taking place. Perhaps they give the families of those who perished innocently some certificate of rehabilitation, some written decision of the party or the government. I don't know; that is also secret. Perhaps the decisions are taken individually for each one, or maybe it's done by age groups, as when recruits are called up into the forces?

Moscow, October 20, 1956

I attended a lunch today given by Marshal Sokolovsky in connection with the visit of our military delegation. Sokolovsky and General Jakšić made the appropriate speeches and everything went off without a hitch. There were no exaggerated declarations on either side. Marshal Sokolovsky's speech was in my opinion acceptable and moderate.

A reception in our embassy was attended by Marshals Sokolovsky, Bagramyan, Moskalenko, Rotmistrov, Sudets, and a large number of Soviet generals. Moskalenko brought apologies from Marshal Zhukov, who was prevented from coming by official duties. The atmosphere at the reception was rather restrained, partly, perhaps, because Marshal Sokolovsky is not a very communicative person and does not appear to be particularly well disposed toward Yugoslavia. Army General Zhadov asked our Colonel Pantelić whether there were any American military advisers in Yugoslavia. To judge from this question, mutual confidence is not running high.

CHAPTER TEN

HUNGARY IN REVOLT. OCTOBER 1956

The crises in Poland and Hungary are resolved in different ways. In Warsaw Khrushchev and Molotov reluctantly accept the Poles' own solution. But the situation in Hungary gets out of hand and Khrushchev threatens the use of force to deal with it. He and Malenkov travel to Yugoslavia incognito to seek Tito's support for their action against Hungary.

Moscow, October 23, 1956

There have been major political developments in Poland resulting in a change of leadership of both party and government. The first secretary of the party is now none other than Władysław Gomułka,[1] who spent five years in prison under the previous leadership. A plenary meeting of the Polish United Workers' [Communist] party was held three days ago, on October 19, in Warsaw, which means that the changes have come about legally.

In Moscow the meeting of the Polish Central Committee and the election of Gomułka has produced something like a state of panic. The changes were preceded by a long period of preparatory moves, but these did not suit the Soviet leaders, and the changes in Poland took place despite Soviet threats that they would oppose them. For more than six months before the present changes the Russians were accusing the Poles, primarily the anti-Stalinists, of "wanting to go West" and "wishing to split Poland off from the socialist camp." Even more than six months ago I did not give much credence to these accusations. The Russians attached the label of anti-Sovietism to us too in 1948, and they think it has the same magical power as it had forty years ago. Anyone who doesn't ac-

---

[1] Władysław Gomułka, b. 1905. Polish Communist leader. General Secretary, Polish Communist party, 1943–48 and again 1956–70. Now living in retirement.

cept Soviet hegemony is immediately declared to be "anti-Soviet." From which it follows that anyone who does accept that hegemony automatically becomes "pro-Soviet." The Russians are deaf to the idea that anyone in the socialist world can be on terms of equality with them and still remain a friend, without being either "pro-" or "anti-" Soviet.

From Western sources we have learned that two or three days ago Khrushchev and Mikoyan suddenly left by air for Warsaw, accompanied this time by Molotov and Kaganovich. Khrushchev no longer goes on his own as he did only a month ago to Yugoslavia. Something is obviously changing in the Kremlin when Khrushchev and Molotov go together to Poland.

We hear from many sides that the Russians went to Poland uninvited, worried about the further course of events. There are some reports that Soviet troops in Poland have been brought to a state of readiness and that the Poles are distributing arms around the factories of Warsaw and forming workers' battalions, a people's army, or something similar, ready to resist the Russians if they try to use force. In the event of a clash with Soviet troops the Polish Army will be on the side of the new Polish leadership.

Now it is apparently Khrushchev who has again adopted the sharpest anti-Polish stand. He is proving, as he did in his speeches and toasts on May Day, that the socialist camp, meaning Soviet domination of Eastern Europe, is as dear to him as it was to any of the well-known Stalinists in the Kremlin. Khrushchev probably thinks that in this way he will strengthen his position and that the Stalinists will not be able to lay the charge against him that the socialist camp began to fall apart under his leadership. If things continue to develop in this way the secret speech at the Twentieth Congress may also be held against him.

The Russian charges that the people now leading Poland want to break up the socialist camp are difficult to believe. Such a policy on the part of the Poles would be equivalent to national suicide. The situation is certainly difficult, but the Russians can make it even more so. The actual danger would be even greater if aggressive circles in the West were to try to interfere in the internal affairs of Poland and other countries of Eastern Europe.

Poland's Minister of National Defense, Rokossovsky,[2] is a Soviet marshal, a citizen of the Soviet Union but a Pole by birth. He was also one of the most successful of the Russian commanders in World War II. He has held the post of Polish Minister of Defense for about seven years, and this

[2] Konstantin K. Rokossovsky, 1896–1968. Marshal of the Soviet Union. One of the leading Red Army commanders in World War II. He was Minister of National Defense in the Polish Government from 1949 to 1956. He returned to Russia and became a Deputy Minister of Defense.

has now become an issue. I believe Rokossovsky is the only Defense Minister of a European country who is at the same time a citizen and marshal of another country. Such things were possible in Stalin's lifetime, in the name of "building socialism" and "proletarian internationalism."

When one thinks of the last partition and utter defeat of Poland on the basis of the understanding between Stalin and Hitler brought about by the pact which Molotov signed with Ribbentrop on behalf of the Russians,[3] then Molotov's presence in Warsaw in the present situation can only be a provocation for the Poles. On the other hand, when you bear in mind that more than 300,000 Russian officers and men perished in battles for the liberation of Poland from Hitler's occupation, then it would seem that any Russian has the right to discuss this matter with the Poles.

Moscow, October 24, 1956

We have received the Yugoslav press for several days back and read in it that our Central Committee and the Yugoslav Government have devoted the greatest attention to the Hungarian party delegation led by Geroe which arrived on an official visit to Yugoslavia on the fifteenth of this month. Several meetings were held in Belgrade and gala receptions were given in the Hungarian embassy and by our government. Apart from Erno Geroe the Hungarian delegation includes the Hungarian Prime Minister, András Hegedűs. Talks between representatives of the two parties and governments went on for several days: They had plenty to say to each other after so many years of conflict. Our top leaders committed themselves to making the Geroe visit as great a success as possible. Tito and Geroe made very optimistic statements at a reception in the Hungarian embassy in Belgrade. The Yugoslav newspaper *Borba* for October 18 carries a statement by Aleksandar Ranković, one of the secretaries of our Central Committee, saying how useful the talks were, that the Hungarians came at the right time and that the result of the talks will be increased cooperation of every kind between our two parties.

A joint communiqué issued at the end of the visit describes what took place very favorably. There was also a very optimistic interview with Geroe, who, perhaps impressed by the Yugoslavs, is now talking of

---

[3] Molotov and Hitler's Foreign Minister, Joachim von Ribbentrop, signed a ten-year Soviet-German treaty of nonaggression on August 23, 1939. Attached to the treaty was a secret protocol recording that the two men had "discussed in strictly confidential conversations the question of the boundary of their respective spheres of influence in Eastern Europe." Article 2 provided for the division of Poland between Germany and Russia and said that the question of whether there was to be an independent Poland in the future would be decided later by "friendly agreement." On September 3 German armies advanced into Poland and World War II began.

greater democracy and the inclusion of all working people in Hungary in the administration of the state.

There are all sorts of rumors going round Moscow about the situation in Budapest, which is said to be far worse than it was in Poland a few days ago. There appears to be widespread disorder. The decision which the Russians took in July to make Geroe, who was Rákosi's first deputy, the leader of Hungary has served to deepen rather than ease the internal crisis. The Russians were ready, on Suslov's proposal, to back Rákosi and through him carry out the "de-Stalinization" of Hungary! When even the Russians realized that such an operation was not possible in Hungary, they chose Rákosi's closest collaborator, instead of picking some less compromised person.

Moscow, October 25, 1956

Western diplomats in Moscow are spreading the most alarming reports about events in Hungary. According to them the people have been out on the streets in large numbers and there have been violent demonstrations against the Hungarian Government. Events quickly took an anti-regime character. Demonstrators are said to have pulled down the great bronze statue of Stalin in Budapest. They are demanding that someone should be made responsible for the murder of Rajk and the others on the principle of "a head for a head." The present Hungarian leadership is under attack as being the same as the old one as far as the main personalities are concerned. There is also talk of the breakup of the Hungarian party, that the population has occupied various buildings and storehouses by force of arms, that Russian troops are on the move to "restore order" in Budapest, and that Geroe and Hegedűs, just back from Yugoslavia, have completely lost any authority they may have had.

We get no information about any of this from the Soviet Foreign Ministry, where they are very tight-lipped indeed. Some Russians can be heard saying that in Hungary the West has embarked on a real war against the "socialist camp" and against the Soviet Union. This is the way the Soviet press presents the situation, saying that the disorder has been provoked by the imperialists and their servants in Hungary, of whom, incidentally, there are said to be very few. Geroe, Rákosi's successor, immediately called for Russian troops to intervene and "restore order," and by so doing further provoked the people to riots and revolt. The new Prime Minister, Hegedűs, resigned and was replaced by Imre Nagy, who was recently expelled from the Hungarian party and has now been readmitted to it.

Western diplomats are the main source of information in Moscow. Nobody takes seriously the Soviet statement about a "plot by the imperialists and their few agents." The Russians also give the impression that they don't believe what is written in *Pravda*.

It might have been possible to find a way of canalizing the demonstrations which broke out at the beginning. But no effort was made to do so. Geroe only fed the flames by talking about the "mob" and turned the greater part of the population against himself. It is difficult to say how it will all finish. It looks like the beginning of the breakup of the socialist camp, which has snapped at its weakest spot. Hungary was never a "pro-Soviet" country; the Hungarians were fighting against the Russians until very recently and anti-Russian sentiments have prevailed there for centuries. You often hear talks now about the way the Hungarians' fight for liberation led by the Hungarian national hero Lajos Kossuth was defeated by the armies of Tsarist Russia more than a century ago. The Russian Tsarist troops then came to the aid of the Austro-Hungarian empire and crushed the Hungarians' struggle for emancipation.

Last night I met Khrushchev in the Kremlin and spoke with him at his request. The principal and practically only subject of conversation was Hungary. Khrushchev looked very worried, to put it mildly. He says that blood has been shed there, accuses the West, and says anti-Soviet elements have taken up arms against the "camp" and the Soviet Union. He alleges that the West is seeking a revision of the results of World War II, has started in Hungary, and will then go on to crush each socialist state in Europe one by one. But he claims that the West has miscalculated. He told me to take a message to Tito about the Soviet view of the situation and the readiness of the Soviet Union to answer force with force. Khrushchev assured me that the Soviet leadership was completely unanimous on this. The Russians would support a political solution in Hungary if such a solution was still possible. But Khrushchev gave the impression that he had no faith in such a solution. He said that we Yugoslavs could now do a great deal for the cause of socialism in Hungary.

I have received permission from Belgrade to leave the day after tomorrow for Yugoslavia. I told Khrushchev this and he appeared to approve the idea of my departure for Belgrade, because he asked me when I would get there, how long I would need for the journey, and appeared interested in my reaching Belgrade as soon as possible so as to convey to Tito his thoughts on the events in Hungary.

Kiev, October 26, 1956

I left on October 26 from Moscow's Vnukovo Airport. We had a normal flight to Kiev, but then difficulties arose. The airport authorities made us leave the aircraft and would not allow us to continue our journey to Lvov and Budapest, obviously because of the situation in Hungary. The Soviet authorities stubbornly refused to give us any idea when we would continue our journey.

I intervened unsuccessfully with the people in command of Kiev Airport, asking them to put me in touch with Moscow. I spoke as one of the passengers and they turned me down like all the others. When I saw it could go on like this till the next day, I told one of the airport officials that I had spent the previous evening with Khrushchev, that I had had an extremely important conversation with him, that that was why I was flying to Belgrade, yet they had held me up here for hours and were thus making it impossible for me to get the message from Khrushchev to Tito. This did the trick. They took me at once to the communications center and I got through straightaway to the marshal of the Air Force, Zhigarev,[4] in Moscow, told him about the fix we were in and suggested he give orders for the Soviet plane to fly to Belgrade across Romania if it was not possible to cross Hungary. With the marshal, too, I played on the message I was taking to Tito. In ten minutes we had Moscow's decision that we would fly via Bucharest, where we arrived late at night. The situation in Budapest had clearly deteriorated, so that even air communications were no longer functioning normally. The situation probably got worse in the course of October 26, because they wouldn't have sold us plane tickets in Moscow if they had foreseen this. Nobody mentioned Hungary, but we all thought the same about the reasons why we were giving Budapest such a wide berth.[5]

[4] Pavel F. Zhigarev, 1900–63. Air Chief Marshal. Commander in Chief, Soviet Air Force, 1949–57.
[5] *Author's note:* In the night of October 23–24, 1956, there were big demonstrations and armed clashes in Budapest. The disorder spread rapidly across the whole country. Under popular pressure Erno Geroe was removed and replaced as first secretary of the Hungarian Workers' [Communist] party by János Kadar, who had been a prisoner of Rákosi from 1951 to 1954, while Imre Nagy, a university professor, scholar, and member of the Communist party of Hungary since 1918, became Prime Minister. The Russian troops reacted immediately to the popular movement by occupying all key points in Budapest in the course of their so-called first intervention. This served only to make the conflict even more violent. The Yugoslav leadership followed closely what was happening in Hungary and condemned the interference by Russian troops in Hungary's internal affairs. On October 29 Comrade Tito sent a message from the Central Committee of the Yugoslav Communist party to the leaders of the Hungarian party expressing concern at the turn of events in Hungary but at the same time supporting the efforts being made to extend democracy in the life of the country. The following is a quotation from the message:
". . . Yugoslav public opinion welcomes unanimously the formation of a new state and political leadership and the declaration of the Hungarian Government on the 29th of this month. The essential points in the political program of the new Hungarian leadership, as for example the democratization of public life, the introduction of workers' self-management and of democratic self-management in general, the regulation of relations between socialist countries on the basis of equality and respect for sovereignty, the steps taken to start talks about the withdrawal of Soviet troops, etc., as well as the realistic assessment of the nature of the events in Hungary given

Belgrade, October 28, 1956

I had my first contacts with senior officials here yesterday and this morning. The situation in Poland and Gomulka's assumption of the leadership of the party against the Russians' will but more especially the events in Hungary have cast into the limbo the idyllic picture of relations between us and the Russians which we had in the Crimea less than a month ago. Our leading people have themselves been preoccupied with the situation in Hungary and have been striving day and night to obtain some accurate information about a situation which has been changing from hour to hour. This it has made it impossible to assess the present situation or to forecast future developments.

The situation in Hungary continues to worsen. As a matter of necessity and not of free choice a new Politburo of the Hungarian party has been formed led by János Kadar, and Imre Nagy, who was until yesterday excluded from the party, is the new Prime Minister. Kadar spent several years in prison as a victim of Stalin's or Rákosi's terror, and he now has to pacify the people in revolt, instead of Geroe, who has simply disappeared from the scene. He has probably taken refuge with the Soviet troops or has been "evacuated" to the Soviet Union. If even three months ago, not to say three years ago, the Russians had got rid of Rákosi and not replaced him by his deputy Geroe but by someone from among the victims of the Stalinist regime, perhaps none of this would be happening. But what's the use of talking about that now!

I learned in Belgrade that Imre Nagy demanded that the Soviet troops should leave the territory of Hungary immediately; actually it appears that this applies only to the territory of Budapest. I have also heard that Nagy lodged a sharp protest with the Soviet embassy at the arrival of more troops in Hungary. The Russians remain silent, say nothing about Imre Nagy's protests, but continue, apparently, to send more troops into Hungary and are now surrounding Budapest.

Belgrade, October 30, 1956

The Russians are trying to do something on the political level, but their main support is armed force. In Moscow they have published a declaration by the Soviet Government concerning relations with the socialist states. It is unusually short, occupying only a column of *Pravda*. The

---

in the declaration, are proof that the policy of the present state and political leadership and the truly socialist and democratic ambitions of the Hungarian working people have fused together."

But unfortunately events later took a quite different course.

content of the declaration is good—it could have been written by us Yugoslavs. It insists on such principles as equal rights, integrity, sovereignty, and the equality of all socialist states, noninterference in the internal affairs of other countries and so forth. But one fears that the declaration has come a lot too late. Most important is the fact that Soviet practice is in complete contradiction to this declaration. There would not have been such a declaration if it hadn't been for the events in Poland and Hungary. I ask myself who in Hungary can be in a position to analyze the contents of any such announcement in the Moscow *Pravda* while Russian troops are streaming into Hungary and surrounding Budapest from all sides.

Crowds of Hungarians are fleeing into Yugoslavia, whose frontier with Hungary was almost hermetically sealed on the Hungarian side. They say there are thousands of them. It is difficult to understand the behavior of the Hungarian Government: The frontier with Yugoslavia still remains closed, while the frontier with Austria, that is with the West, is open, although common sense suggests it should be the other way round, because we are being asked to help Hungary defend the foundations of its socialist system. The immediate danger—people and weapons for the overthrow of that system—comes from the West, from Austria, and not from Yugoslavia.

Reports are also being spread that Imre Nagy wanted Hungary to leave the Warsaw Pact and that this demand of his, like others with which he has approached the West directly or indirectly, has only increased the confusion among what remains of the progressive forces in Hungary, where, it appears, there are very few people who want to defend the existing system; such is the extent to which socialism has been compromised by Stalin through Rákosi. Nor did the visit by Geroe and Hegedűs to Yugoslavia help at all. Instead of us strengthening them, they have weakened us.

Belgrade, October 31, 1956

A furious campaign has started up in the West in support of the "Hungarian uprising." It seems that utterly heterogeneous elements are taking part in the revolt, from the extreme Left to extreme Right or, as ordinary folk in Yugoslavia would say: You can't tell who's drinking and who's paying. As a result of the outbreak of armed conflict in Hungary the situation over Suez has suddenly worsened. Britain and France appear to think that the Russians are now busy with their very pressing worries in Hungary, are interested only in preserving the "socialist camp," and that they can't be bothered now to help Nasser over Suez.

The Island of Brioni, November 3, 1956

Tito's office informed me yesterday that Khrushchev and Malenkov were arriving on Brioni[6] in the afternoon for most urgent consultations with us. They are traveling incognito in a small two-engine Ilyushin-14 plane. It was they who asked to come and insisted on the greatest possible urgency. They also stressed the secrecy of their journey. Tito is expecting them late in the afternoon or during the evening. It will be better as far as secrecy is concerned if they arrive at Pula Airport and on Brioni under cover of darkness.

I was summoned to Comrade Tito at about 4 P.M. Comrades Ranković and Kardelj were already with him. There was nobody from our Foreign Affairs Secretariat. We were all agreed that the Russians were not coming under such conditions for any other reason but Hungary, where the situation is getting ever more chaotic. There is more confusion about the policies of the Nagy government than a few days ago, and Budapest is encircled by Russian troops.

Khrushchev and Malenkov arrived at Pula by plane after six o'clock in the evening and then went by boat to the little harbor near Tito's villa on Brioni. It was pitch-dark outside, you couldn't see your hand in front of your face, there was a howling gale, and it was as rough on the little stretch of water across to Brioni as on the open sea. We went down to the little landing stage: Tito, Kardelj, Ranković, and I to await the unusual guests. Khrushchev and Malenkov looked very exhausted, especially Malenkov, who could scarcely stand up. The Russians kissed us on both cheeks. It was a very strange scene on that little empty quayside. The first thing the Russians said was to complain that it was the worst weather they had ever flown in and that the plane had only just managed to get through in the face of the strong wind. Khrushchev said it had been worse than in the war. Malenkov had not been able even to sit and had lain down for a good part of the trip. It also seemed as though the Russians hadn't had it very easy on the short sea trip. For the sake of "secrecy" the officers from the security service and Tito's guard had brought them from Pula to Brioni by a longer route than they needed, through very bad seas, strong winds, and pitch-darkness, so that Khrushchev and Malenkov had both felt very sick by the end of it.

Our guests were anxious that we should get together as soon as possible, and half an hour later the talks began on the first floor of Tito's villa. Khrushchev and Malenkov were alone, without even their ambassador to Yugoslavia. On our side there was Tito, Ranković, Kardelj, and myself.

[6] Island off the coast of Istria in the northern Adriatic which Marshal Tito adopted as his private residence.

There was nobody else in the room—no notetaker, no interpreter, and no "technicians." Actually this is the only kind of talk that *ought* to be recorded, rather than those which take place during official visits, when there are twenty of us and the Russians at the table and everybody is taking notes, although, more often than not, nobody says anything of importance. There was nothing, not even a scrap of paper, on the table. Nobody made any notes; just occasionally one of us would jot down on a piece of paper what he intended to say or was thinking of asking, and when he had finished he would tear up the paper and drop it into an ashtray. It was as though we were all trying to make sure that no trace should remain of the summit meeting between Yugoslavia and the Soviet Union. Yet a record of that meeting would be more interesting than of any other summit meeting held so far between Russians and Yugoslavs.

It is all very strange. Events are moving as fast as in wartime; there is in fact a war going on which seems to be getting even worse, and it is being waged by the armed forces of the "first and biggest country of socialism" against the people of a "fraternal socialist country" and a member of the "socialist camp." And it is happening for the first time in the history of socialism!

* * *

The talks with Khrushchev and Malenkov lasted from seven o'clock in the evening of November 2 to five o'clock in the morning of November 3.

Khrushchev said at the outset they had come to consult with us about the situation in Hungary, or rather to inform us about what they were preparing to do. They said that on the previous day, November 1, they had spoken with the Poles in Brest. On the Soviet side there had been Khrushchev, Molotov, and Malenkov and on the Polish side Gomulka, Cyrankiwicz, and Ochab. After that Molotov had returned to Moscow, while Khrushchev and Malenkov had gone to Bucharest, where they had spoken with Dej and the Romanians. The leaders of Czechoslovakia, led by Novotný,[7] had joined them. Then Khrushchev and Malenkov had gone to Sofia for talks with the Bulgarians. All these visits had been secret. They had also consulted the Chinese. There had been a delegation of the Chinese Communist party led by Liu Shao-chi[8] in Moscow, and they, like all the others, had been in complete agreement with the Russians on everything. The Poles had had their own views, but even they

[7] Antonín Novotný, 1904–75. Czech Communist leader. First Secretary, Czechoslovak Communist party, 1953–68, when he was replaced by Alexander Dubcek. President of Czechoslovakia, 1957–68.
[8] Liu Shao-chi, 1898–1972. Secretary, Central Committee, Chinese Communist party, 1943–56. Later fell into disfavor.

agreed that the situation in Hungary was turning into a counterrevolution. The Poles knew what the Russians had decided to do and there was no other way out. Khrushchev and Malenkov wanted to inform us about the Soviet Union's decision and to hear our views.

Khrushchev talked about the way events in Hungary were moving toward counterrevolution. He started off emotionally, without giving any serious analysis of the course of events, saying that Communists in Hungary were being murdered, butchered, and hanged. He mentioned Imre Nagy's appeal to the United Nations and the four powers and the withdrawal from the Warsaw Pact. It was a question of whether capitalism would be restored in Hungary. Whether Nagy was just a tool or had himself long been an agent of imperialism was not clear at the moment; what was important was that things had taken this course and that the outcome would be the restoration of capitalism. "What is there left for us to do?" Khrushchev asked, meaning the Soviet Union. "If we let things take their course the West would say we are either stupid or weak, and that's one and the same thing. We cannot possibly permit it, either as Communists and internationalists or as the Soviet state. We would have capitalists on the frontiers of the Soviet Union." He said they had assembled sufficient troops and that they had decided to put a stop to what was going on in Hungary. They still needed a couple of days. He said he had spoken with Bulganin by telephone today, November 2, and the Bulganin had given him the glad news that Ferenc Munnich[9] and János Kadar had succeeded in fleeing from Budapest and were now in a plane on their way to Moscow. Khrushchev said this was tremendously important. He asked whether we knew what had happened to Antal Apro,[10] and said it would be very important if he could get out and be saved. The Russians are doing what they can about this but up to now don't know what has happened to him.

Khrushchev turned again to the question of intervention by the Soviet Army. He said that there were also internal reasons in the Soviet Union why they could not permit the restoration of capitalism in Hungary.

[9] Ferenc Munnich, 1886–1967. Hungarian Communist official. Munnich was taken prisoner in Russia in World War I, took part in the Russian Revolution, returned to Hungary, and participated in the short-lived "Soviet Republic" there. When that collapsed he returned to the Soviet Union, where from 1922 to 1936 he was employed in the economy. He fought in the Spanish Civil War, 1936–39, and in the ranks of the Red Army in World War II. From 1946 to 1949 he was Chief of Police in Budapest and in 1950 became a diplomat. After the Hungarian revolt of 1956 he became a minister in the government and from 1958 to 1961 was Prime Minister and a member of the Politburo of the Hungarian Communist party.

[10] Antal Apro, b. 1913. Hungarian Communist official. Member of Political Committee, Hungarian Communist party, from 1945; Deputy Prime Minister, 1957–71; Chairman, Hungarian National Assembly, 1971.

There were people in the Soviet Union who would say that as long as Stalin was in command everybody obeyed and there were no big shocks, but that now, ever since *they* had come to power (and here Khrushchev used a coarse word to describe the present Soviet leaders), Russia had suffered the defeat and loss of Hungary. And this was happening at a time when the present Soviet leaders were condemning Stalin. Khrushchev said this might be said primarily by the Soviet Army, which was one of the reasons why they were intervening in Hungary.

Khrushchev explained that the military preparations were going successfully. He mentioned Marshal Zhukov and said that the commander of the military operations in Hungary would be Army General Malinin.[11] He said that some Romanian forces might have taken part but the Russians considered it was not necessary. Khrushchev went on to say that in a matter of two days they would halt and crush all resistance in Hungary. He didn't say when it would begin, but it was clear that it would be very soon—and we were the last to be informed. In fact the Russians are not here because they need our agreement. They will do what they have decided to do in Hungary whether we agree with it or not, in spite of the fact the Khrushchev says it is very important that we should "understand them properly."

Khrushchev said that British and French aggressive pressure on Egypt provided a favorable moment for a further intervention by Soviet troops. It would help the Russians. There would be confusion and uproar in the West and the United Nations, but it would be less at a time when Britain, France, and Israel were waging a war against Egypt. "They are bogged down there, and we are stuck in Hungary," Khrushchev said.

Malenkov let it be known that everything in the Soviet Union was ready for the second military intervention against the Nagy government to start right away. It is clear that the Russians are going to intervene frontally and with great force, because they are completely isolated from the Hungarian people; in fact, the population is opposed to the Russians.

Khrushchev mentioned the workers in the Miskolc region, where Hungarian miners had remained loyal though reactionaries were in power. The Czechs had given the miners some arms and it might be possible to try some political action against Nagy with the help of those Hungarian miners or jointly with them. He repeated that everything was ready to be carried out immediately as he had explained, that there was no other way out, and that the situation would be resolved with the greatest speed and firmness. He mentioned incidentally that Hungary had twice fought in coalition with the West against Russia, and he stressed the bad feeling

11 Mikhail S. Malinin, 1899–1960. Army General. Chief of Staff and Deputy Commander in Chief of Soviet troops in Germany, 1945–48; First Deputy Chief of Staff, Soviet Army, 1952–60.

existing in the Soviet Army against Hungary, which wanted again to join the West against the Russians.

On our side we stated at the outset that we had followed the course of events in Hungary with the greatest attention. The revolt and rioting by the people had been an explosion of pent-up dissatisfaction with Rákosi's policy and the faults and crimes of the past. If the right steps had been taken in good time, what was taking place now would have been avoided. Our attitude toward Nagy's first government, after Kadar replaced Geroe, had been explained by us in the message which Tito sent to the Hungarians. (Khrushchev and Malenkov said they agreed with the contents of Tito's letter and referred to the Soviet Government's declaration of October 30, which followed the same lines and was intended basically as support for Imre Nagy.)

We explained that we were also concerned at the swing of events to the right, toward counterrevolution, when we saw the Nagy government allowing Communists to be murdered and hanged. There would have to be intervention if there was a counterrevolution in Hungary, but it should not be based exclusively on the weapons of the Soviet Army. There would be bloodshed, with the people of Hungary fighting against Soviet troops, because the Communist party of Hungary, as a result of what had happened in the past, had disintegrated and no longer existed. We suggested that in the present situation there should be some political preparation, an effort to save what could be saved, and to set up something like a revolutionary government composed of Hungarians who could give the people some kind of political lead.

Khrushchev said they had a proposal that a new Hungarian Government should be formed by Ferenc Munnich, the former Hungarian ambassador in Moscow (who before the revolt had been appointed ambassador in Belgrade). But there was also Kadar. Khrushchev asked what we thought. Tito inquired who Munnich was and Ranković spoke about recent meetings with him. We said it would be better if Kadar and not Munnich formed the new revolutionary government, although we didn't know enough about either of them. The Russians are obviously in favor of Munnich but are not against accepting our proposal.

We pointed out that much depended on what the policy of the new government would be. Some of us suggested that the new government should condemn sharply and categorically the policy of Rákosi and Geroe as well as everything in the past which led to this situation. Khrushchev and Malenkov reluctantly agreed. One had the impression that they would rather talk about the present counterrevolution and the West than about the mistakes of the past, but they agreed. Khrushchev used coarse language about Rákosi and then even worse language about Geroe, who, he said, after being elected secretary went first for a holiday in the

Crimea and then to Yugoslavia. Rákosi telephoned to Moscow offering to go and "help" in Budapest, but Khrushchev told him he could "go down there and the people will hang you there." Rákosi asked for a telephone call to Budapest, but the Soviet operator refused to put his call through. Malenkov said the telephone operator proved himself to be politically more mature than Rákosi, adding: "That idiot doesn't understand the most elementary things."

Khrushchev and Malenkov inquired what points ought to be included in the new government's declaration. The main suggestions from the Yugoslav side were: The new government's program should decisively condemn the past and tell the truth frankly about Rákosi and Geroe. Then it should suggest how the basic achievements of the socialist system can be defended. The program of the new government should aim at establishing democratic relations on equal terms with countries of the socialist camp and arranging for the eventual withdrawal of Soviet troops. Within Hungary it should appeal to the revolutionary committees, the workers' councils, and the working class. Khrushchev agreed with the condemnation of Rákosi and Geroe, and with the prospect of withdrawing Soviet troops, although he was obviously not inclined to stress it.

These talks lasted for about three hours. After ten o'clock we all moved into the next room for supper. At table Khrushchev resumed the discussion about who should form the government. He was clearly not anxious to accept Kadar, who was not his choice. The Russians again praised Munnich. They said they had only just learned that Munnich had always been against Rákosi and that he was an old Communist whom Khrushchev had known twenty years ago: In the thirites they had been officers together in the Soviet Army on maneuvers in Russia, when they had shared the same tent. It appears that the Russians have already formed the government and that Munnich is to be Prime Minister. I said that I knew Munnich and that I had often met him in Moscow and that I could say only the very best things about him. But I explained that there was a major political factor to consider in deciding whether it should be Kadar or Munnich: In Rákosi's time Munnich had been ambassador in Moscow, whereas Kadar had been in prison in Budapest. For every Hungarian this would be decisive in Kadar's favor. Khrushchev withdrew and agreed.

We spoke of the need to find new leaders and stressed that the revolutionary government would have influence insofar as it contained no Rákosi people, condemned Rákosi and Geroe decisively, and really pursued a whole new policy. The Russians seemed to understand and to be reconciled to this, although they had arrived with different ideas about who should lead Hungary. For example, Khrushchev proposed that Istvan Bata take over the Ministry of National Defense in the new government, although he had held the same post in Rákosi's government. When the Yugoslav side said that such a decision would be politically weak, the Russians withdrew it.

There was talk about other Hungarian communists. Khrushchev insisted again that everything should be done to get Antal Apro out. We mentioned Loszonczi[12] as a person who gave the impression of being honest and capable, but Khrushchev and Malenkov reacted coolly. It emerged from the discussion that the Russians know that Loszonczi is in contact with us and regard him as one of Nagy's doubtful characters. There was also a reference to Colonel Maleter,[13] who was appointed head of the Hungarian delegation for discussing the withdrawal of Soviet troops with the Russians. We were not sure who Maleter is; nobody knows him or has any sure information about him. Khrushchev and Malenkov say nothing, although they know Maleter.

After supper, around midnight, the question of political preparations was raised again. Malenkov agreed with our view that this played a very important role. There was further discussion of the principles we had expounded, which Khrushchev and Malenkov once again said they agreed with and would adopt. From what Khrushchev said, one had the impression that the new Hungarian Government's declaration had in fact already been written in Moscow but that it might be changed as a result of these talks and our proposals. When our uncertainty about the Hungarian Communists came up, our comrades said that János Kadar should know them best and that his opinion should be accepted. The Russians agreed.

They again asked what possibilities we had of trying to do something about Nagy. Apart from Loszonczi we mentioned Zoltán Santo, who has already asked for asylum in our embassy because of the danger of reprisals. It seems to us that such people are not to be distrusted, because they are decent folk with good intentions. It was agreed that we would see what we could do in this direction, because the Russians said they had no such possibilities. Khrushchev and Malenkov repeated several times that anything we could do with the Nagy government on the above lines would be of the greatest importance. We pointed out that we didn't know what could be achieved. The Russians still said nothing about when their troops would intervene. We can't ask them, and they don't want to

---

[12] Pál Loszonczi, b. 1919. Hungarian Communist official. Minister of Agriculture, 1960–67; President of Hungary, 1967.

[13] Pál Maleter, 1911–57. General. Maleter was a regular officer in the Hungarian Army and became a Communist after being captured by the Russians in World War II. He was parachuted back into Hungary and became famous as a leader of guerrilla activities against the Germans. In 1956 he was the first Hungarian general to throw in his lot with the uprising, and he commanded the forces based on the Killian barracks in Budapest. He was made Minister of Defense in Nagy's government and was invited by the Russians to discuss the withdrawal of Soviet forces from Hungary.

say. For that reason the time factor remains unclear: We don't know what opportunity we may have to influence Nagy and try to reduce the number of casualties and the amount of unnecessary bloodshed. But we agreed that we would try and influence Nagy.

Khrushchev explained that they had had consultations with everybody, and above all with the Chinese. Only the Albanians were not mentioned. He said they had invited a delegation from China. They knew that Mao Tse-tung[14] would not be able to come, so they had asked for others: Liu Shao-chi, secretary of the Chinese Communist party, and Chou En-lai[15] (who Khrushchev said was a "great diplomat"). The Chinese had agreed and appointed a delegation of six or seven people led by Liu Shao-chi. The Russians wanted to hear the views of the Chinese because they were further away from the events in Poland and Hungary, were not directly involved, and could see things better than the Russians who were affected by inertia and the habits of the past. The Chinese had apparently agreed to everything and had been in contact with Mao Tse-tung by telephone. He had agreed completely with the decision to intervene in Hungary.

Khrushchev said that Marshal Zhukov was dealing with the military side of the matter, praised his ability as a military leader, and said that he had fallen into disfavor during the war in a quarrel with Stalin over plans for military operations. When Stalin said that he, Stalin, bore responsibility for the fate of the Soviet Union, Zhukov replied that he, too, was responsible for its fate.

There was mention of Kadar's statement about the tragic course of events in Hungary. Kadar is afraid that socialism and working-class power will collapse there. Khrushchev said that Kadar is "a good guy." Then there was talk about the terror in Hungary and the arrest of Kadar in Rákosi's day. Farkas'[16] son had distinguished himself particularly in the maltreatment of Kadar. Khrushchev and Malenkov described him repeatedly as "scum."

We said that Kadar, who was in the Hungarian party delegation when it visited Yugoslavia, had made a very good impression. The Russians said Geroe had said that the Hungarian party had had about 900,000 members, but that there was nothing left of it now: It had completely disintegrated.

Several times the Russians mentioned Mikoyan, who had been in Hungary in the summer and again now, but we did not follow up this line of conversation. It must have been clear to Khrushchev and Malenkov that

[14] Mao Tse-tung, 1893–1976. Chairman, Chinese Communist party, from 1935 until his death, and founder of the Communist regime in China in 1949.
[15] Chou En-lai, 1898–1976. Prime Minister of the People's Republic of China, 1949–76.
[16] General Mihály Farkas was Defense Minister and head of the secret police (AVH) under Rákosi. In April 1957 he was sentenced to sixteen years in prison for "serious violations of the law."

the Yugoslavs have a poor opinion of the part played by Mikoyan and Suslov in Hungary.

We then asked what were the views of individual members of the Soviet Presidium about the situation. This took the Russians by surprise. After a short pause Khrushchev replied that there was complete and absolute agreement. Malenkov added that the same degree of agreement had prevailed at all phases of the events and that it still prevailed.

Khrushchev spoke about Poland with some restraint but still critically. He said nothing bad about Gomulka, but declared that the views of some Poles were unacceptable. For example, some of them (he did not know which ones) were talking about the return of Lvov to Poland. Khrushchev said that the Ukrainians and Byelorussians would raise the question of the Curzon Line,[17] and then there was the fact that East Prussia had been divided between Poland and the Soviet Union, so that these territories might also come into question (obviously only the Polish half), but the Poles would not be able to find anyone in Germany to defend their frontiers on the Oder and the Neisse. According to Khrushchev, the Russians had made this clear to the Poles, and Gomulka had said there was no need at all to discuss such questions.

Khrushchev criticized the Poles for the way they thought they could trade: selling coal for cash to the West and asking for grain on credit from the Russians. This was not trading on equal terms, Khrushchev said, but exploitation of the Soviet Union. He explained which of the socialist countries they were giving grain to and how much. They would let the Romanians have it as a loan, and the Romanians would return it next year. Khrushchev was interested to know how much grain Yugoslavia needed to import. We told him of the agreement on this we intended to sign with the United States Government. Khrushchev and Malenkov approved. Khrushchev spoke ironically about the Poles, who had managed to work out that the Soviet Union was in debt to Poland, although the Soviet Union had given them enormous assistance.

At the beginning of the conversation Malenkov demonstrated that from a purely legal and constitutional point of view Imre Nagy's government was not legitimate or properly established by the constitutional bodies, and that its present program was unconstitutional—as though this line of argument made Soviet military intervention any easier—and as if that itself were constitutional!

[17] The eastern frontier of Poland agreed by the great powers following World War II follows roughly the Curzon Line, which was proposed by Lord Curzon, British Foreign Secretary, as an armistice line between the Soviet and Polish forces after World War I. In 1920 the Poles advanced farther to the East into territory which they claimed as Polish. But in 1945 the Russians demanded all the territory up to the Curzon Line, and Poland was allotted territory in the West at the expense of Germany.

As usual when he is talking to Yugoslavs and wants to put them in a good mood, as though he were making some concessions to them, Khrushchev told some unflattering stories about Stalin. This time they referred to Stalin's relations with Rákosi, whom Stalin allegedly could not stand and did not trust. Rákosi used to take his vacation in the Soviet Union in the same place as Stalin, and Stalin was suspicious of this and said he would cure Rákosi of it. At the first opportunity Stalin pressed Rákosi to drink an excessive quantity of alcohol at one gulp. But then they were afraid that Rákosi might die from it and carried him away, although in fact nothing happened to him. Rákosi modeled himself on Stalin to such an extent that he had a steel door made for his office in Budapest as well as some bulletproof clothes to protect him from attempts on his life. Khrushchev and Malenkov concluded by saying that Rákosi never had and still did not have the most elementary understanding of what needed to be done, that he and Stalin had cooked up a porridge in Hungary that the present Soviet leaders now had to eat.

Whenever the question of Imre Nagy came up, Khrushchev would generally repeat, "They are slaughtering Communists in Hungary," as though it was all being done on decisions taken by Nagy's government and carried out by its services. Later, when there was discussion of how much Nagy could do to ease the whole situation, Khrushchev took a different line, did not keep repeating, "They are cutting Communists' throats there," but accepted a quite different assessment of Imre Nagy, agreeing that he could do much to help and to preserve his reputation as a Communist.

* * *

The talks came to an end at five o'clock in the morning of November 3. For some moments there was general silence. It was a rather awkward pause, with no one inclined to attract the attention of the others for further conversation, since there was nothing more to be said on the political questions. Practically no alcohol had been drunk at dinner and none was served during the talks.

Khrushchev and Malenkov had been very mild and restrained, always ready to accept what was said on the Yugoslav side whatever they were really thinking. From this it was clear that they aimed to have the meeting end in agreement, even though throughout the conversation it had been obvious that our views on the reasons for the bloody events in Hungary were completely opposite. This was emphasized several times by the Yugoslav side, particularly when they insisted on a categorical condemnation of Rákosi, which really means the Soviet Union, as the one to blame for the present catastrophe in Hungary. This was the basis for the other points made by the Yugoslav side, such as: Who was to form the new government, what program to draw up, how to influence Imre Nagy before the inevitable second intervention by Soviet troops so as to save what could be saved and reduce the casualties and further bloodshed in Hungary.

Khrushchev and Malenkov left by plane from the airport at Pula early on the morning of November 3. Flying conditions were exceptionally bad.

After we had seen the guests off from Tito's villa I stayed in my hotel room to make notes about this strange meeting which had lasted through the night. It wasn't very easy: I had to reconstruct ten hours of talks from memory.[18]

Our embassy in Moscow is very active, sending reports to Belgrade several times a day. Apart from preparations for crushing the revolt in Hungary by force, the Russians are active in other directions. They have delivered something like an ultimatum to Britain, France, and Israel demanding that they halt all military operations against Egypt and withdraw their troops without delay. They have also delivered a message to Eisenhower informing him of what they have done and even asking for America's cooperation in halting the aggression of the Western powers and Israel. The attitude of the United States in opposing the British-French-Israeli use of force now suits the Russians very well, although for months they have been "exposing" America as the main plotter of aggression against Egypt.

In Moscow the French and British are practically isolated among the Western diplomats, the majority of whom condemn the attack on Egypt. It is not that they have any understanding for Egypt or Nasser but that this "stupid war" makes it impossible for the West to make better use of events in Hungary against the Soviet Union.

The Soviet Presidium has been meeting nonstop for the last few days and nights. Apart from their political and diplomatic activity in all directions, the Russians have carried out military preparations on a large scale, because anything might happen. At one reception Marshal Zhukov referred to the presence of Marshal Koniev in Poland. Angry at the Poles, and with a gesture as if destroying someone with one blow, he said: "And we could have crushed them . . . !" When a Western ambassador

---

18 *Author's note:* Various versions later circulated abroad, some of them malicious with regard to Yugoslavia, concerning the contents of the talks on Brioni on the night of November 2–3, and about other aspects of Yugoslav policy with regard to events in Hungary. At the beginning of 1959 the Yugoslav Government therefore decided to publish a book entitled *Yugoslavia's Policy Towards Hungary and the Case of Imre Nagy* (the so-called "White Book" about Hungary). This includes the most important documents on the subject, including those which confirm what was said at the Brioni talks. The author's notes, which were written immediately after the talks and are reproduced here, coincide exactly with the essential points in the documents published in the "White Book."

asked him: "Who? Do you have in mind the Polish Communists?" Zhukov made no reply. They have sent a Central Committee delegation led by Aristov,[19] a member of the Presidium, to Czechoslovakia. The Russians are rather afraid there may be trouble there, but there are probably no grounds for their concern. If there is anyone in the camp who is firmly on the side of the Russians and against the Hungarians and Poles, it is above all the leaders of Czechoslovakia.

[19] Averki Aristov, b. 1903. Soviet Communist official. Secretary, Central Committee, CPSU, 1955–60; Member of Presidium, CPSU, 1957–61; Ambassador to Poland, 1961–66. Retired.

142

CHAPTER ELEVEN

NOVEMBER 1956. A MONTH OF TROUBLES

The Soviet Army suppresses the revolt in Hungary. Khrushchev presents himself as protector of the Arab world and gloats over the "victory" in Hungary. Imre Nagy takes refuge in the Yugoslav embassy in Budapest, Yugoslavia, is accused of supporting the "counterrevolution," and relations with Moscow take a turn for the worse. Mićunović sees Soviet "public opinion" in action.

On the way to Moscow, November 6, 1956

I am in a Soviet plane on the way to Moscow. I have practically the whole day in front of me, and I will use it to jot down something of what has happened since our meeting with Khrushchev and Malenkov, as far as we could follow events from Belgrade.

Khrushchev and Malenkov left from Pula Airport very early on the morning of November 3. There were no formalities of any kind. There was a suggestion that they were in a hurry to give orders for the second Soviet military intervention in Hungary to begin, though they had not told us when it was to be. The law on military secrecy was in force. I don't know exactly when the Russians gave the command for their troops to move on Budapest, but the Soviet units probably received their orders in the course of November 3.

Soviet troops struck at Budapest, the greater part of which was apparently in the hands of the rebels, in the night of November 3–4, which means less than twenty-four hours after we had seen Khrushchev and Malenkov off from Brioni. This is confirmed by the fact that Imre Nagy and a large group of top Hungarian officials and members of their families made their way to our embassy on November 4 and asked for asylum. I believe there were about forty people altogether.[1] Soon afterward Russian armored units, personnel carriers, and tanks surrounded our embassy building and imposed a complete blockade of it. They checked the identity of every single person leaving or entering our embassy. The windows of the building itself were smashed, and it was very cold on November 4. Among the Hungarian refugees there were some who were sick and in need of a doctor, but the Russian authorities would not allow anyone except Yugoslav diplomats to enter the embassy building. Apart from anything else there was the problem of feeding such a large number of Hungarian refugees. These were new and quite unexpected problems which we had to solve, quite apart from the completely new political situation in which our embassy, and Yugoslavia, suddenly found itself.

Only three days previously Khrushchev and Malenkov had unexpectedly arrived on Brioni as friends but incognito. They behaved in an extremely cordial manner, as never before. This was a premeditated gesture intended to influence our talks and our whole attitude toward them, because it is simply impossible to behave otherwise toward people with whom one has recently been exchanging kisses as with the closest of friends. As I am writing this I still seem to feel Malenkov's fat round face, into which my nose sank as if into a half-inflated balloon as I was drawn into a cold and quite unexpected embrace. We had not exchanged kisses with the Russians at our previous meetings; we hadn't even talked to them for nearly seven years, but now they had decided that we should kiss each other in the difficult circumstances which had arisen—for them, rather than for us. If things had been the other way round, I reckon the Russians would have refused even to talk to us.

It is not difficult to foresee that the Russians and the newly formed Hungarian Government will now start accusing Imre Nagy of things for which he is not to blame. They are already accusing him of betraying socialism, trying to leave the Warsaw Pact, and putting himself under the protection of the West. And Imre Nagy himself, whom they are accusing of counterrevolution, is now enjoying the protection of the Yugoslav embassy in Budapest. It is not far to go from making such accusations against Imre Nagy to extending them to those who have taken him under their wing.

When they seek to find the reasons for the bloody events in Hungary, the Russians will probably follow the same crooked line as they did before these events happened. They are already describing them officially as counterrevolution. So to "defend the revolution" in Hungary they have

---

[1] *Author's note:* It was later confirmed that forty-two persons asked for and were granted asylum in the Yugoslav embassy in Budapest.

sent Soviet troops against Budapest in revolt and are seeking the causes of the revolt from here all the way to America: In their view everyone else is to blame, they alone are in the right!

In such changed circumstances our oral understanding with the Russians and their hugging and kissing with us don't mean much now and will mean hardly anything at all, because the situation has suddenly changed. Now, if it suits Soviet political requirements, we may be accused of having been Nagy's masters and protectors all the time and of being the people really to blame for the "counterrevolution in Hungary." In fact, the principal culprits are the Russians themselves who, through Suslov and then Mikoyan, after ten years of Soviet domination, and through Rákosi and Geroe, without consulting anyone, took such strange decisions about Hungary that they finally provoked the bloody events and the revolt.

Throughout this period and especially in the last few days we have been able to do hardly anything through the Soviet embassy in Belgrade. It simply announced that it was not authorized to deal with anything concerning Hungary and always referred everything to their embassy in Budapest, which has been "out of action" for ten days already. It has not been able to operate normally and the Soviet Government is in fact represented in Hungary by the Soviet troops around Budapest and their command. That the Soviet embassy in Belgrade had been deliberately kept out of everything can be seen from the fact that nobody from the embassy was with Khrushchev and Malenkov on Brioni. I don't know whether, since the new Yugoslavia has existed, a meeting has ever been held at such a high level without the participation and knowledge of the diplomatic representatives of the country whose top leaders were visiting.

It is now simply impossible to talk about the policy of the Twentieth Congress and de-Stalinization when the Soviet Union is restoring order in Hungary by means of armed force and is threatening to do the same for other countries of Eastern Europe. Although Khrushchev is the main instigator of the intervention, I imagine his prestige is on the wane while Molotov's and Malenkov's is on the increase.

Events have followed so fast on one another that I am returning from Belgrade with many more new and complex problems than answers to the questions with which I set out for Belgrade ten days ago.

Moscow, November 6, 1956

The Russians have started to accuse us of protecting the "leaders of the counterrevolution" in our embassy in Budapest. It is obviously not just a matter of their intending to settle accounts with Imre Nagy and the group of his friends who found refuge in our embassy; the Russians also want to make sure that on this occasion Yugoslavia is compromised as much as possible. It is as though they reckoned that Yugoslavia has no way out of the present situation. They have decided to sling mud at Yugoslavia as the organizer of the counterrevolution if we don't hand Imre Nagy and the others over to them. But if we do hand them over, they will then point at us as a country which does not keep its word and which nobody should depend on.

On Brioni they could not have been more accommodating. Whatever we proposed in good faith in an effort to ease their difficulties, so as at least to reduce the bloodshed in Hungary, in the interests of both Russians and Hungarians and ultimately of all of us, Khrushchev and Malenkov accepted at once. But all that is now an embarrassment to them and they would like to disown it all. Comrades in our embassy say that Soviet Foreign Ministry officials behave as though Khrushchev and Malenkov had never been to Brioni and as though the visit, which was to have a substantial effect on relations between our two countries, had never taken place.

While they were preparing the second military intervention in Hungary the Russians were receiving in Moscow delegations from various countries in the East, in the West, and in the neutral part of the world. They appear to be welcoming anybody who wants to come and visit them these days. There have been delegations from Afghanistan, Syria, and Belgium, and on every possible occasion they emphasize the principles which should govern a peace-loving country in its relations with other countries. It is these principles by which, allegedly, the Soviet Union is governed in international relations. So the Russians now proclaim such principles as the sovereignty and integrity of states, noninterference in the internal affairs of other countries, mutual respect, opposition to war, imperialism, etc. They have solemnly signed documents to this effect in the last few days while they have been completing the final preparations for intervening in Hungary, whether there has been a revolution there, as the West says, or a counterrevolution, as the Russians claim.

By doing all this the Russians tried to make it more difficult for the West to attack the Soviet Union because of the second military intervention in Hungary. But the main factor reducing the possibility of joint action by the West over events in Hungary was not Russian diplomacy but the British and French aggression in Egypt. This Anglo-French adventure enjoys no support even in Western diplomatic circles here, where you can often hear outspoken criticisms of the French and British action.

Moscow, November 7, 1956

Gromyko yesterday summoned our chargé d'affaires Božović at one o'clock in the morning for an urgent communication. Just how serious a situation exists is clear from the fact that the Foreign Ministry works through the night, as in Stalin's day, and this creates a very unusual atmosphere in Moscow. Gromyko informed our man as follows:

Khrushchev had sent a letter to President Tito yesterday in which he explained the attitude of the Soviet Union to the situation in the Middle East. The letter refers to documents which Soviet Prime Minister Bulganin has sent about the aggression in Egypt to United States President Eisenhower,[2] the Prime Ministers of Britain and France, Anthony Eden[3] and Guy Mollet, and the Prime Minister of Israel, Ben-Gurion.[4] Shepilov has also sent a similar note to the chairman of the United Nations Security Council.

Gromyko said that the note to Eisenhower called on the United States Government to "take action with our combined military forces against the aggressor and defend Egypt"! The Soviet note says that the United States has at its disposal powerful naval and air forces in the Mediterranean and that the Soviet Union also has powerful naval, air, and other forces in the south and that by joint action they could make aggression impossible, Gromyko said.

* * *

Although this is the Soviet National Day I asked to see Khrushchev, who received me at six o'clock in the evening, which may well have meant that he, too, was interested in seeing me as soon as possible. Although I did not give any reason for asking for the meeting, it wasn't difficult to guess that it was because of Hungary, or, more precisely, because we wanted to resolve the question of Imre Nagy and the other Hungarians who were given asylum in our embassy in Budapest. In this matter, as an independent country, we have obligations of a political and moral character and we must honor the undertaking we have given. When all is said and done, our conduct is in the spirit of our talks with Khrushchev and Malenkov on Brioni. Tito has already sent a letter about this to Khrushchev, who I think knows why I want to see him.

Khrushchev, wearing a dark suit with the two gold stars which he

[2] Dwight D. Eisenhower, 1890–1969. President of the United States, 1953–61.
[3] Sir Anthony Eden (later Lord Avon), 1897–1977. British statesman. Foreign Secretary, 1935–38, 1940–45, and 1951–55; Prime Minister, 1955–57.
[4] David Ben-Gurion, 1886–1973. Israeli statesman. Head of provisional government, 1948–49; Prime Minister, 1949–53, 1955–63.

wears only on special occasions, received me, again along with Malenkov, in the Kremlin close to St. George's Hall, where preparations were afoot for the grand National Day reception, the anniversary of the October Revolution. We talked for about an hour, Khrushchev doing most of the talking. Malenkov said little. I had to reply to a number of attacks by Khrushchev.

Khrushchev began by talking about Egypt and the Western powers. He said they had just heard from New York that Britain and France had informed the United Nations and Hammarskjöld that at midnight tonight they are ordering a cease-fire on the territory of Egypt. This was the direct result of the energetic approach made by the Soviet Union to the three Western powers the day before yesterday. The Arabs had seen who came to their defense at the most critical moment. The Russians had received a note from Nasser which was very moving in its contents. It said that the present generation of Arabs would pass on from generation to generation the fact that the Soviet Union had defended them in their most critical hour.

Khrushchev said they had received identical replies from Eden and Mollet. Eden said that the Soviet note was so insulting that in other circumstances it would have been handed back to the Soviet Government, but that since times were difficult the British would overlook it. The Turks had put their antiaircraft units into a state of readiness, which was ridiculous in view of the strength of the Soviet rocket weapons. Khrushchev went on to say that the role of the United States had been exposed. It had allegedly been against aggression, but when the Soviet Union came forward with its proposal, the United States was exposed as an accomplice in the Western plan to attack Egypt. The defeat of the West was complete. Nasser remained, and the Arabs would be even stronger after this idiotic war-making by the French and British, Khrushchev said in conclusion. He spoke for ten or fifteen minutes, as though he thought that that was the reason for the meeting.

He then spoke about Hungary, saying that it had all gone off better and more quickly than the Russians themselves had reckoned. Apart from two or three points in Budapest the whole thing had been crushed in a single day. People in Moscow had drawn up a plan for the whole operation before Khrushchev and Malenkov returned to Moscow from Brioni. There had been practically no resistance. Kadar was a very good Communist, and he would now extend and strengthen the government. Munnich had declared that this was the first Hungarian Government not to have any Jews in it. It had been reported from East Germany that the Soviet plan had been very well received there, too. Khrushchev said that they had informed Yudin[5] by telephone and that he had passed it on to

[5] Pavel F. Yudin, 1899–1968. Soviet Communist official. Editor of the Cominform journal *For a Lasting Peace*, 1947–50; Ambassador to China, 1953–59.

Mao Tse-tung, who had called a meeting of the Politburo of the Chinese Communist party and invited Yudin to inform all the members about the events. The Chinese had sent a telegram of congratulations to the Russians.

Khrushchev deliberately avoided touching on the main problem: the fate of Nagy and the others. He started telling stories about the war and then the usual talk about Stalin, and it looked to me as if the conversation was going to end there. I pointed out that I had been informed today in the Soviet Foreign Ministry of their reply to our note about Hungary. My personal impression was that such a reply on their part did not resolve the problem that had arisen over the granting of asylum to Nagy and the others, but only made it more difficult for all of us to find a way out of the Hungarian events. I briefly recapitulated the main points from the note which Tito, Kardelj, and Ranković sent to Khrushchev on November 5.

Khrushchev suddenly dropped the friendly tone in which he had so far been holding forth about the great victory of the Soviet Union in Hungary and Egypt. He repeated the arguments from their reply of November 7 and ended up roughly as follows:

–Everything is now in contention again. The Yugoslav attitude to resolving the problem of Nagy will determine whether relations between Yugoslavia and the Soviet Union would continue to develop in a friendly way or in the opposite direction.

–Nobody in the Soviet Union could interpret the failure to hand over Nagy and the other organizers of the counterrevolution otherwise than as evidence that they had long been acting on instructions from Yugoslavia and that Yugoslavia was responsible for what they had done.

–The question of Nagy was a matter between us and the Hungarians, but the Russians were not outsiders in this, and he was telling me what they, the Russians, thought about it. It was the unanimous view of everyone in the Soviet leadership, which had studied the whole affair very closely.

–Although he avoided references to the last Brioni talks, Khrushchev argued that we had agreed about everything there as Communists, and if we were Communists how could we now adopt such an attitude on the question of protecting the leader of the counterrevolution? He quoted Comrade Tito's unfavorable statement about Nagy. He also referred to Ranković's favorable remarks about Loszonczi, who had, however, turned out to be one of the chief "bandits." He said they had accepted our suggestion about exposing Rákosi and had referred to his "clique," which had not been easy. Then he repeated firmly that every aspect of our relations was under review, because nobody in the Soviet Union could understand our insistence on rescuing the leader of the counterrevolution. Instead of making positive statements, Nagy had, right up to the last minute, appealed on the radio for a struggle against the Russians and had then taken refuge in our embassy. What was this leading to: Could it be that we were trying to form a new government opposed to Kadar's? Khrushchev asked in conclusion.

In reply I said the following:

Giving asylum to Nagy and the others in our embassy was the logical consequence of our agreement with Khrushchev and Malenkov about the desirability of reducing the degree of resistance by the Nagy government. Nagy had made no statement and had not resigned, and that was his affair, but it could not be disputed that the fact that the Nagy government had in effect disappeared from the moment it entered the Yugoslav embassy had proved useful and had helped both Kadar and the Russians. Both the Hungarians and the Yugoslavs and the rest of the world as well were witnesses to the fact that this had made things easier for the new government.

As for the idea that Yugoslavia would be held responsible for the events in Hungary because it had offered asylum to Nagy and the others and was demanding a solution of their problems, I said that I personally did not believe that Soviet citizens or anybody else could believe that Yugoslavia bore such responsibility. If we had to go into the question of who was really responsible for events in Hungary, Yugoslavia's conscience was clear, and I believed that we could contribute a good deal to establishing more precisely who was to blame for those events if that was now wanted.

Khrushchev interrupted me and said there was no need for him to scare me or for me to scare him, but that we should talk like Communists and internationalists, and not like nationalists.

I replied that we had agreed on Brioni on a line of action toward those people, that it was true that they were now in our embassy in Budapest, but it was not true that they had been acting on our instructions. I could understand that the situation had changed quickly and that what seemed all right on Friday, on the night of November 2–3, did not appear so good now on Wednesday, November 7. I understood also that Kadar's position was a delicate one, but they should also understand our position. It was not a simple matter for Yugoslavia as a socialist state or for the head of that state to give his word and grant asylum to people, to render any further action on their part impossible and so help the new revolutionary government, and now to go back on their word and hand the people over. Khrushchev repeated that he didn't understand a Communist moral code which protected accomplices of counterrevolution.

During the conversation Khrushchev spoke in a threatening tone about what would happen if they were to announce in Moscow that the leaders of the Hungarian counterrevolution had found asylum in the Yugoslav embassy. I told him that in my personal opinion they could announce it if they wished, because we had not had and still did not have any ulterior motives.

At the reception in the Kremlin, which started immediately after our conversation ended, I kept away from the members of the Presidium, who were very attentive toward the few ambassadors present, since all the Western diplomats boycotted the reception. Malenkov and Kaganovich came up to me and tried to create a normal atmosphere. Later I talked with Bulganin, who asked me how the talk with Khrushchev had gone, because he was not in the picture. I told him briefly, but he was very reserved; he accepted some of my arguments in silence, and repeated that the prestige of Kadar's government had to be raised, not destroyed.

I think we ought to make contact with Kadar and put the problem to him. I have the impression that the Russians are going to be very tough and consider that Yugoslavia ought now to climb down. Either we shall hand over all the refugees and so lose a great deal in the opinion of the world and play a dishonest role in the Hungarian events, or we shall risk a new conflict with the Soviet Union and the others, this time as protectors of Imre Nagy and the other counterrevolutionaries, as the Russians like to describe them.

Moscow, November 8, 1956

Presumably to let me know that there is no longer any special relationship between us, as there was only three days ago, and that everything is now being dealt with exclusively through routine diplomatic channels, I was summoned by Patolichev,[6] one of the assistants to Foreign Minister Shepilov. He invited me to see him on November 7, their National Day, which is unusual except in an emergency. The immediate object of this meeting was probably to inform me officially, before I saw Khrushchev in the afternoon, that their reply to Tito's letter of November 5 about Imre Nagy and the others was entirely negative. Our letter was signed by Tito and Comrades Kardelj and Ranković and was addressed to Khrushchev personally. It was probably thought that in such a form it would be more likely to help resolve the Nagy affair. But the fact that the letter was signed by the three most important people in Yugoslavia has not helped much, since Patolichev informs me of the Soviet reply in the Soviet Foreign Ministry! When Patolichev had given me this "news," he told me that Shepilov wanted to see me. It was clear that this had all been agreed in advance by

[6] Nikolai S. Patolichev, b. 1908. Soviet Communist official. Deputy Foreign Minister, 1956–58; Minister of Foreign Trade from 1958.

the Russians. Patolichev said that Shepilov was ready to see me right away, stood up and offered me his hand, and thus made it impossible for me to say anything, on the excuse that the Soviet Foreign Minister wanted to see me urgently. This, too, wasn't a bad diplomatic device! It is the first time I have come across it in the Foreign Ministry since I arrived in Moscow.

I had asked for a meeting with Shepilov in order to deliver a strong protest to the Soviet Government concerning the armed attack by Soviet troops on our embassy in Budapest and the people who were in it. A Soviet tank had taken up position in the square in front of our embassy building and then without any sort of provocation had suddenly opened machine-gun fire on the windows of the ground floor of the embassy, where there were a lot of people. One of our embassy secretaries, Milovanov, was killed as he sat at his desk. In this way the Russians exerted crude pressure on us and the Hungarian refugees. Apart from that, it appears that the Russians are aiming to make life in the embassy building impossible.

Shepilov did not accept my protest, although the issue was crystal clear: The Russians, unprovoked by anybody, opened fire from machine guns and killed one of our diplomats in the embassy. Shepilov did not even express any regrets. He went through the completely false Soviet version of events, according to which a bomb is supposed to have exploded in the immediate proximity of the Soviet tanks which were maintaining a blockade of our embassy, and it was only then that the Russian tanks opened fire "in the direction from which they had been threatened," i.e., at the Yugoslav embassy building.

Shepilov behaved remarkably arrogantly and let me see that he found the conversation on this subject more than boring and superfluous from the very outset. It was obvious that he had been instructed not to accept my protest and that the Soviet side had invented the story about the explosion of a bomb near a Soviet tank. Shepilov had been Soviet Foreign Minister for about half a year and had never before served in the Soviet diplomatic service. This kind of rude behavior is now required of him and even appears to be an asset.

* * *

I will just record finally that, in the same conversation in which he called Nagy "the leader of the counterrevolution" and demanded that we hand him over to the Russians, Khrushchev spoke of the same person in quite different terms when he discussed his letter to Gheorghiu-Dej of November 3. He then described the contents of Nagy's letter as "very striking" and said it was proof of the isolation and despair of a man whom events had brought to the top and then overtaken, and who now didn't know what to do and was begging Dej for help, almost for salvation, in Khrushchev's words.

In the course of this conversation Khrushchev forced me two or three times to retreat, although even then I did not abandon my original stand. Khrushchev achieved this by turning on me personally, angrily, and threateningly, with the question: Do you really and seriously think like that? I would repeat my reply, using fresh arguments in a rather calmer manner. After that the situation would quiet down, until Khrushchev again put the pressure on. He presumably thought that he would first scare me personally and that I, duly scared, would then frighten everybody else in Belgrade with the alarming news from Moscow.

Moscow, November 10, 1956

While they were preparing their second military intervention in Hungary the Russians published the declaration referred to already about relations between socialist states. The declaration is a step forward by comparison with similar documents produced previously and certainly by comparison with what Moscow is doing in practice. It is not the result of changes in Soviet policy after the Twentieth Congress, nor was it published in time to prevent the events in Hungary; it followed immediately after those events started and was really produced under pressure from them. As it was, the declaration actually played a part in the political preparations for the armed intervention by the Soviet Army in Hungary.

The events in Hungary have caused considerable concern among the people of Moscow, in spite of the fact that the Soviet press has not said anything even approximating the truth about the scale which the events there have assumed. As far as we know, the party and youth organizations have not received any official explanation of what is going on in Hungary. For the moment all you can find in the Soviet press is some brief news stories about attempts to provoke disorder by "counterrevolutionary elements" and their defeat. Since the Soviet information media do not publish any other reports, many people are listening to foreign radio stations, including the Voice of America. This practice becomes all the more popular the less the Soviet Press says about the events.

Of all the organized forces in the Soviet Union now the one which comes most to the fore is the Soviet Army. Without any particular effort being made by military circles in the Soviet Union, the times are such as to stress the role of the Soviet Army above all other institutions in the Soviet state. The more serious the events in Hungary appear and the more unfavorable the situation looks in general, the greater the importance and role of the Soviet armed forces. The British, French, and Israeli attack on Egypt has also resulted in the Soviet Army playing a more important role in current Soviet policy. Khrushchev told us frankly during the talks on November 2–3 that the Soviet Army has been the main factor in reaching a decision about the intervention in Hungary.

There is now a wave of meetings and street demonstrations going on in the Soviet Union against certain Western countries. Everything is planned in advance: what will be said, who has to be condemned and in what terms, what slogans have to be shouted, at which objects bricks can be thrown, and where you can and where you cannot break the windows in some building belonging to foreigners, and so forth. To judge from the demonstrators in Moscow it is mostly workers who take part in these demonstrations organized by Soviet official bodies. Workers are the easiest to gather together, because they are already assembled in their factories. Apart from that, they are supposed to represent what is called "the people," although the number of people who actually take part in this sort of demonstration is very small when you consider how many millions live in Moscow. All this serves further to worsen the atmosphere and relations between the Soviet Union and the West.

The Soviet leaders want at all costs to give the impression that people in Moscow are equally pleased with the outcome of the events both in Hungary and in Egypt. The whole party and state machine is working to this end, and there is endless talk about the defeat of the forces of imperialism in Egypt and of the counterrevolution in Hungary. They continue to link the two together and to describe it as a victory for the Soviet Union, not only in Hungary, where the Russians were most directly involved, but also in Egypt, "which the Soviet Union defended in its most difficult hour." The first to give currency to such interpretations was Khrushchev himself, who now begins to give an impression of much greater self-confidence than when events in Budapest and the war in Egypt first broke out.

Moscow, November 11, 1956

As usual when there is a worsening of relations between East and West, there has been a further tightening up of internal discipline and a strengthening of the "monolithic" organization of all aspects of life in the Soviet Union and in Eastern Europe. It is being made clear both to the peoples of those countries and to people abroad, through speeches and the press, that there would be no wavering here. One reliable indication of the direction in which Soviet political thinking is moving at the moment is provided by the fact that, after a long break, *Pravda* is again giving publicity to such dogmatic and Stalinist representatives of the countries of the "camp" as Enver Hoxha. This is a sign that the Presidium is now adopting attitudes opposed to the policy of de-Stalinization and that at the moment the Russians have need of such an author.

The Moscow *Pravda* and the rest of the Soviet press started yesterday to publish pictures of people being hanged and murdered in Hungary, with captions saying they are Communists and victims of the "white terror." There are no names of the victims. It is not very convincing or clear what it is all about, though the scenes depicted are very grim. It is like some of the propaganda in Yugoslavia during the war ("Hell, or Communism in Montenegro"). You can't make out who killed or hanged whom. It would be a good thing, it seems to me, if the Russians dropped this. But I can't suggest anything like that to them, because, in the psychosis now being created here, it would serve as further "proof" that I was "protecting the counterrevolution in Hungary."

The news of the killing of Milovanov in our embassy in Budapest made a very serious impression on the diplomats here. Many foreign diplomats expressed, in writing and orally, their sympathy and inquired about the circumstances in which Milovanov was killed. But none of the diplomats from the socialist camp expressed any sympathy. The Egyptian told me of his fears about the worsening of our relations with the Soviet Union. This would weaken the Arabs' cause, and that was what mostly interested him.

Diplomats from the East are giving us an ever wider berth. The Chinese do this rather less than the others, although there are plenty of demonstrations of Russian-Chinese brotherhood. *Pravda* and the rest of the Soviet press print everything they can find on the subject. The impression is being created of unity between Moscow and Peking, while what happened between the Russians and the Poles and especially between the Russians and the Hungarians is made to appear unimportant, because the losses there are compensated for by the friendship with the Chinese. A performance by the Chinese theater the night before last was attended by Khrushchev, Molotov, and Malenkov among others, and the applause for the Chinese actors turned into a rather forced Soviet-Chinese friendship rally which went on for an unusually long time. I don't have much to go on, but it strikes me that if the Chinese are going to stick to their "principles" as they did in 1948 when they backed Stalin, the more likely it is that there will be further conflict between us and the Russians.

Moscow, November 12, 1956

Yesterday, Sunday, November 12, Khrushchev received me at my request. After I had apologized on account of it being a Sunday, Khrushchev said he had come to Moscow for the meeting I had asked for and that he would have invited me sooner if he had not been out of town when he was told I wanted to see him. It appeared that Khrushchev had expected me to come with a fresh reply from Comrade Tito, whereas I brought the originals of Comrade Tito's letter of November 9, to which the Soviet Presidium had already sent a reply to Belgrade proposing a new solution of the Nagy affair.

Khrushchev read me their reply from beginning to end. He gave his opinion that their reply was constructive and that the affair ought to be resolved in a satisfactory manner. After our conversation in the Central Committee building Khrushchev invited me and my wife, Miška, to lunch with his family. I spent several hours with Khrushchev and discussed many things.

Although we talked long about Hungary, on neither side was anything substantially new said: The arguments which had been used in our conversation of November 7 were simply repeated. But Khrushchev spoke of Nagy and the others in different terms from those he had used in the conversation with me on November 7, which had been very outspoken and full of open threats on Khrushchev's part. On that occasion I had hardly been able to agree about anything with Khrushchev, apart from approving the description of Rákosi and Geroe as a "clique" and the appointment of János Kadar as Prime Minister. But agreement on that only widened our differences on other subjects.

Khrushchev expects our reply to their latest proposal (letting Nagy go to Romania) to be positive and considers that the compromise solution proposed is the only possible one, that it is satisfactory both to us and to them as well as to the Hungarians (Kadar), while the Romanians have agreed to participate and help. Apart from Nagy, who could not remain in Hungary, Loszonczi is also on the index, probably because the Russians think he had contacts with us and so hastened to compromise and condemn him in the statement made by the Kadar government on November 6. It talks about the "Nagy-Loszonczi group."

Speaking of relations with the West, Khrushchev said there was now going to be a resumption of the cold war, but that wasn't a bad thing for the Soviet Union. They had shown the West that they were strong and resolute. The West was weak and divided. The Russians knew there had been real fear in NATO about the more serious steps the Soviet Army might take in Europe. The Soviet armed forces in Eastern Germany alone were stronger than what NATO had at its disposal at the moment in Europe. This had been stated to a group of NATO experts, Khrushchev said.

The Americans had forbidden any movement of NATO forces in Europe during the latest armed intervention by the Soviet Union in Hungary so as not to provoke the Russians, Khrushchev said. Soviet prestige among the Arabs and in Asia had increased enormously. The weakness of the British and French had been revealed to the whole world. Suez was blocked, and the West had been deprived of its normal supplies of oil, which was important from a military point of view. World trade would suffer a great deal, for which the Anglo-French act of aggression was to blame. Khrushchev said they had finally threatened the West with a statement about sending volunteers, but he didn't think it would come to that. He said in conclusion that the Soviet Union was not thinking of going to war, but that the Soviet Union's latest threats of war had been correct and necessary.

Khrushchev said they were thinking of starting up a new campaign in favor of disarmament. He asked for my views. I spoke in favor of it and of other measures calculated to ease the present tense atmosphere. The question of disarmament was extremely complicated, I said, but I supposed that world public opinion would welcome any move to reduce the threat of the use of force, since the present situation was so difficult. Khrushchev said they would give more thought to the matter.

After the attack on Egypt by the three powers, Nasser had asked for Soviet military advisers, and Khrushchev said they had sent them. They didn't know how many Nasser wanted or how he would use them. The British had especially insisted in seizing the undamaged military equipment which the Egyptian troops had been using, especially the T-54 tank. Perhaps they had succeeded in doing so, Khrushchev said, but it wasn't very important, because today such things quickly became obsolete.

More than ever before Khrushchev assured me of the firm and united Sino-Soviet stand on all questions concerning the present world crisis. They had had discussions with the Chinese and had agreed about everything, from Hungary to the idea of sending volunteers to Egypt. Khrushchev informed me that they had talked about Yugoslavia with the last delegation from the Chinese Communist party, led by Liu Shao-chi, which had come to Moscow secretly at the end of October, and let me understand that the Chinese were in agreement with the Russians. I understood Khrushchev to mean that the Chinese had been told of Soviet reservations about Yugoslav policy and the role played by Yugoslavia in events in Eastern Europe. Khrushchev commented that the Chinese were very different from us and from them, the Russians. They were cautious and wise and acted in their own way, but the present crisis had convinced the Russians that the Chinese were at one with the Soviet Union on all questions.

When he came to Yugoslav-Soviet relations, Khrushchev started by saying that in the plane on the way back from Brioni he had talked at length with Malenkov and that they had both been satisfied with the talks on Brioni. But there were some very clear points of disagreement and a lack of mutual trust in our relations.

Khrushchev then proceeded to give me his opinion of some of the leading people in Yugoslavia, a practice which he and others here still consider their right and is a favorite subject of conversation. When it comes to Soviet relations with other socialist countries this weighing-up of people in other countries and parties is a particularly annoying way the Russians have. After mentioning some of the leading officials in our Foreign Ministry, Khrushchev dismissed them with a gesture of his hand, saying it wasn't worth discussing the extent to which they were "pro-Western." In his view the majority of the members of our diplomatic service were "pro-Western" and "anti-Soviet," and he said it was not an unimportant matter because it concerned a large number of people in the most sensitive places. To convince me of this, he read me a telegram from the Soviet ambassador in Washington, Georgi Zarubin, saying that our ambassador, Leo Mates, had boycotted the Soviet reception on November 7. Khrushchev also criticized our press for its treatment of Soviet affairs and said there had been no changes for the better despite the improvement in our relations.

Khrushchev went on to say that they could not agree with us in our appraisal of Stalin. We were the only people, apart from the West, who were using the terms "Stalinism" and "de-Stalinization." We had started to use these terms in the days of our conflict with the Russians, and we were still making use of them today, and this was bound to have a bad effect on our relations. After all, Yugoslavia did not have anything like as much democracy or decentralization as we gave ourselves credit for. We said that the press in Yugoslavia was free, but we never had any difficulty in making the press write what the government wished. It was just the same with freedom of opinion. "How well you solved the question of Djilas; we can only congratulate you," Khrushchev said.

Khrushchev talked at length about the Chinese, who, he said, had a different way of doing things from the Russians and also from us. They didn't boast about themselves or try to impose their experiences on others, as we Yugoslavs did, or criticize the Russians for doing so, as we were always doing. Khrushchev went on to say that the majority of the intellectuals in Yugoslavia were pro-Western. Even before the war Yugoslavia had boasted of belonging to the West, and after the war, because of what had happened between us, after 1948, those tendencies had become stronger.

This was the first time I had heard such views from Khrushchev. I had the impression that he is deeply convinced that he is right in his attitude and that he quite sincerely voices what he really thinks. There was a certain bitterness in his voice when he spoke several times about our use of the terms "de-Stalinization" and "Stalinism." He said everybody in the East now wanted to measure things by our Yugoslav standards. I said we did not try to impose anything on anybody. We were not to blame if somebody quoted us. As for what terms they were going to use to formulate their views, that was their business, but I considered, despite what had happened in Hungary and elsewhere, that the most successful policy was the one which had been proclaimed as a new policy at the Twentieth Congress in his two speeches.

Khrushchev listened to me with an expression of resignation. He tacitly confirmed what I said about Hungary, making no mention of counterrevolution or the imperialists. When I mentioned the Twentieth Congress and his speeches, Khrushchev commented reluctantly that "there are some people amongst us who think that the new decisions are responsible for everything bad that has happened." He also said that in the Soviet Union they had "eight million Communists, if only they were all Communists."

When Bulgaria was mentioned, Khrushchev said that one of the Bulgarian leaders had come to Moscow asking for help, because they had 100,000 unemployed in Bulgaria, an enormous problem for a small country. The Russians were obliged to help, but how? Khrushchev asked. They could offer the Bulgars to go and work or settle in Siberia, building factories or working on the "virgin lands." "What else can we do?" Khrushchev asked. "We can't offer them Moscow or Kiev, we've got enough of our own problems there already." (Poor things!)

At some moments Khrushchev gave the impression of a very worried man in great difficulties.

CHAPTER TWELVE

TITO'S PULA SPEECH

Tito's defense of Yugoslavia's attitude to the revolt in Hungary and his reference to "Stalinists" in the Kremlin leads to a heated exchange between Mićunović and the Soviet leaders and a strange midnight talk with Khrushchev in a Moscow street. The new Hungarian Government agrees to allow Nagy to return to his home, but he is seized as he leaves the Yugoslav embassy.

Moscow, November 15, 1956

It is nearly ten days since my conversation with Khrushchev about the fate of Imre Nagy and his friends. After that Khrushchev changed his attitude toward me. Instead of going on arguing about Nagy, he invited me to his home on November 11 and was very attentive to me and my wife for several hours, during which he made no reference to Nagy.

We have come to the conclusion that the Soviet leaders are now moving toward a tougher party line at home and a further cooling off of relations with the outside world. It is to be expected that there will be a further retreat from the policy laid down by the Twentieth Congress, since Hungary has now provided further grounds for that.

Moscow, November 17, 1956

Diplomats here—mostly from the West but from the East also—have been asking me for the authentic text of Comrade Tito's speech in Pula. I cannot oblige them because, unfortunately, we still do not have a text of any kind, in our language or any other. I have heard that Tito made the speech on November 11, the very day I went to dinner in Khrushchev's house. The Russians are already suspicious and distrustful, and now they will accuse me of double-dealing because they may believe not only that

I knew that Tito was going to speak and what he was going to say but also that I tried from here to influence the contents of the Pula speech. But even today, November 17, we do not have the text of the speech in the embassy! I hear that the speech sets out Yugoslavia's position on current questions, deals at length with the Hungarian events, and criticizes the policy of the Soviet Union. I have spoken with Khrushchev about all these matters several times in the last few days. He will think that the speech is our reply to everything he has said to me recently. Perhaps he will accuse me of abusing his confidence since the speech is obviously not in the least favorable to the Soviet Union. If it were otherwise, the Western diplomats would not be so anxious to read it.

One of the staff of the embassy spoke with Belgrade by telephone and was told that Tito's speech was printed in the Yugoslav press yesterday. There must be some reason for this: The speech was made a week ago but was published only yesterday. If the Russians don't hold up our newspapers, we should receive the speech the day after tomorrow.

So far the Russians have said nothing. They have not even reported in the press that Tito spoke in Pula. I shall go to the Kremlin today for a reception the Russians are giving for Gomulka and the Poles and there I shall see how the Russians have taken the speech.

* * *

At the reception in the Kremlin for the Poles Khrushchev made a speech attacking the imperialists and their predatory raid on Egypt, after which the NATO ambassadors left the reception demonstratively one after the other.

Not a single Russian, not just from the Presidium but the others, too, wanted to shake my hand or greet me or my wife throughout the two hours that the reception lasted. When it was over, as we left St. George's Hall, I was met by Khrushchev, Bulganin, and Molotov. Without any greeting Khrushchev said they wanted to talk to me, and we went back into the empty hall in a group, and talked for about an hour standing by the wall. My wife sat alone waiting in the hall. Khrushchev then proposed that we should go and sit in the next room and so conceal ourselves from the view of the people who were watching us and were surprised to see us stay so long in heated conversation. In the next room we talked for about another hour. Khrushchev took the lead in the conversation; Bulganin cut in frequently and very sharply. Molotov intervened rarely and calmly, and his contributions were the most restrained throughout this unusual conversation.

Khrushchev began by saying that they were very surprised at Comrade Tito's attack on the Soviet Union. "We are publicly described as

Stalinists, and it is said that it is not a matter of the 'cult of personality' in the Soviet Union, but that the Soviet system itself is Stalinist. That means that nothing has changed here and that the Soviet Union as a whole is under attack. Who needed this, apart from our enemies?" It surprised all of us, Khrushchev went on, especially after Comrade Tito's letter of November 9 on the question of Imre Nagy, which was comradely and friendly. What has happened suddenly to change everything and for Tito to attack us and condemn us openly and before the whole world? They had not expected this and neither had they started a conflict now, but we had, Khrushchev said in a very serious tone which gave the impression that something very bad and unexpected had happened.[1]

Bulganin was aggressive and insulting. He immediately began using the language and "arguments" which were used at the time of the quarrel and bad relations between us. He said: "Now you can look forward to getting credits from the Americans; they will be pleased at what you have done. Comrade Tito referred twice in his speech to Comrade Khrushchev without calling him 'comrade.' That is a public insult which no Soviet person would regard as anything but a deliberate offense." He said that Tito had called them Stalinists, which meant that we wanted to make them responsible for all the bad things in the past that they were now fighting against. Bulganin could not contain himself, saying that we were accusing them of arresting and executing people while we in Yugoslavia had arrested tens of thousands of Communists who had sided with the Cominform. "And you have executed Communists," Bulganin said, unable to control his language so great was his anger and bitterness.

Molotov kept silent, only supporting from time to time what Khrushchev and Bulganin said. They started to count how many months had passed since we had established the friendly relations which had now come to an end. They said they would have to reply to the attack which Tito had made on them. They were not thinking of changing their relations with Yugoslavia on the government level, but we had certainly changed them on the party level.

Any other form of reply could have been expected, Khrushchev said—a letter or something similar—but not a public speech which was now being transmitted round the world. Here in Moscow tomorrow Yugoslav newspapers will be on sale with the Tito speech. We Yugoslavs had acted contrary to our joint party declaration. Dulles and Eisenhower would be pleased, all the more so in view of the difficult situation we had got into after Hungary. They mentioned the million tons of grain we had just received from the United States for foreign currency.

Khrushchev said they would never agree with our opinion of Stalin, whom we wanted to cast into the garbage dump. The foundations of the

[1] For extracts from Tito's Pula speech see the Appendix.

present strength of the Soviet Union had been laid under Stalin, and they were proud of that part of their history. They knew much better than we did all the bad things Stalin had done, but that didn't mean that they could remain silent today when they were attacked in this way. They asked me what I had to say. Khrushchev said he hadn't yet read the whole speech. Bulganin said he had, and he was the most outspoken in the first part of the conversation.

I said I did not have the text of the speech but that I had listened to it on the radio. My impression was that Comrade Tito's speech was constructive and that it did not suggest any breaking off of friendly cooperation between us. The speech examined frankly the causes of the catastrophe in Hungary, and I thought it could only do good if we agreed about that and learned from our experience.

As for the grain from the United States, it was true that we were going to receive a certain quantity in accordance with American and Yugoslav law, but we were eating our own Yugoslav bread. It was sad that we should be talking about this in such a way. We had discussed these matters with them previously, on Brioni, and again here in Moscow in June. We had then been in agreement and nothing new had happened since, yet now I learned that they took a different view.

They asked me what had prompted Tito to do such a thing. I said that I was here in Moscow and that I hadn't yet received the speech ("You'll get it tomorrow in *Borba*," Bulganin blurted out), but that I thought there were some very serious reasons for it. First of all, Hungary. Tito had been obliged to tell our people the reasons for the catastrophe which was a defeat for all of us. None of them had anything to say to this. Apart from that, the word was going round all the parties of Eastern Europe and elsewhere that we Yugoslavs were responsible for the tragedy in Hungary. We were again coming across anti-Yugoslav articles by Enver Hoxha, for which the Soviet Communist party was also responsible, because his article had appeared in *Pravda*. Similar anti-Yugoslav statements were again being made by the French and other Communist parties, as in the past.

All three of them, jumping in one on top of the other, said: Why didn't you reply to Enver Hoxha, the French, and the others who criticized you, instead of Tito attacking us and our system as Stalinist. Bulganin said that if we were against interference in other people's internal affairs, why had Tito interfered in Soviet internal affairs, calling them Stalinists and the Soviet system bureaucratic? Bulganin spoke ironically about Tito's use of the terms "Enver-Hoxhists," "Rákosists" and "Stalinists."

Khrushchev and Bulganin then criticized our attitude toward Albania. Bulganin asked me whether I knew what great-power chauvinism was and said that that was our attitude to Albania. Khrushchev said we were opposed to any monopoly of power among Communist parties, and yet we wanted a monopoly position for ourselves, since we condemned publicly everyone who didn't suit us. Khrushchev said that Tempo[2] had made fun of the Albanian party, an impossible attitude which had quite disgusted the Russians.

I told Bulganin that I had a pretty clear idea of what great-power chauvinism was. I reminded him that we in Yugoslavia had resolved the national question in the course of our war and revolution as well as after the war, that we had had our own direct experience of what it was for one nation to try to dominate others, and that we had no difficulty in recognizing such things. If it had been otherwise, Yugoslavia would not have been able to withstand all the trials she had been through in the last fifteen years. Turning to Khrushchev, I said it wasn't a catastrophe if Tempo had made fun of Enver Hoxha's Marxism on some occasion. Tempo had made a quite contrary gesture when he had embraced Enver Hoxha in Moscow last year, and I didn't think one should draw any far-reaching political conclusions from such gestures.

Bulganin insisted that I should tell them why Comrade Tito interfered in their internal affairs when we were opposed to such interference. I told him that Tito had not interfered in their internal affairs, but had spoken of the causes and consequences of the grave events in Hungary, which also concerned Yugoslavia.

Khrushchev repeated yet again that they were going to reply to this attack, that we would then reply to them, that others would then become involved and who knew what would happen. They had not expected this from Comrade Tito. They knew that the meeting in Pula on November 11 had been specially arranged, which meant that we had decided to act in this way. The consequences would be bad, but the Russians were not to blame; it was we who had violated the Moscow Declaration, Bulganin said. I pointed out that the Declaration had been violated by them immediately after it was signed. How, when, they asked, taken aback. I reminded them of the secret letter from their Presidium in the summer. At this there was an awkward silence. Khrushchev asked whether we had received the letter. I replied that, unfortunately, they had not sent it to us and that we had not been able to get a copy.

Moscow, November 18, 1956 (continuation)

In the presence of Bulganin and Molotov, of whom he took his leave, Khrushchev offered to take me and my wife back to our embassy in his

---

[2] Svetozar Vukmanović-Tempo, b. 1912. Yugoslav Communist official. Minister of Defense, 1948–58; Chairman, Yugoslav Trade Union Organization, 1958–67.

car. While we were talking, my wife had been sitting alone at a table some distance away. She said she had been amazed at what was going on and asked me how it was all going to end.

I accepted Khrushchev's offer. The first part of the conversation, in the car on the way from the Kremlin to our embassy, driving through Moscow's empty streets, was mainly a repetition of what had been said already. We were followed by one or two cars of the security police and stopped at the Yugoslav embassy at 21 Khlebny Street. As she said goodnight to Khrushchev, Miška invited him in for a cup of tea, because it was very cold outside with the temperature ten degrees below zero. Khrushchev thanked her and then kept me in the car and resumed the conversation, which had lasted about an hour. I saw that we were accompanied by several cars full of secret police which had taken up positions in front and behind us so that all traffic on Khlebny Street was stopped.

It was long past midnight, but we continued this unusual conversation in the car. It was Khrushchev who wanted to go on talking and, sitting behind the glass division which separated us from the driver, who could hear nothing, he asked several times, as though thinking aloud, what had made Tito do such a thing.

Khrushchev explained again how much he personally had invested in the establishment of friendly relations between us and recalled the principal events in this connection from 1954 to the present day. Then he said that, unfortunately, he would now have to vote in the Presidium in favor of replying to us publicly and that this would open up a new conflict between the Soviet Union and Yugoslavia. Upset and rather depressed, Khrushchev said: "If you had only seen the written report I made following the talks in Yugoslavia and in the Crimea and knew how I expected relations between us to improve."

To my question as to how they thought of replying Khrushchev said they had yet to agree whether to do it as the Central Committee, as the editorial board of *Pravda*, or in some other way. They would speak about it also at the Central Committee meeting, but they would have to reply before it took place. Once quarrels began it was difficult to keep them within bounds or to stop them, Khrushchev said and repeated that great damage would be done and that people in the West were already delighted. I said that it was not because Tito had made such a speech that the West was pleased but because they expected a new conflict between us. Therefore it was very important what kind of reply they made: upon that depended whether the West would have reason to rejoice or not. I said that the West would not have much reason for rejoicing if the discussion remained within the limits of explaining the points of principle and differences of opinion among Communists. We had sufficient experience of the past conflict between us. But Khrushchev is more of a realist, and he repeated: When quarrels and arguments begin, it is difficult to control and limit them.

I believe they are going to announce that Imre Nagy is in our embassy in Budapest. They have asked me whether I have had any reply from Belgrade about it. I said I hadn't and that I thought it would be better if Nagy and the others could go freely to their homes, and Khrushchev agreed with me.

They were especially upset by the fact that Comrade Tito divided them into Stalinists and non-Stalinists. If anyone else in Yugoslavia had done it, it would have been easier. They knew, Khrushchev continued, that some of our leaders, such as Moša Pijade[3] and Koča Popović, regarded the Soviet Union in the old way. He said that Fierlinger[4] had personally reported that Moša Pijade had advised him in his speeches about Yugoslavia not to stress the role of the Soviet Union as a liberator in the last war in Europe. I said that Moša Pijade's friendship for the Soviet Union was different from and greater than Fierlinger's. I commented that leading people in the countries of people's democracy considered that the best way of winning Soviet confidence was to speak badly about Yugoslavia and to inform on the Yugoslavs to the Russians. They hoped the evidence they produced against us here would be regarded as proof of their devotion to the Soviet Union. This policy was utterly mistaken and destructive. Khrushchev did not agree.

Khrushchev said that we and they had different opinions of people. Thus they were pleased that Chervenkov was in the leadership of the Bulgarian Communist party, but we weren't. He said the same about Ulbricht. I commented that what was decisive was a leader's reputation with the population. People who were responsible for the awful things that had been done in the last ten years could hardly expect, I thought, to stay on in leading positions. No new policy could be pursued through them.

Since neither of us had anything new to say on the main topic, Khrushchev continued the talk in the car by asking me what I thought about their declaration on disarmament which he had told me about on November 11 when I was at his house. I said that I had approved it from the beginning, although I did not think one should expect any practical results now. I argued that there would not be a resumption of the cold war, and Khrushchev agreed, although he had told me on November 11 that the cold war would return and that it would not be a bad thing for them.

At times the atmosphere was very unpleasant. Here in Moscow, unfortunately, we can talk frankly to the Russians only when we are quarrel-

[3] See page 218.
[4] Zdenek Fierlinger, 1891–1976. Czech politician and diplomat. Ambassador to the Soviet Union, 1937–45; Deputy Prime Minister, 1946–53; Member of Presidium, Czechoslovak Communist party, 1948–66.

ing. So it was last night, on both sides. I believe that some of my arguments had an effect. The Russians are really in a bad situation: They don't really want a new conflict with Yugoslavia at the moment, because it will only make the general situation more complicated for them, especially in Eastern Europe. I believe that their first reply to Tito's speech at Pula will be restrained, despite the fact that they are so upset.

Interestingly enough, Khrushchev reckoned that they are now, on the eve of the new conflict which they foresee, politically stronger than they were in 1948. I have the impression that there was an influential group here who wanted to reply to us immediately and in the strongest terms. But the view was accepted that such problems should be resolved more calmly and after solid preparation.

And so came to an end the strangest conversation I have had so far with Khrushchev. More striking than the contents of the conversation were the strange, indeed dramatic circumstances in which it took place: on the street, in front of our embassy, in a car with the temperature ten degrees below zero, well after midnight. These unusual circumstances also reveal how badly Tito's Pula speech has been taken here.

Moscow, November 19, 1956

In today's *Pravda* the Russians replied to Comrade Tito's speech in Pula. They have not dramatized the affair but limited themselves to a report of some two hundred lines on the second page of the paper. It is presented as a report from the TASS correspondent in Belgrade and is not signed. It refers to the text of Tito's speech published in *Borba* on November 16. Although they have tried to make it look like a report from Belgrade, the Russians' reply was in fact written here in the Presidium of the Central Committee, as Khrushchev told me at our last meeting. The Russians will probably explain that they adopted such a tone so as not to make things worse at the moment. But we must expect a further reply from the Russian side and that the December plenum of the Central Committee of the CPSU will take up the question, depending on how things develop in the next ten or fifteen days. Today's reply in *Pravda* is sufficient to indicate what form the Soviet leaders' defense, or rather their accusations against Yugoslavia, will take.

Moscow, November 20, 1956

Khrushchev received me yesterday at half past seven at my request. I read him a telegram from our leaders which was a sort of explanation of Comrade Tito's speech at Pula, and left him a copy in Russian and Serbo-Croat.

Khrushchev interrupted me three times during the reading, although it was a fairly short telegram. He was obviously in the mood for a quarrel. When I read him the passage in which our Central Committee objected to Soviet leaders dividing us into "pro-Soviet" and "anti-Soviet," Khrushchev said it was he alone who had done that personally and no one else, and that that was what he thought now and would go on thinking in the future. He said people were not all the same, either among them or among us. He said he alone did it, quite sincerely, and now we were using it as an argument against the Soviet leadership.

Khrushchev spoke about the Soviet Central Committee's secret letter about Tito's visit which I had mentioned in our last conversation. He said they had acted correctly because they had had reservations about us, and Tito's latest move was the best proof that they had been right. They might have sent their secret letter to us as well, and there had been such a proposal in the Presidium, but they had decided not to. There was nothing of substance in the letter which they had not told us in Moscow during the talks about the party declaration in June. One thing in the letter which might mean something was the criticism of Bulganin (for calling Tito a "Leninist") with which Khrushchev had agreed and which he himself had raised. If he hadn't done it, somebody else would have, Khrushchev said.

Since the Russians are most put out by the charge of Stalinism in Tito's speech, we talked about it again. Khrushchev again went through what they had achieved under Stalin's leadership: industrialization, collectivization of the land, victory in the great patriotic war against fascism. If it comes to that, they are all Stalinists and proud of it. Stalin ruled with an iron hand, and that was what their enemies feared. Now those enemies thought that because they had criticized Stalin, the Soviet Union would be less resolute in the defense of the interests of socialism. Stalin would have his rightful place in history, and all this would pass, as would our attack on them as Stalinists, Khrushchev said.

I said I did not believe that the policy of the iron hand had brought any benefits to socialism as far as the postwar period was concerned. I considered that we had suffered harm from the cold war and from being isolated and that capitalism had benefited from a policy which had speeded the formation of military pacts embracing practically all the Soviet Union's neighbors.

When we spoke about their secret letter, Khrushchev said that they knew we would get to know about it. It was difficult these days to conduct a correspondence in secret, and indeed they knew about letters which we thought had been kept secret. In the conversation of November 17 there was also allusion to some secret correspondence which they know about and to which they now apparently attach great importance.

Khrushchev said that their Presidium was made up of all kinds of people, but they were not divided into Stalinists and anti-Stalinists as we said, nor would they split into factions. They were totally and firmly united in their attitude to us, and so they were as far as Poland and Hungary were concerned. It was true that there were some who would have replied to Yugoslavia as in 1948. Others thought we should go back to where we were in 1954, before the restoration of normal relations between us.

Moscow, November 22, 1956

Ever since the crisis developed in the European part of the socialist camp the Russians have been assuring us repeatedly that the Chinese are in complete agreement with Soviet views and actions. Khrushchev's insistence on Chinese support and identity of views is understandable, since Chinese support for the Russians is the only significant support they have. It would be quite a different matter if the Russians were to say they had the support of the Bulgars, the Albanians, or the East Germans. Even to the Russians it would sound like a joke. But when they talk about Chinese support, that has a different "theoretical and practical" significance. But it has seemed to me in some of my recent meetings with Khrushchev that the Russians tend to embellish and exaggerate the extent of this support.

Today's *Pravda* carries a TASS report from Paris about a meeting of the Central Committee of the French Communist party. Half the article refers quite openly to Yugoslavia and Tito. We are criticized by Raymond Guyot, secretary of the French Communist party, who has been one of the main supporters of the Russians in the conflict with us. In the past Stalin also used to make ample use of the French Communists in the conflict with Yugoslavia. It is not surprising that they are doing it again. There will now probably be similar statements from the other Communist parties, and *Pravda* will "only report" them. At the same time the Russians will tell us they are doing nothing to worsen the conflict but that people were simply free to express their views!

Moscow, November 23, 1956

Agreement has been reached in writing between the Hungarian and Yugoslav governments about ending the asylum for Imre Nagy and the others in our embassy in Budapest. The Hungarian Government has given first an oral and then a written guarantee that all the people who found refuge in our embassy can return freely to their homes. When the text of the agreement was read to them, Imre Nagy and the others themselves decided that they had no further need of asylum. The government of Hungary undertook in writing not to hold them responsible for what they did up to November 4. Imre Nagy and the others left our embassy in Budapest on November 22 in the evening. Our relations with the Russians will be less affected by controversial questions following agreement with the Kadar government over Nagy.

* * *

We rejoiced too soon at the successful solution of the problem of Imre Nagy and the others and their return home. The same evening as they left our embassy they were seized by Soviet troops. It seems either that no one asked the Kadar government about it or that the Russians acted in collusion with them. The agreement signed by the Hungarian Government with the Yugoslav Government has become as usual a scrap of paper. Imre Nagy and the others have been taken off to an unknown destination, somewhere inside Hungary or perhaps in Romania, which the Russians had already involved in the "Nagy affair."

Now official reports about this are being published and we are sending a note of protest to the Kadar government about the way they have broken their promise and crudely violated the agreement. In this way things are taking a new, worse course between the Russians and us and between us and the Hungarians. The Russians had already started to worsen relations with us, and now the process will be speeded up. Relations will also worsen between us and the Kadar government, which has asked for and has been receiving until now political and material help from Yugoslavia, and we have been helping the new "workers' and peasants'" government of Hungary as far as we could. Moscow won't mind, because it suits them better that the Kadar government should continue to be weak, to depend only on the Russians, to quarrel with neighboring Yugoslavia, and to violate the first international agreement it had signed.

Moscow, November 25, 1956

There were long queues of Soviet citizens yesterday at the kiosks waiting to buy the few copies of our newspapers on sale. The Russians permitted a limited number of them to go on sale between *Pravda*'s first and second reply to Tito's Pula speech. The Yugoslav press was immediately snapped up. Because of the shortage of Yugoslav papers, Soviet citizens bought copies of the Polish press in the hope of finding something there.

A lot of people are listening to Radio Belgrade and other foreign radio stations. The present crisis has shown that there is a great demand among Soviet citizens for foreign sources of information, because they want to know what is going on in the world. Some people here complained about this during the events in Poland and later objected to being kept in ignorance about what was really happening in Hungary. Now the same things are being said in connection with Yugoslavia.

The United States ambassador, Charles Bohlen, told me he thought the Russian reply to us fairly restrained, that it was not aimed directly at breaking off diplomatic relations, and that by Soviet standards the language was polite, addressing Tito as "Comrade." He said that the Americans had tried to build reasonable relations with the Russians but had not succeeded, despite their wartime alliance.

My impression is that whoever worked on the second reply in *Pravda* received instructions directly from Khrushchev. Between November 6 and 19 I had several conversations with him and heard from him practically all the arguments and many of the conclusions which later appeared in *Pravda*.

Moscow, November 26, 1956

The Soviet Deputy Minister for Culture summoned me today and proposed that I should speak on Moscow television and radio on the occasion of our National Day! And so the Russians still manage to work out some new moves to surprise us although we think we have foreseen everything. In view of the situation which has developed between us and the Soviet Union we had not the slightest idea that they might ask me to appear on Soviet television. It looks as if the Russians had not thought of it either, because the custom here is to approach ambassadors ten or fifteen days in advance with such invitations, to give them time to consult their governments. They must have made up their minds at the last moment. The situation is rather confused and contradictory. It's a case of: If you agree you'll be sorry and if you refuse, you'll be sorry too, as they say.

I consider it impossible to speak about Yugoslav-Soviet relations and to pass over in silence recent developments and disagreements between us, even if I didn't speak about them explicitly. On the other hand, it will be difficult to explain our stand and outline our policy on the essential issues in a way that would be at all acceptable to the Russians in the present situation.

Personally I have no doubt that the Russian proposal that I should address tens of millions of Soviet citizens about our relations now and in the future was decided in the Presidium and very likely on Khrushchev's initiative. He is the most skillful among them at practicing this policy of the hot and cold treatment. Today they ask me as a friend to speak on Moscow television; only a few days ago they captured Imre Nagy, and now they behave as though nothing at all had happened, as though it didn't concern Yugoslavia in the least.

I couldn't turn the proposal down, and even less could I accept it without Belgrade's knowledge. In both cases it was a decision which an ambassador could not take on his own even in normal circumstances, and certainly not now when our relations with the Russians are in such a bad state.

I asked Belgrade for their views, although I fear I shall get no reply from there because time is too short. The easiest thing would be to turn down the invitation, but even that would be interpreted as a deliberate political move. I would be the first of the ambassadors ever to turn down such an offer by the Soviet Government. Then the Russians would have grounds for asserting that they had offered the hand of friendship and that we refused it.

Moscow, November 28, 1956

As I expected, there is no reply from Belgrade. So I agreed with the comrades in the embassy that I would appear on Moscow television.

I really went through hell composing in Russian a ten-minute speech for this rather difficult occasion. I needed to say something favorable about the improvement of our relations, though they have in fact got noticeably worse recently. I didn't want to criticize the Russians openly for recent events, but at the same time I had to make it clear that we saw things very differently from the way they did. Then I had to point out that the principal documents which we had both signed were still in force although they had been put on one side. I also had to express, even if only in the mildest form, confidence in the future prospects, although mutual distrust is growing and the conflict seems likely to get worse. There were a number of other contradictions which it was impossible completely to ignore. Relations between us at the moment are such that it is impossible to compose the most routine political speech for such a formal occasion and make it acceptable to both Moscow and Belgrade.

I took all this into account as I composed the text of a suitable speech which was to sound very colorless but was on the whole usable and which will probably please neither the Russians nor the Yugoslavs, just as it will not, in the end, please me. However that may be, we must try to make use of all the circumstances connected with our National Day at least to maintain our governmental relations with the Russians. We must try, so to speak, to quarrel with them in a new way, and not as in Stalin's day.

* * *

I attended a reception at the Albanian embassy today. I did not approach the main table and simply hoped that the reception would end without any spectacular scenes in which I might be involved even against my will. When he caught sight of me, Khrushchev broke away from the main table and came up and greeted me with special warmth, and this was noticed by those present. He said with a laugh: "We have quarreled with each other, but we're not going to war." Bulganin was not particularly disposed to talk to me, while Molotov proposed that we drink to "friendship."

At the end of the reception Khrushchev broke away and we talked about the latest developments between us. I asked him his opinion of our reply in *Borba* in the public polemics we are conducting. He said he had received it from TASS and would read it after the reception. He went through everything he had done during the day as if he wanted to convince me that he had really not had time to read our reply. He said he would come to our reception tomorrow and tell me there what he thought of the reply in *Borba*. They also did not want relations to worsen and it was a good thing if the tone of the article was as restrained as I had said, Khrushchev commented.

We talked about Imre Nagy. Khrushchev has again changed his position on Nagy for the worse, condemning him as he did in the conversation of November 7. He said that they could not possibly have permitted Nagy to stay to cause further trouble in Hungary and that it was much better that he was no longer in our embassy. I took the view that this was the worst solution because it weakened Soviet standing in the world and also the position of the Kadar government in Hungary. I said that we had been obliged to publish the notes and the agreement with Kadar which the Hungarians had broken, and that we had no need of Nagy, although we had been obliged to protect him before and after Tito's speech because we had given our word.

I mentioned to Khrushchev the executions which had taken place in the last few days in Albania and condemned them as harmful to the Albanians themselves as well as to everybody else.[5] I said: "When we start a discussion with you about Marxism-Leninism, the Albanians start executing people at home." Khrushchev agreed that it was a mistake, saying: "Instead of being vigilant they start shooting." He repeated that it was essential that the quarrel between us should not get worse. He says now that the June declaration about our party relations was good. This surprised me, because this is not the time to praise that declaration, but he

[5] *Author's note:* According to a report by Radio Tirana carried in *Borba,* on November 20, 1956, Liri Gega, Ndreu Dali, and Petar Bulati (actually Bulatović) were sentenced to death in Tirana and immediately shot. They were accused of having "carried out serious crimes as spies of a foreign state." It was clearly implied that the "foreign state" was Yugoslavia. All three of the victims were organizers of the national liberation war in Albania and high-ranking party leaders. At some point they came into conflict with Enver Hoxha and fell into disgrace. After the Cominform resolution Petar Bulatović was not allowed to return to Yugoslavia and was forced to take Albanian citizenship.

does it probably because he is preparing to accuse us of violating it. When we praised the declaration in the summer, Khrushchev said nothing about it.

I complained to him that the Soviet Ministry of Culture had invited me at the last moment to appear on Soviet television and that I had decided to accept although I have very little time and had not been able to consult with Belgrade about it. Khrushchev said he knew they had asked me to appear, as was right and necessary, and informed me that the Soviet press would be writing about our National Day. I told him about my speech actually so as to dissociate my government from it, because Belgrade has not replied to my telegram. If there is any subsequent trouble, it is better on this occasion that it should concern me personally and not my government, because it can be said that I spoke without their knowledge or approval.

Moscow, November 30, 1956

There were about three hundred guests at our reception on November 29. Our embassy is not large enough to cope with a larger number. The Soviet leaders were present in full force. The whole of the diplomatic corps was also present. I believe we are the only socialist country which, when it comes to diplomatic relations, is not involved in the cold war. They all accept our invitations: the East, the West, and the neutrals. But the Russians and the Western diplomats did not speak to each other. It was more like a truce; because they were on the territory of a "third party," they wanted neither to quarrel nor to be friendly.

We also invited a Romanian delegation led by the Prime Minister, Chivu Stoica,[6] who had been very friendly when we met at the Albanian reception. The Soviet leaders did not turn up all together as usual but in three groups. First to arrive was Marshal Zhukov, then the main body with Khrushchev, Bulganin, and Molotov, and finally Mikoyan and Kaganovich. The Presidium members behaved in a very restrained manner, with Khrushchev making an effort to be more cordial than the others. I asked Khrushchev what he thought of the *Borba* article. He said it had a lot of things in it with which they did not agree, but it did not make for a worsening of the debate and they had decided to make no further reply in the press. They did not want to worsen the dispute and they believed we did not want to either.

Khrushchev went on to explain that he did not agree in particular with our attitude to the question of solidarity with the other countries of the "socialist camp" or with our maintaining a position between the two

[6] Chivu Stoica, 1909–75. Romanian Communist official. Prime Minister, 1955–61. President, 1965–67.

camps. It was now clear that we were in some middle position and he was going to speak about it at their plenum. He was also going to speak about the relationship between their system and the "cult of personality" and our criticisms on that subject. I said that the question of proletarian internationalism as a political slogan and as a definite policy had been a real issue for a hundred years, ever since Marx had propounded it. We were firm supporters of proletarian solidarity only so long as we understood what we were talking about. We were all using the same words but thinking different things. We ought to clear this matter up, and agree what aims we have in mind when we use this slogan. I reminded Khrushchev that Stalin defended his aggressive policy toward Yugoslavia by means of that very slogan about "proletarian internationalism."

I had a long conversation with Bulganin and Mikoyan in the presence of Chivu Stoica. Bulganin said they were a great family and they had been amazed by Tito's speech. They had criticized him, Bulganin, in that family circle for what he had done personally for friendship with Yugoslavia. I told Bulganin that it would be only fair if he were to inform his family and the others of the reasons why Tito spoke as he did. They knew those reasons, and the main ones had been set out in Tito's letter to Khrushchev.

I ended the conversation by saying that however sharp the disagreements were between us now they confirmed that there had been definite progress in our relations and in relations between socialist countries as a whole. Such public and outspoken criticism on both sides as was taking place between us would not have been possible in the recent past and would have led immediately to other consequences. Bulganin supported this energetically, agreed with me, and demanded that we should drink to "friendship." The Romanian Prime Minister, Chivu Stoica, behaved throughout in a very friendly way but did not intervene in the conversation on either side.

On November 30 *Pravda* and *Izvestia* gave a fairly long account of the speech I made on Soviet television the day before, our National Day. Molotov and Mikoyan asked me if I had seen the extracts from my speech and said they agreed with what I had said. Bulganin said the same. I have the impression that they are not really particularly pleased. Some of our comrades in Belgrade will probably also not be pleased. I reckon it is not possible now to speak in such a way as to please both sides at once.

CHAPTER THIRTEEN
DOWNHILL AGAIN

*Khrushchev reacts sharply to a speech by Kardelj, who crit-
ticizes his policy of "maize and potatoes." Mićunović learns
some of Khrushchev's conversational tricks but also finds
that his close contact with the Soviet leader is not always an
advantage.*

Moscow, December 4, 1956

At a reception which the Russians gave for the Romanian delegation in the Kremlin yesterday I had a talk with Khrushchev on his initiative. I will just jot down one or two things from it, because it produced
practically nothing new of any importance.

To my question about when the Central Committee was going to meet,
Khrushchev said it had been put off until the second half of January.
There would also be a plenum of the Central Committee in December,
but not on ideological and political matters as they had earlier thought.
Khrushchev didn't tell me this with any particular pleasure. Nor did he
say that he was going to be the main speaker at the December plenum.
My impression is that these changes are not of Khrushchev's making, but
I may be wrong.

We talked at length again about Imre Nagy. Khrushchev drew attention with some bitterness to a statement by Koča Popović in New York
that they were considering raising the question of Nagy in the General
Assembly of the United Nations. Khrushchev said that Nagy was in
Romania and that in one conversation he had referred to Tito's opinion
of him. The Russians had told him that if he waited a little he would hear
what Tito thought about him. When they arrived at the airport in
Bucharest, Khrushchev said, Nagy had looked to right and left and said it
was Kiev, from which Khrushchev concluded that Nagy was afraid to go
to Russia. It seems to me that Khrushchev is realizing more and more that

they have got themselves into a very unfavorable situation over Nagy. It looks to me as though, under interrogation, Nagy is not replying to questions as they would like. I suggested, purely as my own personal opinion, that it would have been better if Nagy had stayed at home in Hungary. Khrushchev would not accept that. The Russians obviously believe that Nagy's presence in Hungary would be a permanent threat to the process of pacification as the Russians conceive it.

Complaining about our press, Khrushchev referred to a "foul caricature" in the newspaper *Politika* which would make the very worst impression on everyone in the Soviet Union. He claimed that in Yugoslavia the "old machine" from the time of the conflict of 1948 was again swinging into action. I told him I didn't know what he was talking about. He didn't seem to want to explain the affair of the caricature, as though it were insulting enough for anyone in the socialist countries to be caricatured, whatever the point might be. Khrushchev quoted statements made by responsible Yugoslavs in Belgrade and the rest of the world against the Soviet Union, saying they were indisputable facts. I pointed out that the collection of such pieces of information did more harm than good. It had been shown in the past that more often than not the things had been invented. Khrushchev said that they took that into account, that they didn't operate as they used to, that they frequently sent reports back to their intelligence service as untrue, and that they knew themselves how to distinguish between what was fabricated and what was true. Khrushchev quoted as an example the fact that they had had no reports criticizing me from their services and neither had the Westerners here produced anything like that.

Moscow, December 12, 1956

Khrushchev received me today in his office in the Central Committee building. The conversation lasted more than three hours, though I had reckoned on a far shorter meeting. It was Khrushchev who kept the conversation going. I hadn't the slightest idea that I would find Khrushchev so angry with us, because I did not know what had happened again in Yugoslavia to affect Yugoslav-Soviet relations. It turned out that Kardelj had made a speech in our parliament which has done so much to worsen the position between the Russians and us that I found Khrushchev in such a state as I had never seen him in before, not even after Tito's Pula speech.

It seemed as though Khrushchev could hardly wait to see me to give vent to his wrath. He said that it was an unfriendly attack on the Soviet Union as a whole, its leaders, and the system. It was not a question of Hungary but of the Soviet Union. Khrushchev knew that Kardelj was

thinking of him when he "poked fun at the policy of maize and potatoes." Kardelj had condemned everything that had been done in the Soviet Union—industrialization, technical progress, and all the sacrifices
they had made. Khrushchev said the Russians had suffered and gone hun-
gry, they had been alone, and the whole world had been against them.
And now Kardelj, behaving as though he was on some desert island, was
developing a theory according to which nothing existed in the Soviet
Union but bureaucratism and Stalinism. If the Soviet Union had been
built according to such theories, it would not exist. If it were to follow
such theories today, it would collapse, Khrushchev said.

They knew that Kardelj had not been speaking for himself alone but
that the Yugoslav Politburo had approved his speech. For some reason or
other we seemed to want trouble and a fight. As far as party relations
were concerned it would lead to a breakdown and open conflict. Kardelj's speech was not the same thing as Tito's speech in Pula, because
Kardelj had gone further and made the situation worse, Khrushchev said.

They were preparing a reply to Comrade Tito's last letter. There were
plenty of things with which they did not agree, but they considered that
the general sense and purpose of the letter was not aimed at quarreling or
worsening relations but the reverse. But Kardelj's speech had altered
things, and this would be reflected in the reply which they were soon
going to send us.

The day before yesterday, on Khrushchev's instructions, Patolichev
handed me a copy of the Soviet Communist party's secret letter about
Yugoslavia of July 13. Khrushchev asked for my opinion. I said that I
didn't think very highly of the letter. To judge by the way it depicted
our relations with the West, it appeared as though the Soviet Union had
come to the rescue of Yugoslavia. Khrushchev asked if it was a good
thing that they had handed me a copy of the letter. I replied, speaking
for myself, that it seemed to me that this no longer had any particular
significance and that the letter had already played its part. The best thing
would have been for them not to have written it.

About Hungary Khrushchev said that things there were now both
worse and better. They would have to settle accounts once and for all
with the counterrevolution. They had had either to liquidate the territorial workers' councils or hand over power to them and liquidate the government. Territorial workers' councils did not exist even in Yugoslavia.
The workers' councils in the factories would remain.

They had not allowed Hammarskjöld[1] to go to Hungary because it
would have led to fresh demonstrations, disorder, and perhaps bloodshed,
which was why Hammarskjöld wanted to go, or it was what the people
who had proposed his trip wanted. Neither Western propaganda nor the

---

[1] Dag Hammarskjöld, 1905–61. Secretary-General of the United Nations, 1953–61.

United Nations mattered when it came to Hungary. Khrushchev insisted that the Soviet Union had been obliged to carry out the armed intervention there.

Khrushchev asked me several times whether there was any possibility of our reaching a common position on the question of resolving the crisis in Hungary. He said: "Inform Comrade Tito and ask him." This is not in any way an official proposal, Khrushchev said: He was just voicing it in the course of the conversation because he saw that Hungary was the main bone of contention between us; if that could be resolved, everything else could be arranged.

Khrushchev also mentioned Kardelj's lecture in Norway and attempted to minimize the value of Kardelj's ideas. He said that in one part of his talk Kardelj had lectured his audience about the only way socialism could be built and what socialism is, while in another part he had produced contradictory evidence showing what had not been achieved in Yugoslavia, that the living standard was low, and that there were all sorts of economic troubles.

I believe that this deliberate misunderstanding and minimizing of our achievements will find expression in the reply to Kardelj which they are now preparing. It will not be the Central Committee or the government which replies but economists or propagandists from the Soviet party *apparat*. They will not publish Kardelj's speech. When he spoke about it, Khrushchev was more upset and furious than he has ever been at meetings with me. At times he gave the impression of a man who was extremely angry and embittered. Khrushchev told me that their Central Committee would meet on December 17 (they have not postponed it but have changed the agenda). It will deal with economic questions. There are to be changes in the responsibilities of the government planning bodies, with Saburov and Pervukhin[2] and their commissions having greater powers with regard to planning. The Soviet Government will be "relieved" of some of its powers. The main point on the agenda will be changes in the fourth five-year plan. For the time being they will reduce investments in heavy industry and switch financial resources to housing construction, the standard of living, and food supplies. At least that is what they are now going to announce in the press.

Khrushchev asked me not to say anything about this yet because it was confidential. They were obliged to change the plan and were convinced that it was better this way: They would not behave like Stalin, who had forbidden any changes whatsoever in the plan, even when everybody knew it was going wrong.

The Central Committee meeting on ideological questions has been

[2] Mikhail G. Pervukhin, 1904–78. Soviet Communist official. Deputy Chairman, U.S.S.R. Council of Ministers, 1950–57; Chairman, State Committee for Trade Relations, 1957–58; Ambassador to German Democratic Republic, 1958–62.

postponed till the second half of January. Khrushchev again said that he was going to make the main speech at it. To my remark that foreigners here kept on asking me about changes in the Soviet leadership Khrushchev said that he knew all about that, that there was speculation about Molotov, that they were saying that he, Khrushchev, was quitting, and so forth, but that there was no truth in any of it and that there were not going to be any changes.

Khrushchev said many surprising things, including some which I might have taken as a reason for breaking off the meeting and leaving. For example: Geroe had been with a delegation in Yugoslavia when the uprising in Hungary was being prepared—was that just a coincidence? (The visit by a Hungarian delegation led by Geroe was in fact forced on us by the Russians at the meeting in the Crimea.) Or again: Yugoslavia had practically no jet aircraft, yet it had plenty of modern airports—what for? When I asked him whether he really saw things like that, Khrushchev dissociated himself from both questions. About the first one he said: You can hear this sort of thing being said, and about the second one he said that some of their military people noticed these things. He was only telling me how people in Russia now reacted.

By contrast with all the foregoing Khrushchev declared that the Yugoslav party was very strong and had been tested by hard experience, that its leaders were honest and capable, and that the Soviet party was the same. We stubbornly defended our views as the Russians did theirs, but that unfortunately there was a conflict between us and instead of cooperation a fight was beginning. He repeated that they wanted to continue cooperation on the government level.

Moscow, December 17, 1956

I see that for the last few days my notes have been concerned exclusively with my long conversation with Khrushchev on December 12. I think I ought to say something here about the nature of my frequent meetings with Khrushchev. It has now become the usual practice that it is practically impossible for me to get through a reception in Moscow attended by Khrushchev without his getting involved in a long conversation with me. It has often happened that Khrushchev sends one of his bodyguards across to tell me that he would like to talk to me if I am going to stay on at the reception. After that I have been obliged to wait for him. Foreign diplomats are already accustomed to moving away from us and leaving us to talk.

I have already recorded here all the really important matters discussed during these meetings with Khrushchev. At the beginning, when we knew each other much less, Khrushchev forced me on several occasions to retreat and the conversations did not always finish up as I would have liked. Khrushchev usually achieved this advantage in conversation by means of menacing questions: Did I really believe what I had said; or— would I repeat what I had said about something or other? This is what happened when the conversations developed into quarrels and conflicts between us, as happened in July because of the "censorship" of his speech by the Yugoslav press. I wasn't sure what exactly lay behind such loaded questions on Khrushchev's part. I used to think that he might interpret some statement of mine as an insult to the Soviet Government or himself personally. Then everything would have ended in the worst possible way. In the view of both Belgrade and Moscow, irrespective of what had really happened, I alone would have been held responsible. On such occasions Khrushchev several times forced me to withdraw—not actually to change my stand, but to fall back at least on a more careful choice of words and arguments.

After a certain time Khrushchev no longer found it convenient to make use of his advantage in the old way. In reply to his threatening questions I no longer had to make even an apparent retreat because as a rule I would leave the most serious arguments until the end of our conversation and they usually had their effect on the further course of the conversation when it was resumed.

All this established a special relationship between us, which in my opinion it was possible to have with Khrushchev but not with any other person in the Soviet leadership. This kind of conversation has turned out to be acceptable to Khrushchev, despite the fact that I often tell him things which are not particularly favorable to Soviet policy.

I suppose he doesn't have many opportunities of hearing much criticism of Soviet policy, which is *his* policy. Perhaps that is why Khrushchev is interested in having these meetings. If there were no interest on his part, any attempt on my part to establish such relations would be unsuccessful. The more I tried to impose myself, the greater would have been the chances of failure.

It seems to me that Khrushchev is trying to influence Yugoslav policy in the direction which seems to him most useful for the Soviet Union. I think he is confident that I transmit accurately what he says to Belgrade. Indeed, he says a lot of things which are certainly not going to please the comrades in Belgrade. Or it may be that there is much less calculation in the whole situation than I think, and perhaps Khrushchev simply likes talking. One thing is certain: Khrushchev has been interested in having such conversations with the ambassador of Yugoslavia ever since our first meeting in Moscow.

Moscow, December 18, 1956

I soon realized that my frequent encounters with Khrushchev also had their unpleasant, even dangerous, side. In the first place Khrushchev was often unpredictable. You couldn't be sure what questions he was going to raise or how he would react to some of my statements. In the second place Khrushchev began with increasing frequency to refer to me in public before groups of people and later in his speeches to Soviet and foreign guests at various receptions in Moscow, and I had no control over what he might take out of our conversation and use in public as it suited him. He certainly did it with the best of intentions, but the practice itself was unpleasant for me in view of my official position in Moscow. In the third place it wasn't difficult to see that officials in the Soviet Foreign Ministry as well as those in the party and government administration were growing increasingly displeased with the increasingly frequent meetings and conversations between Khrushchev and me.

This latter aspect of the situation I took into account from the very beginning and always tried to be as attentive and as cooperative as possible toward the people from the Foreign Ministry, so that it would not be possible for them to say that I was abusing Khrushchev's attitude toward me. For that reason I tried to deal with matters which fell within the competence of the Soviet Foreign Ministry or any other departments of the Soviet party or government with people from those institutions. I would always approach those bodies or regularly accept their invitations without mentioning on any occasion Khrushchev's name or referring to a conversation of mine with him. But they do not conceal their disapproval, and on one occasion, when he was handing me one of the Soviet Government's routine propaganda notes for transmission to my government, Gromyko commented sourly: "You have already discussed this with Comrade Khrushchev."

When I called on him for my first protocol visit, Khrushchev raised a great many major and very important questions and asked me for my opinion of what he had said. I had then been firmly convinced that I could not reply simply: "I will inform my government and let you have their reply," although some ambassadors do just that. I have been giving Khrushchev my views, with the qualification that I am speaking for myself and am not sure that the comrades in Belgrade would agree entirely with my point of view.

Moscow, December 19, 1956

Yesterday's *Pravda* replied to Comrade Kardelj's speech in an article which took up a quarter of the whole paper, entitled "Whom Does It

Serve?" It was signed by Pavlov, one of the editors of *Pravda*. Here are my first impressions:

Although today's reply is similar to what it wrote about Comrade Tito's Pula speech, *Pravda* has now gone even further in its distortion of the essence of the speech and in misleading the Soviet public. Applying this method, they first give a false account of Kardelj's views and then criticize them. This has now assumed the dimensions of a general attack on the Yugoslav theory and practice of socialist construction.

Of all the known sins *Pravda* accuses Kardelj of revisionism and anarchism in philosophy and of anti-Leninism in the theory of the state in the transitional period, while on the current practical political level it says we are assisting the reaction in Hungary and destroying socialist solidarity. An indication of how far *Pravda* has gone is provided by its quoting Heinrich von Brentano, the West German Foreign Minister, as saying that NATO ought to help Titoism.

At the end *Pravda* says that the Soviet Union sincerely wishes the glorious Yugoslav people success in building socialism "irrespective of what forms of socialist construction the Yugoslav comrades choose." Then follow another couple of sentences developing the thesis that we are setting our form of socialism against all the others and that this is contrary to Marxism, internationalism, and so forth.

These good wishes to the "glorious Yugoslav people" following the worst possible accusations against and condemnation of everything that is being done in Yugoslavia recalls the conclusion of the first Cominform resolution of 1948. There too they sent greetings to the "healthy forces" in Yugoslavia and called on those forces, also in the name of socialism, internationalism, and so forth, to overthrow the legitimate government and leadership of their own country.

Moscow, December 20, 1956

A few days ago I received from our Foreign Minister, Comrade Koča Popović, a letter setting out the position regarding our relations with the Soviet Union. I am trying to get clear what we might be able to do to avoid a further worsening of our relations.

In the course of five or six days, from December 7 to 12, I had eight meetings with Khrushchev, four of them at my own request, on instructions from Belgrade, and the rest on Khrushchev's initiative. Apart from all the bad things that Khrushchev said, trying to turn the conversation into a quarrel and so revealing the Russians' tactics toward us, I had the impression that Khrushchev does not wish the conflict to worsen or to develop into a fresh clash between Yugoslavia and the Soviet Union.

When they talk about not worsening the dispute, they have in mind

183

primarily that things should simply calm down for the present moment, that we should not attack them, and that they should gain time and have to deal with as few enemies as possible at the same time.

There are no real prospects for an improvement in our relations at the moment: The bad experience of the past is still exerting an influence. In 1955 we restored relations between our states, and in 1956 we renewed cooperation between our parties, but now we again have neither one nor the other, and it is not clear where all this is going to lead.

I told Khrushchev frankly on December 3 that, after all that has happened, my impression was that they were still trying to work out how best to draw Yugoslavia into the "camp" and that that was still their strategic aim. This is where they go wrong in their approach to the question of improving relations with Yugoslavia.

Khrushchev did not deny this. The present crisis between us has also a positive side in that it has become clearer to the Russians that they were on the wrong path. It would of course have been much better if they had understood that in June or even later, when peace and "friendship" reigned between us (at the meetings with Khrushchev in Yugoslavia and then in the Crimea), rather than our talking to them now after we have "drawn swords" at each other, as Khrushchev described our present relations in a conversation on November 12.

The Russians have published their offensive and dishonest reply to Kardelj, which has further reduced the likelihood of any solution. It looks as if we shall not get very far with our intention of clearing a way for a new kind of relationship between socialist states which so preoccupied us and which we discussed with them in June and later. Nor will they achieve very much in relations with us in their equally unrealistic intention to drag us into the "camp," which was and remains their strategic aim.

Moscow, December 21, 1956

Three days ago the United States ambassador, Charles Bohlen, came to dinner with me. We had a long conversation about current events.

Bohlen was interested to know whether we expected a general campaign by the Russians against us. I expressed my doubts and ignorance. The Russians had at the beginning given the impression that they did not want that. After the recent worsening of the situation in Hungary and the Russian reply to Kardelj I was no longer sure about it. Bohlen said that a Russian frontal attack on us would further worsen the dangerous situation in Europe. He had not expected such a sharp reply to Kardelj. Compared with *Pravda*'s first reply he thought the situation had taken a turn for the worse.

Bohlen said they were expecting a successful conclusion of the Eisenhower-Nehru talks. He didn't say much about Hungary, as though it had been finally abandoned to the Russians. Apart from such propaganda and political use as the West can make of it, I don't think anything else will happen, whatever the Russians do there. The agreement between the Poles and the Russians about the stationing of troops looks favorable to the Poles and will serve as a precedent for other countries in Eastern Europe.

Bohlen said he has known the Russians for a long time and could well imagine how irritated they were when Kardelj criticized them for their policy of "maize and potatoes," because everybody in the Soviet Union thought of Khrushchev when maize was mentioned. I told him it was a pity that the Russians did not publish anything of ours but distorted everything we said and then criticized us. This Russian way of carrying on a debate served only to disorientate people further and could not clear anything up. Bohlen said that the United States had been for years permanently in a similar situation and that the Soviet leaders systematically depicted American policy in that way.

Moscow, December 22, 1956

Along with the counselors of our embassy and our military attaché I was the guest of the Chinese ambassador and his principal advisers. The ambassador, Liu Siao, is a member of the Central Committee of the Chinese Communist party. Apart from us Yugoslavs there were no other guests at the dinner.

At dinner the Chinese drank a toast to friendly cooperation between our governments and parties. I replied in the same spirit.

In the conversations which followed we raised a number of questions connected with the building of a socialist society and talked about the need for exchanging views as the proper way to express various opinions on the basis of a common socialist doctrine. The People's Republic of China is developing this method within China, primarily in the field of culture, science, and art (the theory of "a hundred schools" and "a hundred flowers").

I raised the question of the present conflict between Yugoslavia and the Soviet Union as a question of principle in relations between socialist states. I said it would be better if I did not go into what had preceded this conflict, and better that he should be informed by the other side. I said that our public disagreement with the Soviet or any other party on a given problem did not mean that we wanted to weaken state or party relations with that country or party. I did not criticize the Soviet point of view. I believed the Russians were not yet accustomed to this kind of public debate. I said that a proof of this was the fact that they had not printed the speeches by Tito and Kardelj and yet they attacked them bitterly in public. I argued the freedom of discussion between Communist parties would sooner or later prevail and that it would serve only to strenghten socialism. The argument that it served the interests of imperialism meant in fact a ban on the free exchange of opinions so long as imperialism existed, and it would exist for a long time yet. Imperialism takes advantage of the serious mistakes which we make and not the freedom of debate and the differences of opinion between us.

Liu Siao agreed with me but went on to say immediately and to my surprise: Imperialism is today on the offensive and the role of the Soviet Union is decisive for the future of socialism—as though the Russians were listening to him, and perhaps they were, as they have been listening in to us for the last ten years. As for our conflict, the Chinese spoke about an eventual meeting of representatives of Yugoslavia and the Soviet Union, and he asked for confirmation that we had indeed published everything the Russians had written against us, while they had published nothing that we had said. At the end he informed me that Chou En-lai was coming here after his visit to India and would stay in the Soviet Union a few days.

The Chinese know very well that this is not the time for such cordial meetings with Yugoslavs in Moscow and that the Russians follow all this very carefully. So why does the ambassador invite me at this particular moment?

CHAPTER FOURTEEN

NEW YEAR'S EVE IN THE KREMLIN

Russians and Chinese draw closer together as Chou En-lai visits Moscow. But relations between Moscow and Belgrade remain cool and the Russians withdraw their promise of a credit for the Yugoslav aluminum industry. The Soviet leaders celebrate a good harvest.

Moscow, January 3, 1957

Pravda for December 30 published the latest declaration of the Communist party of China. As an example of Sino-Soviet unity the Russians point to the Chinese party's criticism of Comrades Tito and Kardelj. Although in their long declaration the Chinese deal with a lot of questions differently from the Russians and even criticize the Soviet Union in their own way, the impression is being created here that Sino-Soviet solidarity is complete. It seems as though the Russians are now in favor of recognizing the Chinese as equal partners of the Soviet Union in the leadership of the socialist camp even if it is at the moment to the Soviet disadvantage. More important now is Chinese support for Soviet policy; the question of prestige can be taken care of later.

This attitude on the part of the Russians became clear at the New Year's Eve party in the Kremlin. The most important event at the party, which was given for the Soviet elite and the diplomatic corps by Bulganin as Prime Minister, was Khrushchev's speech in which he criticized "those who divide Soviet leaders into Stalinists and anti-Stalinists, hoping in this way to cause a split in the Soviet and other Communist parties." He went on to say that they were "Stalinists in the consistency with which they fought for communism and Stalinists in their uncompromising fight against the class enemy, as was Stalin, who devoted his whole life to the victory of the working class and socialism." The high spot of this panegyric to Stalin was Khrushchev's statement in the presence of about a thousand selected guests that he had grown up under Stalin's leadership and was proud of it.

On two or three occasions Khrushchev's remarks evoked a storm of applause from the assembled Soviet elite. I had the impression that the majority of those present were surprised to hear Khrushchev speak in that way and applauded him spontaneously. Although he mentioned Britain and France and their attack on Egypt, Khrushchev did so very briefly and calmly, as though it was all over and done with. His main attack was directed against none other than those "who divide Communists into Stalinists and anti-Stalinists," and that meant the Yugoslavs.

I think this renewed praise of Stalin is a passing tactical move by Khrushchev. The present Chinese stand is particularly important for the Russians in view of the forthcoming meeting of the Central Committee on ideological questions, due to take place this month. As a reply to us the Chinese have thought up the formula that Stalinism is identical with communism, and that that is what is really important about Stalin, not what can be found to criticize about him. The Chinese leaders need this attitude to Stalin primarily for internal use.

The Chinese party declaration can, in my opinion, only serve to weaken the Soviet Union's position as the "center" of world socialism in general and especially with relation to China itself, which is trying in this way to impose itself as a second, parallel "center of world revolution." The trouble is that the theory has been so far that there cannot exist two or more "centers of revolution." In return for recognizing for the time being a second "center of revolution" the Soviet Union has obtained Chinese support for maintaining the unity of the "camp," whether it likes it or not.

Moscow, January 4, 1957

A few more points about the New Year's Eve party in the Kremlin. Bulganin invited foreign diplomats to the party the previous day. The NATO ambassadors boycotted it. The only one who went was the Greek ambassador, who has a trade delegation here and is hoping for a good commercial agreement with the Russians.

After his speech about Stalinism and communism Khrushchev made a striking gesture which was intended to be of symbolic significance. He rose from the table, in the sight of everybody in St. George's Hall, went up to the Chinese ambassador, wished him a Happy New Year, and led him to the Presidium's table. It was a further demonstration by Khrushchev of "Sino-Soviet unity."

I was allotted a place in accordance with the date of my accreditation to Moscow. When the ambassadors went up to greet the members of the

Presidium, I joined them and shook hands with Bulganin, Khrushchev, and Voroshilov. The Russians were strictly formal in their behavior, keeping their lips tightly closed. No one said anything to me except old Voroshilov, who asked me with an air of surprise how I was and kept repeating disbelievingly my reply that I was well. When Bulganin announced that the official part of the evening was over and invited the guests to enjoy themselves, Miška and I left the party.

One always hopes that the new year is going to be better than the old one, which is why one greets it in a good mood and with hope. It is very rarely that you regret the old year, especially if it has produced such poor results as did 1956.

Moscow, January 9, 1957

Chou En-lai's visit to the Soviet Union became a political event even before he arrived in Moscow. It is being talked about in all circles. He is supposed to end his visit to the Soviet Union on January 13, then go to Poland and return again to Moscow. It looks like some kind of mediation between the Russians and the Poles. I don't know whether Chou will go to Hungary. If he does, there will be grounds for supposing that China is playing the role of intermediary and is ready even to play the part of arbiter between the Soviet Union and the other countries of Eastern Europe, primarily those with which the Soviet Union has been in conflict. The news that Chou is going to Poland confirms our first impression that he is not going there on account of bilateral relations between China and Poland but primarily because of Soviet-Polish relations.

The correspondent of the Peking *People's Daily* inquired of our journalists whether Chou En-lai is going this time to Yugoslavia. Our newsmen replied that they had not seen any official statement and knew nothing about it. They replied this time in the Chinese manner, and that was the end of the exchange. But by raising the question among the journalists the Chinese made sure that it would be reported to their ambassadors and that people would start talking about it in Moscow. As a result some Western diplomats came and asked me whether Chou was going to Yugoslavia.

The Russians were at the airport in full force to greet Chou when he arrived. Bulganin welcomed him with a short speech which was relatively moderate and conventional. Chou En-lai replied with a speech which was twice as long, very outspoken and unusual for such a formal occasion. One after the other he attacked Britain, France, Israel, and then the "Eisenhower doctrine," which had been announced the day before. The Chinese referred to the Soviet Union as the leader of the camp and of the "world Communist movement."

At a formal lunch in honor of the Chinese guest Bulganin made a speech, as though he were the leader of the party and not the Soviet Prime Minister, putting the accent on Marxism-Leninism and the building of a Communist society, on interparty relations, and on the everlasting unity of the Soviet Union and China. Bulganin also paid tribute to the Chinese experience as a great contribution to Marxism-Leninism which the Russians were studying carefully. He said the Soviet Union valued highly the position China had adopted with relation to the counterrevolution in Hungary, and added: "Your comradely support and your efforts to expose the aims of the imperialists in Eastern Europe were of great help to us and to the whole international Communist movement."

In his reply Chou went over practically all the main trends which now exist in the working-class movement and laid down the tasks now facing the Communists. He concluded his speech with a sort of war cry: "For victory over the enemy we must strengthen the unity of the socialist camp led by the Soviet Union!"

Moscow, January 10, 1957

One gets the impression here that the Soviet leaders are preparing to carry the conflict between us into the field of interstate relations. The Soviet Government is preparing to cancel or to postpone the largest economic agreement we have signed with them, the one for the so-called aluminum credits.

To judge by the latest agreements which the Soviet Government has concluded with delegations from East Germany and some other countries of Eastern Europe, it has shown itself ready to assume new and additional obligations both at home and in the "camp," and it is only toward Yugoslavia that it is not ready to fulfill its economic obligations. They are obviously doing this purely for political reasons, because of our disagreement over Hungary and not because of a "lack of funds" as they tell me here.

It is interesting to note the attitude of the Soviet Government on the question of selling grain. It seems to me that the Russians are more willing to give you gold, or credit in any kind of currency, not to mention other goods, rather than sell you grain. It is probably a matter of tradition, a fear of possible bad harvests. When anything becomes a tradition with a people, it is not so easily dropped. Consequently the Russians are very tough to deal with when anybody from the "camp" asks them for any quantity of grain, even on the most favorable conditions for the Russians. For the same reasons the Russians are not prepared at any price to publish how many tens of millions of tons of wheat the Americans have so far delivered to other countries, mostly for nothing. There is no way the Russians could explain that to their public, and so they conceal it like some strictly guarded state secret. Khrushchev displayed this same Russian attitude over grain when he told me that they had given the Poles some grain on a short-term credit, as though this was a real Soviet achievement. The same thing was apparent with Mikoyan, when he told me, as something of exceptional importance, that they had given some grain to the East Germans.

Moscow, January 11, 1957

When in May 1955 we were having talks with Khrushchev about restoring normal relations between our two states, the Russians first offered a credit of $200 million for the construction of a new aluminum industry in Montenegro. When they were displeased with our ideological and political views, which we did not alter even after Tito's visit to the Soviet Union in June 1956, they reduced the promised amount by half. Then they reduced this half still further. Of the $200 million which had been provided for they gave the East Germans $50 million so that the Germans could then give it to us as a loan and thus become Yugoslavia's creditors, although we did not have diplomatic relations with East Germany and had not yet recognized it as an independent state. Finally the Russians have now let us know that they are going to postpone for some years the fulfillment of their credit obligations toward us and that, at least for the time being, there will be nothing at all. They are allegedly short of funds, but the real reason is that the Yugoslavs have again opened up a public debate about Marxism-Leninism and relations between socialist states.

As far as we know no reduction in Russian credit obligations toward the countries of Asia and Africa is foreseen this year. On the contrary, countries like Afghanistan and Iran are saying that they will be unable to make use of a good part of the credits which the Russians offer them. It should not be forgotten that the credits which the Russians promised us during Khrushchev's first visit to Belgrade in May 1955 always played a political role in our relations. It was to the Soviet advantage and made it easier for the Soviet Union to resolve some differences with us.

Moscow, January 12, 1957

The East German–Chinese communiqué speaks of the absolute necessity of the unity of the socialist camp "under the leadership of the Soviet Union" as a sure guarantee of the preservation of peace. The formula of "the camp led by the Soviet Union" is being used again after long disuse. The Russians did not dare, either before the Twentieth Congress and certainly not after it, to make use of this formula, which had been law in Stalin's day. Now they have revived it and are putting round the story that the Chinese demanded it. The newspapers *Pravda, Izvestia, Literaturnaya Gazeta,* and others again popularized the formula in their issue of January 10.

Moscow, January 13, 1957

I met Mikoyan three days ago at a reception in the Kremlin for the East Germans. He pointed out to me that we had not yet entered into diplomatic relations with East Germany and that Tito had allegedly told the Russians that we would establish relations before the end of the year, which was now behind us. I told him that as far as I knew it had never been laid down precisely that we were going to establish relations with them by December 31, 1956, and that we now had more important and more urgent questions to deal with than the establishment of relations with East Germany. From this question of Mikoyan's, as from a similar question which Ulbricht recently put to me, it can be seen that we are still as ever on the agenda in talks between the East Germans and the Russians, who have developed a special version of the Yugoslav question for the Germans. It is reasonable to suppose that the Russians have a special anti-Yugoslav version prepared for the Bulgars, one for the Hungarians, one for the Albanians, and so forth.

Perhaps the expulsion from Albania of the first secretary of our legation in Tirana is not unconnected with these various versions. During our earlier conflict the Russians always pushed Albania forward when they needed to provoke Yugoslavia. Albania served the Russians as a toy in their hands, which they used to demonstrate our Yugoslav great-power chauvinism toward a small and undeveloped "socialist" Balkan country, the only one in "capitalist encirclement." It is obvious that among themselves the Russians still regard Yugoslavia as a sort of attachment of the capitalist world and are proclaiming us again to be enemies of socialism.

The Russians are once again so attached to the patterns of behavior they learned in Stalin's day that they believe they won't be able to spoil relations with Yugoslavia "properly" if they don't stick to those patterns down to the last detail! The Russians consider that relations with Yugoslavia will not have been damaged enough unless one of our diplomats is expelled from some country of the "camp" as *persona non grata.* The reasons given are always espionage and sabotage.

Moscow, January 14, 1957

I don't think there has ever been such a mass distribution of medals and orders, in time of peace or war, in any country in the recent or distant past, as is taking place now from one end of the Soviet Union to the other as the result of a decision of the Presidium of the Supreme Soviet. The central Soviet newspapers, *Pravda, Izvestia,* and others, devoted the greater part of their issues for January 13 to lists of collective farmers who have received decorations in Kazakhstan, Uzbekistan, Russia, the Ukraine, the Baltic states, and other regions of the Soviet Union because of last year's good harvest. At the center of attention are the "virgin lands," Khrushchev's gigantic project in Siberia and the republics of Central Asia which is supposed to solve once and for all the grain problem in the Soviet Union. *Izvestia* gave over three quarters of its total space to printing lists of the people who have received decorations, of whom there are 109,647 men and women, including 158 government and party officials.

The papers also report the arrival of Khrushchev in Uzbekistan and of Voroshilov in Kazakhstan. Khrushchev will probably try to make out of this a great political victory. I hear that it was he who demanded that they should distribute tons of orders and medals on a scale without precedent in Soviet history. By means of these triumphal visits to Siberia and Central Asia, the Ukraine, and elsewhere Khrushchev will be trying to change the political situation in the state and party *apparat* in Moscow, since it is difficult to believe that all this is being done for the sake of the state and collective farms which are receiving the awards.

Last year's good harvest in Asia has been exploited here politically for some time now. In view of everything that has happened in the "camp" since the middle of October last year such celebrations are even more necessary to the Soviet system.

This good harvest has to serve as proof of the correctness of the role played by the Soviet state in socialism. It is the Soviet state which has planned and sown and reaped and is now rewarding the farmers on a mass scale. A mood of victory is being generated and proclaimed from the housetops following the recent political defeat in Hungary. It is at the same time a reply to people abroad and especially to the Yugoslavs who dared to criticize the Soviet system and its "policy of maize and potatoes," with which Khrushchev again reproached me at one of our recent meetings.

It is interesting to note that of the two hundred collective farms which delivered the greatest quantity of grain to the state and therefore received the top awards, the greater number of them still bear the name of Stalin —four years after his death and a year after he was criticized in Khrushchev's speech. The relationship between the number of farms bearing the name of Stalin or Lenin is two to one in Stalin's favor, and that in 1957! After Stalin's name comes Molotov's, then Khrushchev's and Lenin's equal, and then Malenkov's, while only one or two bear the names of Kaganovich and Voroshilov. Even such data are important for assessing the positions which members of the Soviet leadership occupy with the people, or rather in the state and party *apparat*.

Moscow, January 15, 1957

The people who deliver lectures at closed meetings on instructions from the CPSU have orders not to mention Yugoslavia explicitly but to put things so that everyone will know that they are talking about Yugoslavia. They are to make a special point of speaking about the Social Democrats as "agents of the bourgeoisie" but also about the "modern revisionists," because while the former have long ago been exposed the latter have not and are therefore more dangerous than the Social Democrats.

Our journalists Čulić and Dužević told me today that the Chinese party declaration, the full text of which has been published here, is being reproduced on a scale unheard-of even for the materials of the Twentieth Congress. First of all the complete Chinese declaration was published by *Pravda, Trud, Izvestia, Komsomolskaya Pravda,* and *Moskovskaya Pravda* (as you can see, there is more than one kind of "*pravda*" [truth] in Moscow) and another fifteen major newspapers in the fifteen republics. Then it was published by *Kommunist,* the Central Committee journal, *Novoye Vremya,* and *Mezhdunarodnaya Zhizn.* Finally the Chinese declaration has been published in a separate booklet, of which a million copies have been printed. Could you ask for any more convincing proof of the extent to which the Russians need the support of the Chinese!

Finally, a very curious incident. Kardelj, whom the Russians are now attacking so much, sent Khrushchev greetings for the new year, to which Khrushchev had not replied. But today, January 14, we received a note from the Soviet Foreign Ministry saying the following:

> The Soviet Foreign Ministry has the honor to enclose the visiting card of the Secretary of the Central Committee of the Communist Party of the Soviet Union, N. S. Khrushchev, with the request that you will send it on to Comrade Edvard Kardelj, vice-president of the Federal Executive Council of the People's Republic of Yugoslavia, and his wife. Moscow, January 14.

Khrushchev's visiting card with his signature was enclosed. Typewritten on the back was: "Thank you for your new year greetings. Best wishes for the new year." I sent this unusual note with its equally unusual enclosure by courier to Belgrade on January 15. This little message has to be regarded as an event of sorts. I am not aware that the Soviet Government has ever sent such a note to the government of any country. The sense of this odd move by the Soviet Government may be that Khrushchev does not wish to maintain with Yugoslavia or its leaders any relations but the most strictly official and only through "government channels," even when it's a matter of a new year's card.

Moscow, January 18, 1957

As in other fields, the Russians are now in a hurry to "bring order" into matters which go under the common label of Ideology. In the sphere of philosophy they call for special vigilance lest any bourgeois ideas should creep in, and it is known in advance which ideas are proscribed and antisocialist and unfriendly. They are not using especially tough language, in Soviet terms, but there is no mistaking the seriousness with which the leaders regard this matter. It is in fact a warning not to indulge in any independent or original treatment of any problems whatsoever, and the subordination of everything done in this field to the current political demands of the state.

Even the theaters have not escaped criticism. They are criticized for putting on translated plays which were once permitted and producers are warned to be careful what they do. The public in Moscow and other Soviet cities who liked the plays which are now being criticized are declared to be "backward" and to have retained elements of a "capitalist mentality," which theaters, publishers, film directors, journalists, and others must take into account. In the field of the graphic arts they criticize everybody who got carried away in their praise of impressionism—an artistic trend which is not supposed to exist in Soviet society. Anyone who has voiced the slightest criticism of "socialist realism" is attacked and openly described as a servant of world reaction.

Even the exact sciences, which are in the nature of things in a rather different position, are not spared criticism. In this field they are criticizing those who started saying that the so-called "party alignment" and involvement of the state machine were hindering the progress of science.

At the same time others are criticized because they "attack the very foundations of the socialist system under the guise of fighting against the cult of personality." This can apply to anybody whom they want to put out of action. Of course, it also puts an end to any opposition to the "cult of personality" unless it has official authorization. It is not very difficult to see how the Soviet state and party use outside events to introduce a tougher line on the domestic ideological front. The cold war penetrates every pore of Soviet society.

Chou En-lai's visit to the Soviet Union only served to increase their efforts in the ideological field. It seems to have been welcomed by certain political forces in the Soviet Union and has spurred them on to be even more rigorous in their work on the ideological front.

195

CHAPTER FIFTEEN

CHINA AS INTERMEDIARY

*After visiting Poland and Hungary Chou En-lai returns to
Moscow and proposes an international conference of Communist parties and invites the Yugoslavs to attend. But relations between Moscow and Belgrade remain cool.*

Moscow, January 19, 1957

Chou En-lai's stay in Moscow continues to occupy first place
among the political events of the week reported in the Soviet press. Receptions in his honor follow one after the other, some given by the Russians, others by the Chinese. It is as though they are trying to outdo each
other with these celebrations. One such occasion was arranged by the
Chinese on January 17, and it will be remembered for the fact that Khrushchev made another speech like the one he made in the Kremlin on New
Year's Eve. He started by saying that he wanted to speak about Soviet-
Chinese friendship, which was such a powerful force that he wanted to
speak about nothing else. And, he continued, so as not to weaken the
quality of his strong emotion, he would not on this occasion speak about
the imperialists and the others. When he got to the point at which he
would stress that he was a Communist, Bulganin interrupted him to say,
loud enough for us to hear some distance away, that "some say he's a
Stalinist." Khrushchev seized on this intervention, which was probably
prearranged, and turned to praising Stalin as he did in his new year toast
in the Kremlin. "They [meaning, no doubt, the Yugoslavs] called us
Stalinists in public, thinking to blacken us, whereas in fact it can only be
for all of us a term of praise and approval." Nobody could wish the Soviet Communist party anything better than that all its members should be
like Stalin in their devotion to the cause of the working class and socialism. "Stalin was a model Marxist-Leninist and a revolutionary and will always remain so in history."

Chou En-lai has been in Warsaw and Budapest, both of which, and particularly the latter, are especially sensitive spots for the policy of the Soviet Union, and by going there the Chinese leader has been probing into open wounds. It is reasonable to suppose that Chou En-lai himself chose to go to those countries in his role as an intermediary.

I had a brief conversation with Chou En-lai at a Chinese reception. He insisted that Yugoslavia must continue to support Nasser and Egypt, and he kept repeating it, as though we were about to change our policy toward Egypt. I was obliged finally to tell him that, as far as I knew, Tito had been the first head of a socialist state to offer unqualified support to Egypt in the most official way and that our friendly relations with Egypt had improved steadily from the day Nasser came to power. I expected him to say something about relations between Yugoslavia and China, which were not good in the past and are not of the best now, but Chou did not say a word on this subject.

There were seven or eight hundred guests at the reception. The main topic of conversation was Khrushchev's speech about Stalin, which was frequently interrupted by applause. On several occasions Chou En-lai was the first to applaud. The party turned into a demonstration of Soviet-Chinese solidarity. The talks between the Russians and Chinese are not yet over.

Moscow, January 20, 1957

There was a rather different atmosphere about the Kremlin reception for Chou En-lai from that prevailing at other affairs organized for the distinguished Chinese guest. Unlike the reception at the Chinese embassy, when the members of the Presidium and Chou En-lai competed with each other in their outpourings of friendly sentiments and when everything echoed with applause and slogans about Soviet-Chinese unity, the reception in the Kremlin was something less of a demonstration of that kind. Bulganin, the host, and Chou En-lai exchanged conventional toasts. Khrushchev did not speak. The atmosphere with which Chou En-lai has so far been surrounded was missing. Some Western diplomats asked me whether I knew the reason for the change.

The reception started with a concert by selected Soviet performers. The principal guest sat in the front row next to Bulganin, but immediately after the beginning of the reception Chou En-lai left his seat next to Bulganin and informed me through a member of the Chinese embassy staff that he wanted to talk to me. So I found myself in the front row, where I would not otherwise have been. Through a Russian-Chinese interpreter Chou En-lai said the following:

In connection with the present situation in certain socialist countries and the state of relations between them it was his opinion that a conference should be organized of representatives of the Communist parties and governments of all the socialist countries. The aim of the conference would be to improve cooperation and unity between the socialist countries and to remove the obstacles to it which had led to serious conflicts. The conference could be held at the end of February or the beginning of March. Chou En-lai asked me to pass this on to Comrade Tito, because he wanted to know if Tito thought that such a conference would be useful or not and whether the date suggested would suit him.

If Comrade Tito considered it useful and if Yugoslavia would participate in the conference, Chou En-lai proposed making an official visit to Yugoslavia after his present visit to Afghanistan and Nepal, for which he was leaving Moscow that evening. If, however, Comrade Tito considered that Yugoslavia could not take part, then Chou would drop the idea of visiting Yugoslavia for the time being. He would go to Yugoslavia at a later date to be agreed by the two governments.

Chou En-lai told me that the details of his proposal were known to the leader of the Chinese parliamentary delegation, P'eng Chen, who was now in Yugoslavia and was authorized to discuss it with Comrade Tito. I promised to inform Comrade Tito, our Central Committee and government about it by cable during the night, and I asked Chou En-lai to clarify certain points for me. Who had taken the initiative in proposing the conference? And would the meeting take place even if Yugoslavia was unable to take part in it?

Chou En-lai was not in the least taken aback by my questions and replied to them more straightforwardly than I had expected. He said the initiative for the conference was Chinese, or more precisely the whole thing came from Mao Tse-tung himself. The proposal had been made after Chou En-lai had been round the countries of Eastern Europe.

He said that every participant would be able to say what he pleased. The aim of the conference would not be to set up new organizations among Communists, nor would it take decisions binding on any participant. Although he was not categorical on this, Chou En-lai gave me to understand that the conference would not take place if Yugoslavia did not take part. Our nonparticipation would be evidence of a weakening of the unity of socialist forces. They did not want that, which was why they were proposing such a conference. Chou also said it would consider the question of starting a new publication for Communist parties.

I told him a couple of things in connection with his visit to Yugoslavia. Our embassy in Peking had been working on the question, which was not, as far as I knew, connected with the holding of any conference, and our government was ready to consider any proposal regarding the date of the visit. I said that, irrespective of the proposal he had now made and whatever the Yugoslav view of the meeting might be, as an official visitor to Yugoslavia he would always receive a friendly welcome both from the people and from the Yugoslav Government. We wanted in all ways to improve cooperation with China and all other socialist countries, despite the present conflicts and irrespective of whether we were going to take part in the conference or not. With the qualification that I was giving my personal opinion and that I was now hearing about the whole matter for the first time, I expressed the fear that the recent course of events was not the best preparation for such a conference.

As for a new ideological publication for the Communist parties, I told Chou En-lai that we had indeed heard, though quite unofficially, that something of the kind was afoot. We had been told nothing about it officially. Chou En-lai said they were against such a move and the question could be discussed at the conference. In the way he talked about this question and about the problem of reaching agreement between the Communist parties one could clearly detect a critical note with regard to Soviet practice to date.

Throughout the conversation there was no reference on either side to the Soviet Union. The conversation lasted nearly half an hour, during which Chou's chair remained empty next to Bulganin. All of which attracted the attention of the Russians and foreigners present, and especially of the foreign journalists.

Moscow, January 21, 1957

Chou En-lai managed even in the inscriptions on the wreaths which he laid on the Lenin-Stalin tomb to reaffirm China's position on the issues in dispute between the Russians and the Chinese. The temporary solution of this quarrel benefits the Chinese Communist party and is contrary to the message of Khrushchev's secret speech. On the wreath to Lenin was written: "To the great teacher of revolution V. I. Lenin." On the other one was: "To the great Marxist-Leninist J. V. Stalin." In this way Chou En-lai again asserted the Chinese view of Stalin as one of the four great names of Marxism-Leninism. This time the Soviet Presidium did not dispute the Chinese point of view.

Moscow, January 25, 1957

Although Chou En-lai's proposal for a conference is to all appearances democratic, it is in fact an attempt to subordinate us to the interests of the great socialist states. While proposing a conference which would allegedly be fair to us, the Chinese are in fact trying to put us in an even worse situation than the one we are in now. If Yugoslavia accepted Chou En-lai's proposal and took part in the conference, whatever degree of agreement was reached, since there could only be agreement on the part of the whole "camp," we would by our very participation be supporting the idea of having a single policy for the whole bloc on the basis of ideology, because there is no other basis (regional, for example) for the conference.

If, however, Yugoslavia rejects Chou En-lai's proposal, the camp will increase for a time its tactical advantage with relation to Yugoslavia on the grounds that they invited us without any conditions to take part in the conference and showed "goodwill" which we did not accept. The situation is different from what it was when we were invited to attend a session of the Cominform in Bucharest in 1948. Although merely on the basis of our participation in this conference they could not "draw us into the camp," because that depends on us and not on them, it is my conviction that the Chinese proposal cannot be accepted in Belgrade although we do not want the present conflict between Yugoslavia and the Soviet Union to continue or get worse.

Moscow, January 29, 1957

I had a long conversation today with the Chinese ambassador and touched on some very interesting topics. Liu Siao said that the cost of keeping Chinese students in the Soviet Union was very high and so was the cost of supporting Soviet experts in China. He asked how we had found this prior to 1948. It looks to me as though the difficulties always start with the Soviet experts; the rest comes later. I told the Chinese that I was leaving for Belgrade, that we were having difficulties in our negotiations with the Soviet Government, which was again postponing the main agreements on credits for Yugoslavia. It did not look as if the Russian attitude was going to change for the better, but rather as though the Russians had already taken a negative decision and that there would be no negotiations at all; it was just that the Russians wanted us to agree with their decision.

The ambassador was at pains not to say anything which might have signified criticism of the Soviet Union, but at the same time he gave the impression that he agreed with me and understood our situation. Yugoslavia is in a worse situation than countries like India or Turkey or Iran, for example. When I tried on one occasion to talk about this to Khrushchev, he told me frankly: "Say publicly that you are like India and similar countries and nobody will touch you." The point is that we too are Communists, and the Russians do not allow that anybody can be a Marxist and not be cut to their pattern or that they do not have an ideological monopoly over everything that is called socialist.

* * *

The British ambassador, Sir William Hayter, has left Moscow for good. He probably left after his hopes of establishing better relations with the Soviet Union had been dashed. He made the best possible impression on me as representative of his country and a person who enjoyed the respect of the majority of the diplomatic corps in Moscow.

Belgrade, February 10, 1957

I have been here in Belgrade for several days, summoned for "consultations" because there have been quite a number of unsatisfactory developments in relations between Yugoslavia and the Soviet Union.

From Belgrade one can see more clearly how much more complicated things between the Russians and us have become. Apart from what one government says to the other through their embassies there is also the regular correspondence, actually a polemic, going on between the Central Committees of the Soviet and Yugoslav Communist parties. And, apart from these parallel party and government tracks running between Moscow and Belgrade, there are also the public statements about each other made in the official organs of the press and in speeches of individual leaders. What is done publicly is more important in its effects than what is said in letters. Although the letters, on both sides, always profess a desire for cooperation and for a joint solution (that is, a solution which suits the author of the letter), letters will not solve anything.

All the various moves undertaken by the Yugoslav and the Soviet side are aimed at enabling each party to the dispute to have its views expressed more accurately. At the root of the conflict lies our criticism of the Soviet Union for its policy of seeking hegemony over the countries of the "camp." We came out in favor of new, democratic, and equal relations between socialist countries, since upon a correct solution of this question depends the further development of socialism. Specifically we criticized the Soviet Union for things done in the camp now and in the past, and in particular for the events which blew up in Hungary.

It is clear that the Soviet Union could not accept our criticism, especially when it was made in public, however justified the Soviet leaders may have known it to be. There have been very few instances in history where a small country has criticized a large one and the latter has publicly admitted it was in the wrong. Instead of our persuading them of the justice of our point of view, or of them persuading us, we are all getting further and further away from each other. And this process is being speeded up by particular acts, such as the latest decision by the Soviet Union to extend the ideological and political dispute into the field of interstate relations.

A plenum of our Central Committee has been called to consider our relations and differences with the Russians. Things between Yugoslavia and the Soviet Union have now reached such a point that it is now practically impossible to stop the correspondence, or polemic, between our two leaderships. It seems to me that if Yugoslavia were to stop this correspondence and all its polemics with the Soviet Union, it could not do it without exposing us to the danger that the next day the Russians would say: You were obliged to end the polemics because you had understood your mistakes. Nevertheless this exchange of letters between the parties will have to stop, because it is quite clear that nothing can be achieved in that way.

The Russians have their own views about the correspondence, and that determines the contents of their letters. The ones to our Central Committee are addressed more to others than to us. More important to the Soviets than stopping further conflict with Yugoslavia is that the leadership of Yugoslavia should be discredited as far as possible in the eyes of the governments and public of the Soviet and other Communist parties and countries. We have heard that the Russians send copies of all the letters they address to us to the leaders of the countries of Eastern Europe, although they have not informed us of this. And the letters to Yugoslavia are marked "strictly confidential."

Belgrade, February 13, 1957

While we were discussing the contents of yet another letter from our Central Committee to the Russians we received information from Moscow about how badly the representative of the Soviet Government has treated our government delegation in the economic talks. Our delegation has been in Moscow for more than a month already, meeting occasionally with the Soviet delegation. But there are grounds for believing that the Russians had decided at the highest level against concluding credit agreements with Yugoslavia even before they invited a delegation from our government to have talks on the subject.

In connection with the exchange of letters between the Central Committees it has been decided that we shall send a copy of our letter to the Soviet Presidium and of the whole correspondence we have had with them to the leaders of the other Communist parties with which we have normal relations. In doing so we refer to the precedent set by the Russians.

We shall not accept the Chinese proposal for a conference because, apart from anything else, we are being subjected to reprisals from the Soviet side in interstate relations and have been subjected to unjustified attacks from the Chinese side as well. This is taken advantage of by the other countries of the "camp," which continue to attack Yugoslavia.

It is decided that I shall return to Moscow in a day or two and seek a meeting with Khrushchev to try and bring about some improvement in the situation. It is not only that Yugoslavia does not desire a further worsening of the conflict between our countries; it is ready to end the conflict, although it still holds to the basic views it held previously.

Moscow, February 16, 1957

I asked to see Khrushchev yesterday and he received me this afternoon. The talk again lasted for more than four hours because Khrushchev kept prolonging it. But there was very little new in what was said.

I conveyed to Khrushchev the views of Comrade Tito, with whom I had spoken in the last few days, about overcoming the difficulties in our relations and the need for a further improvement of our interstate relations. I spoke in some detail about the bad effects which an extension of the conflict would have on relations between our governments. That things were going in the wrong direction could be seen in Shepilov's speech in the Supreme Soviet and in the Russians' postponement—actually their cancellation—of the agreement on aluminum and the other Soviet investment credits. I also mentioned their similar attitude to talks about a barter agreement for this year. They refuse to give us certain articles which they have delivered in large quantities to some of the NATO countries.

I explained our point of view about the socialist camp, to which Yugoslavia is not opposed, since it is the result of historical circumstances, just as Yugoslavia is outside the "camp" as the result of specific circumstances. We discussed quite frankly Soviet efforts to draw us into the "camp" and how unrealistic they were, and I said that we should learn from our experience of that policy and build our relations on the solid foundations of things as they really are.

None of this met with any understanding on Khrushchev's part. He started by talking about our general attitude on controversial issues, beginning with the contents of the last letter from our Central Committee. This was the criterion and the proof that the conflict between us was developing and that there were no signs of a reconciliation. The Russians were going to reply to the letter from our Central Committee, in a negative sense of course, because they regarded it as a further worsening of relations between us.

Khrushchev said he realized that this kind of correspondence was not going to solve anything but would only make the conflict worse. Nevertheless they were obliged to reply to us. If they didn't do so, it would look as though they agreed with us.

As for the credit arrangements, Khrushchev simply said that they were even having to halt the construction of their own plants for lack of funds. That was why they were putting off the construction of plants for us: They had no other choice. I told him that there were, in my opinion, two different things. They could postpone the construction of their own plants or build other ones whenever they pleased; that was entirely their own internal affair in which no one had the right to interfere. But it was a completely different matter to assume obligations toward another state by means of an agreement as they had done in this case with Yugoslavia. In such a case they could not take unilateral decisions as though it were their own internal affair.

Khrushchev said that nobody in the Soviet Union could understand why they should continue to make any economic sacrifices for Yugoslavia. We had attacked them, we criticized the Soviet system, and we did not even recognize that the Soviet Union was a socialist state. Khrushchev said that there could arise exceptional circumstances affecting the fulfillment of economic agreements, such as the events in Poland, Hungary, Eastern Germany, and so forth. The Russians had to give funds to them and not to us.

When I asked him whether the Soviet Government had said all it had to say about this and whether the leader of our government delegation, Minčev, who is already in his second month here waiting in vain for talks, could return home, Khrushchev said he could go back to Belgrade and that nothing could be changed. I commented that our delegation had in fact not conducted any negotiations, but had simply been asked to subscribe to a Soviet decision which had been taken in advance. We could not conduct negotiations in this way.

This discussion was not in the least to Khrushchev's liking. I set out the economic arguments without referring to our "ideological" dispute, and mentioned certain facts concerning the behavior of the Soviet delegation and the harm which this was inflicting on the Yugoslav economy. Khrushchev did exactly the reverse, introducing political arguments all the time and not going into the practical financial side of the credit agreements. In the end he said that my explanation of the bad effect on Yugoslavia of the Soviet Government's decision was probably correct, but they couldn't do otherwise: The Soviet Union was not to blame for the consequences. It was Yugoslavia which had attacked the Soviet Union publicly, and not the other way round.

I also mentioned the other trade talks about an exchange of goods for this year which we are now having in Moscow. The Russians were refusing to sell us goods which they were selling in large quantities even to NATO countries. I pointed out that they had let France have about 2 million tons of oil, but wouldn't sell Yugoslavia even 400,000 tons. People in Yugoslavia would not be able to understand that. I had no objection to them selling oil to France. On the contrary, I thought such a decision by the Soviet Government was only to be welcomed. But I was surprised that they refused at the same time to sell to Yugoslavia.

Khrushchev did not deny this. He said they had to give help and credits to the countries of Eastern Europe, that they bought goods from them which the Soviet Union did not need, and that it wasn't trade on an equal basis on the principle of mutual benefit, but was often to the disadvantage of the Soviet Union. Yugoslavia insisted on the principle of mutual benefit in trade with the Soviet Union. And that was why the present situation arose, Khrushchev said. I came to the conclusion that this means that, of all the socialist countries, Yugoslavia is the only one with which they trade on a basis of equality, and that there was no need for them to drag out the talks with us as they did.

Moscow, February 17, 1957

There were many other questions touched on in that long conversation. Khrushchev spoke at length about how Tito had overestimated his strength and had expected a different effect from his Pula speech, and for that reason had divided them into Stalinists and anti-Stalinists in the Soviet leadership. Seeking to bring up everything he could use to worsen the quarrel between us or to improve the Soviet position, Khrushchev said that Tito had insulted him publicly by not addressing him as "comrade," as was usual both in Russia and in Yugoslavia. He said he was going to speak in the same way in future. He again attacked Kardelj for poking fun at the Russians' "policy of maize and potatoes." He declared that this had also been an attack on him personally, because everyone knew how interested Khrushchev was in agriculture. When he spoke about this, Khrushchev became very excited, giving the impression of a person who was genuinely upset.

I told him that I had spoken with Comrade Tito before and after handing over the latest letter from our Central Committee and told him of Tito's view that it was in the interests of both sides that the conflict should not get worse or be carried over into interstate relations and that we should continue friendly cooperation wherever possible. I reminded him that our latest letter was only a reply to their letter of January 10 and that that was probably how it would be in the future: One letter would lead to another, with no end in sight.

Several times in the course of the discussion Khrushchev agreed eagerly when I spoke about letting us have our system and letting them have theirs, so that each of us could improve our own system as we pleased, while time, the course of events, and goodwill on both sides would have a beneficial effect even where we were now not in agreement. But when I went on to say that a condition for that was that we should not upset our interstate relations, as was the case now with their refusal of credits, Khrushchev changed his attitude and brought up again all the controversial matters.

Khrushchev was angry at the Poles. He said that Gomulka had written to him, despite the November agreement with the Soviet Union, refusing to deliver Polish coal in the quantities agreed in November. "We should have stopped sending them grain; who gives grain on credit today as we've given it to the Poles!" Khrushchev shouted. "The Poles sell their coal to the West for dollars and they fatten their pigs on our Russian grain and then sell them to the British, as though we couldn't do that ourselves," Khrushchev said angrily. "And we haven't stopped sending them grain. Do you call that trade on equal terms? It isn't, because it's a matter of sacrifices on our part. In this case a great power is making sacrifices for a small one—and you and the others say we are murderers," Khrushchev said. Economic relations with the other countries of the "camp" were similarly unequal, to the disadvantage of the Soviet Union. "Much do we need Bulgarian peppers, we can live without them, but the Bulgars haven't got anything else to sell us," Khrushchev went on.

Discussing the new system of management in industry, Khrushchev spoke enthusiastically about the advantages it was going to bring. A plan of the new organization was being prepared which provided for its being introduced by June or July 1957. He would continue to direct all the principal measures in this connection as he had done from the beginning.

After I returned to the embassy late that night Patolichev rang me to ask if I had any objection to their announcing in the press that I had seen Khrushchev. I hadn't. The next day the whole of the central press carried an announcement that I had been received by Khrushchev at my request, and alongside this piece of news they announced that the Chinese ambassador had also seen him and had a "friendly conversation." They made this distinction between the two announcements about the visits so that the Soviet public should not be led by any chance to believe for a moment that my visit had changed Soviet policy toward Yugoslavia.

CHAPTER SIXTEEN

CHANGES IN THE SOVIET ECONOMY

A sudden change of policy affecting the Soviet economy points to continuing disagreements among the Soviet leaders. Gromyko replaces Shepilov as Foreign Minister. Khrushchev's departure on vacation suggests that he feels more secure in the Kremlin.

Moscow, February 19, 1957

It is again apparent that we and the Russians have a different approach to the question of improving cooperation between our two countries. As I have said, the Russians look on it as a sort of preliminary stage in the process of our coming closer together and eventually being included in the "camp." But we have been regarding all this in a different way, hoping that by following this path we shall be doing the maximum to encourage the Soviet Union to abandon its old Stalinist ways as far and as quickly as possible. We thought that by acting in this way we were doing our best to help the Russians to carry out the decisions of the Twentieth Congress and the policy of de-Stalinization in the Soviet Union and Eastern Europe.

Events in Eastern Europe have shown that neither of these two contrary expectations has been fulfilled. What has emerged instead is a relationship of big and small states under socialism, which is not substantially different from the relationship between big and small countries under capitalism. It seems just an illusion to imagine that a small socialist country, in this case Yugoslavia, can have any serious influence on a great socialist country and superpower, in this case the Soviet Union, if that doesn't coincide with the basic interests of the great socialist state.

The experience of our relations with the Soviet Union so far has shown that we don't talk about the differences between us when our relations are good. But when they are bad, we discuss only these differences

207

in public, as though there were nothing else but differences between us and no area in which we could collaborate normally and on equal terms. The outlook for our relations at the moment, for example, is not at all favorable. It will be much more difficult to get the Russians to agree that there are different roads ahead for different countries, all leading to the establishment of a socialist society, than it appeared to us in Yugoslavia at the time of the Twentieth Congress. In the year which has passed since that Congress I do not think the Soviet leaders have ever been further from it than they are now. For the moment the fact that last year it signed with Yugoslavia the Moscow Declaration, in which that point of view was accepted, has not the slightest influence on the Soviet Union.

Moscow, February 20, 1957

On the same day as I returned from Belgrade they published here a decree of a plenum of the CPSU Central Committee of February 14, 1957, about improving the management of the economy. Even the most superficial comparison of the decisions of this February plenum with those of the plenum of last December, which dealt with the same question, raises some unavoidable questions.

An essential feature of the December plenum was a further strengthening of the role of the state in the administration of the economy from a single center. For that purpose new and powerful state bodies were set up, such as the "State Economic Commission" having very important responsibilities such as previously only the Soviet Government itself possessed. That decision was in the spirit of the old Stalinist conception of the all-powerful role of the Soviet state in the administration of the national economy. It signified a further strengthening of the centralist views on the organization and administration of the economy. The decisions of the December plenum were relatively short, which was unusual in view of the fact that as a rule here they pass very long decrees about every conceivable matter. Nothing was said about a speech by the First Secretary of the Central Committee, Khrushchev, which was also surprising in view of his position as party leader and his personal preoccupation with these questions.

The decisions of the February plenum appear to cancel out those of the previous one and proclaim, in a Soviet way, a new economic policy, the reverse of the one approved by the same supreme party body in December. Instead of strengthening the centralized system and setting up new state bodies, the February decisions are based on the idea that the Soviet economy is so advanced and spread out over such a vast area in the Soviet Union that it is inconceivable that it should be administered from one center. There is talk of the "regionalization" of the Soviet economy and of greater responsibilities not only for the republics and regions but also for the local authorities in the management of undertakings and construction sites, of which there are today in the Soviet Union, counting only the big ones, more than 300,000.

If the basic ideas of the February plenum are developed further, it may result in a weakening of the center in Moscow. It is obviously a question of two quite different conceptions, a question of people in the Kremlin who hold such different views and of their relationship with one another.

The most important events which may be connected with this were the decision to appoint Molotov as Minister of State Control, then the conflicting decisions of the two plenums on the economy, the clampdown in the field of culture and art, and so forth. Khrushchev was not active at the December plenum as he was at the last one where he had the initiative in his hands. That is why Khrushchev is constantly referring to the February plenum in conversation but says nothing about the December one. It looks as though it was not Khrushchev but the party that initiated the December decisions, for it seemed as though the government and its machinery were behind the moves. It is said that all the decisions I have mentioned were taken unanimously. This is the way things have long been done here. Even in the case of the present conflict with Yugoslavia the Soviet leaders act unanimously. One cannot speak of any difference between the views of Khrushchev, Molotov, or Malenkov, at least as far as their public activities are concerned. In conversations with me they speak with one voice, and there have been plenty of those conversations, especially since the beginning of November.

These different decisions taken at successive plenums of the CPSU Central Committee can hardly bring the various groups which are known to exist at the Soviet political summit any closer together.

Moscow, February 22, 1957

A few days ago Shepilov was removed from the post of Soviet Foreign Minister. He is returning to his previous job as a secretary of the Central Committee of the party. Khrushchev gave me, but not very convincingly, some reasons for this change at the top of the Foreign Ministry. He said no changes had taken place, that the post of secretary of the Central Committee was above that of Foreign Minister, that the new Minister would be carrying out decisions which the former Minister had announced a week ago, and that the foreign policy of the Soviet Government did not depend on who was the Foreign Minister but was determined by the party and the government. When I first mentioned

Shepilov's removal, Khrushchev said jokingly that they had removed him because of the bad things he had said about Yugoslavia in the Supreme Soviet. He added that Shepilov would be more useful in the Central Committee than in diplomacy.

Andrei Gromyko, one of the First Deputy Ministers, has been put in Shepilov's place. Some Westerners are inclined to think that the choice of Gromyko, a former favorite of Molotov's and a *nyet*-man (a no-man), means a strengthening of the hard line in Soviet foreign policy, in contrast to Shepilov, who came into the job when there was a more relaxed policy which has failed, so that Shepilov has gone alone with the policy.

Other "Sovietologists" in the diplomatic corps assert that the change at the top of the Foreign Ministry means nothing and that no changes in Soviet foreign policy are to be expected. All of them point to the strange story of Shepilov's career as Minister and his almost dramatic appointment in Molotov's place last June on the day before Tito arrived on his official visit to Moscow. In December 1956 the Central Committee released Shepilov from his duties as secretary of the committee and confirmed him in the job at the Foreign Ministry to which he had been appointed in June 1956. Now, six weeks after that Central Committee meeting, Shepilov has been relieved of his duties in the Foreign Ministry and returned to his job in the Central Committee!

Without attaching any special political significance to this change, Gromyko may be expected to be as independent an executor of Soviet foreign policy as was Shepilov, and that control by the Presidium, which means Khrushchev, as First Secretary, can only have been strengthened.

One little aspect of Shepilov's behavior remained in my memory. When Khrushchev went on his famous first trip to Yugoslavia, he took Shepilov with him. On one occasion, at a lunch with Tito, there were about ten of us present, including Shepilov. Khrushchev recounted various good and bad things that had happened to him in the course of his life and would occasionally ask Shepilov whether this or that was true. Shepilov would remove the table napkin which he, like the rest of us, was using, stand up from the table, and, as though he were reporting officially, would reply: "Just so, Nikita Sergeyevich!" and sit down again. I found such behavior on Shepilov's part most unusual, as I did Khrushchev's in tolerating it.

It was not so long ago, less than a year, since the relations between Khrushchev and Shepilov were like those between a general and a soldier. Shepilov was then moving fast up the career ladder, and became unexpectedly Soviet Minister of Foreign Affairs. It looks to me as though Shepilov forgot about that "Just so, Nikita Sergeyevich!" which had helped him reach the top rung. It was that, it seems, apart from his lack of ability, which resulted in his dismissal.

Moscow, February 25, 1957

At a formal reception for a Bulgarian delegation in the Kremlin the Russians were represented by their strongest team, led by Khrushchev. This is the Russians' way of demonstrating that the Bulgars are "on equal terms" with them. I was surprised that Khrushchev and Bulganin offered to sit with me during the concert, especially at a reception for the Bulgars, after the attack on us at the Soviet-Bulgarian friendship meeting.

After we had taken our seats and I found myself next to Khrushchev, he asked me whether I had seen the anti-Soviet caricature in the Belgrade paper *Politika*. He went on to explain that he and Bulganin had been caricatured in connection with Nasser, that it was all very unpleasant—Khrushchev even used the word "disgusting." He said they were deeply insulted, because it was inconceivable in the Soviet Union that anyone should caricature a leader of the party and state of a socialist country.

I told Khrushchev I had not seen the caricature. I don't know how, in the middle of the Kremlin during a concert for the Bulgarian "party-state delegation," *Politika* suddenly appeared in Khrushchev's hands. He passed me the paper like a sort of *corpus delicti* and waited for me to explain to him the sense of the caricature at which he was protesting. Pervukhin, another member of the Presidium, butted in with: "Do you call that a friendly act?"

When I had had a look at the caricature I said that it might not please even our own leaders, but that the Russians were mistaken in believing that it was Khrushchev who was being caricatured. It was not aimed at him but at Eisenhower (both are bald and if badly drawn can look much alike). This surprised Khrushchev, who seemed relieved when he realized that it was not a drawing of him but of Eisenhower and Bulganin. He then explained their mistake to Bulganin, who indicated that he was offended: To be caricatured along with Eisenhower was in a way to be treated as equals in their policy toward Egypt. But Khrushchev calmed down, went into the question of whether it was a good caricature of Bulganin, commented that newspapers published what their editors wished, and that the editors wanted what their superiors demanded.

I tried to explain that there was no sense in making the Yugoslav Government directly responsible for what some Yugoslav journalist wrote or what one of our caricaturists drew. There were articles and caricatures in the papers which pleased some people and didn't please others, and it often happened that our leaders did not agree with what was written or drawn.

Khrushchev noticed that Bulganin was still in a bad mood, and so he again joined in the argument, presumably out of solidarity with Bulganin.

He said we were treating the Soviet Union and America as equal in relations to Egypt by drawing them together in that way. I told him that in any case our Central Committee and government had not composed the caricature or had any connection with it. Pervukhin, when he heard that it was not Khrushchev but Eisenhower who was caricatured, did not say another word.

It was in fact a caricature by Dzumhur[1] in *Politika* for January 17. Irrespective of the fact that this complaint by the Russians—and, what is more, by the leader of the party and the Prime Minister of the Soviet Union—is quite out of place and almost a joke, I think that at least for the present we should try to influence our caricaturists or the editors of the main papers to refrain from caricaturing the Soviet leaders.

I told Khrushchev that the Yugoslav delegation which has been having talks here without success about disputed economic matters (the credits) has returned to Belgrade, but that our trade delegation is still in Moscow. Our people had waited ten days for the Soviet official concerned to invite them to continue the talks and the head of our delegation had been waiting just as long to be received by the Soviet Trade Minister, Kabanov.

Khrushchev put on a look of surprise, gave me to understand that it was not the Soviet leaders' doing, called Mikoyan over and asked him, "How is it possible?" Mikoyan immediately "got the message" from Khrushchev's tone of voice and the expression on his face that he should admit I was right, said that he was hearing about it for the first time and that they had acted "wrongly," and this was repeated by Khrushchev and Pervukhin. Khrushchev said they wanted to trade with us, and that they wanted to have good relations with us but that they were "not going to make any further concessions" to us. I said that we were not in agreement about who had made concessions to whom, but that we had already discussed it and would probably talk about it again.

Khrushchev boasted about the way the talks with the Bulgars had gone. He said they had agreed about everything with a minimum of talk and that there was complete confidence between them. I said that their talks with the Bulgars would have been even more successful if they had not jointly and publicly attacked Yugoslavia. I quoted Yugov's[2] statement at Bulganin's official lunch which was published in the Soviet press. He said that Yugoslavia regretted that an armed conflict had not broken out in Bulgaria as well. I asked Khrushchev what such nonsensical statements meant.

In view of the attacks made by Yugov and the Bulgarian delegation at the receptions I did not approach or shake hands with the Bulgars although I know Yugov personally.

[1] Dzumhur. One of the most talented of Yugoslav political cartoonists.
[2] Anton Yugov, b. 1904. Bulgarian Communist leader. Became Prime Minister of Bulgaria in 1956.

Moscow, February 26, 1957

A few days ago the United States ambassador, Charles Bohlen, asked to come and talk to me. He said he was going off to Washington to report and that before leaving he would like to "check" his opinions.

It is presumably not particularly to the liking of the Soviet Government that the ambassadors of the United States and Yugoslavia should have such meetings. We don't criticize the Russians because their contacts with the Americans are closer than ours and they are trying to increase those contacts as much as possible. But the Russians would like us to break off all contacts with American diplomats insofar as they are not supervised by Moscow.

Bohlen takes a positive view of internal trends in the Soviet Union since the February plenum of the Central Committee, primarily in the economic field. He thinks a return to Stalinism is impossible, although the Russians are taking a harder line on doctrinal and ideological matters. He regards Bulganin as the weakest point in the Soviet leadership. As for changes in the leadership, of which we talked two or three months ago, Bohlen thinks there won't be any. He considers Khrushchev's position has been strengthened since January and especially since the February plenum. He attaches no significance to the removal of Shepilov.

Finally Bohlen said he did not know what exactly to say to John Foster Dulles, with whom in any case he did not get along very well—whether the Russians really desired a gradual improvement of relations with the United States or not. I took the view, on the basis of a conversation with Khrushchev, that the Russians really did want an improvement. I criticized Bohlen for the anti-Yugoslav campaign connected with President Tito's planned visit to America. Bohlen explained it by reference to the specific conditions in America and said the government was not behind it. As though conditions in every other country are not also specific—only in America. It might be said that Bohlen attaches greater significance to the Russians' decision to postpone or cancel the credit agreements with us than to the "ideological" quarrel between us.

Moscow, February 28, 1957

Two days after my conversation with Khrushchev the Soviet Minister of Trade, Kabanov, finally received the head of our trade delegation. The basic questions in dispute, about which the two delegations had been talking for practically a month, were resolved immediately. It was agreed that a fresh trade agreement would be signed.

This time the approach to Khrushchev was successful, which is the most that can be expected in present circumstances.

Minister Kabanov arranged a lunch for our trade delegation at which I was present and spoke. I congratulated the two delegations on their successful work, the conclusion of a new agreement and the development of cooperation between us. Although the new agreement is more than modest, I stressed only its good aspects. The bad things in our relations, which go on along with the signing of the new agreement, were not mentioned by me or by the head of our delegation, Babić, as though they didn't exist.

Khrushchev's efforts to bring about a favorable conclusion of our trade talks and his simultaneous defense of the opposite point of view on the credit agreements show that the postponement of the latter was decided at the February plenum of the Central Committee but the former wasn't. Khrushchev could not have changed that decision even if he had wanted to. The more consistently he carried through the negative decision about the credits, the more strongly he could support the signing of a trade agreement with us for 1957.

In my last conversation with Khrushchev, when he invited me to go with him to the South and the Caucasus so that "we can have a good holiday and catch some fish," Khrushchev looked to me noticeably different, calmer and more self-confident than he had ever been at our meetings in November and December. The very fact that he has decided to leave Moscow for two weeks and to spend them in the interior of the country indicates that he is feeling ever more secure at the summit of Soviet affairs. If it were otherwise, I don't believe Khrushchev would leave Moscow so unconcernedly and go to the Caucasus for political talks.

It may be said that Khrushchev does not strengthen his position by sitting behind the Kremlin walls as did his predecessor and the majority of those now sharing power with Khrushchev. Khrushchev relies more than any other Soviet leader on his appeal to the population. The plan which has been announced for decentralizing the administration of the economy is the most important move in domestic policy Khrushchev has made since he took over the leadership of the Soviet Communist party, apart from his secret speech and criticism of Stalin at the Twentieth Congress. It is a gigantic undertaking, bearing in mind the highly centralized system which has been in force here for decades and the size of the Soviet Union. It will not be a good thing if the policy of economic decentralization follows the same sort of stop-start course and the same waverings as the policy of de-Stalinization.

CHAPTER SEVENTEEN

YUGOSLAVIA UNDER ATTACK AGAIN

*Communist leaders in Eastern Europe join in the campaign
of criticism of Yugoslavia, and a Soviet book on wartime
resistance to the Germans ignores the Partisan movement in
Yugoslavia.*

Moscow, March 10, 1957

Among the most important events in Soviet foreign policy in the
last few weeks was an exchange of letters between Bulganin and Adenauer. With the Federal Republic of Germany playing an increasingly
important role in Western European affairs and with the Soviet Union interested in becoming as deeply involved as possible in European affairs,
the Russians reckon that the difficulties Adenauer is having before the
elections will force him into improving relations with the East without
the Soviet Union having to make any concessions.

A considerable increase in Soviet trade with Western Germany is also
serving as a means of Soviet pressure on Britain and France. This ought
to strengthen the Soviet position as a whole in relation to the West, including the United States. During a visit by West German Foreign
Minister von Brentano to the United States the Russians published a number of articles criticizing the Bonn Government and especially opposing
any linkup between West German and American imperialism, which the
Russians fear more than anything. But I don't think this will have any serious influence on the implementation of those measures on which Bulganin and Adenauer have already agreed in their exchange of letters (increased trade, scientific and technical cooperation).

Russian policy toward Western Europe is becoming steadily subtler
and is making progress despite all the contradictions which led in the recent past to threats of war. If there is a constant in Russian policy in
Europe, it is to preserve at any price the results of World War II, and
that means the preservation of the socialist camp, "led by" the Soviet

Union. This is the strategic aim served by Russian approaches to individual Western European countries.

Moscow, March 11, 1957

In accordance with the decisions of the February plenum of the Central Committee on reorganizing the national economy numerous commissions are now engaged on the preparatory work. It is planned to have the new system worked out in two or three months and for laws to be drafted which the Supreme Soviet will approve at the beginning of July.

The basis of the new system is the division of the country into regions according to where industries are situated and not according to the department or ministry to which they belong in Moscow. The management of industrial plants will be concentrated in such units. Direct control from Moscow over the economy will be maintained in branches which have "all-union significance," such as atomic energy, armaments, defense, research, and the advancement of production and technology. They expect to abolish a large number of economic ministries in the Soviet Government, of which there are now nearly fifty.

This is in a way the beginning of some limitations being put on the absolute power of the *apparat* in Moscow which has been built up, you might say, over the centuries. Now they are seeking to bring the management of industry closer to the republics and the people "on the spot," which should lead to the removal of at least some of the barriers between the leaders and the people in the Soviet Union.

We hear that there are already signs of discontent among ministers who don't know whether their ministries are going to be abolished. There is also said to be resistance on the part of senior officials in the Soviet Union who for years and decades have been occupying top positions and have never dreamed that they might have to leave them in this way. In such circles they are saying that under the *khozyayin* (the "master," as Stalin was known) it was better than under the present leaders.

Moscow, March 12, 1957

At the beginning of March elections were held to the local soviets (councils) in fourteen of the republics of the Soviet Union—all of them except Georgia. It has been announced that 158 of the candidates for deputy to the local soviet failed to secure election, from which one is supposed to conclude that the elections are democratic. But the number of rejected candidates is utterly insignificant. In the Russian republic alone 844,337 deputies were elected exactly as proposed by the party committees. It is normal in the course of all mass production for there to be an insignificant number of "rejects." But here it is a question of millions of candidates proposed and elected, and the 158 who were not elected is proof only of the smooth working and infallibility of the Soviet electoral machine. The elections have not demonstrated anything new; the electoral technique and policy were the same as in the past. It was yet another triumph for that well-tested device of Stalin's—the "bloc of Communists and nonparty people."

Evidence of Khrushchev's growing influence can be seen in the fact that at the February plenum on the reorganization of the economy he was the main speaker, although it would have been more natural for the main speech to be made by someone from the government. Khrushchev's name is now associated not only with the "reclamation of the virgin lands," which is now being celebrated as a great victory: It is also being linked with the planned reorganization of industry. If Khrushchev makes the main speech at the forthcoming Supreme Soviet, then one should be concerned rather about the authority of the Soviet Government than about Khrushchev's authority, which is again in the ascendant.

Moscow, March 13, 1957

A week ago the Congress of Soviet Artists ended in Moscow. There were 579 delegates as well as guests from Eastern Europe. A union of artists has been formed with more than 5,000 members. In Russia every profession must always have people with the status of "candidate," even in cases where it is difficult to imagine such a category. So there are now "candidate" artists and the new union has 1,800 of them.

The principal event at the Congress was a speech by Shepilov. It looks as though the Presidium decided to get rid of the old, compromised cliques, and at the same time, so as to maintain a "balance," to remove the new "extreme" liberal groups which have "displayed anarchism and nihilism," according to the official charges against them. As far as existing works of art and artistic creation are concerned, unconditional respect for the doctrine of "socialist realism" is again demanded.

Shepilov's authoritative speech at the artists' Congress confirms that the new leadership and the party are going to maintain a strict monopoly and control over this field of activity as well.

Moscow, March 15, 1957

A delegation of Yugoslav publishers spent nearly three weeks in the Soviet Union. Unlike many others they arrived in Moscow very well prepared and knowing exactly what they wanted. I believe this was the first serious contact ever to take place between Yugoslav and Soviet publishers.

The Soviet publishers were impressed by the amount of Russian and Soviet literature translated in Yugoslavia. Yugoslavs have translated so far 3,500 Soviet books, while the Russians have translated only about 70 Yugoslav works! The Russians were especially surprised to learn that the translating of Russian and Soviet books had continued in Yugoslavia without a break: We translated them in the old Yugoslavia, and during the quarrel with Stalin, and we are translating them now, in spite of the conflict which is still going on between us.

At a reception which I gave one of the Soviet officials present told me that our delegation had made a better impression in Moscow than similar delegations from Eastern Europe. He told me this in a whisper when nobody else was around, because to say something like that out loud would be dangerous.

Moscow, March 18, 1957

The Soviet leaders have made the very worst impression on us by their behavior on the occasion of the sudden death of Moša Pijade, president of the Yugoslav National Assembly and one of Yugoslavia's most distinguished leaders. He died in Paris, on his way back from Britain, where he had led a delegation to the British Parliament. The attitude of the Soviet Union to this tragic event, which has deeply grieved everybody in Yugoslavia, has been extremely incorrect.

In their issues for March 16 the Soviet newspapers *Pravda* and *Izvestia* gave the news in a single sentence, and this was repeated in *Komsomolskaya Pravda*. In all three papers the sentence appeared on the back page and at the very bottom of it.

The same Soviet papers gave five lines to a report of the funeral in Belgrade and the shortest possible version of the official message of condolence from the Supreme Soviet, less than the minimum demanded by any protocol (Radio Belgrade regularly put the Supreme Soviet message in first place, before all other messages from abroad!). There was not a word about it in the rest of the Soviet press.

I asked the people in the embassy to go through the Soviet papers and compare how the Russians had treated similar events in recent months. We discovered that *Pravda* and *Izvestia* had done exactly the same in the case of the death of the Hungarian fascist émigré the former Admiral Miklós Horthy on March 10, and the death of the former Japanese Foreign Minister Mamoru Shigemitsu on March 3. When the Italian professor Marchesi died on February 14, *Pravda* drew attention to the fact that he was a member of the Central Committee of the Italian Communist party and described his career and work. On the same day as it reported Moša's death *Pravda* reported the death of the President of the Philippines (with which the Soviet Union has no diplomatic relations) and gave three or four times as much space to it. When the Austrian Körner[1] died on January 5, 1957, the Soviet Union sent a special delegation to the funeral, speeches were made, and the Soviet press wrote about it for five days. They did the same when Finnish President Juho Paasikivi died on December 16, 1956. Soviet papers published pictures of him and reported messages from Soviet and foreign personalities.

Our embassy has so far not received a single message of condolence from any official body in the Soviet Union or from any Soviet citizen, officially or privately. We don't know whether there were any other private messages because our mail is examined and such things are confiscated.

There was only one instance of a message of sympathy to the Yugoslav embassy from a private Soviet citizen, but unfortunately it remained anonymous because it was made by telephone from a public phone, and the person who called up did not dare to give his name. He said only that he was speaking on behalf of the students of Moscow University and that they wanted to express their sympathy concerning the death of Moša Pijade, who had been a great revolutionary, a fighter for socialism, and an opponent of bureaucratic rule. When the person receiving the call wanted to continue the conversation, the caller was cut off.

I believe that Moša Pijade was in many ways one of the most outstanding personalities in the European and Soviet working-class movement and not just in the Yugoslav movement. In the old Yugoslavia he spent fourteen years at hard labor in the prisons of the military-fascist dictatorship. During the war and even before it he was one of Comrade Tito's closest colleagues in our national liberation war and socialist revolution. After the war he played a prominent part in the creation of the new state, and it was in the course of that creative work that he died.

We held a memorial meeting in the embassy, at which I made a speech. Evoking memories of the great man, I recounted some events which took place in the prewar period of illegal activity. Moša then worked among the students in Belgrade, and I was among them.

Moscow, March 25, 1957

At a meeting in Leningrad Kadar twice spoke out against Yugoslavia. Apart from giving an incorrect account of Yugoslavia's views on events in Hungary and other questions, he displayed a desire to blacken us in the

---

[1] Theodor Körner, 1873–1957. Austrian statesman. Mayor of Vienna, 1945–55; President of Austria, 1951–57.

eyes of the Soviet public by launching a new attack on Yugoslavia. He compared "the views of Kardelj and other Yugoslav leaders" with the line taken by Radio Free Europe and the Voice of America,[2] which, according to him, also described the Hungarian events of October-November 1956 as a "revolution."

In view of this I do not intend to accept the Soviet invitation to the "Hungarian-Soviet friendship meeting." I think it better not to go than to walk out of the meeting in protest. I shall go to the reception in the Kremlin which Bulganin is giving. If similar slanders against Yugoslavia are repeated I don't think I shall see Kadar off when he leaves, unless Belgrade thinks differently.

After the delegation led by Yugov the Russians have now involved Kadar and the Hungarians in the offensive against Yugoslavia. Today's *Pravda* appears eager to include Albania in the campaign as soon as possible. All these countries are immediate neighbors of Yugoslavia.

I believe that it is of especial importance for the present foreign policy of the Soviet Union toward us, which is based on isolating Yugoslavia from its neighbors, to do everything possible to worsen relations between Yugoslavia and Hungary. The present clash between the Russians and us started over the question of Hungary and these speeches of Kadar's are intended to show that Hungary condemns Yugoslavia's policy.

Moscow, March 26, 1957

On instructions from the Central Committee of the CPSU Patolichev today handed me Khrushchev's letter to the Presidium about the changes in system for managing industry and Khrushchev's speech at the February plenum. He did it on Khrushchev's explicit instructions.

At a time when attacks on us are extending to the government level and are being made by visiting delegations from the "camp," it is interesting that Khrushchev should make such a gesture at this very moment, since it has quite the opposite political significance.

The whole of the Soviet press today published in full the speeches made by Bulganin and Kadar at the Soviet-Hungarian friendship meeting. Both of them attacked Yugoslavia. Unlike the anti-Yugoslav campaign to date, which has been carried on mainly in the newspapers and magazines, the whole affair was raised yesterday to the level of the heads of government of the two countries, and in the presence of leading representatives

[2] Radio Free Europe. An American-financed radio station based in Munich which has broadcast since 1949 to the countries of Eastern Europe in their own languages in an attempt to overcome the effects of censorship of the press in Communist regimes.

The Voice of America is an entirely American broadcasting organization directed from Washington and broadcasting to the whole world.

of the parties and governments of the Soviet Union and Hungary. And so in a way Soviet action against Yugoslavia to date becomes the official policy of the Soviet Government with Hungary involved as well.

Moscow, March 29, 1957

A few days ago the correspondent of the American CBS,[3] Daniel Schorr, returned from Warsaw with a sensational report to the effect that the second armed intervention by the Soviet Army into Hungary took place only after agreement on it had been reached between the Soviet Union and Yugoslavia. He also said that a Pole told him in Warsaw that Khrushchev had made a secret trip to Yugoslavia to reach agreement with Tito.

This American correspondent is telling this to all his friends among the foreign correspondents in Moscow. He also told the local correspondent of the Agence France Presse, Schirey, who told us. The Frenchman told us as a friend, not in order to verify the report but simply so that we should know what was being said. He regards the report as true. As I have already explained at length, the Russians had in fact already taken the decision to intervene with their troops in Hungary and they had no need of Yugoslav agreement to do it. It was rather a case of getting agreement that there would not be a public conflict between us because of their armed intervention.

Moscow, March 30, 1957

I don't believe that anybody except the Russians knows what are the results of the investigation into the case of Imre Nagy. In the past Communist leaders accused of political offenses in the Soviet Union and the countries of the "camp" would make, under interrogation and in court, any statements the Soviet prosecutors demanded. In this way the most fantastic accusations were concocted. During our first conflict with the Soviet Union such "irrefutable proofs" provided the basis not only for a propaganda campaign against Yugoslavia but for tearing up all the international agreements which the Soviet Union and the countries of Eastern Europe had with Yugoslavia. I don't think anything similar is going to happen now, although they are talking about Nagy, now under arrest, as they once did about László Rajk in the same situation.

Having dragged Bulgaria, Hungary, and Albania into the anti-Yugoslav campaign, the Russians may try to do something similar with the Romanians, too, even though they will find this more difficult. In

[3] The Columbia Broadcasting System. One of the principal American radio and television networks.

Romania there is a widely held conviction that the more they criticize Yugoslav independence the less independence the Romanians themselves will have in relations with the Russians. Apart from that, Yugoslavia's relations with Romania are good by tradition. One of the most difficult problems in our foreign policy and one of its greatest failures—despite the fact that Yugoslavia is not alone responsible for those failures—is the unsatisfactory state of our relations with practically all our neighbors, and not only with those which belong to the "camp." The Russians will no doubt try to maintain such a situation on the borders of our country.

There can be no question of Bulganin's latest attack on Yugoslavia at the Soviet-Hungarian friendship meeting having been a piece of improvisation. Everything he said was published next day in the Soviet press. Perhaps Bulganin is trying in this way to atone for the things for which the Presidium criticized him last July? Maybe he was given the job against his will precisely because he lavished such praise on us in public last year? However that may be, by what he has done Bulganin has lost whatever remained of his reputation in Yugoslav eyes. Now there will be no more opportunities for us to talk as we did in the Crimea last October. Even if such an opportunity again offered itself, it would be difficult for me to "make it up" with Bulganin, because his "dirty words" about Yugoslavia are being repeated in circumstances in which even in the Soviet Union no one should be able to force anyone to make such speeches, as it was possible to do in Stalin's time. Would it really be possible to put such "dirty words" into the mouth of the Soviet Prime Minister if he were not ready himself to say them?

Moscow, March 31, 1957

In view of the removal of the editorial board of the main Polish newspaper, *Trybuna Ludu*, and the way the new Polish leadership is making more and more compromises with the reactionary and Stalinist elements in Poland, Belgrade asked us how it all looked from Moscow. With all reservations we told Belgrade that it seems to us here that Gomulka is coming more and more to terms with the Russians. He is doing this on the grounds that he has sure information that the situation in the Soviet Union is getting more difficult all the time and that they, the Poles, would not wish to make it even more difficult. As though Polish influence over Soviet internal policy is strong enough to determine its course! I consider this to be a one-sided and exaggerated argument. But it suits Gomulka very well to explain his unpopular political moves at home by reference to the demands of foreign policy.

The Polish argument that everything they are doing is aimed at keeping the present Soviet leaders and Khrushchev personally in power suggests a certain criticism of the behavior of the Yugoslavs, who, unlike the Poles, are said not to be inspired by "higher interests."

Moscow, April 1, 1957

In conversation with Khrushchev at a Kremlin reception for the Hungarians I asked him to explain to me why they had introduced the practice of using the presence here of government delegations from the countries of Eastern Europe for demonstrations against Yugoslavia. I said it seemed as though the most important issue in relations between those countries and the Soviet Union was to attack Yugoslavia in public in the presence of the highest Soviet officials and even along with them. We had absolutely nothing against Soviet friendship with those countries, but why were the Russians behaving as though that friendship was founded on those countries' hostility toward Yugoslavia and as though, if they failed to declare themselves against us, they could not be friends with the Russians? Khrushchev again asserted that we were waging a campaign against them and the "camp," that what we were doing caused them more harm than the propaganda of the imperialists, and that the Russians were defending themselves. As an example he said that Svetozar Vukmanović-Tempo had recently attacked them in the presence of the Egyptians, who had immediately informed the Russians.

It was easy to see that Khrushchev felt uncomfortable when I mentioned Bulganin's speech. On this occasion I made use of the phrases which Khrushchev used against us in November and December—whom does it benefit, why is it necessary, why are you worsening relations between us, we never expected anything like this, and so forth.

Maybe the way they are now linking Yugoslavia with Imre Nagy is a result of what they have achieved in the investigation they are carrying out in prison, nobody knows where, of Nagy and the other arrested Hungarians. This may also explain Bulganin's reference to "irrefutable proof" that it had been "confirmed beyond all question" that Nagy had long been "in foreign service." The language Bulganin used resembled that in the indictments made in the thirties at the famous show trials in the Soviet Union and the more recent ones in Eastern Europe. The situation of Imre Nagy and the others is, to all appearances, extremely serious. It looks as though the Russians are handling the affair in such a way as to obtain from Nagy and the others statements to justify as far as possible the Russian armed intervention in Hungary.

223

Moscow, April 3, 1957

A few weeks ago the most important of the Soviet publishing organizations, *Gospolitizdat*,[4] issued a book entitled *What Is "People's Democracy"?* by Alexander Ivanovich Sobolyev. Two hundred thousand copies have been printed. The first chapter heading is: "The Heroic Struggle of the Working Masses of Central and Southeastern Europe for the Establishment of 'People's Democracy.'"

When writing about the "heroic struggle of the countries of Central and Southeastern Europe" against Hitler, the author cites data about all the countries except Yugoslavia. As "evidence" of the liberation struggle in Czechoslovakia, for example, he quotes leaflets and proclamations issued by the Czechoslovak Communist party, describes in detail the destruction of the village of Lidice[5] and the arrest of one or two members of the Central Committee, and then gives the number of Czechs who were interned. Yet the number of people who perished in Yugoslavia amounted to 1.7 million, and there is not a word about that!

About Bulgaria it says that the Bulgarian partisans waged more than 1,600 battles(!) against the fascist armies in 1943 alone. In the course of the winter and spring of 1943 the Bulgarian partisans are supposed to have thrown back attacks by fascist armies amounting to twenty divisions! There were allegedly 18,000 Bulgarian partisans fighting those twenty divisions, helped indirectly by 200,000 Bulgars. It is taken to such absurd extremes and invented from beginning to end, and yet the world will now learn about it all for the first time from this Soviet book. There can be no talk here of facts: It is a case of pure invention and the crudest falsification of history.

In a number of places there is reference to the heroic struggle of the popular masses of Hungary against fascism! How could anyone write anything like that about the Hungarians, who fought on Hitler's side right up to the moment when their capital, Budapest, was taken by the Russians. The Red Army lost, in dead alone, more than 100,000 officers and men in the liberation of Hungary. That was the Hungarians' "heroic struggle," but it was *against* the Russians and their armed forces.

The book also talks about Romania's heroic struggle, although the Romanians were also allies of Hitler and Romanian armies fought their way, along with Hitler's armies, all the way to the Volga and Stalingrad.

---

[4] The State Political Publisher, responsible for issuing all major political works in the Soviet Union.
[5] Lidice was a village in Bohemia with a population of about 2,000 which the German occupying forces razed to the ground in 1942 as a reprisal for the assassination of Reinhard Heydrich, the German "protector" of Bohemia. The entire male population was massacred and the women and children were deported.

Then they began to be annihilated by the Soviet armed forces. So far the Russians have not dared to invent anything about the "heroic struggle" of the East Germans against fascism.

There is nowhere any mention of Yugoslavia either during the war or in the postwar period, although Yugoslavia and Albania were the only countries in the "area of Central and Southeastern Europe" which fought against the fascist invaders as allies of Russia. In the primitive way in which it falsifies history, especially the history of the war, and in its general level from the point of view of propaganda, even Soviet propaganda, this book is like the worst kind of Cominform literature that was produced in Stalin's lifetime. I don't think it will have much success either in Soviet or in East European circles among ordinary people. The average reader is surely more aware of the truth than the author of this book and those who passed it for publication.

Moscow, April 5, 1957

The extent to which the Russians are sensitive to anything which has any connection whatsoever with Yugoslavia is apparent in the way the Soviet press is treating some of our sportsmen now visiting Russia. They are obviously far better than the Soviet players whom they outplayed and defeated. The Soviet press does not want to report the facts correctly but, writing about our player Harangoz, they put things the other way round. They say he did not lose a single match but do not say that he won, because it is not permitted to say that a Yugoslav defeated the Russians!

CHAPTER EIGHTEEN

SOVIET POLICY, CHINA AND YUGOSLAVIA

Marshal Zhukov criticizes the downward trend in Soviet-Yugoslav relations. The Chinese suggest that their relations with the Russians are not as satisfactory as appears in public pronouncements. Enver Hoxha takes a tough line with Yugoslavia. The Russians withdraw another credit.

Moscow, April 6, 1957

When I spoke recently to Bulganin about Albania, with the intention of persuading the Russians to make less use of the Albanians against us, Bulganin listened attentively to my argument that such behavior by the Albanians might have serious consequences for the Albanians themselves. I explained that the internal situation in Albania was not of the best and that the international position of the Albanian state had a measure of security only thanks to Yugoslavia, which guaranteed Albanian independence and its territorial integrity. But for years now Albania has been replying only with unfriendly acts to this policy of Yugoslavia's.

The same evening Marshal Zhukov indicated that he would like to talk to me about Yugoslav-Soviet relations. When Bulganin criticized Tempo's speech criticizing the Soviet Union in the Middle East, Zhukov agreed with Bulganin and said that he, Zhukov, could have attacked Yugoslavia in India and Burma but that he had refused to say a single word against us there. "Why should I do so—would it have helped us to understand each other better or to reach some agreement?" he asked. Then Zhukov criticized Koča Popović's speech in the Yugoslav National Assembly because, according to Zhukov, he had adopted the same attitude toward both the United States and the Soviet Union, in other words to each military alliance.

When I was left alone with Marshal Zhukov, he changed his manner of talking. He said he wanted to speak to me sincerely and frankly and explain to me his opinion of our relations. He said he had recently spoken to Khrushchev on the subject and that he "would say it openly to any of those"—at which point Marshal Zhukov pointed to Bulganin, Molotov, and Malenkov, who were standing in a group near us. Zhukov said he didn't agree with the way relations between Yugoslavia and the Soviet Union were developing. One made a public attack on the other, the other replied and made a worse attack on the other side, and so things went from bad to worse between us. Each was concerned primarily with the question of his own prestige, instead of working the other way round and trying to find some solution. "If we go on a bit longer like this, we'll be pulling bayonets on each other, and what good will that do us and whose interests will it serve?" Zhukov asked.

I did not interrupt Zhukov, but gave him to understand that I agreed with him. He went on: It is the task of politicians not to permit such a development. There is no sense in it, and something serious must be done to get our top people together or to find some other way of putting things right between us.

I didn't criticize the Soviet side for worsening relations between us, because I would only have driven Zhukov to defend his own people and to attack us. I have had plenty of such conversations here and very little good has come of them. So I agreed with Zhukov and said that we also wanted to find the way out he talked about. It appeared from the conversation, which we broke off when Bulganin approached us, as though Zhukov does not agree with Bulganin about Yugoslavia and does not approve of his latest attack on us.

Moscow, April 11, 1957

United States Ambassador Charles Bohlen called on me for a farewell visit. He said he had wanted to stay here another year, but it would then have been impossible for his successor, Llewellyn Thompson, to come. In conversation with Westerners Bohlen does not hide the fact that he is very displeased that John Foster Dulles has appointed him ambassador to the Philippines, which is practically equivalent to being exiled. Many people are surprised that Bohlen accepted the appointment. The Russians are pleased for two reasons: first, I think they couldn't bear Bohlen because he knows too much about the Russians; second, they are glad that the Americans can also take a decision which is a form of exile. The French, Swedish, Canadian, and other ambassadors say that Bohlen had a good understanding of the policy of the Soviet leaders and had a good influence on Dulles and Eisenhower. They disapprove of his removal from Soviet affairs. The story had been going round here that Bohlen was going as ambassador to Yugoslavia.

Bohlen considers that things in the Soviet Union have not yet been stabilized since the failure in Hungary. He thinks the Russians are not so worried about the general course of events as might be concluded from their statements. He says the Soviet Union, with which he has been dealing for twenty years, has made tremendous progress in technology and industry, but that the political administration is out of date and contrary to the needs of society. Ideologically he thinks the Russians are terribly behind.

Moscow, April 14, 1957

Officials of the Chinese embassy have been telling us for the first time some of the difficulties they are having with the Russians. It is a question of problems in the field of economic and scientific-technological collaboration.

The Chinese told us again that they have to bear what are for them very high costs of training Chinese students in the Soviet Union. The training of one Chinese student here costs between twenty-five and thirty times as much as when they train in China. It is difficult to believe there is such a difference in the cost. They think of not sending any more to study in the Soviet Union and of allowing only a few to come for specialized training and then for a specific job and a limited period. This will result in a drastic reduction in the number of Chinese in training in the Soviet Union, and China has taken this decision although it will lead to a considerable decline in cultural and scientific cooperation between the two countries.

The Chinese are nowadays especially interested in how we pay the Soviet experts in various fields who are now working in Yugoslavia and "what are our experiences with them." We told them that for the time being we don't have any experience of them, because we don't have any Soviet experts. They say they are paying the Soviet experts far too much, incomparably more than they pay their own people. Soviet experts working in China are paid more than the very same experts working in the Soviet Union. The Chinese also complained to us of the exaggerated demands made by the Soviet experts and of the additional difficulties they cause them.

The night before last Voroshilov left for Peking. It was noticeable that he was not accompanied by a single member of the Presidium or by any political personality of the first rank. To judge by the composition of the delegation the visit will not include any serious political talks.

We might draw the conclusion from this that conflicts with the Soviet Union begin first over the question of Soviet experts working in other countries. This was the case with Yugoslavia. I don't know whether something similar will happen in the case of China. These two great powers have plenty to quarrel about even without the question of the Soviet experts. And here, too, as was the case with us, it can serve as an excuse to cover up more substantial causes of conflict.

There is still talk about the "monolithic unity" existing between the Soviet Union and China. It is not clear how the first country of socialism is going to develop collaboration on a basis of equality with the second great socialist power, when it wasn't able to do so with a small European country such as Yugoslavia.

Moscow, April 16, 1957

I went yesterday to the reception given by the Albanians for their Soviet hosts on the occasion of a visit by an Albanian party and government delegation to the Soviet Union. I kept a long way away from the head table where the Albanian delegation and members of the Soviet Presidium were sitting. There were about a thousand guests at the reception, and I got myself lost in the crowd, which filled the largest hall in the Sovietskaya Hotel. Enver Hoxha and Khrushchev made speeches. Hoxha did not refer to Yugoslavia directly and his speech was relatively moderate. Khrushchev devoted about half of his speech to Yugoslavia, but what he said was very restrained and conciliatory, not only toward us but toward everybody. He made a very good impression, and some Western ambassadors congratulated him on his speech.

When Khrushchev came to speak about Yugoslavia and the Soviet Union's desire to improve relations between us as well as to establish friendly relations between Yugoslavia and Albania, he referred to me by name, pointing out, in the presence of some thousand people, that I was a long way away from them and that they wished that "Comrade Mićunović would be closer to us." At the end of his speech Khrushchev invited me to join them at the head table, for which he received a storm of applause from the majority of those present. I accepted his invitation and had to make my way through lines of guests to join them.

In the presence of Khrushchev, several members of the Soviet Presidium, and the Albanians Enver Hoxha said that they wanted to improve relations between us, that it was in our common interest, and so forth. The Russians added their piece and applauded. I agreed with what Hoxha had said and said that these had been and still were the views of the Yugoslav Government. Hoxha ended practically every sentence about their desire for an improvement in our relations with the words: "Tell that to Comrade Tito." Khrushchev expressed his view that we and the Albanians should establish cooperation between our parties and states, that we should do it gradually, and that the Russians sincerely desired good relations between Yugoslavia and Albania. Khrushchev reproached me jokingly for standing close to the exit, saying that I had probably expected an attack on Yugoslavia and had stayed there so that it would be easier for me to quit the reception, and yet they really wanted to be friends.

Mikoyan and Malenkov also made some comments about the need for friendly relations between us, and Bulganin joined in, saying it was the sincere desire of the Russians. I had the impression that they had discussed what I said to Bulganin on April 4 about his speech and Kadar's and the policy of the Albanian Government and that yesterday's conciliatory speech by Khrushchev was to a large extent a result of that. Khrushchev's remarks about Yugoslavia were the most important part of his speech. He said only a few sentences about Albania, so that the Albanians had double reason to be displeased.

Even before Khrushchev spoke, the other members of the Presidium were strikingly attentive to me. Khrushchev asked to talk to me and abandoned the Albanians. Shepilov forced a way through the group of guests to greet me "because we haven't seen each other for so long." The Presidium left the reception, as usual, in a group. Khrushchev and Malenkov returned to the hall to take their leave of me. It is not so long since none of the Russians wanted to shake hands with me or my wife, even at a reception to which they had invited us in the Kremlin—and now what a fuss they make! The main political event at the Albanian reception was the unexpectedly friendly attitude of Khrushchev and the others to Yugoslavia.

Moscow, April 18, 1957

At a reception for the Albanians on April 17 in St. George's Hall in the Kremlin Khrushchev came up to me and invited me to talk with the head of the Albanian delegation, Enver Hoxha. I accepted this mediation by Khrushchev. It was so arranged that Hoxha and I were between Khrushchev and Bulganin, who did not intervene throughout the conversation. After twenty minutes, which is what the conversation with Hoxha lasted, the others came up—Molotov, Malenkov, Kaganovich, Shepilov, Furtseva, Pospelov,[1] and Marshal Zhukov, as well as members of the Albanian delegation. The conversation with the Albanians and the Russians continued in this large group. The whole thing was played out in the presence of the diplomatic corps and the foreign journalists. I was unable to avoid this performance. There will probably be all sorts of commentaries. Such

[1] Petr N. Pospelov, b. 1898. Soviet Communist official, historian. Director of the Marx-Engels-Lenin-Stalin Institute, 1949–52, and of the Institute of Marxism-Leninism, 1961–67. Secretary, Central Committee, CPSU, 1953–60.

scenes as this, organized by the Russians in public places when they think it can benefit them, are becoming more unpleasant every time they occur.

In the conversation with Hoxha, which Khrushchev and Bulganin were able to follow, he told me "as a friend and a Communist" the following:

The Albanians desire good relations with Yugoslavia and will strive to improve our relations "on the basis of Marxism-Leninism and proletarian internationalism." As soon as Hoxha started off like this I realized that there wasn't going to be any real conversation. Our minister in Tirana, Arso Milatović, was playing a very negative role in relations between Albania and Yugoslavia, Enver Hoxha went on. Two months ago Milatović had taken a photograph of the military airport near Tirana, a fact which had been confirmed beyond question by the security officer who knew our minister personally. Milatović had traveled without the permission of the Albanian authorities to Berat, which was a forbidden zone for foreigners. In both cases, said Hoxha, the Albanian authorities had not reacted to this violation of Albanian laws. At receptions in Tirana officials of our legation had said things about him and Shehu,[2] the Albanian Government and party, and held conferences in the same spirit in the houses of Albanian citizens in Tirana. Hoxha attributed all this to our present minister, Arso Milatović, who, he said, was a greater enemy of Albania than was our previous minister, Predrag Ajtić, although Ajtić was in Tirana when relations between us were worse.

As can be seen, Hoxha started in such a way that it could not end well, while there were some things which could not be passed over in silence. It was quite clear that no agreement on the controversial issues between us would be achieved.

I expressed doubt about the charges against Milatović and rejected the assertion that he was an enemy of Albania, because I had known him very well for a long time. As for taking pictures of military objectives and traveling to forbidden areas, I did not believe that any of our people in Tirana would do so, let alone the minister. I knew for certain that our Central Committee had several years ago explicitly forbidden such activity in countries of the "camp" including Albania.

Speaking in support of the Albanians, Khrushchev recounted that when Comrade Tito visited the King of Greece one of the Greeks present had spoken "as a joke" about dividing Albania between Yugoslavia and Greece. I said that neither Tito nor any other Yugoslav could influence what the Greek King or anyone in his suite might choose to make a joke about, in good or bad taste. I rejected any suspicions that might be directed at Yugoslavia in this connection. I pointed out that at the peace conference in Paris, and not in the form of a joke but officially

[2] Mehmet Shehu, b. 1913. Albanian Communist official. Member of the Politburo, Albanian Communist party, from 1948 and Prime Minister from 1954.

through their representative, Tsaldaris, the Greeks had proposed to the Yugoslav delegation that they should discuss the partition of Albania. Our representative, the late Moša Pijade, had exposed the Greek plan and Tsaldaris publicly at the conference. In Stalin's time and later, despite the bad state of Yugoslav-Albanian relations, we had always defended the territorial integrity and independence of Albania, as we continued to do today.

Moscow, April 21, 1957

Khrushchev informed me yesterday that the Soviet Government had decided to postpone the agreement about credits for the construction of a nitrogen plant in Yugoslavia. I expressed my surprise, for only a few days ago we issued visas to a large group of their specialists who had gone to Belgrade to draw up the plans with our experts. Khrushchev told me they had already recalled their fertilizer specialists who were now on their way back to the Soviet Union.

I asked him for the reasons. He said they were economic. I pointed out the political harm that this would do to our relations. I feared that no one in Yugoslavia, or in the Soviet Union or in the world at large, would interpret this otherwise than as a political decision of the Soviet Government. I mentioned his own statements of a few days previously about their desire to improve our relations as well as the fact that they were distributing right and left millions and billions of rubles of credit while postponing unilaterally, or rather canceling, an agreement with Yugoslavia for the construction of a medium-size plant—and in the middle of completing the agreement.

The postponement of the fertilizer plant in addition to the aluminum plant represents a further stiffening of the tough line toward us. This negative decision has been made easier for the Russians to some extent by the agreement on economic aid and credits between Yugoslavia and the United States Government. The Russians consider that our agreement with the United States will be sufficient justification in the eyes of the Soviet public for postponing the agreement on credits for the fertilizer plant.

Khrushchev informed me that the Soviet Government would hand me a note about this matter. I gained the impression that he does not personally approve the decision, but that there is a solid majority at the top of the Soviet system which is against Yugoslavia and that Khrushchev has no intention of pitching himself against that majority when it comes to things like this.

Moscow, April 21, 1957

In a speech at a reception in the Polish embassy Khrushchev again mentioned me by name. He said I had reproached him because the Russians were not buying agricultural produce from Yugoslavia as they did from other countries of the "camp," and that I had commented that of course "Bulgarian peppers are tastier than the Yugoslav variety, which are hotter." Khrushchev went on: "Yes, the Bulgarian peppers are more to our taste . . ." and so forth. There was a general laughter and murmuring among the five or six hundred Soviet guests, the diplomatic corps, journalists, and others.

Khrushchev quoted me accurately on the whole, but not fully. I had told him that I knew that our Yugoslav peppers were too hot for the Russians, that they liked the Bulgarian ones and so they bought from the Bulgars. I could understand that, but I could not understand why they made difficulties for us over oil which they were selling anyway in large quantities to members of the NATO alliance. But Khrushchev did not mention this.

When Khrushchev referred to their successful talks with the Albanians, I told him that on April 17 in the Kremlin, when he invited me to talk with Enver Hoxha, I had expected the conversation to be of some use. Unfortunately I had heard only accusations against Yugoslavia: that we wanted to include Albania as the seventh republic in Yugoslavia, to partition it with Greece, and to destroy the Albanian minority and so forth. Khrushchev did not take up this point.

At a reception in the Syrian embassy I spoke with Marshal Zhukov. After telling me he had been to the south of Russia he said: Have you seen how things are beginning to improve between us?—thinking of Khrushchev's speech of April 15. He told me he had spoken with Khrushchev after talking to me on April 4, and that he would speak with him again. There had been no results so far, but he hoped there would be in the future.

I expressed regrets about Suslov's speech at the meeting on April 16. I tried to explain that it was going to be difficult if it went on like this: to make unfounded accusations against Yugoslavia in a public speech and to follow it with statements about the desire for collaboration and so forth. Marshal Zhukov replied that they did not regard Yugoslavia as being "revisionist"; only a few individuals did. The conversation was broken off here.

CHAPTER NINETEEN

KHRUSHCHEV IMPROVES HIS POSITION

Khrushchev pushes through his economic reforms despite opposition from other Soviet leaders and the entrenched Soviet bureaucracy. The Soviet press snipes at Yugoslavia over its acceptance of American military aid. Mićunović visits Mongolia and sees the clash of Russian and Chinese influence.

Moscow, May 3, 1957

Following the May Day parade in Moscow the Central Committee of the CPSU organized a lunch as it did last year. Apart from members of the Presidium and the Central Committee it was also attended by the ambassadors from all the countries of Eastern Europe. I was also invited. The lunch did not take place as usual in the Kremlin but in the grounds of the Central Committee's villa about twenty miles from Moscow, which produced a less official, more easygoing atmosphere. Khrushchev wasn't the only host in the strict sense of the word; others also proposed toasts. Most of the speeches, of which there were about a dozen, dealt with Soviet domestic policy. Some of Khrushchev's remarks were interesting and fitted well into the general atmosphere. He spoke mainly about the country's economic problems, saying that the old system was outdated and stressing the benefits which the new system would bring to the economy.

They did not pay special attention to China or mention the countries of the socialist camp by name, because then they would have had to speak about Yugoslavia in particular, and it wasn't the occasion to attack us since they had invited me to the lunch, and there was of course no question of praising us. After the lunch Khrushchev and Furtseva came up to me and we were joined by the Polish ambassador, Tadeusz Gede. Khrushchev invited us to go with him to his country house which was nearby, where Gede and I remained for about four hours. Around midnight we went back to Moscow with Khrushchev in his car.

Before Gede joined us the following questions came up:

I asked Khrushchev whether he had had the opportunity to read Comrade Tito's latest speech at the meeting of our Socialist Alliance on Brioni. Khrushchev was rather reserved in his reply. He said he didn't agree with certain points of view which Tito had expressed, but that his opinion of the speech was in general favorable, because Tito said he was anxious to improve our relations and that was fundamental. Ranković's speech pointed in the same direction, and that was also a positive sign.

In a rather bad mood, insofar as the festive atmosphere permitted, Khrushchev told me that our leaders were completely misinterpreting certain moves made by Soviet leaders and himself and were drawing quite mistaken conclusions from them. He referred to reports they had that in conversations with certain Western ambassadors Comrade Tito had commented on the frequent conversations which Khrushchev (and other members of the Presidium) had with me at diplomatic receptions in Moscow. Comrade Tito had reportedly been explaining to Western diplomats that the Soviet leaders, and primarily Khrushchev himself, talked with me in that way in order to upset Yugoslavia's relations with the West and to create in the public mind a false impression of the state of Yugoslav-Soviet relations. By so doing the Soviet leaders allegedly wanted to indicate to the Westerners that something confidential was going on between us and that the public dispute was something agreed between the two countries. Khrushchev insisted that he had conversations with me because he was striving in this and other ways to put our relations right.

Khrushchev takes an optimistic view of the development of the internal situation in the Soviet Union. He again talked to me about the February plenum, saying that the decisions taken there were of the greatest historical significance and that this could be seen better now than when the idea of reorganizing the economic system first came up. He said they were reckoning on making a number of personal changes among the top people, not just in the all-union ministries which were being abolished, but even higher than that. All these measures would facilitate the introduction of the new system. People who for years and decades had been wallowing in the old system could not introduce the new one. The majority of the present ministers whose ministries were being abolished would be put in charge of departments in the State Planning Committee.

The results already achieved on the economic front and those which would be achieved under the new system would show that Yugoslav criticisms of the Soviet system were unfounded, Khrushchev said. "You must understand that the Soviet Union would be ruined if it worked according to Yugoslav rules." He went on to comment that the new open dispute

between us had benefited the Soviet Union and strengthened the links between the Russians and the countries of Eastern Europe. Similarly our attack on the Soviet leadership had had a good effect in consolidating the
internal situation in the Soviet Union, and we had expected the reverse,
Khrushchev said, when we divided them into Stalinists and anti-Stalinists.
Now the situation was different even in the other socialist states, which
were free to take their own line, criticize Yugoslavia, and defend themselves. They had not been able to do this following our joint declaration
in Belgrade and Moscow. "We had to keep on telling those countries not
to criticize Yugoslavia," Khrushchev said, looking really pleased with the
way things were going.

I expressed our satisfaction with the decentralization and other changes
in the Soviet economy, and said we were informing our public about it. I
then spoke about the favorable development of our economy, which their
magazine *Kommunist* had recently considered to be in the last stages of
collapse, and I described some of the plans for further economic expansion in Yugoslavia. Then I commented unfavorably on the reports they
had from Belgrade about our conversations which I described as an in-
trigue "on the highest level."

The conversation was conducted in a fairly friendly tone which neither side wanted to upset, even though what was said was not always
very agreeable. In this spirit I commented at the end that the public dispute between us appeared to have been of benefit both to the Soviet
Union and to Yugoslavia and, as I gathered, to the countries of the
"camp." According to that we ought not to be trying to end the dispute
as we were doing all the time! Khrushchev took this well and there was
laughter on both sides. The conclusion of all this was that we could argue
in public and still have friendly conversations.

Moscow, May 4, 1957

At the May Day lunch Khrushchev was much more reserved once the
Polish ambassador joined us. He stopped raising any fresh political topics
and did not once criticize the Poles, which suggested that there was a
certain coolness and distance between them.

Khrushchev drank a toast to "Comrade Tito and Comrade Gomulka,"
and that was the first time Khrushchev had drunk to Tito's health since
the new conflict broke out between us. It was the same when he inquired
about Tito's rheumatism. He said he was convinced that Tito would
derive benefit from treatment in one of the Soviet spas. He mentioned a
number of medicinal baths in the Soviet Union, told me to tell Comrade
Tito about them, so that he could decide for himself. They would be
very glad to do everything necessary to arrange a visit by Comrade Tito

sometime. Khrushchev later returned to the question of a visit by Comrade Tito to the Soviet Union and finally said more precisely that it would be a very good thing if Tito and Gomulka came to the Soviet Union privately for a holiday. It looks as though Khrushchev has hit on a cover—medical treatment—which could be used in the event of Tito's coming to the Soviet Union in present circumstances. It is also interesting that he thinks of Gomulka coming as well. He probably reckons that this might make it easier for Tito to come, since he might agree to come at the same time as Gomulka. On the other hand Khrushchev was certain that Gomulka would support the Soviet side in any discussion of the differences between us.

We spoke about the late Moša Pijade. I believe that even the Russians, and above all Khrushchev, have realized that it was wrong of them to take revenge on Moša even when he was dead. They know about the memorial meeting in our embassy and what I said about Moša and our indignation at the Russians' behavior. It seems as though they would now like to put things right to some extent. Khrushchev told me that they had not been able to pass over Comrade Moša's "anti-Soviet" attitude even after the normalization of our relations. For my own part I did not want to add heat to the discussion while I was in Khrushchev's home, so I spoke about Moša's merits and the loss which his death meant to the revolutionary movement, not only in Yugoslavia.

Moscow, May 6, 1957

I paid a call on Marshal Zhukov yesterday and informed him about the visit of our State Secretary for Defense, General Ivan Gošnjak. Marshal Zhukov agreed that the visit should take place in the first half of June as we had proposed. He pointed out that it would not be really satisfactory if our military delegation were to consist only of one general, one colonel, and a junior officer, since the delegation would have to have some meetings with senior officers of the armed forces of the Soviet Union. He explained that it would be better if there were, say, three generals, three colonels, and some other officers from various branches of the services. Zhukov jotted down a list of ten people and said there could be more if we thought it necessary. The conversation was full of good wishes on both sides and much more agreeable than what we encounter in the Foreign Ministry.

Marshal Zhukov told me that it would not be possible to show our people the atomic installations belonging to the military, which were subject to special controls and were not accessible to senior Soviet military and other personnel who had no need to know about them. I took Zhukov's explanation as his personal desire to assure me that it was not a matter of some special treatment for Yugoslavs but that the situation was indeed as he said.

Even if our relations were better than they are, Marshal Zhukov would probably have been just as interested in this visit. Our links with the Russians had been in fact strongest in the military field. It is our armies which in the main carried on our joint struggle and which symbolize the comradeship in arms and the close links which were formed in the past, especially during the last war. Such links are not easily forgotten; they enter into a people's history and it is impossible to erase them from the memories of contemporaries or from the minds of the rising generation.

The Russians are very strong in the manufacture of weapons and military equipment, and it is this, more than anything else, that can put us into a position of dependence in view of our need of armaments and of Soviet ability to produce them. In addition to the high position he occupies in the state, Gošnjak is also a member of the top party leadership in Yugoslavia, which makes his visit all the more important, in the eyes not only of the Russians but of others too. This is the first visit of a member of the Politburo of our party to Moscow since the outbreak six months ago of the open dispute between us. Perhaps they will treat him here primarily as one of our party leaders and only afterward as a minister in the government. With things as they are now between us I do not believe that it would be possible to have such a high-level visit to Moscow in any other field. It is all the more significant in that the host to our Defense Secretary is none other than Marshal Zhukov, a person enjoying the highest reputation both in the Soviet Union and in Yugoslavia.

I advised Belgrade to accept Marshal Zhukov's suggestion about the composition of our delegation, because this would undoubtedly be well received on the Soviet side and is in line with our practice.

Moscow, May 13, 1957

The speech on the reorganization of the Soviet economy in the Supreme Soviet was made by Khrushchev. The Russians keep on insisting that the decentralization of the economic system which they are bringing in now is different from what we are doing in Yugoslavia, that they are doing it "according to Lenin," while we are not keeping to his principles. Nevertheless it remains a fact that this is the beginning of change in the life of the Soviet Union and that they could not continue with things as they were in Stalin's day, even if the decentralization is not following the Yugoslav pattern. Even in the Soviet Union it is impossible to imagine a further expansion of their industrial production without some changes in the organization of the economy. The Russians continue to defend the all-powerful role of the state, but not as they did in the past.

The man who initiated all these changes is Khrushchev, who insists that no one should think that the plan for reorganizing the economy was worked out by Gosplan, the Soviet Government, or anybody else. Even three months ago Khrushchev started to make changes in some of the biggest government bodies, abolishing some of them and putting new and relatively unknown people into top positions. In this way he took all the real power away from the State economic commission, which had been set up only at the end of the year. Nor was the creation of a committee of state control to be headed by Molotov ratified, although it was expected to be an important department in the Soviet Government.

The composition of the Soviet Government was strengthened significantly at the end of last year following the Hungarian events. The majority of the members of the Presidium were brought into the government. Khrushchev remained secretary of the Central Committee, where he prepared the decentralization program, which ought to have been the task of the Prime Minister rather than of the First Secretary of the Communist party. It wasn't like that last November or even later. Khrushchev was not able then himself to represent the Presidium as a whole but was always accompanied by Malenkov and Molotov, whereas now he speaks in the name of the party and the government and himself proposes the most important measures. The other members of the Presidium do not go out of their way to support him, not even Bulganin, let alone Malenkov, Molotov, and the others who remain silent during his public discourses on the new system in the economy.

Moscow, May 16, 1957

In a conversation with us Banik, counselor of the Polish embassy, spoke in favor of a private visit to the Soviet Union by Comrades Tito and Gomulka. The Polish ambassador has obviously discussed Khrushchev's idea with his colleagues and now the counselor tries to persuade us that the visit would be "very important for all three countries." Perhaps the Russians have given the Poles the job of working on us in this sense. Banik thinks that the visit should be secret and completely informal. This would make it much easier to discuss existing problems and differences because the talks would then be really open and frank. The Poles have certainly obtained Gomulka's agreement for such a meeting of the three leaders and are therefore now working on us to put Khrushchev's plan into practice.

Our experience with the Russians teaches us to oppose secret meetings and secret agreements, whether with the Russians or any of the others. Irrespective of what agreements we might come to and what we might agree about, the very fact that the visit and the agreements were not announced publicly can be only to our disadvantage and limit our freedom of action in foreign policy. For that reason I think that nothing like this should be contemplated. We have no need of any such secrecy, which may not be observed even if we were to agree to it. It would be sufficient simply for it to get around that there had been a secret visit for people on all sides to start looking suspiciously at our foreign policy. The basic advantage of that policy lies precisely in its being conducted publicly. That is why it gained the support of the people even in difficult situations, as in 1948.

Izvestia has ended the calm which has reigned over our relations with the Russians for the last few weeks. On May 16 it published a report entitled "American military supplies for Yugoslavia." A similar report appeared today in all the central military newspapers.

In a situation like this the publication in the Soviet press of the American version of the new military supplies to Yugoslavia is aimed at creating as bad an impression as possible among the Soviet public. The same purpose is served by certain phrases in which, quoting the Americans, they say that Eisenhower's decision to provide armaments for Yugoslavia "should be in the national interests of the United States." This statement was welcomed by the Russians as a means of further discrediting Yugoslavia. In accordance with the way in which the public here has been trained for years to know what opinion to have about particular foreign political events, the Russians now "prove," with the aid of a quotation from Eisenhower, that the sale of American arms to Yugoslavia has always been the other side of the "ideological" quarrel between us and the Soviet Union, and this is now being "exposed."

The Soviet public will be more disposed to believe what Eisenhower says than what is said by some Soviet leader in the dispute with Yugoslavia. The Russians simply ignore our statement on the same question and make sure that nobody in the Soviet Union publishes it. The Russians have planned it so that it appears as though it is the United States Government and not the Yugoslavs who interpret the policy of the Yugoslav Government. It is no longer just a question of disagreement about "modern revisionism" and "proletarian internationalism" but about the further deliveries of American arms to Yugoslavia, and the Soviet public is far more sensitive on this question.

Moscow, May 20, 1957

In Moscow and probably in other places in the Soviet Union people continue to complain about the reorganization of the economic administration and about the speed with which it is being put into practice. We hear that there were demands that the session of the Supreme Soviet of

May 7 should be postponed because there was not enough time to prepare for it. Yet the session not only took place but was even shortened and all the measures proposed became law in accordance with Khrushchev's speech.

The opponents of Khrushchev's policy and his economic reform are putting round the story that it is "Trishka's caftan." There was once a man called Trishka who had a fine caftan but who started altering it to make it even better and went on doing so until his caftan was completely ruined. Khrushchev is said to be doing the same with the Soviet economy. His opponents use against him the same devices as he employs—anecdotes and popular proverbs. One hears comments that Khrushchev's plan will not produce anything new because, instead of providing material incentives for the working people and their enterprises, it is concerned only with altering the responsibilities of Moscow and some of the republics and other instruments of authority.

Moscow, May 22, 1957

It is characteristic of the complicated way the Soviet Government conducts its foreign policy in relation to the West that the Russians start from the assumption that the consequences of the war in the Middle East and of the Soviet armed intervention in Hungary must be removed and that the atmosphere in international relations which prevailed in 1955 and the first half of 1956 must be restored. They say that the atmosphere then was favorable primarily because of the peaceful policy of the Soviet Union. The Russians are now offering each of the Western powers opportunities for contacts and talks both to improve bilateral relations and to resolve some unsettled world issues. They expect to get some results from this campaign, and then they would go over to the second phase, keeping to the same basic objective—the preservation of peace—and at the same time maintaining the status quo above all in Europe. This policy of maintaining the status quo does not hold for Asia and still less for Africa. There the political map is constantly changing: New independent states are being formed on the territory of the former colonies and at the same time Western colonial possessions are being reduced in size. That is why the Russians are for the status quo in Europe and at the same time for the liquidation of colonialism in Asia and Africa.

Moscow, May 23, 1957

Miška and I leave together this evening for Mongolia, where I have been accredited as Yugoslav ambassador with permanent residence in Moscow. We are being accompanied by Raif Dizdarević, secretary in our

Moscow embassy. We have tried to read up, as far as possible from a couple of books and a reference book in Russian, about this distant, strange land. We are still unable to rid ourselves of the feeling that we were going into the unknown. We are taking with us some gifts for top Mongolian officials. There is something strange about this: I am going to Mongolia to present my letters of accreditation, bearing "gifts" for the Head of State, the Prime Minister, and the Foreign Minister as in the old times.

Ulan Bator, June 3, 1957

We have been extremely well received in Mongolia and treated as official guests of the Mongolian Government. Through the Mongolian embassy in Moscow we had reserved rooms in a hotel in Ulan Bator, but when we arrived we found we had been accommodated in a government villa outside the city, provided with the most competent servants they have, and given special food. In Mongolian terms this represented the maximum that they were able to offer foreign guests.

The ambassadors from Asian countries as well as those from Eastern Europe did not get such treatment when they arrived in Mongolia, and the attitude of the Mongolian Government toward us has not been well received by some of the East European ambassadors. The Czech ambassador told me how he had succeeded in "obtaining permission" to spend a couple of weeks in this villa last year when he was seriously ill.

Immediately after our arrival we spoke to the protocol department of the Mongolian Foreign Ministry about payment for the cost of our stay in Ulan Bator. Although the expenses were considerable the Mongolians insisted that we were the guests of their government and that there could be no question of our paying for anything except the formal reception which I gave for the Mongolian leaders, which had naturally to be at our expense.

The Mongolian Government went out of its way to facilitate my presentation of letters of accreditation and fulfillment of other official duties. The Foreign Minister received me shortly after my arrival and I presented my letters the next day. The same day I was received by the Prime Minister and the secretary of the party. The chairman of the Presidium of the Supreme People's Hural—which corresponds to the Supreme Soviet in the U.S.S.R.—paid special tribute to Comrade Tito and this was later reported in the Mongolian press. The Prime Minister, Tsedenbal, and the party secretary, Damba, also sent greetings to Comrade Tito.

From all the conversations I had I was left with the impression that the Mongolian leaders expect the establishment of relations with Yugoslavia to assist them greatly in their efforts to assert themselves in international affairs. They were trying to give the first official representative of Yugoslavia the best possible reception. Throughout our week-long visit the Mongolian press gave it front-page publicity.

Moscow, June 6, 1957

It is not difficult to observe how the interests of Mongolia's two giant neighbors, Russia and China, clash on its territory. Each one has its own different conception of the way Mongolia should develop. The Russians consider that the development of Mongolia cannot be solved by increasing the number of foreign workers (which means in practice the import of Chinese workers) but by training local, Mongolian skilled workers in all fields, by expanding the country's productive capacity, and developing industry and mining.

Contrary to the Russians, the Chinese believe that the People's Republic of Mongolia would develop much more quickly if manpower were imported from China, since the underpopulation of those vast areas and the shortage of workers is, in the Chinese view, Mongolia's main problem. There are now in Mongolia about 8,000 Chinese workers and 5,000 members of their families, according to what the Chinese ambassador told me. He is annoyed at the strict quotas imposed on them by the Mongolian Government. The Chinese are ready at once to send hundreds of thousands of workers, but the Mongolian authorities are against it and prefer to put up with the lack of manpower and the underpopulation of whole regions.

Since they have to choose between the contrary plans of their two great neighbors, who both profess themselves interested in Mongolia's "rapid internal development," each in his own way, the Mongolians have plumped for the Russians. This is understandable, not only because they are dependent on the Russians for everything and the Soviet program takes account of the expansion of Mongolian potentials but also because there is no prospect or danger of the Russians settling in Mongolia. With the Chinese it is the reverse. Apart from their memories of an unhappy past, when the Chinese occupied Mongolia and later were enemies of the new Mongolian Government until the victory of the revolution in China in 1949, the Mongolians reckon quite realistically that in the course of time they would become a national minority in their own country if they were to agree to Chinese plans for "rapid internal development" and allow uncontrolled immigration by the Chinese.

Both the Chinese and the Russian embassies in Ulan Bator have very large staffs, but it is the Russians who play the decisive role in the development of Mongolia. It was Soviet troops who protected the Mongolian frontier in the east and south—that is, the frontier with China—right up to 1949. I don't know what the situation is now. The victory of the revolution in China improved the prospects for developing Sino-Mongolian relations. But the Russians are becoming more deeply involved. There are also signs that the Mongolians would like to be more independent.

Moscow, June 8, 1957

In the vicinity of Ulan Bator we visited an old Mongolian temple in which the priests still remained. It was Miška who asked for the visit, although the Mongolian official who accompanied us didn't like it very much. Religious belief played an important part in the life of old Mongolia, with power resting for centuries in the hands of the priests of the Lamaist religion, a Tibetan variation of Buddhism, which is as far as I could make out one of the most backward religious sects in the world. Those ten priests were far more revealing of what Mongolia must have been like in the past than anything that can be read in books. They were conducting some kind of service when Miška, Dizdarević, and I arrived. The ritual looked awful, and so did the priests. We reckoned their average age at around seventy. Most of them had no hair and the shape of their bald skulls was deformed and some of them bore scars. Some were unnaturally fat, others were exceptionally thin, and they were smeared with some kind of fat and dressed in robes of reddish-yellow cloth. They didn't look at all attractive. The temple was heavy with the spirit of the past and it was an effort to remain inside it for more than ten minutes.

I kept thinking what an unfortunate past the Mongolians had had, being ruled by such a priesthood until the revolution of 1921. I seem still to have ringing in my ears the banging of the cymbals which the priests used during their prayers. One of the dogmas of this priesthood was to forbid any "harm" to the earth, which meant that nothing could be done on the earth, no digging or cultivating, because that inflicted wounds on the earth. That was why there was no agriculture or mining in Mongolia. At one time they did not even bury the dead so as not to "harm" the earth. They put their faith in their "sanitary inspectors"—the carrion eagles which still circle over inhabited places in Mongolia.

Stalin ordered the introduction of the Cyrillic alphabet into Mongolia as early as 1942! The ancient Mongolian script was simply banned. They told us that the Cyrillic alphabet was actually introduced only five years later, because of the opposition to Stalin's order. But when I presented my letters of accreditation, the Mongolian President made a speech and I could see that it was not written in the official Cyrillic alphabet but in the classical Mongolian script in which the characters are written vertically from the top to the bottom of the page. I thought that the old script was still used only by a few old people, and yet there he was using it. I was mistaken. The journalists present, who were all very young people, also took their notes in the old Mongolian script.

Moscow, June 8, 1957

For a long time Mongolia was dominated by the Chinese. Then it was taken over by the Russian Tsars as a sort of protectorate. Then came the Mongolian revolution of 1921—according to the Russian reference books and school textbooks which I read in Moscow—and under Soviet protection Mongolia achieved a sort of independence as far as the Chinese were concerned. I think Mongolia is primarily of military importance to the Soviet Union, for the security of its southeastern frontiers. It was like that in the past in Tsarist times, and it was like it between the wars with relation to Japan and China. Now it is only a question of China since Japan created the present-day Mongolia and kept it as a sort of buffer state between the Soviet Union and China. I believe Mongolia is beginning to assert a sort of independence, especially since the death of Stalin and Khrushchev's assumption of the leadership of the Soviet Union. However that may be, the fact is that, although Mongolia is today under Soviet domination, it has in the course of a few decades achieved greater social, economic, and cultural progress than it had done previously in the course of several centuries. For us Yugoslavs the sort of independence that Mongolia enjoys would not mean much. We quarreled with Stalin when he tried to impose a similar kind of "independence" on our country. But, while our opposition to Stalin and conflict with the Soviet Union was the only right course for Yugoslavia, by force of circumstances different rules apply to Mongolia.

CHAPTER TWENTY

YUGOSLAV-SOVIET RELATIONS IMPROVE

A Yugoslav military delegation is well received in Moscow, although the Soviet marshals remain concerned about the American military mission in Belgrade. Khrushchev commits Soviet agriculture to overtaking America in the production of basic foodstuffs.

Moscow, June 9, 1957

A Yugoslav military delegation led by General Gošnjak arrived on an official visit to the Soviet Union yesterday at Marshal Zhukov's invitation. It is significant that the Russians have used Marshal Zhukov—that is to say, the Soviet armed forces—for improving relations with Yugoslavia and in so doing have practically left both our Foreign Ministry and theirs out of the picture. Marshal Zhukov is the best person the Russians could have chosen for such a task. On the Yugoslav side there was no hesitation about accepting the Soviet proposal for reestablishing the links between the representatives of the armed forces of our countries which were broken off in 1948. It is certainly a move which has far greater political significance than the mere establishment of routine contacts between the two Ministries of Defense.

Moscow, June 10, 1957

Our military delegation has been very well received in Moscow. The arrival at Vnukovo Airport was attended by Marshal Zhukov and an impressively large number of Soviet marshals and generals. The Soviet Army provided a guard of honor and the national anthems were played. Marshal Zhukov gave me to understand that they had accorded Gošnjak the maximum honors, more than was customary. (Ministers do not get a military guard of honor nor the playing of anthems; these are reserved for heads of state and government.)

Last night Marshal Zhukov gave a formal dinner at the Ministry of Defense in honor of the Yugoslav guests. It was attended by senior officers of the Soviet armed forces now in Moscow, more than twenty of them, headed by a group of seven or eight marshals and some army generals. Zhukov's speech of welcome was full of recognition and praise of our Army and people, and politically it was moderate and unobjectionable. The whole of the Soviet central press today published a special communiqué, referring to "talks between Marshal Zhukov and Gošnjak" and saying that I was also present. In fact there were no talks at all apart from an exchange of greetings and the taking of photographs which is customary when there is a desire to create a better atmosphere. This all indicates that the Russians are trying to push things a little too fast politically. They don't seem to have the patience to let the visit follow the very good program which has been arranged and to wait until the time comes for talks.

A meeting with Marshal Zhukov had been planned for today. But the Russians avoided it and simply dropped it from the program, telling our people that certain items in the program were being "changed." In the course of conversation after the dinner, which was in fact the first opportunity for getting to know each other, the Russians proposed to take our delegation back to Belgrade in their TU-104 jet aircraft. Gošnjak thanked them but did not accept the offer. The delegation came from Belgrade to Moscow in a small slow twin-engine Dakota, which looks like a toy alongside the modern TU-104 jet plane which the Russians boast about not only to us but to the West as well. They would like to appear in Belgrade with this plane as soon as possible. Here again they were impatient and made their offer to take Gošnjak back to Belgrade right at the beginning. The plane that our delegation came in is being taken care of at Vnukovo Airport where it will stand for more than a fortnight under constant guard. We cannot boast that our State Secretary for Defense traveled to Moscow in a particularly prestigious aircraft.

Marshal Zhukov's attitude toward Gošnjak and the other Yugoslavs is very correct and friendly. Each meeting with him leaves our people with a pleasant impression on account of the direct and straightforward way he behaves and talks. But I must record here some statements Zhukov made on a previous occasion when we were alone, preparing for the arrival of our delegation. I don't think that what he said is politically especially topical today, but coming from such a person as Marshal Zhukov it is certainly worth recalling because it shows the way he thinks.

Marshal Zhukov was summing up our conflict in 1948. Declaring that nothing like it should be allowed to happen again, he said that even then it was not a conflict between one nation and another but between the government of one country and another government, that it was all a result of Stalin's arbitrary rule, and we had replied in kind. There were personal ambitions involved on both sides, but the people themselves did not quarrel, Marshal Zhukov said. I did not agree with him, but it seemed better to pass it over than to argue about who attacked whom in 1948 and why. He went on to say that they were a great power with powerful armed forces and that in 1948 they could have forced us to submit in a matter of three days! I found this too much to swallow. I said that the conflict between us came about for many reasons which there was no need to go into since they were well known. As for the suggestion that the Soviet Union could have "forced us to submit in three days," I did not believe that was so because experience had shown that even the Germans, when they were at the very height of their military strength, had not been able to conquer us, not just in three days but in four years. "You know very well," I told Marshal Zhukov, "what German military strength was in 1941, yet we succeeded not only in holding out but in growing steadily stronger and were in the end victorious along with the Soviet Union and the other allies."

This was by no means the best subject for conversation. But I didn't choose it or start it and I did my best to bring it quickly to an end. Zhukov said that our resistance movement had been possible and successful thanks to the battles fought by the Soviet Army. I did not contradict him, but commented that it was true and said it was a pity that the same had not applied to other peoples like the Czechs, Romanians, Bulgars, Hungarians, and others who had not taken advantage of the efforts of the Soviet Army. If they had fought they would have made the Russians' war effort easier, reduced the losses suffered by the Soviet Army in liberating their countries, and possibly had the effect of shortening the duration of World War II. To this Marshal Zhukov said that the war would have lasted just as long as it did last and that no resistance movement in those countries would have made any serious difference.

Moscow, June 12, 1957

I was visited in our embassy by an official of the *apparat* of the Central Committee of the CPSU by the name of Medvedev. He is an important *apparatchik* who deals with all exchanges between the Soviet Central Committee and our party. He previously "kept in touch" with our Cominform émigrés and probably still does. The fact that he came to see me with friendly messages and good news confirms that our relations with the Soviet Union are improving. His visit was of course the result of a decision at the highest level to pass on to us some good information.

This must be taken as a sign that the Soviet leaders have set course in the direction of improving our relations. This time it is a question of contact and collaboration on the party level, which must have a specific political significance.

Medvedev handed me two friendly letters from the Central Committee of the Communist party of Greece which is under Soviet influence. Although I did not ask about it, Medvedev raised the question of our party archives, assured me that they were still working on the matter and that it was a job that required a lot of time. Medvedev talked about the improvement of relations between our parties and as confirmation he passed on the decision of the Soviet Central Committee, which has already been communicated to our people in Belgrade through the Soviet Ambassador, to invite twenty to twenty-five of our party and government officials for a holiday in the Soviet Union. "Comrade Kardelj has expressed the desire to come and so did Comrade Ranković. Comrade Tito said he would certainly come next year," Medvedev said.

In this way the Russians have taken a decisive step to bring an end to the conflict between us, and have done it in a way that must be apparent to everyone. I think the fundamental fact here is that it is Yugoslavia which is sending its leaders to the Soviet Union "on holiday" and not the other way round. It is as though for the Russians this decision has politically a "retroactive effect" with relation to our last conflict, and all the more so since it concerns Comrades Tito, Kardelj, and Ranković. The Russians are very pleased about all this.

Moscow, June 17, 1957

Two days ago I gave a dinner in honor of Marshal Zhukov and his colleagues to mark the official visit of General Gošnjak and our military delegation. It was attended, apart from Marshal Zhukov, by a large group of Soviet marshals: Rokossovsky, Malinovsky, Bagramyan, Moskalenko, Sudets, Rotmistrov, Biryuzov, Generals Antonov, Sokolov, and other distinguished Soviet military leaders. The Russians stayed for about three and a half hours and the evening passed off in a friendly atmosphere, although there were some exchanges which were not, in places, very agreeable to either side. A general air of formality imposed itself on both us and the Russians and prevailed throughout.

I welcomed Marshal Zhukov and the other guests with a specially written speech, although it is not the custom in our embassy, as the Russians know, to make speeches on such occasions, and this made it all the more formal. This was how the Soviet side understood it, since Marshal Zhukov also replied with a written speech, which is not the Russian custom except when they want to give the whole affair a strictly formal character. In Moscow, when such formality is the order of the day, it is at the expense of cordiality, as though the two things cannot go together.

I believe Marshal Zhukov and the majority of the Soviet marshals and generals present were not particularly enthusiastic about my rather restrained speech. Zhukov placed great emphasis on our alliance in the war and on the necessity for "friendship" between us and all the "countries of the socialist commonwealth." Among the specific issues which Zhukov raised in conversation was the question of the American military aid which Yugoslavia was receiving, and he asked us: What's the good of American aid to you? Such aid was harmful for Yugoslavia both militarily and politically. There was today no reason for us to receive it since there was no threat to us from the East and the Russians had never thought that we could be enemies. The American military mission in Yugoslavia was damaging to our real interests and jeopardized our sovereignty in view of the right of inspection of our Army which the mission had. (So now the Russians are concerned about our sovereignty!) The United States military mission in Belgrade had been from the outset a center of intelligence activity against the Soviet Union and the "camp," as well as against Yugoslavia. How could the Russians give us, for example, military equipment (Zhukov mentioned particularly the MIG-17 aircraft) if it was all going to be accessible to the Americans in Yugoslavia?

From a military point of view American military aid was aimed ultimately at weakening Yugoslavia and not strengthening it, Marshal Zhukov continued. The Americans had given us, for example, the F-86 jet aircraft, yet these planes had long been out of service in America. They were now training aircraft and were fit for the scrap heap. The same could be said of other weapons, and then there was the question of spare parts and our complete dependence on the United States.

Along with this Zhukov mentioned the Balkan Pact,[1] which we had "signed not so long ago," and its connection with NATO. Our position, both political and economic, was not essentially opposed to military blocs, since Yugoslavia was in fact linked with the Western bloc. Marshal Zhukov said they were not in favor of our joining the Eastern bloc, but it was a question of solidarity among Communists. He was clearly urging us to refuse American military aid and to quit the Balkan Pact. If Yugoslavia were to change its policy in that way, it would find itself left in the lurch between the two blocs and on bad terms with both of them.

Neither Marshal Zhukov nor the other Soviet marshals and generals present made any reference at all to the conflict of 1948, because of

[1] The Balkan Pact was concluded between Greece, Turkey, and Yugoslavia in February 1953 and provided for close cooperation between the three countries in political, defense, economic, and cultural matters. With the restoration of normal relations between Yugoslavia and the Soviet Union after 1955 interest in the pact declined and it never developed into an effective alliance.

which Yugoslavia had been obliged to accept American military aid and to join the Balkan Pact.

It was mainly Gošnjak who replied to Marshal Zhukov. I intervened only very occasionally since I have already had plenty of opportunities to discuss these topics with Zhukov. Although we had agreed not to raise the question from our side, Gošnjak was obliged to refer to 1948. We no longer needed American military aid (as Tito had told Khrushchev last June) and it was only a question of agreeing with the United States Government about ending it. Yugoslavia had to make sure that it could buy from others what it needed in the way of arms and military equipment, but it had so far not received any such assurance from anybody.

The Russians appeared to be relieved that they had raised various questions which had previously been referred to only in the course of the quarrel between us. On this occasion it had not resulted in a quarrel and things had been discussed quite normally. It had been made clear where we agreed and where we didn't and what were the reasons. Everybody had stuck to his point of view. And still we parted friends with both sides talking of the need for establishing better relations. I believe this is the principal political significance of the evening and the talks we had at it.

Marshal Zhukov several times used the same arguments and practically the same words as Khrushchev in his talks with me. They had obviously agreed what Marshal Zhukov would say.

Moscow, June 19, 1957

The visit of our State Secretary for Defense continues successfully and the delegation is meeting an ever larger circle of Russian senior officers. Marshal Zhukov has proposed that General Gošnjak should extend his stay in the Soviet Union by two days, on the grounds that from June 22–24 they are going to celebrate the 250th anniversary of Leningrad. We hear that the whole party Presidium is going there. This would involve certain changes in the program so that Khrushchev and Bulganin would be able to receive our military delegation only after the Leningrad celebrations. I advised Belgrade to accept Marshal Zhukov's proposal.

Moscow, June 21, 1957

I gave a reception on June 19, in connection with the visit of our military delegation, for the top Soviet leaders, for Marshal Zhukov and senior officials of the Defense Ministry and for the diplomatic corps in Moscow. I invited all the members of the Presidium and left it to them, on the advice of the Soviet protocol department, to decide which of them would come. I invited the diplomatic corps for political reasons, although there is no strict rule about inviting foreign ambassadors for the visit of a Defense Minister. It seemed to me better to invite my colleagues as well as all the military attachés so that they should see, as far as it was possible, that there was nothing secret on our side about our relations with the Russians. I knew the Russians were not particularly enthusiastic about my inviting the ambassadors and military attachés of Western and other countries. They even let me know that they had expected the evening to include only Soviet and Yugoslav guests. But I could not accept the Russians' advice, because by so doing I would have been supporting their one-sided interpretation of the nature of the visit.

Khrushchev, Bulganin, and Mikoyan came from the Presidium. Then there was Marshal Zhukov and Gromyko as well as the great majority of the Soviet marshals we invited: Koniev, Sokolovsky, Bagramyan, Moskalenko, Yeremenko, Malinovsky, Sudets, Rotmistrov, Budenny, and numerous generals of the Soviet Army. The number of diplomats who accepted was beyond all expectations. All the Western ambassadors, including those from the NATO countries, turned up as well as those from Eastern Europe. There were also representatives of the Arab countries as well as the Asians, Africans, and Latin Americans. We had the impression that the reception went off better than anyone had expected. Our decision to invite the foreign ambassadors and military attachés was proved correct because interest in our delegation's visit is very great.

Unfortunately our embassy building is small and unsuitable for such an occasion. We can use only one medium-size salon and two other rooms, into which we have to find room for all the guests. Consequently we always have a crush at a reception if we invite more than two hundred guests. This time there were more than three hundred and, although it was a very successful affair, the majority of the guests will probably remember it for the terrible crush and difficulty of moving about. Bulganin was cross and gruff, didn't utter a single word, went into the room to which I invited him, and then spent the whole time in the company of Russians, showing no desire to talk to Gošnjak or with the members of our delegation or even with Khrushchev and the other members of the Presidium. I don't know how to explain this. Never since I arrived in Moscow have I found Bulganin in such a bad mood, so lacking in courtesy and ready for a quarrel.

Khrushchev behaved differently, almost cordially. He thanked Comrade Tito for the gift he had sent him (a shotgun). First Mikoyan and then Khrushchev informed me that the Soviet ambassador in Belgrade had just been the guest of Comrade Tito and had been very well received and that they in Moscow were very pleased with his reception and the talks he had had with Comrade Tito on Brioni.

The Russians took advantage of the reception again to put pressure on us with regard to the further stay in Yugoslavia of the American military mission now there. Marshal Malinovsky told a member of our military delegation, General Veljko Kovačević, that the Russians would neither give us nor sell us any military equipment as long as there was an American military mission in Yugoslavia. Malinovsky said this in connection with a discussion about the Soviet T-54 tank, in parts of which our people had shown some interest. The Russians repeated this categorically; I think it was easier for them to do so since they know that the American military mission is leaving Yugoslavia shortly and that the military aid is coming to an end.

The Russians now want to speed things up and to create the impression that it has come about under pressure from them. But such behavior on the part of the Russians only makes it more difficult for us to agree with the United States Government about resolving this question together. We think that the rejection of American military aid should not come about as a result of a unilateral decision by the Yugoslav Government. But that is what the Russians are actually pushing us into and what we must certainly avoid. If we were to act in the way the Russians are demanding, it would mean rejecting American military aid at the cost of switching to Soviet military aid, which is out of the question.

Moscow, June 25, 1957

I had a talk a few days ago with Gromyko about the latest death sentences passed in Hungary and the campaign which has started up in this connection in some countries of the West against both Hungary and the Soviet Union. I had not received any instructions from my government to discuss this with the Soviet minister, but Gromyko apparently assumed that I had, as though people can't talk about anything, especially when it's a question of an ambassador and a Foreign Minister, unless they do it on instructions from the governments they represent.

With the qualification that I had not got all the necessary facts, I told Gromyko that it seemed to me politically mistaken and lacking in humanity to start up again with death sentences in Hungary which was only just setting out on the road to political stability. The campaign waged against Hungary from abroad had started to die down. But now two Hungarian writers had been condemned to death, according to what I had read recently in *Le Monde*. Western public opinion was again being roused. The people concerned about this question were not, in my view, simply reactionary cold-war elements in Western countries. It wasn't a matter simply of a campaign against Hungary which was being revived but of whether these people ought in any case to be condemned to death and whether such sentences did anything to bring order into the situation in Hungary or the reverse. The answer, I thought, was clear!

Gromyko reacted as though he were giving an official reply to a question in Parliament or some similar gathering, saying: "It is a matter for the Hungarians themselves"—he did not wish to interfere in their internal affairs.

I had not expected to receive such an official and "correct" reply. I told him that it was certainly a matter which was primarily of interest to Hungary, but that it interested me and other friends of Hungary, although I didn't want to interfere in the "internal affairs" of Hungary or any other country. I thought that it wasn't a matter of indifference to Hungary's friends whether some Hungarian problem which had foreign political consequences was resolved in one way or another, though the Hungarians would certainly know best what to do.

Moscow, June 26, 1957

Gošnjak has invited Marshal Zhukov to visit Yugoslavia. Zhukov appears to have counted on this and accepted the invitation at once with pleasure, saying that he would be able to stay with us about eight days, and mentioned September as the time which would suit him. He later suggested that we might invite Khrushchev as well at the same time. To judge by the readiness with which he accepted the invitation and went into the details of his stay in Yugoslavia, and especially his suggestion that we invite Khrushchev as well, it is reasonable to conclude that Marshal Zhukov had agreed about all this in advance with Khrushchev.

Khrushchev and Bulganin received Gošnjak and me yesterday at three in the afternoon. Just before we left for the meeting we were informed by the Soviet side that there would also be journalists and photographers present, which we had not counted on. The room in the Kremlin looked as though it had been specially prepared for formal talks between the two delegations. Apart from Khrushchev and Bulganin there were Marshals Zhukov, Koniev, and Sokolovsky, General Antonov, and Ambassador Firyubin. No talks in fact took place.

Bulganin did not say a word throughout the proceedings. When he realized that such behavior on his part was attracting attention, Bulganin told me that he was not feeling well, unbuttoned his jacket, and showed me that he was covered in perspiration. But his behavior was quite different from what it was at our reception when he had also been indisposed but was ready for a row with us. Last night he was also in a bad mood, but his silence did not suggest a readiness to quarrel; he was noticeably withdrawn.

After the "talks," which lasted no more than fifteen minutes, we sat down to a lunch at which the atmosphere was very good. This was mainly due to Khrushchev, who was in a very good mood and had a similarly cheering effect on most of us. He proposed two or three toasts as in the "good old days." After lunch Firyubin told me confidentially and, as he said, "in secret" that he believed that our government's request for military supplies would be dealt with favorably on their side and that we should not delay with our official approach to the Soviet Government. It had obviously been agreed by the Soviet leaders that he should tell me this. It was apparent that the Russians, especially Khrushchev and Marshal Zhukov, were pleased with this meeting.

Moscow, June 27, 1957

Our military delegation left for Yugoslavia on June 26. We and the Russians regard the visit as having been very successful. It might be said that on this occasion Marshal Zhukov took over Gromyko's role as Soviet Foreign Minister and played it very well. The Russians did everything they could in terms of official honors and treated it like a visit by a head of government. By so doing they achieved the maximum in the way of building up a friendly atmosphere and have not committed themselves to anything at all.

Moscow, June 30, 1957

We have learned from the Soviet press that neither Khrushchev nor Bulganin nor any member of the Soviet Presidium went to the celebrations in Leningrad, although it was explicitly because of that that Marshal Zhukov asked us to postpone the departure of our military delegation for two days. Khrushchev received us on June 24 in the Kremlin along with Bulganin and gave a dinner in our honor. Khrushchev was in a very good mood, but Bulganin seemed very worried and complained of being ill. During the conversation I asked Khrushchev about the celebrations in Leningrad and he replied that they had thought of going there in the first place, but they had had to abandon the idea and send A. A. Andreyev,[2] an old member of the party Central Committee, to represent them. I didn't talk about it further to Khrushchev, although his reply was not particularly convincing in view of the fact that members of the Presidium usually go to much less important celebrations than the one in Leningrad. It is clear that the members of the Presidium were prevented

[2] Andrei A. Andreyev, 1895–1971. Soviet Communist official. Member of Politburo, CPSU, 1932–52.

from taking part in the celebrations by some important matter, and that there was no real need for us to extend the visit of our military delegation.

Moscow, July 1, 1957

In the course of a recent speech about the progress of Soviet agriculture Khrushchev launched the slogan "to catch up with and overtake America in the production of meat, milk, and butter per head of the population." Agriculture is one of the weakest points in the Soviet economy, although it is the branch with which Khrushchev is mostly concerned and about which he most frequently speaks in public. He is probably right when he talks about the colossal resources and reserves which Soviet agriculture has at its disposal. Apart from natural resources, however, there is a need for human resources, which in the Soviet Union means the state, to put those favorable natural conditions to use.

I believe that the Russians produce something between 6 and 7 million tons of meat a year, while the Americans produce around 19 or 20 million tons. A difference like that cannot be wiped out in the course of three or four years, as Khrushchev suggested. I have already heard a good deal of criticism not only from foreigners but also from Russians about this claim.

As for the production of milk, Khrushchev was even more impatient, or more unrealistic, and suggested that the Soviet Union should "catch up and overtake America" already next year. This would mean that in such a short period the Soviet Union would have to increase the production of milk by about 20 million tons, which is the amount by which it lags behind America—and this seems to me impossible. When this is put to people in Gosplan, they do not want to comment or else they look very uncomfortable.

I believe that it is not just a question of "catching up with and overtaking America" in the quantity of this or that article produced, although the actual production is of course a major factor. At the same time they need to solve all the other problems connected with the regular supply of goods to the people, not just in Moscow and the other big centers but throughout the country. We have come across students and their professors in Moscow, for example, who buy up sugar here and take with them enough to cover a whole excursion down the Volga all the way to Astrakhan, because they are not sure of finding any sugar on the way, although they pass through several large Soviet cities! Moscow has absolute priority in the supply of goods, because it is a sort of permanent Soviet shop window for the world. But neither Moscow nor the rest of Russia has any trade in the proper sense of the word, but something more like government centers for the distribution of specific articles of which there are usually not enough and which are mostly exactly the same in all these shops or distribution centers. There is no choice of styles and qualities. The purchaser is usually offered one kind of article in just one version, and it's a case of "take it or leave it." When they talk about "catching up with and overtaking America," all this and a lot more besides has to be considered.

The worst of it is that Khrushchev has not simply said this in a speech; it has been formally declared to be the task of the party and the government. I don't know what consequences this may have, but I believe the fact that such an aim cannot be achieved is apparent to the majority of people. Russia is drawing close to America in, for example, the production of steel. Perhaps it would have been better to take this or some similar article as a matter for competition with America, but not meat and milk, in which America is far ahead of the Soviet Union. The Americans have the highest income per head of the population in the world, while the Soviet Union is still among the countries with a medium national income and will surely remain so for a long time to come.

I also think it is dangerous for Khrushchev to set precise dates by which the building of socialism is to be completed in the Soviet Union and the building of communism is to begin, how long that is going to last, and when—in which year—we can expect the building of communism to be completed. This is even more questionable and unrealistic than the speed at which the Russians are supposed to catch up with and overtake America in the production of the basic products of agriculture. It is not in the least surprising that America is far ahead of Russia in the production and consumption of the greatest numbers of goods. America is ahead of many other countries in this respect and in some products it produces alone as much as the rest of the world. It is all explicable, and the explanation does not discredit the Soviet Union, when you bear in mind the historical conditions in which the two countries existed in the past. There are surely other ways in which the Soviet Union is ahead of America, as for example in such things as the distribution of wealth, the rate of growth of its industrial production, the social and health services provided for the population, the country's natural resources, and so forth.

This race to "catch up and overtake America" does not seem to me to be a happy idea at all. I would like to talk to Khrushchev about it, even though it is hardly practicable, because it will result in unnecessary disputes, and we have enough and more of our own Yugoslav disputes with the Russians already.

CHAPTER TWENTY-ONE

SETTLING ACCOUNTS IN THE KREMLIN

Khrushchev defeats an attempted coup by Molotov and Malenkov and, with the backing of Marshal Zhukov, expels the "antiparty group" from the Soviet leadership. He gives Mićunović the inside story of how he brought off his victory.

Moscow, July 3, 1957

I was summoned today by Patolichev, one of Gromyko's deputies, to the Soviet Foreign Ministry, where I found gathered the diplomatic representatives of the countries of the "socialist camp." They were already sitting in their places as though the conference was going to last some time. In a half-hour statement Patolichev informed us of the decisions taken at a special plenary meeting of the Central Committee. The majority of the ambassadors spent the whole of the conference busily taking notes and looked to me rather like shorthand reporters. Patolichev informed us that on July 2 everything that he was going to tell us had been communicated to the governments of our countries, but that he had been given the task of informing us here so that we should hear what had happened from an official source in Moscow. Patolichev first read from a text and then spoke without notes at some length. Here is what he said:

The plenum of the Central Committee of the CPSU had not been a regular meeting called by the competent party authorities but had been summoned on the basis of a written request by a quorum of members of the Central Committee, as laid down in the party rules. This procedure was adopted in abnormal circumstances, and the circumstances had been abnormal because of the antiparty action by the Malenkov-Kaganovich-Molotov group which had been joined by Bulganin, Saburov, and Pervukhin, and at the beginning old Voroshilov as well, and which had thus had a majority in the Presidium.

Patolichev did not tell us what exactly happened at the beginning when the antiparty group had a convincing majority nor how long it lasted, but turned immediately to the plenum of the Central Committee at which he said 216 members had asked to speak and about 60 of them had actually taken the floor. The remainder had not been able to speak because there had not been enough time and they had made their contributions in written form. The plenum had been unanimous in its condemnation of the M-K-M antiparty group "which had been preparing a plot" against the general policy of the party and state. Members of the group had spoken three times during the plenum, apart from some brief interventions. They had had complete freedom in this respect.

Apart from being expelled from the Presidium and the Central Committee, Malenkov, Kaganovich, and Molotov had also been removed from their positions as Deputy Prime Ministers. All those who had so far been candidate members of the Presidium had been promoted to full membership, with the exception of Shepilov, who had joined the antiparty group and had been expelled from the Central Committee. The party secretaries in Gorky, Stalingrad, and Byelorussia, as well as the existing secretaries of the Central Committee, Belyaev,[1] Pospelov, and Aristov,[2] had been similarly promoted.

Bulganin, Prime Minister and a member of the Presidium, had been punished by a reprimand with a final warning, but remained a member of the Presidium. Patolichev gave us to understand that this decision was partly the result of the fact that Bulganin was Soviet Prime Minister and that had he not been, he too would have been expelled from the Presidium. I took it that Bulganin remains there only on sufferance and that it is only a matter of time before he will lose his party and government positions in the Soviet leadership. Maksim Saburov has been expelled from the Presidium but remains a member of the Central Committee. Pervukhin's punishment is to be reduced from full to candidate membership of the Presidium. The party's reprimand to Bulganin will not be announced because of his position as Soviet Prime Minister. Patolichev begged us to treat this as confidential, but I doubt whether it will remain so now that it has been passed on to fifteen people from ten countries. It simply means it won't appear in the press.

What Patolichev said appeared to me as the greatest surprise to the majority present. A deathly silence reigned. Nobody had any questions to ask. It seemed to me that the complete silence on the part of the fifteen of us was not right and that it might even seem as though we had some reservations about what Patolichev had told us. Since he seemed to be wait-

[1] Nikolai I. Belyaev, 1902–66. Secretary, Central Committee, CPSU, 1955; Member of Presidium, 1957.
[2] Averki B. Aristov, 1903–73. Secretary, Central Committee, CPSU, 1955–60; Member of Presidium, 1961; Ambassador to Poland, 1961–66.

ing for something, I asked to say a few words. I wished the Soviet party and government the greatest success in their further political work. I said no more than this one sentence. After me the Polish ambassador, Gede, spoke and repeated more or less word for word what I had said. Patolichev also told us that the members of the party were taking the decisions of the Central Committee well and that party meetings at which the decisions were being explained were taking place throughout the Soviet Union.

Moscow, July 4, 1957

Foreigners in Moscow are making every effort to get in contact with us, on the assumption that we are better informed about affairs than we are in fact, because Khrushchev, Bulganin, Mikoyan, Zhukov, the Soviet marshals and generals, Gromyko and others had been at our reception on June 19 and stayed there nearly two hours, and we had been talking to them without any other foreigners being present. They probably think we were talking about the Central Committee plenum and what was happening in the Kremlin.

We were later received by Khrushchev and Bulganin in the Kremlin on June 24 and spent about two hours with them, and it was then, between our reception and the one the Russians gave, that this truly historical plenum of the Central Committee was held. This has increased still further the foreigners' conviction that we were informed about what was going on, because the Soviet press made a point of reporting our meetings with Khrushchev and the others. Many ambassadors will certainly not believe that I don't know much more than has appeared in the papers.

In the light of the events which have now been revealed we have tried, here in the embassy, to reconstruct every detail of the behavior of Khrushchev, Bulganin, and the others when they came to us on June 19 and when we met them again in the Kremlin. We had no difficulty now in explaining Bulganin's behavior, which struck us all, first because of his gruffness and lack of interest in our military delegation and also because he seemed so apathetic and depressed to the point of illness.

On June 19 Khrushchev seemed to be almost his usual self, although there had been something different about him too. It is only now clear to us, for example, why on that day he did not talk to a single foreign ambassador in the way we have become accustomed to. The ambassadors were in one room, while Khrushchev and the most important Soviet guests were in another room ten paces away. As for his general disposition, Khrushchev tried to be in as good a mood as possible although he did not always succeed. It is now clear to us that on that day Khrushchev was in a minority at a meeting of the Presidium and that he had to make a great effort not to let us know what was going on. In the course of some two hours he did not exchange a single word with Bulganin, for the first time since I arrived in Moscow.

If it is possible now to draw any conclusions, we can do it only on the basis of what Patolichev told us yesterday in the Foreign Ministry and what the Soviet press has written in the last two days. It is certainly significant that Patolichev announced Bulganin's punishment to some fifteen foreign diplomats from Eastern Europe and Yugoslavia. We learn that it is also being announced at the party meetings, which are attended by thousands of people. So it is easy to imagine what sort of a situation the present Soviet Prime Minister is in.

The problem of replacing Bulganin is very complicated. His removal, in addition to Molotov, Malenkov, Kaganovich, Shepilov, Saburov, and Pervukhin, would be too much for the Soviet Union and for Khrushchev personally. It would make it more difficult to get through the present crisis. I believe it is only for that reason that Bulganin remains and that this is only a temporary solution. It is not possible for him to remain long in the post he now occupies.

By joining the "antiparty group" Bulganin has seriously upset and angered Khrushchev, who proposed him for Prime Minister when Malenkov was removed. Bulganin turned out to be politically quite unequal to the position. He hasn't shown himself to be any better as far as moral qualities are concerned; he has betrayed Khrushchev with whom he has been a political friend for decades. If Malenkov had succeeded in his attempted coup, because that's what it really was, I don't believe Bulganin would have remained in power but would have lost his position in a very short time.

As for who is to replace him there is at the moment not much of a choice, if you don't count Khrushchev himself. Although the new Presidium has been increased in membership to fifteen, we can now see the extent to which Stalin destroyed people of ability and training and kept new people out of the Soviet leadership. Apart from Khrushchev, Marshal Zhukov, and up to a point Mikoyan, it seems to me that there is nobody who could take over easily the post of Prime Minister. Marshal Zhukov is a military man and has never been concerned with the administration or the economy, and apart from that it would not be a good idea from the point of view of foreign reaction to make Marshal Zhukov Prime Minister. Mikoyan is an Armenian, and since Stalin, it is out of the question to have a non-Russian at the head of the Soviet Union. Khrushchev is First Secretary of the party, and surely they will not again unite these two top positions? However that may be, I believe Bulganin's removal is only a matter of time.

I think that the most difficult question for the Soviet Union will be that of Molotov. That is why he has been put in the third place, although in my opinion Molotov is the real leader of the group and not Malenkov, who was half liquidated already in 1955 when he was removed from the post of Prime Minister. Malenkov succeeded nevertheless in preserving a certain popularity among the peasantry and a part of the urban population. The people remember that "it was better under Malenkov," since it would have been better for them under anybody else after Stalin.

Kaganovich means practically nothing at all, although he has been put second in alphabetical order before Molotov. His name may mean something to the most backward part of the Soviet population, primarily because he was at Stalin's side in the Soviet leadership for thirty years. There are stories about how Kaganovich is "beyond space and time" when a political speech has to be made or when one talks to him about anything. I don't say that he has become senile; indeed he does not look old physically, he looks very fit and is even said to go skiing regularly near Moscow. They now talk about a list of more than a hundred railwaymen which Kaganovich sent to Stalin with the explicit demand that they be executed. His request was not only satisfied: For this and similar acts he was held up as a model "Bolshevik."

In any case I think it will be easier to expose the antiparty group in view of the fact that Kaganovich was in it.

But it is a different matter with Molotov. He is a name and practically a legend for the party and the Soviet public. He is one of the few surviving Soviet leaders about whom there are documents to show that he was active in Lenin's day and under Lenin's leadership. Later he was in the Soviet leadership and for three decades was Stalin's right-hand man. The course of events following the Twentieth Congress seemed to show that Molotov was right and that some of his pessimistic forecasts had come true. The crisis of foreign policy in the "camp" and the setbacks which the Soviet Union suffered last year, especially the changes in Poland and the events in Hungary and the renewed conflict with Yugoslavia, strengthened Molotov's position. It might even be said that Khrushchev was forced to make concessions to Molotov after Hungary.

The arrangement of the names in this order—Malenkov, Kaganovich, and finally Molotov—is in my opinion Khrushchev's way of suggesting that Malenkov was the leader of the group and is also a sort of argument against Molotov, who allowed himself to be led by Malenkov and a person like Kaganovich. Molotov will not only be the most difficult for the new Soviet leadership and Khrushchev to deal with; he is the most stubborn of the lot. He was after all, according to the official version, the only one who refused to vote in favor of the plenum's decisions, while all the others indulged in "self-criticism," as is the custom here.

It looks as though one of the things which may have united Molotov and Malenkov, who are known to be friends or close colleagues, was in fact their unwillingness to tolerate Khrushchev as leader of the party or of the Soviet state. Molotov and Malenkov did not agree with Khrushchev's ideas, nor could they put up with him personally. And this all goes back far into the past and came to light only after Stalin's death: through the removal of Malenkov first from the post of First Secretary of the party in 1953 and then from the post of Prime Minister in 1955. I believe that it was their objection to Khrushchev as Soviet leader, and not just a difference of views that brought Malenkov and Molotov together to achieve a common aim: the overthrow of Khrushchev.

As far as I have been able to observe them and talk with them since I have been in Moscow, Malenkov managed to conceal his intolerance of Khrushchev better than Molotov. Even now I can recall last year's May Day lunch in the Kremlin, when Khrushchev as host proposed ten toasts or more, while Molotov sat for many hours at the table, mostly in silence and apparently finding it all very difficult to bear.

In my view the Soviet public is more surprised by Bulganin's conduct than by the M-K-M group. Khrushchev had been in conflict with all three of them in the past to some extent or other, but he had never quarreled with Bulganin.

Moscow, July 5, 1957

Our embassy is continuing to study the results of the recent specially summoned plenum of the Central Committee of the CPSU which frustrated an attempt by a group of Soviet political leaders to remove the leadership of the country from power illegally and put their own people in its place. The Molotov-Kaganovich-Malenkov group tried to do this in the Soviet Union according to the rules by which putsches are carried out in other countries, though adapted to Soviet conditions. Here they don't call it by its proper name—an attempted coup d'état—but the action of an "antiparty group," as though it is impossible to have anything like coups d'état or putsches in the Soviet Union or under socialism.

In my opinion there have already been in the Soviet Union, in the three or four years since Stalin died, two coups d'état of a kind and now this third attempted coup, which is the most far-reaching. The organizer of the first two putsches was, I believe, Khrushchev himself. The first one was in 1953 when, by means of a conspiracy among a very small circle in the Kremlin, Beria was taken by surprise and liquidated along with his closest collaborators. The second, bloodless coup was also carried out by Khrushchev when he removed Malenkov from the post of Prime Minister. That was in 1955. It was characteristic of these two coups that, among other things, they were both organized at the very summit of the Soviet system in the Presidium of the Central Committee by its First Secretary, who was thus able to present the Soviet Communist party and the country as a whole with an accomplished fact.

Now the others, Malenkov, Kaganovich, and Molotov, have tried to carry through an even bigger coup, this time against Khrushchev himself, the legally elected first leader of the party. This third putsch was also organized, like the two which preceded it, among a small number of top leaders. Not even all the members of the Presidium knew about it, since it was a conspiracy by one group against another. The plotters intended simply to inform the Central Committee and the Soviet Government about what had already been decided by the putsch, while the people of Russia would not be told anything very much about it, as was the case on the first two occasions. A major role in their defeat was played by the loyalty of the Soviet Army and Marshal Zhukov to the policy represented by Khrushchev. But what stands out most in this clash is the dynamic, courageous, and politically gifted personality of Khrushchev himself, whose popularity with the people has been increasing in recent months.

In some places the M-K-M group are still called "comrades," but only rarely. They are more often called fractionalists and an antiparty group. As time passes I think these latter labels will predominate. Such is the logic of political battles in Soviet society and under socialism in general from what we know about it so far.

No exceptional security measures appear to have been taken in Moscow. There are rather fewer people on the streets than usual. People tend to gather around the bulletin boards where newspapers are displayed, but only read them without comment. In the queues outside the shops people talk about everything except the most important news. We have carried out a sort of "opinion poll." A taxi driver said: "Russia is finished—they're fighting for power at the top." "Molotov is an old Bolshevik." An old woman said resignedly: "The same as it ever was!" A man in the street: "Malenkov is liked by the people." Another one said: "Who knows who's right and who's wrong? In Russia the people never know." People do not appear to believe the official explanation of the affair. I think this is the result of many long years during which they kept on giving the people false reasons for getting rid of political leaders in the time of the "purges." That is why people here long ago lost faith in official statements "from above."

Western diplomats are behaving as though they knew nothing before the announcement was made. Perhaps most of them really knew nothing, like us. The East European diplomats are very worried. They are afraid that this isn't the end of the affair, but only the beginning of a settling of accounts with the Stalinists. It may spread to their countries, where there are still many Stalinists in top positions in the party and government. Some European journalists, when they are somewhere where they dare speak, are saying: Now we should recall Tito's Pula speech. And we have even heard some Russians say: Now it can be seen whether there were Stalinists among our leaders, as Tito said, or not, as our people claimed.

* * *

The American reception on July 4 was the first occasion for the political elite of Moscow to get together since the stormy events and the liquidation of the Malenkov-Kaganovich-Molotov group and of "Shepilov who joined them"—as the Moscow press invariably describes him. It is as though Shepilov now has a new first name. The Russians observe this rule so strictly that it is simply impossible for his name to be mentioned in the press without it being preceded by "who joined them." The Russians themselves are now calling Shepilov "the man with the longest first name in Russia."

The Moscow diplomatic corps attended the Americans' party in full strength. The Soviet guests were very carefully selected. Of the top leaders Mikoyan, Shvernik, and Gromyko appeared at the reception. Khrushchev did not come. There was nobody from among the well-known Soviet military leaders, apart from some people from the department dealing with foreign military missions. Mikoyan is one of the few members of the old Presidium who has managed not only to "survive" (as always until now) but also to appear at the American reception. The choice of Shvernik seemed to be a good one for the occasion since he is so uncommunicative and foreigners tried in vain to draw him into a political discussion.

I spoke at length with Mikoyan who was himself eager to talk. He said that the members of the antiparty group had themselves chosen the moment to provoke a crisis and go over to the offensive. They had probably come to the conclusion that they could wait no longer since time was not on their side. When, under the guise of an attack on Khrushchev, they openly attacked the general line of the party, the other part of the Presidium demanded a meeting of the Central Committee as the only body competent to resolve the dispute. Mikoyan said that it was Bulganin who caused Saburov and Pervukhin to waver. If Bulganin had not been won over by Malenkov, the other two would have remained with the party.

I asked Mikoyan what led Shepilov to join the group. He said it was not the first time Shepilov had been at odds with the party. Even in 1955 after they returned from Yugoslavia Shepilov had said that the Yugoslav views were pure Menshevism. Later he had disagreed with the current plan for reorganizing the economy. He regarded his functions in the government as his own private preserve and treated diplomatic notes and speeches as his own "works," having them published at government expense as his own pamphlets. I commented that it had seemed to us that Shepilov had risen too quickly, from being the editor of a newspaper to becoming overnight a secretary of the Central Committee and then Soviet Foreign Minister. Mikoyan said that was one of the reasons for his fall.

I said, on my behalf since I still had no instructions from Belgrade, that I thought it very good that the Central Committee had presented the affair to the Soviet public and the world at large as a purely political question. I thought that this was the best and most convincing way to do it.

The foreigners saw that I was having a long conversation alone with Mikoyan and did not approach us. But afterward they crowded round me, though I directed them to Mikoyan, who was still at the reception. I made some favorable comments, especially about the foreign political aspects of the Soviet statement, saying that all the rest was the Soviet Union's internal affair. A considerable number of the Western diplomats pointed out that we had now come to the end of "collective leadership" because there was no longer a balance of forces or rather of one man. The Western diplomats behaved as though they still knew nothing about Bulganin, which one cannot of course believe.

Moscow, July 6, 1957

Late last night I sent a letter to Comrade Tito about my conversation with Khrushchev concerning the stormy events which took place in Moscow between June 17 and 29:

Moscow July 5, 1957

Dear Comrade Tito,

I am sending you this letter with an account of the conversation I had with N. S. Khrushchev on July 5, 1957.

I asked to be received on July 4 in the evening, and Khrushchev received me on July 5 at midday in the Central Committee building.

In view of the fact that Khrushchev is exceptionally busy because of all that has been happening I was prepared for the meeting to last only five or ten minutes. In fact Khrushchev kept me in conversation for an hour and a half. He was very frank, adopted a friendly and cordial manner, and in the course of an hour-long statement he acquainted me with the course of events and with the battle in the Presidium of the Central Committee and later in the Central Committee session, which lasted from June 17 to 29 and ended with the complete defeat and liquidation of the powerful Stalinist group of Molotov, Malenkov, and Kaganovich.

In this letter I will set out for you as precisely as possible the course of my conversation with N. S. Khrushchev, so as to acquaint you with the facts as Khrushchev presented them to me and with everything that was mentioned in the course of the conversation.

Even as I greeted him I congratulated Khrushchev on the important historic victory of their party and the principles of Marxism-Leninism, and wished the greatest success to the Soviet Union and to Khrushchev personally. I thanked him for receiving me and then read him the text of your message. Khrushchev listened seriously, expressed his thanks, spoke of his satisfaction that you had understood them correctly and had adopted such an attitude to the decisions of the Central Committee, declared that they would continue to do their utmost to build communism, and asked me to convey to you his cordial greetings.

Khrushchev then said he did not know whether Firyubin had informed you about the plenum, though he had been instructed to do so. Then Khrushchev gave me the following details.

He said that even during his stay in Finland he had felt that there was something wrong with Bulganin. Bulganin's behavior toward him was unusual and there was a feeling of intolerance as sometimes happens between people. Khrushchev did not attach any special importance to this. He assumed that it was because Khrushchev had often criticized him. When they returned from Finland to Moscow, the affair began to develop. One afternoon Bulganin phoned him to say that the Presidium of the Central Committee must be called together urgently. Khrushchev was at home, but Bulganin was in the Kremlin, where there is a dining room for members of the Central Committee so that they can lunch there between 1 and 2 P.M. when they have things to do immediately after the lunch break. Khrushchev's reply to Bulganin was that he had summoned the regular meeting of the Presidium and that he saw no reason for calling one on June 18. Bulganin replied "we demand" and so forth. Khrushchev asked him who are "we." Bulganin replied: "a group which is here having lunch." Khrushchev replied that according to the party rules and the practice of the Presidium there was no "lunching group in the Central Committee" and that the meeting should take place as arranged. Bulganin became even more categoric in his demands, at which Khrushchev replied that he would come from his home to the Kremlin dining room and lunch there so that they could talk things over.

There Khrushchev found: Bulganin, Voroshilov, Molotov, Malenkov, Kaganovich, Pervukhin, and Mikoyan; that is, the whole Presidium. Suslov was not in Moscow but on his annual holiday, Saburov was in Warsaw at a meeting of Comecon, and Kirichenko was in the Ukraine. Khrushchev continued the discussion which Bulganin had started on the telephone—and the clash of views immediately became sharper. Malenkov, Molotov, Pervukhin, and Voroshilov demanded a meeting of the Presidium. Khrushchev tried to explain that there could not be a meeting that day because the Presidium had decided that Khrushchev should receive a delegation of Hungarian journalists, after which he had to give an interview to a Japanese journalist, that it had all been agreed and they would have to wait till the next day. They refused, and everybody except Mikoyan began to attack Khrushchev: Why should he receive the Hungarians alone, they would all go. Khrushchev said that they could all go if the Presidium so decided but that he thought it was abnormal that the whole Presidium should receive a single journalists' delegation. This didn't help; they had made up their minds and, in fact, they all went, including the candidate members of the Presidium.

Even during this first conversation the atmosphere became extremely strained. It was actually an explosion and an attack which had been long in preparation. Khrushchev was alone, except for Mikoyan (and my impression is that at this point Mikoyan was passive and neutral). Even then, on June 18, the Stalinists put forward their first demand: that Khrushchev should not preside over the meeting of the Presidium which they demanded. Khrushchev tried to resist this demand by referring to earlier proposals of his: In fact, he had previously proposed that they should all preside in turn, but they had rejected this at the time and had laid it down that he, Khrushchev, should preside. Now they wanted to get rid of him and for that reason were going back on their own decisions. Khrushchev's resistance was not successful. Malenkov or Molotov proposed that Bulganin should conduct the meeting, which was to lead to the victory of the Stalinists, according to their plans. Khrushchev was forced to give in, and Bulganin presided. Khrushchev succeeded only in getting it agreed that they should summon Saburov, Suslov, and Kirichenko to the meeting. Khrushchev hoped that those three would correct the balance of forces in the Presidium, and in addition he wanted to gain time in the face of a bitter attack by a majority which had planned the affair so that it would all be played out and finished in the Presidium, where a resolution would be passed and everything would be imposed on the party and the country.

The majority agreed to send for the three people mentioned. Suslov and Kirichenko came out firmly in support of Khrushchev, but Saburov, unfortunately, made it clear that he had already been won over before his departure for Warsaw, so that he backed the majority in the Presidium.

The Stalinists' demands were aimed at liquidating Khrushchev. This was in fact a device for taking over power in the party and the country as a whole. At the outset they did not put forward any political program but aimed by tactical moves to settle accounts with Khrushchev as quickly as possible over minor questions, because that was easier. They succeeded in putting Bulganin to preside over the meeting, and that was already a great deal.

Their charges against Khrushchev amounted roughly to the following:

Under Khrushchev's leadership there is no unity either in the Presidium or in the party and this must be changed: Why does Khrushchev himself do as he pleases—traveling around the Soviet Union, interfering in everything, and conducting foreign policy? Tomorrow they are supposed to go all together to the Leningrad celebrations, and it had been decided that Khrushchev should speak. That ought to be changed; others should speak.

They raised the question of restricting Khrushchev's freedom of speech at the Leningrad gatherings. Khrushchev imposes his will on the majority. This should be condemned and a resolution passed in the Presidium.

The whole affair became steadily wider in scope and more violent in tone. The Stalinists raised the question of the Ministry of Internal Affairs and the removal of Serov[3] and accused Khrushchev of having members of the Presidium "bugged." They also attacked Khrushchev's campaign aimed at "catching up and overtaking America" in the production of milk, meat, and butter. They criticized Khrushchev for forcing himself on foreign delegations, and so forth.

Khrushchev put up a stubborn defense from the outset. In fact, although he was in the minority, Khrushchev was the one who did the attacking and from the start told them who's who, what's what, and where they are going. When Malenkov raised the question of the trip to Leningrad, Khrushchev says he told Malenkov that perhaps he had better not go there. He had good reason to fear going to Leningrad, since he was smothered in the innocent blood of the Leningrad Communists he had killed. He, Malenkov, was directly to blame for the shooting of Kuznetsov, and Malenkov had strangled Voznesensky. "You have reason to be afraid to go there; the Petrograd workers may ask you about it," Khrushchev told Malenkov. The latter began to make a scene: This is scandalous—do you hear what he says, comrades? —and so forth. Khrushchev said something similar about Molotov.

Khrushchev's basic tactical idea was: "The Presidium cannot pass any resolutions about anything. Let us go to the Central Committee," where everything would be settled. Khrushchev kept up his resistance and pursued his tactical ploy so as to gain time and mobilize the Central Committee. One example of Khrushchev's successful tactics: He was basically opposed to any idea of putting a resolution to the Presidium because that would have meant defeat for him. At the same time, so as to gain time, he agreed to the setting up of a commission to draw up the text of a resolution for the Presidium. They discussed and fought over the question of the commission for a long time. The Stalinists proposed Molotov, among others, as the leader of their group, "and Khrushchev can lead the other one." But he was against this and said: "If Molotov and I are going to be in the same commission, I can tell you no draft resolution can come out of it." They agreed with him and then fought over other members of the commission. Khrushchev took part in this, although, as he himself explained to me, there was no point in any of it. There could not be any resolution: It was simply that Khrushchev wanted to drag the affair on so as to gain an hour or a day more to prepare the Central Committee.

Another example of Khrushchev's tactics: The day after the row in the Presidium there arrived a group of twenty members of the Central Committee from Moscow led by Marshal Koniev and, I believe, Ignatov, secretary of the Gorky regional committee. They demanded to be present at

[3] General Ivan A. Serov, b. 1905. On staff of Soviet Ministry of Internal Affairs, 1946–54; Chairman, KGB (secret police), 1954–58.

the session of the Presidium. The group waited outside the door, while the Stalinist majority in the Presidium attacked Khrushchev, saying that it was putting pressure on them, that it was splitting the party, and so on. Old Voroshilov, who was with the Stalinists, said excitedly: "You can even bring up the tanks." To which Marshal Zhukov, who was present as a candidate member of the Presidium, said that that had nothing to do with the matter, that tanks moved on his, Zhukov's, instructions, and that there were members of the Central Committee and not tanks at the doors! (The sessions of the Presidium, which lasted from morning till evening, were attended also by the candidate members.)

Khrushchev said to Malenkov and the others: "There you have your very own Central Committee, yet you are afraid to face its members." He then reminded them of an old practice in the leadership, even under Stalin until the mass executions started, that every member of the Central Committee had the right to attend meetings of the Politburo without asking anyone for permission. Khrushchev said that he had often made use of this practice when he was secretary of the city committee in Moscow, yet the Stalinists were now refusing to admit twenty members who wanted to be present. Nevertheless the majority did not yield. Instead of letting in the group of twenty who, it was easy for them to guess, were all opposed to them, the Stalinists decided to appoint somebody from the Presidium to go out and "explain" to them what was going on. The majority chose Bulganin. Khrushchev would not agree, demanded and persuaded them that he should go out, too. According to Khrushchev, Bulganin muttered a few sentences which did not satisfy the members of the Central Committee and then Khrushchev himself spoke. The whole business worked out greatly to Khrushchev's advantage, because his argument was that the full Central Committee was the only competent body, and so forth.

And so it went on. Another group of thirty members of the Central Committee arrived and demanded the same as the first one. After that the Presidium, which was then meeting for the fourth day, received a written request from eighty-three members of the Central Committee who no longer demanded that the Presidium should receive them but that the Presidium should go to them in the Sverdlov hall of the Kremlin and explain what was going on, because the full committee was the only body authorized to take decisions. At that point Khrushchev was already in sight of victory. But the Stalinists' morale was still high. When the affair took this turn, they started to prepare to fight for a majority at the Central Committee plenum.

There the Stalinists found a completely different atmosphere. Instead of continuing with their accusations against Khrushchev, the plenum turned the tables and demanded that the Stalinists should speak and explain what they were cooking up and what they wanted. Molotov, Malenkov, Kaganovich, and Shepilov spoke. They were faced by an angry plenum and they found themselves in the position of an insignificant minority: the situation had changed fundamentally. More than 60 members of the

Committee spoke and another 150 put their names down to speak, and there was a demand for the whole group to be expelled from the party and to be tried.

Khrushchev took complete command of the plenum. From what he told me it is apparent that he displayed, in my opinion, extraordinary political and tactical skill. He was worried about how to save old Voroshilov. The plenum was already demanding that Voroshilov should explain his position and then they would have included him among the Stalinists, because in the Presidium Voroshilov had sided with them. Khrushchev used his influence with Voroshilov, made it easier for him in the plenum, so that Voroshilov split away from them and made a satisfactory speech. (Khrushchev had spoken in his favor before he spoke to the plenum; he said Voroshilov was an old wolf, the others had dragged him into the mud, but had realized what had happened, backed out, and got away.) In the same sense and, in my opinion, objectively and rightly he said of Voroshilov that he is an "old man," that he does nothing and is capable of nothing but thinks he's still a young Communist; he didn't know himself where they were leading him. "What is important is Voroshilov's name; it carries weight, so he had to be dragged out of it," Khrushchev said.

The conversation then turned to the question of Bulganin. Khrushchev is very cross with Bulganin and speaks of him with revulsion. Khrushchev says: He's a fool, he always was and always will be. Khrushchev says he told Bulganin that to his face during the meeting of the Presidium when Khrushchev was still in the minority and while Bulganin was presiding, that he swore at him and told him to bring it up at the plenum as an argument against him, Khrushchev. But after the tables were turned in the plenum Bulganin came up to Khrushchev and asked for his help. Khrushchev told him he should help himself first and only then could Khrushchev help him. Bulganin promised to do so.

But Bulganin's first two speeches were not satisfactory. Then Saburov asked to speak and he brought everything into the open. After that Bulganin spoke again and confirmed what Saburov had said. Saburov made clear the real sense of everything that was happening. It was a question of changing the leadership of the party and then of the government. (Khrushchev said to me: "Bulganin, the fool, didn't realize that they would have got rid of him the next day if they had succeeded.") It had even been decided (by the antiparty group) to give Khrushchev the agricultural ministry as a first, transitional step. Bulganin was to be allowed, as a bribe and a bait, to keep the premiership and to take over the Committee for State Security until a final decision was reached. That was proposed by Saburov, about whom Khrushchev said that he was an honest man but that he had been led astray by Bulganin. Pervukhin, who had also been won over by Bulganin, spoke in similar terms to Saburov, but after him.

That was already the end of the affair. The saving of Voroshilov proved easy and the plenum took it well, because people really value the "old man" and were ready to forgive him. With Bulganin it was more difficult: The plenum demanded his removal and there were some very harsh things said about him. This is now being repeated at meetings of Communists before thousands and thousands of people. At one meeting in Moscow there were 3,500 people. Bulganin spoke, indulged in self-criticism, said he had shown himself to be an idiot, and Khrushchev said that people naturally concluded that "the post of Prime Minister of the Soviet Union is not intended for an idiot." Khrushchev says that at both the plenum and the mass meetings of workers he had to convince people that for Bulganin to remain as Prime Minister was for the time being in the best interests of the Soviet Union, although it was clear to everyone that Bulganin deserved to go.

Khrushchev went on to say that Mikoyan spoke at the plenum for about three hours. The first part of his speech was rather academic, even didactic. This did not please the plenum and there began to be interruptions. Then came the end of the day's session. Khrushchev warned Mikoyan that the atmosphere was different from what it was during the first part of his speech, drew attention to the interruptions but did not ask him what he was going to say or how he would say it. Mikoyan agreed and spoke the next day for an hour and a half. The plenum gave him a very good reception and Khrushchev considers he made a good speech.

Khrushchev gave me a few details about the decline in morale and the cowardice of the Stalinists when they found themselves at the plenum and people began to tell them the truth. Kaganovich and Malenkov excelled in cowardice and baseness. Molotov stood firm—he is a real leader, says Khrushchev. This benefited Malenkov, because of Molotov's prestige, age, and reputation. Otherwise Malenkov had been the most active in the first phase of the struggle in the Presidium. At that time the situation was such that individual members of the Central Committee from Moscow were coming up to Khrushchev and saying: "Don't give in, we'll back you up, don't surrender."

About the strength of the plenum Khrushchev spoke to me in the following terms: "Since Lenin's day there has never been anything like it in the party, neither such a battle nor such unity of everybody against a single group." Khrushchev says he cannot remember anything similar in the course of his party and political career. He is very pleased with the way the decisions of the plenum are being received throughout the country. He says the group did not play any real part in the actual life of the party or the country and that from this point of view there is no loss (here Khrushchev gave Kaganovich as an example). About Shepilov he expressed himself in very harsh terms. Khrushchev admitted at the plenum that he was to blame for the mistake of pushing Shepilov forward: He had thought him to be an honest and capable Communist, but Shepilov had turned out to be unworthy. At the plenum he had made a disgusting speech, and the plenum gave him an especially bitter reception (probably precisely because Shepilov had come to the very top of the Soviet Union in just a year and had now shown what sort of a man he was).

Khrushchev says that after June 29 they had informed all the Communist parties about what had happened. They are now receiving from all sides the most positive reactions. Khrushchev mentioned the French and some of the European parties in the camp. He did not mention the Chinese and I didn't ask him about them.

In the course of Khrushchev's statement I put only a few, very short questions to make it as factual and as clear as possible (and so as not to interrupt him). At the end we had a short discussion. I told Khrushchev roughly the same as I said to Mikoyan yesterday at the Americans. I commented favorably on the foreign policy decisions of the plenum, saying that they should increase the prestige of the Soviet Union and reduce the hostile activities of reactionaries in the West. This would also have a calming and constructive effect on public opinion as a whole, at home and abroad, and would make it easier to get rid of the dogmatists.

I also told Khrushchev that in my opinion a very positive aspect of the affair was that the plenum had explained the events to the Soviet public and the world at large as a purely political matter, that is, without any suggestion that any of the Stalinists had served foreign interests. I told him that was something new for the Soviet Union and that it would be of tremendous importance for convincing people and for Soviet prestige. Khrushchev agreed.

Saying that I was speaking personally and that I might be criticized in Belgrade when they got to know about it, I told Khrushchev that I thought it would be a good thing if the public were informed officially as soon as possible about the personal fates of Molotov, Malenkov, Kaganovich, and Shepilov. I told him I had already heard from foreigners here and from Soviet citizens on the street all sorts of suggestions about what might have happened to Molotov, Malenkov, and the others. I think it would be only in the interests of the Soviet Union if it were said officially as soon as possible, for example, that one of them had been pensioned off, or that he had been given some job or other. I apologized to Khrushchev for meddling in this matter, which I was doing, not as ambassador of Yugoslavia, but as a Communist and a friend of the Soviet Union who wanted to see the decisions of the plenum of the Central Committee carried out.

Khrushchev took very well what I put to him on my own behalf, saying that he agreed with me and that they were already thinking about it. At the same time I voiced the opinion that it might be a good idea if Saburov were to appear somewhere and take part in some action connected with the plenum. Many people had asked me what had happened to Saburov because, as far as I could see, there had been something said in the Soviet press about everybody except him, and enemies could make use of this. I think it would be a good thing if the newspapers, when eventually they report some statement by Saburov, mention that he is a member of the Central Committee, and that would put everything right. Khrushchev said that he was going to give Saburov the job of handling economic relations between the Soviet Union and the countries of the camp.

Khrushchev told me today that he was going to travel to Leningrad with a large number of members of the Presidium. Only now are they going to do what they should have done on June 22–24, to celebrate the 250th anniversary of the city, which the developments in the Kremlin prevented them from doing. On Monday, July 8, he is going with Bulganin with a government-party delegation to Czechoslovakia. He no longer gets on with Bulganin, but such are the demands of politics. After Czechoslovakia he will return through Eastern Germany. It seems to me he will make some sort of statement there in support of Eastern Germany so as to weaken Adenauer's chances in the election.

Khrushchev informed me of their attitude to our proposal for a party meeting on the Danube. He said they agreed on condition that the Romanians were in agreement because it concerned their territory. I may be mistaken, but I have the impression that Khrushchev would prefer the meeting to take place somewhere else, without involving other countries.

Several times in the course of his statement Khrushchev mentioned one or other of the speeches made by Zhukov against the M-K-M group—and the majority of the Presidium. Even before the row boiled up in the Presidium Malenkov had said in conversation with Zhukov that they would have to "discuss what's going on," that it couldn't go on like this, that he was telling him this as a friend and a comrade, and so forth. Kaganovich, who has a country house next to Zhukov, told him it was wrong that Zhukov was only a candidate member of the Presidium, that he was a political figure and not just a soldier, that he was a famous military leader, and so on. Zhukov rejected these propositions of both of them on the spot and pretty clearly. This later served as a strong argument against the fractionalists.

As for the final outcome of the events Khrushchev was optimistic. Unlike the Molotov-Kaganovich-Malenkov group, who in a typically Stalinist way tried to settle everything within four walls, behind the back of the Central Committee, Khrushchev displayed tremendous faith in the Central Committee, and so in the party and people. He said in the course of his battle with M-K-M that they don't know where they are living or what they are doing, that they have no contact with reality, that the Central Committee could elect at least three Presidiums which would not be worse than the one they have today.

When the Stalinists said that they were being bugged and wanted in that way to discredit Khrushchev and remove Serov, Khrushchev demanded a commission to investigate the matter; if it proved to be correct, then whoever ordered the bugging should pay with his head. If it turned out to be untrue, then those who spread the story should pay the same price. Khrushchev proposed a commission headed by Pervukhin, who had been with the Stalinists.

The fractionalists took fright and this argument of theirs was rejected. Khrushchev told me they had wanted to remove Serov and get their hands on his job primarily so that they could destroy the archives that are there to condemn them. When I said that it would be a good thing to inform the public as soon as possible about the personal fates of M-K-M,

Khrushchev told me how, when it was all over, Kaganovich telephoned him in his office in the Central Committee. In tearful tones Kaganovich had told him that he hoped that he was not going to revert to the ways of the past which Khrushchev had so strongly condemned (he was thinking of reprisals, prison, and executions). Khrushchev replied that it was in order to prevent the past being repeated that he, Kaganovich, and the others had been thrown out of the Central Committee.

That is, by and large, basically what Khrushchev told me today about the stormy events in the Presidium and the Central Committee of the CPSU and which were made public yesterday. Although this report is made up of disconnected details which reveal the external aspects of the affair and not the entirety of a major crisis, I think it will be of use to you as a supplement to reports of all the events that took place.

I apologize for the lack of order in this letter. I am writing in great haste because in a few hours I am leaving Moscow by air for the Black Sea to meet Comrades Marko [Ranković], Bevc [Kardelj], and the others. I have not copied the letter to anyone else at home; you will know best whether anyone else should be informed. I will recount the main points to Marko and Bevc.

With many comradely greetings and wishing you good health,

Veljko Mićunović

I sent the letter to Conrade Tito by courier; it was so long and I had no time to shorten it, because its contents were such that I couldn't have decided what to leave in and what to cut out of it.

CHAPTER TWENTY-TWO

THE AFTERMATH OF THE JUNE PLENUM

Kardelj and Ranković spend a "holiday" in the Soviet Union, only to discover that the defeat of the "antiparty group" has done little to improve Soviet-Yugoslav relations.

Sochi, July 7, 1957

I am down in Sochi on the Black Sea coast awaiting the arrival of Kardelj, Ranković, and the other comrades who have accepted the Soviet leaders' invitation to take a fortnight's "annual leave" in the Soviet Union. After they return to Yugoslavia our comrades will have to take another holiday to recover from this "holiday." During their stay in the Soviet Union they will spend two or three days in Moscow and have talks there with the Soviet leaders.

Even before the dramatic events took place in the Presidium on June 17 we had practically restored Yugoslav-Soviet relations to normal. The Central Committee of the CPSU had already invited twenty or twenty-five of our party leaders to "come on holiday in the Soviet Union." Comrades Kardelj and Ranković are coming as a result of that invitation.

It may appear to those who do not have the full facts that it is not pure chance that the visit of Kardelj and Ranković to the Soviet Union coincides with the defeat of the Malenkov-Kaganovich-Molotov group. The top Yugoslav leaders are arriving in the Soviet Union, so to speak, on the day after the group was removed. Yugoslav-Soviet friendship is being re-established at the same time as a powerful group of Stalinists in the Soviet leadership have been defeated. Khrushchev received me immediately after these events so that I could convey Tito's greetings to him and he could give a detailed account of what happened to me, probably the first foreigner in Moscow to hear it. But the fact remains that Yugoslav-Soviet relations had already been restored to normal independently of what happened later in Moscow, although the timing of the two developments has given the public a different impression.

I believe there can be no talk of any direct effect of the "Yugoslav factor" on the course of events here or of our having any foreknowledge of what was going to happen. Something similar happened last year when Tito came on his official visit to the Soviet Union and Molotov was suddenly and to our great surprise removed from the post of Foreign Minister only twenty-four hours before Tito arrived in Moscow. Yugoslavia is regarded as having played an active part in all that.

One thing is certain: After all that has happened here Comrades Kardelj and Ranković will now arrive in the Soviet Union in much happier circumstances than they thought they would about a month ago when they decided to make this trip.

Sochi, July 8, 1957

Comrades Kardelj, Ranković, and Veselinov[1] have arrived, and I have given them as detailed an account as possible about events in Moscow. Afterward we discussed the possible reasons for the attempt of the Stalinist group to overthrow Khrushchev. There were lots of suggestions, but we were agreed that the profound crisis which Stalin bequeathed to his successors in the Soviet Union and the international Communist movement has not yet been resolved, even though the defeat of the Stalinist group is a major contribution. It is obvious that the Soviet Union can no longer be governed as in Stalin's day. But it is less obvious how the new political order which is to replace what we call Stalinism is to be established.

I gave it as my opinion that Khrushchev had been at his weakest just over six months ago, following the Hungarian events. The extent to which he then felt he was going to lose his position in the Presidium can be judged from the way he made himself out in public to be a greater Stalinist than Molotov and Malenkov.

In the course of conversation I recalled that Khrushchev had gone over from the defense to the attack, that he had remained silent at the December meeting of the Central Committee and had then summoned the February plenum at which he put forward his program for decentralizing the administration of the Soviet economy and by so doing had in fact canceled out the decisions of the December plenum. This created fresh enemies for Khrushchev among the top Soviet bureaucrats whose interests were threatened by Khrushchev's plan. I am inclined to believe that it was on this issue that the long friendship between Khrushchev and Bulganin came to an end, that this made it easier for Molotov and Malenkov to swing Bulganin against Khrushchev, and that he then won over

[1] Jovan Veselinov, b. 1906. Yugoslav Communist official. Member of Presidency of League of Communists, 1966; Chairman, Serbian National Assembly from 1955.

Saburov and Pervukhin. All of them except Khrushchev supported the decisions of the December plenum and opposed Khrushchev's plan for decentralizing the economy. The dogmatic forces were sure that they had the central government *apparat* on their side, while Khrushchev was relying more and more on the party leaders in the republics as well as the party and state *apparat* outside Moscow.

The fact that Khrushchev had Marshal Zhukov and the leaders of the Soviet armed forces on his side turned out to be of decisive importance. Apart from that Khrushchev also had on his side the men in charge of the Soviet state security service. The M-K-M group was deeply convinced that it would not come to a trial of strength and that the secure majority which they had in the Presidium was sufficient for them to carry through their whole plan. It looks as if they were so certain of the success of their coup that they had not felt it necessary to organize some support in the armed forces or in the security service, let alone to win some backing among what is called the "social basis," in other words the Soviet population. The M-K-M group was mainly concerned right up to the last moment with making sure that their planned coup remained completely secret. When it comes to coups d'état in general and in the Soviet Union especially, the population is simply not a factor to be considered, it is presented with an accomplished fact.

It was important for us that in this new situation Yugoslavs were again coming to the Soviet Union as friends. It was not only a victory for Khrushchev but also for the Yugoslav line which was emphasized particularly by the fact that the Soviet side had officially labeled Molotov, Malenkov, and Kaganovich as Stalinists, and the Yugoslavs had clashed with the Soviet Union because they had asserted publicly that among the Soviet leaders there were still people who were unable to rid themselves of Stalinist ideas and methods.

After remaining in Sochi from July 7 to 10 Kardelj, Ranković, and the others are due to leave for the Caucasus and Georgia. They will spend several days there and then go to Moscow, where they will spend two days before going on to Leningrad.

Moscow, July 11, 1957

Khrushchev was so frank and, I believe, at certain moments so utterly sincere during the two hours on July 5 when he recounted to me the stormy events in the Kremlin that he even gave me his own opinion about Mikoyan's conduct in the affair. He said there had been two parts to Mikoyan's speech at the Central Committee. If events had taken the opposite course it was not impossible that the second part of his speech, which he left deliberately until the second session of the plenum next day, would have been adapted to suit such a turn of events.

I do not know the whole story of Mikoyan's maneuverings during the crises which followed Stalin's death, let alone the many crises during Stalin's lifetime. I am thinking of the arrest and execution of Beria in 1953, the removal of Malenkov in 1955, Khrushchev's secret speech and criticism of Stalin at the Twentieth Congress in 1956. I know that in Stalin's day, like the others who survived the terror, Mikoyan did his very best to keep in the good graces of the great dictator.

Last year I received anonymously from some Russian the first two pages of a copy of *Pravda* of some years ago with Mikoyan's speech on the occasion of Stalin's birthday. The speech had been underlined in red pencil as an example of toadying and of the glorification of Stalin, which deserves to be placed in a museum as an outstanding example of a eulogy of the "cult of personality."

The anonymous Russian wrote to me roughly the following: In just the same way as he spoke in praise of Stalin yesterday he is ready to say it all again in favor of anybody else tomorrow; in this Mikoyan has not changed. I am sorry I didn't keep that anonymous letter.

Judging from Mikoyan's actual behavior during the present crisis I don't think he behaved very differently in earlier crises. He probably waited to see which side was going to win. Under a socialist system, as under the capitalist system, a man who behaves in this way does not have to have much firmness of character or strength of convictions. Such qualities can only be a hindrance. It is all the more important for such a man to have skill and talent. Mikoyan has undoubtedly displayed both in the last forty years, for a good thirty of which he managed to hold a position in the Soviet leadership and under Stalin. Now he is on the side of Khrushchev, who has come out on top. Mikoyan's talents will probably find further employment in the Soviet Union.

Mikoyan is now going round Moscow speaking at party meetings and is having much success exposing the antiparty group and assuring Soviet Communists of the correctness of the party's line—and of course of his own, too!

In the last few days we have had contacts with Soviet citizens from a variety of regions: Tashkent, Vitebsk, the Baltic states, Siberia, Bashkiria, Saratov, and other places. It is interesting to note that the majority of them are inclined to forgive and take pity on the former leaders rather than to want to see them punished. Only in a few cases did we come across people who supported the plenum's decisions. The majority had reservations about them and some were afraid that enemies abroad would take advantage of this internal settling of accounts in the Soviet Union.

For many years now the Soviet practice has been to liquidate physically not only anyone in an official political position who did not agree but even those who were suspected of being potential opponents of the official policy. There were such physical eliminations even after Stalin's death in the case of Beria. But now a debate with Molotov and the others has been carried on for nearly three weeks and the "antiparty group" even remains in the party! I believe it is to Khrushchev's credit that he has introduced a way of settling accounts between political leaders which is the very opposite of the criminal acts committed for decades under Stalin.

Moscow, July 14, 1957

A few days ago Khrushchev and Bulganin left with a government delegation for a visit to Czechoslovakia. The Czechs at their embassy here know the fully story of the way Bulganin behaved during the June events; they say they are not too happy that Bulganin is now going to be their guest. In this way some Czech diplomats here try to show that they are not scared to criticize a leader—in Bulganin's position.

Khrushchev has made a speech in Czechoslovakia at some factory, his first political speech in a country of the "camp" since the elimination of the M-K-M group. It was in my opinion one of his worst speeches. For that reason even the Soviet press published only a shortened version. But even so there were plenty of allusions and attacks which can refer only to Yugoslavia. The greater part of Khrushchev's speech is in contradiction with the decisions of the June plenum of the Central Committee. It looks as though the same thing is happening now as happened after the speech about Stalin at the Twentieth Congress. It is as though the people here are afraid of their own anti-Stalinist decisions. Khrushchev seems to feel the need to demonstrate that he is not a revisionist and talks as the members of the "antiparty group" used to talk. Meanwhile Khrushchev now shows himself to be less consistent than those whom yesterday he was criticizing, saying again that the revisionists are now the main danger for Communist parties, although it was the Stalinists here who only yesterday acquired a majority in the Presidium and he only just managed to save not only his position but possibly his head as well. This behavior of Khrushchev's cannot be viewed apart from the system which prevails in the Soviet Union. By acting in this way Khrushchev is trying, consciously and subconsciously, to be the best spokesman for that system.

Moscow, July 15, 1957

The day before yesterday I sent a letter to Comrades Kardelj and Ranković, who are still in Georgia and will arrive here in four or five days. Here is the letter:

Dear Comrades,

I am sending you our press and the *Tanjug* bulletin for the last week. It is not my intention to spoil your holiday with these pounds of paper, but I believe you will be interested in this "literature," and above all in the *Tanjug* material, on the eve of your arrival in Moscow. Apart from that I have sent the courier to you for the following reasons:

1. Comrade Veljko Zeković has sent the following telegram from Belgrade to Comrade Kardelj:

"Some republics are proposing to hold elections to the people's committees in October. We agree with this and suggest that the others do the same. Please reply urgently whether you agree. Zeković."

2. The Finnish ambassador here has informed me of his government's wish that you should be their guest during your stay in Finland. I thanked him and gave him a few preliminary facts about your movements and told him of the very limited time you had at your disposal. He will come and see me again about it.

3. Khrushchev is in Czechoslovakia and on July 11 made a very bad speech in the Stalingrad factory. You will see extracts from it in *Pravda* for July 12.

It is rather like what happened after the Twentieth Congress with all the inconsistencies, confusion, and mistakes now being committed by Khrushchev, who appears to think that his main task now is, by attacking Yugoslavia, to win over the supporters of Molotov in the Soviet Union and the "camp" and in this way avoid a political battle and "preserve the unity" of the party and the country.

Khrushchev paid tribute to the Communist party of Czechoslovakia in the struggle against the revisionists and for its internationalism during the Hungarian events, and appealed three or four times to those present to strengthen the "camp." But he did not say a word about dogmatism or the reasons for the removal of the Molotov-Kaganovich-Malenkov group. In the shortened text of the speech published in the Soviet press Yugoslavia is nowhere mentioned, which is very typical, since it was the main point of the speech which Khrushchev made on July 11. But there were plenty of allusions to Yugoslavia.

His speech was in fact even worse than it appeared from the Soviet press. On July 12 Radio Belgrade reported that Khrushchev had attacked the Yugoslav attitude over the question of Hungary, our acceptance of military aid from the United States, and finally he criticized the workers' councils. Western news agencies seized on what Khrushchev said about Yugoslavia as the most important points in his speech. Everybody stresses that he spoke without a prepared text.

After this bad speech of July 11 Khrushchev made another one on July 12. According to the Soviet press he again referred to Yugoslavia, this time in a positive way, declaring categorically that "Yugoslavia is a socialist country and nobody can get away from that."

Taken all together this is, in my opinion, negative and harmful, primarily for Khrushchev himself and the Soviet Union. It shows that the Russians were not able to remain faithful even for a week to the Central Committee statement. In this way they actually weaken their own positions. Khrushchev's speech at the Stalingrad factory caused much disappointment not only in Yugoslavia, Poland, and elsewhere in the world but also in the Soviet Union itself.

4. The Soviet Government replied on July 10 to our note of May 9 about the aluminum and fertilizer plants. They agree with our new proposals; for their part they suggest fresh talks in Moscow beginning around July 15. We have agreed; Hasan Brkić will arrive shortly with a delegation. This was agreed in Belgrade before Khrushchev's speech at the Stalingrad plant.

5. The Soviet Foreign Ministry informed us on July 10 that their atomic scientists are asking whether Comrade Ranković would like to go round some of the Soviet atomic institutions while he is here.

6. I have just been informed by Belgrade that Comrade Tito thinks we should not take any steps on the international level concerning Khrushchev's speech of July 11 or attach any special significance to the whole affair. . . . Comrade Tito's idea is that you should talk about this in Moscow, that Khrushchev's remarks were not directed specifically against Yugoslavia, which has supported without reservations the latest decisions of the Soviet Communist party, and that the whole affair will do more harm to Khrushchev and the Soviet Union than to us.

With comradely greetings to all of you,

Moscow, July 13, 1957   V. Mićunović

Moscow, July 19, 1957

Kardelj and Ranković were received today by Khrushchev. I went along with them. We agreed in advance not to bring up thorny questions from the past. If Khrushchev were to raise them, however, we agreed that we would maintain our point of view while at the same time trying not to make the situation worse. We reckoned that recent events in Moscow would be at the center of attention and that Khrushchev would probably talk more than the rest of us put together.

The talk lasted for about two and a half hours. Khrushchev raised, among other things, the question of his speech in Czechoslovakia. He had heard our opinion of it. He said he had thought the speech would not be published—he had said that only journalists from the socialist countries could be present, but that some Western newsmen had pushed their way in and reported it in the world's press. Khrushchev's explanation sounded more like an effort to defend himself than to defend the contents of the speech, which he did not refer to or try to defend. Kardelj and Ranković offered no comments.

On the question of American military aid Kardelj referred to the talks which Tito had had previously with Khrushchev. Nothing of real importance had happened in the meantime and our attitude on the subject had not changed. We hoped that the Soviet attitude had not changed either. Khrushchev confirmed this, but talked about the visit of our military delegation, said we had established contacts on this important level but that it was going to be difficult to get real cooperation going so long as the American military mission remained in Belgrade. He did not see any particular obstacle in this, but some of their military leaders did and they would make difficulties for us.

As for the June plenum and the "antiparty group," Khrushchev did not go beyond generalizations, saying that they were now united, strong, and so forth. He did not appear disposed to discuss this matter at length, since it would have supported the Yugoslav thesis concerning the existence of a powerful group of Stalinists and dogmatists in the Soviet leadership, something which Khrushchev firmly denied throughout last year, right up to the June plenum of the Central Committee.

We counted on continuing the talks in the evening in a wider circle of Soviet leaders at the dinner to which Khrushchev had invited us. We were sure that it was going to be just a Yugoslav-Soviet evening, a sort of friendly conclusion to our comrades' visit to the Soviet Union.

The dinner took place in the Central Committee's villa in the countryside near Moscow. As we approached the house, walking along a narrow path toward the entrance of the villa, I was bringing up the rear of our group. Kardelj led the way. On entering the house, uncertain with whom to shake hands, Kardelj went up to Enver Hoxha, who, to my surprise, was standing near the entrance and exchanged greetings with Kardelj. Kardelj obviously thought he was shaking hands with one of the Russians. I was unable to make my way forward to tell him it was Enver Hoxha and that I could also see Todor Zhivkov in a group of Russians waiting for us. Without informing us in advance, Khrushchev had brought Zhivkov and Hoxha along to the dinner. Although this was a very unpleasant trick for the Russians to play on us, we could do nothing but pretend not to be taken by surprise and that we regarded it as natural to find ourselves with the Bulgarians and Albanians. But the atmosphere at the table could scarcely be relaxed or agreeable. This gradually made itself felt to all those present.

Toasts were proposed by Khrushchev, Zhivkov, and Hoxha. It was apparently not such a surprise for them as for us—they had agreed about it all in advance. They didn't say very much about friendship with Yugoslavia, but spoke more in praise of the Soviet Union, while Zhivkov and Hoxha made a special point of extolling the virtues of Khrushchev personally, as they had until recently spoken about Molotov, Malenkov, and the rest. It seemed to me that both they and the Russians were leaving it to us to say something of current political significance in the toasts which we were to propose, and that they would then determine whether we had spoken "correctly" or "incorrectly." Kardelj and Ranković made the speeches on our side but without saying any of the things the Russians, Bulgars, and Albanians expected. Kardelj was unable to conceal his displeasure and kept his speech short. Ranković's speech was appreciably longer and reflected Yugoslav attitudes. They would certainly not have spoken in that way if only the Russians had been present. It was only after the toasts proposed by Kardelj and Ranković that there was no applause. The Russians did not applaud, and Zhivkov and Hoxha followed suit.

Toward the end of the evening some of the Russians had in their hands the text of an official announcement about the dinner. It gave all the names and positions of the people present and then stated that there had been talks between the four countries in an atmosphere of friendship, etc. Kardelj was very upset by all this but made no effort to alter in any way the text of the statement which was to be published on the front pages of the Soviet press the next day, as though it were a really important event—it was the first such meeting of representatives of Albania, Bulgaria, the Soviet Union, and Yugoslavia for many years. The rest of us did not interfere either, and the Russians simply interpreted this as meaning that we had no comments to make on their text and that we agreed that it should be published as planned.

We expected people to be surprised, both in Yugoslavia and abroad, and that we should have some explaining to do to our people as well as to foreigners about how it all came about and how it actually finished up. It would be a mistake to regard it as a political event of any special significance. Some of our people reproached us for accepting a joint communiqué, saying that there was no need to do so, and that we were now having meetings, dinners, and communiqués forced on us without being informed in advance and without having agreed to them, and that the Russians should be told frankly about it to discourage them from repeating that sort of thing in the future. We agreed not to take any special steps, since it would soon be obvious that the whole affair had been laid on without our agreement.

We all recalled that Khrushchev had done much the same in the Crimea last October, when, to our surprise, he produced Geroe and the Hungarians at a lunch and then wished on us an official visit by Geroe and a Hungarian delegation to Yugoslavia in the middle of October 1956. Khrushchev believed that in that way he would best be able to stabilize the situation in Hungary, and it all ended up in disaster and the Russian armed intervention. Khrushchev is now behaving again in the same way, tricking us into a meeting with representatives of other states and publishing communiqués to make a political event of it. The Russians imagine that in this way they can change to their advantage and that of the countries of Eastern Europe the character of Yugoslavia's relations with those countries. We knew that, like other people, Khrushchev could make a political mistake. But we had thought that he would not make the same mistake a second time, yet that is exactly what he has now done. We were obviously in too much of a hurry, following the elimination of the "antiparty group," to achieve some success in foreign policy as far as the relations of the Soviet Union and Eastern Europe with Yugoslavia are concerned.

Moscow, July 20, 1957

The whole of the Soviet press for July 19 gave front-page publicity to the official communiqué about the "friendly meeting of representatives of four countries." The reaction to the report about the dinner in the Moscow countryside has been quite considerable, especially in the foreign press and, of course, in the Moscow diplomatic corps.

CHAPTER TWENTY-THREE

TITO AND KHRUSHCHEV MEET AGAIN

*A meeting between Tito and Khrushchev in Romania is
followed by an improvement in relations between Russians
and Yugoslavs. Molotov is appointed ambassador to Outer
Mongolia.*

Belgrade, July 27, 1957

I have been here in Belgrade for about a week now working on
preparations for the meeting between Tito and Khrushchev and delegations from our two parties. We have had some problems in arranging the
meeting. Khrushchev told me several times that this time they would not
come to Yugoslavia and that it was now our turn to go to the Soviet
Union. We went into the possibility of having the meeting on the
Danube, on a Soviet or Yugoslav boat. But Khrushchev wasn't very enthusiastic about that idea. It seemed to him very complicated from the point
of view of protocol. He proposed instead that the meeting should take
place in a frontier area, or better still in one of the countries of Eastern
Europe having frontiers with both Yugoslavia and the Soviet Union. We
finally agreed to have the meeting in Romania, after learning that the
Romanian leaders were happy to play the part of hosts. I presume that
the Russians are pleased that the meeting will not take place in Yugoslavia
but in one of the countries of the "camp," where they will at least feel
more "at home" than the Yugoslavs.

Belgrade, July 28, 1957

We have received good news from our embassy in Moscow. The Soviet Government has accepted our proposal to resume talks about the decisions which the Russians took about the credits. They agree to improve

the terms of the agreements and tell us explicitly that the matter was decided at the highest level.

We learn from Moscow that meetings are taking place there every day with the leaders of one of the various Communist parties which are visiting the Kremlin one after the other and proclaiming their solidarity with the Soviet leaders. It looks as though a secret meeting of all the parties of the socialist camp has been held, because all the leaders have been in Moscow. This was presumably aimed at helping the Russians on the domestic political scene. The same purpose is served by the international youth festival now being held in Moscow.

Belgrade, July 29, 1957

We are due to leave soon for Bucharest and the meeting with Khrushchev. We shall travel by boat, which makes it seem more like an excursion and a pleasant trip down the Danube than a journey connected with important political negotiations.

I think it should be said that on this occasion as far as protocol is concerned the Yugoslavs have not only gone to meet the Russians "halfway" but have done more than that. We have recently had many delegations in the Soviet Union, including the "holiday" which Kardelj and Ranković spent there. All this made it possible for Khrushchev to remain faithful to his statement last autumn that "next time we shall not go to Yugoslavia." When it comes to considering why the meeting in Bucharest is taking place sooner than expected, by no means the least important factor is the Soviet experience that their influence with us always increased when our relations were good, just as their influence dropped to its lowest point when those relations were at their worst. Following the removal of the M-K-M group, the conditions were created for improving relations between the Soviet Union and Yugoslavia. In this way the Russians improve their prospects of increasing their presence and prestige in Yugoslavia.

I believe that we are in a stronger position politically on the eve of this meeting than seemed likely a short time ago. Six months ago some people found it possible to criticize our leaders because of the renewed conflict between Yugoslavia and the Soviet Union, when we asserted publicly that there were Stalinists in the Soviet leadership. But today this is seen in many circles as a sign of Yugoslav farsightedness and our accurate forecasting of what was going to take place in Moscow.

Bucharest, August 2, 1957

The conference of delegations from the Soviet and Yugoslav Communist parties held at Snagov, near Bucharest, ended today. It was attended on the Soviet side by, apart from Khrushchev, Mikoyan, and Kuusinen,[1] both members of the Presidium, and then Ponomarev, Andropov,[2] and Firyubin. On the Yugoslav side, apart from Comrade Tito, there were Edvard Kardelj, Aleksandar Ranković, Veljko Vlahović[3] and myself. There was less need for detailed negotiations on particular questions in view of the fact that the Russians had already announced that it was a "party" and not a "government" meeting. In the Soviet draft communiqué which the Russians handed us yesterday all the participants in the meeting are given only their party functions, implying that these are more important than their government posts—and as though it were in any case possible to separate one from the other.

The Russians consider a party agreement to be more lasting and, for us, more binding, because "government" agreements can be concluded with countries with a different ideology and a different social system, as Khrushchev explained on one occasion last year.

The Russians made up their delegation in accordance with their understanding of the character of the meeting. Mikoyan was there so that he could if necessary act as representative both of the Soviet party and of the Soviet Government, while the majority of the others gave the delegation a "party" character. There was old Kuusinen, who followed the greater part of the talks in silence but whose presence underlined the fact that the talks were between parties and not between governments. The presence of Ponomarev in the Soviet delegation was intended to ensure the orthodoxy, or the "correctness," of the decisions reached.

The talks themselves were smoother and more friendly than any we have had so far. In fact it might be said that the meeting was necessary to register the latest improvement already achieved in relations between Russians and Yugoslavs, rather than to bring about such an improvement. For this reason the joint communiqué was easily agreed and very brief, consisting of less than a dozen sentences.

The communiqué was drawn up by the Russians, as can be seen from the style and vocabulary. The Yugoslavs would not have formulated some points as they did, but the Soviet version was accepted. The Russians would be able to say that the Yugoslavs had at last accepted the Soviet view on the necessity for strengthening cooperation between the Communist and workers' parties of all the socialist countries, and it could be argued in the Soviet Union that our latest conflict had broken out for

[1] Otto V. Kuusinen, 1881–1964. Soviet Communist official of Finnish origin. Member of the Presidium, CPSU, 1952–53 and 1957–64.
[2] Yuri V. Andropov, b. 1914. Soviet Communist official. Ambassador to Hungary, 1954–57; Secretary, Central Committee, CPSU, 1962–67; Chairman, Committee for State Security (KGB), 1967; Member of Politburo, CPSU, 1973; Army General, 1976.
[3] Veljko Vlahović, 1914–75. Yugoslav Communist official.

that very reason, and that we had now "come round." Of the particular issues mentioned, very important was our agreement regarding aid and support for János Kadar's government, which was all the more important in view of the fact that it was over Hungary that we clashed with the Soviet Union last year.

To the Russians it appeared that they had again drawn Yugoslavia closer to the socialist camp. To the Yugoslavs, on the other hand, it appeared as a reaffirmation that they were a factor in the situation when it came to the internal political struggle in the Soviet Union, as was the case at the June plenum of the CPSU, and that Khrushchev would now put the policy of de-Stalinization into practice with greater determination.

The Bucharest meeting was of especial importance in that friendly personal relations were reestablished between Tito and Khrushchev. In addition, by referring to the Belgrade and Moscow declarations, we expressed our agreement to develop our relations on the basis of equality, mutual aid, and respect for sovereignty, independence, and noninterference. In this way Yugoslav-Soviet relations, after the unsatisfactory state into which they lapsed at the end of last year, are again on the upgrade. But this latest normalization of our relations will probably not be the last, and neither will the conflict which preceded it.

Snagov is where the meeting of the Cominform was held at which, on Stalin's orders, the famous resolution of June 28, 1948, was passed expelling Yugoslavia from the "community of socialist states" and the Communist party of Yugoslavia from the "family of fraternal parties." This was followed by a policy of aggressive pressure on Yugoslavia by the Soviet Union, the "camp," and the Communist parties throughout the world. Between that meeting of the Cominform and the present meeting on the outskirts of Bucharest nine years have elapsed, which is both a short and a long time. In the history of the advance of socialism in the world it is too short a period. On the other hand, bearing in mind everything that has happened between Yugoslavia and the Soviet Union and in the international working-class movement, one could say that in the course of those nine years a whole stage in the further development of socialism as a worldwide process has been traveled.

All the participants in the meeting were well aware of the associations of which I speak. But they all appeared nevertheless very pleased that the meeting had taken place in Snagov. Khrushchev appeared pleased because he had managed to get himself elected as the only and unchallenged leader of the Soviet Union at the June plenum of the CPSU. The Yugoslavs appeared pleased with the latest turn of events, since, apart from anything else, it recognized that Belgrade had been right in the quarrel with Moscow. The Romanian leaders, led by Gheorghiu-Dej, who were present at the lunches and dinners we had together, say they are pleased that the meeting between Tito and Khrushchev took place in Romania.

Belgrade, August 5, 1957

The meeting between Tito and Khrushchev in Bucharest received great publicity round the world, especially in the West. In the countries of the "camp" the publicity was carefully controlled. Although there was no reference in the official communiqué after Snagov to any specific agreements between the Russians and us, it could be presumed that specific matters had been discussed and that agreement had been reached. And that is what actually happened. The Russians proposed that we should draw up a sort of short note of the most important points covered in the two days of talks and that the two heads of delegation should sign it. To make this new procedure more acceptable to us, since we did not show ourselves very enthusiastic at the outset, Khrushchev said that there was no need to sign it "but only to initial the record"—as though that made any real difference. It was also pointed out that the record had not been drawn up in order to force each other to carry out what we had agreed—that was taken for granted and beyond question—but because it would serve as a sort of reminder of the matters we had agreed on at the meeting. These explanations made it easier for us to agree, and so the "reminder" was drawn up and initialed.

Although this record of the talks did not amount formally to a secret diplomatic document between the governments of two countries but was in the form of a memorandum, it did represent an agreement between the Yugoslav and Soviet governments on the questions recorded in it. We would not like to have this sort of relationship between our government and the government of any other country. I believe we should not have agreed to it on this occasion either, though not because the document contained anything contrary to our foreign policy, since we had reason to support Khrushchev following the stormy events in Moscow in June and the political liquidation of the M-K-M group. It was agreed on our side that for these reasons it would not be right for us to allow Khrushchev to go back to Moscow without our having reached agreement on the matters we discussed. For that reason we agreed to initial the document about the Snagov meeting.

Belgrade, August 6, 1957

From the many conversations I have had in Yugoslavia I have the impression that a considerable number of people here are inclined to exaggerate the part played by Yugoslavia in the formation of Soviet policy.

Notwithstanding the importance which the Russians attach to relations with our country, I do not believe that Yugoslavia has played the part in Soviet policy which some of our comrades imagine. At the June plenum of the CPSU the question of Yugoslavia could have had only marginal significance. According to my information, nobody mentioned Yugoslavia as one of the reasons for the conflict in the Soviet Presidium.

This does not mean that Yugoslavia does not have an important political role to play in the countries of Eastern Europe today. It is natural for those countries to continue striving for a greater degree of freedom and independence than their membership of the camp of socialism "headed by" the Soviet Union permits them. But Yugoslavia's influence on the situation in those countries is the result of the successes achieved so far by the people of Yugoslavia in their struggle for their own independence and not of any interference by the Yugoslav Government in the internal affairs of those countries. This sort of influence, based on the Yugoslav experience confirmed by daily practice, cannot be prevented by government decisions, just as influence over another country cannot come about simply because you happen to wish it. As long as Yugoslavia remains an independent and free country its influence can only serve to weaken foreign domination over socialist countries. The Russians are constantly aware of this, and that is why they were so persistent in their efforts to move Yugoslavia from its position of self-reliance and to reduce Yugoslav independence as far as possible to the state in which the countries of the socialist camp find themselves. The imposition of limitations on Yugoslav independence in domestic and foreign policy has been the central issue in all the quarrels which have so far taken place between the Soviet Union and our country. It will probably be the same in the future, but that does not mean that the dispute between our two countries on this basic question will be permanently in a state of acute conflict.

Some time ago, when I was discussing Khrushchev's arrival in Belgrade in 1955, I wrote that the Russians then found it necessary to have the "Yugoslav clearance" in addition to all the material and military resources at their disposal, and to be able to use that "clearance" to perform successfully on the international scene. After the meeting with Khrushchev on August 1 I had the impression that he finds that "Yugoslav clearance" today far less necessary than it was two years ago when Khrushchev arrived in Belgrade to discuss the restoration of normal Yugoslav-Soviet relations.

Moscow, September 13, 1957

A few days ago I arrived back in Moscow with Miška and our child from our annual holiday in Yugoslavia. I also took a holiday from keeping this diary, which I am now resuming after a break of several weeks.

In our embassy they tell me that the Soviet officials with whom we have dealings changed their attitude for the better the very next day after the meeting in Bucharest. For example, at the beginning of August a World Youth Festival took place in Moscow. The day after the joint communiqué about the Bucharest meeting was published Shelepin[4] and Semichastny,[5] the first and second men in the Soviet Komsomol, began to take a close and friendly interest in our representatives' impressions and placed themselves at the disposal of the Yugoslav youth delegation. Radio Moscow also changed its attitude to Yugoslavia. Instead of broadcasting our traditional folk songs and music it is now broadcasting Yugoslav Partisan songs. There were even instances of their broadcasting some of our wartime songs about Comrade Tito! Until then it was songs from Czechoslovakia which had priority over a similar program from Yugoslavia. Now the Czechs have dropped back into second place in these programs!

In the diplomatic corps the Bucharest meeting has been regarded in a variety of ways. Some Western diplomats make very little effort to conceal their displeasure at the meeting. The French ambassador, Dejean, is as usual the least reserved and appears not to be surprised at all. The Chinese ambassador, Liu-Siao, is reserved, although he might have been expected to be among the first to welcome an improvement in Yugoslav-Soviet relations. Hitherto the Chinese have been telling us of their concern at the unsatisfactory state of our relations with the Soviet Union.

The most satisfied of the diplomats in Moscow appear to be the Arabs. They say that if our collaboration with the Russians improves, theirs does, too; so they welcome any move which improves Yugoslav-Soviet relations.

The Bulgarian and Albanian ambassadors, on the contrary, have not discussed the meeting with us although it was the most important item of news, above all for the socialist countries. The Romanian and the Pole expressed pleasure at the improvement in Yugoslav-Soviet relations. The Bulgarians appear to be dissatisfied both with the state of their own relations with the Russians and with the improvement in the Russians' relations with us. It also seems as though they are not very enthusiastic about internal developments in the Soviet Union. Perhaps they expected more from Khrushchev in the way of Soviet help over Bulgaria's economic difficulties, whereas Khrushchev only offered them Siberia to provide

[4] Aleksandr N. Shelepin, b. 1918. Soviet Communist official. Secretary, Communist Youth Organization (Komsomol), 1952–58; Chairman, Committee for State Security (KGB), 1968–71; Secretary, Central Committee, CPSU, 1961–67; Chairman, Soviet Trade Union Organization, 1967–75; Member of Politburo, CPSU, 1964–75. Following his dismissal in 1975, he disappeared from public life.
[5] Vladimir E. Semichastny, b. 1924. Secretary, Communist Youth Organization (Komsomol), 1950–59; Chairman, Committee for State Security (KGB), 1961–67.

jobs for the unemployed in Bulgaria. The internal changes which have taken place in Bulgaria are the reverse of what has happened in the Soviet Union. While in Moscow it is the dogmatists and Stalinists who have been removed from the leadership, in Bulgaria it is the most progressive people who have been turned out of the Central Committee.

The Albanian ambassador does not conceal his displeasure at the changes in Yugoslav-Soviet relations. The Albanian leaders were also displeased with the decisions of the June plenum. For similar reasons they are also against the policy of peaceful coexistence which Khrushchev stands for. That policy cannot be fitted in with the continuous Albanian campaign of hatred and hostility toward Albania's neighbors.

It is interesting that the Russians, as far as we know, have taken no special steps to influence the political line which is being pursued continually in Tirana and for some time in Sofia and which differs from the Moscow line. Moscow is interested primarily in having Bulgaria and Albania declare themselves firmly for the socialist camp "headed by" the Soviet Union and criticize Yugoslavia whenever Moscow wants them to.

Moscow, September 15, 1957

The Ministry for Foreign Trade, the Committee for Cultural Relations with foreign countries, the Soviet youth organizations, and other Soviet institutions are now treating our representatives very much better than in the past. They have taken the initiative in again developing contacts between us so as to improve our relations in practice, in accordance with the principles proclaimed at the Bucharest meeting. Foremost in this has been the Komsomol organization which was very friendly toward a large group of our young people at the World Youth Festival in Moscow. For example, the representative of our youth organization Vejzagić complained to Shelepin about the bad impression our young people had been left with because the jury had awarded our choir only a bronze medal. Shelepin's immediate reaction was to phone the Soviet Minister of Culture, Mikhailov, and demand that the bronze medal should be replaced by a gold one! The minister agreed at once, and our choir was awarded a gold medal! Shelepin not only changed the bronze into gold and quashed the verdict of the Soviet jury, which had already been announced; he also apologized to our representatives and showered them with praise!

We have come across an interesting list of questions which Russians were provided with at the beginning of the World Youth Festival for use when they met young people from Yugoslavia. The list contains the following questions: Why do you accept American planes? Why do you permit a flood of American films in Yugoslavia? Why are there no collective farms in Yugoslavia? Is Russian taught in your schools? Workers' councils which have been forced on other socialist countries lead to anarchy; why does Yugoslavia not join the socialist camp? Why does Yugoslavia not improve relations with Albania? Why do you permit the cult of Tito in Yugoslavia? This list was drawn up during the conflict between us last year and was distributed throughout the Soviet Union. It has now been officially withdrawn, but there are occasional signs that it is still being used.

At the end of August a government delegation from the People's Republic of Mongolia, led by the Prime Minister, Tsedenbal, visited Yugoslavia. I accompanied the delegation for the four days it spent in our country. I think it was a very successful visit and our Mongolian guests seemed to be genuinely pleased with the attention they were shown and the number of things they saw in our country. It was the first time the Mongols had been outside the "camp" in Europe and they are naturally interested in coming out onto the international scene. Our government and Comrade Tito gave them the sort of attention normally reserved for delegations from countries with which we have much closer relations.

Moscow, September 16, 1957

Even last month the Russians started to discuss with us and with some of our delegations preparations they are making for celebrating the fortieth anniversary of the October Revolution. The Presidium has already taken its decisions about the main features of the celebrations. They are expecting delegations from the parties and governments of all the countries of the "camp," led by the heads of government and party. They are also expecting to have delegations on the highest level from the Communist parties outside the camp.

Mao Tse-tung has agreed to take part in the celebrations in Moscow and will arrive here in the first days of November. The Chinese have revealed this well in advance so as to exert pressure on others to send their top people to Moscow. This confirms the view that the October anniversary celebrations are to be the occasion for holding the conference of Communist parties about which Chou En-lai spoke to me last January.

A special contribution to the celebrations of the fortieth anniversary of the October socialist revolution is to be made by the Russian Orthodox Church! It is also celebrating a fortieth anniversary of its own, "independently" of the party and government celebration of October, and is inviting Orthodox churches abroad to send their delegations to Moscow. The church celebrations are to begin a fortnight after the party celebrations and will last two weeks. The Russian Patriarch, Alexius, has already sent an invitation to the Serbian Patriarch, Prodanov, as well as to the patriarchs of Istanbul [Constantinople], Alexandria, Antioch, Jerusalem, Greece, and to the archbishop of Cyprus.

In this way the gathering of Orthodox priests in Moscow, which is being organized by the Soviet Government and the department in charge of the Russian Orthodox Church, will make its contribution to the celebration of the October socialist revolution and the conference of Communist parties which will be taking place about the same time in Moscow! One might have thought that if some church festival in Moscow really did coincide with the October celebrations the Russians should have postponed it so as not to spoil the October affair. On the contrary, the Russians arrange for both to take place in parallel! In the Soviet view it is not simply that the church festival does not interfere with the Communist party celebrations; the two simultaneous celebrations in Moscow seem to supplement one another very conveniently.

Moscow, September 19, 1957

The appointment of Molotov as ambassador to Mongolia confirms reports that the Presidium has decided not to pension off the members of the antiparty group but to require them to carry on working at "their own speciality." Molotov has been received by the Mongols with exceptional attention and is still the principal subject of conversation in Ulan Bator.

The Mongols have not, of course, shown that they do not approve the decisions of the June plenum. Like the others in the "camp" they supported those decisions and criticized the antiparty group in public. Nevertheless the attention they are paying to Molotov leaves people rather confused. In the Foreign Ministry in Ulan Bator they told Dizdarević that it is not so simple for people to take in all at once the difference between Molotov as he was yesterday, one of the great men, and what he is today. The Mongols have the excuse that they are showing respect for the ambassador of the Soviet Union! It is more difficult for the Russians to explain why they have put the Mongols in such a position: first they send them Molotov as ambassador and then they expect the Mongols to treat him in the spirit of the June plenum.

The man who preceded him as Soviet ambassador, Pisarev, who was doyen of the diplomatic corps, has now been reduced in rank, through no fault of his own, to that of minister-counselor under Molotov! This is also a sort of anomaly.

I believe that Malenkov, Kaganovich, and Shepilov are less of a problem for the Soviet leaders than Molotov. They will get lost in the vast spaces of the Soviet Union and do not come into daily contact with foreigners as is the case with Molotov. It seems likely that Khrushchev will still have trouble with Molotov, who behaves as though he still resists the decisions of the June plenum.

Moscow, September 24, 1957

We have a visit here of a delegation from our Veterans' Alliance, led by Velja Stojnić, which is going very well. I have agreed with Stojnić that the delegation will not lay a wreath at the Lenin-Stalin tomb in Moscow, as the Russians have already suggested. Instead I proposed that they should lay wreaths at the memorials to the defenders of Leningrad and Stalingrad when they are in those cities. I think this will be better, because it is impossible to work out an inscription for a wreath on the tomb without getting into political difficulties. If we declare explicitly that the wreath is only for Lenin, we shall only irritate the Russians and the whole affair will have the opposite of the desired effect. It is not possible for every one of our delegations to follow the example of the Yugoslav Government delegation led by Comrade Tito, which last year laid a wreath with an inscription saying that it was for Lenin.

Unlike the majority of states, the Soviet Union does not have in Moscow a national or state monument (to an unknown hero or something similar). This makes it difficult for us, as for all other countries outside the "camp," to carry out our obligations toward the Soviet Union on formal occasions. This is damaging to the Soviet Union and the countries concerned. Perhaps it would not be a bad idea if I were to talk to Khrushchev about this on some suitable occasion. It would make it easier for us and for others to behave normally; above all it would make it easier for the Russians themselves to limit the use made of the Lenin tomb and not create difficulties and dilemmas for foreign delegations.

Moscow, September 30, 1957

The current Soviet plan for the development of the economy has already been substantially modified, first at the December plenum of the Central Committee and then, two months later, at the February plenum. Now, only nine months later, changes are being made in the plan for the third time: the sixth five-year plan is actually being abandoned, although this is not admitted officially. There is to be a new long-term plan for 1959–65.

Western ambassadors in Moscow are already talking about the "collapse of the sixth five-year plan" and saying that the part of the program of the Twentieth Congress dealing with the internal development of the Soviet Union has turned out to be unfeasible and unrealistic. It seems to us that this Western interpretation of the situation is not altogether correct, although it is true that the current plan, approved by the Twentieth Congress, has not been fulfilled in a number of economically very important fields (coal, steel, cement, etc., about which I have heard from Khrushchev and Mikoyan).

It seems to us that Soviet official documents do not mention all the main reasons for the major changes now taking place. The reorganization of the economy, which is being carried out according to Khrushchev's program, has probably revealed numerous weaknesses in the present plan which was drawn up on the basis of the old centralistic way of running the economy. Many of the organic weaknesses of the Soviet economy are handed on from year to year and from one plan to another: the unprofitable operation and backwardness of a number of branches, the low productivity of labor, the high cost of production, and the technological backwardness compared with the West over a wide field. This is why the latest reorganization cannot even begin to be introduced successfully simply by dividing the country up into new economic regions.

For decades in Russia heavy industry, or "group A," has been favored at the expense of light industry—"group B." This latter group includes not only all kinds of light manufacturing industries but also agriculture, cattle raising, and everything which concerns the people's standard of living. The most positive aspect of Khrushchev's reorganization, in my opinion, is that it aims to raise the standard of living. This is actually the same policy as was proposed immediately after Stalin's death by Malenkov, who fell from grace, I believe, for other reasons, and not because he favored "group A" at the expense of "group B," although this was given as one of the reasons for removing him.

Since June other economic decisions have been taken which the Soviet leaders are sure will be well received by the population. Among them is the decision to abolish the tax on the peasants' private plots. Moreover the Soviet Government has announced its intention of solving the housing question in the next ten or twelve years. Although this was favorably received in the first place, it was followed by skepticism. I don't believe the Russians will be able to solve this problem in a single decade or in several decades to come. The setting of such impossible targets is presumably Khrushchev's doing.

Altogether I think we can believe Soviet claims that the country's economic potential looks better now than it did a year ago, when they introduced the plan which they are now largely abandoning.

When it is a question of revising Soviet economic plans, one must not forget the constant pressure exerted on economic growth in this country by the huge cost of equipping the Soviet Army. Although the total cost is nowhere revealed completely, there is good reason to suppose that it is very high and that it is rising rather than falling. The burden of this expenditure falls more heavily on the Soviet Union than on the United States and the advanced capitalist countries with which the Soviet Union is trying to keep pace in this field.

CHAPTER TWENTY-FOUR

THE FIRST SPUTNIK
AND THE END OF ZHUKOV

The Russians launch the first sputnik and make exaggerated claims about Soviet strength. Yugoslavia establishes diplomatic relations with the government of East Germany, and West Germany breaks off relations with Yugoslavia. Immediately following a visit to Yugoslavia Marshal Zhukov is removed from the party leadership and replaced as Minister of Defense.

Moscow, October 2, 1957

Andropov, a member of the Central Committee of the CPSU, invited me to call on him. He handed over to me part of the archives of the Communist party of Yugoslavia which remained in Moscow. We signed a brief record of what he gave me.

At the same time he informed me about the forthcoming conference of Communist parties and the October celebrations and said they were considering the possibility of holding a mass meeting in Moscow on November 8 at which those Communist leaders could speak who had not been able to do so at the session of the Supreme Soviet. The conference of Communist parties would begin on November 9. Following the conference there would be trips to various parts of the Soviet Union for the delegations.

Andropov did not say a word about Comrade Tito's illness,[1] or the fact that he will not be leading our delegation or coming to Moscow. I have the impression that the Russians believe the illness is a "diplomatic" one

[1] The official news agency Tanjug announced in Belgrade on October 29 that Tito was suffering from an "acute attack of lumbago" and that he would be unable to go to Moscow or to make a planned trip to Asia during the winter.

and that we have decided for political reasons that Tito will not come to Moscow on this occasion.

Our delegation will take part in the October celebrations, but it is not yet clear whether we will take part in the conference. Andropov did not ask me about this. We discussed only technical questions connected with the celebrations and the conference and did not touch on the key question of our participation or nonparticipation. Andropov obviously had instructions in that sense.

We shall have to prepare ourselves properly for the forthcoming events in November. There is a fairly widespread belief among our people that Yugoslavs know everything that is going on in the Soviet Union and that we understand the Russians better than anyone else. How exaggerated this view is can be seen from the fact that the majority of Yugoslavs who arrive here believe that they even know the Russian language! For this reason whole delegations arrive to do business here—but without an interpreter! The most stubborn among them even dare to make speeches "in Russian"—which they have never studied or spoken in their lives and which, of course, they don't know. The Russians are unable to understand such people and this occasionally leads to really laughable situations.[2]

Moscow, October 9, 1957

I have been in hospital for the last week, and so was unable to attend the Soviet celebrations connected with the launching of the first artificial satellite, the sputnik, into orbit round the earth. The whole world has been writing and talking about it for several days now. By means of a powerful rocket vehicle the Russians launched the sputnik on October 4 and under the force of gravitation it went into orbit and transmitted regular radio signals. This is no longer just Soviet propaganda but an unpleasant reality for the rivals and opponents of the Soviet Union.

The world appears really to have been taken by surprise by this epoch-making Russian technical and scientific achievement. Most put out are the advanced Western countries headed by the United States, because it was rather from them than from the Soviet Union that the world expected this sort of historic feat. Soviet prestige is suddenly on the increase everywhere in the world, among the more advanced nations who well know what this achievement means as well as among the backward nations, who understand it less.

[2] Serbo-Croat is one of the Slav languages and related to Russian, with which it has many common features. In Serbia it is written in the Cyrillic alphabet, similar to that used in Russia. But Russians and Yugoslavs cannot easily understand each other's speech.

THE FIRST SPUTNIK AND THE END OF ZHUKOV

The launching of the Soviet sputnik is important in many ways; it is not just a scientific achievement, opening a new era in the exploration of the cosmos, but is of military importance as well. The Russians have demonstrated in practice that they possess powerful rockets with which they may tomorrow launch an atomic bomb to any place on the world's surface. This will undoubtedly have an effect on the present balance of forces, military and in other ways, between the Soviet Union and the United States.

I believe there is no reason to doubt that the West and first of all the Americans will succeed in launching their own "sputnik" sooner or later. . . . But this time the Americans have to catch up with the Russians.

I don't need to point out that the timing of this Soviet achievement is exactly what the Russians must have desired—a month before the celebration of the fortieth anniversary of the October Revolution and the conference of Communist parties. During celebrations of the current geophysical year the Russians have been claiming that they had long since achieved important results in the manufacture of rockets and they refer to the scientist Tsiolkovsky[3] as the father of Soviet rockets. I have to admit that I had never heard of Tsiolkovsky before: He died a long time ago. I am probably not alone in my lack of knowledge of the development of rocket motors and of the Russian contribution in this field. From now on, it would seem, we laymen are also likely to have opportunities to learn about this subject.

Moscow, October 11, 1957

My stay in hospital prevented me from taking part in an event of importance for our relations with the Soviet Union: Marshal Zhukov's departure for his official visit to Yugoslavia. So I sent him the following letter from hospital:

Dear Comrade Zhukov,

I greatly regret that a sudden illness has prevented me from wishing you well in person on the eve of your departure for a friendly visit to Yugoslavia. Since I am not able to do it in any other way—I am in the Kremlin clinic—permit me to wish you in this way a safe journey and a very pleasant stay in our country, which is expecting you with a feeling of sincere friendship and deep respect for the Soviet Union as well as for yourself personally.

I am convinced that your friendly visit to Yugoslavia will be another

---

[3] Konstantin E. Tsiolkovsky, 1857–1935. Russian scientist and pioneer in the field of rockets and the theory of space travel.

major contribution to the joint efforts of our peoples to develop friendship and cooperation in all fields between our countries.

With sincere respect,

Ambassador of the F.P.R. of

Yugoslavia in the Soviet Union

Veljko Mićunović

I can say that on this occasion I was not simply meeting the requirements of protocol with regard to the Soviet Government, because I have the most sincere respect for Marshal Zhukov from the time of World War II when, as Yugoslav partisans, we admired the successes of one of the greatest military leaders of the Soviet patriotic war and of World War II as a whole.

Moscow, October 12, 1957

I have come across a booklet written by Enver Hoxha, the First Secretary of the Albanian [Communist] party of Labor, which has been published here as part of the publicity connected with the forthcoming October Revolution celebrations. The booklet is entitled "The Influence of the Great October Revolution on Albania" and is published by Gospolitizdat, the Russians' most authoritative publisher for such works, with a note that Enver Hoxha wrote the booklet at the request of the Soviet publisher. A hundred thousand copies have been printed. It was passed for printing on August 27, 1957, or nearly a month after our meeting with Khrushchev in Bucharest.

The booklet is written in the usual language employed by the Albanian Communist leaders. For example, Enver Hoxha describes the retreat of the Serbian troops across Albania in 1915 as follows:

> The chauvinist government of Serbia seized upon a favorable opportunity for carrying out its expansionist aims and sent its armed forces into Albania in June 1915, where they annexed the northern and central parts of the country and introduced everywhere a brutal regime of murder and plunder. After 1916 the Serbian troops were replaced by units of the Austro-Hungarian imperialists.

Lenin said that the battle fought by Serbia and Montenegro in World War I, of which Enver Hoxha now writes, was a war of national liberation and a just war. The Serbian troops fought heroically in the defense of their country against the attack by Austro-Hungary and Germany. They were forced to retreat in the face of a far superior enemy. The only possible direction in which they could retreat to avoid annihilation and to carry on the fight was into Albania and onto the Mediterranean, yet Enver Hoxha calls this a "favorable opportunity" for Serbia and describes the retreat of the remnants of the Serbian troops across Albania as "carrying out its expansionist aims" into Albania!

There is not a word about the help or cooperation which Yugoslavia extended to Albania during World War II in the fight against the fascist invader—though it is well known that the Yugoslav resistance movement gave continual help to the liberation fight in Albania. On the other hand Hoxha claims that, after the liberation of Albania toward the end of the war, the Albanian national-liberation army "carried on the fight against the Nazis in Yugoslavia and so fulfilled its international duty."

It is not surprising that Enver Hoxha should make such a typical "contribution" to the celebrations of the Revolution anniversary. What is surprising is the fact that the Russians should publish such a booklet in a hundred thousand copies on the eve of the celebrations and the conference of Communist parties, and should even reveal that Enver Hoxha wrote the booklet for Soviet readers at the request of Gospolitizdat!

Let me add just this: The Russians cannot have the slightest doubt as to our opinion of such a booklet, which is seething with hatred and slander of the people of Yugoslavia. If there is anything to reflect on in all this, then it is the Soviet attitude rather than what Hoxha has written.

Moscow, October 17, 1957

Yugoslavia has decided to recognize East Germany and this has created a real commotion among the Western diplomats in Moscow. I have spoken in the last few days with the ambassadors of France, Sweden, Greece, Poland, Switzerland, and East Germany, as well as with Khrushchev. The Western diplomats have become suddenly very reserved in their contact with us, while the Russians haven't become any less reserved than they were when Yugoslavia did not recognize East Germany. To judge from the reactions of diplomats from East and West so far, it looks as though Yugoslavia has lost more in the eyes of some than it has gained in the eyes of others.

Criticizing our recognition of the German Democratic Republic, Western diplomats reproach Yugoslavia for having done a service to the Soviet Union without receiving anything in return, and has thus inflicted serious harm not only to the West but also to its own political interests in the world. In this way we have ourselves, Western diplomats assert, destroyed our politically midway position which made it possible for us to have good relations with both sides.

We in this embassy have not tried to defend ourselves and even less to justify ourselves. We have not agreed with our interlocutors that to form an opinion of a political move by Yugoslavia it is sufficient to know what Moscow or Washington thinks about it. We have not agreed that our recognition of the G.D.R. means a policy of "striking a blow" against West Germany or anybody else. On the contrary, it could be only in the interests of international cooperation. The fact that there are two German states is not to be laid at the door of Yugoslavia and its recognition of the G.D.R.—that was the result of World War II and the policy which the great powers have pursued so far with regard to Germany.

I met Khrushchev and mentioned the fuss which was being made in the West about our recognition of East Germany. He said he did not expect West Germany to break off diplomatic relations with us, and that the present dramatization of the situation would pass. It is interesting to note that Khrushchev did not attach any particular significance to Yugoslavia's decision. He made no particular comment about it, as though it stood to reason that we had to recognize East Germany and that we should have done so a lot sooner.

The Russians and East Germans are now behaving as though they did not obtain anything resembling a concession out of Yugoslavia but rather what was due to them, and now they are interested in obtaining further concessions and more things they consider due to them. The Russians will continue to exert pressure on us; our recognition of the G.D.R. has changed nothing in that connection and has in fact not reduced the prospects that the pressure will increase.

Moscow, October 19, 1957

The government of West Germany has decided to break off diplomatic relations with Yugoslavia because of our recognition of East Germany. The Russians are behaving as though they had not expected this and criticize the West German Government's move. In fact they are not very grieved by this decision; they are, I would say, pleasantly surprised that Bonn has broken off relations with Belgrade.

Nielsen, the Moscow correspondent of the West Germans news agency, told our correspondent Milićević, apparently on instructions from his superiors, that the West German Government does not intend to spoil relations with Yugoslavia although they were obliged to break them off. Minister von Brentano cited twenty-two states which might have followed Yugoslavia's example and which had been waiting to see how Bonn reacted. Those states would now refrain from doing what Belgrade had done. The German correspondent repeated that it was the wish of the West German Government that relations with Yugoslavia should remain as they have been till now in the field of trade, war claims, tourism, and so forth.

A commentary in the Soviet press criticizes not only the West Germans for this decision but the Americans as well. It is as though the Soviet press welcomes what has happened so as to be able to attack the United States and West Germany; it is less interested in what suits Yugoslavia's interests. We have information in the contrary sense, that the Americans advised Bonn not to break off relations with us, and not that they encouraged Bonn to do so, as the Russians say.

The story is going round the diplomatic corps that the embassies of a number of countries have reported from Belgrade their view that Belgrade had not counted on relations being broken off and that Yugoslavia was taken by surprise. People are convinced that we miscalculated. In those Western circles here which were not badly disposed toward us one can hear comments to the effect that in this case the Yugoslavs have made the first serious mistake in their foreign policy for a long time.

I cannot rid myself of the impression that the Russians and especially the East Europeans are pleased with the move made by Adenauer's government. It is as though they are saying: As soon as you Yugoslavs adopted a "correct stand" on the recognition of the G.D.R., which you avoided doing for years, you saw what happened.

Moscow, October 26, 1957

At a reception given by the Iranian ambassador this evening Khrushchev informed me that this afternoon, from half past two till nearly eight in the evening, the Presidium had been discussing the conduct of Marshal Zhukov following the June plenum. He mentioned the following examples of Zhukov's antiparty behavior:

At the time of the events in June connected with the Molotov-Kaganovich-Malenkov group Marshal Zhukov told certain people that he, Zhukov, would call out the Army and the people and settle accounts with M-K-M if it should be necessary. Zhukov had thus been speaking in a manner which could not be tolerated in a Communist and a leader, because what, Khrushchev asked, was the position of the Central Committee and the party, if Zhukov had such an opinion of himself and of the way the Army could be used.

In connection with the visit of a Soviet Government delegation to East Germany in August this year it was later decided in Moscow that Bulganin should not go. But Zhukov is alleged to have intrigued and to have told Bulganin that he ought to go. Zhukov also told Marshal Grechko, commander of the Soviet troops in the G.D.R., that there was no need for him to meet Khrushchev and the delegation but to leave it to the Germans. Grechko did not agree to this and informed Khrushchev about it.

As Minister of National Defense Marshal Zhukov was deputy to the head of the secret Military Council of National Defense, that is to

Khrushchev, who as First Secretary of the party has the leading position on the council. Zhukov, who never called any meetings of the council, proposed to reorganize it in such a way that the party leaders would have been pushed right out, including members of the Presidium, in favor of military officers.

Khrushchev said that in the campaign which the West deliberately worked up about the role of Marshal Zhukov in the June events Zhukov allowed himself to be influenced by that campaign, forgetting the party and the people and overestimating the importance of his own person.

Because of all this, Khrushchev went on, the Presidium has today, in the presence of those members of the Central Committee who were in Moscow, decided that Marshal Zhukov should be removed from the post of Minister of Defense. Marshal Malinovsky has been appointed in his place, as will be announced on the radio this evening and in the press tomorrow. On Monday next there will be a plenum of the Central Committee which will decide on the question of Zhukov. Khrushchev told me that the plenum would probably remove him from the Presidium, but from the way he spoke it is not impossible that some more severe penalty may be imposed.

Khrushchev assured me that the whole affair had nothing at all to do with Zhukov's stay in Yugoslavia and that the Presidium today recorded the fact that Zhukov's trip to Yugoslavia had been successful and useful for the development of friendly relations between our countries.

Marshal Zhukov arrived in Moscow today at about two in the afternoon. According to Khrushchev, it appears he went straight from the airport to the meeting of the Presidium which was already in session and waiting for Zhukov to arrive.

I talked to Khrushchev for a long time about what was for me surprising news. After saying that my comments might perhaps be thought out of place, I mentioned the shadow which this incident would cast over the forthcoming celebration of the October Revolution. People in the world outside would try to find in this affair further proof of a lack of unity in the Soviet leadership. I wondered aloud whether a week before the October celebrations was the best time to take such decisions?

Khrushchev replied that they had thought about all these factors but there had been no alternative. On Monday it would be approved by the plenum, then the party would be informed and finally the public at large. I then returned to the question of Zhukov's visit to Yugoslavia. Khrushchev assured me that everything had been all right there and that they had no criticisms to make. At the end of the conversation Mikoyan and Bulganin came up and Khrushchev told them he had informed me what had happened. They both in turn said it had nothing to do with Zhukov's visit to Yugoslavia.

Khrushchev wanted Tito and the other comrades to understand correctly the entirely sound party motives which had made it essential to resolve the question of Marshal Zhukov in this way. He again talked about the monolithic nature of the Central Committee and the party, which would deal in this way with Zhukov and with anybody else who got out of step with the party.

As for reaction abroad, in Khrushchev's view, there would be all sorts of commentaries, but the foreigners would on the whole be pleased, because they would be freed from the fear that the military leaders, the marshals, might take power in the Soviet Union and so increase the danger of war. On the other hand, foreigners would see that the Soviet party was strong, taking the sort of decisions that only a really strong person takes. Khrushchev then said that he had never agreed with Stalin over his attitude to Marshal Zhukov.[4] The fact that Zhukov behaved well at the June plenum did not alter the necessity for the present treatment of him. Khrushchev asked me to regard some of the things he told me as confidential.

Moscow, October 27, 1957

In the course of our conversation yesterday I told Khrushchev that I was surprised at the length of time Zhukov had spent in Albania, where he had stayed almost as long as in Yugoslavia. The implication was clear: They had kept Zhukov ten days in Albania and as much again in Yugoslavia to give them time here to prepare for his political liquidation. Khrushchev now says this was a mistake, and that one would normally stay in Albania for such a visit for two or three days and not ten!

In the latter days of Zhukov's stay in Albania the Soviet press suddenly stopped printing any reports about it. This was explained on the grounds that they had nothing to report. Interestingly enough, Marshal Zhukov himself agreed with the program for his stay in Yugoslavia and Albania. From which one might conclude that the marshal had not the faintest idea of what was being cooked up for him in Moscow.

I asked Khrushchev what Zhukov had to say about what had happened. Khrushchev replied that Zhukov had said that the Presidium's decision to remove him from the post of Defense Minister was understandable if the Presidium had such an opinion of his behavior. Khrushchev said that the party could never permit a person who had such an opinion of himself as

[4] After the victory over Germany in 1945 Marshal Zhukov became commander in chief of Soviet troops in Germany, 1945–46, and then Commander in Chief of Soviet ground forces and Deputy Defense Minister. But in 1946, either because he was jealous of Zhukov's popularity or because he wanted to cut the Soviet military down to size, Stalin gave Zhukov the relatively obscure post of commander of the Odessa military district, where he remained until Stalin died in 1953.

Marshal Zhukov, who considered that it depended on him alone when the Army should be called on to intervene in domestic affairs, to be minister of the armed forces of the Soviet Union. If in June he threatened to call out the Army and "restore order," that meant that he was capable of using the troops against Molotov and Malenkov today and of using the same troops against someone else tomorrow. But what about the Central Committee, which had to decide everything, and what about the party and the people? Khrushchev kept asking.

Khrushchev assured me that the military had been especially upset by Marshal Zhukov's behavior. He quoted the example of some admiral in Sevastopol who suffered from asthma and who had said that he could now "breathe more easily." Khrushchev spoke very highly of the new Defense Minister, Marshal Malinovsky.

News of Marshal Zhukov's removal has come as a big sensation here. . . . But no special security measures appear to have been taken in Moscow.

Moscow, October 28, 1957

The extent to which Zhukov's removal took Soviet people by surprise can be judged from the fact that some of them interpret it as a preparation for his appointment as Prime Minister in place of Bulganin, who compromised himself in June. There is talk of Zhukov's popularity and naturally people expect him to be promoted and do not realize that he has been eliminated politically. Similar explanations were offered even by some East European and other Communist journalists!

I have asked Belgrade to inform the Foreign Ministry and our State Secretariat for Defense what has happened, because many of our people are still causing us trouble. Today, on an open telephone line, which the Russians, Hungarians, and others listen in to, someone in the second department of our General Staff reproached our military attaché for not letting Belgrade know anything, yet he cannot have anything new to tell them, since I alone inform Belgrade, and the comrades there pass the information on to those who need it.

I tried to find out how Khrushchev thinks of dealing with the Zhukov affair publicly. Since it was impossible for me to put the question directly, I talked about Zhukov's wartime services, said he was well known to the British and Americans and to everybody else in the West and the East, and that this should be treated realistically even though Zhukov's position was now fundamentally changed. Khrushchev immediately grasped what I was implying and said that they respected Zhukov's wartime achievements and that nobody thought of questioning them. He went on to praise Marshal Malinovsky as a military man and a politician.

Malinovsky is evidently Khrushchev's choice as successor to Zhukov. According to Khrushchev, before the war he only just escaped being executed by Stalin as a foreign agent.

Khrushchev, Bulganin, Mikoyan, and many other top Soviet officials turned up at the Turkish ambassador's reception, to the great surprise of everybody present and especially the ambassador himself because throughout October the Soviet attitude to Turkey has been almost threatening on account of Syria.[5] The Russians would probably not have turned up had it not been for the Zhukov affair. Khrushchev is trying to do everything possible to allay the fuss about this sudden development. When there is a crisis in the Kremlin, Khrushchev does not withdraw from public view but appears at diplomatic receptions and in public, carries on conversations right and left, and tries to give the impression of calm and self-confidence. This reveals him as a skillful political tactician and as a man who knows how to face up to political difficulties and does not try to evade them.

Moscow, October 30, 1957

Patolichev called in the ambassadors of the socialist countries to inform them about the Zhukov affair. He said that the Central Committee plenum met for two days, October 28 and 29, and that the report on improving party-political work in the Soviet Army was delivered, on behalf of the Presidium, by Suslov. Information about Zhukov's mistakes had already been received from party sources in the armed forces. The Presidium had ordered an inquiry to be made in certain military regions on October 19 and this had revealed the scope and seriousness of the mistakes, after which it was decided to hold a plenum, Patolichev said.

It is clearly not true that it was only on the basis of this inquiry that they decided to call the plenum. It was all decided much earlier. In fact I believe no "inquiry" was carried out, nor is it possible in the Soviet Union to carry out such an inquiry, either secretly, as this one was, of course, or in public in the matter of a few days and in such circumstances.

Patolichev said that Marshal Zhukov had performed great services in the war with Germany, as had been confirmed at the plenum, but so had other Soviet marshals, and the greatest contribution had been made by the party and the people who had done the fighting. Among those mar-

[5] From mid-September 1957 tension rose in the Middle East following Soviet and Syrian allegations that Turkey was concentrating troops on the Syrian border with the object of overthrowing the existing regime in Syria with American help. The Americans and Turks denied the allegations, drew attention to Soviet supplies of arms to Syria, and accused the Russians of trying to convert Syria into a Soviet satellite.

shals whose merits were no less than Zhukov's, Patolichev mentioned Malinovsky, Rokossovsky, and Koniev.

As evidence of a campaign aimed at creating a cult of Zhukov's personality Patolichev mentioned a film in which Zhukov is shown as the great victor of the 1941–45 war. At the end of the film Zhukov appears, more than life-size, on a white charger against a background of the ruins of the Reichstag in Berlin. Another similar film shows Zhukov against the background of the damaged Brandenburg Gates in Berlin. These films were run through at the Central Committee. I have never before heard of films being shown, here or anywhere else at Central Committee meetings, as evidence against someone about whom the meeting has to take a political decision.

Patolichev particularly insisted that the affair was a strictly internal matter for their party and could not have anything to do with Zhukov's visits to "our fraternal socialist countries, Yugoslavia and Albania." The ambassadors present put to Patolichev a lot of largely pointless questions. Only the Chinese ambassador and I did not ask anything. When we shook hands, Patolichev commented that I had known about it all already because of my talk with Khrushchev.

On my way back from the meeting I reflected on what Patolichev had said. It seems to me that he was most successful in the part where he talked about the films showing Zhukov as the great victor on a white horse. I recalled seeing another film about Zhukov which was made by Moscow television during the marshal's visit to Leningrad in July. I think it was at the time of Khrushchev's visit to Czechoslovakia, immediately after the June plenum and the elimination of the Molotov-Malenkov group. Zhukov was filmed, not in Berlin, but on the Nevsky Prospekt in Leningrad, and not on a white horse but in an open ZIS limousine, which was moving slowly, as though at a review of troops, along the street lined by more than a million Leningraders who were cheering the famous Soviet marshal, bedecked in his orders and medals.

In those days Zhukov was the only person in the Soviet Union (it was not the case with Mikoyan or any other member of the Presidium) who was "authorized" to make outspoken speeches about the antiparty group, which had only just been defeated with his decisive assistance. The impressive welcome he received in Leningrad was transmitted by Moscow television, and his outspoken statements about Molotov and Malenkov were reported by the whole of the central Soviet press. I do not know whether cuts from that Leningrad film were shown at the October 29 plenum.

I imagine Khrushchev was not at all pleased with these Leningrad films when he returned from Czechoslovakia. I also believe he didn't like Zhukov's sharply worded speeches about the antiparty group or the fact that in Khrushchev's absence Zhukov was the only speaker in the Soviet Union to raise the matter in public. One cannot conceive of the Soviet system without a single, unchallenged leader to personify both party and state. That's how it was in Stalin's lifetime, and after his death it was unclear who would finally take over the role of undisputed leader, since there were plenty of pretenders for the position. June 1957 saw the defeat of Molotov and Malenkov, who made a bid for the leading role, although they tried to share it for a time just to get it away from Khrushchev. In their defeat Marshal Zhukov came very much to the fore, and his prestige in the Soviet Union was, in my opinion, even before June, greater than that of any other Soviet personality. It looks as though this circumstance did not work in Marshal Zhukov's favor.

Moscow, October 31, 1957

The epoch-making scientific and technological achievements of the Soviet Union in launching the first sputnik and producing intercontinental ballistic missiles has had a very powerful effect on Soviet society. It will soon be a month during which the subject has not left the front pages of the Soviet press. Films have been made about it and popular scientific meetings are being held throughout the country which are developing into a campaign to glorify the Soviet state and society. At the same time they reveal a tendency to suggest that the sputnik is in itself sufficient to make up for all the weaknesses in the Soviet Union, as though it could provide the answer to everybody who has criticized the Soviet Union in any field.

Nationalistic slogans are reappearing from earlier days: not just about the Soviet genius but about the Russian national genius as well in the field of scientific and technological discovery. Thus the central Soviet newspapers have printed leading articles about what the Russians have invented in modern times: The Cherepanovs invented the steam engine; Mozhaisky invented the airplane; Popov invented radio; and Yablochkov invented the arc lamp.[6]

This was first published by the *Literaturnaya Gazeta* and then repeated

[6] The Cherepanovs—Yefim (1774–1842) and Miron (1803–49)—father and son, were both inventors and responsible for constructing in 1834 the first locomotive for use in the Russian mining industry.

Aleksandr F. Mozhaisky, 1825–90. Russian engineer and inventor who is said to have completed the construction of an airplane in 1882, but there is no record of its having flown.

Aleksandr S. Popov, 1859–1905. Russian scientist who demonstrated a radio receiver in 1855, before Marconi invented radiotelegraphy.

Pavel N. Yablochkov, 1847–94. Russian electrical engineer who invented the first electric arc lamp.

by the president of the Soviet Academy of Science, Nesmeyanov,[7] at a gathering of scientists in Moscow in October!

Khrushchev has said that the development of the sputnik means that bombers could now be put on the scrap heap. This tends to obscure the scientific and technological aspects of the achievement and to put too much stress on its military significance. The sputnik is being used as evidence of Soviet superiority over the West in the armaments field. This is probably being pushed on account of the tense international situation, which has to some extent damped down the enthusiasm within the Soviet Union about the sputnik because it increases the fear of war. The Soviet press has been writing about that fear throughout October, as well as writing about the sputnik.

[7] Alexsandr N. Nesmeyanov, b. 1899. Russian organic chemist. President, Soviet Academy of Science, 1951–61.

CHAPTER TWENTY-FIVE

THE ANNIVERSARY OF THE REVOLUTION
AND THE PARTY CONFERENCE

The Russians are annoyed by Tito's failure to lead the Yugoslav delegation to the celebration of the fortieth anniversary of the Revolution and by the Yugoslavs' refusal to sign the "declaration" approved by the other parties. Mikoyan's strange reaction to Mao Tse-tung's speech suggests that all is not well between the Russians and Chinese. The Yugoslav delegation calls on Mao Tse-tung.

Moscow, November 3, 1957

The Soviet Communist party's "theses" published in connection with the celebration of the fortieth anniversary of the October Revolution contain its official assessment of the achievements of the Soviet party and state over the forty years as well as the Soviet view of the major problems of the day. These views are set out in "theses" which are in many respects contradictory. It is as though the Soviet authors had tried to make it possible for every one of the foreign parties to find something in the theses to suit its needs and to ignore the rest, and so find it easier to agree with the Russians. Thus, for example, the theses include acceptance of the idea of various paths to socialism, but at the same time socialism is treated as though it coincides with the countries in the Soviet orbit and socialism cannot exist outside it. The theses include some new approaches to world events, but also quite a few of the old views and rules which operated in Stalin's day.

I believe that this document, like every other presented to the forthcoming conference of Communist parties, should be examined from one basic point of view: Does it or does it not provide answers to the questions raised by the present state of the revolutionary movement in the

313

world? I will mention only two or three of the questions which have been demanding solution for some years now:

–Will the individual Communist parties be free to determine their own policies in accordance with the situation of the working class and people of their own country, or will they be guided and led from one center, as has always been insisted to date?

–Do the socialist forces in the world coincide in the main with the state frontiers of the countries of the "socialist camp" or do they embrace a far wider area irrespective of those frontiers?

–Are we to accept the theory, or rather the existing reality in the world, that there exist different paths in different countries, all leading to socialism, but depending on the specific historical, economic, cultural, and other conditions in each country, or do we have to agree that socialism can be built only on the Soviet model in all countries without distinction?

So long as there existed only one socialist country, the Soviet Union, the question of relations between socialist states did not arise as it does today, when there are many socialist states in the world, from the smallest, Albania, to the largest, which is China. Are the socialist countries building a new type of international relations based on the principle of the independence and equal rights of every country, which would have a positive effect on international relations, or is the world of socialism to be subject to the domination of the strong powers over the less strong, the great over the small, and the rich over the poor—as is the case in the capitalist world?

To judge from the insistence on the monolithic character and unity of the socialist camp, into which they are trying to drag independent Yugoslavia—for that is the political sense of these theses—it might well be said that the Moscow conference is not intended to provide new answers to these questions.

Moscow, November 5, 1957

The welcome for our delegation at the Soviet frontier went off all right, and so did the dinner which the Ukrainian Government and Communist party gave for the delegation in Kiev. Kardelj, the leader of our delegation, made a very friendly speech about the Soviet Union and the Ukraine and I had the impression that it was well received. To judge from this, one might conclude that everything will go off well in Moscow. But nice speeches in Kiev are one thing, and what is now awaiting us in Moscow quite another.

During the train journey to Moscow I tried to acquaint Comrades Kardelj and Ranković, as well as Veljko Vlahović, who knows Moscow well from the war years, with the general mood in Moscow which is not going to be particularly favorable for us. This was not news for the comrades, who had already come to some definite conclusions about the Russians' attitude in the course of discussions with Ponomarev and Andropov, who went recently to Belgrade on behalf of the CPSU to try to reconcile with the Yugoslavs their views about the declaration which the Presidium wants the Moscow conference of Communist parties to approve. Our people did not agree and told the Russians so, so that they returned to Moscow not only with empty hands but also with bad news about Yugoslavia's attitude. Soviet displeasure with us is on the increase, and so the cordial welcome at the frontier and the dinner in Kiev do not reflect the Russians' real attitude.

On our arrival in Moscow the Russians did not conceal their displeasure. The delegation was met by Mikoyan, Suslov, and a group of minor officials, mostly from the government service. Mikoyan and Suslov escorted Kardelj and Ranković by car to their residence. In the ten minutes during which they were together there was no talk of political questions. Immediately on arriving our people asked for a meeting with Khrushchev. They were told only in the evening that Khrushchev was busy but that he could meet them tomorrow, November 6, during the break in the session of the Supreme Soviet.

The Russians are convinced that Tito's illness is a "political" one. When we raise the question on our side, the Russians avoid talking about it and so demonstrate their displeasure.

Moscow, November 7, 1957

I believe that Kardelj's speech at the special session of the Supreme Soviet was among the best suited for this occasion. Kardelj and Gomulka were the only ones to speak in Russian, the other East Europeans speaking in their own languages, presumably because they don't know Russian and because they are so devoted to their native tongues. The Soviet public could follow them only through the interpreter and for the most part missed the more striking parts of their speeches, although some of the East European party leaders shouted as though they were addressing an election meeting. Todor Zhivkov in particular spoke at the top of his voice.

The speeches by Kardelj and Gomulka were listened to by some ten thousand Russians who were present and received significantly more applause than the other leaders from the "camp." So it turned out that the Soviet public gave a better reception to the speeches of the "Yugoslav revisionists" and the Poles than to those of the "true Marxist-Leninists" and the "proletarian internationalists" from the other countries of the "camp."

I don't believe the Russians expected Kardelj's speech to be so friendly toward the Soviet Union or so full of the ideas of the October Revolution and of recognition for Lenin and the Russian people who started the Revolution and carried it through to victory. In the interval which followed Kardelj's speech a group of Russians came up to me, said the speech had made the best possible impression, and congratulated me on "Kardelj's brilliant speech." These people appeared to be genuinely surprised and enthusiastic. I thanked them for their congratulations, shook hands with five or six of them, and said that the speech was nothing special, that Kardelj had spoken in that way about the October Revolution in the past and that he always spoke about it like that in Yugoslavia.

Moscow, November 8, 1957

The Russians are displaying their annoyance with us by operating a sort of boycott of our delegation. This affects other delegations who don't want to upset the Russians and so they avoid us too and make our situation even less pleasant. The Poles are an exception: They talk to us normally, although even they take care not to spend too long in our company. We have told Gomulka that we are not going to sign any joint document, such as a declaration obliging all the parties to follow the same course, because we are opposed in principle to signing such documents. Gomulka informed us that the Russians want at any price to have such a joint document approved.

Things took a further turn for the worse at the dinner which our delegation had with the Russians at Khrushchev's invitation. Mikoyan, Suslov, Ponomarev, and Andropov were also present. On the Yugoslav side were Comrades Kardelj, Ranković, Koliševski, and Vlahović. Without wasting time on polite speeches Khrushchev immediately took the floor and informed us that a meeting was to take place of representatives of the Communist parties of the socialist countries and that they had agreed to publish a joint declaration without the Yugoslavs. Khrushchev said he was sorry it had turned out like that, but that the matter was in our hands and they were not in any way responsible for the fact that our relations were again going to be disrupted, since it had been our choice and not theirs.

Kardelj and Ranković spoke for us. They put forward the same arguments as had been set before Andropov and Ponomarev in Belgrade. The longer the discussion went on, the more heated it became. Khrushchev's behavior contributed a good deal to the worsening of the atmosphere.

Some of his remarks were plainly insulting and he made no effort to avoid this.

Our delegation has the impression that the events of recent months have prompted the Russians to take this tough line and exert such strong pressure on us. There was talk about our last meeting in Bucharest. The Russians now interpret that in their own way—to suit their needs—suggesting that we are not carrying out something that we promised. This again confirms that it is best not to sign anything with the Russians that is not going to be published. Khrushchev was tougher than previously, and it looks to us as though he was easier to talk to so long as Molotov and Malenkov or Marshal Zhukov were still in the Soviet leadership.

On the first evening Khrushchev tried by means of a sort of frontal assault to break down our opposition to signing a joint declaration. When this tactic of the "surprise attack" produced no results, the Russians adopted gentler tactics, again through Khrushchev. He said that Tito's article in the American magazine *Foreign Affairs* was excellent and that after all that had happened they were now even more surprised that we refused to sign the declaration. All the parties have apparently accepted the Soviet draft. Many did so by telegram before their delegations arrived in Moscow, Khrushchev said. They were now putting the final touches to the draft along with the Chinese and they wanted to come out with a joint declaration. The Chinese are now insisting on inserting into the draft the phrase "the camp led by the Soviet Union." The Poles are also going to sign. In fact, there is not going to be any conference of Communist parties at all. Instead of a conference or any kind of discussion there will be a number of more or less formal and identical statements in support of the joint document.

We find quite unacceptable Khrushchev's advice that we should approve the declaration in essence but express our reservations on specific issues. By doing that we should provoke confusion on all sides. Then neither in the camp nor in the rest of the world would anybody know what our attitude was and, most important, there would be confusion in Yugoslavia itself. It would appear that we did not in fact have a stand of our own, but accepted the line of the Russians and the camp, though not entirely, as if we wanted to preserve some room for relations with the other, Western bloc, of which the Russians accuse us anyway. The solidarity of the Communist parties represented in Moscow with the ideas inspired by the October Revolution and the support which they give to the Soviet Union in this way is very strong. But the Russians themselves actually weaken this support, which we all give them by taking part as friends, when they insist on pushing through a joint declaration which they have drawn up themselves and with which we do not agree.

Nor can we act in accordance with Belgrade's suggestion that we should put forward our own draft declaration. This would only be an open provocation which would lead to a break between us and the Soviet Union and others in the camp. The only realistic thing is for us to sign the "peace appeal" which the Poles have proposed, on condition that we get the draft in good time and that we agree with it. We shall not take part in the party conference when the declaration is being passed but only at the meeting which is to approve the "peace appeal."

Moscow, November 10, 1957

Our delegation asked to be received by Khrushchev and Voroshilov on the day they arrived in Moscow, but they saw them only yesterday. These were planned as courtesy visits, but it was agreed that if the Russians again raised controversial questions our people were ready once again to talk and inform them of our unchanged point of view.

Although our people had already met Khrushchev and the others at the Supreme Soviet and again at the dinner with Khrushchev and had already had talks with the Soviet delegation, they behaved yesterday as though we were meeting for the first time. Our people handed over Comrade Tito's greetings to the Soviet officials and commented that the very successful Supreme Soviet session had made a deep impression on those present. In all its forty years the Supreme Soviet has probably not held a single session outside the walls of the Kremlin, but this time it was held in Luzhniki Stadium on the outskirts of Moscow in a hall capable of holding ten thousand people and which was practically full. It is something new for the Russians to go outside the Kremlin for such an occasion. But it was more suitable for the celebration of October and made a greater impression on the foreign delegations and the Soviet public.

Because of our refusal to sign the declaration, we have no contacts at all with Soviet officials at other levels and we are surrounded by an unpleasant atmosphere. Our comrades while away the time in the house they have been provided with on the Lenin Hills. Time passes slowly and our people mostly stay at home playing cards on these long November evenings, not because they are so keen on the game but so as to avoid talking, because they know the Russians are listening in to them. It is consequently very quiet in the residence.

We have told the Poles about our talk with Khrushchev. Although the Polish delegation has not said explicitly that they agree with us, their attitude is essentially the same as ours. This can be deduced from the text of their "peace manifesto" which will be put forward in the "second part" of the conference. The Polish text seems perfectly acceptable to us, so

318

long as the Russians don't "improve" it, as the Chinese "improved" the Soviet draft of the declaration.

Moscow, November 12, 1957

Our delegation met with Khrushchev again today. Kardelj explained that we are unable to sign the declaration for reasons which were already well known to Khrushchev. The text did not correspond with what we had agreed in Bucharest but went a lot further. We thought that it would be best for our relations with the Soviet Union and the others if we did not take part in the conference. There could be no question of our signing the declaration with reservations, because that would only add to the confusion which we and they would then have to explain, and that was altogether undesirable. In our press we would support those points in the declaration with which we agreed, Kardelj said.

Khrushchev did not get excited or raise his voice as he did at the last meeting, but used essentially the same arguments. He tried to give his own interpretation to everything that had happened as well as to our meeting in Bucharest. He threatened that there would now be a rift in our relations and that we ourselves had chosen such a course. He said our enemies would now be pleased because it had been shown that we were not united. Molotov might send us congratulations for such conduct, Khrushchev said. Our people did not react to what Khrushchev said in the same spirit. They tried to have a reasonable discussion with him, explaining the reasons why we were opposed in principle to the revival of a new international organization of Communist parties, which such a declaration implies.

Khrushchev explained that Mao Tse-tung had demanded that the declaration should include the words "the camp headed by the Soviet Union" and that the Soviet party should be given written authority to call a similar conference in the future. They foresee having such conferences every two years. Mao Tse-tung was so insistent over these proposals that he had said that they must be included in the declaration "even if it were signed only by the Chinese and the Russians."

Kardelj and Ranković restrained themselves so as to avoid more heated arguments. They argued that our refusal to sign the declaration ought not to affect the good relations between our governments. The meeting ended in a relatively tolerable mood. Although our people made it clear that this was our last word and that there was no point in returning to the question, Khrushchev said the matter would have to be further considered and so gave us to understand that pressure would be put on us for the third time.

Moscow, November 14, 1957

When we reached the point of having to take a final decision about whether we would stick to the view we have held from the beginning—not to sign the declaration or to take part in the conference—our delegation decided to have one more meeting in the embassy building where, as it seemed to me, we could speak more freely. For this purpose we did not use any of the main rooms in the embassy, although we had already destroyed the Soviet "bugging" system, having found nineteen microphones all wired up and installed in all the rooms either under the parquet floors or in the ceilings. It seemed to me better to have the meeting in a small passageway which is not generally used and where there is no electric current. I thought that there we might be less likely to be listened to by the Russians.

Those who took part in the meeting were Comrades Kardelj, Ranković, Veljko Vlahović, Lazar Koliševski, Ugleša Danilović, and myself, as members of the delegation. We also invited Comrade Djuro Salaj, who was on his way through Moscow. We only just managed to squeeze into the space around a small table, and since there was no electricity we had a candle burning in the middle. I doubt whether since World War II any of us had been present at such a meeting in semidarkness at a round table with a lighted candle in the middle. We kept our voices as low as possible to a background of music coming from the next room.

The meeting lasted for about an hour. Being in a sense the host, although I was the youngest member of the delegation, I spoke first and briefly: I said that although Khrushchev expected us to give him our final views once again, nothing new had happened to cause us to change the stand which our leaders had already taken up and of which the delegation had already informed the Russians several times.

All the members of the delegation spoke, some of them very briefly, simply repeating in fact what they had agreed before arriving in Moscow. Kardelj and Salaj spoke rather longer. Kardelj spoke about the situation which might arise after our failure to sign the declaration, which was taken for granted. On the credit side would be our signing of the "peace appeal," which all the parties were signing, our speech in the Supreme Soviet, which had been published and was available in the Soviet Union and elsewhere, and our statement at the end of the conference, and —no less important than all that—was the Soviet interest in not immediately straining relations with Yugoslavia to the limit—as we hoped.

We accepted the final text of the "peace manifesto," which was not ideal but better than the declaration and had a different role to play as a political document. Neither the Soviet texts nor this document had managed to rid themselves of Soviet clichés: accusing the West and the United States of conducting a cold war policy and so forth, and presenting the Soviet bloc exclusively in the opposite, favorable light. The style and vocabulary of the draft are pure "camp" language and in the spirit of the other propaganda documents published here. The conference of the twelve parties will begin without us. We shall take part in the second conference with all the parties and not just those from the "camp." We shall make a short statement about signing the "peace appeal" and explain our stand on the basic issues.

Moscow, November 17, 1957

Complete agreement has been reached between our delegation and the comrades in Yugoslavia about our conduct here, which Tito and the other comrades there support completely. This has a good effect on the mood in our delegation, in which there really is unanimity even when it comes down to details. And this unity in the delegation also, I believe, has a good effect on the comrades at home. This all creates a healthy atmosphere in which one must feel good.

The Russians have made their own contribution to this by sticking rigidly to their old fundamentally hegemonistic attitude. If they had not demanded such uniformity and had been more flexible and if they had not put forward the Twelve-party Declaration as a sort of set of ideological principles for all the Communist parties of the countries of the socialist camp, into which they wanted to push Yugoslavia as well, it would not have been so easy for us to decide not to take part. The second conference of the sixty-four parties started yesterday in St. George's Hall of the Kremlin around a huge rectangular table, with the Russian and Chinese delegations facing each other in the middle. The Soviet delegation distributed in good time the text of the report to be made by Suslov, a whole book of seventy pages, but on a very low level for such a gathering. Suslov spoke very briefly, simply to point out the official nature of the report distributed to us and to warn us that what it said was not for publication.

The conference continued today and, as we expected, the most interesting speech was Togliatti's. He polemicized indirectly with everyone who supported the old ideas, especially with the French delegate Duclos.[1] This was less painful and much easier for him to do than to criticize the Russians or anybody else in the "camp." Togliatti was categorically opposed to any idea of setting up a new international organization of Com-

[1] Jacques Duclos, 1896–1975. Secretary, French Communist party, 1931–64.

munist parties like the old Cominform. At the same time he made a strong appeal for developing cooperation between the parties. The stronger his support for such cooperation, the more decisively he criticized the formation of any new international organization. He supported the Twelve-party Declaration, because if he had not done so he would not have been able to say the positive things he did.

Moscow, November 19, 1957

Here are a few notes about the speech which Mao Tse-tung made at the conference the day before yesterday and in which all the delegations were greatly interested. Mao was the only speaker at the conference not to go on to the tribune from which the others spoke. He spoke sitting down in his place. When he began to speak, he explained that he was a sick man and that it was "in the head," according to the way the interpreter translated it, which, it seemed to me, came as a surprise to the majority of those present. Mao spoke for about an hour through an interpreter. It was a speech which seemed to me to be full of clichés and propaganda and crammed with Chinese proverbs and pieces of wisdom, and which did not give a true picture of the modern world, either socialist or capitalist or the one between them.

As Mao spoke from his place at the table and his speech was interpreted into Russian, there was a good deal of movement in the Soviet delegation, and then Mikoyan reacted ostentatiously to what Mao Tse-tung was saying. At one point, without any particular warning, Mao said that there had been a clash in the Soviet Union between "two different groups" in the leadership of the party and that "the tendency led by Khrushchev had won the day." That was how the interpreter translated his words. What exactly he said nobody except the Chinese knew.

Mao Tse-tung's statement identifying the antiparty group of Malenkov, Molotov, and Kaganovich with the CPSU, which he called the second group, produced a deathly silence among the several hundred people present in St. George's Hall. Mikoyan rose demonstratively from the table and, with an expression on his face which was anything but friendly, stood there looking at the speaker and the group of Chinese sitting directly opposite the Soviet delegation. At times Mikoyan turned his back on the speaker and appeared to be reading the names of the Tsarist regiments and Russian soldiers who had won the order of St. George, which are inscribed in letters of gold on the walls of the hall.

None of the Russians sitting near Mikoyan as he made his demonstration tried to stop him or urged him to sit down. The whole hall was watching and I believe that this was why Mikoyan continued to listen to

Mao Tse-tung standing, now turning round to look at him as though listening to his words, then looking out of the window with his back to the speaker. After such a speech by Mao Tse-tung and Mikoyan's demonstrative reaction, as well as the glacial silence which reigned in the Soviet delegation, statements about the "monolithic unity" of the Soviet Union and China which we hear here at every step do not sound particularly convincing. The Chinese behaved throughout as though nothing was happening and that it was all quite normal.

Veljko Vlahović made a short statement on behalf of the League of Communists of Yugoslavia and our delegation. Unlike Mao Tse-tung, who spoke sitting in his place, Veljko went up to the rostrum at the end of the hall, despite the fact that he has only one leg and was seriously wounded in the Spanish Civil War. His statement was well received by a large number of delegations, but the Russians did not conceal their displeasure and did not applaud. With that our delegation's work in Moscow was at last finished and it was free to return to Yugoslavia after a long stay in Moscow and resistance to the Russian pressure.

Moscow, November 20, 1957

Our delegation left Moscow by train today for Belgrade. I believe all of them felt that we had done the best we could in Moscow and that we had done a good job in the circumstances. We had never for a moment had the slightest hesitation about whether to sign the Twelve-party Declaration or not. The decision on that was already taken in Yugoslavia. All we had to do here was to put the decision into practice and at the same time do everything in our power not to let differences with the Russians go to extremes or to let Yugoslavia be isolated from the other delegations.

The resistance which we put up successfully to all the various pressures was not especially difficult, although Soviet pressure was very strong. We had the feeling that the leadership of our party, led by Tito, was unwavering in its determination that we should remain independent, both as a state and as a force for socialism in Europe and the world irrespective of the way things went in Moscow. At the same time we felt that our line enjoyed the active support of millions of people in Yugoslavia, Communists and non-Communists alike, and that the great majority of our citizens believed our party delegation in Moscow could not act differently.

* * *

I omitted to write about our delegation's reception by Mao Tse-tung. When the conference was nearing its end and the Twelve-party Declaration had already been signed without Yugoslavia, on Comrade Kardelj's advice our delegation asked to make a courtesy call on Mao. If he refused to receive the delegation, which we considered quite possible after our final refusal to sign the declaration, we decided to leave it to the Chinese to consider whether that was the best thing to do.

Chinese Ambassador Liu Siao replied to my request very quickly and in the affirmative. Mao would be very glad, I was told, to receive our delegation that very day. It almost looked as though the Chinese had only been waiting for us to ask for a meeting. Mao shook hands cordially with each of the Yugoslavs and was an extremely amiable host throughout the hours which our delegation spent talking to him. The conversation dealt with various questions about conditions in Yugoslavia and our comrades tried to give Mao as accurate a picture as possible. But we had the impression that he knew nothing about the basic facts concerning the internal situation in Yugoslavia. Perhaps this was a mistaken impression, because it is difficult to guess what a Chinese knows or doesn't know when you are talking to him.

It was interesting to find that Mao Tse-tung gave no sign of being displeased that we had not signed the Twelve-party Declaration. When we tried to explain to him briefly our reasons for not signing, Mao said simply that he didn't see any problem, that we hadn't signed this declaration, but that we would sign some other declaration in fifteen or twenty more years. Our people were surprised by such a reply. Mao reacted similarly when our comrades tried to explain why Yugoslavia was still lagging behind in agricultural production. When we told him that we had so far been investing mainly in industry and the towns and that the countryside had therefore fallen behind but that we would begin to improve the situation in two or three years, Mao commented: Why in two or three years? Maybe it will need twenty or thirty years or more.

At the end, as he took leave of our delegation, Mao found a few carefully chosen words for Yugoslavia and its people, to whom he sent cordial greetings and best wishes. Apart from the other obvious differences between the Chinese and us, it was obvious that we had an entirely different view of the time factor in our foreign and domestic policy.

The conference concluded with a lunch, also in St. George's Hall, during which Mao Tse-tung took a glass of wine and went round all the guests at the huge table, exchanging greetings with them and occasionally stopping briefly to talk. He made about six such stops as he went right round the hall. When he came to where I was sitting, he stopped because his escort from the Chinese embassy introduced me. He said he wanted to drink to friendship between us and added a few polite words. He then continued to make his way round the guests, occasionally stopping and greeting those present by inclining his head to left and right.

Moscow, November 21, 1957

When I saw our delegation off from the Kiev station, the comrades wished me good luck but without very much conviction that I was going to have it. We all expected relations with the Russians to get worse and that the ups and downs would continue. I don't know how deep the present dip will be, but it looks as though we can't arrive at a stable situation so long as the Russians keep trying to limit our independence and to push us into the socialist camp and we keep resisting their efforts.

Everybody at the embassy feels in a much weaker position following the departure of our party delegation, which spent some twenty days with us. We had got used to having them here; they increased the strength of Yugoslav representation in Moscow many times; now we have again been reduced to more modest proportions. If our relations with the Soviet Union withstand this latest—probably not the last—conflict, then it will be possible to say that Yugoslavia is in this way promoting the establishment of relations with the Soviet Union and the other socialist countries on a new democratic basis of equality, even if it has taken such a conflict to bring it about.

We still remain alone in our efforts: Only Yugoslavia refused to sign the declaration of the twelve Communist parties reaffirming the old relations of inequality. I don't know how much our example may influence other countries for whose equality of status we are also striving, but I am sure that Yugoslavia has sufficient political strength to continue on this path. By remaining faithful to the struggle we been waging for the independence and equal status for the socialist and all other states, we are not reducing our political prestige but can only increase it. I think this is the result of our refusal to sign the declaration of the twelve parties.

CHAPTER TWENTY-SIX

THE END OF ANOTHER YEAR

*Under treatment in hospital, Mićunović records some re-
vealing anecdotes told him by Khrushchev and, as the year
draws to an end, reflects that there has been more conflict
between the Russians and the Yugoslavs in the past year or
two than friendship and cooperation.*

Moscow, December 1, 1957

On our National Day the Soviet Government gave the impression
that relations with Yugoslavia are continuing to develop normally. Khrushchev, Bulganin, and Mikoyan all came to the reception in our embassy.
Mikoyan said that our press had not given sufficient publicity to the
Twelve-party Declaration, and cited *Borba*, the official organ of our
party, which he said had "censored" the declaration and published only
an insignificant part of the original text. Khrushchev and Bulganin joined
in, saying they had never expected us to behave in such a way.

Khrushchev said he was acquainted with what had been said at a recent
conversation between Koča Popović and the United States ambassador to
Yugoslavia, James Riddleberger. In the way he has of delivering judgment about everything that anybody else does, especially if it concerns
Yugoslavia, Khrushchev said that Popović's contribution to the conversation was good. This was one of the rare occasions on which Khrushchev
offered a favorable opinion of anything that Koča Popović has done.

Moscow, December 4, 1957

In Soviet military circles in various parts of the Soviet Union we have
come across an attitude, with regard to the November events in Moscow,
that is anything but friendly toward Yugoslavia. Comrade Tito is attacked openly and Yugoslavia's policy is described as "inconsistent and

hypocritical." One high-ranking Soviet officer in a large group of people asked: "Why is Tito sitting on two stools? Is he for the Soviet Union or the United States? Why doesn't he make up his mind?" And again: "What is this Yugoslav socialism? There can't be any other socialism apart from the one being built in the Soviet Union."

A great number of Soviet Communists, including some members of the Presidium, take the view that Yugoslavia has to choose between the Soviet Union and the United States. This is based on the assumption that anyone who does not go along with the Soviet Union in everything is against it and in favor of the policy of the United States. This cold-war concept of the Soviet Communists does not take into consideration the possibility that Yugoslavs stand above all for Yugoslavia.

The commander of a large Soviet military unit in Kherson told a Soviet citizen on November 7 that he had stopped wearing his Yugoslav war decoration. Was it not clear that Tito had refused to attend the celebrations in Moscow and that Yugoslavia's policy was not sincere and could even be unfriendly to the Soviet Union? We have heard of similar reactions by five or six senior Soviet officers in various places.

Moscow, December 16, 1957

Comrades in the embassy learn from Soviet sources that the people here are beginning to come to the conclusion that Soviet propaganda about the first Soviet sputnik has gone too far. The exaggerated propaganda about the strength and technical superiority of the Soviet Union in this field, which is primarily the field of armaments, is beginning to have the reverse effect from what they wanted to achieve. In America and other countries of the West the question of the West being behind the East, or rather of America being behind the Soviet Union in this field, has come suddenly to the fore. This situation can be quickly changed by means of vastly increased investments aimed at catching up with the Soviet Union as soon as possible and at depriving it of the monopoly it enjoys for the moment. Although Soviet propaganda is directed at preserving peace, it has had the opposite effect in a world where the fear of war and of Soviet military superiority has increased. It will now not be at all difficult for Eisenhower to obtain from the American Congress the sums necessary—and they run into billions of dollars—to overcome the apparent difference between the Soviet Union and the United States.

We hear that the Presidium has decided to correct these mistakes. A directive has been issued through the party *apparat* that nothing further is to be published about Soviet superiority in the field of rockets and that the propaganda machine is to revert to the question of peaceful coexistence. That is why the present moment has been chosen for sending messages of peace to Nehru, Eisenhower, and others.

Moscow, December 19, 1957

One of the questions we often discuss is that of the unsatisfactory state of our relations with practically all the countries surrounding Yugoslavia. In the embassies of some of the neighbors of Yugoslavia they have again begun criticizing Yugoslavia because we refused to sign the Twelve-party Declaration.

Nowhere in Europe, and probably nowhere in the whole world, is there such an interplay of interests or so many neighboring countries with conflicting aims in such a small space as we have in the Balkans. The many centuries of foreign occupation and the days when great powers ruled over the Balkan peoples are past and have now passed into history. What has not yet passed, however, is the domination of the great powers over the small countries of the Balkans. This domination is now accomplished in modern ways, through the "construction of socialism" in one group of Balkan countries, or through the "defense of the free world" in another. These two groups of states now belong to the opposing and, as it appears, irreconcilable military blocs of the great powers. Some Balkan countries, like Yugoslavia, do not belong to either military bloc and adopt an independent position. It stands to reason that a better future for all the Balkan peoples depends on their emancipation from the great powers and in their independent and voluntary cooperation with all countries on a basis of equality, which is what the best representatives of all the Balkan peoples fought for in the past, as they do today.

Moscow, December 23, 1957

I shall be out of the hospital in a few days. But since I am still bedridden and unable to follow or record current events, I will note down a few of the conversations I have had at my meetings with Khrushchev, of which there have been many, both at bad times and on more agreeable occasions. Upon the circumstances depended the mood and atmosphere between us, but it was always quite informal, thanks to Khrushchev's attitude toward me. He knew how to be interesting and witty, with his original and picturesque way of recounting things. But I am recording here some of the things he told me which are not only interesting as stories but may also help toward an understanding of his complex and dynamic personality.

When he told me on July 5 how certain members of the Presidium had behaved in the political crisis in the Kremlin, he dwelt for a time on the behavior of Voroshilov and told the following story about the "old man":

As nominal head of state Voroshilov had the task of receiving the credentials of foreign ambassadors newly appointed to the Soviet Union, and a couple of years ago he had received them from the Iranian ambassador, Dr. Ansari, who had been appointed to the post by the Shah of Iran, Riza Pahlevi. Dr. Ansari spoke Russian very fluently, so that there was no need for an interpreter during the ceremony.

In accordance with the rules of protocol, the first to speak was the new ambassador, who began by handing over messages and personal greetings for Voroshilov from the Shah. In so doing the ambassador several times referred to "His Majesty," meaning the sovereign in whose name he spoke. After he had mentioned "His Majesty" a few times, Voroshilov appeared suddenly to wake up and started asking the ambassador: "What's that, what's that, did you say His Majesty?" When the ambassador, somewhat taken aback, confirmed this and explained which "His Majesty" he was referring to, Voroshilov commented: "We had a 'His Majesty' here in Russia, the Tsar, just scum, riffraff, and we just chopped his head off, and see what a powerful state we created after that!"

The Iranian ambassador was taken aback. The Russian diplomats present tried to gloss over what Voroshilov had done, but it was impossible. Finally they agreed, Khrushchev told me, not to tell a soul what had happened. The Russians had good reason not to talk, because by so doing they could avoid compromising themselves, meaning their head of state. The Iranian ambassador had reason not to tell anyone about it so that the Shah should not get to know. That would have meant his recall from the post in Moscow and might have led to unforeseen complications in relations between the two neighboring states.

This dialogue between Voroshilov and the Iranian ambassador would be memorable in itself even if the scene had not been described by such a gifted storyteller as Khrushchev. I did not report it to Belgrade because I was sure that it would become too widely known and that Soviet Intelligence would report it back to Moscow, which could only make trouble for us there.

* * *

On another occasion Khrushchev told a very colorful story about the partition of Germany, aimed at "proving" that there was no such thing as a "German problem." At the same time it showed that Khrushchev was not too choosy about the sort of jokes he told.

At a reception in the Kremlin last spring, when we found ourselves alone and discussed some matters concerning Germany, Khrushchev asked me whether I had heard the latest comment at the expense of Adenauer[1] and the German question. When I said I hadn't, Khrushchev told the following joke, which has since become very popular in Moscow:

Adenauer likes to speak in the name of the two Germanies and to raise the German question in Europe as though we couldn't survive without accepting what Adenauer proposes. But Adenauer himself does not reveal the true state of affairs and himself demonstrates that what he says is not true. If you strip Adenauer naked, Khrushchev said, and look at him from the rear, then you can see clearly that Germany is divided into two parts. But if you look at Adenauer from the front, then it is equally clear that his view of the German question "never did stand up, doesn't stand up, and never will stand up."

*　　*　　*

Just before Tito's visit to the Soviet Union in June last year Khrushchev explained to me the situation which arose in Russia in Stalin's day with relation to Yugoslavia, when they wrote and spoke their worst about our country. Since they kept on repeating it day after day the population began to believe it, although the charges laid against Yugoslavia were fictitious. The situation, Khrushchev said, was like the one with the Moslem priest who came to believe the lies which he himself invented. Khrushchev said he had told Tito the story in 1955 and asked me if I had been present. When I said I hadn't been, he seemed pleased because it gave him an opportunity to tell once again a story "with a moral," which obviously gave him a lot of pleasure. Here is his story:

Once upon a time in Russia, in Central Asia, a Moslem priest was walking through the town when he had the idea of misleading the people he met in the street. He started telling them that at the other end of the town pilaf (the Moslems' favorite dish) was being given away free, and the news spread quickly from one end of the town to the other. Then people started to rush up to the priest and tell *him* that the pilaf was being given away free at the other end of the town. Finally the priest turned around, gathered up his robes, and said to himself: Maybe they really are giving away the pilaf!—and he joined in the general rush. So Khrushchev ended his tale. It was like that in the Soviet Union during the conflict with Yugoslavia, he said. The most serious accusations were invented by Stalin, and they were then spread around the whole country and it went on for years without a break. Finally those who had invented the false charges against Yugoslavia also began to believe them.

If it were possible to explain Soviet policy toward Yugoslavia after

[1] Konrad Adenauer, 1876–1967. Founder and Chairman of the German Christian Democratic party, 1945–66; Chancelor of the Federal Republic of Germany, 1949–63.

1948 by means of stories and jokes like this, then I think few people could do it as successfully as Khrushchev. He is clearly much more familiar with stories to illustrate the experience and wisdom of ordinary people than he is with quotations from Marx and Lenin.

Moscow, December 24, 1957

I will recount yet another conversation with Khrushchev in which he got the better of me but which is so typical of Khrushchev and so effective, even though it is to my disadvantage, that I have not been able to refrain from telling it to others many times.

Some time ago now *Pravda* published an unusually long article against "modern revisionism." There had just been a meeting of the Central Committee of the CPSU and the article really had an official character, resembling a formal pronouncement or a party resolution, although it was not signed. You didn't have to be an expert on ideological matters or Soviet foreign policy to see at once that it was in fact a serious attack on Yugoslavia, although it was nowhere referred to by name. The article also criticized "national communism," people who opposed "proletarian internationalism," people who "receive credits from the imperialists," and so forth, so that there was no chance that even the dullest of readers would have any difficulty in realizing what it was about.

On the same evening I met Khrushchev at a reception in the Kremlin and told him I was surprised at this unsigned, and therefore more official, article by means of which they were trying to discredit Yugoslavia, that it was only making our relations worse quite unnecessarily, and that the Yugoslavs would now have to reply to the attacks. Khrushchev promptly inquired: What article are you talking about? to which I replied that I was talking about the article in *Pravda*. He then went on: Nobody has said anything about Yugoslavia there; we write an article criticizing modern revisionists, and you say we are attacking Yugoslavia. Both Russians and foreigners know that it is about Yugoslavia, I said, trying to expose this transparent Soviet trick. But to strengthen his argument Khrushchev, laughing, told me the following story:

Before World War I a group of Russian students were traveling by train and talking politics. They were opponents of the regime and were too loud in their comments about Tsar Nicholas II,[2] calling him the worst of names, such as murderer, bloodsucker, fool, and so on. They were overheard by agents of the secret police, who arrested the student who had talked in this way about the Tsar. When he was before the investigator, the student tried to argue that, when he had used those expres-

[2] Nicholas II, last Tsar of Russia, 1868–1918. Abdicated in 1917 and was shot by the Bolsheviks in July 1918.

sions, he had not been thinking of Tsar Nicholas but of Kaiser Wilhelm II.[3] To which the investigator replied: When you say that the Tsar is an idiot, a murderer, a fool, and so forth, that could only be Tsar Nicholas and nobody else. It's the same with you, said Khrushchev, very pleased with himself. *Pravda* attacks national communism and modern revisionism and you cry: Why are you attacking Yugoslavia! He laughed very loud, and I was no longer able to go on criticizing *Pravda* but joined in his laughter and allowed his story to have the effect it deserved. I admitted that his joke was first-class, but that would have been better still if *Pravda* had not published such an attack on "modern revisionists."

* * *

Khrushchev showed many times that he was deeply interested in the part of Russian history connected with the Cossacks and knew a great deal about their past. He was always ready to make use of some story of far-off days, especially if he could discover a suitable contemporary peg to hang it on. When Tito visited the Soviet Union last year, he traveled to southern Russia, to the Don and the Kuban, and stayed there along with Khrushchev and the rest of us in a Cossack village. Khrushchev could not have felt himself more at home and showed us something of what the Cossacks had preserved from their ancestors. He showed that he knew plenty of Cossack songs, and as we traveled through those parts of Russia he sang very well some of their old tunes. Khrushchev would be in that sort of mood when he was "among the people," whether we were going around a factory, village, or collective farm. But the mood usually left him when the time came for official meetings with us.

Moscow, December 26, 1957

I have left the hospital, where the Soviet doctors did their best to help me and succeeded. The comrades in the embassy—the minister-counselor Zvonko Perišić, the counselor Božović, secretaries Dizdarević, Božić, and Pelicon, the military attaché Savo Popović, my secretary, Božo Frank, and others—visit me at home, as they did in the hospital, to discuss various matters, since I shall not return to work until the end of the year—just four days away.

On the Soviet side they are carrying on with the double game they play with Yugoslavia: The official Soviet departments behave normally and in a businesslike way to the majority of their Yugoslav opposite numbers and deal with current matters. Occasionally Yugoslav and Soviet representatives even make plans for the future without reference to the

[3] Wilhelm II, German Kaiser, 1859–1941. Abdicated following Germany's defeat in World War I.

ideological and party rifts which have widened since the November conference. On the other hand, through the Soviet Communist party and various other means they continue the campaign of lectures, confidential instructions, and so forth inside the Soviet Union with the aim of discrediting Yugoslavia in various ways. They talk about Yugoslavia as they did during the last public conflict between us and describe our party as revisionist, opportunist, nationalist, and even, in certain situations, anti-Soviet.

The Soviet Government is not able to give its public an objective account of Yugoslavia's policy, especially of our relations with the United States. The recent agreement, reached on Yugoslav initiative with the United States Government about the cessation of American military aid to Yugoslavia, is presented by *Pravda, Izvestia,* and other Soviet papers as though it were a question of American initiative, as though the U. S. Government had decided to stop further military aid to Yugoslavia, and not that the Yugoslav Government proposed to the U. S. Government that the aid should be stopped by agreement. As it is reported in the Soviet press one has the impression that Yugoslavia would have liked to go on receiving American military aid but that the United States Government cut it off!

Moscow, December 29, 1957

As I come to write the last lines this year about the state of Yugoslav-Soviet relations I cannot unfortunately boast of a particularly favorable balance. There seem to have been more conflicts between us than friendship and cooperation in the past two years, not to mention the last ten. We hoped that relations between Yugoslavia and the Soviet Union would develop differently and better after the agreement to restore normal relations of June 1955. It has not been like that. The Russians throw the blame on us for the bad state of Yugoslav-Soviet relations, and we throw the blame back at the Russians, because nothing has changed in our policy. The trouble is, it seems, that nothing has changed in Soviet policy either, and that it remains fundamentally just as it was. And because nothing has changed on either side, conflicts arise between us.

What has happened in the last two years in Soviet-Yugoslav relations confirms that, in spite of the major changes in the methods it uses to carry out its policy, the Soviet Union has not abandoned, as far as Yugoslavia is concerned, its strategic political aims with which we are familiar from the past.

In the periods when conflicts blew up between us I told Khrushchev that in my opinion the fundamental mistake in Soviet policy toward Yugoslavia was that they were unable to accept us as we are, but are constantly trying to make out of Yugoslavia a different country to suit their taste and to include us in the Socialist camp. Now again, following our refusal to sign the declaration of the twelve parties, this question is at the root of our conflict with the Soviet Union. It is most likely to remain so for the foreseeable future. There will be bigger or smaller quarrels between our countries as long as the Soviet Union continues to insist on its own policy based on a "socialist camp," and so long as Yugoslavia continues to resist that policy as it has done till now.

Here it is not just a question of the line pursued in foreign policy by an independent Yugoslavia. It is also a question of domestic policy, of the development of socialist relationships within Yugoslavia, which is following a path independent of the Soviet and East European model of socialism. The differences between Yugoslavia and the Soviet Union may even be greater in the field of domestic politics than in foreign policy. In my opinion the Russians are not bothered so much by Yugoslavia's independent moves in international relations, although they are not enthusiastic about them, as by Yugoslavia's independent road to socialism, which is very often quite different from the path the Russians have followed.

With regard to the basic foreign policy of the Soviet Union and Yugoslavia, which is aimed at peaceful coexistence between all states, there is also a difference between Moscow and Belgrade, and it seems to me that the Soviet formula here is not sufficient. To be precise: The Russians are at great pains always to put the stress of the peaceful coexistence of states with different social and political systems. This must mean that the policy does not apply to states with the same or similar social systems like, for example, the socialist states of Europe. I raised this question in some talks I had with Khrushchev, and he stuck stolidly to the view that Yugoslavia "has no right" to have such a policy, because Communists are in power in Yugoslavia and therefore different rules apply from those which apply, for example, to India, Iran, or Turkey! As long as the Russians continue to insist on this point of view, it will be a sign that they have not abandoned their idea of a "camp" as far as relations between socialist states are concerned. According to this view those states do not benefit from the principles of peaceful coexistence.

CHAPTER TWENTY-SEVEN

THE "PEACE OFFENSIVE" CONTINUES

As the new year begins Khrushchev moves to improve relations with America, and a Soviet-American cultural agreement is signed. But the launching of the American earth satellite upsets Khrushchev.

Moscow, January 3, 1958

This year the Soviet Government again organized a New Year's Eve party in the Kremlin as they did last year. But unlike last year, when the party served to intensify the cold war, the atmosphere this year was incomparably better, even festive and friendly. Khrushchev proposed four toasts: to the diplomats, with special emphasis on the ambassadors of the countries of the wartime anti-Hitler coalition, then to the Soviet Army, then a special toast to representatives of the socialist countries, and finally one to the Soviet Communist party.

All Khrushchev's remarks were very conciliatory toward the representatives of the West, especially what he said about the anti-Hitler coalition which, he said, "had collapsed the day after we had routed Hitler together." It is a long time since there was any reference here to the wartime coalition. Khrushchev has created a precedent, but he immediately singled out the United States, to which he devoted the greater part of his speech, thus revealing Soviet interest in resolving the basic world issues with the Americans alone. He insisted that such a Soviet-American understanding could be only to everybody's advantage and would not harm third powers. He ended his speech with a toast to Eisenhower, President of the United States. At that point American Ambassador Thompson crossed the room to the Presidium's table to exchange greetings with Khrushchev and the other Soviet leaders. President Eisenhower was the only person to be referred to by name and to whom a toast was drunk by the Soviet side, thus stressing the interest which the Russians have in a Soviet-American understanding. Practically all countries, including the big and the strong, in the West and the East, have their doubts about such an arrangement.

Khrushchev did not even mention the socialist camp, nor did he say anything about NATO or attach any special importance to the neutral countries of Africa and Asia in an anti-Western sense. His toast was responded to by the doyen of the diplomatic corps, the Swedish ambassador, Sulman, who took the same line as Khrushchev. The two speeches had probably been agreed beforehand. Some Western ambassadors who have served a long time in Moscow said it was the most successful party to be held in the Kremlin since they arrived here.

From Khrushchev's attitude it might be concluded that the Soviet leaders are more anxious to find some way of getting out of the cold war than they are to win it. Claims to have "won a victory" in the cold war could be made only by its most fervent supporters, such as John Foster Dulles or Adenauer—and the champions of a cold-war policy on the Soviet side. Khrushchev gave the impression the night before last that the Russians are becoming convinced that there can be no victors in the cold war, and for that reason he pointed to the paths which might lead to a way out of the cold war as the Soviet leaders see it.

Moscow, January 21, 1958

Eisenhower's reply to Bulganin's message of January 9[1] has been received in Moscow, and it is, as expected, negative. The Russians have published in their press only a few sentences from the American reply. They have done the same with the replies from British Prime Minister Macmillan, and from the French and Italian governments, which were probably similar. There are so many of these diplomatic exchanges being prompted by the Soviet Government now that they can be published in the press here like a series of articles "to be continued." The fact that only a few sentences of Eisenhower's reply were published upset the American ambassador, because it has not given the Soviet public a true idea of what Eisenhower said. Ambassador Thompson reproaches the Russians for not being able to publish at least one sentence in which the United States declares categorically that they will never be the aggressor and will not aid any act of aggression committed by any of its allies. At first sight the Soviet side appears to be the one which has twice "proved" that it is in favor of East-West negotiations, because they have published here the Soviet notes in which such talks are proposed, while Eisenhower and the other governments of the West do not agree with the Soviet pro-

---

[1] Proposing an East-West conference.

posals. The Soviet press thus demonstrates to its readers that it has again been "confirmed beyond doubt" that the Soviet Union is in favor of peace while the other side is not ready for such a policy.

Moscow, January 24, 1958

The Soviet press has given very little publicity to Sukarno's[2] official visit to Yugoslavia, although Yugoslavia is the only socialist country in Europe except the Soviet Union which Sukarno has visited so far and at a very difficult time for Indonesia. The old rule is still in force here according to which nothing is published about Yugoslavia which might lead to an increase in our country's prestige and role in international relations. The Soviet press has not attacked us for some time now. Yugoslavia is now largely ignored.

* * *

The Mongolian ambassador, Bata, handed me an invitation from the Central Committee of the Mongolian party to send a delegation from the League of Communists of Yugoslavia to their Thirteenth Congress in March. This is the first time any of the countries of the socialist camp has invited representatives of the LCY to its party congress, and this comes only a few months after Yugoslavia's refusal to sign the Twelve-party Declaration. I passed the invitation on to Belgrade, and I am sure in advance that the comrades there will accept it with pleasure.

Moscow, January 26, 1958

I had a talk with Khrushchev at a reception given by the Indian ambassador. In response to a question I told him that, as far as I could judge, his speech in Minsk, in which he made a violent attack on the United States and West Germany, had evoked various comments and that those circles in the West who were opposed to talks would make use of his speech to spoil the atmosphere further. Khrushchev said that he had had to state frankly what could and what could not be done today in international relations, that the sharp words used on both sides would soon be forgotten, and that we would see what each side stood for and what sort of an understanding was today possible between East and West.

Mikoyan, who was also present, went out of his way to criticize the attitude of the Americans, who, he said, still cherished illusions about being able to change the social and political system which had been established in Eastern Europe, and that this applied also to Yugoslavia and not just to the "socialist camp." Khrushchev said that recognition of the present sta-

[2] Ahmed Sukarno, 1901–70. President of the Republic of Indonesia, 1949–67.

tus quo in Europe was the essential condition for any talks and that this must be made quite clear to the West. I put forward the opinion, or rather stated the fact, that that status quo had already existed and had been affecting international relations throughout the postwar period. That was the only basis on which any talks could be held today, but I saw no need for anyone now to demand that the West formally recognize the present status quo, because that would mean postponing the talks themselves. If, however, successful talks took place, that would imply acceptance of the present situation by the West, even though nobody actually referred to it. Khrushchev agreed emphatically with my comments.

Moscow, January 29, 1958

Soviet Deputy Foreign Minister Patolichev came to me for dinner last night, and to my question about how their exchanges with Western and other states was going he said that there would not be any meetings or talks now because America was not ready for them. He said that the inferiority of the United States in the field of rocketry had weakened their position and that the balance of forces had swung to the Soviet advantage. The Americans did not want to have negotiations now from a position of weakness. Following the delivery of intercontinental missiles to the Soviet Army and the launching of the sputnik any agreement now would be to the disadvantage of America. Instead of coming to an understanding, the Americans would first do everything they could to restore the balance of forces. This was an unusually frank conversation for a Soviet official to have with me on these matters.

Patolichev went on to talk about the conflicting interests of Western Europe and America, and also of those between certain of the countries of Europe, which is a favorite topic for Soviet officials when they discuss international affairs. It is obvious that the Russians are betting heavily on the contradictions which exist between Great Britain and the continent of Europe, as well as on the conflicting interests of France and Germany, and finally on those between all the countries of Western Europe on the one hand and America on the other. This old formula is still not forgotten here, although times have changed fundamentally, and so indeed have the nature and significance of contradictions between the countries of Western Europe.

Unlike his reaction to Eisenhower's reply, Patolichev praised Nehru's. The Russians were especially pleased that Nehru talked only of a meeting between the United States and the Soviet Union and not of all the countries belonging to the two blocs. This conversation confirmed that the Soviet leaders want more than anything else to have direct negotiations and an agreement with the United States.

Moscow, February 1, 1958

The Soviet press has become very clever at reporting half-truths and publishing sentences torn out of speeches by Yugoslav leaders and other foreign statesmen when they do not agree with the Russians. Because of this one cannot go to the Soviet Foreign Ministry and protest that the sense of speeches by our people has been distorted because they will reply that the Soviet press has only published quotations from the Yugoslav press and that we should therefore direct our anger at our own journalists. That is how *Pravda* and *Izvestia* handled Tito's latest speech. The Russians make use of various tricks, including inaccurate translations and picking out the ambiguous statements which suit their book. For example, Tito said that Yugoslavia was struggling to be able as soon as possible to "stand on her own feet," but the Russians translated this as though Tito had said that Yugoslavia wanted to "become independent" as soon as she could. In the same context they write about the cessation of American military aid so as to produce the utterly wrong sense—that Yugoslavia was not previously independent and that this had been "admitted" by no less a person than Tito himself at a congress of Yugoslav youth!

Moscow, February 3, 1958

The Russians have just signed an agreement with the United States Government concerning cultural and scientific cooperation. Statements by Eisenhower and Bulganin have stressed the political importance of the agreement.

Apart from the general political motives which lead them to establish contacts and understandings with the Americans, the Russians have on this occasion shown the greatest interest in American economic and technological achievements. The Americans were concerned more with creating opportunities to enable the Soviet public to be informed regularly about American achievements. The Americans are especially interested in the following Soviet fields: radio, film, television, and the sale in the Soviet Union of the magazine *Amerika* in Russian. But the Russians tried to get an agreement which would protect them as far as possible from this American interest. For example, immediately after the signing of the agreement the Americans offered to sell the Russians about thirty American films. But the question of the distribution of *Amerika* has still not been resolved, because the Americans are not satisfied with the present system which does not allow the magazine to get into the hands of the population.

In view of the fact that the agreement has been published after Khrushchev's speech in Minsk, in which there was a lot of talk of relying on force, this has strengthened the conviction in Soviet circles that the strength factor is not an obstacle to reaching such agreements, but the reverse. First impressions gathered here are that both Russians and Americans are pleased with the agreement but that some of America's allies are not so pleased. The reactions of Russia's allies and whether they approve or disapprove are not recorded or taken into account.

Moscow, February 4, 1958

At yesterday's reception in the Romanian embassy I spoke to Khrushchev about the launching of the first American artificial earth satellite. This event has caused surprise and disappointment among the Russians. Even as I arrived at the reception and was putting my coat in the cloakroom I met the secretary of the Presidium of the Supreme Soviet, Georgadze, who asked me whether I had heard the "bad news" about the launching of the American "sputnik." Although the Russians had counted on not remaining for long the only country with a monopoly in this field, they had not expected the Americans to catch up so quickly.

I found Khrushchev in a bad mood. It was apparent that he was surprised and cross. But the Russians themselves prepared the ground for this disappointment. They boasted too much about being first in the world in rocketry, of being first to launch an artificial satellite, and of being so far ahead of other states in this field. Since space research has a clear military significance, it might be said that the Russians based East-West relations too much on this. I think it reasonable to say that the Russians are now the victims of their own propaganda of four months ago and that they have thus only increased the political and psychological effect which the American achievement is having on the Soviet public and the Soviet leaders.

To put Khrushchev in a better mood I said that the United States might have been expected to launch a sputnik even sooner and that the delay was an unpleasant surprise for their friends in the world, and that other advanced nations would probably also succeed in launching their own sputniks. I behaved as though, unlike the Russians present and Khrushchev, I was not in the least impressed by the American accomplishment. Still moody and depressed, he told me that the Americans had not launched their sputnik by means of a ballistic missile such as the Russians have but by means of something different and less powerful. He went on to explain what the difference was and to say it was to the Soviet advantage.

Khrushchev spoke scornfully of the size of the American sputnik. It was only about a thirtieth of the weight of the Soviet one—"about as big as an orange," he said. "Tomorrow we'll show them," Khrushchev said, clenching his fist, "we'll launch a sputnik weighing over a thousand kilograms."

I said that it was undoubtedly of great importance that the Soviet Union could launch another sputnik of such a weight, but it seemed to me better to let the American "orange" go on circling the earth to see how it works and then to send a greetings telegram to Eisenhower and the American scientists, engineers, and workpeople on the launching of their sputnik.

I drew Khrushchev's attention to the first commentaries on the event, particularly in Britain and America, suggesting that after the launching of the American sputnik the United States might agree to talks with the Soviet Union, since they would no longer have a feeling of inferiority.

I believe that what I said had some effect on Khrushchev; he livened up noticeably when I suggested sending a telegram to Eisenhower.

Moscow, February 9, 1958

By February 8 members of the Presidium had been proposed as candidates in the forthcoming election to the Supreme Soviet as follows: Khrushchev has been selected as a candidate in 110 electoral districts, Voroshilov and Mikoyan each in 40, Kirichenko in 27, Suslov in 21, Shvernik[3] in 17, Furtseva in 15, Aristov, Ignatov,[4] and Brezhnev each in 13, Kuusinen in 11, and Mukhitdinov[5] in 10. Finally Kosygin, Pospelov, and Belyaev[6] have been put forward each in 2 or 3 districts. Bulganin has been chosen as a candidate in only 8 districts. The process of choosing candidates continues. In the end the members of the Central Committee will decide which candidatures they will accept and will leave the rest to the second choices whose election is also guaranteed. This is the way they arrange the electoral rights of members of the Presidium and of citizens of the Soviet Union, who propose them as candidates in a number of different places and reveal in this way the relative standing of each leader. Everything is fixed in advance and planned down to the last detail. A member of the Soviet leadership not only has no need to fight to be chosen; he himself decides which constituency he will honor by accepting the mandate.

[3] Nikolai Shvernik, 1888–1970. Chairman, Presidium of Supreme Soviet, U.S.S.R., 1946–53; Member of Presidium, Central Committee, CPSU, 1957–66.
[4] Nikolai Ignatov, 1901–66. Member of Presidium, CPSU, and Secretary, Central Committee, 1957–60.
[5] Nuritdin Mukhitdinov, b. 1917. Uzbek Communist official. Member of Presidium, CPSU, 1957–61. Removed from all leading positions in 1968 and made Ambassador to Syria.
[6] Nikolai Belyaev, 1903–66. First Secretary, Communist party of Kazakhstan, 1957–60.

Moscow, February 17, 1958

I have heard from Belgrade that they are going to invite a delegation from the Soviet Communist party to the Seventh Congress of the LCY and that the invitation will go through the Soviet ambassador in Belgrade. It is not yet clear how this will turn out, because our Seventh Congress has among other things to approve a new program for the League, and the program has already been criticized by the Soviet Presidium. I asked to be received by Khrushchev on Saturday, February 15, and he saw me today in the Central Committee building.

I handed him a letter from our Central Committee concerning our decision not to take part in the meeting which is going to take place in Prague on March 7–8 to arrange for the publication of a theoretical magazine for the Communist movement. I read him a Russian translation of our Central Committee's reply, which lasted a couple of minutes. Khrushchev said he already knew about our reply because Kardelj had informed the Soviet ambassador in Belgrade about it. Khrushchev also informed me what Kardelj had told their ambassador about our party congress. I said we were expecting a delegation from the CPSU, at which Khrushchev commented that they had not yet received the invitation. But he didn't tell me how they would react to our invitation.

The following questions came up later in the conversation:

I asked Khrushchev whether East-West talks were to be expected and what were the prospects of success in them. He said that talks would probably take place this year, but that the prospects were not very good for agreement on major issues. The West did not want such agreements. The Soviet Union was interested in talks, or rather for agreement on various questions, and considered this might be a starting point for better understanding in the future.

I mentioned the report that I read yesterday in the BBC bulletin[7] that the United States was preparing to conduct a new series of explosions of nuclear weapons in the Pacific. I expressed my personal conviction that this move by the Americans would be badly received in the world, and that American military strength would not be greatly increased by this series of tests, just as it would not have been reduced if the United States had refrained from testing. I voiced the opinion that in the present situation, when there is a prospect of East-West talks at which the question of banning atomic explosions will be on the agenda, the Soviet Union would gain tremendously in the world if it were to announce its intention of *not*

[7] The British embassy in Moscow recorded the daily news bulletins broadcast by the British Broadcasting Corporation and made them available in printed form to other embassies in Moscow.

carrying out any experimental explosions before the East-West meeting. I asked Khrushchev for his opinion.

Khrushchev said they were ready to renounce testing on the condition that others did the same, but that a unilateral renunciation by the Soviet Union would give the Americans an advantage. The purpose of the tests was mainly to make the A- and H-bombs cheaper because it would be possible to produce two, three, and even more bombs for the same cost, Khrushchev said. The Soviet Union was not so interested in further tests, because it had been established that ten bombs would be sufficient to annihilate Great Britain, so what was the point of producing forty? Khrushchev repeated that the tests meant a saving of billions of rubles, and that moreover a unilateral renunciation by the Soviet Union would be interpreted by the world as a sign of weakness in that the Soviet Government would appear to have yielded to public opinion.

There appears to be very little prospect of the Russians accepting the proposal to stop nuclear tests. It is apparent that Khrushchev has a very pronounced complex about strength and weakness, quite apart from the actual value of these atomic test explosions.

There was mention of the Supreme Soviet elections and the government changes to follow them. After a brief pause for reflection or hesitation Khrushchev told me that Bulganin would be removed from the position of Prime Minister after the elections. The basic reason was the way he had behaved in June and, apart from that, Khrushchev said, he was not capable of handling the job. They had put up with him so far but there was no reason to go on doing so. For example, Khrushchev said, in the current exchanges with the West, Bulganin had signed the Soviet proposals and when they were published in the Soviet Union, the outside world people talked about "the Bulganin proposals" and "Bulganin's policy." This caused discontent in the Soviet Union and they were reproached for it, because people knew how Bulganin had come to be Prime Minister. Khrushchev said that Bulganin had not even read the third note sent over his signature to Eisenhower because he had been sick, tired, or just absent. Khrushchev said he was sure that an absolute majority of the Central Committee would be in favor of replacing Bulganin and that it would be decided at the Central Committee on the eve of the Supreme Soviet session at the beginning of April, but that until then things would remain as they were.

Khrushchev raised the question of Voroshilov's visit to Yugoslavia, saying that we had brought it up again. They now agreed to it. Last year in Bucharest they were not in favor of Voroshilov going to Yugoslavia as representative of the Soviet Union immediately after the June plenum at which he had behaved so badly.

I inquired casually how Voroshilov would stand up to the journey physically, because the program on such occasions was always very full and demanding. Khrushchev said Voroshilov would stand up to it very well and added: "Ever since the October Revolution and the Civil War Voroshilov has been mainly taken up with making visits." Khrushchev said Voroshilov would remain president of the Presidium of the Supreme Soviet. "Why change him?" Khrushchev asked. "The old man" didn't do anything anyway; at the present moment it was better for the Soviet Union if he remained in his job. He could stand for something different so long as Molotov, Kaganovich, and Malenkov were in the leadership; they were the ones who had pushed Voroshilov forward and won him over to their side. But the situation was quite different today, Khrushchev said. He believed that Voroshilov would be well received in Yugoslavia and that Yugoslavia would make a good impression on him. "He will come back here as one of your agents," Khrushchev said jokingly.

I was not able to ask Khrushchev directly who the new Prime Minister would be because that would have been going too far. In any case I had been too curious about their elections and internal changes.

When we came to talk about our party congress, I got the impression that Khrushchev was rather concerned about the eventual bad effect the congress might have on our relations and the general situation in the "camp" over ideological questions. Although the official Soviet attitude toward us is in accordance with Khrushchev's statement at the Supreme Soviet in December (our failure to sign the Twelve-party Declaration is a negative element, but ideological differences between us are less than before and it is hoped that they will disappear entirely in the future), one senses serious reservations among the Russians about what the Seventh Congress of the LCY will produce. They are just waiting.

The atmosphere during the conversation with Khrushchev was as usual good.

CHAPTER TWENTY-EIGHT

KHRUSHCHEV IN UNIFORM.
MOLOTOV IN MONGOLIA

The Russians agree to attend the Seventh Congress of the League of Communists of Yugoslavia. Mićunović attends the Mongolian party congress and pays a call on Molotov, now ambassador to Mongolia, who is the subject of public attacks in Ulan Bator. Khrushchev becomes Prime Minister.

Moscow, February 23, 1958

Yesterday evening a meeting was held to celebrate the fortieth anniversary of the founding of the Red Army. The Russians went too far in using the occasion to serve current political requirements. They introduce too much of what happens to suit their needs into their accounts of past events, at the expense of the history which they rewrite and amend. This is what they did yesterday with the history of World War II. The Russians have no need to minimize the contribution made by their Western allies to the victory over fascism or to magnify their own contribution. The Soviet Union unquestionably made the greatest and the decisive contribution. Nevertheless, in an article in *Izvestia*, Marshal Grechko referred to the great anti-Hitler coalition which won the war in the following fashion:

> The armed forces of the states of the anti-Hitler coalition made a contribution to the great victory over the sworn enemy of humanity—German fascism—in the final stage of the war.

When the Russians say, for example, that Great Britain contributed to the victory over fascism only "in the final stage of the war" it can only cause anger in Britain and elsewhere because it is obviously not true. From 1939 to 1941 the Soviet Union remained neutral and carried out its treaty obligations to Nazi Germany; but, after the fall of France, Britain fought alone against Hitler for more than a year. But the Russians are now displeased with the attitude of Great Britain and the other Western powers on various international issues and so they rewrite history.

This is altogether the reverse of what Khrushchev said in his speech on last New Year's Eve in the Kremlin, some six weeks ago. This is the best guide to the direction in which the general situation has been "evolving" in that short period.

At the meeting in Luzhniki Stadium there was another unexpected novelty: Khrushchev turned up and took his seat on the platform in the uniform of a lieutenant colonel, the rank which he had in the Soviet Army in the last war. We were sitting quite a long way away from him and could not make out what rank he had. But someone produced a pair of binoculars and everyone was relieved to see that he was not wearing the uniform of a Soviet marshal, as the word had gone round at the beginning. The meeting ended with a mass dance of "friendship" beneath the national flags of the twelve socialist countries which signed the Declaration. The Yugoslav flag was not there.

Moscow, February 24, 1958

Another nuclear explosion of many megatons has been carried out in the Soviet Union in the last few days. It took place on the same day as the Red Army anniversary meetings were being held throughout the country. The Russians have not reported the explosion; it took place at a time when Soviet diplomats are working on preparations for a meeting with the West about the preservation of peace!

The Russians, and the Americans, too, attach far more importance to atomic explosions than to the letters about peace which they exchange. And the public in many countries can now see that the exchange of letters is not of primary importance, since in both East and West they are accompanied by fresh nuclear explosions which serve as the main arguments. In this way the Soviet Government is replying not only to America, which wishes, like Russia, to talk from a position of strength, but also to "liberals" like the Japanese parliamentarians who appealed to the Soviet Union to stop nuclear testing for the time being.

Moscow, March 7, 1958

The Soviet leaders have decided to send a delegation to the Seventh Congress of our League of Communists, and they have appointed Pospelov to lead it. To judge by the position occupied by its leader the Soviet delegation will not be top-level. Pospelov belongs to that group of Soviet leaders who spend their days in offices sorting out papers and establishing what is and what is not correct according to the writings of Marx, Engels, Lenin, and Stalin. Pospelov had much greater political importance in Stalin's day than he has now. I cannot recall that he ever said or wrote a single word in favor of Yugoslav-Soviet cooperation, even when it was more the fashion to do so than it is today.

Moscow, March 8, 1958

At the end of last year the Russians started setting up "friendship societies" between various countries and the Soviet Union, and this has continued at an even greater pace this year. In the course of January and February friendship societies have been set up between the Soviet Union and Finland, Czechoslovakia, Italy, and Hungary and a preparatory committee is working on one with India. Since it is an important political action by the Soviet Government, a conference of all the "Soviet friendship" societies formed so far was held here in February.

I have heard that a Soviet proposal is being drafted for the founding of such a society for Yugoslavia as well. This whole operation is in my opinion politically very questionable.

The Soviet press is emphasizing that Nina Popova, a party worker, is the initiator of the movement to "form friendship societies with the Soviet Union." They do this probably to give the impression that the whole business is not connected with the Soviet state machine, although the very opposite is the case.

We are in favor of developing the greatest possible friendship with the Soviet Union on a basis of equality, because only people who are equal and independent can be friends, while those who are not in a position of equality cannot possibly be. Then it is a relationship between superior and subordinate and not between friends. The whole concept of "friendship societies" does not please us or suit us. What is the sense of having such societies in Czechoslovakia, Hungary, Bulgaria, and the other countries of Eastern Europe when all social and political organizations in those countries, and indeed all organizations without distinction, *have* to be on friendly terms with the Soviet Union, while all organizations which are not friendly toward the Soviet Union are banned by law? What is the point of setting up "Soviet friendship societies" in those countries?

In Yugoslavia's case it is an especially sensitive question. In the first place, we are opposed to having friendship with the Soviet Union handled by a special organization "responsible for friendship with the Russians." Instead of that we shall all be working on that friendship, including the Central Committee of the LCY and the Yugoslav Government. In the second place, to set up such a society in this situation would be like dividing our citizens into those who are friends of the Soviet

Union and those who are not. We would then not have far to go to start looking on it as a sort of pro-Soviet organization which might gradually take up an ever more independent position and start pushing its own policy of "friendship with the Soviet Union."

In my opinion the Russians should be setting up this kind of society in countries like America, West Germany, Great Britain, and similar countries where various anti-Soviet organizations are free to operate. Let "friendship societies" work to popularize the Soviet Union in those countries and to develop friendly contacts between the peoples of those countries and the Russians.

Apart from all this, Yugoslavia cannot behave in this respect differently toward the Soviet Union from the way it behaves toward the rest of the world. That means that tomorrow we should have to permit the formation of such friendship societies with America, Britain, Japan, and any other country if we permitted the Russians to do something like this. I hope that the Russians will not try to rush this in the case of Yugoslavia, because we have discouraged them here, although that may not have any effect.

Moscow, March 12, 1958

In two days' time I am leaving for Mongolia to attend the party congress there. Mongolia is, so to speak, 100 percent under Soviet influence and yet it invited the League of Communists of Yugoslavia to send a delegation to its party congress. I don't believe the Mongols could have done anything like that without the knowledge of the Soviet Union or without Soviet approval. Does it mean that the Russians are going gradually to accept our independent status and that they are not going to insist, as they have done so far, on including Yugoslavia into the socialist camp? One may have one's doubts in view of Soviet behavior in other directions.

Perhaps the Russians have not yet ceased to hope that they can influence us by pretending not to notice what we are doing and by not preventing the Mongols from inviting us to their congress. I am particularly interested in having another meeting with Molotov, who is now Soviet ambassador to Mongolia. Although I have no advice from Belgrade about how I should behave toward him, I hope our meeting will be interesting; I believe we shall have more time to talk in Ulan Bator than when we used to meet in other circumstances.

Moscow, March 26, 1958

I returned from Mongolia on March 25 after spending ten days in the country. The Yugoslav delegation consisting of Comrade Krste Crvenkovski[1] and myself was received in a very friendly manner by the Mongolian Government and their party congress. The other foreign delegations were led mostly by ambassadors accredited simultaneously in Moscow and Ulan Bator. I think we did better, in that the leader of our delegation arrived directly from Yugoslavia and not from Moscow as the others did.

The actual congress was in every respect like Communist party congresses in the Soviet Union and the countries of Eastern Europe: very long speeches, an organized debate, nothing to liven the atmosphere or to suggest anything new, certainly not anything like a conflict or even a free exchange of views. The speeches and the debate were strictly "correct" and "on the line."

The Mongolian leaders informed me that they are going to send a party delegation to our Seventh Congress. If they do that it looks as though cooperation between some countries of the socialist camp and the LCY may gradually develop in spite of our refusal to sign the Twelve-party Declaration.

I handed the Mongols an invitation from our government to send their students for training in Yugoslavia, on a very modest scale for a start. The Mongols accepted this enthusiastically and said that they now had about a thousand students being trained in the Soviet Union and another hundred in the other countries of the "camp." We agreed that we and they should try to make up for what has so far been neglected in cooperation in all possible fields and above all in cultural matters.

I paid calls on the heads of diplomatic missions in Ulan Bator, which wasn't particularly difficult in view of the fact that there are only four ambassadors residing permanently here in the Mongolian capital: the ambassadors of China, North Korea, Czechoslovakia, and Molotov, the Soviet ambassador. The Soviet delegation behaved very badly toward Molotov, ignoring him and boycotting him and even preventing him from attending formal occasions on which the Soviet delegation met top Mongolian leaders at which an ambassador's presence was essential. Even at the congress itself he was discriminated against compared with the other diplomats who were constantly in the company of Mongolian leaders or their delegations. Molotov was not permitted to be with either, and he was never to be seen except in the seat allotted to him at the congress.

There will probably be a lot of stories about my talks with Molotov which will be magnified many times over by the time they reach Moscow. In fact the Russians could have made a fuss if I had not called on Molotov, since I called on all the other ambassadors in Ulan Bator. They

[1] Krste Crvenkovski, b. 1921. Macedonian Communist official. Chairman of League of Communists in Macedonia, 1966–69, and later member of the leadership of the LCY.

could have said that I had insulted the Soviet Union by not paying a courtesy visit on the Soviet ambassador. However, it is more likely that the Russians will be displeased with my long conversation in Ulan Bator with Molotov alone. For that reason I decided to tell Khrushchev about the meeting at the first opportunity. I will tell him as much as possible about how the situation around Molotov looked on the spot.

Moscow, March 27, 1958

At the Supreme Soviet session which took place this afternoon the composition of the new Soviet Government was announced. Khrushchev was appointed Prime Minister, and the crisis which has lasted since last June has been resolved. He has now formally united the supreme power of the state and the party in his own hands. It will no longer be possible for one of the Soviet leaders to build up a position for himself in the government to compete with a rival who has built up a position in the party, or the other way around. Something like that took place in the course of the few years following Stalin's death. Malenkov, and later Molotov, Kaganovich, Bulganin, and the others tried to strengthen their positions in the state administration, while Khrushchev did the same thing in the party *apparat*. It was more or less from these party and government positions that the bitter political struggle at the top of the Soviet political system took place last June.

It may be that in the Soviet political system it is essential to have both those top positions concentrated in the hands of one person. The system which Stalin built up over the decades is inconceivable except as one of unlimited power in the hands of one person. The present Soviet system is, subject to certain adjustments connected with the rule of law and the cult of personality, what Stalin bequeathed. The choice of Khrushchev in such circumstances is nonetheless the most logical solution because he is today the only one of the leading personalities in the Soviet Union who is in many respects far superior to all the other members of the Presidium.

Moscow, March 28, 1958

During my stay in Ulan Bator I had to deal with the problem of arranging a meeting with Molotov, because I had none of the younger members of our embassy with me who could have gone to the Soviet embassy to propose a meeting. I was also unable to ask anybody from the Mongolian Government to help me fix a meeting, because it was too delicate a matter: the Mongolian Government arranging a meeting between Molotov and the Yugoslav ambassador! A simple thing like this immediately gets complicated once you set off on those lines.

350

I saw that I should have to do it myself somehow, and I did it at the Mongolian party congress. During an interval I waited for Molotov in the corridor along which he was regularly escorted by the head of the protocol department of the Mongolian Foreign Ministry to a separate room where he had to remain during the break, not mixing with the foreigners and Mongolians, who passed the time in conversation in the lobbies or just strolling around them. The Mongolians would do this only after we had all left the hall and would detain Molotov and make it impossible for him to meet any of us. I stayed in the corridor waiting for Molotov and his escort to approach me, because there was no other way they could pass, and I went up to Molotov, shook hands, and was warmly received. Molotov appeared to me to be sincerely pleased when he saw me waiting in the corridor and showed a desire to rid himself for a moment of the guard who had been attached to him "as a mark of respect." I walked with him into the lobby where the delegates and guests had gathered and there we stayed talking. Not one of the several hundred people present came up to us. In fact they formed a circle round us at a distance of several meters, and Molotov and I remained in friendly conversation in this state of "siege" for fifteen minutes.

The delegations from the countries of Eastern Europe followed the example of the Soviet delegation and boycotted Molotov until I had my meeting with him. When we parted, the first to approach me were the ambassadors of the "camp" in Moscow to ask me about my meeting with Molotov. I told them that I paid regular calls on all my colleagues when I visited Mongolia and would, of course, call on the Soviet ambassador like the rest. After that the Polish ambassador summoned up the courage to go up to Molotov and shake hands with him although he had avoided doing so previously. The other East European ambassadors from Moscow did not approach Molotov even then; nor did the members of the Soviet delegation. I arranged to call on Molotov the next day in the Soviet embassy in Ulan Bator.

Since I was accredited to Mongolia before Molotov he was insistent that he should make the first protocol call on me, thus observing the rules in force in the diplomatic service in Ulan Bator. He gave way only when I told him that I had nowhere to receive him and that I was staying along with all the foreign delegates in one big building and had only a bedroom in the hostel. Molotov received me very kindly in the Soviet embassy. We talked for nearly two hours, during which we were served with tea, but drank Georgian wine at Molotov's suggestion. The meeting continued although I stood up two or three times and made to leave, but stayed on longer at his insistence.

We were overheard throughout by the leader of the Soviet delegation,

Nikolai Ignatov, who was also in the embassy building. As for what we discussed and how Molotov behaved, I started with an inquiry about his health. When he said he was feeling well, I said I did not feel very well there and talked about the severity of the Mongolian climate. Molotov said he kept fairly well but that his wife was ill and had been operated on a few days previously in Ulan Bator for something connected with the stomach, and apart from that she suffered from her heart. He was worried about his wife's health because she had been feeling unwell before: "If she went to Mongolia she'd have a heart attack, if she went to Moscow she'd have one there; now there's this operation, but maybe she'll get over it," Molotov said.

"And how is Moscow?" was Molotov's first question. He looked more interested and brightened up when I told him about the new American ambassador, Thompson. He said he had known him in Vienna. Then he asked what were the real prospects for an East-West meeting and what would come out of it. I replied in general terms.

I asked Molotov about Mongolia: whether he had spent the whole time since his appointment as ambassador in Ulan Bator or had traveled round the country. Molotov said he had done a great deal of traveling and talked about his impressions. Once out in the steppes he had come across a group of nomads and asked them how they lived. They replied: We live with our cattle, and how they live so we live. Those people, Molotov said, could not have any other attitude toward life, and it was difficult to say who was in charge of whom: whether they were in charge of the cattle or the cattle were in charge of them. When, for example, the icy winds start to blow from the north the cattle turn tail and flee southward, sometimes for hundreds of kilometers. There had been cases where the cattle and the people crossed over into China.

Molotov told me he had gone into a nomad's tent and asked the couple living in it what they wanted to be. One said he wanted to become a lama (priest) but the other wasn't sure whether he wanted to be a priest or to join a stock-raising cooperative—"just imagine the choice," Molotov said. The Mongolian leaders had been very cross to hear the peasants give such answers.

During the conversation, possibly because he felt he had been too critical, Molotov said the Mongolian leaders were making great efforts and that they had some successes, but again he talked about negative aspects: that the training of skilled people was the country's main problem; they had enough doctors, teachers, and veterinary surgeons ("even the Foreign Minister is a veterinary surgeon here," he said sarcastically), but they had no trained technicians.

Moscow, March 29, 1958

This is a continuation of the account of my conversation with Molotov on March 18.

Molotov said it was important that the Soviet Union had been first to launch a sputnik. This might make the Americans and the West more realistic, since they may have underestimated the state of science, technology, and industry "on the other side." The United States would now take a more sober view of military adventures than it had previously. He told me that the United States had that day launched a second sputnik, that it had been a very small one, and that somebody had told him about it at Ulan Bator Airport where he had been meeting his daughter, who had come because of her mother's illness.

Molotov once mentioned Voroshilov during the conversation, in connection with the climate and Voroshilov's visit to Mongolia last year. But he did not mention any other Soviet personality. He did not even refer to the Soviet Government when talking about the Soviet proposal for an East-West meeting and the launching of the sputnik. He always found some other expression, as though he refrained deliberately from saying "our proposals" or "the Soviet Government's proposals." This seemed to me to reflect Molotov's psychological state: He did not on this occasion dare to associate himself with the government of his country (even when he agreed with its policy).

As for life in Mongolia, Molotov appeared to have forgotten that he had told me at the outset that he felt well there. He spoke about the difficult climate, showed me the bowls of water they stood in the rooms to humidify the air, said that in some parts of Mongolia the severity of the climate was made still worse by radiation, because the sun shines constantly throughout the year, and that this had an especially disastrous effect on women, that nobody had really gone into the question of the effect of living in Mongolia and Ulan Bator on non-Mongolians (illnesses, reaction to the water, air, etc.), that wolves and wild animals came right into the outskirts of Ulan Bator, and so forth. From these remarks one could tell how difficult Molotov was actually finding life in Mongolia.

But he behaved extremely politely toward me and restrained me two or three times when I moved to go. As we talked he proposed the first toast: "To Belgrade and Moscow." Then we drank to our health and I expressed the wish that his wife should recover from her serious illness. Then Molotov drank a toast "to our friendship." It was some time before we came to the last glass and it appeared that he was leaving the toast to me. I proposed that we drink to "the prosperity of the Soviet Union and the success of the latest Soviet efforts to reach agreement with the West, and to peace in the world," in which Molotov very gladly joined and added "to Yugolsavia."

Molotov said that the Chinese were helping Mongolia more and more and asked me if I had seen the new Chinese embassy building in Ulan Bator, which was, he said, very large and well built. Compared with it the Soviet embassy was a small and rather old building. (I later called on the Chinese and found the embassy really enormous, including an eight-hundred-seat cinema and room to entertain two thousand people. All the material, including the bricks, had been brought from China. I believe the Chinese embassy in Mongolia now has the most impressive and largest building of any Chinese embassy abroad. They are now building a hospital with one hundred beds for the embassy staff. This is altogether typical of the extent of Chinese plans to install themselves in Mongolia.)

As he was seeing me off, Molotov said several times, "Come back again," and I promised to do so, but I was unable to do so because it would have been more than the official minimum which served as my excuse for the one call which I made. Molotov wanted to return my call. I thanked him and explained that on this occasion I was not in a position to receive a return call. I said I would come to Ulan Bator again in July and there would then be an opportunity for a meeting.

Moscow, March 30, 1958

With regard to our visit to Ulan Bator I want to record that the way they are treating Molotov there made an unpleasant impression not just on our delegation alone. One felt uncomfortable at Molotov's presence at the congress in such circumstances, especially when the leader of the Soviet delegation, Ignatov, made a sharp attack on Molotov in his speech of greetings. He used the familiar phrases from the Soviet party decisions on the antiparty group, twice referring to Molotov as a factionalist and an antiparty element, and saying that the Molotov-Malenkov group had been defeated in the CPSU, with which "the Mongolian revolutionary party had fully agreed." When Ignatov referred to Molotov as a factionalist the first time, many of the delegates in the hall as well as the foreigners started turning round to look at the place where Molotov had been sitting (during the congress he had been among the first to stand up and always remained standing and applauding right to the end when there was something to applaud). Molotov was not in his seat. Ignatov's words had a bad effect on the whole congress.

After Ignatov's speech there was a break in the proceedings. For the first time the Soviet delegations found themselves alone and isolated in the hall; nobody approached them and the three of them did not even talk among themselves. For the first time a rather unpleasant atmosphere came over the gathering. The Polish ambassador came up to me and said he was surprised at what Ignatov had done, which was damaging for the congress and for Mongolia, but not for Molotov. One could feel that the Mongolians were also put out. Altogether it harmed Soviet prestige (primarily in the eyes of the Mongolians). A country, its government, party, and congress were being made use of to carry on the internal quarrels of the Soviet leadership.

I believe the appointment of Molotov as ambassador to Mongolia was a bad move from the outset, if they planned to continue criticizing him publicly as a factionalist. And on this occasion it was reduced to absurdity. The Russians reckoned that the Mongolian congress—with Molotov present—was a unique occasion for again venting their wrath on him. In so doing the Soviet delegation completely ignored the Mongolians as an interested party and paid no attention to the foreign delegations who watched it all.

Some illustrations of how Molotov is being treated: Unlike all the other ambassadors in Ulan Bator, Molotov was not allowed to meet his country's party delegation when they arrived or to attend protocol meetings between the delegation and the Mongolian Government. They invited Molotov to be present on the first day of the Congress and then kept him away on the second day when Ignatov criticized him, and then brought him to the Congress again on the fourth day. Then the Mongolian press published Ignatov's speech attacking Molotov, and finally Molotov was invited "as ambassador" to the gala reception, but he was unable to sit down—although the foreign delegations and the Mongolian leaders were sitting—but he had to stand up the whole time some distance away from us. There were similar scenes every day. There are many other ways in which this situation could have been handled, any of which would have been better in my opinion for the Soviet Union and Khrushchev than the one they used. On the fourth day after they arrived Molotov went with trepidation up to the second member of the Soviet delegation, Shtykov, and the last member, Vinogradov, to exchange greetings with them at a reception, as I saw with my own eyes.

Ignatov and the Soviet delegation left for Moscow on March 24. At the reception on March 23 he shook hands with those present but did not offer his hand to Molotov as he walked past him.

On the day of my meeting with Molotov I found myself entering the Congress hall along with Ignatov, the leader of the Soviet delegation. When I told him that I had been with Molotov, he replied that the conversation had been "strained" and not natural and spontaneous like my talks with Khrushchev. He thus confirmed that during my conversation with Molotov in the Soviet embassy he had been in the next room and listening throughout our conversation. As soon as the conversation was over Ignatov rushed out to his car as I did to mine, so that we arrived at the congress at the same time.

Ignatov then mentioned Molotov's bad attitude toward Yugoslavia in the past. I said I knew about it. I couldn't discuss with Ignatov how he had behaved to Molotov, because I had the impression that he would not be able to understand the affair except in the sense that I was "backing Molotov" and "against the CPSU" and that he would inform Moscow accordingly.

After my return to Moscow I found that the great majority are reproaching Khrushchev for what Ignatov did. Some foreigners who are well disposed toward Khrushchev's policy cannot understand why he had to attack Molotov at the Mongolian congress as though the June plenum had taken place yesterday; they say that by so doing Khrushchev himself is magnifying the importance of the M-K-M group, bringing his own successes into question and throwing doubt on the degree of stabilization achieved in the party and the country.

As for Molotov himself, I remain convinced that he no longer thinks of supporting or opposing the policy of Khrushchev or of anybody else in power in the Soviet Union. But perhaps that is just an impression based on the present situation.

Last year Molotov, along with Kaganovich and Malenkov, tried to bring about illegally a change of leadership in the Soviet Communist party. I believe that everybody who knows how people used to be dealt with in the Soviet Union when political accounts were settled, even up to the present day, may say that in this matter Khrushchev has carried out a real revolution. Irrespective of all the criticisms of Soviet behavior, Khrushchev has readily shown such lenience in his handling of the leaders of the opposition as has not been known in the Soviet Union since Lenin's day.

CHAPTER TWENTY-NINE

CONFLICT OVER THE NEW PROGRAM

The new program of the Yugoslav League of Communists does not meet with the Russians' approval, and they refuse to send their delegation to the congress. Mićunović is treated insultingly by Suslov.

Moscow, April 1, 1958

The new Soviet Prime Minister—Khrushchev—has kept practically all the ministers who served in Bulganin's government. The few changes made have no political significance. An exception is the appointment of Kozlov[1] as First Deputy Prime Minister. It looks to me as if the Russians wanted to emphasize that the "collective"—all of them except Bulganin—were fully in support of the party line and that there was no need to move anybody. The appointment of Frol Kozlov is a promotion which was expected. Mikoyan has, as always, kept his position, although there are signs that Kozlov is ahead of him and not only alphabetically.

Bulganin has retained the rank of a member of the government but he is now the forty-fourth out of forty-five. He has been made director of the Soviet State Bank. Bulganin began his career in banking and the job he has now been given he held more than twenty years ago.

The first politically significant move by Khrushchev's government was to pass a resolution about the temporary cessation of nuclear testing by the Soviet Union. The Supreme Soviet approved Gromyko's proposal about this with enthusiasm and the vote turned into a strong demonstration of support. Moreover foreign reaction here is favorable and could not be otherwise. The Russians hope to extract some political advantage out of their unilateral decision, whether the West follows them or not. If the West doesn't, and it probably won't, the Russians will make the opposite move from today's and resume nuclear explosions, accusing the West of responsibility for not following their example.

[1] Frol Kozlov, 1908–65. Member of Presidium, CPSU, 1957–64.

357

Moscow, April 4, 1958

I paid a call today on Voroshilov, who was again elected president of the Supreme Soviet a few days ago. I handed him our latest Draft Program for his visit to Yugoslavia. I renewed our invitation to him and his wife and told him that it also extended to his son and daughter-in-law. Voroshilov was not sure whether his wife could go, because her health is not good, but was pleased to have the invitation for his son, saying it would be a good thing for his son to "accompany the old man to Yugoslavia."

* * *

At a reception given by the Hungarian ambassador I talked to the Deputy Ministers of Foreign Affairs, Kuznetzov and Patolichev, and later with Mikoyan about our league's Draft Program. As in the case of all the reactions we have noted here in conversations with Russians at all levels, Kuznetzov and Patolichev were reserved, excused themselves on the grounds that it was a long document, a whole book, that they had not yet read it, and so on. As far as the length was concerned Kuznetzov quoted a Russian saying, "better shorter but better." The extreme reserve shown by both of them usually means in Soviet terms a negative attitude, and the only question is when will they state it publicly.

Mikoyan said that they hoped that our program would not be as it appears in the draft, that we had taken a step backward by comparison with what we agreed and signed at the meeting in Romania last year. He said this so decisively that there could be no doubt that he was expressing the opinion of the Soviet leadership.

Four days ago Dizdarević asked for a meeting with Medvedev, head of the Yugoslav section in the Soviet Central Committee *apparat* "concerning the departure of the delegation from the CPSU to the Seventh Congress of the LCY." Medvedev did not say when Dizdarević should come to see him and still has not done so, although four days have passed. Previously we have normally been received for such meetings in a matter of hours. I intend to arrange with the leader of the Soviet delegation, Pospelov, for a dinner to mark the delegation's departure for Yugoslavia. There is still no word from the Central Committee of the CPSU. Before I talked to Mikoyan about the Draft Program I told Patolichev that we were expecting the arrival of a delegation from the CPSU at our congress. Patolichev did not comment.

It looks as though they have suddenly reviewed the question of our congress and that their conclusions about it are negative. Maybe they

have changed the decision they had already taken about sending a delegation from the Soviet party to the congress?

Moscow, April 7, 1958

There are signs that the Russians have informed the leaders of the
other parties of the "camp" of their disapproval of the Draft Program of
the LCY, although they have still said nothing to us about it. During the
first days of April they started a more intensive campaign against "modern revisionists." This is a sign that the Russians are preparing to attack
our Draft Program in public. Some of the East European ambassadors are
already starting to do so, certainly on instructions from their capitals.

The publication of our Draft Program in the form of a book and its
translation into foreign languages has been taken here as a challenge by
Yugoslavia and as the beginning of an offensive against the Soviet model
of socialism, which they again tried to impose as the only pattern at the
November meeting in Moscow last year. Our Draft Program now plays
the part of another, opposite political line to the one agreed in Moscow
last November and is being published in foreign languages for mass
distribution under the title of Draft Program of the LCY. This looks inevitably like opposition to the Moscow Declaration of Twelve Communist
Parties not only because it coincides in time with it but because on a
large number of basic current issues our program puts forward different
solutions from the ones proposed in the Twelve-party Declaration.

In a brief conversation with Mikoyan last week it became quite clear
that the Russians do not regard the program as something intended only
for the League of Communists of Yugoslavia but ascribe much more ambitious aims to it. They are of the opinion that the Yugoslavs are trying
by means of their program to carry on an active struggle inside the international working-class movement against the "Soviet model of socialism"
which Yugoslavia has been opposing now for a whole decade. The relative calm which has reigned over Yugoslav-Soviet relations from November till a few days ago will now probably be replaced by a new open
conflict between the Soviet Union and Yugoslavia. The conflict will not
be limited just to the field of theory and ideology but may have more
far-reaching consequences for Yugoslav-Soviet relations.

The Russians will now accuse us of failing to observe the "generally
accepted principles" and of thus causing discord in the international revolutionary movement; we shall accuse the Russians of not permitting any
revolutionary movement to develop outside Moscow's control. It looks as
though the experience of our ten-year struggle for independence and
equality in international relations has not been of any particular benefit

here. The very same questions over which we clashed with the Russians back in Stalin's day are once again on the agenda.

* * *

I was summoned today by Mikoyan in connection with the conversation we had at the Hungarian reception about the LCY Draft Program. The Soviet Foreign Ministry informed me that Pospelov, who has been appointed to lead the Soviet delegation to our Seventh Congress, would be with Mikoyan.

I called on Mikoyan and Pospelov in the Central Committee building. Mikoyan read me a letter from the Central Committee of the CPSU to our Central Committee declaring that our Draft Program (which they treat already as the approved program) is unacceptable for the following reasons: (a) it is opposed to the idea of the unity of the international working-class movement; (b) it represents a retreat on our part from the positions we took up during the talks in Romania; and (c) it represents a retreat by us from the ideas in the "peace manifesto" which we signed in Moscow.

For these reasons they are canceling the delegation which the Central Committee had appointed for our Seventh Congress. The Russians talked vaguely about the possible attendance of their ambassador at the congress as an observer. There followed a long discussion which produced no results. In his attacks on us Mikoyan made use of the Draft Program and some works of Lenin from which he quoted some sentences. A new clash between us appears inevitable.

Moscow, April 9, 1958

Last year I was elected to the LCY commission for drawing up the Draft Program. But since I was all the time in Moscow I was not able to take part in the work of the committee in Belgrade, so I have sent my comments in writing. Since there is so little time left before the congress I have sent my comments in the shortest and most down-to-earth form, indicating specific parts of the program which ought in my opinion to be dropped and suggesting what should replace them. And as briefly as possible I have given the reasons for my proposals.

The Russians are not going to wait for the Seventh Congress or for us to approve the new program; they have decided already to attack us openly. This will probably take place "frontally" in the Soviet press next week. Once again they regard themselves as being responsible for everything that happens; they decide what each party will adopt as a political program for its country and they already arrogate to themselves the right to decide whether something to be agreed at the Yugoslav or some other party congress is "correct." And "correctness" still depends upon whether what is decided at the congress of a Communist party strengthens or weakens the Soviet monopoly of power in the international working-class movement.

It will be useless for us to try and explain to the Russians that we did not write the program for them or for anyone else, but for ourselves. The Russians look upon the Yugoslav Draft Program from here as a danger of international dimensions, and not just a national or Yugoslav affair, and they have decided to oppose that "danger."

Moscow, April 15, 1958

I was received today by Khrushchev and handed him Comrade Tito's letter concerning our congress, after which we talked at length about the Draft Program of the LCY. Khrushchev said that our letter was not convincing, that we were insisting on things which had produced the present state of affairs, and that some of the things said in the letter could be regarded as insulting.

Khrushchev repeated some of the arguments from their letter and then the ones which Mikoyan and Pospelov had used in their talk with me. He referred to what Comrade Tito had said in 1955 about the need to drop all our old ways of conducting relations and claimed that we had now deviated from this rule. The Russians were going to publish an article criticizing Yugoslavia and our Draft Program in *Kommunist*, their "theoretical" journal. Khrushchev said they had thought of publishing it in the daily press, because Radio Belgrade was broadcasting the text of our draft program for Russian listeners, and the Russians ought therefore to use corresponding means of informing the public when they did not agree with the draft. The article being published in *Kommunist* would be signed by a group of Soviet authors, which was a milder form than leaving it unsigned.

Khrushchev said that the Chinese had sent us a "more outspoken" letter, but that the Russians had had our Draft Program printed and distributed to all members of the Central Committee of the CPSU and to all secretaries of republican and regional party organizations, so that they could acquaint themselves with the draft and so understand better the criticisms of it when they were published here. In this way party officials would be better able to direct discussion of the matter at meetings of party members. Khrushchev concluded this part of his statement by saying that not only were they not sending a delegation to our congress; they would not send greetings either.

I told Khrushchev that we had not expected such disagreement on their part, because our Draft Program was actually the most positive document of that kind with regard to the Soviet Union which had been published in Yugoslavia since 1948. I asked why they were taking all these steps now and preparing to attack us before the congress which still had to decide what the new program of the LCY would be. I said that, quite apart from the criticisms which they were going to make in their letter, there would be lots of comments about the program in Yugoslavia, and there already were, as we had expected. I told him that Comrade Ranković had told me that the Seventh Congress would probably not be able to draw up the new program and that a commission would probably have to work on it for at least a month after the congress. I asked Khrushchev whether he really thought that Yugoslavia could accept some of the things proposed in the Soviet criticism of the draft in the face of their refusal to send a delegation to the congress? Was it to be expected that in the full view of the Soviet public we would now dress up the Draft Program of the LCY in accordance with their demands?

I went on to say that all the Social Democratic parties had refused to take any part in our congress, and now the Russians were following suit. Opinions about our program in the West were very critical on account of our "rapprochement with the Soviet Union," as the West put it, yet in the Soviet Union itself they were preparing to attack our program and congress in this way!

After much talk and repetition of largely the same arguments Khrushchev framed a question, which he put personally for his own part and not on behalf of the Soviet leadership: Would we issue a statement that on account of the large number of amendments to the Draft Program that had been submitted we would not be able to do everything necessary before the congress; in other words, would we postpone the matter? If we issued such a statement they would delay in making their criticisms public. Khrushchev also referred to the possibility of postponing the congress itself.

I gave him my personal view that such an alternative did not seem possible. The commission working on our party program could not now issue any such statement or decide what the congress was in a position to do or not to do. In Yugoslavia there were no grounds for postponing the congress, apart from which other Communist parties were beginning to take up the same critical attitude, and to carry on a debate about it all in public would inflict fresh harm on Yugoslavia. More than once I referred to the expressions "hegemony," "spheres of influence," "two blocs," on which they base their criticisms, and I said that some expressions could be changed, but that they must leave us to work things out in our own way, while they should reverse their decision not to send a delegation and stop attacking us in advance. Khrushchev did not agree with this conclusion of mine, repeated that we had printed and distributed the Draft Program, that we were already taking action and yet demanding that they should not speak. The concession which they were ready to make, Khrushchev said, consisted in being willing not to publish their critical article before the congress, but on condition that we publish a statement postponing the program.

Although I told him repeatedly about the amendments to the program and the comments already received about it in Yugoslavia, this had no effect on Khrushchev, nor did there appear to be any possibility that they would drop what they planned to do. Khrushchev talked about a conflict between us which might go further than anyone wanted. I had the impression that the Russians are not really interested in amending particular passages in the draft because they have already created an abnormal situation between us; they have mobilized all the other Communist parties against our Draft Program and they didn't even wait for us to reply. It seems to me that a statement by us now to the effect that we are ready to change certain passages would not alter the present Soviet decision not to send a delegation and to publish the article. Apart from that Khrushchev said they now had political obligations and could not alter their stand.

The question is whether from the outset, irrespective of our program, the Russians ever had any intention of sending a delegation to our congress. I am not sure that there would now be any point in our taking any extraordinary steps, such as handing the amended text of our program to the Russians alone. If there are no prospects of changing the Soviet attitude, we can easily make the situation worse.

Moscow, April 15, 1958

At a reception in the Kremlin last night I spoke again with Khrushchev, Kozlov, Mikoyan, and Kirichenko. Nothing essentially new was said on either side. Khrushchev expounded his idea about the postponement of the congress rather more clearly. I rejected it as an abnormal move.

Khrushchev touched on the following themes: He said that, even when they dealt only with Yugoslavia and did not refer directly to foreign countries, speeches and articles by our leaders invariably included claims to impose our political system on other countries and held up our "model of socialism" as the only right one. That was why we were now broadcasting our Draft Program by radio and in Russian. If we didn't have such pretensions, what was the purpose behind such broadcasts?

When I commented that they hadn't even published Tito's reply to their letter about the cessation of atomic tests and yet regularly published replies from other statesmen, Khrushchev got angry, phoned *Pravda* in my presence, reprimanded them, and then admitted that it was their mistake but not his. I said that I was not proposing that they should publish this or that about Yugoslavia, let them do as they pleased, I was only pointing to the facts. Today both *Pravda* and *Izvestia* published Comrade Tito's letter to Khrushchev.

Once again Khrushchev was unable, or did not wish, to refrain from giving his unfavorable opinion of Kardelj, saying that such a Draft Program was his work and that Tito himself had not given enough of his time to studying the whole affair. Khrushchev also repeated the story of the soldier who claimed that he was the only one in his company marching in step. We were behaving as though we were the only ones in step, he said. He had once told Koča Popović that he didn't know which was the company and which was the soldier. This meant that Yugoslavia was setting itself up against the whole international revolutionary movement. "Now we shall see who's who," Khrushchev said.

When we talked of finding ways out of the situation that had arisen, it became obvious that the Russians want to get us to take steps which would make it quite clear that we had publicly abandoned our own Draft Program. Their idea of postponing the congress is aiming in the same direction. I believe the result in either case would be to provoke a crisis in Yugoslavia and not to improve any passages in our Draft Program.

Moscow, April 16, 1958

I received instructions from Belgrade to ask for a meeting with Khrushchev or any other member of the Soviet Presidium and to inform him of the amendments and additions made in Yugoslavia to our Draft Program of the LCY. A special courier flew from Belgrade with the amended version.

The Russians had not in fact thought of the possibility of amending passages in our program; that was not the point. Moscow is against our program as a whole, and it seems to me that by discussing this with the Russians we may weaken our general position and that the Russians may see in this a readiness on our part to bargain with them over certain passages.

In response to my request Khrushchev replied immediately that he was busy and could not receive me. This is the first time since I have been in Moscow that Khrushchev has flatly refused to see me. This was already a sign that everything is going badly; the Russians probably knew why I was asking for a meeting and that was the reason for Khrushchev's avoiding it. The Russians have already taken up a negative attitude concerning amendments to our Draft Program, which are in any case fairly unimportant.

After the Soviet Central Committee had informed me that Khrushchev could not receive me they offered me a meeting with Mikhail Suslov. This was another sign that nothing useful was going to come out of the meeting. When it comes to a conversation with Suslov, all possibility of agreement between Yugoslavs and Russians is excluded, even if it concerned a less controversial matter than the program of the LCY.

I went to the meeting with a whole pile of papers, and found Suslov in his office barely visible behind the mass of papers and books on his desk. As soon as we had greeted each other he started to raise his voice and to criticize our program in sharp terms. At the beginning I was unable to get a word in edgeways. Suslov appeared to be so angry and furious that he was unable to restrain himself. It didn't occur to him even to offer me a seat; he stood behind his desk and I stood opposite him and listened to his bitter attacks on our program. He behaved so angrily that it was not in fact a conversation; I listened to his attacks on Yugoslavia as they followed one after the other, spoken as though I or some other Yugoslav had insulted Suslov or his family personally. When I managed to get a word in, still standing and with the bundle of papers in my hand, I told Suslov that we were talking about a program for the Yugoslav and not the Soviet Communists. I then made as though to abandon any further conversation and to leave. Only then did Suslov offer me a seat and indicated a readiness to listen to me.

After this unpleasant beginning I handed Suslov our "comments" on the program and the original of Comrade Tito's letter, a copy of which I handed Khrushchev yesterday. I explained to Suslov that the commission working on the program would submit the changes to the congress on the basis of comments and proposals made by Yugoslav Communists, and that the commission reckoned on having to do more work on the original text because they had already received several hundred comments.

Suslov attacked the draft more sharply than anyone here has done so far: The Draft Program was calculated to set Yugoslavia against the Soviet Union and all the other Communist parties. It was not just a matter of the first three chapters (the ideological or foreign policy part of the draft) but of the program as a whole. No amendments or additions could improve the essence of the program which claimed for the LCY a leading role in the international working-class movement. All the other parties were marching in step, but we Yugoslavs were going in the opposite direction and were seeking to get others to follow us.

In our Central Committee's letter we say that we have been reproached by Yugoslav Communists for the way the program deals with Stalin (that it is too favorable to him). It was clear that there must be such letters, because the general attitude we have taken up in the Draft Program has actually turned Communists against the Soviet Union, Suslov said.

He asked why there was not a single reference in the draft to the United States of America as the principal enemy of socialism, as they were described in the sixty-four-party "peace manifesto" which we had also signed.

As far as that part of the draft program dealing with Yugoslav internal affairs was concerned, Suslov said: "We have not devoted any attention to that, but even there the line of attacking the Soviet Union and the fraternal parties is constantly stressed." Wherever there is talk of "étatism" and the role of the state, it is all directed against the Soviet Union, Suslov said.

In the course of a tense exchange which might at any moment have ended with the refusal, on Suslov's part or on mine, to continue the conversation and with our parting in an even worse atmosphere than when we met, I told Suslov the following:

We are talking about a program for the Yugoslav and not for the Soviet or any other Communist party. Therefore the changes which were now being proposed and which were to come were not to be understood as a change in the substance of our draft, as he suggested, nor were we ready to produce some other quite different program in place of the present one. His view that our program was aimed at achieving Yugoslav hegemony in the international working-class movement was unfounded and in contradiction with our whole draft whether it was changed or not. As for the argument that the whole world Communist movement was marching "in step," that we were going the opposite way, and that this proved how wrong our policy was, I told Suslov I thought it would be better if we did not rely on such arguments but discussed the affair in concrete terms ("You'll get it in concrete terms," Suslov chipped in). Back in 1948 all the Communist parties had been "in step," I went on, and the Soviet Communist party was there with them, too, and we didn't march "in step," but I wouldn't have brought this up now if he had not started it ("Things are different now," Suslov said).

The "peace manifesto" which Suslov had referred to was not just a Soviet party document, since the LCY had signed it as well, and his assertion that we were afraid of America was not true since the whole of our Draft Program was against imperialism.

Today, like Khrushchev yesterday, Suslov reproached me because no publicity had been given in Yugoslavia to the Twelve-party Declaration and because we had censored it in *Borba*. I told him it had been published in full in *Kommunist* for November 29, and I was surprised they didn't know that.

I tried not to allow the sharpness of our exchanges to go to extremes, because that was what Suslov was out for, not even avoiding plain insults ("You are friendly with Americans"). He glanced at some of the amendments which I had given him and belittled their significance.

Moscow, April 17, 1958

Not only has the meeting with Suslov not changed the situation; it has made it worse. I believe that the Russians are pleased about what Suslov said to me and that our "amendments" have had the opposite effect of confirming the Russians in their stand. Our people in Belgrade can be at ease because my conversation with Suslov has shown goodwill on Belgrade's part and a readiness to agree with the Russians about anything on which agreement is possible.

I have referred here to Comrade Tito's letter to Khrushchev about the general Soviet attitude to our Draft Program and Seventh Congress. It had already been announced that the Russians had refused to send their delegation to the congress when Comrade Tito wrote the letter. He tried to influence the Soviet leaders to adopt a more tolerant attitude toward the Yugoslav program and congress. It was no misfortune if we didn't agree about everything, Tito said in his letter, but it was not a good thing for us to quarrel in public and attack each other on account of the differences existing between us instead of discussing those differences calmly. There would be nothing very terrible about a critical analysis of our program being published in some Soviet paper or magazine. But it would not be a good thing if there were a frontal attack on Yugoslavia, which would be a sign of a fresh general campaign against our country.

There are many places in our Draft Program where there is clear criticism of the theories and the practice which Stalin applied for so long in the Soviet Union and the international working-class movement. The Russians just couldn't take it. Apart from anything else, this shows how much influence Stalin's legacy still has over the policy of the present Soviet leadership and how strong is the policy of Soviet hegemony both in the socialist camp and in the international working-class movement. It will show in fact just how correct is the line taken in our program on those very questions. Yugoslavia still has the political strength to resist such a policy on Moscow's part, although we are trying at the same time to be on the best possible terms with the Soviet Union—but as an independent and equal country.

Moscow, April 18, 1958

Today the Russians have launched an attack on the League of Communists of Yugoslavia because of our new program. Doubtless other East

European parties—the Albanians, Bulgarians, East Germans, and others—will sharpen up some of the Soviet criticisms of Yugoslavia. The Soviet article provides a starting point for a campaign which, as has always happened in the past, will go a good deal further than what the Russians began with.

CHAPTER THIRTY

THE YUGOSLAV CONGRESS
WITHOUT THE RUSSIANS

The Russians enforce a partial boycott of the Yugoslav congress by other Communist parties. The congress is followed by a scurrilous attack on the Yugoslav Communists in Pravda. *The Yugoslav Communists close their ranks.*

Moscow, April 19, 1958

I am setting off for Belgrade with bad news. Soviet disapproval in the field of party affairs will probably be carried over into other aspects of Yugoslav-Soviet relations before we shall be able to hope for an improvement in party relations again.

The Russians have not burned all the bridges as far as further cooperation is concerned. They have appointed their ambassador in Belgrade to be an observer at our congress. For the moment one cannot speak of a complete break in party relations, which is what they threatened me with originally in Moscow. But now the presence of the Soviet ambassador as an observer must represent a softening to some extent of the Soviet attitude. The other countries of the socialist camp will probably follow the Soviet example and appoint their ambassadors in Belgrade as observers. Observers can have their reservations about what happens at the congress, but their very presence is a quite favorable sign in the given circumstances. It would be worse if the Russians and the "camp" had decided not to send them. After all, even through their observers the Soviet Union and the other countries will in a sense be taking part in the work of the congress.

We gather that the Russians have succeeded in dissuading most Communist parties from attending the Yugoslav congress. But it is obvious that the support which the other Communist parties are giving to the Soviet Union is not as wholehearted as it was ten years ago. After all, the attitude of the Soviet Union and the countries of Eastern Europe is also not so unbending as it was in 1948.

Ljubljana, April 20, 1958

The open attack on our program came out of Moscow on April 18 just before our congress[1] opened. It took the form of a very long and officially inspired article which declared that the program of the LCY contained many statements which did not correspond with the practice of Marxism-Leninism (according to the Soviet interpretation). This applied, the article said, especially to the Yugoslav assessment of the present international situation, to the views expressed concerning the existence of two world systems, and to the summing up of the experience of socialist construction in various countries, above all in the Soviet Union. Then came an attack on our theory concerning the role of the state and our attitude to "proletarian internationalism." Our views concerning equal status and independence in relations between socialist states and Communist parties were also attacked. But at the end the article said that such criticism of our Draft Program should not be an obstacle to the further development of relations between our countries.

This conclusion was to be welcomed, however unacceptable everything that preceded it appeared. We couldn't have asked for anything more, and there were many among us who had not expected as much.

The only question is whether the Russians will be able to maintain this attitude when it comes to open polemics. Even now the *Kommunist* article supports the principle of a Soviet monopoly in the field of theory and of Soviet hegemony in the matter of relations between socialist countries. The clock has been turned back with regard to the joint Yugoslav-Soviet documents of recent years.

It seems to me that we ought to do nothing to turn Yugoslav public opinion against the Soviet Union. On the other hand it will be necessary for our government and party leaders to make a special effort to maintain the spirit of cooperation and not to destroy the prospects of a further improvement in our relations following the latest Soviet attacks. It is not so simple a matter for the Yugoslav Government to try to inspire confidence in the Soviet Union when every year the Russians again make unfounded attacks on Yugoslavia. After 1948 the Soviet Union lost absolutely all the confidence which Yugoslavia had placed in it, and it is certainly not going the right way to restore that confidence.

[1] The Seventh Congress of the League of Communists of Yugoslavia took place in Ljubljana, capital of Slovenia, from April 22 to 26, 1958.

Ljubljana, April 21, 1958

The Seventh Congress of the League of Communists of Yugoslavia was opened this morning by Comrade Tito to stormy applause from the participants and guests who filled one of the largest halls in Ljubljana to overflowing. After opening the Congress Comrade Tito had the opportunity to welcome the small group of various left-wing parties from different continents who had not obeyed the Soviet or the Social Democratic suggestion that they should boycott our congress. They included the Communist parties of Denmark and Norway, probably the two Communist parties in Europe with the least political influence in their own countries, and some socialist parties from Asia, Africa, and Latin America. Then there was a rather larger number of representatives of foreign Communist parties attending as observers, and a third group composed of ambassadors from Eastern Europe "led by" the Soviet Union who were also attending as observers. Albania, Czechoslovakia, and China did not even send observers to the congress.

It had been hoped that the Italian Communists, who play a very important political role in their country, would send a party delegation to our congress. But the Italian Communists, even now, ten years after the clash with Stalin, did not dare to act differently from the present successors to Stalin. The second largest Communist party in the West, the French party, did not do even that much; they didn't send even an observer. In this way, unexpectedly, the French Communists revealed themselves to be "more Catholic than the Pope."

Ljubljana, April 22, 1958

The fact that the countries of Eastern Europe sent their ambassadors as observers evoked a good deal of criticism among a certain number of our delegates, because the congress is a party and not a government gathering. For this reason a large number of the delegates quite spontaneously paid greater attention to the socialists from Chile and the representatives of the national liberation movement in the Cameroons than to the observers from the "camp." This will probably be interpreted in Moscow as indicating that an "anti-Soviet atmosphere" predominated at the congress, although that was not the case. It will not occur to anybody in Moscow that they themselves demonstrated their anti-Yugoslav stand in the most official way by their attack on our Seventh Congress even before it opened.

Anyone who is in favor of equality among states, socialist or otherwise, who defends the idea of equality and independence among Communist parties, who demands recognition of the fact that there are different paths to socialism according to the specific conditions in each country, who strives for the independence and sovereignty of his own country and fights against the hegemony of great powers over other countries—such a person cannot be anti-Soviet. It is on precisely these principles that the new Draft Program of the LCY is based, and that is why Soviet allegations that our Draft Program is "anti-Soviet" miss the mark.

Ljubljana, April 23, 1958

Although it is not stressed at the congress, it is a fact that there are major differences between the program of the LCY and the Soviet Communist party on a whole series of issues. There are also significant differences on a number of important questions between the LCY program and the Twelve-party Declaration. These two programmatic documents reflect in many ways two different concepts of the present state of the world and of the problems involved in the further struggle for socialism.

But the draft of our party program was not intended as a document to be different from or to be set in opposition to the Twelve-party Declaration. Nobody in Yugoslavia had the slightest desire, by approving the new program, to get into conflict with the Soviet Union and the "camp." Ten years ago Yugoslavs were driven to resist Stalin's theory and practice by Stalin's own attack on Yugoslavia. Something similar might be said about the present situation.

Ljubljana, April 25, 1958

What looked at the outset like an unpromising political state of affairs —that the congress was being held in conditions of noticeable isolation, exposed to open attacks by numerous Communist parties—also has another side to it. The Yugoslav Communists are once again revealing some of that fighting spirit which they demonstrated at the Fifth Congress in 1948.[2] Now as then they are trying to get on with their own business without permitting foreign interference in their own Yugoslav internal affairs. Pressure from abroad again appears as a factor strengthening our internal unity.

The open Soviet attack on us has, in my opinion, only increased the in-

[2] The Fifth Congress of the Yugoslav Communist party took place from July 21 to 28 in Belgrade, a month after the Cominform Resolution which expelled the Yugoslav Communists from the Communist movement. It turned into a demonstration of the party's support for Tito in his resistance to Stalin.

ternational significance of our program. The main Soviet argument: that our Draft Program is openly set against the Twelve-party Declaration serves only to arouse international interest in the program.

Belgrade, April 28, 1958

There was yet another matter which did not suit the Soviet Union in connection with our congress. Just before it began a group of former Četnik quislings,[3] including two or three former Social Democrats, were put on trial in Belgrade for antistate activities. Because they had at one time belonged to a group which was a member of the Second International, although in the war they had been on the side of Draža Mihailović's Četniks, the Western European Social Democratic parties, which belong to the Second International, boycotted the LCY Congress.

When, ten days ago in Moscow, I told Khrushchev about this and said that, to our great regret, the Russians were now following the Social Democrats' example, Khrushchev didn't like it. Perhaps this influenced the Russians to decide at least to send their ambassador as an observer.

The boycott of our congress by those who count themselves on the left wing of the working-class movement as well as by those who make up the right wing of the movement gave our congress even greater balance. The Russians found themselves for once in the same position as the Social Democrats with regard to our congress. Merely to register this fact weakened the Soviet position in the eyes of the Yugoslavs. By boycotting our congress the Social Democats upset Soviet plans to some extent.

The Seventh Congress of the LCY ended yesterday in good order. If one can talk about historic decisions being taken, then the most important was the decision to adopt the new LCY program. The draft has become the program of the LCY; there is nothing more of importance to be changed, and there is certainly no more talk of postponing it for another occasion as Khrushchev suggested in April. We consider it a step forward in the advance toward socialism.

The last act of the congress was to elect a Secretariat of the Executive Committee, i.e., the highest party organ of the LCY. Comrades Tito, Kardelj, Ranković, Svetozar Vukmanović-Tempo, and Ivan Gošnjak were elected unanimously. Finally all the participants and guests attended

[3] They were: Dr. Alexander Pavlović (seventy-three), former vice-president of the Serbian Socialist party; Bogdan Krekić (seventy), founder of the Serbian Socialist party and former secretary of the Yugoslav Trade Union movement; Dr. Milan Žujović (fifty-eight), brother of a leading Četnik; and Dr. Dragoslav Stranjaković (fifty-six), an associate of Professor Jovanović, Prime Minister of the Yugoslav government-in-exile in London. They were found guilty of conspiring to overthrow the government of Yugoslavia and sentenced to long prison terms.

a joint reception given for all of us in Ljubljana. I believe a great many comrades stayed at the party the whole night, but I didn't notice a single person misbehaving.

Moscow, May 6, 1958

The Seventh Congress was followed by the May Day holiday which I spent with comrades in Belgrade. One gets so quickly out of the everyday routine to which I had been accustomed in Moscow that it sometimes seemed as though I had never left Belgrade.

Immediately before leaving Belgrade I received a greetings telegram for May Day from Molotov in Ulan Bator, Mongolia, addressed to me in Moscow:

> On this First of May, on behalf of the staff at this embassy and myself personally, I send greetings to you and through you to all the members of your embassy on the occasion of the international festival of solidarity of all working people. I wish you and all the members of your staff good health and further success in your work, aimed at developing friendship between the peoples of our countries, and the consolidation of peace and socialism. V. M. Molotov.

After everything that had happened between our countries I had not expected a telegram from any Soviet official, least of all from Molotov. It was possible that Molotov was not "in the know" or that he had not been informed by Moscow that our relations had taken a turn for the worse. The telegram had been sent by the normal postal service and the Soviet authorities had apparently overlooked it. I did not have an opportunity in Belgrade to consult with anyone about how to reply to Molotov, but there was no particular need to do so, since it was only a question of returning Molotov's good wishes in similar terms. Without further reflection I sent a reply to Molotov, also through the open post:

> To the Embassy of the Soviet Union, Ulan Bator,
> Comrade V. M. Molotov.
>
> Best thanks for your greetings for May Day, the international festival of working-class solidarity. On behalf of the members of our embassy and myself personally I send you and the whole staff of the embassy of the U.S.S.R. cordial May Day greetings with wishes for every success in your work.
>
> V. Mićunović

I don't know whether Molotov will receive the telegram and I shan't have a chance to find out unless I go to Mongolia again. But there is not much likelihood of that. Comrades joked about my "correspondence" with Molotov after my relations with Khrushchev had been upset. However that may be, Molotov was not only the Soviet ambassador but the only Soviet citizen in any political post to send me friendly greetings on May 1, 1958. All the other Soviet officials made it clear that they were well aware of the new conflict between Yugoslavia and the Soviet Union.

Moscow, May 7, 1958

Two days ago the Moscow *Pravda* published an attack by the Chinese Communist party on Yugoslavia. Today the Russians have published a similar attack by the Czechoslovak Communist party. The next few days will probably bring further anti-Yugoslav articles by the Communist parties of other countries to suit the requirements of the Soviet leaders.

With a minimum of goodwill on the Soviet side the Seventh Congress, the congress resolutions, and Comrade Tito's closing speech could have been taken as a desire on our part not to worsen relations. But the Russians don't have that minimum of goodwill. As far as the uninformed Soviet public is concerned, it looks as though it is Yugoslavia which is making things worse. For the Russians a conciliatory attitude is a sign of weakness, just as the violence of the language used in the articles published in their press and the arrogance of their behavior are signs of strength. That is why, following our conciliatory gestures, the Russians increase their pressure on us instead of acknowledging them. If they go on behaving like this, they will probably start publishing even sharper attacks on us, because they believe that by so doing they show people in the Soviet Union and elsewhere that they are not worse Marxist-Leninists than the Chinese or others who have attacked us more brutally than the Russians.

* * *

We have again inquired at the Soviet Foreign Ministry about Voroshilov's visit, and again we have no answer even about matters which have already been agreed by the Soviet Government. It seems as though they would rather like us to cancel the visit, so that the Soviet Government could find in that clear proof that, apart from breaking off party relations, we had also broken off governmental relations and even insulted the Soviet Union.

Moscow, May 9, 1958

Today's *Pravda* publishes the decisions of the Central Committee of the CPSU about the expansion of the Soviet chemical industry. The announcement is given in two or three sentences on the front page. But on the third and fourth pages there is an unsigned article which is in fact the

Central Committee's pronouncement against Yugoslavia. Its title: "Constant unity of the Marxist-Leninist parties is the guarantee of further victories by the world socialist system." The article is divided into six parts. Although it doesn't say explicitly that it is a formal pronouncement by the Central Committee of the CPSU, it is obvious to everyone who reads it that that is what it is and that it, and not the routine resolution about the chemical industry, was the main business of the plenum. *Pravda*'s anti-Yugoslav declaration is not signed; it is to be regarded as a party directive, although the Soviet Central Committee cannot be accused of having drawn it up since it did not sign it!

The Soviet opinion of Yugoslavia and our Seventh Congress, as well as of our government's policy and ideology, is extremely hostile. Moreover, there are many places in the article where we are said to be taking up the same position as the American imperialists toward the Soviet Union and the socialist "camp" and to have revealed ourselves not as critics of their policy but as falsifiers and slanderers of it!

Unlike the other documents which the Soviet Central Committee has published recently about Yugoslavia and contrary to the discretion which Soviet propaganda has so far shown, Comrade Tito and his speech at the Seventh Congress are now the central point in the Russians' criticism of Yugoslavia. This has a special political significance for Yugoslav-Soviet relations. The Russians have thus come into the open, no longer maintaining as before that our top leaders are divided into "pro-Soviet" and "anti-Soviet." Hitherto, when the Russians interfered in this way in Yugoslav internal affairs, Tito was not usually classed among the "anti-Soviets," but now this has also changed.

The Soviet declaration against Yugoslavia is written in provocative and offensive language, and in this respect resembles documents of Stalin's time. It is probably the Soviet Government's intention to make Yugoslavia's relations with the Soviet Union and the countries of Eastern Europe and other Communist parties as bad as possible, so as to provoke us to make an even sharper reaction in public. That is why they have set out in *Pravda* the precise amount in American dollars for which Yugoslavia has sold its ideology to the Americans in the last two years.

Thus, according to *Pravda*, for Comrade Tito's speech in Pula, which the Russians call anti-Soviet, Yugoslavia received from the United States Government in November 1956 no less than $98.3 million. At the end of December of the same year we are supposed to have received a further check from the American Government for $6 million which the Americans had at their disposal in Yugoslavia. Then *Pravda* alleges that Yugoslavia received $60.5 million from the United States for refusing to sign the Twelve-party Declaration. For our Seventh Congress, according to *Pravda*, Yugoslavia is due to receive from the United States Government an appropriate reward in dollars. This reveals to what depths *Pravda* has sunk in its attacks on Yugoslavia's policy.

The sort of shock which, by the violence and crudeness of its language, the Soviet attack on Yugoslavia produced here can be judged by the fact that some well-intentioned but uninformed Russians, in an effort to explain their Central Committee's action, have been saying that we are on the brink of a third world war! Otherwise, they say, many things would not have been said and published in this way. I am not sure whether this is not put out by Soviet black propaganda so as to make this serious Soviet attack on Yugoslavia more easily accepted.

There is something more than twenty-four hours left before Voroshilov's visit to Yugoslavia, officially agreed at many meetings between our governments, but the Yugoslav Government can still not obtain a reply from the Soviet Government whether Voroshilov and his delegation are going to Yugoslavia or not. So far I have been to the Foreign Ministry and asked the Soviet Government eight times.

I hear from visitors that they have already started in Belgrade to put up banners where Voroshilov is due to pass and to decorate the streets with flowers and flags. But it is difficult to imagine that this or any similar visit could take place in the present atmosphere. That is clear both to us and the Russians, though the Soviet Government will not inform us of its decision until the last minute. They want all the preparations to be completed in Belgrade and then to cancel the visit themselves at the last moment.

Moscow, May 10, 1958

The Czechoslovak ambassador gave a big reception last night, at which there were about fifteen hundred guests, the diplomatic corps, and, of course, the Soviet leaders led by Khrushchev.

I hesitated about whether I should attend. There were plenty of reasons for not going. The Soviet press has published the Czech attack on our Seventh Congress, falsifying the Yugoslav attitude and then condemning it on the Soviet pattern. Apart from that, the serious attack on the whole of Yugoslav policy in *Pravda*, according to which Yugoslavia sold its policy for American dollars, was reason enough for my not going to the reception.

Nevertheless, I went. But I kept myself quite apart, far away from the head table where Khrushchev, Mikoyan, and the other Soviet leaders were sitting. I didn't want to meet them or any of the Soviet leaders, because it could easily have led to an unpleasant argument about the *Pravda* article.

But, after having just spoken with Khrushchev, Mikoyan moved away from the head table and made his way through the crush of guests to join me. He then invited me on Khrushchev's behalf to go up to the head table where the Soviet leaders were sitting with their Czech hosts. Khrushchev's idea was, I believe, to put on a rather special show. With the Yugoslav ambassador sitting beside him on the same day as *Pravda* had published the worst possible attack on Yugoslavia, who knows how Khrushchev would have tried, in the speech he was about to make, to exploit the situation. I thanked Mikoyan and refused to go to the head table.

But things didn't end with the invitation and refusal. There followed a long conversation about what *Pravda* and the Soviet Central Committee had done today. I am sure Mikoyan would not have approached me if he had thought he would get involved in such a conversation. Even though the ring formed around us was at quite a distance, some of the Russians and foreigners present who know Russian may have been able to hear something of this extremely unpleasant argument.

I asked Mikoyan how they could write such an article about Yugoslavia and why they had set out to compromise the many years of effort on both our parts to improve Yugoslav-Soviet relations? Mikoyan replied that we had started the quarrel and that their reply in *Pravda* was moderate and cautious. These are the terms the Russians usually use when there is a quarrel between us. But this time I couldn't let Mikoyan get away with it. I asked him whether he was joking when he talked about moderation and caution. When he replied that it was his serious opinion, I asked him how he could say that to me seriously when they had today informed the whole world in *Pravda* that Yugoslavia had sold its honor and ideology to the Americans for a certain number of dollars every time we had not agreed with the Soviet Union? They had also said that Yugoslavia would be similarly rewarded in American dollars for the Seventh Congress and the new program of the LCY. Was this really their Marxism-Leninism; was this the result of the efforts which had been put into establishing new and better relations between us?

Mikoyan did not say anything for a time, because the waiter came up and offered us a glass of wine. Then, after a few moments of silence, he continued the conversation by saying that we were counting on aid from the United States and were adapting our policy accordingly. I reminded him that we invariably heard this Soviet reproach whenever there was a worsening of relations between us. I recalled the meeting in the Kremlin in June 1956 and went through the list of the people present, including him, when Khrushchev stated that they not only had nothing against Yugoslavia taking American credits and accepting American aid, but that the Soviet Union was also ready to take American credits on the same terms. Khrushchev had said the same thing a year previously at the meeting of our two delegations in Belgrade at which Mikoyan had again been present. Now, in the name of the Central Committee, they had announced officially that Yugoslav policy was not independent, as we claimed, but was being sold for American dollars.

Mikoyan said nothing in reply. We were both holding a glass of wine in our hands, but neither of us wanted to drink. When there was a brief pause Mikoyan tried to drink a toast with the usual words: "Your health," to which I replied, not very courteously: "To *your* health," but refrained from drinking. We repeated this again and neither of us even sipped his wine but just kept holding our glasses aside so that it was obvious that neither had any intention of accepting the other's toast.

The silence was broken by Mikoyan, who said that we had agreed last August in Bucharest not to attack each other in public. I replied that, unfortunately, no agreements made with them had any meaning, as had been shown in our relations so far, and that today they had trampled publicly on everything we had agreed about. I pointed out to Mikoyan that the resolution of our Seventh Congress was friendly toward the Soviet Union, yet they were today saying that Yugoslav Communists were being paid by the Americans. Mikoyan said he hadn't read the resolution of the Seventh Congress. I asked him whether it was really possible that he had not read the most important document of our whole congress and yet at yesterday's plenum here they had condemned our congress and Yugoslavia in that way? Mikoyan realized immediately that he had made a mistake. He tried to put it right by saying he had read the speeches made at the congress. I told him I was amazed that he had not read our most important congress document and at the same time found it possible to support the stand taken by their Central Committee with regard to that same Yugoslav congress, the resolution of which he had not read.

After that Mikoyan became noticeably more nervous. The conversation turned again to relations between Yugoslavia and the United States and I quoted some of the worst and more insulting passages from the *Pravda* article. I said to Mikoyan, applying their method used by *Pravda*, that they had given Yugoslavia credits to the extent of something over $200 million; nevertheless they had not been able to buy a single sentence in the Yugoslav party program, let alone Yugoslavia's whole policy—which meant they must be bad businessmen.

This was going too far on my part. Apart from anything else, Mikoyan was Soviet Minister of Trade and that had been his main occupation for decades, so that my remark struck a personal note. Mikoyan said that I was upset, at which I asked him what he expected from me after everything they had done to Yugoslavia. I said I believed that there were very few people in the world who would approve such methods, quite apart from the effect their attitude would have in Yugoslavia. To which

Mikoyan replied that I was mistaken when I talked of their being isolated and that it was in fact we Yugoslavs who were isolated, because all the Communist parties were on the side of the Soviet Union while Yugoslavia was alone. I told Mikoyan that we had been through it all once before in Stalin's day and that everyone knew how it ended.

While this conversation was going on Khrushchev was waiting for Mikoyan to return and report to him the results of his "mission," so that he could make his speech. After leaving me Mikoyan drew Khrushchev a few paces aside and became engaged in a lively conversation with him. I presume he was talking about the argument he had had with me, that our conversation couldn't have been less agreeable, and that I had turned down Khrushchev's invitation to go to the head table. Khrushchev then made the speech which all those present had been waiting for. He seemed to find it difficult to speak, although he usually proposes toasts at such receptions with great facility. He referred to the Central Committee plenum and the prospects for expanding the Soviet chemical industry, but not a word about Yugoslavia. It was a rather confused speech—I imagine not what he had planned to say before his talk with Mikoyan. When Khrushchev started to be ironic at the expense of those who said the Soviet Union was exploiting Czechoslovakia, Mikoyan took his glass and started to throw in slogans about Soviet-Czechoslovak friendship and solidarity, and with that Khrushchev's speech came to an end without being properly rounded off.

I still believe that I adopted the only correct attitude in conversation with Mikoyan and that I was right to turn down Khrushchev's invitation to join him. Anything else would have been damaging to Yugoslavia's prestige. I believe I upset Khrushchev's plan. There was every reason to believe that he intended to make a speech in support of the Central Committee's decision on Yugoslavia but in the event he didn't mention Yugoslavia at all. I may be mistaken, but I believe Mikoyan dissuaded him following such an exchange of words as an ambassador rarely has with the Deputy Prime Minister of the country to which he is accredited.

Quite a few foreign diplomats from neutral and Western countries came up to me after I had been talking to Mikoyan, but not one of them asked me what we had been talking about. I imagine that some of them who know Russian had heard something of what we said. For the rest, it was sufficient for them to watch us and to guess what we were discussing. The majority expressed their disagreement with such offensive treatment of Yugoslavia in *Pravda*. Among others the Polish ambassador, Gede, came up and started to tell me that there had been no need for us to talk as we had about Stalin in our program. I cut him short and told him to tell it to Khrushchev and not to me, and with that the conversation ended.

Moscow, May 11, 1958

Belgrade's first reactions to the worsening situation in Moscow were, in my opinion, of a rather routine nature. They contained quite a lot of old arguments which have been overtaken by events and which are not sufficient to explain such behavior by the Soviet leaders or by Khrushchev personally, who is now head of both party and government in the Soviet Union. I sent a letter in reply to a message from Belgrade which repeated some of our old arguments about the "pressure by Stalinists on Khrushchev" which we heard a couple of years ago. I said I was unable to accept the view that even today somebody apart from Khrushchev himself was determining the Soviet attitude toward Yugoslavia or that Khrushchev was still obliged to adapt himself and make concessions to someone else.

Khrushchev imagined that he could publish such an anti-Yugoslav pronouncement in *Pravda* on May 9 and that on the same day at the Czechoslovak reception in the presence of fifteen hundred people, the diplomatic corps, and the foreign and Soviet press, he could have the Yugoslav ambassador sitting beside him and, referring directly to him, say that the Soviet Union wanted to have good relations with Yugoslavia. Reports of that scene, so damaging to Yugoslavia, would have gone round the world and the Soviet leaders' anti-Yugoslav behavior would have continued. At least I had deprived Khrushchev of that pleasure.

I know we cannot look at the question of our relations with the Soviet Union simply in the light of one article in *Pravda,* however anti-Yugoslav it might be. I tried to set out my views on the present situation in a letter I sent to Koča Popović today. Among other things, I said in this personal letter that I no longer had any doubt in my mind that the principal initiator of the current anti-Yugoslav moves by the Soviet Government was Khrushchev himself.

There is no reason to believe that the so-called Stalinists, the Chinese, and others have any serious influence on Khrushchev's policy. Only uninformed people think like that, out of inertia and habits of the past when the relationship of forces in the Soviet leadership was different. The Soviet Intelligence service (Khrushchev is its supreme head) makes no effort to counter such mistaken views in their everlasting efforts to deceive and misinform the "enemy," which is the favorite trick of Khrushchev, the great tactician.

After June 1957 Khrushchev made sure that he personally wielded the decisive influence in the leadership of the Soviet Union. In the course of a year he carried out numerous changes in the party and government *apparat,* ending up with a new party Presidium, Supreme Soviet, and gov-

381

ernment. He cleared out both the big people and the small upon whom he couldn't rely, and not just those who were Stalinists.

In the course of this it was often the non-Stalinists and the anti-Stalinist decisions of the Twentieth Congress of the CPSU which suffered. I am sure that the removal of Marshal Zhukov came about exclusively on Khrushchev's initiative and not as a result of some battle between Stalinists and non-Stalinists, since both Khrushchev and Zhukov were in their own ways both one and the other. The influence of the so-called Stalinists, if one thinks in terms of definite groups and persons, ceased to be a serious factor in Khrushchev's policy after June 1957. But no essential change came about in the Soviet Union because of the removal of the Molotov-Malenkov group. Khrushchev determined Soviet policy by adapting his Marxist-Leninist convictions and ideas to Soviet reality and on the basis of his unchallenged power in the Soviet Union. One cannot reasonably assert, for example, that, immediately after getting rid of the Molotov-Malenkov group, it was under the influence of the so-called Stalinists that Khrushchev took action to counter the positive results of the Twentieth Congress on the cultural, artistic, and ideological front and stepped up control in that sphere as in the old days. It is paradoxical but it is a fact that the situation in that field got worse after the Stalinists had been liquidated, and it was done on instructions from the non-Stalinist Khrushchev.

There is something superficial, outdated, and inaccurate in any attempt to divide the present Soviet leaders precisely into Stalinists and non-Stalinists. It is no longer possible to use those categories as it was possible to do some years ago. It is even less possible to explain Khrushchev's present policy against Yugoslavia by reference to some influence which the Stalinists have over Khrushchev or some compromise he has made with them.

These were the arguments I set out in my letter to Koča Popović.

Until the June plenum Khrushchev frequently made use of the existence of an opposition in the Presidium whenever he wanted to exert pressure on Yugoslavia or Poland, threatening that the Stalinists might come to power if something that Moscow wanted was not done. Similar ideas are still being put around even now, the sense of which is that we should back Khrushchev lest somebody worse should take his place. The Poles in particular are always ready to use this argument, so that Gomulka's opportunism may even appear progressive.

My impression is that Khrushchev's actual political influence in the Soviet Union has declined in recent years, although it was in those very years that he emerged as absolute master of the Soviet Union: First Secretary of the party, Prime Minister, commander in chief of the Army, and head of the State Security Service.

Khrushchev is often inconsistent in foreign and domestic policy and one cannot avoid the conclusion that the supreme distinguishing feature of his ideology and practice is opportunism. That is why he was more of a Stalinist than Molotov or Malenkov in domestic policy immediately after their removal. And it is much the same with his never-ending tactics of "hot and cold" toward Yugoslavia, and other countries, too. Apart from that, Khrushchev's prestige among the people suffered badly as they became ever more aware of the fact that he was fighting skillfully and stubbornly for his own absolute personal power. The way he got rid of Marshal Zhukov had a very bad effect among the people and the Army as far as Khrushchev was concerned. This latest move of Khrushchev's with regard to Yugoslavia may result in a further decline in his prestige. But none of this is to be explained by the influence of Stalinists, and even less by a linkup of Soviet and Chinese Stalinists—which in my opinion never came about—but by the very complex set of problems Soviet domestic and foreign policy faces and the efforts being made by Khrushchev, sometimes a Stalinist and sometimes not, in his own way to keep in step with the demands of a changing situation.

There is objectively a profound antagonism between Yugoslavia and the Soviet Union and the "camp" on many issues. At times it has been concealed and at others it has come to the surface; moreover, our efforts to bring about a new relationship coupled with Soviet hopes of getting us into the "camp" frequently obscured the real nature of Yugoslav-Soviet relations. The LCY program is open confirmation of the contradictions existing between them and us. In the Soviet Union both Stalinists and non-Stalinists—although this way of dividing them is outdated—are convinced that the Soviet Union would disintegrate if it tried to follow Yugoslavia's example. Khrushchev was the first to reach that conclusion and still believes it. They are also convinced that the "camp" would fall apart if Poland and the other countries were to follow Yugoslavia. The ring of American atomic bases around the Soviet Union and the possibility of war breaking out strengthens these convictions and their belief in the "danger" which Yugoslav socialism represents for the Soviet Union and the "camp" which has been consolidated by new and better methods on the old, fundamentally Stalinist principles of Soviet hegemonism.

After the Twelve-party Declaration it was only to be expected that Khrushchev would eventually turn to attacking us. This has now come about on the excuse that we have attacked them and the "camp." It was not only the Soviet leaders' way of looking at the world as a great power and master of the "socialist camp" which played a part in this but also Khrushchev's well calculated choice of the tactical moment and the fact that he had managed somehow to get all the Communist parties together to sign the Declaration.

I still have no doubt that the person who initiated the latest attack on us was Khrushchev himself, and of his own free will, not under pressure from anyone else. Perhaps it is because I am influenced by the Soviet attack on us on May 9 that I now stress only some of Khrushchev's qualities and do not talk about some of the more positive aspects of his policy. But this is not an attempt to give a complete picture of Khrushchev's policy; it is rather a note in a diary about the present moment in Yugoslav-Soviet relations, written while still under the impression left by that brutal attack on Yugoslavia.

CHAPTER THIRTY-ONE

THE CAMPAIGN AGAINST YUGOSLAVIA

*No tricks are too mean for the Russians to use in their cam-
paign against "revisionist" Yugoslavia. There are further
delays over the question of Soviet credits for Yugoslav industrial development, but the Russians are eager themselves
to expand trade with the capitalist world.*

Moscow, May 14, 1958

The campaign against Yugoslavia continues. Every day the Soviet
press publishes statements by different Communist parties criticizing our
program and our Seventh Congress. Today *Pravda* printed an article
which appeared in the East German *Neues Deutschland* four days ago
under the headline "Out of Step with Marxism-Leninism" and the sub-
title "The Seventh Congress of the League of Communists of Yugoslavia."

The extent of this Soviet campaign can also be judged from a *Pravda*
report of May 14 headed: "Conference of Scholars on the Struggle
Against Revisionism." Here is the text:

> In the Soviet Academy of Science today the Academy of Social Sci-
> ences held a session to consider the struggle with revisionism at the pres-
> ent time. The meeting began with an introductory speech by member of
> the Academy K. V. Ostrovityanov.[1] A report on the main issues involved
> in the struggle was delivered by Professor B. N. Ponomarev. The session
> was followed with great interest by scholarly circles in the capital. More
> than a thousand people will take part in the work of the session which
> will last two days.

Of the two people referred to as conducting this conference I know
Ponomarev much better than Ostrovityanov. I have already mentioned

[1] Konstantin Ostrovityanov, 1892–1969. Russian academician, economist. Vice-
president, Soviet Academy of Science, 1953–62.

that he still has a portrait of Stalin in a prominent place in his office two years after Khrushchev made his secret speech.

I do not believe that there exists in other societies and systems a profession like the one which is followed by Suslov, Ponomarev and the army of party and government officials at their service in Soviet society and the "camp." Their judgments on matters of theory and ideology in socialism, as in the case of their present campaign against our program and the LCY Congress, are final and irrevocable. Their disagreement with our program does not resemble criticism but is more like the anathema which used to be pronounced upon heretics and those who strayed from the truth and the true faith.

The countries and parties of the "camp," who also have their Suslovs and Ponomarevs, as well as the majority of the world's Communist parties who support the Soviet line, are actively engaged in the same business. One has to admit that Yugoslavia's position is not easy.

Although the Soviet Government has not canceled the agreement it concluded with the Yugoslav Government for the sale of a certain number of copies of our newspapers in the Soviet Union, our papers are again nowhere to be obtained. The issues containing our replies to the Chinese have not been seen anywhere in Moscow. They have probably been confiscated.

On the basis of an earlier agreement with the Soviet Government one of our naval squadrons paid a courtesy visit here. The Soviet officers obviously had orders 'to treat our sailors in a friendly way, as people "who were not responsible for the Seventh Congress." The Russians will probably behave similarly toward a delegation of our university professors who are due to arrive the day after tomorrow. When there is a conflict between us and the Russians, they do not hesitate to try and create a good impression on some of our better known people. They surround them with an atmosphere of friendship so that later they can try and set them against their own government. Apart from that the Russians' influence in certain Yugoslav circles varies, a circumstance of which they are well aware here and try to turn to their own advantage.

Everybody here knows that Voroshilov's visit to Yugoslavia, which had been agreed officially down to the last detail, was canceled unilaterally by the Russians at the last minute. When we are asked about it by foreigners, we confirm this. But we do not discuss the insulting method which the Soviet Government used in refusing to give us any explanation by diplomatic channels. We learned of the Soviet Government's decision from its statement in the Soviet press.

THE CAMPAIGN AGAINST YUGOSLAVIA

Moscow, May 17, 1958

Diplomats from the socialist "camp" have ceased altogether to talk politics with me. The Asians in the "camp" are now better than the Europeans and the one among them who behaves most correctly is the Mongolian ambassador, Bata. Unlike the other East European diplomats, Polish Ambassador Gede has kept up his earlier relationship with me. On May 15 he brought me the *Trybuna Ludu* article about the Seventh Congress. Although the language and style of the Polish article are different from that used in the campaign in the Soviet press, it still fits in with that campaign and criticizes us in the same way as the Russians, though in more polite language and without being offensive.

Moscow, May 22, 1958

Conferences of the countries of Eastern Europe have been taking place here one after the other, mainly on economic matters. The Russians are trying to bring about as great a degree of economic integration as possible among the countries of the "camp" by means of a greater and more precise division of labor among them. This increases their interdependence and has the final result of leading to greater unity of the "camp." The "monolithic unity" of the camp would be more firmly assured on this economic basis than what has been achieved so far by means of political and party pressures and "ideological" measures taken with regard to first one and then another member of the camp.

The authorities in Moscow confiscated *Borba* for May 17, which contained our reply to *Pravda*'s attack of May 9.

Moscow, May 24, 1958

The confidential TASS bulletin[2] for May 22 printed an article headed "American Economic and Military Aid to Yugoslavia." It reads as follows:

New York (TASS). Allen, correspondent of the New York *Post*, reports from Washington that Tito is now trying to obtain more economic and military aid from the U.S.A. Allen states that the Yugoslav Government is making "careful preparations" through diplomatic channels to investigate the possibility of such aid and will begin official talks if the American Government indicates willingness for them. In the State Department and the Pentagon, Allen writes, there are signs that the

[2] The TASS agency prepares bulletins of daily news items not published in the Soviet press which are distributed for the confidential information of Soviet officials.

extension of further aid to Yugoslavia will be approved. Allen says that Yugoslavia will receive a long-term credit of $300 million for the purchase of heavy machinery and other industrial equipment in the U.S.A. and Western Europe and also permission to buy "limited quantities" of American arms, especially spare parts for the military equipment which the Americans have already supplied to Yugoslavia.

This report in the New York *Post* was most probably written by the Russians themselves and reprinted "objectively" from there in the confidential TASS bulletin. Allen's report contains everything Moscow needs to support the open attacks they made on Yugoslavia in *Pravda* of May 9. I have previously come across instances where the Russians themselves write reports about Yugoslavia and publish them exclusively in the Western press and then pick them up in the confidential TASS bulletin, thus "informing" their key people in the spirit of what they write and say about Yugoslavia.

I believe that there are quite a few members of the Central Committee of the CPSU who think such reports by Soviet "black propaganda" in the confidential TASS bulletin are quite genuine. A fortnight ago *Pravda* published the Soviet Communist party's estimate, supported by figures, of how many American dollars Yugoslavia had received for its independent, or as they call it here "anti-Soviet," policy in the course of the last five years. Now it is a question of the exact sum in dollars "which Tito has asked the Americans for." That means to say that what *Pravda* said in its article against Yugoslavia on May 9 has proved to be true and the Soviet Central Committee's forecast to be correct. The "proof" is provided by the confidential TASS bulletin with the New York *Post* report.

Moscow, May 26, 1958

The Russians continue to "play politics" with regard to Yugoslavia and are not acting as Stalin did, as Khrushchev pointed out to me when the quarrel broke out over the Hungarian events in November 1956. So to-day's *Pravda* prints greetings telegrams sent by Khrushchev and Voroshilov to Comrade Tito for his birthday. But the same copy of the paper also contains a report by the Chinese news agency about the decisions taken by a meeting of the Chinese Congress which has just been meeting. It passed three resolutions of which the second was mainly devoted to criticism of the Yugoslav League of Communists and "modern revisionism."

In the flood of articles directed against "modern revisionists," which means against Yugoslavia, there is never any reference to one of the fundamental points in our program: our insistence that relations between socialist countries and Communist parties must be based on the principles of equality of status and rights. I would say that it is that which bothers the Soviet Union most of all in the LCY program. The Russians are not especially concerned about whether the Yugoslavs are wrong in their interpretation of Marx or Lenin or any other question. What provokes their anger is the Yugoslav criticism of the unequal relationship existing between socialist countries and Communist parties and of Soviet domination in those relations and our demand that such a legacy of the past should be removed as one of the main obstacles to the further advance of socialism in the world.

Moscow, May 28, 1958

In a note received yesterday the Soviet Government has unilaterally postponed for another five years the Soviet-Yugoslav agreements on credits for the creation of a new Yugoslav aluminum industry, a fertilizer plant, and some other enterprises. It is not the first time.

Before handing me the note Gromyko, with a very serious face, said that by what it was doing the Soviet Government was concerned not to worsen but to improve our relations! The Soviet Government had allegedly taken this decision bearing in mind Comrade Tito's statement that economic relations between Yugoslavia and the Soviet Union were based on the principle of mutual benefit.

I expressed regret that they were again refusing to carry out intergovernmental agreements simply because there were ideological differences between us which had existed for some time. I said we had much greater differences with other states, but that they did not refuse unilaterally to carry out agreements which they had signed with Yugoslavia. The matter assumed the character of economic reprisals on account of ideology. Under such conditions it was not possible for an independent country to maintain normal relations with another country. We had reached agreement on these matters with the Soviet Government when normal governmental relations were restored three years ago. We now realized that they thought differently and had gone back on what we agreed in June 1955.

Gromyko returned several times to Comrade Tito's statement about "mutual benefit" in the development of our economic relations, saying that they, the Russians, now wanted to put relations between our countries onto such a basis. I had to listen again to Gromyko's statement that the Soviet Government, in handing us such a note, did not wish to see our relations worsen! He stopped when I said to him that the Soviet Government had said in its note what it really wanted and that their note did not leave room for the least doubt in that respect.

Moscow, May 31, 1958

At a reception given by the Soviet Government in the Kremlin yesterday Khrushchev had a long conversation with me. I listened fairly calmly to him as he went through, one after the other, as he has done so many times before, the various charges against Yugoslavia: that we are to blame for the present conflict between the Soviet Union and Yugoslavia, that the Russians don't want to worsen but to improve relations between us, that Tito broke the agreement reached in Bucharest in 1957 about not attacking each other in public, that Tito had spoken highly of American aid, saying that it was given unselfishly, and that he had said that economic relations between Yugoslavia and the Soviet Union were based on "mutual benefit," and so forth.

Khrushchev then went on to say that he had gone to Belgrade in May 1955 in difficult circumstances in the desire to reestablish friendship with Yugoslavia but that we had on several occasions caused open clashes between us. At the LCY Congress Tito had made use of certain statements out of Khrushchev's secret speech on Stalin, although he had no authority to do so, since we had received the speech in confidence from the Soviet Communist party only for our information, that it was John Foster Dulles who had printed it in his own version so as to inflict as much harm as possible on the Soviet Union and socialism, and that we had started to sling mud at the Soviet Union. Then Khrushchev said that we were isolated, that the world Communist movement was united and marching in step, that Yugoslavia alone was out of step, and that we were wrong in our assessment of Stalin, as if the Soviet Union were a desert in which we saw only Stalin's faults ("And where were we then?" Khrushchev asked).

I replied to Khrushchev on one or two points. But on this occasion I left most of what he said unanswered because we have discussed these questions more than once since I arrived in Moscow. Instead of arguing further about Stalin and Dulles I asked Khrushchev whether they really had to break their interstate agreement on credits. I told him that Yugoslavia would not collapse without the Soviet credits, as it wouldn't collapse without American credits either, but that we were amazed that the Soviet Government should take the initiative in worsening relations between our governments after a month of ideological campaigning against the Yugoslav League of Communists.

Khrushchev appeared disinclined to discuss this "because it is a question of economics, not politics." When I said that it was certainly the policy of the Soviet Government toward Yugoslavia, Khrushchev changed his tone, declared that the financial resources involved were theirs and not ours, and that the governmental agreements had to be dropped when Tito had declared at our party congress that Yugoslavia's economic relations with the Soviet Union were based on the principle of "mutual benefit."

I don't think the conversation served any good purpose. To Khrushchev's request that I should inform Belgrade that it was now up to Yugoslavia to put our relations right I said that very little depended on us because we were not refusing to carry out agreements reached between our governments while they were, and that I would inform Belgrade what we had been talking about.

Moscow, June 1, 1958

Western businessmen are arriving in Moscow ever more frequently, and they are being well received by the Russians. At the last plenum of the Soviet Central Committee Khrushchev talked about the Soviet Union's economic cooperation with the West, but at the same time he never stops criticizing Yugoslavia for doing the same. We hear that the Russians are telling trade delegations from the West that cooperation with a country like Yugoslavia is practically negligible because Yugoslavia is small and poor, and that the real prospects for expanding the economy are in the West, with the establishment and development of cooperation between the Soviet Union and Western governments, for which there exist real prospects and almost unlimited opportunities. They obviously apply one criterion to the "camp," another to the neutral countries, and a third to member countries of the NATO bloc, to which the Russians continue to propose talks on the highest level.

Moscow, June 6, 1958

I drew Belgrade's attention to the proposal which Khrushchev made in a message to Eisenhower on June 2 for talks aimed at developing American-Soviet economic and scientific-technical cooperation. I believe this Soviet move to promote trade relations between the Soviet Union and the United States should be given publicity in our press, especially since Khrushchev raises the question of American credits for the Soviet Union "on the usual terms" and speaks of repaying the credits "by installments." According to his letter it appears they are thinking of long-term credits. Moreover, in my opinion, publicity should be given in the Yugoslav press to those passages in Khrushchev's message in which he talks of granting concessions to foreign enterprises and accepts in advance the idea that the Soviet Union will have a negative trade balance in the early stages of the opening up of Soviet-American trade relations as Khrushchev now imagines them.

It would be good for our public to be informed objectively about Khrushchev's real stand on the question of their relations with the United States. In that way people will be able more easily to distinguish Soviet propaganda "against American imperialism" from the Soviet policy of expanding trade and all other kinds of relations between the Soviet Union and the United States. The Russians have been attacking us for ten years now, and are doing so again today, for taking credits from the West and the United States—exactly the same sort of credits as Khrushchev is today asking Eisenhower for. When Yugoslavia is obliged to take such credits from the West, and on terms unfavorable to us, the Russians then make out that we have practically abandoned the basic principles of socialist ideology. It is in fact the Russians' main "argument" against our foreign policy. But when Khrushchev proposes to Eisenhower that America should extend credits to the Soviet Union, this is then put forward as an example of the policy of peaceful coexistence and cooperation between states.

Khrushchev's message is in my opinion a major political and propaganda move with regard to the United States and the West. One should not exclude the possibility of practical results, although I don't believe Khrushchev now expects to receive American credits. But Soviet-American cultural contacts are steadily increasing and so are scientific, technological, and business links, although there is still no normal trade between the Soviet Union and the United States. Khrushchev's present policy toward the West as a whole can only benefit from his latest move. The other Western powers, especially West Germany, will probably not be entirely indifferent to what Khrushchev has said. I don't think it is just a matter of Soviet propaganda but of a real Soviet need for Western technology in a number of fields, which is going to affect Soviet policy for a long time.

Pravda for June 5 reprinted the full text of a Chinese article consisting mainly of insults and crude comments about Yugoslavia.

Moscow, June 7, 1958

Radio Belgrade reported a few days ago that I have been appointed a member of the LCY Commission for International Relations, which makes it clear to everyone in Moscow and Belgrade that I shall soon be returning to Yugoslavia, because it is not possible to be at the same time ambassador in Moscow and a member of that commission in Yugoslavia. As usually happens, the diplomats are always among the first to get to know when an ambassador is being moved and they have already started asking me how much longer I am going to remain in Moscow.

I have not heard anything from Belgrade about being moved or about when I am to leave Moscow. It will probably be fairly soon; otherwise I don't suppose they would have announced my new job in the press.

I would start making my farewell calls here in a week's time. I think I will ask to call on the Soviet leaders at the beginning of next month so that I can leave about July 15. If I get no special instructions from Belgrade about it, I think I shall ask to call on the same leading Soviet personalities as I made courtesy calls on at the beginning of 1956 when I arrived in Moscow. What interests me by far the most, of course, is how my farewell call on Khrushchev will go off, if in fact it ever takes place.

Moscow, June 10, 1958

I had a conversation a few days ago with United States Ambassador Thompson and asked him what he thought about Khrushchev's idea of America giving the Soviet Union long-term credits on favorable terms. Thompson said he thought Khrushchev's message had three aims: to strengthen the Soviet position with relation to the West, presenting the Soviet Union as the initiator of better trade relations. Second, the Russians come up with this kind of proposal now not simply for political reasons but also because they overestimate the significance of America's economic troubles and think this is a good moment to address such a message to Eisenhower. Third, if there are no results as far as the Americans are concerned, the Russians think they are strengthening their position with the other Western governments which the Russians have already offered big business deals. In this connection Thompson mentioned West Germany, which is in a better position than any of the countries of Western Europe to meet Soviet requirements in introducing new technology.

I asked Thompson jokingly whether he could say what advice he had given Washington about Khrushchev's proposal. He said there would not be any American Government credits for the Soviet Union. But as for American private firms that was another matter; they could take up Khrushchev's proposals if they were interested. In any case the American ambassador also thinks the Russians have a real and substantial need for foreign involvement in their chemical industry, for which they announced ambitious plans at the last Central Committee meeting but do not have either enough resources or enough technological know-how, of the kind that exists in the United States and the West.

CHAPTER THIRTY-TWO

THE EXECUTION OF IMRE NAGY

The execution of Imre Nagy shocks the Yugoslavs and leads to a further worsening of relations with the Russians. Mićunović sees how the Russians organize "spontaneous" demonstrations in Moscow.

Moscow, June 18, 1958

On June 17 the Soviet newspapers carried a report about the execution of Imre Nagy and his companions.[1] Under the terms of an agreement which the Yugoslav Government signed with the Hungarian Goverment that they would not be held responsible for what was done before November 4, 1956, these people voluntarily left our embassy in Budapest in November 1956. Soviet troops then seized them by force and took them off to an unknown destination. In that way the Russians, along with the Hungarians, showed their contempt for the first agreement the new Hungarian Government had signed with another government, in this case with Yugoslavia.

The Icelandic ambassador gave a reception yesterday in Moscow at which the news of Nagy's execution was the main subject of conversation. People are shocked and indignant. The majority of the diplomats are asking why Moscow had to make such a move when they knew in advance what an extremely bad effect it would have in the world for the Soviet Government and its international prestige. Although the Soviet Government is trying to create the impression among the public that it is not its affair but Hungary's, commentaries by the great majority of foreigners lay Nagy's execution at the Soviet Union's door. Everything that the Russians have been saying and writing in recent years about the inde-

[1] *Author's note:* According to an official communiqué published in Hungary on June 16, those sentenced to death apart from Imre Nagy were Pal Maleter, Miklos Gimesi, and Dr. Joszef Szilagy. Another five were sentenced to from five years to life imprisonment. All those sentenced were members of Imre Nagy's government.

pendence, sovereignty of the countries of Eastern Europe and about noninterference in their internal affairs has once again been shown to be false.

Even at some of the trials in Stalin's day, though only in a formal sense, there was greater respect for the law than there has been in the case of the execution of Nagy. In Stalin's day there were at least some members of the public present at the trials, whoever they may have been. There are suggestions that Nagy had already been executed much earlier or had died while under interrogation, and that the news of his execution has only now been released.

Some of the charges which are laid against Nagy can apply to us: his appeal for the "liquidation of military blocs" and his support for "national communism," as the West used to describe the internal system in Yugoslavia. Nagy is also accused of setting up workers' councils in Hungary. He is described as an agent of imperialism with a party card in his pocket, as a splitter of the socialist camp, as a man who disguised his treachery with socialist slogans, and so on. Before saying that he has been condemned to death the communiqué gives Nagy's main political label as "revisionist." All these charges have already been made many times in public against Yugoslavia in one way or the other. The Yugoslav embassy in Budapest which gave asylum to Nagy and his comrades has been the subject of criticism throughout the last two years and it is now starting up again. All this will have the effect of worsening relations not only between Yugoslavia and the Soviet Union but also between Yugoslavia and Hungary.

I have noticed in conversation that a considerable number of foreigners who arrived here after November 1956 are not aware of the agreement signed by János Kadar's government with the Yugoslav Government concerning the voluntary departure from our embassy in Budapest of Nagy and his comrades. Yesterday the BBC from London gave a questionable version of the arrangement, not mentioning the agreement but saying that Nagy left the Yugoslav embassy "after receiving assurances about free passage." This could be interpreted as meaning that Nagy and the others were tricked by us and not that Soviet troops violated the first international agreement signed by Kadar's government and seized Nagy and the whole group.

At yesterday's reception Mikoyan and the other Soviet representatives were more or less isolated. Foreigners did not go up to them as usual or did not stay long in their company. The Hungarian diplomats stood apart so as to avoid a boycott by the majority of the diplomats present. Because of this event the general political atmosphere in Moscow has worsened.

Moscow, June 19, 1958

I asked yesterday to see Khrushchev and he received me today. I handed him our Central Committee's reply of June 14. He pointed out that it was a long document, put it on one side, and said he would study it carefully later. It was apparent that he did not reckon that the contents of our letter, written before the announcement of Nagy's execution, might change our relations substantially for the better.

We talked for more than two hours in the unpleasant atmosphere caused by Nagy's execution. Khrushchev started by saying that the Soviet Union had not intended to quarrel with Yugoslavia. They had appointed a delegation from the Soviet Communist party to attend our Seventh Congress. They had also accepted our invitation for Voroshilov to pay an official visit to Yugoslavia. Neither they nor the other parties had attacked us when we refused to sign the Twelve-party Declaration. Thus all the familiar matters from the past were presented in a manner to suit the present situation. In the course of a long conversation each of us stuck to his point of view and the conversation was in fact fruitless.

I raised the question of Nagy's execution. I told him that the whole world was shocked, that an irreparable mistake had been made, and that it would be difficult for anyone to conceive anything worse for the Soviet Union and Hungary. Nagy had meant less and less politically in Hungary, but they had now liquidated him physically but had resurrected him politically. It was obviously a disagreeable subject for Khrushchev. He said it was Hungary's affair and not the Soviet Union's, but that he personally approved what the Hungarians had done and would have done the same himself. He reproached me as a Communist for referring to world public opinion, saying that Communists have other, class criteria in such matters.

Changing the subject, Khrushchev then talked about how well their industry was working, what a wonderful harvest they were going to have this year, and so forth. I said that would make it easier for them to reserve their negative attitude on the question of the credits for us. Khrushchev rejected this, started to reflect on the meaning of Tito's statement about "mutual benefit," and said that they were adapting themselves to our view. Then he said: "If at the Seventh Congress Tito had said just one word about the Soviet Union's aid to Yugoslavia by means of credits it wouldn't have come to this." The barter deals with us are also going to be based on the principle of "mutual benefit."

I brought up the matter of his speech in Sofia and of *Pravda*, which for the last six weeks, day after day, has been printing articles from other parties directed against Yugoslavia. I asked whether they were going to stop doing it. Khrushchev said that it was very significant that all the Communist parties in the world were against us, and that they would go on publishing the articles. I pointed out that at the Congress of the Czechoslovak Communist party yesterday, even before he announced the Congress agenda, Široky[2] had attacked Yugoslavia, that Kirichenko would probably do the same in Prague as Khrushchev did in Sofia, and that this showed that they were not interested in calming things down but in doing the reverse. Khrushchev said that the Czechs were free to make up their own minds and that he could answer only for the CPSU. He added that Kirichenko was not going to say very much and that he would go himself to the party congress in East Germany at the beginning of July and reply to Tito's speech in Istria.[3]

In a quite different tone Khrushchev then said that he knew that our leaders enjoyed great prestige among the people of Yugoslavia, both now and in the past. But we were mistaken if we thought that they also did not enjoy prestige in the Soviet Union; and it was not true to say that the Soviet people were not completely in agreement with them with relation to Yugoslavia. Nor were we right in believing that the very friendly welcome Tito received in Soviet cities in 1956 was contrary to the wishes of the Soviet leaders. Khrushchev said that some people in Moscow were now saying that he had been wrong to put his faith so quickly and so lightly in the Yugoslavs, and that Molotov had had better judgment. Khrushchev asked what I thought: Did it suit him better personally that things had taken the turn they had between us? I said that people in Yugoslavia were also reproaching Tito for moving too fast toward full support of the Soviet Union and that we were now seeing repeated something we thought was over and done with.

[2] Viliam Široky, 1902–71. Slovak Communist official. Prime Minister of Czechoslovakia, 1953–63.

[3] In a speech at Labin, Istria, on June 15 Tito replied both to recent Chinese attacks on Yugoslavia and to what Khrushchev had said in his speech in Sofia on June 3. On the question of American aid to Yugoslavia Tito said:

"I fully agree that the Americans are not giving us aid so that socialism may triumph in Yugoslavia, just as in 1921 and 1922 they gave assistance to the Soviet Union, not in order to strengthen the Soviet Government, but because there was famine there. . . .

"Comrade Khrushchev often repeats that socialism cannot be built with American wheat. I think it can be done by anyone who knows how to do it, while a person who doesn't know how to do it cannot build socialism even with his own wheat. Khrushchev says we live on charity received from the imperialist countries in the form of goods that could not be placed elsewhere. But American wheat, cotton, and fats are of very high quality and could be placed anywhere. American wheat is no worse than Soviet wheat, which we do not receive anyway. . . . What moral right have those who attack us to rebuke us about American aid or credits when Khrushchev himself has just tried to conclude an economic agreement with America? This is the height of cynicism. . . ."

Moscow, June 20, 1958

Khrushchev said that we were saying that he was returning to Stalin's policy, that we were shouting: See how in Sofia Khrushchev has revived the first Cominform resolution, Khrushchev is reverting to Stalin's policy. None of that was true, Khrushchev said. "In the first place you Yugoslavs don't want to hear anything about Stalin apart from the worst that happened in 1948, before and after that, but that isn't all," he said. "We in the Soviet Union know much more than you do about Stalin's mistakes, but there is another side to the matter. When today I hear people around the world saying that I am like Stalin, in a certain sense it rejoices my heart," Khrushchev said. "That's as it should be, and let the Western capitalists know that we shall fight consistently for communism. Stalin certainly had his faults, but I cherish the greatest respect for the other, positive side of his character."

Khrushchev said he knew that the Yugoslav leaders were greatly respected by the people—that was an undoubted fact. Their wartime services had been tremendous, and he had always said so. But now our leaders were not taking the correct line, and the Soviet leaders, Khrushchev said, would fight against it. Khrushchev then put to me in the form of a question "confidentially" that a "very serious comrade" had said that it was not true that in Yugoslavia Kardelj was the principal defender of Yugoslav policy, that Kardelj and Ranković had been ready to sign the Twelve-party Declaration, but that Tito had sent them orders from Belgrade not to sign. "You know best whether that is what happened; but it came as a surprise to me," Khrushchev said, "because I was always able to come to an understanding with Tito with a minimum of talk. Later somebody spoiled this, and things often didn't work out as Tito and I had agreed."

I said that I could tell him, also "in confidence," that his information was not correct. I had been a member of the Yugoslav delegation at the November celebrations in Moscow and all the exchanges between Ranković, Kardelj, and Tito had passed through me, and I could tell him that there had been absolute unanimity between them from beginning to end. Khrushchev said: "You know best, it must be so." (The sense of this "information" which we had exchanged "in confidence" was clear both to Khrushchev and to me. What is most important, in my opinion, is that in the present crisis in our relations the Russians have abandoned their former favorite tactic of singling out Kardelj for criticism, while praising Tito and Ranković, and that they now claim to "have information" that it was Tito who was "against signing the Declaration.")

As he has done frequently in the past, Khrushchev spoke at length about our efforts as Yugoslavs to impose ourselves as leaders of the international Communist movement, saying that we claimed to be the only ones who understood Marxism in the modern world, that we were always in the right, that we were too proud, and that once we had said something we would never modify it or correct it. Then he talked about a panic in Yugoslavia, about the arrests of Cominform supporters and people fleeing to Hungary and Albania. The real reason why Khrushchev does not like this is that it is a clear proof of Yugoslavia's firm stand in the present conflict. I calmed him down by saying that there was no panic in Yugoslavia, that I had also heard of the arrest of some Cominformists, and that the people concerned were well known to me. Perhaps there was panic among a few individuals who had something to hide, but that was also natural.

Khrushchev said that we had immediately seized on his letter to Eisenhower of June 2 and were using it as an argument against him. He asked me whether I seriously believed that he was expecting to obtain credits from the United States. No, the letter had been written only for political reasons; there could be no credits, that at least was clear—the Lord preserve the Soviet Union from drawing up plans on the assumption of receiving American credits. If there were no credits there would be trade with Britain, West Germany, France, and Japan. "And if that doesn't come off, we can manage on our own; we shall be a year late with expanding the chemical industry, that's all," Khrushchev said. He confirmed that the Soviet press would continue to publish "criticisms" of the LCY. The Soviet Government would soon reply to the note about the credits. It was "impossible" for them to change the stand they had taken. Khrushchev said that relations between our countries would be "good neighborly"—quite distinct from the relations they have with the countries of the "camp" and even with the neutral countries.

We spoke about American aid to Yugoslavia. Although he was not quite precise on this, Khrushchev said that they would have had nothing against our accepting the aid if our relations with the Soviet Union had been different—based on the "principles of proletarian internationalism." Here Khrushchev was not clear: At times he spoke in the above sense, at others he repeated his suppositions about why the United States was helping us. I had the impression that he now wanted to "explain" what he was thinking two years ago when he said he agreed with us about American aid. But it was by no means clear, and probably not just because of us but because of the Poles as well, who are receiving aid according to the formula mentioned above, which also doesn't please the Soviet Union either.

The Soviet Foreign Ministry asked me how my meeting with Khrushchev should be reported, as a party or a government meeting or both, in view of Khrushchev's different functions. I said we had talked about all sorts of things and that they could report it as they wished, I had no objections.

Our conversation lasted more than two hours. Khrushchev was more considerate than he has often been when our relations were incomparably better. The Soviet press today reported my meeting very prominently immediately after a report of the Central Committee resolution. The Russians were interested in having me meet Khrushchev as soon as possible. It suits their purpose to give it prominence, among other things because it took place the day after the announcement that Imre Nagy had been executed.

Moscow, June 21, 1958

Khrushchev and the other top Soviet leaders yesterday attended a reception given by the King of Nepal, who is here on an official visit. Foreign diplomats did not approach them. A group of Western ambassadors left the reception after a short stay as a sort of demonstration.

The atmosphere here is becoming steadily more tense. The Danish embassy was damaged after the Soviet press published Gromyko's protest to the Danish Government because of similar action against the Soviet embassy in Copenhagen. Danish young people and ordinary people in Copenhagen did that as a protest at the news of Nagy's execution. Gromyko demands that the security of the Soviet embassy is guaranteed, and then for two hours Soviet "demonstrators" here, under the protection of the Soviet police, break the doors and windows of the Danish embassy building and do everything of which Gromyko accuses the Danes!

The Soviet press is writing about the "justified wrath of Soviet working people" but calls the demonstrators in Copenhagen provocateurs and hooligans and attacks them as hirelings of NATO. In my opinion the Russians are afraid there will now be a wave of demonstrations and attacks on Soviet embassies in various countries in the West and they are trying in this way to prevent it. They have damaged the Danish embassy here to let others know what to expect.

The news of Imre Nagy's execution continues to be the main topic of conversation in the diplomatic corps here, and the most divergent views are expressed. If Nagy did not succumb because of the torture to which he was subjected, there are suggestions that the Soviet conflict with Yugoslavia influenced the Russians to decide on his execution. If relations between the Soviet Union and Yugoslavia had been better, the Russians, it is suggested, would not have risked spoiling relations with Yugoslavia on account of Nagy, and Nagy might still be alive. It is also being suggested that Nagy was liquidated a long time ago but that it has been announced only now lest we Yugoslavs should announce it, since we are supposed to have known all about it and the Russians were afraid lest we announced it first. If Nagy died under interrogation, as some people suggest, the Russians would have preferred to announce that he had been condemned to death and shot than that he had died in prison. By so doing they are showing a "firm hand," primarily for the benefit of the countries of the "camp," and whether he died in prison or was shot Nagy remains "on their conscience."

There has been a return to something like the atmosphere that prevailed between the Russians and Western diplomats in October and November 1956 at the time of the intervention in Hungary. Although this is to the disadvantage of the Russians, they don't appear especially worried; it appears that Hungary is safely in the camp and that the present indignation about Nagy's execution will pass as it did in 1956, as Khrushchev told me at our last meeting.

* * *

After Khrushchev's secret speech about Stalin at the Twentieth Congress, in which he condemned his predecessor primarily because of the number of innocent people executed in the Soviet Union in the decades of his absolute personal power, I don't think there have been in the Soviet Union or in the other Communist countries any political show trials or any executions of politicians, except in Albania. In any case one of the main points in Khrushchev's speech was that Stalin's crimes would never be repeated again, that there would never be any killings of politicians with or without a trial, and that the Soviet Union was reverting to "socialist legality," i.e., the rule of law, about which so much has been written here since the Twentieth Congress.

Now they have executed Nagy and inflicted serious harm on their own political interests and have betrayed once again the hopes raised by the Twentieth Congress.

Moscow, June 23, 1958

The Soviet press continues to take the view that the Nagy affair should not be given much publicity. It prints two or three sentences each day about the enthusiasm with which the Hungarian workers are approving Nagy's execution, as well as a few sentences about how Hungarian émigrés, along with Eisenhower and Dulles, are condemning it. According to the Soviet press the rest of the world approves what has been done. In fact the Russians want to rid themselves of any direct responsibility in the eyes of the public, since there have so far been no official Soviet commentaries on Nagy's execution.

Moscow, June 24, 1958

The Russians could not leave the Hungarian Government to deal with the situation. The campaign going on in the world, especially in the countries of the West, is growing in volume. So today's *Pravda* printed the first official Soviet commentary about Nagy's execution. It contains no reference to "modern revisionism" or to Yugoslavia, but replies to the campaign in the West and declares Soviet solidarity with the Hungarian Government which is formally responsible for the affair. The majority of the foreign diplomats here are rather surprised that Yugoslavia has not been referred to at all.

In Moscow a fairly small group of demonstrators, under the protection of the Soviet police, smashed up the building of the West German embassy. This is the Soviet Government's reply to the demonstrations in Bonn in front of the Soviet embassy. The police guarded the group until they had made a good job of smashing the windows and doors of the building. The Soviet demonstrators wrote slogans on the walls of the embassy, including "Remember Stalingrad," which got the West German diplomats here on the raw. The West German ambassador, Krol, who has told everybody how well he has been received here and what good relations he has with Khrushchev and who says he is acting in Moscow directly in Adenauer's name, was found sitting in a state of deep depression near a pile of broken glass, bricks, and other rubble which the demonstrators left behind. A West German journalist, with no particular sympathy for his ambassador, said he had "come across his ambassador sitting dumbly on a heap of faded illusions."

The Soviet authorities completely ignore the fact that people abroad who demonstrate in front of Soviet embassies are not protected in this way by their own police as is the case in Moscow, and that in the majority of countries in the West the police do their best to protect the Soviet embassy buildings. Here a certain party organization and some government departments are given the job of producing a "demonstration" against a particular country and to damage the country's embassy building to an extent which is precisely laid down. When the job has been done, the "demonstrators" depart quietly. This is one of the new forms of cold-war account-settling between East and West.

The public here keep repeating the Soviet official line that such demonstrations here and in the West are practically the same, and the Russians intend to go on replying to Western countries in this way. Meanwhile the Soviet Government will send the Western governments its notes of protest and reject similar notes from the West. Relations between Western diplomats and the Soviet Government continue to worsen. In conversation with me Khrushchev condemned these attacks on embassies in the West and in the East. But he says the Russians are forced to do it because of the attacks on Soviet embassies around the world.

Moscow, June 27, 1958

The Norwegian Ambassador, Brodland, who before coming here represented his country in Belgrade and with whom I have been on friendly terms, told me that he made a farewell call on Khrushchev on June 25. When the question of Hungary came up, Khrushchev told him that Yugoslavia had been interfering in Hungary's internal affairs through the Imre Nagy group. Brodland said he questioned this statement and that this part of the conversation was not at all agreeable to Khrushchev who did not want to continue it. He closed the subject with the statement that it was "Hungary's internal affair" and that there were not and would not be any political trials in the Soviet Union.

* * *

The demonstrations which "broke out" here under the protection of the Soviet official organs in front of the United States embassy are connected with the new hostile atmosphere which is developing along a wide front in relations between the Soviet Union and the West. The whole business is so well organized that it seems almost comic. The Americans here say that they were informed unofficially in advance by the Soviet side that "demonstrations" were going to be held, but that "everything would be all right," that is to say there would be no stone throwing or smashing of doors and windows as was the case with the embassies of some other Western countries toward which the Russians did not show such consideration as they did toward the Americans. While the "demonstrations" were taking place in front of the embassy building, members of the embassy staff stood on the balconies and at the windows and some of them shot films of the whole course of the "demonstration of Soviet workers." They even asked the "demonstrators" to look at them so that they could get good pictures. Some of them did so. The Americans now say that they have an "interesting documentary film" of the demonstrations.

Moscow, June 30, 1958

Gomulka criticized Yugoslavia publicly in a speech on June 28 which Moscow reprinted on June 30. Gomulka's criticism of Yugoslavia is more valuable to the Russians than anything that may be said about us in any other country of the "camp." As a former victim of Stalin's policy and an opponent of the Cominform who spent several years in jail in Poland in Stalin's day, Gomulka enjoyed the reputation of being more of a "friend of Yugoslavia" than any other East European Communist leader. That same Gomulka is now trying to give the campaign against Yugoslavia some new moral and political features and to justify it. Gomulka's arguments are that, unlike 1948, Yugoslavia is now exclusively responsible for the conflict, that Yugoslavia is indeed a socialist state, but that it is now acting to the advantage of the imperialists, that there is still some hope that we will abandon our revisionist line, and so forth. The Polish criticism completes the present campaign against Yugoslavia in the "camp" and will be exploited much more than the attacks made by the Bulgarians, Albanians, or Czechs on our country.

The tenth anniversary of the Cominform Resolution, June 28, has been marked in Yugoslavia by articles recalling our decision to stand up to Stalin and his aggressive policy toward Yugoslavia. On the Soviet side it looked as though there was no intention to mark the day in any way. It turned out differently, however. On that very day Gromyko handed me the second Soviet note in which the Soviet Government definitively refuses to extend credits to Yugoslavia. I believe the Russians were not aware of this coincidence and that, if they had been, they would not have handed over such a note recalling the times of our earlier quarrel on that very day. What is now happening in Yugoslav-Soviet relations will have the effect of a further destruction of illusions on our part, since the foreign policy of a superpower toward independent Yugoslavia can be changed so quickly and so lightly although circumstances have changed and the methods by means of which that policy is applied are different.

Moscow, July 4, 1958

I was struck today by what *Pravda* has written on the occasion of the fifteenth anniversary of the most difficult battle fought by the Yugoslav Partisans in the course of the war, the battle on the Šutjeska[4] in June 1943. The line taken by this Soviet article, which was probably approved by the Soviet Presidium, assumes that our fight for national liberation was the result of an elemental and centuries-long brotherhood of the peoples of Yugoslavia and Russia. Unlike Great Britain and the United States,

---

[4] In the spring of 1943, after having narrowly escaped destruction in the German "Fourth Offensive," Tito gathered his main striking force in a mountainous region near Mount Durmitor on the border between Bosnia and Montenegro. The Germans then launched their "Fifth Offensive," with a five-to-one advantage in manpower, which was intended to encircle the Partisan forces and annihilate them. But Tito and his commanders succeeded in deceiving the Germans, crossing the Maglić Massif and the Šutjeska River and, despite heavy losses, reaching the comparative safety of eastern Bosnia. It was probably the most critical battle of the war for the Partisans.

which, they say, supported the treacherous clique of Draža Mihailović, the Soviet Union throughout actively helped our struggle and equipped units of our liberation army. In fact Great Britain was the first of the great powers, and of our wartime allies, to send a military mission to our supreme H.Q. in the spring of 1943. The British began to help the Yugoslav Partisans first with weapons and equipment and organized for that purpose special bases in Cairo and Bari practically a year before the Soviet Union managed to send us a group of Soviet liaison officers, let alone send us aid in the form of arms.

We do not, of course, reproach the Soviet Union for not being able in the first years of the war to provide any direct aid for the Yugoslav peoples' war of liberation. At the same time it is not possible to pass over in silence the rewriting of recent history to suit the needs of *Pravda*.

Moscow, July 7, 1958

A well-informed neutral diplomat told me "in confidence" at the beginning of July that there had been spontaneous signs of displeasure and hostility with regard to Khrushchev. My interlocutor told me that Soviet sources (meaning more than one) had assured him that there was no organized opposition, but that there were spontaneous outbursts of discontent on account of the continual surprises which Khrushchev caused them by his decisions and changes of line, now in one direction, now in another. Khrushchev was too much and too often concerned with matters of foreign policy, which he dealt with in public practically every day, either in the press or in his speeches or at the many diplomatic receptions in Moscow. He would give his views on every possible question, including those which were not part of his "speciality"; people found it impossible to follow him even if they wanted to. They were not used to this after decades in which a quite different kind of rule had prevailed. People were losing their sense of security and did not know what might happen next day to the policy being pursued today or to their jobs and the work they were now doing. This was why there were signs of lack of confidence. A certain number of people did not agree with Khrushchev's decisions; others were unable to understand him properly or to support him as he wanted them to.

All this was, of course, felt at the last meeting of the Central Committee. My informant said that the sources of his information were Soviet intellectuals. A large number of them had not been very fond of Khrushchev previously and took especially badly his policy speeches about the situation and the party's tasks in the field of culture and art, which were much less suited to Khrushchev than many other of his speeches in which he also played the supreme judge.

As far as I can judge about Khrushchev's position in the Soviet Union, I think he lost a good deal of personal prestige by his political liquidation of Marshal Zhukov. Khrushchev told me, as an aggravating circumstance in Zhukov's case, that immediately after returning home after the Presidium meeting at which his expulsion from it was proposed he picked up the telephone, called Khrushchev, and said: "Comrade Khrushchev, what's going on? You know me; we're friends; I can't understand any of this!" Citing this as a sort of proof of his objectivity and lack of prejudice, Khrushchev said he told Zhukov that he had absolutely no desire to talk to him except at the forthcoming meeting of the Central Committee. Such, in Khrushchev's own words, was his reply to the friendship to which I am sure Marshal Zhukov appealed sincerely at that moment. I don't know whether there were any further conversations between these two "except at the meeting of the Central Committee."

Immediately after the June plenum when he told me with such great satisfaction about the complete defeat of the "antiparty group," Khrushchev told me how, when it was all over, he had been rung up in a tearful voice by Kaganovich. I have already recorded here what Khrushchev replied to him. That reply greatly pleased me at the time. But I did not feel the same when Khrushchev himself made similar comments about this other telephone conversation—with Marshal Zhukov.

CHAPTER THIRTY-THREE

ANOTHER CRISIS IN THE MIDDLE EAST

*The crisis in the Middle East produces further "demon-
strations" in Moscow. Khrushchev objects to the Yugoslav
government's decision to recall Mićunović to Belgrade. But
the Soviet press continues sniping at Yugoslavia.*

Moscow, July 12, 1958

Khrushchev has been more prominently and more frequently involved in the campaign against Yugoslavia than any other top Soviet
personality and most of the other Communist leaders in the world. This
may be because Khrushchev was much more deeply involved personally
in the restoration of normal Yugoslav-Soviet relations in 1955. When that
normalization did not produce the results Khrushchev expected, as others
in the Kremlin doubtless persuaded him, and Yugoslavia continued with
its independent policy, Khrushchev felt obliged, in order to forestall
attacks by the others, to take the initiative and be the most outspoken in
the "ideological" campaign against Yugoslavia.

On the basis of Khrushchev's speech in Berlin it could be said that he
regards as bad for the Soviet Union everything which suggests that the
present campaign in the "camp" against Yugoslavia is a continuation of
the anti-Yugoslav policy conducted by Stalin and the Soviet Union after
1948. In East Berlin Khrushchev reviewed our relations over the last ten
years to show that he was not reverting to Stalin's policy toward
Yugoslavia. The propaganda services in the Soviet Union and other countries of the "camp" will probably now be directed to supporting this argument of Khrushchev's. I recall that in our conversation following the
Hungarian events of 1956 Khrushchev said that he would "fix" us, that
they "would not behave toward us as Stalin did" but that they would
deal with Yugoslavia by political means.

Moscow, July 14, 1958

In our personal contacts Khrushchev has maintained the same relations with me as in the best time in the past. A few days ago, at a Kremlin reception for Novotný and a Czechoslovak delegation, when I went up to Khrushchev to exchange greetings he drew me to one side and took out of an inside pocket of his jacket a piece of crumpled paper and said he wanted to give me the text of the historic "letter from the Cossacks to the Sultan" which inspired the artist Repin[1] to paint his famous picture. Holding the paper in his hand he read out some parts of the letter, but some of the words he did not say out loud but pointed to them because they were Cossack expressions which he would not dare to use in St. George's Hall even in a whisper. This was all observed by foreign journalists and other guests without their knowing what it was all about. Some of the journalists reported that same evening that Khrushchev at a Kremlin reception had shown the Yugoslav ambassador the text of the Soviet-Yugoslav declaration due to be published the next day. People had to think up something!

* * *

I had a conversation with Mikoyan again at a reception given by the Mongolian ambassador on July 11. He had recently returned from Belgium, where he visited the international exhibition in Brussels.[2] He said he had visited the Yugoslav pavilion and that he had been impressed by it as well as by the friendly reception he had received from our people there. We discussed briefly the unsatisfactory state of our relations. I said that we were not replying to the many attacks being made on Yugoslavia, that we didn't wish to make the conflict worse, and I referred to Comrade Tito's recent speech which had been moderate and in my opinion calculated to smooth things over. Mikoyan said they had taken note of this and were bearing it in mind and that they also did not want to worsen relations with us. This was the first faintly tolerable exchange I have had with Mikoyan since the conversation which was so very unpleasant for both of us on May 9.

Mikoyan asked me whether it was true that I was leaving the Soviet Union for good, as he had heard. I confirmed this and said that I had already paid a farewell call on the doyen of the diplomatic corps and a

---

[1] The painting by the Russian artist Ilya Repin (1844–1930) shows the Zaporozhian Cossacks composing a letter to the Sultan of Turkey, defiantly rejecting demands he has made on them. It is said to have been couched in the crudest language, though no text survives.

[2] The International Exhibition, held in Brussels from April to October 1958, was the first to be held after World War II.

number of ambassadors and that I would get through them all fairly quickly because it was now the "dead season." Mikoyan expressed displeasure, saying that "Belgrade has made a mistake" by transferring me because I had "got to know them all very well" and could do more than any new person who would have first to get used to the post. He described my transfer as a further proof of our "ill will," because if we had no intention of worsening Yugoslav-Soviet relations I would not have been moved from Moscow. Mikoyan asked me to pass this view on to Belgrade. I promised to do so, but did not do it immediately. I waited to hear Khrushchev's speech, which turned out to contain the very opposite of some of the things Mikoyan had said.

Moscow, July 16, 1958

I called on Khrushchev twice today, not on account of Yugoslav-Soviet relations but because of Nasser's trip to Yugoslavia and then in connection with Nasser's proposal for a meeting with the Russians somewhere on Soviet territory. Khrushchev received me on both occasions immediately I asked to see him: The Russians knew what I wanted to see him about. The Soviet leadership took decisions acceptable to Nasser and Khrushchev informed me of them at the first meeting.

Khrushchev said that they had learned of the events in Iraq[3] from the papers and radio and had not known what was about to happen. He paid tribute to the Iraqi nationalists, and said it was a pity that there had been arrests in Jordan as a result of pressure from the Western powers because, but for those preventive measures, there would have been a revolution there, too. The West's hostile attitude toward the Arab nationalists who had carried out the coup in Iraq and toward the Arab countries where the Arab nationalists were in power would serve only further to compromise Western policy in the Near and Middle East. Khrushchev said that the Soviet Government would publish today its statement on the events in the Middle East and announce its recognition of the new government of the Republic of Iraq led by Kassem. The new Iraqi Government would be recognized by all the countries of the socialist camp.

The Soviet Government has taken other steps to help the new Arab regimes. In order to reduce pressure from the West the Russians have given

[3] *Author's note:* On the morning of July 14, 1958, a military coup took place in Baghdad in which King Faisal II and several members of his family were killed, the monarchy was overthrown, and a republic was proclaimed, headed by General Abdul Karim el Kassem. Fearful of similar attempts to overthrow them, the right-wing government in the Lebanon and King Hussein of Jordan appealed to the governments of the United States, Great Britain, and France to send them military assistance. Marines of the American Sixth Fleet landed next day in Beirut and a British parachute brigade was sent from Cyprus to Aman. Extreme tension reigned throughout the area.

orders for troop movements and military maneuvers to take place in the area of the Caucasus, close to Turkey, which will be directed by Marshal Grechko, as well as in Turkmenia opposite Iran, to be directed by Marshal Meretskov. They have arranged for similar maneuvers by Bulgarian forces with the participation of the Soviet Air Force close to the Turkish-Bulgarian frontier. Marshal Sokolovsky (in the absence of Marshal Malinovsky) and V. V. Kuznetzov (in the absence of Gromyko) were working in the next room on preparations for these military operations, and Mikoyan and Suslov were also present, according to Khrushchev.

Khrushchev greeted me with the remark that the events in Iran and the American moves in the Middle East had caught them at a time when many of the Soviet leaders were on holiday and such developments had not been expected. I told him that something similar had been the case in Yugoslavia, where they had also learned of the coup in Iraq from the radio, although Nasser had been visiting our country. I told Khrushchev what was in the first Yugoslav Government statement. He commented that our attitudes were the same, although we had not agreed them beforehand and, he added jokingly, "in spite of your revisionism." Then he talked about preparations for the military moves directed at the members of the Baghdad Pact and awaited some comment from me. I told him that some people would certainly understand such military arguments better than others. I asked him what he thought the prospects were of the conflict reaching dangerous dimensions. He did not give me a direct answer but I had the impression that he does not foresee the worst happening.

Like Mikoyan a few days ago, Khrushchev raised the question of my departure from the Soviet Union in the near future. He said that by withdrawing me Yugoslavia would be worsening relations with the Soviet Union despite statements to the contrary and that anyone who did not want to worsen relations with his country would not change ambassadors in such circumstances. He said that he and the whole Soviet Presidium had treated me with the greatest trust and frankness on all occasions since I had arrived in Moscow, and he went on to say that I knew all of them well and that all their doors were always, like his own, open to me.

I said there was no connection between the present bad state of our relations and my transfer back to Yugoslavia and that our new ambassador would do everything in his power to restore good relations. Khrushchev did not accept this but quoted the example of their decision to withdraw their ambassador, Firyubin, from Belgrade following our quarrel over events in Hungary but that they had changed their minds and left him in Belgrade until relations improved. It was apparent from what

Yugoslavia was doing, which was the reverse, that we were not counting on a speedy improvement in our relations.

When I was with Khrushchev yesterday morning, he informed me "as the representative of revisionism"—as he said jokingly—that he was going on holiday on August 15, that Gomulka and Kadar were coming to the Ukraine, and that they were going to spend some time there hunting before all three of them went on to the Crimea.

At the second meeting yesterday afternoon, when we agreed about Nasser's visit to the Soviet Union, Khrushchev told me to convey his greetings to Comrade Tito, adding with a smile "the revisionist," and to tell him that their hunt in the Ukraine would be very interesting, that he knows the terrain very well and that it would be pleasant if Tito could join them in the shoot. Instead of replying I asked him what they were going to hunt, and Khrushchev then told me about the various possibilities and the rich areas for hunting in the Ukraine and about his own trophies. Khrushchev repeated his invitation for Tito to join Gomulka and Kadar in the Soviet Union and said they would all be his personal guests. Khrushchev was in a good mood.

Moscow, July 19, 1958

A further worsening of the general situation is apparent in Moscow. Soviet political organizations, or, to be more precise, the Soviet authorities, yesterday organized further demonstrations of workers and young people in front of the United States embassy. This time the demonstrations were more serious. Windows were smashed and the "demonstrators" competed to see who could throw a brick or something else to break the highest windows. To create an even more serious atmosphere the Soviet authorities informed foreign embassies in Moscow through the Foreign Ministry that all permission for foreigners to make any trips in the southern parts of the Soviet Union had been canceled until further notice.

Moscow, July 20, 1958

Belgrade has changed the decision about my early return to Yugoslavia and has decided that I should remain at my post in Moscow "until further notice." Our people are thus showing goodwill with regard to the Russians' request that I should not leave Moscow for good at the moment. They have told me I am to stay here for an indefinite period. This has put me in a rather unusual situation, because I have already taken my leave of the doyen of the diplomatic corps and of half the ambassadors here. There will be all sorts of comments when I again meet ambassadors of whom I have already taken leave, and whose guest I have been at farewell lunches and dinners, at which I have made farewell speeches.

I am also in a very awkward position personally. My family is already in Yugoslavia and I was due soon to join them. Suddenly everything is changed. Belgrade invited me to take my annual holiday in Yugoslavia, but I was unable to do so. I hope that my stay in Moscow will not be extended by more than a few months. I think it is more important to be here now. We must see how this latest, certainly not the last, crisis in the Middle East finishes up.

Moscow, July 24, 1958

I am taking up again matters which I am supposed to deal with here and meeting again with ambassadors to whom I have already said goodbye, which provides material for various humorous comments. It seems to me that the majority of the ambassadors here attribute my remaining in Moscow to changes which are about to take place in Yugoslav-Soviet relations or which have already taken place.

* * *

At a reception given by the Polish ambassador Khrushchev left the head table at which he had been sitting with his Polish hosts, sat at the table of United States Ambassador Thompson, and stayed there for more than an hour. The Canadian ambassador, who was sitting in the same company, told me that throughout the time Khrushchev did not raise a single political topic but succeeded by this gesture in creating a certain impression on about a thousand guests, demonstrating that he desired to change for the better the general atmosphere prevailing between the Soviet Union and the West. The people here are inclined to dramatize the present situation and to exaggerate in different, often opposite, directions and in the course of only two or three days.

Moscow, July 31, 1958

The newspaper *Sovietsky Flot* [The Soviet Fleet] has published an article headed: "Forthcoming Naval Maneuvers with the Participation of Yugoslavia and Member-states of NATO"—meaning Italy and Britain.

The article is an instance of misinformation and provocation of the kind that used to appear in the Soviet press at the time of our conflict with Stalin. I suppose it is the work of the Soviet intelligence service which first found a way of having this false report published in the West German paper *Der Mittag* and having it quoted in *Sovietsky Flot,* so that the whole thing might appear credible to the Soviet reader. They have chosen one of the Soviet armed forces newspapers because it is "competent" when it comes to questions of movements of a country's navy and is more likely to be believed by the Soviet public when it publishes a report like this which will surprise the average Soviet citizen: that the Yugoslavs are carrying out naval maneuvers along with members of NATO! This has a much more powerful effect on the average Russian than articles put out by the propaganda department of the Soviet Communist party about "Yugoslav modern revisionism." It is interesting to note the moment which the Soviet Intelligence chose to place this canard in the Soviet press (the Middle East crisis and the Anglo-American armed intervention in Jordan and the Lebanon). This was calculated specially to compromise Yugoslavia's armed forces in the eyes of the Soviet public at which it is directed. In Western Germany, Italy, and elsewhere in the West the public was immediately made aware that the report was false and treated it accordingly. But here that was impossible.

Although the Russians know that they have published a false report and a slander about Yugoslavia, our people have tried in vain to get *Sovietsky Flot* or any other Soviet paper to issue a correction, even though the Yugoslav embassy in Moscow and the Yugoslav Government in Belgrade have requested this officially. Even before the press published this false report the Soviet Government was well aware that the Yugoslav Government had issued a categorical denial of the report in the foreign press as long ago as July 17 through our Tanjug news agency. It is of no importance to the Soviet authorities what the Yugoslav Government publishes officially, but only what the Soviet intelligence service has published, first in *Der Mittag* and then in *Sovietsky Flot*.

I think we should protest to the Russians either in Belgrade or here. Everything should be done to make the Soviet public understand that its press spreads lying reports and slanders about Yugoslavia and about other countries as well. Whether or not Belgrade agrees with our proposal to protest to the Soviet Government, I have said that, in the name of the embassy, I shall write a letter to the editors of *Sovietsky Flot* saying that their report does not correspond with the truth and that, if they are interested in the truth, an official statement on the subject was issued in Belgrade some time ago.

* * *

The Prime Minister of the Russian Federation, Polyansky,[4] said he had been informed that the Yugoslav Government had changed its decision

[4] Dmitri Polyansky, b. 1917. First Deputy Prime Minister of the Soviet Union, 1965–73; Minister of Agriculture, 1973–76; Member of Politburo, CPSU, 1966–76. In 1976 appointed Ambassador to Japan.

about my leaving Moscow, that they welcomed this, and that Khrushchev said at the last meeting of the Presidium that I was staying in Moscow "until further notice." According to Polyansky this was well received in the Presidium and that was why he was telling me. This conversation with Polyansky took place before *Sovietsky Flot* reported the alleged maneuvers of our Navy with the Italian and British navies in the Adriatic. If the Russians intend to go on publishing false reports about Yugoslavia as in the case of *Sovietsky Flot*, then I don't think there was any need for us or the Russians to discuss the extension of my stay in Moscow.

CHAPTER THIRTY-FOUR

END OF A MISSION

Mićunović is recalled after all, and makes preparations to leave.

Moscow, September 2, 1958

Our government has decided in spite of everything that I am to return home for good. The postponement decided on in July following my talk with Khrushchev and Mikoyan was premature, and our government has reverted to its earlier decision that I should leave Moscow and return to Belgrade to take up my duties as a Deputy Foreign Minister. I returned recently from Yugoslavia, not to prolong my stay in Moscow but to continue with my farewell calls. The Russians are repeating their original comments to the effect that my departure from Moscow is a sign of the poor state of our relations with the Soviet Union.

Moscow, September 11, 1958

The Soviet leaders have announced that they are going to hold a Twenty-first "extraordinary" Congress of the CPSU, and I have the impression that their decision has caused some surprise among a number of Soviet citizens and not only among the diplomats in Moscow. The only item on the agenda is "the expansion of the national economy in the period 1959–65." Hitherto such questions were usually decided at meetings of the Central Committee of the party or of the Soviet Government and were then proclaimed as law at sessions of the Supreme Soviet. The government and the Supreme Soviet play the part of "transmission belts" for carrying out party decisions in such cases. It is now probably not so much a question of approving the economic plan as of having the policy Khrushchev has been pursuing so far confirmed by this "extraordinary" party congress.

In view of the settling of accounts which took place among the Soviet leaders in June 1957 and later, this Twenty-first Congress of the CPSU is intended, even if indirectly and without actually mentioning those matters, to confirm the new course and serve as the ultimate sanction for all the changes which have taken place since the proclamation of "collective leadership" at the Twentieth Congress in 1956. The years which have passed since then have already been proclaimed as "the most important and decisive stage in the Soviet people's struggle to fulfill their world-historical tasks" (*Pravda*, yesterday). All this is connected directly with Khrushchev. He is the person who decided to hold the Congress, he will make the speech on the only item on the agenda, and he is the author of the ambitious economic plans for Soviet internal development over the next seven years.

The present Congress has been preceded by the political liquidation of exactly half the members of the Soviet Presidium chosen at the Twentieth Congress. That was followed by the removal of other prominent persons. All this is also directly connected with Khrushchev personally. Therefore, apart from approving the plans for further economic expansion, the Twenty-first Congress of the CPSU has to serve as a powerful demonstration of the new "monolithic unity" which has been established under Khrushchev's leadership.

Moscow, September 13, 1958

For some time now the Soviet press has been using a new device in its propaganda against Yugoslavia. Instead of the long articles by Soviet "doctors of science" about the "modern revisionism" of the Yugoslav Communists, in which the Soviet people were not greatly interested, the Russians have now taken to publishing "reports" about specific events in Yugoslavia. An example of this was a recent article in *Pravda* about the Zagreb trade fair, about the security measures taken when Comrade Tito visited it, about how the public were not allowed into the fair while Tito was there, and finally about the Soviet pavilion and the fulsome comments which Yugoslav visitors are said to have written in the visitors' book.

Such reports make a greater impression on Soviet citizens than incomprehensible and enormously long dogmatic articles about Marxism-Leninism and Yugoslav revisionism such as have been appearing here on and off for years. The present Soviet attacks are directed at various organs of authority in Yugoslavia, most frequently the police, customs officials, the state security service, and so forth. The one idea running through all this is to turn our people against the organs of authority in Yugoslavia.

END OF A MISSION

Moscow, September 23, 1958

It is already ten days since I have written anything in this diary. I have spent my time making farewell calls on members of the diplomatic corps and attending the usual farewell lunches and dinners at which speeches have to be made before departing. All these occasions are more or less the same and there are so many of them that it can be said that I am pretty well exhausted physically. I am repeating what I did on arriving in Moscow.

Instead of writing about these farewell calls I will record just one meeting which was not a farewell call. One of the Soviet Deputy Foreign Ministers, Firyubin, summoned me to the ministry on September 22 and handed me a note from the Soviet Government about the credit agreements which they have canceled unilaterally, or rather for which they have set new terms and then invited the Yugoslav Government to accept them, which we refused to do. Now the Soviet authorities want to depict all this in another light: They are trying to provide documentary proof that it is the Soviets who on this occasion are observing the normal international practice and the Yugoslav Government which is allegedly not respecting that practice and refusing to negotiate.

Before handing me the note, which meant that the whole affair had been decided once and for all by the Soviet side at Yugoslavia's expense, it is interesting to record how Firyubin introduced the matter.

Without having informed me why he wanted to see me Firyubin inquired after the health of Comrades Tito and Ranković and then told me he had several times sent Comrade Tito from Moscow some "Siberian cranberries," a very rare and healthy fruit which grows beneath the snow in the Siberian tundra. Firyubin then asked my opinion as to whether he should send Comrade Tito some more "Siberian cranberries"; he wanted to consult with me while I was still here to know how it would be taken in Belgrade. I told him that I believed it could only be taken now as it was understood before—as a friendly gesture and sign of concern on his part—and that his official and personal relations with Comrade Tito had been, as far as I knew, very good. Firyubin then said he would like to send them with me and asked me to convey his greetings to Comrade Tito.

After such a friendly introduction it was to be expected that the Soviet note which Firyubin had to hand me would contain something different. But it turned out, unfortunately, the other way. There was no more talk about "Siberian cranberries" but about the Soviet Government's policy toward Yugoslavia. I don't expect there to be any parcels such as Firyubin said he wanted to send with me to Belgrade.

Moscow, October 6, 1958

As I was going through the list of Soviet officials upon whom I should ask to make a farewell call, I was in some doubt about whether to call on certain members of the Soviet Presidium whom I have often met in Moscow and also whether to take my leave of some of the top Soviet military leaders, the Soviet marshals, including the Minister of Defense, Marshal Malinovsky. Among the party leaders, I planned to call on Leonid Brezhnev, Nikolai Ignatov, Yekaterina Furtseva, Dmitri Polyansky, and a few others.

I have met Leonid Brezhnev on a number of occasions. When Comrade Tito visited the Crimea in 1956, Khrushchev invited a number of Soviet leaders who were apparently very close to Khrushchev and on whom he relied in the new distribution of positions of authority in the Soviet Communist party. Among those leaders who were rising steadily in the Central Committee was Brezhnev, along with Kirichenko, Furtseva, Marshal Grechko, and some others.

Brezhnev was the one whom I later met most frequently, but not on official business. He was one of the secretaries of the Central Committee, and there was no reason for the Yugoslav ambassador in Moscow to meet him officially. Brezhnev's duties as a secretary of the Central Committee were of an internal nature and he had no official business with foreigners. At Kremlin receptions and when there were official guests of the Soviet Government all the members of the Soviet Presidium attended, led by Khrushchev, and Brezhnev would often be in Khrushchev's company at such receptions and at my conversations with Khrushchev. On other occasions Brezhnev would move away from us when Khrushchev let it be known that he wanted to talk to me alone. After such conversations Brezhnev, who would have been standing to one side, sometimes for quite a long time, would usually ask me how the conversation had gone, to which I would reply that it went very well, and that would be the end of it.

There were other, unofficial circumstances which led to my having more contact with Brezhnev than with some other members of the Soviet Presidium with whom I had official relations. Brezhnev knew, for example, that our son had been born just after my arrival in Moscow and he would always greet me and Miška with the question: "How is our little boy?" so that we knew in advance to expect this question whenever we caught sight of Brezhnev at some reception. And finally Brezhnev is an inveterate smoker, as I am myself, and he is very fond of Yugoslav cigarettes. If he does not approve of our form of socialism, he approves at least of our tobacco. As a smoker it always gave me pleasure to offer

Brezhnev a cigarette or to have him beat me to it and ask me for one. It gave me pleasure also to send Brezhnev a large collection of Yugoslav cigarettes and later to receive a similar gift from him.

In spite of these considerations which favored my making a farewell call on Brezhnev, I refrained from doing so, although I believe he would glady have received me, even though relations between our two countries were not good. I also refrained from asking to call on other members of the Soviet Presidium or on the military leaders. Our cooperation on the military side has not yet begun to develop seriously or to be a major factor in our relations.

I decided to stick to the government level. Apart from a visit to Khrushchev, which is by far the most important, and to officials in the Soviet Foreign Ministry, there was nobody left on the list except Voroshilov, the nominal head of state, and Mikoyan, member of the Presidium and deputy Soviet Prime Minister, whom I had called on when I arrived in Moscow. Since then a great deal has changed and many prominent people have disappeared from Soviet public life who had occupied leading positions for decades.

CHAPTER THIRTY-FIVE

A LAST MEETING WITH KHRUSHCHEV

Mićunović spends a whole day with Khrushchev on the Black Sea coast and finds him still anxious to be friendly and ready to improve relations with Yugoslavia but unable or unwilling to understand the Yugoslav Communists' stand. As he leaves the Soviet leader, Mićunović reflects on some of his many contradictory qualities.

On the way to Gagri, October 8, 1958

I left for the Black Sea shortly before midnight on October 7 in a special plane put at my disposal by the Soviet Government. It was an Ilyushin-14 in which were, instead of seats, just a bed and some armchairs, making it look like an ordinary bedroom. As we were preparing to take off I established the fact that I was the only passenger. The security officer accompanying me on the trip offered to prepare the bed for me to sleep in because it was more than five hours' flight to the airport at Adler on the Black Sea coast. I found myself for the first time in the unusual situation of getting ready for bed, just as if I were at home, in a plane which had just taken off from Vnukovo Airport and set course for the south.

I very nearly refused. It seemed to me so strange to take off my shoes and walk about barefoot in a plane, to put on my pajamas and to get into bed. What if something happened to the plane? But I hesitated only for a moment, having come to the conclusion that it was all the same to me whether the plane crashed while I was in bed or while I was sitting in a chair.

I was soon lying in bed listening to the monotonous, soothing drone of the plane's engines as we flew through the dark night. It all seemed to me so strange, especially to be lying in bed with a table lamp at my side, studying the notes I had made for my meeting next day with Khrushchev.

At last I dropped off to sleep in my flying bedroom. It occurred to me that this was the first and would probably be the last time that I would ever make such a journey by plane. When the Soviet official woke me and told me to prepare for the touchdown, the sun was shining and I could feel the warmth outside, so different from the winter weather we had left behind in Moscow.

We landed at Adler Airport, close to the town of Gagri on the Caucasian coast of the Black Sea, just after six o'clock in the morning. After I had left the plane the Soviet crew informed me in military style that the plane would remain at my disposition. A chauffeur was waiting to drive me to Gagri, where I was installed in a tastefully furnished villa above the town and advised to take a rest. An hour later I was told that Khrushchev would receive me that morning at ten o'clock at his summer residence close-by.

Gagri, October 8, 1958

I found Khrushchev strolling in the grounds of a modest house down on the shore of the Black Sea in the middle of a pine forest. He was alone and he gave me a warm welcome. He asked me whether I knew to whom the villa in which I had been put had belonged. It had been Beria's villa, he said, adding the comment that "the scoundrel knew how to arrange his life."

"So now the Yugoslav ambassador is staying in Beria's villa!" Khrushchev said with a smile.

My "farewell call" on Khrushchev lasted practically the whole day, in the course of which we had three meetings with no one else present, not counting lunch with Khrushchev's family. The first conversation I had with him was in the morning, in the garden of his villa. After that Khrushchev proposed that we should go swimming in the sea before lunch. The second conversation was after lunch, down on the beach in a tent, and that lasted nearly three hours. The third meeting was back at his house over tea, and that lasted about an hour, until we were joined by Nina Petrovna. If you include the time taken for lunch, I spent about eight hours with Khrushchev on October 8, 1958, and I left Gagri the same day as night fell over the pine forest and Khrushchev's house and the open sea beyond.

Khrushchev was full of praise for this part of the Black Sea coast and claimed that it was in some ways better than the coast in the Crimea. He said it was the warmest part of the Black Sea, which made it possible to swim even in October, which was why he was not taking his holiday here. I believe this is the second villa, in addition to the old one at Yalta, which he has at his disposal on the Black Sea. He later talked about Stalin's villas in these parts. They were now empty, Khrushchev said, and neither he nor anybody else ever went into them.

Referring to this year's harvest in the Soviet Union, which they were still hoping would be a good one, Khrushchev said that the figures for the grain deliveries would be accurate, and that they would not permit, as they did last year, the shortfall in deliveries to be compensated for by grain equivalents (in fact, potatoes) in order to "fulfill the plan." He said he had insisted that they should have the true facts irrespective of whether the plan was fulfilled.

The conversation turned to this year's harvest in China, which was going to be a record one according to reports. The world was amazed at the high yields the Chinese achieved. Khrushchev stressed that the Chinese made up by hard work (the human factor) for their lack of financial resources and machinery in agriculture: They worked "just like ants."

When he was in China recently, Khrushchev said, Mao Tse-tung had told him that they didn't know what to do with the grain, they had so much. "I told him," Khrushchev went on, "that I hoped China would be best able to solve that problem herself and that they would have no need of Soviet experts." He revealed a certain skepticism about the Chinese data concerning their yields and quoted the figures with the comment "if they are accurate."

We spoke about China's situation in Asia and the world, about China's relations with her neighbors, about the commune system in China and other innovations in the present-day China. Taking a historical view, Khrushchev argued that it was no accident that the Russians had taken the north and the Chinese the south of Asia, that life was easier in the south, and that the two great powers were "protecting each other's rears." The Chinese would discover new ways of organizing their society and they should not be judged by our criteria. As for overpopulation, Khrushchev said, China would find at home new ways of dealing with the question of her huge and rapidly growing population.

As we were talking about China I said the diplomatic corps in Moscow was a source of all kinds of speculation on the subject. Khrushchev took up this subject and replied to a number of questions by reference to Marxism-Leninism. This appeared to lead to the conclusion that relations between the Soviet Union and China would continue to be as they have been till now so long as both sides observe those principles. "They try to frighten me with China," Khrushchev said. But he relies on Marxism-Leninism, on the basis of which one must conclude that such things as happened in the past between these two great countries can never happen again. The conversation about China lasted about an hour, during which Khrushchev did not once attempt to change the subject.

* * *

Khrushchev then looked at his watch and said it was time to go for a swim before lunch and invited me to join him. He encouraged me by saying that there was no need to think about the Moscow climate or about the winter clothes in which I had traveled down. But I did not accept his invitation, saying that in Moscow, where it was still cold, I still had several days to go and many official duties to carry out before I left, that I was afraid of catching cold and just could not risk getting ill at the moment. Khrushchev was not pleased with this and said jokingly: "As you wish: Let everybody have his own kind of socialism." Even this was counted as a Yugoslav "peculiarity." I realized that I would have done better to accept his invitation straightaway, but I still tried to get out of it, saying I had nothing to swim in. At that Khrushchev offered me something from his wardrobe. Ten minutes later I had chosen one of his bathing suits, which, although it didn't fit me, was good enough for the occasion.

We were soon in the sea, which was really for me, a "Muscovite," amazingly warm for the time of year. Khrushchev also invited a party secretary from Novosibirsk, who had come on Khrushchev's instructions to inform him about the situation in Western Siberia, to join us. Khrushchev said that he was himself a poor swimmer and that the doctors had advised him not to overtire himself. For that reason he wore a cork life belt while he was in the sea.

We swam about fifty meters from the shore. I kept a certain distance away from him and a little farther off there was a boat with an officer of the security service in civilian clothes who apart from anything else kept looking at his watch to make sure that we remained in the water exactly the length of time that Khrushchev had been prescribed by his doctors. I didn't swim close to Khrushchev because of one of the stories he had told me in Moscow last year about how in the autumn of 1956 he had been on holiday in the Crimea with Marshal Zhukov and had noticed that, as he swam, the marshal kept coming very close to him. As we were swimming away from the shore yesterday this story came into my mind as well as the question, which he said he had then asked himself as he watched Marshal Zhukov: "Why does he come so close to me?" Swimming slowly, I kept about ten meters away from Khrushchev and at that distance we could talk normally. The party secretary from Novosibirsk, keeping the same distance from Khrushchev, joined in this part of the conversation.

423

* * *

When we had had our swim, Khrushchev invited us to lunch, at which we were joined by Nina Petrovna, Khrushchev's son-in-law and his wife, Khrushchev's daughter, and the party leader from Western Siberia. Political topics were largely avoided during the conversation. We recalled Tito's visit to the Soviet Union in 1956 and the exceptionally friendly atmosphere which prevailed on that occasion. There were also pleasant memories of Khrushchev's visit to Yugoslavia the same year. Every time he mentioned Tito, Khrushchev called him "Tovarishch Tito" (Comrade Tito). We exchanged very short toasts: Khrushchev drank to Yugoslavia and Comrade Tito. The atmosphere over lunch was friendly and intimate.

On the way to Moscow, October 9, 1958

I am continuing with the account of my farewell visit to Khrushchev.

After lunch he suggested that we should go and talk in the tent on the sands by the sea. When we had settled ourselves in the tent which protected us from the sun, Khrushchev remained silent, thus leaving it to me to start the conversation. I asked him to allow me on this occasion to make use of my notes. It was not actually essential for me to do so, but it seemed to me necessary because I started the conversation by transmitting to Khrushchev a message from Comrade Tito and our leaders dealing with the present state of Yugoslav-Soviet relations.

It was our wish, I told Khrushchev in conclusion, that our relations with the Soviet Union should be of the best; in this respect nothing in Yugoslavia had changed. We did not want relations between us to deteriorate and were trying gradually to improve them. There was still a good deal of room for cooperation, of which we were only at the very beginning in practically all fields. I told Khrushchev I thought any further worsening of our relations should be halted and that this would be in our common interest, despite the different views we had on certain questions. I tried to argue that this could easily be done, as it appeared to us. Fundamentally it was a question above all of stopping the anti-Yugoslav campaign in the "camp."

Khrushchev replied that our basic argument was not correct. This time Yugoslavia had attacked the Soviet Union and the other socialist countries; the new program of the LCY was to blame for the latest quarrel between us. Everything would have been all right between us if we had not published our program and we ought finally to understand that. We were to blame for the worsening of our relations with the Soviet Union, which had also led to the cancellation of the credit agreements which they had wanted to discuss with us but we had refused to do so.

We knew, Khrushchev went on, the extent to which he had committed himself in the Presidium and how he had fought for the Soviet credits to Yugoslavia from the very beginning. They had been opposed at the time by Molotov, even more by Voroshilov, as well as by Kaganovich and Pervukhin. He, Khrushchev, had managed to save the credits after the conflict between us over Hungary in 1956. Now we had again attacked the Soviet Union and the "camp" publicly in our new LCY program.

"In such conditions it was impossible to go on supporting the idea of Soviet credits for Yugoslavia. People in the Soviet Union really began to question whether the Soviet leaders were obliged to endure Yugoslav criticism and still have to provide Yugoslavia with money," Khrushchev said.

As the final unhelpful move on our part Khrushchev cited Tito's remark about the "mutual benefit" derived from economic relations between Yugoslavia and the Soviet Union and the "unconditional aid" when it was a question of economic relations between Yugoslavia and the United States. Khrushchev said that such an attitude was incorrect and unacceptable to them.

"If the Soviet Union gives credits to Yugoslavia or anybody else, we have to snatch the means out of our own mouths," Khrushchev said. "Ours is a planned economy and we have no need to export capital as countries in the West do; we can invest everything here at home without exporting a single kopek abroad. That's the way it is now and that will be the situation for a long time to come, as far as our needs are concerned. But we are giving help to Egypt, Indonesia, and other countries. We do it by making sacrifices on our part and not for our 'mutual benefit' as you tell us. India, Egypt, and the others realize that and don't attack us as you Yugoslavs do."

It was the first time during our meeting that Khrushchev used such language and gave the impression of being genuinely upset and indignant. Finally he said that if it had not been for the new LCY program the present quarrel between us would not have come about.

I tried to explain to him that his interpretation of Comrade Tito's speech about the principle of the "mutual benefit" deriving from our economic relations was not correct. After all, the Soviet Union also had some economic benefit from the credits which it gave Yugoslavia: We had to return the credits over a definite period with interest and on the basis of the credits the Soviet Union would provide work for its industry producing machinery for our enterprises, while we would have to use the credits in the Soviet Union. Which meant that even from this form of collaboration they would derive benefit and not suffer a loss. As for our party program I referred to conversations I had had many times in Moscow, especially with Mikoyan, Suslov, and Pospelov, and pointed out that we had accepted all the criticisms we found it possible to accept. It was another matter that they were against any program of the Yugoslav League of Communists, even though it was a program for Yugoslav Communists and not for the Soviet Communists or any others.

We then talked about how the authorities in Yugoslavia and the Soviet Union had treated citizens of the other country. Khrushchev complained that the Yugoslav authorities had behaved in an unfriendly manner on a number of occasions. He quoted the case of the arrest of a young Soviet Communist who had gone to visit her relatives in Yugoslavia and had been held in prison there for sixty-eight days without good reason. Then he mentioned the agreement between our government and the United States Government on a number of questions concerning the Middle East and about which our press had written essentially like the New York *Times*, criticizing the policy of the Soviet Government. Finally he cited the case of the Albanian Hasan Spata who had been killed by members of our security service near Belgrade. Khrushchev referred to articles in the Soviet press in connection with all three cases.

I knew personally the Soviet "Komsomolka." The Soviet police tried very hard to get her into our embassy. They tried to involve her with my family and with me by having her offer to take our children for a walk every day and to teach them Russian. When they didn't succeed in this in Moscow, the Ministry of the Interior sent her to Yugoslavia. There she provoked her own arrest and then the whole story was published in detail in the Soviet press as an example of Yugoslavia's unfriendly treatment of Soviet citizens. I recounted all this to Khrushchev and expressed regret that the officials of the Soviet young Communist organization had behaved in that way. (Khrushchev's son-in-law A. Adzhubei was editor of the *Komsomolskaya Pravda*.) I urged Khrushchev to look into the matter more closely and said that he could easily confirm that I had told him the true state of affairs.

I told Khrushchev that I was also acquainted with the case of the death of the Albanian émigré, Spata, near Belgrade. I told him that we regretted the accident despite the fact that the man killed had collaborated with the Fascists in his day and had more recently been working to destroy good relations between Yugoslavia and Albania. The government in Tirana was really glad he had been killed; it was their agencies which had arranged things so that Hasan Spata should lose his life, and now Albanian diplomats were holding press conferences in their embassies around the world about the reign of terror in Yugoslavia. The Albanian ambassador in Moscow had also, unfortunately, held such a press conference to describe the terrible things happening in our country.

Finally I said that *Pravda* had not acted correctly when it tried to present Yugoslavia's stand with relation to events in the Lebanon and Jordan —the withdrawal of the Anglo-American troops—as a pro-American attitude. The Soviet Foreign Ministry had been aware from the outset of Yugoslavia's attitude to these questions, which was very well received in the Arab world because it was to their advantage. *Pravda* was now trying to discredit Yugoslavia in that area, too.

Khrushchev did not attempt to defend *Pravda*. He said that all the three cases he had quoted were not so important in themselves; what was more important was the "bad blood" which was being introduced into our relations day after day, which he very much regretted because he was personally interested in seeing our relations develop in the best possible way. In fact, Khrushchev dropped all three charges against Yugoslavia which the Soviet "special service" had prepared for him so inadequately for this meeting. The thing which caused him least pleasure was my reference to the cooperation between *Komsomolskaya Pravda* and the Soviet state security service which was revealed in the case of the "Komsomolka" arrested in Yugoslavia.

The conversation on these subjects put Khrushchev in an awkward position, because it had been mainly a matter of facts which he quoted against Yugoslavia, but which I knew about in greater detail than he did. He was not in a position either to contest or to accept my explanations, and so he switched the conversation to "general questions." There he felt himself on much safer ground; it was much more like a discussion of principles, and here the Soviet attitudes seemed rather more substantial. Khrushchev proceeded to accuse Yugoslavia of specific things which could not be denied by simply saying they were incorrect, as, for example, his assertions that there was still "anti-Sovietism" in Yugoslavia, that Yugoslavs still regarded the Soviet Union "in the old way" and that we could see nothing but bureaucratism and Stalinism in the Soviet Union.

Khrushchev criticized what the Yugoslav press had written about the celebrations of the fortieth anniversary of the breakthrough on the Salonika front as well as the celebrations themselves, which, he said, had a nationalist spirit about them. For Yugoslavia to introduce such a spirit into relations with its neighbors, especially a socialist country, could not fail to have a bad effect on our relations with those countries (meaning Bulgaria), Khrushchev said. This gave me the opportunity to recount the historical facts about Bulgarian policy from the time when the Russians liberated them from Turkish oppression in the wars of 1876–77, which required no comments from either side. I mentioned some Russian Tsarist generals who had commanded forces in battles for the liberation of Bulgaria, for which Russian troops then sacrificed their lives. I then went on to recall that immediately after their liberation the Bulgarians put an Aus-

tro-Hungarian dynasty into power, and in every European crisis from
then right up to the last war Bulgaria had been an ally of Germany and
Austria. Finally I pointed out that in the last war Bulgaria had been an
ally of Hitler against Yugoslavia and Russia, so that in the course of only
thirty years in modern times Bulgaria had fought on the side of the
enemy, attacking Serbia and Montenegro and later Yugoslavia, and had
always been Germany's ally in those wars.

In Yugoslavia we do not speak or write publicly about the mass war
crimes committed by the Bulgarians as Hitler's allies from 1941 to 1944 in
Macedonia, Serbia, and other parts of Yugoslavia. Those crimes were just
as cruel and bloody as those committed by the German invaders. We
could remain silent about it today, but the people of Yugoslavia knew all
about it and it was impossible for us now to depict Bulgaria as a friend
and an ally in the wars of the past.

As for the celebrations of the breakthrough on the Salonika front and
the battle with the Bulgarian armies which were then fighting on the side
of the Germans, I told Khrushchev that we should probably have more
celebrations like it in Yugoslavia as long as such occasions were celebrated under socialism. I mentioned Lenin's opinion that the war of
1914–18 had been a war of liberation for the independent Balkan states—
Montenegro, Serbia, and Greece—who had been fighting against the Central Powers and their Bulgarian ally. It was the same in World War II.
This past of theirs did not today suit the Communists in Bulgaria. They
were now in power and would like the past to be forgotten as though it
had never happened, to be erased from people's memory, but it was all
historical truth and there was nothing we could do about it. After 1945
we had not demanded from Bulgaria the war reparations which we
would have been awarded by any international court against present-day
Bulgaria.

Khrushchev did not interrupt me. It seemed to me that the facts about
Bulgaria had made an impression on him. He had not expected to hear all
that; otherwise I don't think he would have raised the question of Bulgaria. He was particularly impressed by my reference to Lenin about the
emancipatory character of the wars of the Balkan states against the Central Powers—and Bulgaria. I had the impression that he was not aware of
Lenin's view on this question, and it had a special effect on him; he might
have contested everything I said but not the quotation from Lenin.

Replying to my criticisms of statements by Bulgarian leaders who keep
saying that the Macedonian people are historically, culturally, and eth-
nically the same as the Bulgarian people and that Macedonia is Bulgarian
territory, Khrushchev inquired about the republic of Macedonia, asked
whether there were Macedonians in Bulgaria and how many. Wanting to
bring the conversation about Bulgaria to an end, he said he didn't know

what the Bulgarians had said, but that it was now silly to talk about changing state frontiers in Europe. There were national minorities, bigger or smaller, in all socialist states, but it was one thing to recognize them and quite another to make territorial demands for anybody's frontiers to be changed. Khrushchev said he had told this to everybody in the "camp" and that he would tell them again; he mentioned the Bulgarians, the Albanians, and the Hungarians and said he had said it once to the Poles.

"If we were now to raise the question of making territorial changes on account of national minorities, there would have to be changes everywhere, in the Soviet Union and in Yugoslavia; the whole of Eastern Europe is full of them. These questions should not be raised," Khrushchev said. He said he would talk to Todor Zhivkov about these matters the next time he saw him.

When we came to talk about the press, I said that there was an essential difference between the Soviet and the Yugoslav press: We were printing lengthy reports about the Soviet Union every day, whereas they wrote about Yugoslavia mostly to attack us. Khrushchev said that, probably because of the bad relations now existing between us, some people were willing only to criticize us. "You think it's all done on Khrushchev's instructions, but I don't know anything about it. There are many things I hear about only after they've happened," Khrushchev said.

After we changed the subject Khrushchev asked me what would happen about the plants which were to have been built with the Soviet credits. Would the Americans now offer us credits? I said I didn't know, but that we would certainly take steps to complete the fertilizer plant in Pančevo and some smaller projects, and we would probably manage to obtain some credit from somewhere. But I did not believe we would obtain a credit for building the aluminum industry in Montenegro, because large sums were involved. It looked as though nobody wanted socialist Yugoslavia to have a new aluminum industry.

Khrushchev raised the question of the foreign policy of the Soviet Union and Yugoslavia, saying that we agreed on many things. He listed a number of major issues on which Yugoslavia and the Soviet Union were in agreement and said that it was only on the question of the socialist camp that we did not agree. He said Yugoslavia was in active opposition to the "camp," unlike, for example, Poland, with which they also didn't agree on everything but didn't quarrel. The Poles adopted the basic "class" approach to the essential questions and stood firmly along with the countries of the camp, unlike Yugoslavia. Even if the Soviet Union had made the mistakes of which we accused them, Khrushchev said, nevertheless the basic "class" approach was not to be denied, and that was what we Yugoslavs did. I tried to turn the discussion to concrete examples of what he had in mind. Khrushchev again referred to our press and our boasting, saying that we were always stressing our own merits, while others had their merits, too. We did not quarrel over all these things: I simply said that in Yugoslavia, for example, even in Stalin's day we had never contested the decisive role played by the Soviet Army in World War II and that we had always stood up for it in public. But today in the Soviet Union Yugoslavia's war of national liberation and revolution were not being truthfully depicted.

Talk about World War II provided Khrushchev with an excuse for saying something about the strength of the Soviet armed forces today—that they were incomparably stronger than they had been. He said that last month they had had a conference in the Crimea about the state of the Soviet Navy and its armament. They were no longer going to build the classical type of navy. Everything was decided by missiles, with which they had complete control, not only over certain important targets such as the Turkish straits, but far more than that. Today the Russians could seal off the Bosporus and the Dardanelles completely.

Khrushchev went on to say that some Soviet "sailors" were still opposed to opening places like the Crimea to tourists. Kirichenko and some others had proposed that he should introduce special passes, but he had turned that down. It would be better not to open the Crimea to tourists than to introduce a system of special passes. Khrushchev said that their military leaders had been absolute masters in the Crimea because of the naval base in Sevastopol and other military installations. The same situation was to be met with today in other places in the Soviet Union. "If we were to keep vast areas like the Crimea closed, we wouldn't have any tourism," Khrushchev said.

Moscow, October 11, 1958

More about my farewell visit to Khrushchev.

In the conversation which we had in the tent on the beach Khrushchev said toward the end that there was a lack of trust developing between us and that was the last thing he wanted. He quoted the example of some Soviet atomic expert who had recently warned the Soviet Government that the reactor which the Russians had built along with the Yugoslavs near Belgrade contained some different and better device than what comparable American reactors had, and that the Soviet side should bear this in mind since the reactor was now in Yugoslav hands. Khrushchev said he had reproached the Soviet expert and asked him if he thought the Yugoslavs were going right away to call the Americans in to show them the reactor.

Khrushchev said he had intervened several times with *Pravda* to suggest they should publish some more positive articles about Yugoslavia. He said the lack of trust between us kept growing, and implied that we were responsible for this. I pointed out that, apart from the sort of thing that was being written in the Soviet press, the Soviet Academy of Science was now being brought into the campaign against "revisionism," i.e., against Yugoslavia, and that that would be another step backward in our relations. It was already clear that the newspaper articles served no good purpose, and what they were doing with the Academy of Science and the writing of books against "modern revisionism" would make things even worse.

* * *

Khrushchev reproached us for "arresting Communists in Yugoslavia," saying he had heard that some former émigrés had been arrested after having been repatriated on the basis of the agreements between the Soviet and Yugoslav governments. I appealed to Khrushchev to realize that it was not friends of Russia who were being arrested in Yugoslavia but people who were actively hostile to Yugoslavia and that it was purely incidental whether they praised or criticized Russia. I said that that was the way it would be in the future and that no changes were to be expected in this matter.

* * *

Accusing us of having a one-sided and entirely negative opinion of Stalin, Khrushchev said that in the Soviet Union they knew much better than we did all Stalin's faults, but that history would weigh the whole picture up according to the truth and to his merits, because there was also a positive side to Stalin's work. I said that we had nothing to quarrel about there and that during my stay in the Soviet Union I had not once discussed Stalin with any Soviet person. At the Seventh Congress of the LCY Tito had dealt with this question and presented an objective picture of Stalin. This had considerable political significance in view of our relations. Khrushchev said he didn't know about it.

* * *

As for the general situation, Khrushchev said he did not count on a worsening of East-West relations, and certainly did not believe there was danger of a serious conflict breaking out. He said that capitalism was getting steadily weaker. Africa was at the center of the struggle between socialism and imperialism.

"If we weren't strong, what do you think: Would it really be possible for Nasser, Sukarno, or the new government in Iraq and elsewhere to

431

hold on to power? The United States would send troops in, and through armed intervention and force would again subjugate those peoples. The Soviet Union will continue to fight stubbornly for peace, which we have especial need of for the next fifteen or twenty years. After that no one will be able to go to war even if he wants to. The United States doesn't yet want any relaxation in Europe because that would lead to a general relaxation, would weaken the system of American domination in vast areas around the world, and would weaken the American military alliances and their military bases, and that would in turn produce political problems at home," Khrushchev said.

Khrushchev said in conclusion that in the Soviet Union they were very satisfied with the development of the situation both internally and in foreign affairs. He mentioned certain events which were of special importance for the relation of forces on the world scene and said that all of them had been bad for imperialism and the Americans. He then listed them: the nationalization of the Suez canal, the defeat of the West in its attack on Egypt, the defeat of the uprising in Indonesia, the United Nations decision concerning the withdrawal of the Americans and British from Lebanon and Jordan. Khrushchev said that that had been only formally a diplomatic solution; in fact it was exactly the same as though the Anglo-Americans had been driven out of there by force. Then there had been the revolution in Iraq and the compromising of the Americans in the Far East, where the United States was forced to defend Chiang Kaishek and to pretend they were ready to go to war on account of the Chinese offshore islands, although it was obvious that the United States would not go to war for either Taiwan or the islands.

* * *

Khrushchev reduced the question of improving Yugoslav-Soviet relations to the possibility of a meeting of representatives of our two countries, adding the remark that there was no question this time of the Russians going to Yugoslavia. From this one might conclude that the Yugoslavs would have to come to Moscow if they wanted to change our relations for the better. Khrushchev did not talk specifically about having another meeting, but he clearly had something like that in mind.

On two occasions during our conversation Khrushchev asked, as though thinking aloud, how we could straighten out our relations. I said roughly the following: In view of the campaign which has been going on in the Soviet Union and the "camp" for six months already and the bad effect it had had on our interstate relations, I did not see any way in which our relations could make a sudden turn for the better or how everything could be changed at one stroke. Certain socialist countries which were neighbors of Yugoslavia, encouraged by the campaign against us, had started talking about having territorial claims on our country. Although I could not see any magic wand that would put everything on the right road at one stroke, I could not imagine a state of continual and endless quarreling between us. I considered it essential for the tension to be taken out of the situation and for the campaign against Yugoslavia to be halted, or at least for the tone and language, as well as the aims pursued by the articles, to be modified. At the same time they should write something positive about Yugoslavia. This would in time create a better climate between us and then it would be easier to find a way of improving our relations.

It was clear to Khrushchev that at the moment we were not suggesting a meeting. He kept repeating that we were responsible for the present state of affairs. He repeated that he personally would be ready to do something to improve the situation, but didn't see what he could do. In a sort of summing up he said that they for their part would not do anything to worsen relations or attack Yugoslavia and that collaboration between our governments would continue. I told him I was sure that his assurance about not worsening our relations would be received with pleasure in Belgrade. It was apparent that he was not particularly pleased with such a conclusion, which confirmed in fact that each side had stuck to its own point of view. Perhaps he expected Yugoslavia to ask for a top-level meeting and that that was why I had come from Moscow to the Black Sea. But nothing came of it and one could assume that the poor state of our relations was going to continue.

Apart from this, Khrushchev remained in a good mood throughout. As it was already five o'clock in the afternoon I again thanked him for the friendly reception and asked to take my leave. Khrushchev would not agree and again invited me to his house for tea. There the conversation continued but without touching on any essentially new topics. It was again established that there was no question of any special steps to be taken to improve our relations. I again said that we ought to stop the attacks on each other and other unpleasant things which damaged our relations. Khrushchev repeated that we were the ones to blame, and recalled that in the summer he had asked that I should stay on in Moscow, that first he had been informed that his request had been agreed to in Belgrade, and that later this decision had been changed again and I was called back home. Khrushchev asked me whether I myself had asked to leave the Soviet Union. I didn't answer the question directly but told him that it was not important and that I would continue to deal with the same matters although I would not be in Moscow. We drank tea and Khrushchev offered me Hungarian apples, which he said had been sent him by János Kadar. He expressed himself in glowing terms about Kadar.

Finally before dinner I thanked Khrushchev for a very friendly visit and apologized for having taken up his whole day. Khrushchev asked me to convey his greetings to Comrades Tito, Kardelj, and Ranković. I tried to say good-bye to Khrushchev and Nina Petrovna in front of the house, but he would not let me. After we had reached the car and I had thanked him once again, I took my leave of Nina Petrovna. For the first time since I have been in the Soviet Union I addressed Khrushchev in the more familiar Russian manner, using his first name and patronymic—"Nikita Sergeyevich." I waved my hand to Khrushchev and Nina Petrovna until the car went round the first bend in the road.

On Khrushchev's advice I spent the night of October 8 in the former Beria villa above Gagri. It was already about seven o'clock in the evening when I reached it and found seven or eight top officials of the Soviet Government there. They had come down by plane from Moscow at Khrushchev's invitation and had arrived that morning. They told me they had been waiting half the day to be received by Khrushchev. Some of them I knew already, but the majority of them were noticeably cold in their attitude to me, in tune with the bad relations now prevailing between Moscow and Belgrade.

One of the Russians with whom I was better acquainted, Leonid Ilyichev, a secretary of the Central Committee of the CPSU, commented jokingly that I had "ruined their working day," because they had been kept waiting for hours "because of me." I said I was sorry that they had been wasting their time and expressed my satisfaction with the conversation I had had with Khrushchev. None of the other Soviet officials showed the slightest wish to talk to me, and I withdrew to my room.

The attitude of these Soviet officials toward me had an even more unpleasant effect on me in view of the friendly and cordial behavior of Khrushchev, whose guest I had been that day—a fact which obviously did not please this group of senior Soviet officials. Perhaps their behavior toward me reflected more accurately the Soviet Government's true attitude toward Yugoslavia than did Khrushchev's friendliness. In any case it served as a useful corrective and complement to the way I had been treated by Khrushchev. I tried to explain to myself why a group of top Soviet officials should behave so coldly toward a Yugoslav ambassador about to leave their country. But their behavior could not erase the impression I had gained in my friendly talks with Khrushchev.

The Soviet press reported my farewell visit on its front pages but without saying anything about the friendly atmosphere that prevailed or that Khrushchev gave me lunch. Two or three days previously the Chinese ambassador, Liu Siao, had visited Khrushchev, and the Soviet press reported that Khrushchev gave him lunch and that everything went off in a "friendly and cordial atmosphere." A few days ago an American film producer visited Khrushchev in the same house, and it was reported that he was asked to lunch. I remained, at Khrushchev's insistence, the whole day with him, was invited to lunch with Khrushchev and his family, and received an exceptionally cordial and friendly welcome. But the Soviet press is silent about all that, but said, on the other hand, that I had seen Khrushchev "at my own request"—as though you could make such a visit at someone else's request!

Moscow, October 12, 1958

As I was preparing to leave the Soviet Union for good, I gave a lot of thought, as I had done many times before, to the unusual personality of Khrushchev. In spite of various forecasts made by both Russians and foreigners, he has succeeded in four years in getting rid by various means of all his rivals, of whom there were not a few.

Khrushchev saw far more clearly than the majority of his rivals and colleagues the necessity of abandoning Stalinist ways, and he made a number of moves in that direction which were of great significance for internal developments in the Soviet Union and for increasing the part played by the Soviet Union in the world.

One of Khrushchev's most important decisions was to make his secret speech criticizing Stalin at the Twentieth Congress. This had the greatest significance not only for the Soviet Union but also for the further advance of the international relations as a whole. It was that congress which laid the foundations for the emergence of a new principle, which had been rejected by Stalin and which accepted the idea that there are different roads to socialism. Because of that the "Soviet model" of socialism began to lose its universal and compulsory application, although even today Moscow has not admitted this explicitly.

It was of historic significance that Khrushchev clearly turned the foreign policy of the Soviet Union and the "camp" in the direction of the peaceful coexistence of states with different social systems. This opened up the prospect of abandoning the cold war and removing the danger of nuclear war. Khrushchev also started to reintroduce the rule of law in the Soviet Union with a policy of respect for "socialist legality"; he rehabilitated numerous Soviet citizens who had been innocent victims and liberated the survivors from the concentration camps which had been for decades an integral part of the system under Stalin.

Thanks to Khrushchev's dynamic personality—he spoke in public more often than anyone else in the Soviet leadership—a certain movement began to be apparent in some circles in the Soviet Union quite unlike the apathy and passivity that had marked Stalin's dictatorship. Khrushchev opposed the official ideologists and theoreticians in the Soviet Communist party and state who can still only repeat the old Stalinist slogans about socialism and communism. Khrushchev called such theoreticians in the Soviet Union "parrots," according to a *Pravda* report.

One of the first major steps taken by Khrushchev in the direction of changing Stalin's policy toward Yugoslavia was his visit to Belgrade in May 1955. After talks with Comrade Tito and other Yugoslav leaders the Belgrade Declaration was then signed, signifying the restoration of normal governmental relations between Yugoslavia and the Soviet Union. The same purpose was served by Comrade Tito's visit to the Soviet Union in June 1956, on which occasion the Moscow Declaration, signifying the normalization of Yugoslav-Soviet party relations, was signed.

Under Khrushchev's leadership the Soviet Union also adopted a different policy toward the new independent states of Africa and Asia. The Soviet Union became directly involved in Egypt and in other countries in Africa and Asia. Unlike the attitude adopted in Stalin's time, when the leaders of those countries—Nehru, Nasser, Sukarno, and others—were described in Moscow, if not as agents of Western imperialism, at least as "bourgeois nationalists," Khrushchev directed Soviet foreign policy onto new paths of cooperation with those national leaders and their countries.

Khrushchev does not rule Russia simply by means of "decrees" of the Soviet Presidium and he has not cut himself off from the Soviet people behind the walls of the Kremlin and the State Security Service. He doesn't derive his information about conditions in the Soviet Union from films which have been made for him and doesn't avoid contact with people—in a word, he behaves in a new and completely different way from his predecessor.

On the other hand one can draw up a list of quite a few things which drag Khrushchev back into the past, to Stalin's days, of which Khrushchev has not been able to rid himself. Khrushchev is a fervent supporter of Stalin's policy of consolidating the "socialist camp" and Soviet domination over it. He intervened by force of arms in Hungary in 1956 when there was a danger that the "socialist camp" would disintegrate. He then made several public speeches in praise of Stalin as a great Marxist-Leninist, forgetting that at the Twentieth Congress of the CPSU he had said the reverse and was the author of a policy of de-Stalinization. In 1958 he spoke out in favor of the execution of Imre Nagy and his comrades. Khrushchev continues to take the view that the international working-class movement should be led from one center and that the "socialist camp" must unquestionably be "led by the Soviet Union."

The decentralization of the management of the Soviet economy and the other new measures which Khrushchev introduced in that field are administrative in nature and do not affect fundamentally the essential principles governing social relations in the Soviet system. Even after the reorganization of relations between the people directly engaged in production, both in the towns and on the farms, the organs of the Soviet state have not changed essentially. The strictly centralized Soviet system tolerates with difficulty, and in fact cannot assimilate, the innovations which Khrushchev is introducing in this field.

Although Khrushchev took the initiative to restore normal relations with Yugoslavia, even after they were normalized Soviet policy led to fresh political conflicts between our countries on grounds similar to those which led to quarrels in the past. In these new disputes Khrushchev has as a rule been sharper in his criticisms of Yugoslavia than the other Soviet leaders and has attacked us from dogmatic and conservative positions. As in the recent past, in the conflicts between us the Soviet side did not pay much attention to facts or principles or the agreements which we had concluded; the aim was to compromise Yugoslavia at all costs. This was particularly apparent in *Pravda*'s, that is, the CPSU's, brutal attack on Yugoslavia on May 9, 1958.

Even after the normalization of Yugoslav-Soviet relations Khrushchev's attitude to our émigrés and deserters in the East remained fundamentally unchanged, and he continued to call them "Communists and internationalists."

In all these instances Khrushchev acted as though he was making a special effort to "appease" the dogmatic and Stalinist elements in the Soviet Union whose existence and influence he had to take into account. He continued to do this even when, after June 1957, there were no more known Stalinists in the Soviet leadership.

At the Twentieth Congress of the CPSU Khrushchev was inclined to accept the principle that each country would follow a different path to socialism, but in practice he was not able to apply that principle or to deal with relations between socialist states and Communist parties on the basis of independence and equal status. And even when he did accept that principle for a time, as in the case of Yugoslavia, the Soviet Union under Khrushchev's leadership was not able to apply that policy consistently. The Soviet leaders obviously regarded it as a tactical move.

Certain steps which he is taking in domestic politics, curtailing the omnipotence of the state and party *apparat*, as well as some policy statements having a purely programmatic character and which clearly cannot be realized, are undermining Khrushchev's position in the Soviet Union.

Following the Twentieth Congress of the CPSU it was to be expected that the climate with regard to freedom of artistic creation would be more bearable. But nothing of the sort took place. Official party doctrine and state control continued to increase in strength in this field as well.

Although he lived for such a long time so close to Stalin and later reached the top of the Soviet pyramid of power, Khrushchev never tired of insisting that he had improved on the situation which he had inherited from Stalin. But Khrushchev himself had been too long involved in the building of that system, and it was actually the system which formed him as a politician. Nobody, not even Khrushchev, can change his spots, and that is why we have in him to deal with the old and the new in one person.

It is in the light of such contradictory circumstances that Yugoslav-Soviet relations have to develop, periodically lapsing into a state of crisis. Although it might be said, in my opinion, that Khrushchev was not in the least pleased with this state of our relations, he was not prepared, or he was not able, as Soviet Prime Minister, to seek a new way out of the crisis in the spirit of the Belgrade and Moscow Declarations or to resolve the issues in dispute between us as equal with equal, as it was laid down in those declarations. Instead of that, Khrushchev relied on rules inherited from the past and on the Soviet idea of the "socialist camp" to which, in Khrushchev's opinion, Yugoslavia ought to belong as a socialist and an East European country in which Communists were in power.

My farewell visit to Khrushchev may serve in its way as a particular illustration of Khrushchev's unpredictable behavior toward Yugoslavia.

* * *

On my last days in Moscow I made farewell calls on Voroshilov and Mikoyan. Our conversations were formal and empty. Both of them inquired how my talks with Khrushchev had gone.

A week after my meeting with Khrushchev on the Black Sea coast I left Moscow for Belgrade. It was October 14, 1958, when I finally left the Soviet Union with Miška and the children.

A POSTSCRIPT

Belgrade, September 14, 1971

Nearly fifteen years have passed since I wrote this diary. I will add a few pages to round the record off.

On September 9, 1971, Nikita Sergeyevich Khrushchev died. As I write these words I feel as though I am actually present at his funeral in Moscow.

On the very day before he died I left Moscow along with my family, having completed my second term as Yugoslav ambassador to the Soviet Union.

I agreed with Miška that we would send a telegram to Khrushchev's widow, Nina Petrovna, to express our deep sympathy. On September 13 in my office in Belgrade I had drawn up the short text of a telegram to be typed out and then sent to the Khrushchev family in Moscow by the normal postal service. Meanwhile I read in the *Tanjug* bulletin the text of a report by TASS saying that the Central Committee of the CPSU and the Soviet Government had announced Khrushchev's death in one single sentence, with the words: "N. S. Khrushchev, distinguished pensioner of the Soviet Union, has died." And nothing else!

I took my telegram back and wrote another one, as follows:

Nina Petrovna and the family of N. S. Khrushchev, Moscow.

We are with you in your deep sorrow on the death of Nikita Sergeyevich. Our grief is all the greater because during a long stay in your country we had the honor and the good fortune to enjoy personally the friendship and hospitality of that great man.

We are convinced that there are millions of people in Yugoslavia and throughout the world who are thinking of you today and who will cherish the memory of N. S. Khrushchev and his work. Nikita Sergeyevich's name will always be remembered in the history of the people's fight for a better life, for cooperation and friendship between nations, and for peace and progress in the world. May this be a consolation to the friends and admirers of that exceptional man and those who were closest to him in this painful and sudden loss.

A POSTSCRIPT

Please accept our deepest sympathy.

> Belgrade, September 13, 1971
> Budislava and Veljko Mićunović

Somebody on the staff of the biggest Belgrade daily paper, *Politika*, learned of our telegram and reported it on the front page on September 14. Perhaps they thought our telegram was sent officially? Even if *Politika* did not think it was official, I am sure the Soviet authorities did.

Belgrade, September 15, 1971

Comrade Tito, President of Yugoslavia, again appointed me ambassador to the Soviet Union in 1969. This was following the armed intervention in Czechoslovakia by the Soviet Army and the armed forces of another four members of the Warsaw Pact in August 1968. That intervention was carried out on the basis of the so-called "doctrine of limited sovereignty" of the socialist countries belonging to the Warsaw Pact. The main argument used to support that doctrine concerned the "overriding interests of socialism" or "proletarian internationalism" in the Soviet and East European interpretation. But that is quite another story, and a long one.

What I have to say about my second term as Yugoslav ambassador in the Soviet Union concerns Khrushchev. To my surprise, on October 14, 1964, at a meeting of the Central Committee of the CPSU, he was deprived of all his functions in the party and government. I had then already been more than two years in Washington as Yugoslav ambassador to the United States, and I had never dreamed that I might go to Moscow again after Khrushchev had been removed and pensioned off in that way.

While I was in Washington I did not have the opportunity to follow closely, as I had done for many years before, the course of Yugoslav-Soviet relations, and I was able to pay even less attention to Khrushchev's domestic policies. But even at that distance one could see clearly how difficulties were piling up around Khrushchev on the domestic and the foreign front. The latter had been marked recently by two major failures in the two main areas of Soviet foreign policy, or at least of Khrushchev's foreign policy: the conflict with China in the East and the Cuban missile crisis in the West.[1]

---

[1] Toward the end of the 1950s the differences between Moscow and Peking, which Mićunović had earlier detected, became more serious. In June 1959 the Russians revoked an agreement to provide the Chinese with assistance in the manufacture of nuclear weapons. In 1960 the dispute came into the open in articles and speeches, and in July the Soviet Government announced the withdrawal of all Soviet technical advisers and aid from China.

In October 1962 the Americans became aware that the Russians were engaged in the construction of missile sites on Cuba and were shipping missiles across the Atlantic. Resolute action by President John F. Kennedy forced Khrushchev to halt the missile shipments and to abandon the Cuban project.

I do not believe that the rift with China, however new and disturbing a factor it was in Soviet foreign policy, was decisive in bringing about Khrushchev's fall. His successors probably had very few illusions about being able to improve Sino-Soviet relations if they got rid of Khrushchev, although they gave the opposite impression at the beginning.

Although right up to the moment of his fall Khrushchev had not fully recovered from the blow which the Cuban crisis of 1962 inflicted on him, I also do not consider that this defeat in foreign policy played a decisive role in his removal. Internal Soviet reasons were decisive for Khrushchev's fall. His failures in foreign policy only added to the accumulation of Soviet internal factors which worked toward his removal. Although all the failures were laid at Khrushchev's door, people in the Soviet Union knew very well that Khrushchev alone had not been responsible for Sino-Soviet relations or for United States policy toward the Soviet Union, and that Khrushchev's successors would not be able to change that policy any more than Khrushchev had been. That internal reasons were decisive in bringing about his fall is shown by the fact that his successors continued Khrushchev's foreign policy.

Belgrade, September 26, 1971

On my second term of service in the Soviet Union I remained in Moscow for nearly two years, from 1969 to 1971. The general conditions in which I had to work this time were not at all agreeable.

A fresh conflict arose between Yugoslavia and the Soviet Union because of the Soviet armed intervention in Czechoslovakia. Apart from that, there had been certain changes in the attitude of Soviet official bodies toward the diplomatic corps in general and toward me in particular. Nevertheless I cherished the hope that I would have the opportunity of meeting Khrushchev again. But to my very great sorrow it was not possible for me to visit the man whose hospitality I had so often enjoyed in the period 1956–58.

If I had asked for such a meeting through official Soviet channels, I might as well have packed my bags at once and returned to Belgrade. Such a thing is still quite inconceivable in the Soviet Union.

As is always the case in the Soviet Union, Khrushchev's dismissal meant at the same time his condemnation and permanent fall from grace. In this way Soviet leaders who are dismissed find themselves automatically under a sort of modern anathema and in a state of excommunication. This practice of excluding people completely from society is still applied in a socialist system, although there is no provision for anything like it in Soviet law.

Despite this state of affairs, it has to be stressed that on this occasion the decision to make changes in the leadership of the Soviet Union was made by a vote at a full meeting of the Central Committee of the CPSU. Similar decisions made in the decades of Stalin's dictatorship were carried out in such a way that people dismissed from leading positions lost both their jobs and their heads. The person most responsible for the fact that Khrushchev was not dealt with in the same way was Khrushchev himself. It was he who, as long as he led the CPSU and the Soviet state, did most to see that the practice of Stalin's days became a thing of the past.

Realizing that we were not going to be able to visit Khrushchev, Miška and I tried on several occasions to send our greetings and good wishes to him and his family through senior Soviet officials who had at one time been counted as Khrushchev's friends. I doubt whether we succeeded in this. Those Soviet officials and their wives who, we hoped, might do something for the sake of friendship looked the other way and avoided our company when they realized what we wanted. Needless to say, even if I had had another meeting with Khrushchev, our relations with the Soviet Union would not have suffered in the slightest; indeed, there were good reasons for expecting the contrary. Unfortunately, neither Yugoslav-Soviet relations nor the Soviet system itself could tolerate such a meeting.

Belgrade, September 27, 1971

As I am writing about Khrushchev's dismissal all sorts of thoughts pass through my mind about that not-so-distant past in the Soviet Union when Khrushchev was dismissing his rivals and opponents and removing them from the path along which he was forcing his way to the Soviet political summit. It was not he who took the initiative in the political liquidation of the three prominent Soviet leaders of Stalin's time. Molotov, Kaganovich, and Malenkov tried to get rid of Khrushchev and lost a battle which they joined only when they believed it had been won.

The members of the "antiparty group" were removed from Soviet public life, but they continued to do less important jobs in their own field. I believe Khrushchev's position—since he was not sent off to distant Mongolia like Molotov, or to Siberia like Malenkov, but remained in his country house near Moscow—was more like what I have called "anathema and excommunication" than the situation of the members of the "antiparty group." I believe that his "exile" under house arrest near Moscow is a worse fate for Khrushchev than the jobs which Molotov and Malenkov were given, even though they were thousands of miles from Moscow, which they could visit only with special permission.

As well as being dismissed, Khrushchev was in fact also condemned to a sort of permanent house arrest. In view of his dynamic temperament this was probably the severest punishment he could have suffered: He had to spend the last years of his life in solitude and cut off from people, yet it was in conversation with people that he had spent his whole life.

The majority of those who voted for a new leader appear to have been sure that they would no longer have to suffer the various sudden changes, innovations, and ideas which did not fit in with the established Soviet system and which were typical of Khrushchev's style of leadership. The new Soviet leaders appear to have set themselves the aim of directing the Soviet Union again along proven paths and away from the surprises and innovations which Khrushchev produced for them. The organized forces in the Soviet state and society—the party, the Soviet Army, the State Security Service, and the other organs of power—saw in Khrushchev's further retention of power dangers to which they were not prepared to expose themselves.

Belgrade, September 29, 1971

There is a great similarity between the way Khrushchev removed Marshal Zhukov in October 1957 and the way Khrushchev himself was dismissed seven years later. The "technique" used on both occasions was practically the same: Both of them were dismissed when it appeared that they were at the very summit of their power. Both Khrushchev and Zhukov—and others, too—were taken completely by surprise and had not the slightest idea of what was being prepared for them by the Central Committee, to which Khrushchev had done something to restore to a position of supremacy in the party and the country.

Immediately after Marshal Zhukov returned from his highly successful official visits to Yugoslavia and Albania he was taken from Vnukovo Airport in Moscow, where he had been given an official welcome, straight to a meeting of the Soviet Presidium, where he was informed of the quite unexpected decision to remove him from all his functions in the Soviet party and government. On that occasion it was Khrushchev who took the initiative in having him dismissed.

Seven years later Khrushchev, not suspecting what awaited him, was taken by Mikoyan straight from Moscow Airport, where he had been brought from his holiday on the Black Sea coast, to a meeting of the party Central Committee which he did not know had been summoned, although he was its First Secretary and leader of the party. There he was informed of the decision to remove him from all his government and party functions. On the surface the two cases were practically identical. When it came to removing Khrushchev, the Central Committee had a precedent in his removal of Marshal Zhukov. It looked then as though Khrushchev had consolidated his position in the Kremlin. It turned out later that he hadn't.

As we know, Marshal Zhukov was one of the decisive factors in Khrushchev's victory at the June plenum in 1957; it was thanks to him that the Soviet Army was on Khrushchev's side in those events. Seven years later it turned out, among other things, that Khrushchev had lost the support of the Soviet armed forces, although that was not the only factor determining whether Khrushchev remained in power.

However great were the differences in the reasons for the numerous dismissals of top Soviet leaders in Khrushchev's time, and later for the removal of Khrushchev himself, it is interesting to recall that in all these events the man who made the speech for the prosecution was always the same—Mikhail Suslov. It was he who made the speech condemning Molotov, Malenkov, and Kaganovich at the Central Committee plenum in June 1957. It was he again who appeared as the "prosecutor" at the Central Committee meeting at the end of October 1957 when Marshal Zhukov was removed. And it was Suslov who did the same job as prosecutor on behalf of the Central Committee at the meeting in October 1964 when Khrushchev was dismissed.

Belgrade, September 30, 1971

During my second period of service in Moscow the new Soviet leadership's relations with me were very cool and strictly in accordance with the rules of protocol, for which the principal reason was the fact that Khrushchev had been so friendly toward me during my first stay in the Soviet Union. This was very well known to the new Soviet leaders, by whom I was regarded, quite correctly, as a friend and admirer of Khrushchev's. Some of the Soviet leaders actually pointed this out to me when I arrived in Moscow again as Yugoslav ambassador.

These details indicate the sort of atmosphere which reigned over Yugoslav-Soviet relations at that time, although the dismissal of Khrushchev was a Soviet internal affair, irrespective of how popular Khrushchev and Zhukov had been in Yugoslavia.

Belgrade, October 4, 1971

During my second period of service in Moscow I heard that Khrushchev was able occasionally to meet the peasants who lived in a nearby village not far from the country house near Moscow in which he spent the last years of his life. I heard that he sometimes went fishing with them in the river close-by. It was also said in Moscow that Khrushchev often talked with the peasants about farming and all sorts of other topics. He thus continued in those conditions to deal in a way with the subject which had been one of his main preoccupations throughout his life.

Khrushchev was allowed after his dismissal to appear in public once when he visited an exhibition and again when he went to vote in the elections in Moscow, where he had always voted in the past. This was probably intended to show that Khrushchev was not under anything like an anathema or excommunication. For that reason they even allowed him to be photographed and shown on television as he "carried out his duty as a citizen under socialism," as they say in Moscow.

When he appeared for the second time in these circumstances at the polling center in Moscow, there was a quite large group of people waiting to see him and they applauded spontaneously as soon as he got out of his car. But inside the polling booth it turned out that Khrushchev had no means of identification or any other documents with him, and this set the election officials a problem because Soviet law lays down that a voter has to identify himself in order to vote. The official in charge was a woman, and she exchanged cordial greetings with Khrushchev, adding that the whole of Russia knew him and had confidence in him, even without an identity card. What Khrushchev and this woman said received worldwide publicity, both in words and pictures.

After that "incident" Khrushchev was never again allowed to appear in public, whether to vote or for any other reason. He continued to live in his family circle behind the walls of his dacha near Moscow. He was allowed out only when he was obliged to move for a time to a Moscow hospital.

Belgrade, October 5, 1971

A few days ago I received the following telegram from Nina Petrovna and the Khrushchev family in Moscow:

Dear Comrades Veljko and Budislava Mićunović,

Most heartfelt thanks for the warm and friendly sentiments which you expressed about our dear Nikita Sergeyevich and for your sympathy in our grief.

Your telegram was a great comfort to us. We wish you every happiness.

Moscow, September 20, 1971
Nina Petrovna Khrushchev and
the whole Khrushchev family

445

A POSTSCRIPT

Belgrade, October 8, 1971

Finally, as I come to complete these notes, I want to say that it was not such a bad thing that Khrushchev fell from power in October 1964. He had, after all, been the leader of the Soviet Union for a long time—a whole decade. What I find bad about the dismissal of Khrushchev is that it confirmed once again that in the "first and greatest land of socialism" everything in a man's life continues to be linked with his retention of power: his personal prestige, his political influence, his position in society, the assessment of his past services, and even the material circumstances in which he lives. To be removed from power means to disappear from public life, to fade into anonymity, to become, so to speak, an unperson. It even goes as far as a tacit ban on any public mention even of the name of the man who has thus been excluded from society. In addition, such a person is very often subjected to a regime of isolation.

Such a regime is permanent and is part and parcel of the removal of someone from power, although it is not written into any Soviet laws. Khrushchev was subject to such a regime right up to the day of his death. It might be said to have continued afterward, when the Soviet press was permitted to publish just one sentence about his death.

The same spirit governed the manner in which the "distinguished pensioner" was seen off from this world. Khrushchev was not buried on the Red Square beside the Kremlin where Lenin's tomb stands, where the new Soviet leaders have erected a tombstone to Stalin, and where the mortal remains of other distinguished Soviet leaders have been buried from the October Revolution to the present day. Khrushchev was buried in the presence of his family and a group of friends in the cemetery of the Novodevichi monastery in Moscow.

APPENDIX

Extracts from Tito's Pula Speech[1]

Borba for November 16, 1956, gave two pages to the speech Comrade Tito had made in the Army Club in Pula on November 11, in which, referring to the events in Hungary, he said:

"We saw that things were going to be pretty difficult, because the Soviet leaders had a mistaken and faulty view of relations with those countries, with Poland, Hungary, and the others. But we didn't take that so tragically, because we saw that it was not a matter of the whole Soviet leadership, but only of some of them, who had to a certain extent imposed that attitude on the others. We saw that the attitude had been imposed by people who had long stood and were still standing on Stalinist positions.

"To call out the troops of one country to teach a lesson to the people of another country, even if there has been some shooting, is a great mistake. It enraged the people even more and so led to a spontaneous uprising in which Communists found themselves against their will along with various reactionary elements. The latter intervened in the uprising and exploited it for their own purposes. . . .

"The question now is: Was the Soviet intervention necessary? The first intervention was not necessary. The first intervention, which took place in response to Geroe's appeal, was absolutely mistaken. . . .

"I have to say that the situation in Hungary assumed such proportions that it was obviously going to lead to a frightful slaughter, to a frightful civil war, in which socialism might be completely buried and which might lead to a third world war. . . .

". . . we shall always say that we are against intervention and the use of outside armed force. But what was the lesser evil? Was it to be chaos, civil war, counterrevolution, and another world war, or intervention by the Soviet troops which were on the spot? The former would be a catastrophe, the latter was a mistake. And, of course, if it saves socialism in Hungary then, comrades, then we shall be able to say that, although we

[1] See page 162.

447

are against intervention, the Soviet intervention was necessary. But had they done everything they should have done earlier there would have been no need for any military intervention. The mistake was made because, unfortunately, they still think that armed force can resolve everything. But it can't. Look what a fierce resistance the people are putting up with their bare hands when they have a single aim—to free themselves and be independent. They no longer care what sort of independence it will be, whether the bourgeoisie and a reactionary system will be restored, so long as they have national independence. That is what dominated the people's mind. Of course I can now say that the first possibility was the worst thing that could happen, while the second—intervention by Soviet troops—was also bad, but if it leads to the preservation of socialism in Hungary, i.e., to the further building of socialism in that country and peace in the world, then one day it will appear as something positive, on condition that the Soviet troops withdraw the moment the situation in Hungary is settled and peaceful."

INDEX